Information Theoretic Methods for Future Communication Systems

Information Theoretic Methods for Future Communication Systems

Editors

Onur Günlü
Rafael F. Schaefer
Holger Boche
H. Vincent Poor

MDPI • Basel • Beijing • Wuhan • Barcelona • Belgrade • Manchester • Tokyo • Cluj • Tianjin

Editors
Onur Günlü
Linköping University
Sweden

Rafael F. Schaefer
Technische Universität
Dresden
Germany

Holger Boche
Technische Universität
München
Germany

H. Vincent Poor
Princeton University
USA

Editorial Office
MDPI
St. Alban-Anlage 66
4052 Basel, Switzerland

This is a reprint of articles from the Special Issue published online in the open access journal *Entropy* (ISSN 1099-4300) (available at: https://www.mdpi.com/journal/entropy/special_issues/future_communication).

For citation purposes, cite each article independently as indicated on the article page online and as indicated below:

LastName, A.A.; LastName, B.B.; LastName, C.C. Article Title. *Journal Name* **Year**, *Volume Number*, Page Range.

ISBN 978-3-0365-7364-9 (Hbk)
ISBN 978-3-0365-7365-6 (PDF)

Contents

About the Editors

Onur Günlü

Onur Günlü received a B.Sc. degree (Highest Distinction) in Electrical and Electronics Engineering from Bilkent University, Turkey in 2011, and M.Sc. (Highest Distinction) and Dr.-Ing. (Ph.D. equivalent) degrees in Communications Engineering, both from the Technical University of Munich (TUM), Germany, in October 2013 and November 2018, respectively. He was a Working Student in the Communication Systems division of Intel Mobile Communications (IMC) in Munich, Germany between November 2012 and March 2013. He worked as a Research and Teaching Assistant at the TUM Chair of Communications Engineering between February 2014 and May 2019. Onur has made many research visits to top universities and companies, including visits to the TU Eindhoven, Netherlands and later to Georgia Institute of Technology, USA. He was a Research Associate and Dozent between June 2019 and September 2020 and was a Research Group Leader and Dozent between October 2020 and March 2021 at TU Berlin, and he held the same academic titles at the Chair of Communications Engineering and Security at the University of Siegen, Germany from April 2021 until September 2022. Onur has been working as an ELLIIT Assistant Professor at Linköping University, Sweden, as the head of the Information Theory and Security (ITS) group within the Information Coding Division (ICG) since October 2022. He has received the prestigious VDE Information Technology Society (ITG) 2021 Johann-Philipp-Reis Award, was selected by the IEEE Communications Society as 2021 Exemplary Reviewer of the IEEE Transactions on Communications (TCOM), and received the 2023 ZENITH Research and Career Development Award. His research interests include information-theoretic privacy and security, coding theory, statistical signal processing for biometrics and physical unclonable functions (PUFs), private (federated) learning and function computations, and doubly exponential (secure) identification via channels.

Rafael F. Schaefer

Rafael F. Schaefer is a Professor and head of the Chair of Information Theory and Machine Learning at Technische Universität Dresden. He received a Dipl.-Ing. degree in Electrical Engineering and Computer Science from the Technische Universität Berlin, Germany, in 2007, and a Dr.-Ing. degree in Electrical Engineering from the Technische Universität München, Germany, in 2012. From 2013 to 2015, he was a Post-Doctoral Research Fellow with Princeton University. From 2015 to 2020 he was an Assistant Professor with the Technische Universität Berlin, Germany, and from 2021 to 2022 a Professor with the Universität Siegen, Germany. Among his publications is the recent book *Information Theoretic Security and Privacy of Information Systems* (Cambridge University Press, 2017). He was a recipient of the VDE Johann-Philipp-Reis Award in 2013. He received the best paper award from the German Information Technology Society (ITG-Preis) in 2016. He is currently an Associate Editor of the *IEEE Transactions on Information Forensics and Security* and of the *IEEE Transactions on Communications*. He is a member of the IEEE Information Forensics and Security Technical Committee.

Holger Boche

Holger Boche received a Dipl.-Ing. degree in Electrical Engineering, a graduate degree in Mathematics, and a Dr.-Ing. degree in Electrical Engineering from the Technische Universität Dresden, Germany, in 1990, 1992, and 1994, respectively. In 1998, he received the Dr. rer. nat. degree in Pure Mathematics from the Technische Universität Berlin, Germany. From 2002 to 2010, he was a Full Professor in Mobile Communication Networks with the Institute for Communications Systems, Technische Universität Berlin, Germany. In 2004, he became the Director of the Fraunhofer Institute for Telecommunications (HHI). He is currently a Full Professor at the Institute of Theoretical Information Technology, Technische Universität München, Germany, which he joined in October 2010. Since 2014, Prof. Boche has been a member and Honorary Fellow of the TUM Institute for Advanced Study, Munich, Germany, and since 2018 has been a Founding Director of the Center for Quantum Engineering, Technische Universität München, Germany. Since 2021, he has been jointly leading the BMBF Research Hub 6G-life with Frank Fitzek. He was elected a member of the German Academy of Sciences (Leopoldina) in 2008 and to the Berlin Brandenburg Academy of Sciences and Humanities in 2009. He is a recipient of the Research Award "Technische Kommunikation" from the Alcatel SEL Foundation in October 2003, the "Innovation Award" from the Vodafone Foundation in June 2006, and the Gottfried Wilhelm Leibniz Prize from the Deutsche Forschungsgemeinschaft (German Research Foundation) in 2008. He was a co-recipient of the 2006 IEEE Signal Processing Society Best Paper Award and a recipient of the 2007 IEEE Signal Processing Society Best Paper Award. He was General Chair of the Symposium on Information Theoretic Approaches to Security and Privacy at IEEE GlobalSIP 2016.

H. Vincent Poor

H. Vincent Poor received his Ph.D. in EECS from Princeton University in 1977. From 1977 until 1990 he was on the faculty of the University of Illinois at Urbana-Champaign. Since 1990, he has been on the faculty at Princeton, where he is currently the Michael Henry Strater University Professor. From 2006 to 2016, he served as the Dean of Princeton's School of Engineering and Applied Science. He has also held visiting appointments at several other universities, including most recently at Berkeley and Cambridge. His research interests are in the areas of information theory, machine learning, and network science, and their applications in wireless networks, energy systems, and related fields. Among his publications in these areas is the recent book Machine Learning and Wireless Communications. (Cambridge University Press, 2022). Dr. Poor is a member of the U.S. National Academy of Engineering and the U.S. National Academy of Sciences, and is a foreign member of the Chinese Academy of Sciences, the Royal Society, and other national and international academies. He received the IEEE Alexander Graham Bell Medal in 2017.

Preface to "Information Theoretic Methods for Future Communication Systems"

Information theory provides powerful tools that can help to eliminate bottlenecks in future communication and computation systems. Eliminating such bottlenecks requires low latency operations with large amounts of data to take advantage of data-driven methods for improving services and providing reliability and other benefits. A collection of highly significant results, provided in this book, shows how information theory can provide a fundamental understanding of the limits of the reliability, robustness, secrecy, privacy, resiliency, and latency of such systems. Thus, we are happy to share these fundamental insights to contribute to the research and development of future systems.

Onur Günlü, Rafael F. Schaefer, Holger Boche, and H. Vincent Poor
Editors

entropy

Editorial

Information Theoretic Methods for Future Communication Systems

Onur Günlü [1,*], Rafael F. Schaefer [2,3], Holger Boche [4,5,6,7] and H. Vincent Poor [8]

1 Information Coding Division, Linköping University, 58183 Linköping, Sweden
2 Chair of Information Theory and Machine Learning, Technische Universität Dresden, 01062 Dresden, Germany
3 BMBF Research Hub 6G-Life, Technische Universität Dresden, 01062 Dresden, Germany
4 Lehrstuhl für Theoretische Informationstechnik, TUM School of Computation, Information and Technology, Technical University of Munich, 80333 Munich, Germany
5 CASA: Cyber Security in the Age of Large-Scale Adversaries Exzellenzcluster, Ruhr-Universität Bochum, 44780 Bochum, Germany
6 BMBF Research Hub 6G-Life, Technical University of Munich, 80333 Munich, Germany
7 Munich Center for Quantum Science and Technology (MCQST), Schellingstr. 4, 80799 Munich, Germany
8 Department of Electrical and Computer Engineering, Princeton University, Princeton, NJ 08544, USA
* Correspondence: onur.gunlu@liu.se

Citation: Günlü, O.; Schaefer, R.F.; Boche, H.; Poor, H.V. Information Theoretic Methods for Future Communication Systems. *Entropy* **2023**, *25*, 392. https://doi.org/10.3390/e25030392

Received: 13 February 2023
Accepted: 15 February 2023
Published: 21 February 2023

It is anticipated that future communication systems will involve the use of new technologies, requiring high-speed computations using large amounts of data, in order to take advantage of data-driven methods for improving services and providing reliability and other benefits. In many cases, information theory can provide a fundamental understanding of the limits to the reliability, robustness, secrecy, privacy, resiliency, and latency of such systems. The aim of this Featured Special Issue has been to develop a collection of top information and coding theoretic results that provide insight into future communication and computation systems.

The top-notch quality contributions to this Featured Special Issue consist of 11 articles, one of which is a review article. The topics touched upon include a multi-layer grant-free transmission method [1], a direct transform-coding approach that maps the delay-Doppler domain to the time domain [2], degree-of-freedom bounds for multi-antenna, multi-user, and frequency-selective interference channels with an instantaneous relay with or without coordination [3], new coded caching methods to reduce latency with user cooperation and simultaneous transmission [4], and a low-resolution downlink precoding method for multi-input single-output channels with orthogonal frequency-division multiplexing [5]. Furthermore, machine learning methods are discussed in the context of knowledge graphs for semantic communications [6] and in a review of the state-of-the-art coding methods for large-scale distributed machine learning [7]. Focusing on coding theory over rings, a new weight that extends the traditional Hamming weight used for algebraic structures is proposed and its properties are analyzed in [8]. Moreover, security aspects for future communication and computation systems are considered to analyze Gaussian wiretap channels with a jammer that overhears the transmissions [9], to propose new polynomial codes that enable straggler-tolerant secure matrix multiplication [10], and to illustrate the private-key rate regimes observed when reconstructing source sequences at another node with side information under privacy and security constraints [11]. It is expected that these contributions will have a significant impact on the applications of information and coding theory to future communication and computation systems.

Acknowledgments: The Guest Editors are grateful to all authors, anonymous reviewers, and the *Entropy* Editors for their great contributions to this Featured Special Issue. Our work was partially supported by the German Federal Ministry of Education and Research (BMBF) within the national initiative on 6G Communication Systems through the research hub *6G-life* under Grants 16KISK001K and 16KISK002, which motivated and greatly assisted the Guest Editors in putting together this Featured Special Issue. Moreover, this Featured Special Issue was also supported by the ZENITH Research and Career Development Fund, ELLIIT funding endowed by the Swedish government, and U.S. National Science Foundation (NSF) Grant with no. CCF-1908308.

Conflicts of Interest: The authors declare no conflict of interest.

References

1. Zohdy, M.; Tajer, A.; Shamai, S. Broadcast Approach to Uplink NOMA: Queuing Delay Analysis. *Entropy* **2022**, *24*, 1757. [CrossRef] [PubMed]
2. Lampel, F.; Joudeh, H.; Alvarado, A.; Willems, F.M.J. Orthogonal Time Frequency Space Modulation Based on the Discrete Zak Transform. *Entropy* **2022**, *24*, 1704. [CrossRef] [PubMed]
3. Abdollahi Bafghi, A.H.; Mirmohseni, M.; Nasiri-Kenari, M. Degrees of Freedom of a K-User Interference Channel in the Presence of an Instantaneous Relay. *Entropy* **2022**, *24*, 1078. [CrossRef] [PubMed]
4. Huang, Z.; Chen, J.; You, X.; Ma, S.; Wu, Y. Coded Caching for Broadcast Networks with User Cooperation. *Entropy* **2022**, *24*, 1034. [CrossRef] [PubMed]
5. Nedelcu, A.S.; Steiner, F.; Kramer, G. Low-Resolution Precoding for Multi-Antenna Downlink Channels and OFDM. *Entropy* **2022**, *24*, 504. [CrossRef] [PubMed]
6. Jiang, S.; Liu, Y.; Zhang, Y.; Luo, P.; Cao, K.; Xiong, J.; Zhao, H.; Wei, J. Reliable Semantic Communication System Enabled by Knowledge Graph. *Entropy* **2022**, *24*, 846. [CrossRef] [PubMed]
7. Xiao, M.; Skoglund, M. Coding for Large-Scale Distributed Machine Learning. *Entropy* **2022**, *24*, 1284. [CrossRef] [PubMed]
8. Gassner, N.; Greferath, M.; Rosenthal, J.; Weger, V. Bounds for Coding Theory over Rings. *Entropy* **2022**, *24*, 1473. [CrossRef]
9. Chou, R.A.; Yener, A. Gaussian Multiuser Wiretap Channels in the Presence of a Jammer-Aided Eavesdropper. *Entropy* **2022**, *24*, 1595. [CrossRef] [PubMed]
10. Byrne, E.; Gnilke, O.W.; Kliewer, J. Straggler- and Adversary-Tolerant Secure Distributed Matrix Multiplication Using Polynomial Codes. *Entropy* **2023**, *25*, 266. [CrossRef]
11. Günlü, O.; Schaefer, R.F.; Boche, H.; Poor, H.V. Private Key and Decoder Side Information for Secure and Private Source Coding. *Entropy* **2022**, *24*, 1716. [CrossRef] [PubMed]

entropy

MDPI

Article

Low-Resolution Precoding for Multi-Antenna Downlink Channels and OFDM †

Andrei Stefan Nedelcu [1], Fabian Steiner [2] and Gerhard Kramer [2,*]

1 Optical and Quantum Laboratory, Huawei Munich Research Center, 80992 Munich, Germany; andrei.nedelcu2@huawei.com
2 Institute for Communications Engineering, Technical University of Munich (TUM), 80333 Munich, Germany; fabian.steiner@tum.de
* Correspondence: gerhard.kramer@tum.de
† The results of this paper have been presented in part at the Workshop on Smart Antennas (WSA) 2018.

Abstract: Downlink precoding is considered for multi-path multi-input single-output channels where the base station uses orthogonal frequency-division multiplexing and low-resolution signaling. A quantized coordinate minimization (QCM) algorithm is proposed and its performance is compared to other precoding algorithms including squared infinity-norm relaxation (SQUID), multi-antenna greedy iterative quantization (MAGIQ), and maximum safety margin precoding. MAGIQ and QCM achieve the highest information rates and QCM has the lowest complexity measured in the number of multiplications. The information rates are computed for pilot-aided channel estimation and data-aided channel estimation. Bit error rates for a 5G low-density parity-check code confirm the information-theoretic calculations. Simulations with imperfect channel knowledge at the transmitter show that the performance of QCM and SQUID degrades in a similar fashion as zero-forcing precoding with high resolution quantizers.

Keywords: massive MIMO; precoding; coarse quantization; coordinate descent; information rates

Citation: Nedelcu, A.S.; Steiner, F.; Kramer, G. Low-Resolution Precoding for Multi-Antenna Downlink Channels and OFDM. *Entropy* **2022**, *24*, 504. https://doi.org/10.3390/e24040504

Academic Editor: Syed A. Jafar

Received: 13 February 2022
Accepted: 27 March 2022
Published: 4 April 2022
Corrected: 3 March 2023

1. Introduction

Massive multiple-input multiple-output (MIMO) base stations can serve many user equipments (UEs) with high spectral efficiency and simplified signal processing [1,2]. However, their implementation is challenging due to the cost and energy consumption of analog-to-digital and digital-to-analog converters (ADCs/DACs) and linear power amplifiers (PAs). There are several approaches to lower cost. One approach is hybrid beamforming with analog beamformers in the radio frequency (RF) chain of each antenna and where the digital baseband processing is shared among RF chains. Second, constant envelope waveforms permit using non-linear PAs. Third, all-digital approaches use low-resolution ADCs/DACs or low-resolution digitally controlled RF chains. The focus of this paper is on the all-digital approach.

1.1. Single-Carrier Transmission

We study the multi-antenna downlink and UEs with one antenna each, a model referred to as multi-user multi-input single-output (MU-MISO). Most works on low-cost precoding for MU-MISO consider phase-shift keying (PSK) to lower the requirements on the PAs. For instance, the early papers [3,4] (see also [5]) use iterative coordinate-wise optimization to choose transmit symbols from a continuous PSK alphabet for flat and frequency-selective (or multipath) fading, respectively. We remark that these papers do not include an optimization parameter (called α below, see (8)) in their cost function, which plays an important role at high signal-to-noise ratio (SNR), see [6,7]. This parameter is related to linear minimum-mean square error (MMSE) precoding.

Most works consider discrete alphabet signaling. Perhaps the simplest approach, called quantized linear precoding (QLP), applies a linear precoder followed by one low-resolution quantizer per antenna [8–15]. Our focus is on zero forcing (ZF), and we use the acronyms LP-ZF and QLP-ZF, respectively, for unquantized ZF and the QLP version of ZF.

More sophisticated approaches use optimization tools as in [3,4]. For example, the papers [16–18] use convex relaxation methods; Refs. [19–25] apply coordinate-wise optimization; Refs. [26–28] develops a symbol-wise Maximum Safety Margin (MSM) precoder; Refs. [29–32] use a branch-and-bound (BB) algorithm; Ref. [33] uses a majorization-minimization algorithm; Ref. [34] uses integer programming; and [35,36] use neural networks (NNs). These references are collected in Table 1 together with the papers listed below on orthogonal frequency-division multiplexing (OFDM). As the table shows, most papers focus on single-carrier and flat fading channels.

Table 1. References for quantized precoding.

		Precoding Algorithm			
Modulation	**Fading**	**QLP**	**Convex Relaxation**	**Coord.-Wise Optimization**	**Other (MSM, BB, NN, etc.)**
1 Carrier	Flat	[8–15]	[16–18]	[19–25]	[26,27,29–36]
	Freq.-Sel.				[28]
OFDM	Freq.-Sel.	[37]	[38]	[39–41]	[42,43]

1.2. Discrete Signaling and OFDM

Our main interest is discrete-alphabet precoding for multipath channels with OFDM as in 5G wireless systems. Precoding for OFDM is challenging because the alphabet constraint is in the time domain after the inverse discrete Fourier transform (IDFT) rather than in the frequency domain. We further focus on using information theory to derive achievable rates. For this purpose, we consider two types of channel estimation at the receivers: pilot-aided channel estimation via pilot-aided transmission (PAT) and data-aided channel estimation.

Discrete-alphabet precoding for OFDM was treated in Ref. [37], who used QLP and low resolution DACs. A more sophisticated approach appeared in Ref. [38], who applied a squared-infinity norm Douglas-Rachford splitting (SQUID) algorithm to minimize a quadratic cost function in the frequency domain. The performance was illustrated via bit error rate (BER) simulations with convolutional codes and QPSK or 16-quadrature amplitude modulation (QAM) by using 1–3 bits of phase quantization.

The paper [39] instead proposed an algorithm called multi-antenna greedy iterative quantization (MAGIQ) that builds on [19] and uses coordinate-wise optimization of a quadratic cost function in the time domain. MAGIQ may thus be considered an extended version of [4] for OFDM and discrete alphabets. Simulations showed that MAGIQ outperforms SQUID in terms of complexity and achievable rates. Another coordinate-wise optimization algorithm appeared in [40,41] that builds on the papers [21,22]. The algorithm is called constant envelope symbol level precoding (CESLP) and it is similar to the refinement of MAGIQ presented here. The main difference is that, as in [38], the optimization in [40,41] uses a cost function in the frequency domain rather than the time domain. We remark that processing in the time domain has advantages that are described in Section 3.1.

The MSM algorithm was extended to OFDM in [42]. MSM works well at low and intermediate rates but MAGIQ outperforms MSM at high rates both in terms of complexity and achievable rates. Finally, the recent paper [43] uses generalized approximate message passing (GAMP) for OFDM.

1.3. Contributions and Organization

The contributions of this paper are as follows.

- The analysis of MAGIQ in the workshop paper [39] is extended to larger systems and more realistic channel conditions;
- Replacing the greedy antenna selection rule of MAGIQ with a fixed (round-robin) schedule is shown to cause negligible rate loss. The new algorithm is named quantized coordinate minimization (QCM);
- The performance of QLP-ZF, SQUID, MSM, MAGIQ, and QCM are compared in terms of complexity (number of multiplications and iterations) and achievable rates;
- We develop an auxiliary channel model to compute achievable rates for pilot-aided and data-aided channel estimation. The models let one compare modulations, precoders, channels, and receivers;
- Simulations with a 5G NR low-density parity-check (LDPC) code [44] show that the computed rate and power gains accurately predict the gains of standard channel codes;
- Simulations with imperfect channel knowledge at the base station show that the achievable rates of SQUID and QCM degrade as gracefully as those of LP-ZF.

We remark that our focus is on algorithms that approximate ZF based on channel inversion, i.e., there is no attempt to optimize transmit powers across subcarriers. This approach simplifies OFDM channel estimation at the receivers because the precoder makes all subcarriers have approximately the same channel magnitude and phase. For instance, a rapid and accurate channel estimate is obtained for each OFDM symbol by averaging the channel estimates of the subcarriers, see Section 4.1. Of course, it is interesting to develop algorithms for other precoders and for subcarrier power allocation.

This paper is organized as follows. Section 2 introduces the baseband model and OFDM signaling. Section 3 describes the MAGIQ and QCM precoders. Section 4 develops theory for achievable rates, presents complexity comparisons, and reviews a model for imperfect channel state information (CSI). Section 5 compares achievable rates and BERs with 5G NR LDPC codes. Section 6 concludes the paper.

2. System Model

Figure 1 shows a MU-MISO system with N transmit antennas and K UEs that each have a single antenna. The base station has one message per UE and each antenna has a resolution of 1 bit for the amplitude (on-off switch) and b bits for the phase per antenna. All other hardware components are ideal: linear, infinite bandwidth, no distortions except for additive white Gaussian noise (AWGN).

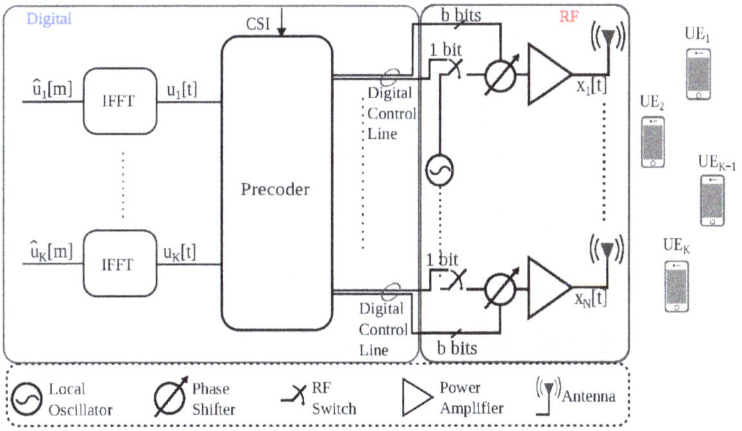

Figure 1. Multi-user MIMO downlink with a low resolution digitally controlled analog architecture.

2.1. Baseband Channel Model

The discrete-time baseband channel is modeled as a finite impulse response filter between each pair of transmit and receive antennas. Let $x_n[t]$ be the symbol of transmit antenna n at time t and let $\boldsymbol{x}[t] = (x_1[t] \ \dots \ x_N[t])^T$. Similarly, let $y_k[t]$ be the received symbol of UE k at time t and let $\boldsymbol{y}[t] = (y_1[t] \ \dots \ y_K[t])^T$. The channel model is

$$\boldsymbol{y}[t] = \sum_{\tau=0}^{L-1} \boldsymbol{H}[\tau]\boldsymbol{x}[t-\tau] + \boldsymbol{z}[t] \tag{1}$$

where the noise $\boldsymbol{z}[t] = (z_1[t] \ \dots \ z_K[t])^T$ has circularly-symmetric, complex, Gaussian entries that are independent and have variance σ^2, i.e., we have $\boldsymbol{z} \sim \mathcal{CN}(\boldsymbol{0}, \sigma^2 \boldsymbol{I})$. The $\boldsymbol{H}[\tau]$, $\tau = 0, \dots, L-1$, are $K \times N$ matrices representing the channel impulse response, i.e., we have

$$\boldsymbol{H}[\tau] = \begin{pmatrix} h_{11}[\tau] & h_{12}[\tau] & \dots & h_{1N}[\tau] \\ h_{21}[\tau] & h_{22}[\tau] & \dots & h_{2N}[\tau] \\ \vdots & \vdots & \ddots & \vdots \\ h_{K1}[\tau] & h_{K2}[\tau] & \dots & h_{KN}[\tau] \end{pmatrix} \tag{2}$$

where $h_{kn}[.]$ is the channel impulse response from the n-th antenna at the base station to the k-th UE. For instance, a Rayleigh fading multi-path channel with a uniform power delay profile (PDP) has $h_{kn}[\tau] \sim \mathcal{CN}(0, 1/L)$ and these taps are independent and identically distributed (iid) for all k, n, τ.

The vector $\boldsymbol{x}[t]$ is constrained to have entries taken from a discrete and finite alphabet

$$\mathcal{X} = \{0\} \cup \left\{ \sqrt{\frac{P}{N}} \, \mathrm{e}^{\mathrm{j}2\pi q/2^b}; q = 0, 1, 2, \dots, 2^b - 1 \right\}. \tag{3}$$

The transmit energy clearly satisfies $\|\boldsymbol{x}[t]\|^2 \le P$ and we define $\mathrm{SNR} = P/\sigma^2$. The inequality is due to the 0 symbol that permits antenna selection. Antenna selection was also used in [45] to enforce sparsity. Our intent is rather to allow antennas not to be used if they do not improve performance.

2.2. OFDM Signaling

Figure 1 shows how OFDM can be combined with the precoder. Let $T = T_F + T_c$ be the OFDM blocklength with T_F symbols for the DFT and T_c symbols for the cyclic prefix. We assume that $T_F \ge L$ and $T_c \ge L-1$. For simplicity, all T_F subcarriers carry data and we do not include the cyclic prefix overhead in our rate calculations below, i.e., the rates in bits per channel use (bpcu) are computed by normalizing by T_F.

Consider the frequency-domain modulation alphabet $\hat{\mathcal{U}}$ that has a finite number of elements, e.g., QPSK has $\hat{\mathcal{U}} = \{\hat{u} : \hat{u} = (\pm 1 \pm \mathrm{j})/\sqrt{2}\}$. Messages are mapped to the frequency-domain vectors $\hat{\boldsymbol{u}}[m] = (\hat{u}_1[m], \dots, \hat{u}_K[m])^{\mathrm{T}}$ for subcarriers $m = 0, \dots, T_F - 1$ that are converted to time-domain vectors $\boldsymbol{u}[t]$ by IDFTs

$$u_k[t] = \frac{1}{T_F} \sum_{m=0}^{T_F-1} \hat{u}_k[m] e^{\mathrm{j}2\pi mt/T_F} \tag{4}$$

for times $t = 0, \dots, T_F - 1$ and UEs $k = 1, \dots, K$. For the simulations below, we generated the $\hat{u}_k[m]$ uniformly from finite constellations such as 16-QAM or 64-QAM. We assume that $\mathrm{E}[\hat{u}_k[m]] = 0$ for all k and m. Each UE k uses a DFT to convert its time-domain symbols $y_k[t]$ to the frequency-domain symbols

$$\hat{y}_k[m] = \sum_{t=0}^{T_F-1} y_k[t] e^{-\mathrm{j}2\pi mt/T_F}. \tag{5}$$

2.3. Linear MMSE Precoding

To describe the linear MMSE precoder, consider the channel from base station antenna n to UE k:

$$\boldsymbol{h}_{kn} = (h_{kn}[0], \ldots, h_{kn}[L-1], \underbrace{0, \ldots, 0}_{(T_F - L)\text{ zeros}})^{\mathrm{T}} \tag{6}$$

and denote its DFT as $\hat{\boldsymbol{h}}_{kn} = (\hat{h}_{kn}[0], \ldots, \hat{h}_{kn}[T_F - 1])^{\mathrm{T}}$. The channel of subcarrier m is the $K \times N$ matrix $\hat{\boldsymbol{H}}[m]$ with entries $\hat{h}_{kn}[m]$ for $k = 1, \ldots, K$, $n = 1, \ldots, N$. The linear MMSE precoder (or Wiener filter) for subcarrier m is

$$P[m]\hat{\boldsymbol{H}}[m]^{\dagger}\left(P[m]\hat{\boldsymbol{H}}[m]\hat{\boldsymbol{H}}[m]^{\dagger} + \sigma^2 \boldsymbol{I}\right)^{-1} \tag{7}$$

where $P[m] = \mathrm{E}[|\hat{u}_k[m]|^2]$ is the same for all k, $\hat{\boldsymbol{H}}[m]^{\dagger}$ is the Hermitian of $\hat{\boldsymbol{H}}[m]$, and $\boldsymbol{I}$ is the $K \times K$ identity matrix. The precoder multiplies $\hat{\boldsymbol{u}}[m]$ by (7) for all subcarriers m, and performs N IDFTs to compute the resulting $\boldsymbol{x}[0], \ldots, \boldsymbol{x}[T_F - 1]$. We remark that ZF precoding is the same as (7) but with $\sigma^2 = 0$, where $\hat{\boldsymbol{H}}[m]\hat{\boldsymbol{H}}[m]^{\dagger}$ is usually invertible if N is much larger than K.

3. Quantized Precoding

We wish to ensure compatibility with respect to LP-ZF. In other words, each receiver k should ideally see signals $u_k[t]$, $t = 0, \ldots, T-1$, that were generated from the frequency-domain signals $\hat{u}_k[m]$, $m = 0, \ldots, T_F - 1$. Let $\boldsymbol{u}[t] = (u_1[t] \;\ldots\; u_K[t])^T$ and define the time-domain mean square error (MSE) cost function

$$\begin{aligned} G(\boldsymbol{x}[0], \ldots, \boldsymbol{x}[T-1], \alpha) &= \sum_{t=0}^{T-1} \mathrm{E}_{\boldsymbol{z}[t]}\left[\|\boldsymbol{u}[t] - \alpha \boldsymbol{y}[t]\|^2\right] \\ &= \sum_{t=0}^{T-1}\left\|\boldsymbol{u}[t] - \alpha \sum_{\tau=0}^{L-1} \boldsymbol{H}[\tau]\boldsymbol{x}[t-\tau]\right\|^2 + \alpha^2 T K \sigma^2 \end{aligned} \tag{8}$$

where $\mathrm{E}_{\boldsymbol{z}[t]}[\cdot]$ denotes the expectation with respect to the noise $\boldsymbol{z}[t]$. The optimization problem is as follows:

$$\begin{aligned} \min_{\boldsymbol{x}[0],\ldots,\boldsymbol{x}[T-1],\,\alpha} \quad & G(\boldsymbol{x}[0], \ldots, \boldsymbol{x}[T-1], \alpha) \\ \text{s.t.} \quad & \boldsymbol{x}[t] \in \mathcal{X}^N,\ t = 0, \ldots, T-1 \\ & \alpha > 0. \end{aligned} \tag{9}$$

The parameter α in (8) and (9) can easily be optimized for fixed $\boldsymbol{x}[0], \ldots, \boldsymbol{x}[T-1]$ and the result is (see [18] Equation (26))

$$\alpha = \frac{\sum_{t=0}^{T-1} \mathrm{Re}\left(\boldsymbol{u}[t]^{\mathrm{H}} \sum_{\tau=0}^{L-1} \boldsymbol{H}[\tau]\boldsymbol{x}[t-\tau]\right)}{\sum_{t=0}^{T}\left\|\sum_{\tau=0}^{L-1} \boldsymbol{H}[\tau]\boldsymbol{x}[t-\tau]\right\|^2 + TK\sigma^2}. \tag{10}$$

For the MAGIQ and QCM algorithms below, we use alternating minimization to find the $\boldsymbol{x}[0], \ldots, \boldsymbol{x}[T-1]$ and α. For the linear MMSE precoder, we label the α in (10) as α_{WF}.

Observe that we use the same α for all K UEs because all UEs experience the same shadowing, i.e., all K UEs see the same average power. For UE-dependent shadowing, a more general approach would be to replace α with a diagonal matrix with K parameters α_k, $k = 1, \ldots, K$, and then modify (8) appropriately.

3.1. MAGIQ and QCM

For multipath channels, the vector $\boldsymbol{x}[t]$ influences the channel output at times t, $t+1, \ldots, t+L-1$. A joint optimization over strings of length T seems difficult because of this influence and because of the finite alphabet constraint for the $x_n[t]$. Instead, MAGIQ splits the optimization into sub-problems with reduced complexity by applying coordinate-wise minimization across the antennas and iterating over the OFDM symbol.

For this purpose, consider the precoding problem for time t' starting at $t'=0$ and ending at $t'=T-1$. Observe that $\boldsymbol{x}[t']$ influences at most L summands in (8), namely the summands for $t=(t')_T, \ldots, (t'+L-1)_T$ where $(t)_T = \min(t, T-1)$. To compute the new cost after updating the symbol $x_n[t']$, one may thus compute sums of the form

$$\sum_{t=(t')_T,\ldots,(t'+L-1)_T} \left\| \boldsymbol{u}[t] - \alpha \sum_{\tau=0}^{L-1} \boldsymbol{H}[\tau]\boldsymbol{x}[t-\tau] \right\|^2 \tag{11}$$

for $t'=0,\ldots,T-1$. In both cases, one computes a first and second sum having the old and new $x_n[t']$, respectively. One then takes the difference and adds the result to (8) to obtain the updated cost.

We remark that the time-domain cost function (8) is closely related to the frequency-domain cost functions in [38,40,41]. However, the time-domain approach is more versatile as it can include acyclic phenomena such as interference from previous OFDM blocks. The time-domain approach is also slightly simpler because updating the symbol $x_n[t']$ in (8) or (11) requires taking the norm of at most L vectors of dimension K for each test symbol in $\mathcal{X}$ while the frequency-domain approach in ([40] Equation (17)) takes the norm of T_F vectors of dimension K for each test symbol. Recall that $T_F \geq L$, and usually $T_F \geq 10L$ to avoid losing too much efficiency with the cyclic prefix that has length $T_c \geq L-1$.

The MAGIQ algorithm is summarized in Algorithm 1. MAGIQ steps through time in a cyclic fashion for fixed α. At each time t, it initializes the antenna set $\mathcal{S} = \{1,\ldots,N\}$ and performs a greedy search for the antenna n and symbol $x_n[t]$ that minimize (8) (one may equivalently consider sums of L norms as in (11)). The resulting antenna is removed from $\mathcal{S}$ and a new greedy search is performed to find the antenna in the new $\mathcal{S}$ and the symbol that minimizes (8) while the previous symbol assignments are held fixed. This step is repeated until $\mathcal{S}$ is empty. MAGIQ then moves to the next time and repeats the procedure. To determine α, MAGIQ applies alternating minimization with respect to α and the precoder output $\{\boldsymbol{x}[t] : t=0,\ldots,T-1\}$. For fixed $\boldsymbol{x}[.]$ the minimization can be solved in closed form, see (10) and line 22 of Algorithm 1.

Simulations show that MAGIQ exhibits good performance and converges quickly [39]. However, the greedy selection considerably increases the computational complexity. We thus replace the minimization over $\mathcal{S}$ in line 9 of Algorithm 1) with a round-robin schedule or a random permutation. We found that both approaches perform equally well. The new QCM algorithm performs as well as MAGIQ but with a simpler search and a small increase in the number of iterations.

Finally, one might expect that α is close to the α_{WF} of the transmit Wiener filter [6,7] since our cost function accounts for the noise power. However, Figure 2 shows that this is true only at low SNR. The figure plots the average α of the QCM algorithm, called α_{QCM}, against the computed α_{WF} for simulations with System A in Section 5. Note that α_{QCM} is generally larger than α_{WF}.

Algorithm 1 MAGIQ and QCM precoding.

1: **procedure** PRECODE(Algo, $H[.], u[.]$)
2:    $x^{(0)}[.] = x[.]_{init}$
3:    $\alpha^{(0)} = \alpha_{init}$
4:    **for** $i = 1 : I$ **do** // iterate over OFDM block
5:      **for** $t = 0 : T - 1$ **do**
6:         $\mathcal{S} = \{1, \ldots, N\}$
7:         **while** $\mathcal{S} \neq \varnothing$ **do**
8:           **if** Algo = MAGIQ **then**
9:             $(x_{n^\star}^\star, n^\star) = \mathrm{argmin}_{\tilde{x}_n \in \mathcal{X}, n \in \mathcal{S}}$
10:             $G\Big(x^{(i)}[0], \ldots, x^{(i)}[t-1], \tilde{x},$
11:             $x^{(i-1)}[t+1], \ldots, x^{(i-1)}[T-1], \alpha^{(i-1)}\Big)$
12:           **else** // Algo = QCM
13:             $n^\star = \min \mathcal{S}$ // round-robin schedule
14:             $x_{n^\star}^\star = \mathrm{argmin}_{\tilde{x}_{n^\star} \in \mathcal{X}}$
15:             $G\Big(x^{(i)}[0], \ldots, x^{(i)}[t-1], \tilde{x},$
16:             $x^{(i-1)}[t+1], \ldots, x^{(i-1)}[T-1], \alpha^{(i-1)}\Big)$
17:           **end if**
18:           $x_{n^\star}^{(i)}[t] = x_{n^\star}^\star$ // update antenna $n^\star$ at time t
19:           $\mathcal{S} \leftarrow \mathcal{S} \setminus \{n^\star\}$
20:         **end while**
21:      **end for**
22:      $\alpha^{(i)} = \dfrac{\sum_{t=0}^{T-1} \mathrm{Re}\left(u[t]^{\mathrm{H}} \sum_{\tau=0}^{L-1} H[\tau] x^{(i)}[t-\tau]\right)}{\sum_{t=0}^{T} \left\| \sum_{\tau=0}^{L-1} H[\tau] x^{(i)}[t-\tau] \right\|^2 + TK\sigma^2}$
23:    **end for**
24:    **return** $x[.] = x^{(I)}[.], \alpha = \alpha^{(I)}$
25: **end procedure**

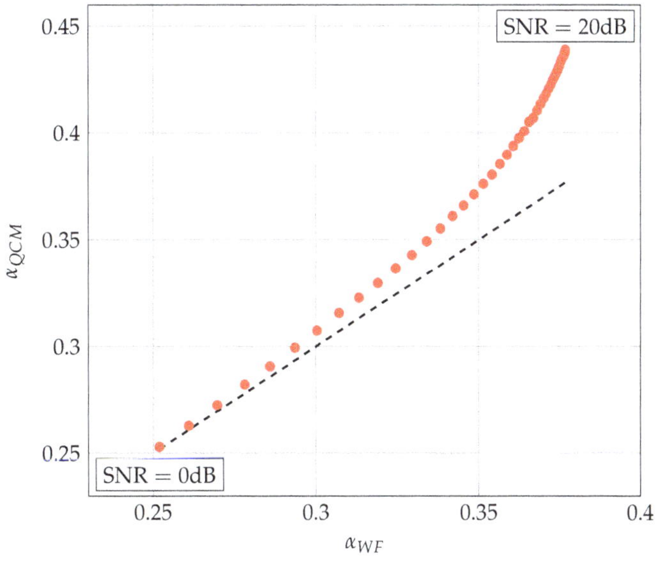

Figure 2. α_{QCM} vs. α_{WF} for System A of Table 2 and 64-QAM.

Table 2. System parameters for the simulations.

System	N	K	$T = T_F + T_c$	L	Constellation	b	Fading Statistics
A	128	16	$270 = 256 + 14$	15	$\{16, 64\}$-QAM	2, 3	Flat and Rayleigh uniform PDP
B	64	8	$35 = 32 + 3$	4	{4-32}-PSK	2	Rayleigh uniform PDP
C	80	8	$277 = 256 + 21$ $286 = 256 + 30$	22 varies	16-QAM	2	Rayleigh uniform PDP Winner2 NLOS C2 urban
D	128	16	$410 = 396 + 14$	15	64-QAM	2	Rayleigh uniform PDP

4. Performance Metrics

4.1. Achievable Rates

We use generalized mutual information (GMI) to compute achievable rates [46,47], (Ex. 5.22) which is a standard tool to compare coded systems. Consider a generic input distribution $P(\boldsymbol{x})$ and a generic channel density $p(\boldsymbol{y}|\boldsymbol{x})$ where $\boldsymbol{x} = (x_1, \ldots, x_S)^T$ and $\boldsymbol{y} = (y_1, \ldots, y_S)^T$ each have S symbols. A lower bound to the mutual information

$$\mathrm{I}(\boldsymbol{X};\boldsymbol{Y}) = \sum_{\boldsymbol{x},\boldsymbol{y}} P(\boldsymbol{x})p(\boldsymbol{y}|\boldsymbol{x}) \log_2\left(\frac{p(\boldsymbol{y}|\boldsymbol{x})}{\sum_{\boldsymbol{a}} P(\boldsymbol{a})\, p(\boldsymbol{y}|\boldsymbol{a})}\right) \tag{12}$$

is the GMI

$$\mathrm{I}_{q,s}(\boldsymbol{X};\boldsymbol{Y}) = \sum_{\boldsymbol{x},\boldsymbol{y}} P(\boldsymbol{x})p(\boldsymbol{y}|\boldsymbol{x}) \log_2\left(\frac{q(\boldsymbol{y}|\boldsymbol{x})^s}{\sum_{\boldsymbol{a}} P(\boldsymbol{a})\, q(\boldsymbol{y}|\boldsymbol{a})^s}\right) \tag{13}$$

where $q(\boldsymbol{y}|\boldsymbol{x})$ is any auxiliary density and $s \geq 0$. In other words, the choices $q(\boldsymbol{y}|\boldsymbol{x}) = p(\boldsymbol{y}|\boldsymbol{x})$ for all $\boldsymbol{x}, \boldsymbol{y}$ and $s = 1$ maximize the GMI. However, the idea is that $p(\boldsymbol{y}|\boldsymbol{x})$ may be unknown or difficult to compute and so one chooses a simple $q(\boldsymbol{y}|\boldsymbol{x})$. The reason why $p(\boldsymbol{y}|\boldsymbol{x})$ is difficult to compute here is because we will measure the GMI across the end-to-end channels from the $\hat{u}_k[m]$ to the $\hat{y}_k[m]$ and the quantized precoding introduces non-linearities in these channels. The final step in evaluating the GMI is maximizing over $s \geq 0$. Alternatively, one might wish to simply focus on $s = 1$, e.g., see [48].

We study the GMI of two non-coherent systems: classic PAT and data-aided channel estimation. For both systems, we apply memoryless signaling with the product distribution

$$P(\boldsymbol{x}) = \prod_{i=1}^{S_p} 1(x_i = x_{p,i}) \cdot \prod_{i=S_p+1}^{S} P(x_i) \tag{14}$$

where the $x_{p,i}$ are pilot symbols, $1(a = b)$ is the indicator function that takes on the value 1 if its argument is true and 0 otherwise, and $P(x)$ is a uniform distribution. Joint data and channel estimation has $S_p = 0$ so that we have only the second product in (14). At the receiver we use the auxiliary channel

$$q(\boldsymbol{y}|\boldsymbol{x}) = \prod_{i=1}^{S} q_{\boldsymbol{x},\boldsymbol{y}}(y_i \mid x_i) \tag{15}$$

where the symbol channel $q_{\boldsymbol{x},\boldsymbol{y}}(.)$ is a function of $\boldsymbol{x}$ and $\boldsymbol{y}$. Observe that $q_{\boldsymbol{x},\boldsymbol{y}}(.)$ is invariant for S symbols and the channel can be considered to have memory since every symbol x_ℓ or y_ℓ, $\ell = 1, \ldots, S$, influences the channel for all "times" $i = 1, \ldots, S$. The GMI rate (13) simplifies to

$$\sum_{\boldsymbol{x},\boldsymbol{y}} P(\boldsymbol{x})p(\boldsymbol{y}|\boldsymbol{x}) \sum_{i=S_p+1}^{S} \log_2\left(\frac{q_{\boldsymbol{x},\boldsymbol{y}}(y_i \mid x_i)^s}{\sum_a P(a)\, q_{\boldsymbol{x},\boldsymbol{y}}(y_i \mid a)^s}\right). \tag{16}$$

One may approximate (16) by applying the law of large numbers for stationary signals and channels. The idea is to independently generate the B pairs of vectors

$$\boldsymbol{x}^{(b)} = (x_1^{(b)}, \dots, x_S^{(b)})^T$$
$$\boldsymbol{y}^{(b)} = (y_1^{(b)}, \dots, y_S^{(b)})^T$$

for $b = 1, \dots, B$, and then the following average rate will approach $\mathrm{I}_{q,s}(\boldsymbol{X};\boldsymbol{Y})/S$ bpcu as B grows:

$$R_{\mathrm{a}} = \frac{1}{B}\sum_{b=1}^{B} R_{\mathrm{a}}^{(b)} \tag{17}$$

where

$$R_{\mathrm{a}}^{(b)} = \frac{1}{S}\sum_{i=S_p+1}^{S} \log_2\left(\frac{q_{\boldsymbol{x}^{(b)},\boldsymbol{y}^{(b)}}\left(y_i^{(b)} \mid x_i^{(b)}\right)^s}{\sum_a P(a)\, q_{\boldsymbol{x}^{(b)},\boldsymbol{y}^{(b)}}\left(y_i^{(b)} \mid a\right)^s}\right). \tag{18}$$

We choose the Gaussian auxiliary density

$$q_{\boldsymbol{x},\boldsymbol{y}}(y|x) = \frac{1}{\pi\sigma_q^2}\exp\left(-\frac{|y - h \cdot x|^2}{\sigma_q^2}\right) \tag{19}$$

where for pilot-aided transmission (PAT) the receiver computes joint maximum likelihood (ML) estimates with sums of S_p terms:

$$\begin{aligned} h &= \frac{\sum_{i=1}^{S_p} y_i \cdot x_i^*}{\sum_{i=1}^{S_p} |x_i^2|} \\ \sigma_q^2 &= \frac{1}{S_p}\sum_{i=1}^{S_p} |y_i - h \cdot x_i|^2. \end{aligned} \tag{20}$$

For the data-aided detector we replace S_p with S in (20). Note that for the Gaussian channel (19) the parameter s multiplies $1/\sigma_q^2$ in (16) or (18), and optimizing s turns out to be the same as choosing the best parameter σ_q^2 when $s = 1$.

Summarizing, we use the following steps to evaluate achievable rates. Suppose the coherence time is S/T_F OFDM symbols where S is a multiple of T_F. We index the channel symbols by the pairs (ℓ, m) where ℓ is the OFDM symbol and m is the subcarrier, $1 \le \ell \le S/T_F$, $0 \le m \le T-1$. We collect the pilot index pairs in the set $\mathcal{S}_p$ that has cardinality S_p, and we write the channel inputs and outputs of UE k for OFDM symbol ℓ and subcarrier m as $\hat{u}_k[\ell, m]$ and $\hat{y}_k[\ell, m]$, respectively.

1. Repeat the following steps (2)–(4) B times; index the steps by $b = 1, \dots, B$;
2. Use Monte Carlo simulation to generate the symbols $\hat{u}_k[\ell, m]$ and $\hat{y}_k[\ell, m]$ for $k = 1, \dots, K$, $\ell = 1, \dots, S/T_F$, and $m = 0, \dots, T-1$;
3. Each UE estimates its own channel h_k and $\sigma_{q,k}^2$, i.e., the channel estimate (20) of UE k is

$$\begin{aligned} h_k &= \frac{\sum_{(\ell,m)\in\mathcal{S}_p} \hat{y}_k[\ell, m] \cdot \hat{u}_k[\ell, m]^*}{\sum_{(\ell,m)\in\mathcal{S}_p} |\hat{u}_k[\ell, m]|^2} \\ \sigma_{q,k}^2 &= \frac{1}{S_p}\sum_{(\ell,m)\in\mathcal{S}_p} |\hat{y}_k[\ell, m] - h_k \cdot \hat{u}_k[\ell, m]|^2. \end{aligned} \tag{21}$$

For the data-aided detector, in (21) we replace $\mathcal{S}_p$ with the set of all index pairs (ℓ, m), and we replace S_p with S;

4. Compute $R_{\mathrm{a}}^{(b)}$ in (18) for each UE k by averaging, i.e., the rate for UE k is

$$R_{\mathrm{a},k}^{(b)} = \frac{1}{S} \sum_{(\ell,m)\notin \mathcal{S}_p} \log_2 \left(\frac{q_{\hat{\boldsymbol{u}}_k,\hat{\boldsymbol{y}}_k}(\hat{y}_k[\ell,m] \mid \hat{u}_k[\ell,m])^s}{\sum_a P(a)\, q_{\hat{\boldsymbol{u}}_k,\hat{\boldsymbol{y}}_k}(\hat{y}_k[\ell,m] \mid a)^s} \right) \tag{22}$$

where $\hat{\boldsymbol{u}}_k$ and $\hat{\boldsymbol{y}}_k$ are vectors collecting the $\hat{u}_k[\ell,m]$ and $\hat{y}_k[\ell,m]$, respectively, for all pairs (ℓ,m). For the data-aided detector we set $\mathcal{S}_p = \emptyset$ in (22);
5. Compute R_{a} in (17) for each UE, i.e., the average rate of UE k is $R_{\mathrm{a},k} = \frac{1}{B}\sum_{b=1}^{B} R_{\mathrm{a},k}^{(b)}$;
6. Compute the average UE rate $\overline{R}_{\mathrm{a}} = \frac{1}{K}\sum_{k=1}^{K} R_{\mathrm{a},k}$.

Our simulations showed that optimizing over $s \geq 0$ gives $s \approx 1$ if the channel parameters are chosen using (21).

4.2. Discussion

We make a few remarks on the lower bound. First, the receivers do not need to know α. Second, the rate R_{a} in (17) is achievable if one assumes stationarity and coding and decoding over many OFDM blocks. Third, as S grows, the channel estimate of the data-aided detector becomes more accurate and the performance approaches that of a coherent receiver. Related theory for PAT and large S is developed in [49]. However, the PAT rate is generally smaller than for a data-aided detector because the PAT channel estimate is less accurate and because PAT does not use all symbols for data.

We remark that blind channel estimation can approach the performance of data-aided receivers for large S. Blind channel estimation algorithms can, e.g., be based on high-order statistics and iterative channel estimation and decoding. For polar codes and low-order constellations, one may use the blind algorithms proposed in [50]. We found that the PAT rates are very close (within 0.1 bpcu) of the pilot-free rates multiplied by the rate loss factor $1 - S_p/S$ for pilot fractions as small as $S_p/S = 10\%$.

Depending on the system under consideration, we choose one of $T_F = 32{,}256{,}396$, one of $T = 35{,}270{,}277{,}286{,}410$, one of $S = 256{,}1584$, and $B = 200$. For most simulations we have $T_F = S = 256$ and estimate the channel based on individual OFDM symbols, see Section 1.3. For example, for $T = 270$ and a symbol time of 30 ns (symbol rate 33.3 MHz) the coherence time needs to be at least $(30\text{ ns}) \cdot T = 8.1\ \mu\text{s}$. Of course, the transmitter needs to know the channel also, e.g., via time-division duplex, which requires the coherence time to be substantially larger. The main point is that channel estimation at the receiver is not a bottleneck when using ZF based on channel inversion. Finally, for the coded simulations we chose $T_F = 396$ and $S = 4T_F = 1548$ because the LDPC code occupies four OFDM symbols.

4.3. Algorithmic Complexity

This section studies the algorithmic complexity in terms of the number of multiplications and iterations. The complexity of SQUID is thoroughly discussed in [38] and Table 3 shows the order estimates take from [38] (Table I). Note the large number of iterations.

Table 3. Algorithmic complexity.

Algorithm	Multiplications per Iteration	Iterations	Pre-Processing Multiplications
QLP-ZF	$\mathcal{O}(TK^3 + TK^2N)$	1	-
SQUID	$\mathcal{O}(8KNT + 8NT\log T)$	20–300	$2T \cdot (\frac{5}{3}K^3 + 3K^2N + (6N - \frac{2}{3})K)$
MSM	$\mathcal{O}(4KNT^2 + 4KT + 2NT)$	≈8400	$4KNT$
MAGIQ & QCM	$\mathcal{O}(KNTL + KNL\lvert\mathcal{X}\rvert)$	4–6	$KNT + 4NT\log T$

The complexity of MSM depends on the choice of optimization algorithm and [42] considers a simplex algorithm. Unfortunately, the simplex algorithm requires a large number of iterations to converge because this number is proportional to the number of variables and linear inequalities that grow with the system size (N, K, T). An interior point algorithm converges more quickly but has a much higher complexity per iteration.

For MAGIQ and QCM, Equation (8) shows that updating $x[.]$ requires updating L of the T terms that each require a norm calculation. The resulting terms $||u[t]||^2$ do not affect the maximization; terms such as $||\alpha Hx||_2^2$ can be pre-computed and stored with a complexity of $NKL|\mathcal{X}|$, and then reused as they do not change during the iterations. On the other hand, products of the form $\alpha u^{\mathrm{H}} Hx$ must be computed for each of the L terms for each antenna update and at each time instance, resulting in a complexity of $\mathcal{O}(NKLT)$. The initialization requires KNT multiplications and one must transform the solutions to the time domain. We neglect the cost of updating α because the terms needed to compute it are available as a byproduct of the iterative process over the time instances.

4.4. Sensitivity to Channel Uncertainty at the Transmitter

In practice, the CSI is imperfect due to noise, quantization, calibration errors, etc. We do not attempt to model these effects exactly. Instead, we adopt a standard approach based on MMSE estimation and provide the precoder with channel matrices $\tilde{H}[\tau]$ that satisfy

$$H[\tau] = \sqrt{1-\varepsilon^2}\tilde{H}[\tau] + \varepsilon Z[\tau] \tag{23}$$

where $0 \le \varepsilon \le 1$ and $Z[\tau]$ is a $K \times N$ matrix of independent, variance $\sigma_h^2 = 1/L$, complex, circularly-symmetric Gaussian entries. Note that $\varepsilon = 0$ corresponds to perfect CSI and $\varepsilon = 1$ corresponds to no CSI. The precoder treats $\tilde{H}[\tau]$ as the true channel realization for $\tau = 0, \ldots, L-1$.

5. Numerical Results

We evaluate the GMIs of four systems. The main parameters are listed in Table 2 and we provide a few more details here.

- System A: the DFT has length $T_F = 256$ and the channel has either $L = 1$ or $L = 15$ taps of Rayleigh fading with a uniform PDP. The minimum cyclic prefix length for the latter case is $T_c = 14$ so the minimum OFDM blocklength is $T = 270$;
- System B: MSM is applied to PSK. However, the MSM complexity limited the simulations to smaller parameters than for System A. The channel now has $L = 4$ taps of Rayleigh fading with a uniform PDP. The $T = 35$ OFDM symbols include a DFT of length $T_F = 32$ and a minimum cyclic prefix length of $T_c = 3$;
- System C: System C is actually two systems because we compare the performance under Rayleigh fading to the performance with the Winner2 model [51] whose number L of channel taps varies randomly. For the Winner2 channel, the choice $T_c = 30$ suffices to ensure that $T_c \ge L - 1$. The Rayleigh fading model has $L = 22$ taps with a uniform PDP, where L was chosen as the maximum Winner2 channel length that has almost all the channel energy;
- System D: similar to System A but for a 5G NR LDPC code with code rate 8/9 and 64-QAM for an overall rate of 5.33 bpcu. The LDPC code uses the BG1 base graph of the 3GPP Specification 38.212 Release 15, including puncturing and shortening as specified in the standard. The code length is 9504 bits or 1584 symbols of 64-QAM; this corresponds to 4 frames of $T_F = 396$ symbols.The codewords were transmitted using at least $T = 410$ symbols that include a DFT of length $T_F = 396$ and a minimum cyclic prefix length of $T_c = 14$.

The average GMIs for Systems A–C were computed using $S = 256$, $B = 200$, and a data-aided detector. The coded results of System D instead have $S = 1584$ symbols to fit the block structure determined by the LDPC encoder. For System D we considered both PAT and a data-aided detector. For all cases, the GMI was computed by averaging over the sub-carriers, i.e., channel coding is assumed to be applied over multiple sub-carriers and OFDM symbols. The MAGIQ and QCM algorithms were both initialized with a time-domain quantized solution of the transmit matched filter (MF).

Figures 3 and 4 show the average GMIs for System A with $b = 2$ and $b = 3$, respectively. In Figure 3, MAGIQ performs four iterations for each OFDM symbol while QCM performs six iterations. Observe that MAGIQ and QCM are best at all SNRs and they are especially good in the interesting regime of high SNR and rates. The gap to the rates over flat fading channels ($L = 1$) is small. SQUID with 64-QAM requires 100–300 iterations for SNR > 15 dB and a modified algorithm with damped updates, otherwise SQUID diverges. In addition, we show the broadcast channel capacity with uniform power allocation and Gaussian signaling as an upper bound for the considered scenario [52,53]. Figure 4 shows that QCM with three iterations operates within $\approx$0.2–0.4 dB of MAGIQ with five iterations when $b = 3$, which shows that QCM performs almost as well as MAGIQ.

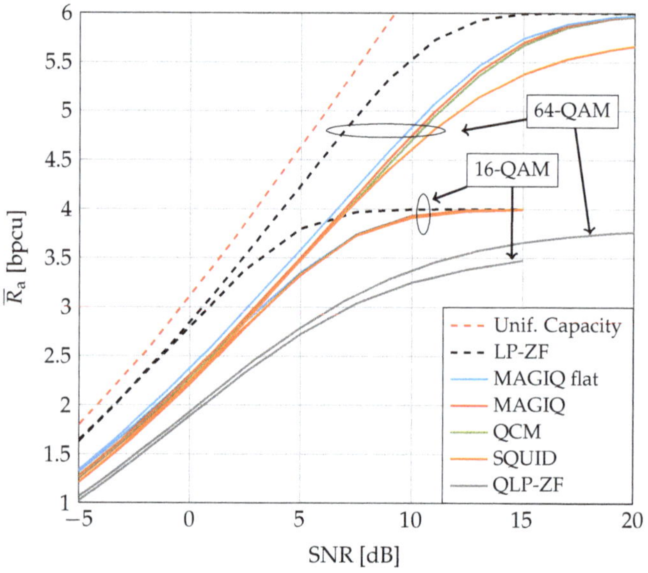

Figure 3. Average GMIs for System A and $b = 2$.

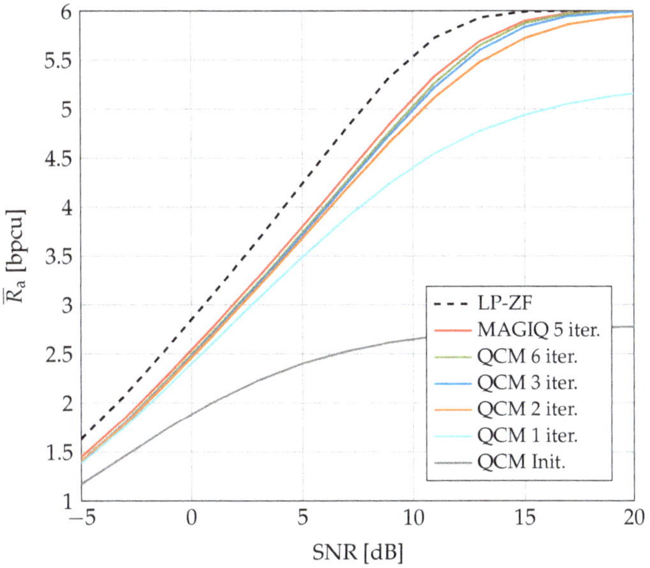

Figure 4. Average GMIs for System A with 64-QAM and $b = 3$.

Figure 5 compares achievable rates of QCM, SQUID, and MSM for a smaller system studied in [42]. We use PSK because the MSM algorithm was designed for PSK. The figure shows that MSM outperforms SQUID and QCM at low to intermediate SNR and rates, but QCM is best at high SNR and rates. This suggests that modifying the cost function (8) to include a safety margin will increase the QCM rate at low to intermediate SNR, and similarly modifying the MSM optimization to more closely resemble QCM will increase the MSM rate at high SNR. We tried to simulate MSM for System A but the algorithm ran into memory limitations (we used 2 AMD EPYC 7282 16-Core processors, 125 GB of system memory, and Matlab with both dual-simplex and interior-point solvers).

Consider next the Winner2 non-line-of-sight (NLOS) C2 urban model [51], which is more realistic than Rayleigh fading. The model parameters are as follows.

- Base station at the origin $(x, y) = (0, 0)$;
- 100 drops of 8 UEs placed on a disk of radius 150 m centered at $(x, y) = (0, 200\,\mathrm{m})$; the locations of the UEs are iid with a uniform distribution on the disc;
- 8×10 uniform rectangular antenna array at the base station with half-wavelength dipoles at $\lambda/2$ spacing;
- 5 MHz bandwidth at center frequency 2.53 GHz;
- No Doppler shift, shadowing and pathloss.

Figure 6 shows the average GMIs for LP-ZF and MAGIQ. At high SNR, there is a slight decrease in the slope of the MAGIQ GMI as compared to LP-ZF. This suggests that one might need a larger N or b. The performance for the Rayleigh fading model is better than for the Winner2 model but otherwise behaves similarly.

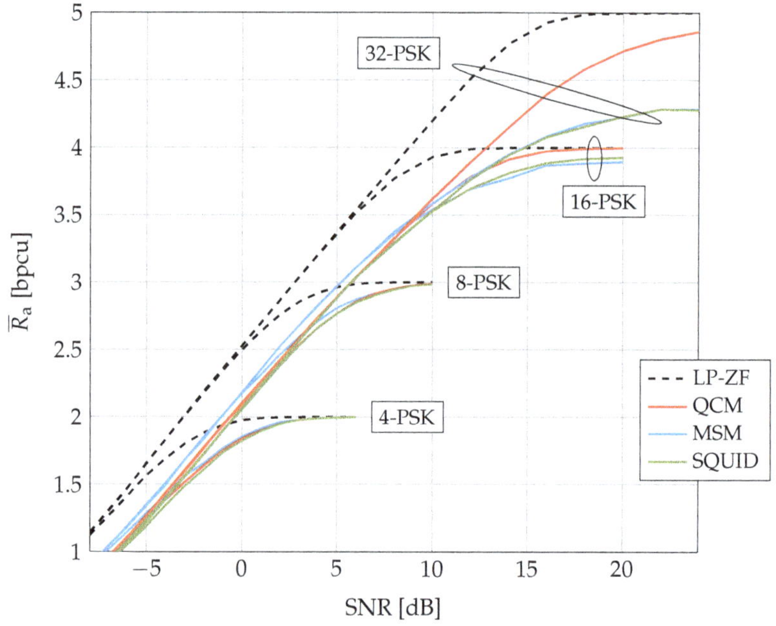

Figure 5. Average GMIs for System B.

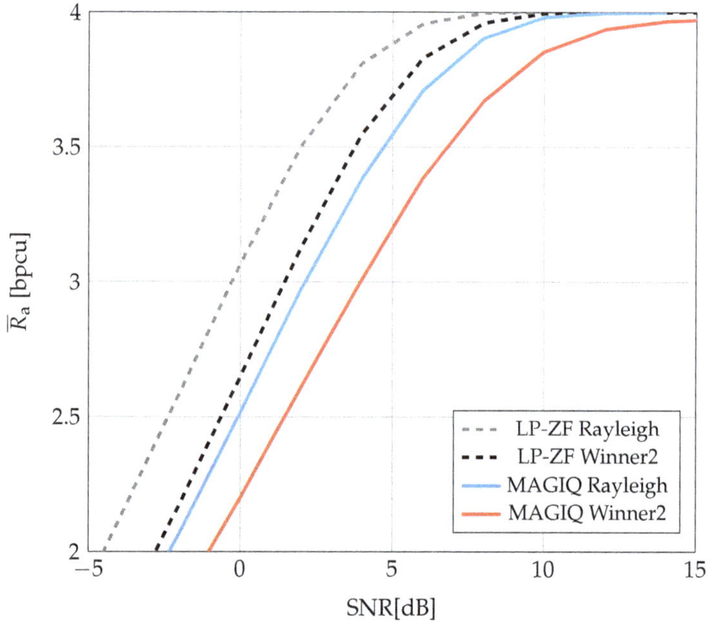

Figure 6. Average GMIs for System C.

Figure 7 shows BERs for the LDPC code with 64-QAM. Each codeword is interleaved over 4 OFDM symbols, all 396 subcarriers, and the 6 bits of each modulation symbol by using bit-interleaved coded modulation (BICM). The interleaver was chosen randomly with a uniform distribution over all permutations of length 9504. The solid curves are for data-aided channel estimation and the dotted curves show the performance of PAT when the fraction of pilots is $S_p/S = 10\%$. The pilots were placed uniformly at random over the four OFDM symbols and 396 subcarriers. A good blind detector algorithm that performs joint channel and data estimation should have BERs between the solid and dotted curves.

The dashed curves in Figure 7 show the SNRs required for the different algorithms based on Figure 3. In particular, the rate 5.33 bpcu requires SNRs of 9 dB, 12.9 dB, and 15.2 dB for LP-ZF, QCM, and SQUID, respectively. SQUID is run with 300 iterations and QCM is run with 6 iterations. Each UE computes its log-likelihoods based on the parameters (20) of the auxiliary channel. The GMI predicts the coded behavior of the system within approximately 1 dB of the code waterfall region, except for SQUID, where the gap is about 2 dB. The gap seems to be caused mainly by the finite-blocklength of the LDPC code, since the smaller gap of approximately 1 dB is also observed for additive white Gaussian noise (AWGN) channels. The sizes of the gaps are different, and the reason may be that the slopes of the GMI at rate 5.33 bpcu are different, see Figure 3. Observe that LP-ZF exhibits the steepest slope and SQUID the flattest at $R_a = 5.33$ bpcu; this suggests that SQUID's SNR performance is more sensitive to the blocklength.

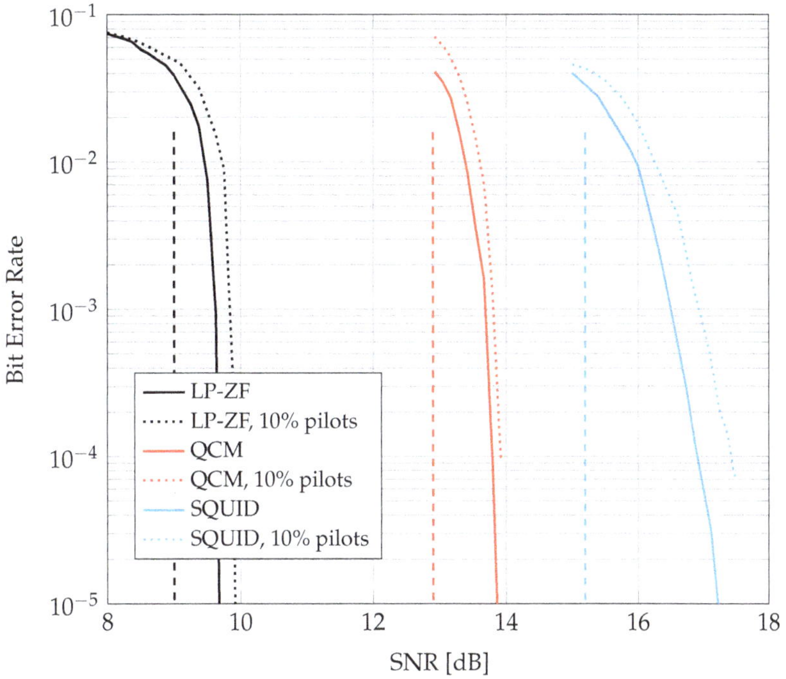

Figure 7. BERs for System D and a 5G NR LDPC code. The dashed vertical curves show the SNRs required for long random codes, see Figure 3.

Figure 8 is for System A and shows how the GMI decreases as the CSI becomes noisier. The behavior of all systems is qualitatively similar. However, the figure shows that the QCM rate is more sensitive to the parameter ϵ than the SQUID rate when ϵ is small.

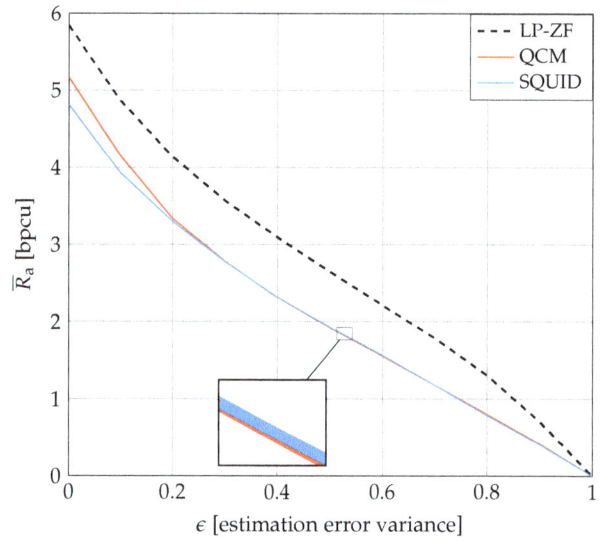

Figure 8. Average GMIs for System A and imperfect CSI at SNR = 12 dB.

6. Conclusions

We studied downlink precoding for MU-MISO channels where the base station uses OFDM and low-resolution DACs. A QCM algorithm was introduced that is based on the MAGIQ algorithm in [39] (see also [19]) and which performs a coordinate-wise optimization in the time-domain. The performance was analyzed by computing the GMI for two auxiliary channel models: one model for pilot-aided channel estimation and a second model for a data-aided channel estimation. Simulations for several downlink channels, including a Winner2 NLOS urban scenario, showed that QCM achieves high information rates and is computationally efficient, flexible, and robust. The performance of QCM was compared to MAGIQ and other precoding algorithms including SQUID and MSM. The QCM and MAGIQ algorithms achieve the highest information rates with the lowest complexity measured by the number of multiplications. For example, Figure 4 shows that $b = 3$ bits of phase modulation operates within 3 dB of LP-ZF. Moreover, BER simulations for a 5G NR LDPC code show that GMI is a good predictor of the coded performance. Finally, for noisy CSI the performance degradation of QCM and SQUID is qualitatively similar to the performance degradation of LP-ZF.

Author Contributions: Investigation, A.S.N., F.S. and G.K.; Software, A.S.N.; Writing—original draft, F.S.; Writing—review & editing, A.S.N. and G.K. All authors have read and agreed to the published version of the manuscript.

Funding: This research was funded by Deutsche Forschungsgemeinschaft through the grant KR 3517/9-1, and by Nokia Solutions and Networks through the project "Low Cost Booster Arrays for Massive MIMO Precoding" in 2017.

Acknowledgments: The authors wish to thank M. Staudacher, W. Zirwas, B. Panzner, R. S. Ganesan, P. Baracca, and S. Wesemann for useful discussions.

Conflicts of Interest: The authors declare no conflict of interest.

References

1. Marzetta, T. Noncooperative cellular wireless with unlimited numbers of base station antennas. *IEEE Trans. Wirel. Commun.* **2010**, *9*, 3590–3600. [CrossRef]
2. Ngo, H.Q.; Larsson, E.; Marzetta, T. Energy and spectral efficiency of very large multiuser MIMO systems. *IEEE Trans. Commun.* **2013**, *61*, 1436–1449.
3. Mohammed, S.K.; Larsson, E.G. Per-antenna constant envelope precoding for large multi-user MIMO systems. *IEEE Trans. Commun.* **2013**, *61*, 1059–1071. [CrossRef]
4. Mohammed, S.K.; Larsson, E.G. Constant-envelope multi-user precoding for frequency-selective massive MIMO systems. *IEEE Wirel. Commun. Lett.* **2013**, *2*, 547–550. [CrossRef]
5. Mohammed, S.K.; Larsson, E.G. Single-User beamforming in large-scale MISO systems with per-antenna constant-envelope constraints: The doughnut channel. *IEEE Trans. Wirel. Commun.* **2012**, *11*, 3992–4005. [CrossRef]
6. Joham, M.; Utschick, W.; Nossek, J.A. Linear transmit processing in MIMO communications systems. *IEEE Trans. Signal Process.* **2005**, *53*, 2700–2712. [CrossRef]
7. Björnson, E.; Bengtsson, M.; Ottersten, B. Optimal multiuser transmit beamforming: A difficult problem with a simple solution structure. *IEEE Signal Proc. Mag.* **2014**, *31*, 142–148.
8. Mezghani, A.; Ghiat, R.; Nossek, J.A. Transmit processing with low resolution D/A-converters. In Proceedings of the 2009 16th IEEE International Conference on Electronics, Circuits and Systems—(ICECS 2009), Yasmine Hammamet, Tunisia, 13–16 December 2009.
9. Mezghani, A.; Ghiat, R.; Nossek, J.A. Tomlinson Harashima Precoding for MIMO Systems with Low Resolution D/A-Converters. In Proceedings of the ITG/IEEE Workshop on Smart Antennas, Berlin, Germany, 18–20 February 2009.
10. Usman, O.B.; Jedda, H.; Mezghani, A.; Nossek, J.A. MMSE precoder for massive MIMO using 1-bit quantization. In Proceedings of the 2016 IEEE International Conference on Acoustics, Speech and Signal Processing (ICASSP), Shanghai, China, 20–25 March 2016.
11. Saxena, A.K.; Fijalkow, I.; Swindlehurst, A.L. Analysis of one-bit quantized precoding for the multiuser massive MIMO downlink. *IEEE Trans. Signal Proc.* **2017**, *65*, 4624–4634. [CrossRef]
12. Kakkavas, A.; Munir, J.; Mezghani, A.; Brunner, H.; Nossek, J.A. Weighted sum rate maximization for multi-user MISO systems with low resolution digital to analog converters. In Proceedings of the International ITG Workshop Smart Antennas, Munich, Germany, 9–11 March 2016.
13. Li, Y.; Tao, C.; Swindlehurst, A.; Mezghani, A.; Liu, L. Downlink achievable rate analysis in massive MIMO systems with one-bit DACs. *IEEE Commun. Lett.* **2017**, *21*, 1669–1672. [CrossRef]
14. Swindlehurst, A.; Jedda, H.; Fijalkow, I. Reduced dimension minimum BER PSK precoding for constrained transmit signals in massive MIMO. In Proceedings of the 2018 IEEE International Conference on Acoustics, Speech and Signal Processing (ICASSP), Calgary, AB, Canada, 15–20 April 2018.
15. Saxena, A.K.; Mezghani, A.; Heath, R.W. Linear CE and 1-bit quantized precoding with optimized dithering. *IEEE Open J. Signal Proc.* **2020**, *1*, 310–325. [CrossRef]
16. Jedda, H.; Nossek, J.A.; Mezghani, A. Minimum BER precoding in 1-bit massive MIMO systems. In Proceedings of the 2016 IEEE Sensor Array and Multichannel Signal Processing Workshop (SAM), Rio de Janeiro, Brazil, 10–13 July 2016.
17. Jacobsson, S.; Durisi, G.; Coldrey, M.; Goldstein, T.; Studer, C. Quantized precoding for massive MU-MIMO. *IEEE Trans. Commun.* **2017**, *65*, 4670–4684. [CrossRef]
18. Wang, C.-J.; Wen, C.-K.; Jin, S.; Tsai, S.-H. Finite-alphabet precoding for massive MU-MIMO with low-resolution DACs. *IEEE Trans. Wirel. Commun.* **2018**, *17*, 4706–4720. [CrossRef]
19. Staudacher, M.; Kramer, G.; Zirwas, W.; Panzner, B.; Ganesan, R.S. Optimized combination of conventional and constrained massive MIMO arrays. In Proceedings of the ITG Workshop Smart Antennas, Berlin, Germany, 15–17 March 2017; pp. 1–4.
20. Shao, M.; Li, Q.; Ma, W.-K. One-bit massive MIMO precoding via a minimum symbol-error probability design. In Proceedings of the 2018 IEEE International Conference on Acoustics, Speech and Signal Processing (ICASSP), Calgary, AB, Canada, 15–20 April 2018.
21. Tsinos, C.G.; Kalantari, A.; Chatzinotas, S.; Ottersten, B. Symbol-level precoding with low resolution DACs for large-scale array MU-MIMO systems. In Proceedings of the 2018 IEEE 19th International Workshop on Signal Processing Advances in Wireless Communications (SPAWC), Kalamata, Greece, 25–28 June 2018; pp. 1–5.
22. Domouchtsidis, S.; Tsinos, C.; Chatzinotas, S.; Ottersten, B. Symbol-level precoding for low complexity transmitter architectures in large-scale antenna array systems. *IEEE Trans. Wirel. Commun.* **2019**, *18*, 852–863. [CrossRef]
23. Li, A.; Masouros, C.; Liu, F.; Swindlehurst, A.L. Massive MIMO 1-Bit DAC transmission: A low-complexity symbol scaling approach. *IEEE Trans. Wirel. Commun.* **2018**, *17*, 7559–7575. [CrossRef]
24. Li, A.; Masouros, C.; Swindlehurst, A.L.; Yu, W. 1-Bit massive MIMO transmission: Embracing interference with symbol-level precoding. *IEEE Commun. Mag.* **2021**, *59*, 121–127. [CrossRef]
25. Li, A.; Liu, F.; Liao, X.; Shen, Y.; Masouros, C. Symbol-level precoding made practical for multi-level modulations via block-level rescaling. In Proceedings of the IEEE International workshop on Signal Processing advances in Wireless Communications, Oulu, Finland, 4–6 July 2022; pp. 71–75.

26. Jedda, H.; Mezghani, A.; Nossek, J.A.; Swindlehurst, A.L. Massive MIMO downlink 1-bit precoding with linear programming for PSK signaling. In Proceedings of the 2017 IEEE 18th International Workshop on Signal Processing Advances in Wireless Communications (SPAWC), Sapporo, Japan, 3–6 July 2017; pp. 1–5.
27. Jedda, H.; Mezghani, A.; Swindlehurst, A.L.; Nossek, J.A. Quantized constant envelope precoding with PSK and QAM signaling. *IEEE Trans. Wirel. Commun.* **2018**, *17*, 8022–8034. [CrossRef]
28. Jedda, H.; Mezghani, A.; Nossek, J.A.; Swindlehurst, A.L. Massive MIMO downlink 1-bit precoding for frequency selective channels. In Proceedings of the 2017 IEEE 7th International Workshop on Computational Advances in Multi-Sensor Adaptive Processing (CAMSAP), Curacao, 10–13 December 2017.
29. Landau, L.T.N.; de Lamare, R.C. Branch-and-bound precoding for multiuser MIMO systems with 1-bit quantization. *IEEE Wirel. Commun. Lett.* **2017**, *6*, 770–773. [CrossRef]
30. Jacobsson, S.; Xu, W.; Durisi, G.; Studer, C. MSE-optimal 1-bit precoding for multiuser MIMO via branch and bound. In Proceedings of the 2018 IEEE International Conference on Acoustics, Speech and Signal Processing (ICASSP), Calgary, AB, Canada, 15–20 April 2018.
31. Li, A.; Liu, F.; Masouros, C.; Li, Y.; Vucetic, B. Interference exploitation 1-bit massive MIMO precoding: A partial branch-and-bound solution with near-optimal performance. *IEEE Trans. Wirel. Commun.* **2020**, *19*, 3474–3489. [CrossRef]
32. Lopes, E.S.P.; Landau, L.T.N. Optimal and suboptimal MMSE precoding for multiuser MIMO systems using constant envelope signals with phase quantization at the transmitter and PSK. In Proceedings of the International ITG Workshop on Smart Antennas, WSA 2020, Hamburg, Germany, 18–20 February 2020; pp. 1–6.
33. Shao, M.; Li, Q.; Ma, W.; So, A.M.; A framework for one-bit and constant-envelope precoding over multiuser massive MISO channels. *IEEE Trans. Sig. Proc.* **2019**, *67*, 5309–5324. [CrossRef]
34. Sedaghat, M.A.; Bereyhi, A.; Müller, R.R. Least square error precoders for massive MIMO With signal constraints: Fundamental limits. *IEEE Trans. Wirel. Commun.* **2018**, *17*, 667–679. [CrossRef]
35. Balatsoukas-Stimming, A.; Castañeda, C.; Jacobsson, S.; Durisi, G.; Studer, C. Neural-network optimized 1-bit precoding for massive MU-MIMO. In Proceedings of the 2019 IEEE 20th International Workshop on Signal Processing Advances in Wireless Communications (SPAWC), Cannes, France, 2–5 July 2019; pp. 1–5.
36. Sohrabi, F.; Cheng, H.V.; Yu, W. Robust symbol-level precoding via autoencoder-based deep learning. In Proceedings of the ICASSP 2020—2020 IEEE International Conference on Acoustics, Speech and Signal Processing (ICASSP), Barcelona, Spain, 4–8 May 2020; pp. 8951-8955.
37. Jacobsson, S.; Durisi, G.; Coldrey, M.; Studer, C. Linear precoding with low-resolution DACs for massive MU-MIMO-OFDM downlink. *IEEE Trans. Wirel. Commun.* **2019**, *18*, 1595–1609. [CrossRef]
38. Jacobsson, S.; Castañeda, C.O.; Jeon, D.G.; Studer, C. Nonlinear precoding for phase-quantized constant-envelope massive MU-MIMO-OFDM. In Proceedings of the International Conference on Telecommunications and Communication Engineering, Beijing China, 28–30 November 2018; pp. 367–372.
39. Nedelcu, A.; Steiner, F.; Staudacher, M.; Kramer, G.; Zirwas, W.; Ganesan, R.S.; Baracca, P.; Wesemann, S. Quantized precoding for multi-antenna downlink channels with MAGIQ. In Proceedings of the International ITG Workshop on Smart Antennas, WSA 2018, Bochum, Germany, 14–16 March 2018; pp. 1–8.
40. Tsinos, C.G.; Domouchtsidis, S.; Chatzinotas, S.; Ottersten, B. Symbol level precoding with low resolution DACs for constant envelope OFDM MU-MIMO systems. *IEEE Access* **2020**, *8*, 12856–12866. [CrossRef]
41. Domouchtsidis, S.; Tsinos, C.G.; Chatzinotas, S.; Ottersten, B. Joint symbol level precoding and combining for MIMO-OFDM transceiver architectures based on one-bit DACs and ADCs. *IEEE Trans. Wirel. Commun.* **2021**, *20*, 4601–4613. [CrossRef]
42. Askerbeyli, F.; Jedda, H.; Nossek, J.A. 1-bit precoding in massive MU-MISO-OFDM downlink with linear programming. In Proceedings of the International ITG Workshop on Smart Antennas, WSA 2019, Vienna, Austria, 24–26 April 2019; pp. 1–5.
43. Mezghani, A.; Heath, R.W. Massive MIMO precoding and spectral shaping with low resolution phase-only DACs and active constellation extension. *IEEE Trans. Wirel. Commun.* **2022**. [CrossRef]
44. Bae, J.H.; Abotabl, A.; Lin, H.-P.; Song, K.-B.; Lee, J. An overview of channel coding for 5G NR cellular communications. *APSIPA Trans. Signal Inf. Proc.* **2019**, *8*, e17. [CrossRef]
45. Zhang, J.; Huang, Y.; Wang, J.; Ottersten, B.; Yang, L. Per-antenna constant envelope precoding and antenna subset selection: A geometric approach. *IEEE Trans. Signal Process.* **2016**, *64*, 6089–6104. [CrossRef]
46. Kaplan, G.; Shamai, S. Information rates and error exponents of compound channels with application to antipodal signaling in a fading environment. *AEU. Archiv Elektr. Übertrag.* **1993**, *47*, 228–239.
47. Gallager, R.G. *Information Theory and Reliable Communication*; John Wiley & Sons, Inc.: Hoboken, NJ, USA, 1968.
48. Arnold, D.M.; Loeliger, H.A.; Vontobel, P.O.; Kavcic, A.; Zeng, W. Simulation-based computation of information rates for channels with memory. *IEEE Trans. Inf. Theory* **2006**, *52*, 3498–3508. [CrossRef]
49. Meng, X.; Gao, K.; Hochwald, B.M. A training-based mutual information lower bound for large-scale systems. *arXiv* **2021**, arXiv:2108.00034.
50. Yuan, P.; Coşkun, M.C.; Kramer, G. Polar-coded non-coherent communication. *IEEE Commun. Lett.* **2021**, *25*, 1786–1790. [CrossRef]
51. Kyösti, P. IST-4-027756 WINNER II D1.1.2 V1.2. 2007. Available online: https://www.cept.org/files/8339/winner2%20-%20final%20report.pdf (accessed on 1 February 2022).

52. Viswanath, P.; Tse, D.N.C. Sum capacity of the vector Gaussian broadcast channel and downlink-uplink duality. *IEEE Trans. Inf. Theory* **2003**, *49*, 1912–1921. [CrossRef]
53. Vishwanath, S.; Jindal, N.; Goldsmith, A. Duality, achievable rates and sum rate capacity of Gaussian MIMO broadcast channel. *IEEE Trans. Inf. Theory* **2003**, *49*, 2658–2668. [CrossRef]

entropy

Article

Reliable Semantic Communication System Enabled by Knowledge Graph

Shengteng Jiang, Yueling Liu *, Yichi Zhang, Peng Luo, Kuo Cao *, Jun Xiong, Haitao Zhao and Jibo Wei

College of Electronic Science and Technology, National University of Defense Technology, Changsha 410073, China; jiangshengteng@nudt.edu.cn (S.J.); zhangyichi13@nudt.edu.cn (Y.Z.); pengluo.eric@outlook.com (P.L.); xj8765@nudt.edu.cn (J.X.); haitaozhao@nudt.edu.cn (H.Z.); wjbhw@nudt.edu.cn (J.W.)
* Correspondence: liuyueling16@nudt.edu.cn (Y.L.); caokuo18@nudt.edu.cn (K.C.)

Abstract: Semantic communication is a promising technology used to overcome the challenges of large bandwidth and power requirements caused by the data explosion. Semantic representation is an important issue in semantic communication. The knowledge graph, powered by deep learning, can improve the accuracy of semantic representation while removing semantic ambiguity. Therefore, we propose a semantic communication system based on the knowledge graph. Specifically, in our system, the transmitted sentences are converted into triplets by using the knowledge graph. Triplets can be viewed as basic semantic symbols for semantic extraction and restoration and can be sorted based on semantic importance. Moreover, the proposed communication system adaptively adjusts the transmitted contents according to channel quality and allocates more transmission resources to important triplets to enhance communication reliability. Simulation results show that the proposed system significantly enhances the reliability of the communication in the low signal-to-noise regime compared to the traditional schemes.

Keywords: semantic communication; knowledge graph; semantic extraction; semantic restoration

Citation: Jiang, S.; Liu, Y.; Zhang, Y.; Luo, P.; Cao, K.; Xiong, J.; Zhao, H.; Wei, J. Reliable Semantic Communication System Enabled by Knowledge Graph. *Entropy* **2022**, *24*, 846. https://doi.org/10.3390/e24060846

Academic Editors: Onur Günlü, Rafael F. Schaefer, Holger Boche and H. Vincent Poor

Received: 26 April 2022
Accepted: 18 June 2022
Published: 20 June 2022

1. Introduction

In recent years, wireless communication technology has developed rapidly, bringing great convenience to human life. Fifth-generation (5G) wireless communication technology has played an important role in smart cities, autonomous driving, telemedicine, and other fields [1]. However, with the gradual increase in the communication rate, the explosive growth of data has created enormous challenges for wireless communication technology [2]. According to the forecast from the International Telecommunication Union (ITU), the annual growth rate of the global mobile data stream will reach up to 55% by 2030 [3]. Moreover, the transmission rate of existing communication technologies has gradually approached the Shannon capacity [4], which cannot meet the continuously growing communication demands in the future 6G era. In the future, the 6G communication system will play an important role in remote holography [5], digital twin [6], and other application fields. Therefore, the sixth-generation wireless communication system needs to provide an ultra-high peak rate, ultra-large user experience rate, and ultra-low network latency, which will consume more limited available spectrum and power and bring huge challenges to communication technology. Semantic communication is one of the effective techniques used to overcome these challenges [7].

Semantic communication, as a revolution against traditional communication, is a new communication paradigm [8]. The concept of semantic communication was first proposed by Weaver (1949) [9]. After Shannon (1948) put forward the classical information theory [4], Weaver proposed that communication should be divided into three different layers, namely the technical layer, semantic layer, and effectiveness layer. The technical layer represents traditional communication, focusing on "how to accurately transmit communication symbols".

The semantic layer focuses on "how to accurately convey the meaning of communication symbols"; the effectiveness layer focuses on "how the received meaning effectively affects the receiver's behavior". Compared with traditional communication, semantic communication aims to reduce the uncertainty of message understanding between the transmitter and the receiver. Moreover, semantic communication mainly transmits semantic-relevant information, which greatly reduces the amount of redundant data. Therefore, semantic communication is a suitable technology (against the scenarios) with limited communication bandwidth and a low signal-to-noise ratio (SNR) [10,11].

However, some fundamental problems of semantic communication have not been effectively solved. One of them is semantic representation, which limits the development of semantic communication [7]. Regarding semantic representation—existing research studies tend to use transmitted content features to represent the semantics. This representation lacks human language logic and cannot be interactive verification with human understanding [12]. To solve this problem, we considered using the knowledge graph instead of features to represent semantics. The knowledge graph can decompose text into multiple semantic units without losing semantics [13], ensuring the accuracy of semantic representation. The basic structure of the knowledge graph is a triplet in the form of an "entity-relation-entity" [13]. From the linguistic point of view, a single entity may have multiple types of semantic information. The specific semantic information can be determined after a relationship is formed between entities, so the triplet in the knowledge graph can be regarded as the smallest semantic symbol. There have been some research studies exploring the relationship between the knowledge graph and semantics. Jaradeh et al. (2019) proposed that the knowledge graph was the next-generation infrastructure for semantic scholarly knowledge [14]. Mosa (2021) proposed that the knowledge graph could help with semantic category prediction [15]. Zhou et al. (2022) combined the knowledge graph with semantic communication to improve the validity of communication [16]. Thus, the knowledge graph can effectively represent semantics; we investigated the semantic communication system based on the knowledge graph (SCKG) for improving communication reliability. The main contributions of this paper are summarized as follows:

- A semantic extraction method is proposed to extract triplets from transmitted text to represent its core semantic information, reducing the information redundancy of the transmitted text.
- A semantic restoration method based on text generation from the knowledge graph is proposed, which completes the semantic restoration process by reconstructing the text structure between entities and relations.
- A novel semantic communication system was developed, which can sort triplets based on semantic importance and adaptively adjust the transmitted contents according to the channel quality.

The rest of this paper is organized as follows. Section 2 briefly reviews the related work. Section 3 details the proposed system and the semantic extraction and restoration methods used in the model. Experimental results are presented in Section 4 to verify the performance of the proposed model. Finally, Section 5 concludes this paper.

2. Related Work

2.1. Semantic Communication Development

Due to technical limitations in the early stage of communication development, researchers have focused on solving engineering problems at the technical layer and postponed the study at the semantic layer. However, this does not mean that the research on semantic communication will be shelved. With the advancements in technology, the semantic problem has become an urgent problem that needs to be solved in the communication field [17].

In terms of theoretical research, Carnap et al. (1954) first proposed the concept of the semantic information theory to supplement the classical information theory [18]. They thought that the semantic information contained in the sentence should be defined based on the logical probability of the content of the sentence. Floridi (2004) proposed a theory of strongly semantic information [19] and pointed out the problem that sentence contradictions will have infinite information. Bao et al. (2011) put forward a general model of semantic communication, using a factual statement in the propositional logic form to represent semantics [20]. Moreover, the semantic entropy, semantic noise, and semantic channel capacity were defined in [20]. Based on the literature [20], Basu et al. (2012) provided a detailed explanation of the relationship between semantic entropy and information entropy, and they defined the concepts of semantic ambiguity and semantic redundancy [21]. In [22], Lan et al. (2021) proposed that semantic communication can be divided into human-to-human, human-to-machine, and machine-to-machine sub-areas, which broadened the scope of semantic communication.

On the other hand, the rapid development of neural networks and artificial intelligence technology promotes the progress of technical research in semantic communication. In terms of semantic coding, the authors of [23] proposed a joint source-channel coding for semantic information with a bidirectional long short-term memory model (BILSTM). As an extension of the literature [23], Rao et al. (2018) presented a variable-length joint source-channel coding of semantic information [24]. In [25], Liu et al. (2022) proposed a semantic encoding strategy based on parts-of-speech and context-based decoding strategies, which enhanced communication reliability from the semantic level. Based on the semantic communication framework, Xie et al. (2021) proposed a deep learning-based semantic communication model [26], which used word embedding technology to map text to semantic space and then performed source-channel joint encoding for semantic information by using the transformer framework [27]. Furthermore, the authors of [28] proposed a lightweight distributed semantic communication system for the application scenario of the internet of things (IoT), which reduced the cost of IoT devices. The authors of [29] proposed a semantic communication model based on reinforcement learning to investigate the impact of noisy environments on semantic information. In different information forms, Weng et al. (2021) proposed a semantic communication model for speech transmission [30]. In [31], Hu et al. (2022) proposed a robust end-to-end semantic communication system to combat the semantic noise for image transmission. Moreover, a semantic communication model based on multi-information modalities was developed in [32]. Regarding semantic representation, Zhou et al. (2022) used the transformer for semantic extraction and semantic restoration [33].

2.2. *Performance Metrics*

Semantic communication, different from traditional communication systems, does not emphasize the perfect recovery of the transmitted message, but rather on the receiver correctly understanding the message in the same way as the transmitter. As a result, performance metrics commonly used in traditional communication systems (e.g., bit error rate and symbol error rate) are no longer suitable for semantic communication. Hence, this paper uses the bilingual evaluation understudy (BLEU) score [34], a metric for evaluation of translation with the explicit ordering (METEOR) score [35], and the semantic similarity score [36], as performance metrics.

2.2.1. BLEU Score

BLEU is currently the most commonly used metric in text evaluation [37]. It evaluates the similarity by counting the number of the same n-grams between transmitted and received texts, where n-gram means n consecutive words in the text. The formula can be expressed as

$$\log \text{BLEU} = \min\left(1 - \frac{l_{\hat{s}}}{l_s}, 0\right) + \sum_{n=1}^{N} \omega_n \log p_n \tag{1}$$

where s and $\hat{s}$ denote the transmitted sentence and restored sentence, respectively. l_s and $l_{\hat{s}}$ are the lengths of the transmitted sentences s and restored sentence $\hat{s}$, respectively. ω_n represents the weight of n-grams, and p_n denotes the precision of n-grams.

2.2.2. METEOR Score

METEOR extends the synonym set by introducing external knowledge sources, such as WordNet [38]. Furthermore, it uses precision P_m and recall R_m to evaluate the similarity between transmitted and received texts. The formula is given as follows

$$F_{\text{mean}} = \frac{P_m R_m}{\alpha P_m + (1-\alpha) R_m} \tag{2}$$

$$\text{METEOR} = (1 - \text{Pen}) F_{\text{mean}} \tag{3}$$

where α is the hyperparameter according to WordNet, F_{mean} represents the harmonic mean combining P_m and R_m, and Pen is the penalty coefficient.

2.2.3. Semantic Similarity Score

The semantic similarity score converts text into vectors by using the BERT model [39]. It evaluates the semantic similarity between sentences by comparing the degree of similarity between vectors. For the transmitted sentence's vector $\boldsymbol{v}(s)$ and the received sentence's vector $\boldsymbol{v}(\hat{s})$, the semantic similarity score can be expressed as

$$sim_{\text{v}}(s, \hat{s}) = \frac{\boldsymbol{v}(s) \cdot (\boldsymbol{v}(\hat{s}))^T}{\parallel \boldsymbol{v}(s) \parallel \cdot \parallel \boldsymbol{v}(\hat{s}) \parallel} \tag{4}$$

All the performance metrics introduced above take values between 0 and 1. A higher score given by the performance metrics means that the received text's semantic is closer to the transmitted text's semantic; 0 means semantically irrelevant; 1 means semantically consistent.

3. System Model

As shown in Figure 1, the structure of the proposed system consists of a semantic extraction module, traditional communication architecture, and semantic restoration module. The proposed system can be divided into two levels, which are the semantic level and the technical level. The structure of the technical level is the same as that of the traditional communication system; thus, we mainly introduce the details at the semantic level. At the transmitter, the semantic extraction module can extract the knowledge graph (KG) of the transmitted sentence to represent its semantics. More importantly, the knowledge graph is sorted according to semantic importance. At the receiver, the semantic restoration module can recover the transmitted sentence according to the received knowledge graph.

Figure 2 shows examples of the proposed semantic communication system in different channel qualities. At the transmitter, the transmitted sentence is first converted into the knowledge graph through the semantic extraction module. Next, the transmitter adjusts the knowledge graph according to the channel quality. Then, the knowledge graph is transmitted through the channel. With the noisy knowledge graph received, the semantic is recovered through the semantic restoration module. In Figure 2a, when the channel quality is good, the transmitted sentence and the restored sentence convey the same semantics although they have different sentence structures. When the channel quality is poor, all triplets cannot be transmitted correctly. Therefore, the proposed semantic communication system chooses to transmit the most important triplet. When it comes to Steve Jobs, people tend to care about his relationship with Apple rather than the college he graduated from. As shown in Figure 2b, the transmitter only sends "< Steve Jobs-founder-Apple" when the channel quality is poor.

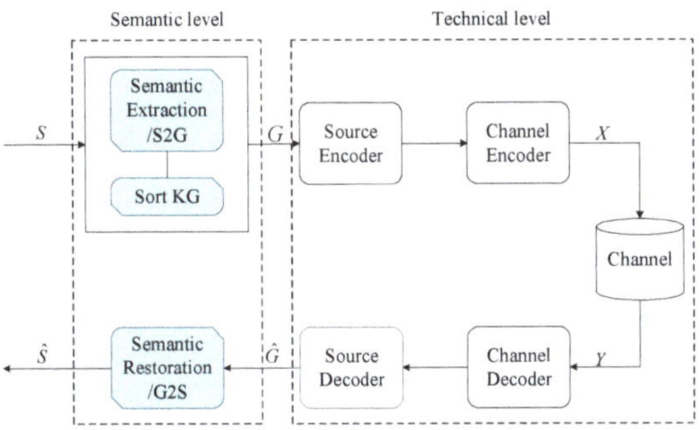

Figure 1. The structure of the proposed semantic communication system based on the knowledge graph, including the semantic extraction module, traditional communication architecture, and semantic restoration module.

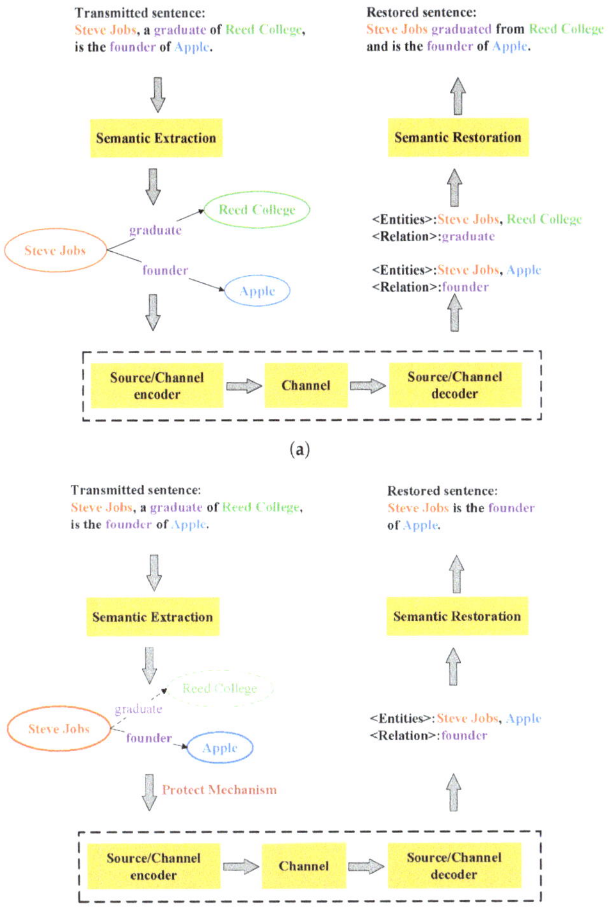

(b)

Figure 2. Examples of the proposed semantic communication system in different channel qualities. (**a**) An example of the proposed semantic communication system when the channel quality is good. (**b**) An example of the proposed semantic communication system when the channel quality is poor.

3.1. Semantic Extraction Method

To represent the semantic information correctly, the semantic extraction module at the transmitter uses a deep learning network to extract the knowledge graph from the transmitted sentence. Let $S2G_\theta(\bullet)$ be the function of the proposed semantic extraction method, which takes the sentence $S = [w_1, w_2, \cdots, w_m]$ as input and its corresponding output is the knowledge graph G, where w_m is the mth word in the sentence. The deep learning network structure for the semantic extraction method is shown in Figure 3.

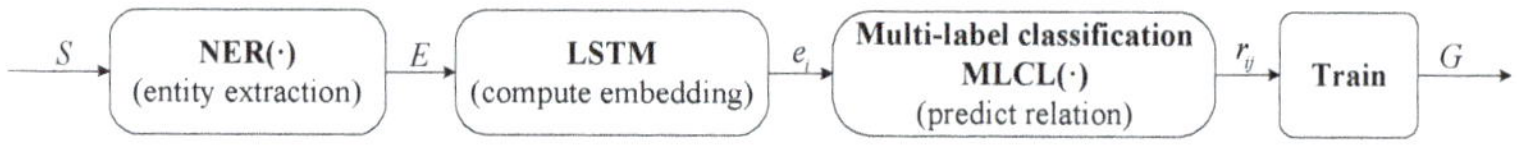

Figure 3. The deep learning network structure for the semantic extraction method.

In particular, we used the pipeline method to extract the knowledge graph, which means extracting the entities in S and then predicting the relations between entities. Firstly, we used a well-established named entity recognition model (NER) to extract the entities [40]. This model is based on the conditional random field classifier and Gibbs sampling. The conditional random field classifier combines the characteristics of the maximum entropy model and the hidden Markov model, and it is often used to deal with sequence labeling tasks, such as parts-of-speech tagging and named entity recognition. Gibbs sampling is a method of generating Markov chains that can be used for Monte Carlo simulations. Based on the conditional random field classifier and Gibbs sampling, NER is trained by using a large amount of manually annotated text and can recognize entities from given sentences. Therefore, the entities in the transmitted sentence can be expressed as

$$E = [en_1, en_2, \cdots, en_i, \ldots, en_L] = \text{NER}(S) \tag{5}$$

where en_i represents the ith entity in the sentence, L is the total number of entities contained in the sentence.

After extracting entities from S, we predict the relations between the two entities. Firstly, the embedding of each word w_j in the entity en_i is averaged to obtain the entity's embedding. The embedding of w_j can be obtained by using a long short-term memory model (LSTM) [41] to encode w_j and its context. The formula is given as follows

$$\text{emb}(w_j) = \text{LSTM\_encode}(w_j, w_{<j}, w_{>j}) \tag{6}$$

Therefore, the ith entity's embedding e_i can be represented as

$$e_i = \frac{1}{\text{Len}(en_i)} \sum_{w_j \in en_i} \text{emb}(w_j) \tag{7}$$

where $\text{Len}(en_i)$ is the number of words in the entity en_i.

Then we feed the entity embeddings into a multi-label classification layer $\text{MLCL}(\bullet)$ to predict the relations. The multi-label classification layer $\text{MLCL}(\bullet)$ can take in two entities and predict the possible relation set. To prevent these two entities from being irrelevant, the relation set includes the "no-relation" type. The relation set between the ith entity and the jth entity can be represented as

$$r_{ij} = \text{MLCL}(e_i, e_j) \tag{8}$$

Since the knowledge graph is made of entities and relations, the probability of extracting a graph from a given sentence is equivalent to the product of the probability of extracting the relation set given any two entities. The formula can be expressed as

$$p(G \mid S) = \prod_{i=0}^{L}\prod_{j=0}^{L} p(r_{ij} \mid e_i, e_j, S) \tag{9}$$

Based on the probability $p(G \mid S)$, we can denote the loss function of the proposed semantic extraction method by using the negative log-likelihood loss, which can be formulated as

$$\begin{aligned}\mathcal{L}_{S2G}(\theta) &= \mathbb{E}[-\log p(G \mid S;\theta)] \\ &= \mathbb{E}\left[-\log \prod_{i=0}^{L}\prod_{j=0}^{L} p(r_{ij} \mid e_i, e_j, S;\theta)\right]\end{aligned} \tag{10}$$

where θ is the network parameter set of the deep learning network, which is shown in Figure 3.

Utilizing the loss function $\mathcal{L}_{S2G}$, the optimal parameter set θ^* can be easily found using the gradient descent method. Consequently, the details of the proposed semantic extraction method can be summarized in Algorithm 1.

Algorithm 1 The proposed semantic extraction method

Input: the transmitted sentence S

1: Build entity set E by Equation (5)
2: **for** each $en_i \in E$ **do**
3: Compute the embedding e_i by Equations (6) and (7)
4: **end for**
5: Construct the relation set according to Equation (8)
6: Compute loss function $\mathcal{L}_{S2G}(\theta)$ according to Equation (10)
7: Train $\theta \rightarrow \theta^*$

Output: The knowledge graph G

3.2. Semantic Restoration Method

The proposed semantic restoration method—similar to the proposed semantic extraction method—uses deep learning to generate sentences from the received knowledge graph. The generated sentence can help the receiver understand the semantics of the transmitted sentence. Let $G2S_{\varphi}(\bullet)$ be the function of the proposed semantic restoration. The input of $G2S_{\varphi}(\bullet)$ is the received knowledge graph $\hat{G}$ and its output is the restored sentence $\hat{S}$. The deep learning network structure for the semantic restoration method is shown in Figure 4.

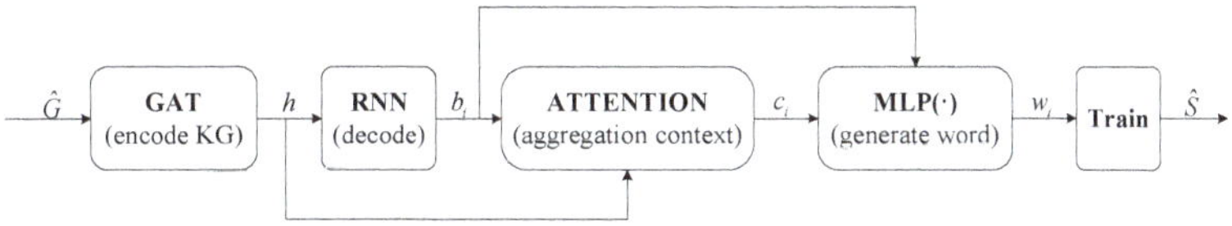

Figure 4. The deep learning network structure for the semantic restoration method.

At first, we encoded the received knowledge graph $\hat{G}$ to convert it to the embedding, which could be processed by the deep learning network. Specifically, we used the graph attention network (GAT) [42] to calculate the embedding of the received knowledge graph $\hat{G}$. GAT is a representative graph convolutional network that can encode the knowledge graph by introducing the attention mechanism into the knowledge graph. Therefore, the embedding of $\hat{G}$ can be represented as

$$h = \text{GAT}(\hat{G}) \tag{11}$$

After obtaining the embedding h, we used the recurrent neural network (RNN) and the attention mechanism to generate the sentence word by word. Each step of RNN can produce a word embedding. In the ith step, the embedding b_i can be represented as

$$b_i = \mathrm{RNN}(b_{i-1}, w_{i-1}) \tag{12}$$

where w_{i-1} is the $i-1$th word in the generated sentence, b_{i-1} is the embedding produced in the $i-1$th step. To improve the accuracy of the generated sentence, the attention mechanism was used to obtain the embedding of contextual information. The formula can be described as

$$c_i = \mathrm{ATTENTION}(b_i, h) \tag{13}$$

where c_i denotes the contextual information of the ith word. Then we fed the word embedding b_i and the contextual information c_i into a multilayer perceptron (MLP) to generate the ith word w_i.

Consequently, the generation of w_i based on the received knowledge graph $\hat{G}$ and all previously generated words $w_{<i}$ was fulfilled by predicting the word w_i through MLP with the assistance of the word embedding b_i and the contextual information c_i. Thus, the probability of recovering word w_i can be represented as

$$p(w_i|w_{<i}, \hat{G}) \propto \exp(\mathrm{MLP}([b_i; c_i])) \tag{14}$$

In summary, the probability of generating a sentence from the received knowledge graph $\hat{G}$ is equivalent to the product of the probability of generating each word. The probability can be described as

$$p(\hat{S}|\hat{G}) = \prod p(w_i \mid w_{<i}, \hat{G}) \tag{15}$$

Similarly, we used the negative log-likelihood loss to denote the loss function of the proposed semantic restoration method according to the probability $p(\hat{S}|\hat{G})$. The loss function can be represented as

$$\begin{aligned} \mathcal{L}_{G2S}(\varphi) &= \mathbb{E}[-\log p(\hat{S} \mid \hat{G}; \varphi)] \\ &= \mathbb{E}[-\log \prod p(w_i \mid w_{<i}, \hat{G}; \varphi)] \end{aligned} \tag{16}$$

where φ is the network parameter set of the deep learning network, which is shown in Figure 4. Finally, the gradient descent can be used to find the optimal parameter set φ^* for minimizing the loss function $\mathcal{L}_{G2S}(\varphi)$.

The details of the proposed semantic restoration process are summarized in Algorithm 2.

Algorithm 2 The proposed semantic restoration method

Input: the received knowledge graph $\hat{G}$
1: Compute the embedding of $\hat{G}$ by Equation (11)
2: **while** w_i is not the satisfied end feature **do**
3: Compute b_i by Equation (12)
4: Compute the contextual information c_i by Equation (13)
5: Generate word w_i according to Equation (14)
6: **end while**
7: Compute the loss function $\mathcal{L}_{G2S}(\varphi)$ according to Equation (16)
8: Train $\varphi \to \varphi^*$
Output: the knowledge graph $\hat{S}$

3.3. System Process

In this section, we introduce the overall process of the proposed semantic communication system. Let $S = [w_1, w_2, \cdots, w_m]$ be the transmitted sentence, where w_m is the mth word in the sentence. As shown in Figure 5, with the help of the proposed semantic extraction method $S2G_\theta(\bullet)$, the transmitter converts the transmitted sentence S to the knowledge graph G, which can be represented as $G = S2G_\theta(S)$. The knowledge graph G consists of n triplets and it can be formulated as $G = [g_1, g_2, \cdots, g_n]$.

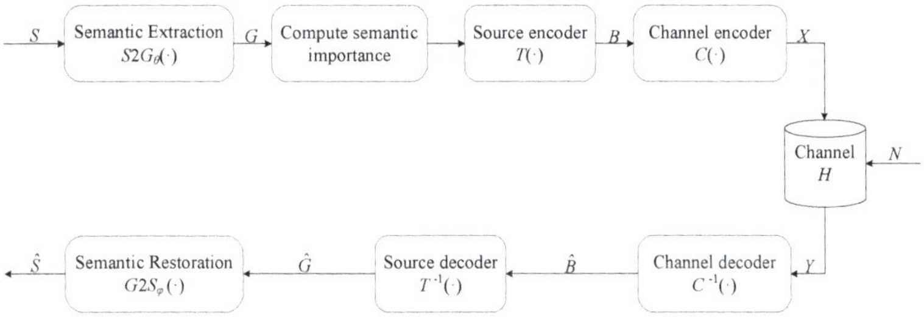

Figure 5. The overall process of the proposed semantic communication system based on the knowledge graph, combining the proposed semantic extraction method, the proposed semantic restoration method, and the traditional communication architecture.

Using the proposed semantic extraction method, the transmitted sentence is converted into a series of triplets. In this process, the semantics of the transmitted sentence are extracted without losing semantics [13]. During transmission, these triplets are independent of each other, which means that errors in some triplets will not affect other triplets. However, in Markov models, once there is a transmission error, the whole transmitted sentence will be affected. Therefore, the proposed semantic communication system is more robust under a low SNR. Moreover, different semantic basic symbols (triplets) have semantic importance in semantic communication, unlike bits or symbols that are treated equally in traditional communication, such as longer-range models and Markov chain-based probabilistic models. These triplets (with semantic importance) should be treated differently. The triplets with important semantics should be allocated with many time slots and bandwidth resources. When the channel quality is extremely poor, instead of transmitting all triplets, which cannot be guaranteed by the channel, it is better to ensure that the most important triplet can be transmitted correctly. When the channel quality is better, the system can adjust the sending content according to semantic importance. Motivated by the different triplets with semantic importance, we sort these triplets according to their semantic similarity scores:

$$sim_{\mathrm{v}}(s, g_i) = \frac{\boldsymbol{v}(s) \cdot (\boldsymbol{v}(g_i))^T}{\| \boldsymbol{v}(s) \| \cdot \| \boldsymbol{v}(g_i) \|} \tag{17}$$

where g_i denotes the ith triplet in G. Table 1 shows an example of semantic importance. From Table 1, "< Steve Jobs – founder-Apple>" is more important than "< Steve Jobs – graduate-Reed College >", which is also in line with human perception.

Table 1. An example of semantic importance.

Sentence	Triplets of Knowledge Graph	Semantic Similarity
Steve Jobs, a graduate of Reed College, is the founder of Apple	Steve Jobs – graduate-Reed College	0.56
	Steve Jobs – founder-Apple	0.73

Based on the sorted triplets, we can adaptively adjust the number of transmitted triplets according to the channel quality. When the channel quality is extremely poor, we only transmit the most significant triplet and use the communication resources of triplets not transmitted to protect it. As the channel quality improves, we increase the number of transmitted triplets.

After the transmitted knowledge graph G is obtained, the transmitter first maps it into a binary bit stream $B = T(G)$, and then feeds the binary bit stream into the channel encoder to cope with the effects of channel noise and distortion. Therefore, the whole process of the transmitter can be represented as

$$X = C(T(G)) \tag{18}$$

where $T(\bullet)$ and $C(\bullet)$ denote the source encoder and the channel encoder, respectively. If X is sent, the received signal can be represented as

$$Y = HX + N \tag{19}$$

where H is the channel coefficient and $N \sim \mathcal{CN}(0, \sigma_n^2)$ denotes the additive white Gaussian noise.

After obtaining the received signal, the receiver will decode it to recover the transmitted knowledge graph. Defining $C^{-1}(\bullet)$ and $T^{-1}(\bullet)$ as the channel decoder and the source decoder, respectively, the received knowledge graph $\hat{G}$ can be represented as

$$\hat{G} = T^{-1}\left(C^{-1}(Y)\right) \tag{20}$$

Then we use the proposed semantic restoration method $G2S_{\varphi}(\bullet)$ to obtain the restored sentence $\hat{S}$.

$$\hat{S} = G2S_{\varphi}(\hat{G}) \tag{21}$$

The process of the proposed semantic communication system is shown in Algorithm 3.

Algorithm 3 Process of the proposed semantic communication system.

Input: The transmitted sentence S

Transmitter:
- Extract the knowledge graph by Algorithm 1
- **for** $i = 1$ to n **do**
  - Compute the semantic importance of g_i by Equation (17)
- **end for**
- Sort the knowledge graph according to the semantic importance
- Adjust the number of transmitted triplets according to the channel quality
- $C(T(G)) \rightarrow X$
- Transmit X over the channel

Receiver:
- Receive Y
- $T^{-1}(C^{-1}(Y)) \rightarrow \hat{G}$
- Restore the sentence $\hat{S}$ by Algorithm 2

Output: The restored sentence $\hat{S}$

4. Experimental Results

In this section, we compare the proposed SCKG with other traditional models under different channels, including the AWGN channel and the Rayleigh fading channel to verify the effectiveness of SCKG. In Table 2, we introduce the models used in the experiments, including their general features and technical methods. It is worth noting that the traditional communication models are not the only ones mentioned in Table 2. The source coding can also choose arithmetic coding, L–Z coding, and other coding methods. Identically, the channel coding can also choose turbo code, polar code, and other coding methods.

Table 2. Introduction to the proposed model and other traditional models.

Model	General Features	Technical Methods
SCKG	(1) Adding the semantic extraction module and semantic restoration module into traditional communication architecture. (2) Using triplets as semantic basic symbols for semantic extraction and restoration.	(1) Semantic extraction—network structure using NER + LSTM. (2) Semantic restoration—network structure using GAT + RNN + ATTENTION.
Huffman [43] + LDPC [44]	(1) Using the traditional communication architecture from Shannon's information theory. (2) Using Huffman coding as source coding and using LDPC coding as channel coding.	(1) Convert transmitted sentences to bit sequences by using Huffman coding. (2) Using LDPC coding to combat channel distortion.
DeepNN [23]	(1) Using the deep neural network for source-channel joint coding. (2) Replacing source encoding and channel encoding with the encoder of the deep neural network. (3) Replacing source decoding and channel decoding with the decoder of the deep neural network.	(1) Encoder—network structure using BILSTM. (2) Decoder—network structure using LSTM.

4.1. Experimental Settings

In the simulation, the adopted dataset was the WebNLG dataset [45], which is usually used to generate sentences from knowledge graphs. Each data in the dataset consists of multiple triplets and their corresponding sentences. After preprocessing the dataset, we obtained 12,597 training data, 1746 validation data, and 2493 test data. The training and testing environment was Ubuntu16.04+CUDA10.1, the selected deep learning framework was PyTorch 1.6.0. The training settings of the semantic extraction method and the semantic restoration method are shown in Table 3.

Table 3. Training settings for semantic extraction and restoration method.

Type	Parameters for Semantic Extraction Method	Parameters for Semantic Restoration Method
Epochs	50	50
Batch size	32	32
Optimizer	Adam	Adam
Learning rate	5×10^{-5}	2×10^{-4}
Drop	0	0.1

In the experiment, the test data of WebNLG were transmitted sentence-by-sentence to the transmitter. Then we obtained the restored sentences by using the above-mentioned methods at the receiver. After the restored sentences were obtained, the experimental results could be calculated according to the performance metrics.

For the benchmark, we adopted the traditional communication architecture with source coding and channel coding, where source coding could use Huffman coding, arithmetic coding, L–Z coding, etc., and channel coding could use LDPC coding, turbo code, polar code, etc. For simplicity, we adopted the combination of Huffman coding and LDPC coding (named "Huffman + LDPC"). Moreover, we considered another two methods as ablation experiments to validate the effectiveness of the proposed model. One involved using the proposed model without adaptive transmission and semantic restoration (named the "Proposed model without AT and SR"), and the other involved using the proposed model without adaptive transmission (named the "Proposed model without AT").

4.2. Experimental Result Analysis

4.2.1. Performance of the Proposed Semantic Communication System

First, we investigated the effects of the number of triplets on the semantic performance under different SNRs. Here, we considered three strategies, one strategy was to send the first triplet (named "Send the 1st triplet"), and the other two schemes involved sending 50% triplets (named "Send 50% triplets") and 100% triplets (named "Send 100% triplets"), respectively. Moreover, we compared these three strategies with the benchmark and an end-to-end deep learning-based communication system proposed in [23] (named DeepNN). Figure 6 shows the performance of the semantic similarity versus the SNR in this experiment. From Figure 6, "Send the 1st triplet" has the best semantic similarity under a low SNR because it uses the most resources to protect the first triplet. With the SNR becoming better, "Send 50% triplets" has better performance because "Send the 1st triplet" transmits limited semantics, and the accuracy of the scheme "Send 100% triplets" cannot be guaranteed due to the channel distortion. The semantic similarity of "Send 100% triplets" is above the others at a high SNR, which is reasonable due to the error-free transmission when the channel quality is good. Meanwhile, all three strategies outperformed the benchmark and DeepNN in their superior SNR regions. According to Figure 6, it is reasonable to send the most important triplet in the low SNR region, send 50% triplets in the medium SNR region, and send 100% triplets in the high SNR region.

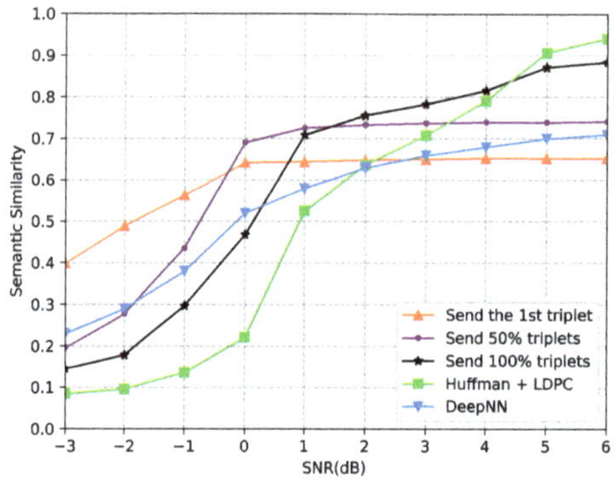

Figure 6. Semantic similarity versus the SNR under the AWGN channel, with send the 1st triplet; send 50% triplets; send 100% triplets; Huffman + LDPC; DeepNN.

Figure 7 demonstrates the relationship between the SNR and the BLEU score under the AWGN channel. From Figure 7, the proposed model performs better under a low SNR in terms of the 1-gram BLEU score or 2-gram BLEU score due to the protection of important triplets. Moreover, after converting the received triplets into sentences by using the proposed semantic restoration method, "Proposed model without AT" outperforms "Proposed model without AT and SR" for all SNR regimes. However, the performance of the proposed model is inferior to the traditional communication system in the high SNR region in Figure 7. This is because the proposed semantic restoration method attempts to recover the same semantic rather than the same sentence structure. For example, the transmitted sentence is "Steve Jobs was the founder of Apple", and the restored sentence is "Steve Jobs founded Apple". Although the two sentences are semantically consistent, the BLEU score of the proposed scheme is poor.

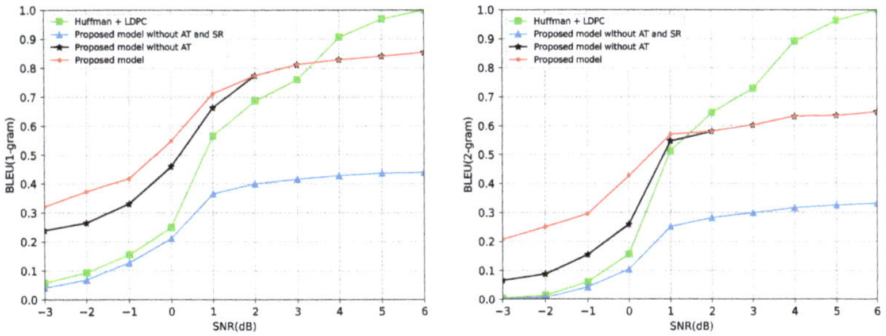

(**a**) (**b**)

Figure 7. BLEU score versus the SNR over the AWGN channel. (**a**) BLEU(1-gram) score over the AWGN channel. (**b**) BLEU(2-gram) score over the AWGN channel.

Figure 8 shows the relationship between the SNR and the BLEU score under the Rayleigh fading channel. All scores in Figure 8 are lower than the scores in Figure 7 because of the severe impacts of Rayleigh fading. However, the proposed model significantly improves performance compared to the benchmark. From Figure 8, the proposed model outperforms the benchmark across the SNR range over the Rayleigh fading channel, either the 1-gram BLEU score or the 2-gram BLEU score. It reflects that our proposed model is more robust to complex communication environments. Meanwhile, since "Proposed model without AT" and "Send 100% triplets" are identical in the high SNR region, the results of the proposed model and "Proposed model without AT" are the same when the SNR is higher than 2 dB.

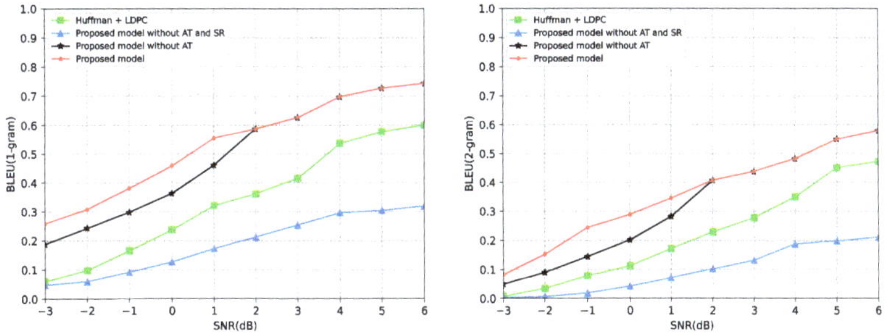

(**a**) (**b**)

Figure 8. BLEU score versus the SNR over the Rayleigh fading channel. (**a**) BLEU(1-gram) score over the Rayleigh fading channel. (**b**) BLEU(2-gram) score over the Rayleigh fading channel.

Since BLEU is an evaluation metric that calculates scores based on word matching, sentence sizes can affect the performance of our proposed model. To research this, we divided the transmitted sentences into three groups—sentence length between 0 and 15, sentence length between 15 and 30, and sentence length greater than 30. Figure 9 shows the relationship between the SNR and the (1-gram) BLEU score under the AWGN channel and the Rayleigh fading channel, respectively. From Figure 9a, "Sentence Length (0, 15)" is significantly higher than the other two groups. This is because the proposed model only transmits the most important triplet in the low SNR, and the length of the restored sentence is limited. In the low SNR region, the BLEU score decreases as the sentence length increases. With the SNR increasing, the number of the transmitted triplets increases, and the gaps between the different groups narrow. In Figure 9b, the gaps between the different groups are not obvious due to the effects of Rayleigh fading.

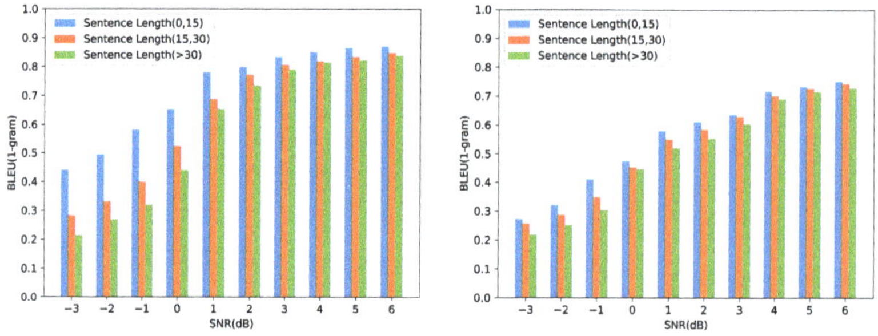

(a) (b)

Figure 9. BLEU (1-gram) score versus the SNR with sentence length (0, 15). Sentence Length (15, 30); sentence length (>30). (**a**) BLEU (1-gram) score over the AWGN channel. (**b**) BLEU (1-gram) score over the Rayleigh fading channel.

Figure 10 shows the METEOR score versus the SNR over the AWGN channel and the Rayleigh fading channel. From Figure 10a, the score of the benchmark is close to 1 and higher than our proposed model when the SNR is above 4 dB. This is because the few errors that occurred during the transmission were corrected by the channel coding at a high SNR; the benchmark could restore the transmitted sentence without distortion. However, our proposed model discards the information of sentence structure during transmission. When the SNR is less than 4 dB, the channel coding cannot correct all errors during transmission. In this situation, the METEOR score of the benchmark degrades rapidly. However, the proposed model reduces the number of transmitted triplets and protects important triplets in this case, which leads to a better performance in the low SNR region. From Figure 10b, even under the Rayleigh fading channel, our model outperforms the benchmark in all SNR regions.

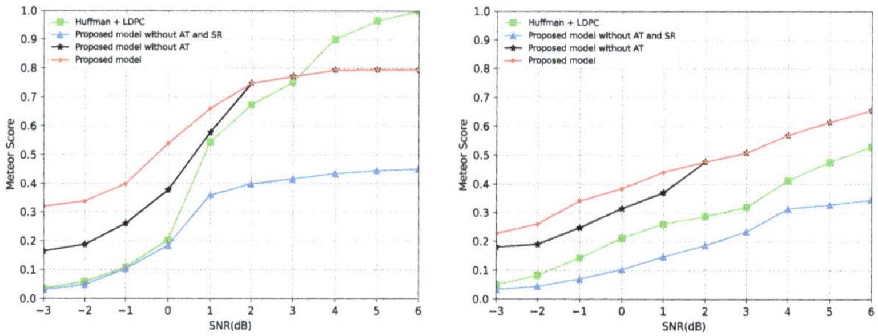

(a) (b)

Figure 10. (**a**) METEOR score versus the SNR over the AWGN channel. (**b**) METEOR score versus the SNR over the Rayleigh fading channel.

Figure 11 draws the relationship between the SNR and the semantic similarity under the AWGN channel and the Rayleigh fading channel. From Figure 11, the "Proposed model without AT and SR" outperforms the benchmark in the low SNR region under the AWGN channel, while it outperforms the benchmark in all SNR regions under the Rayleigh fading channel. This is because our proposed model splits the transmitted sentence into multiple independent triplets, leading to that, the wrongly transmitted triplets will not affect the semantics of other triplets. However, the benchmark model transmits the sentence as a whole, and if errors occur in the transmission, then the semantics of the sentence are affected. Therefore, when the channel quality is poor, our proposed model can preserve partially correct semantics. Meanwhile, since the semantic similarity based on the BERT model can capture semantic relationships among words, the proposed scheme obtains a higher similarity compared with the BLEU score and METEOR score.

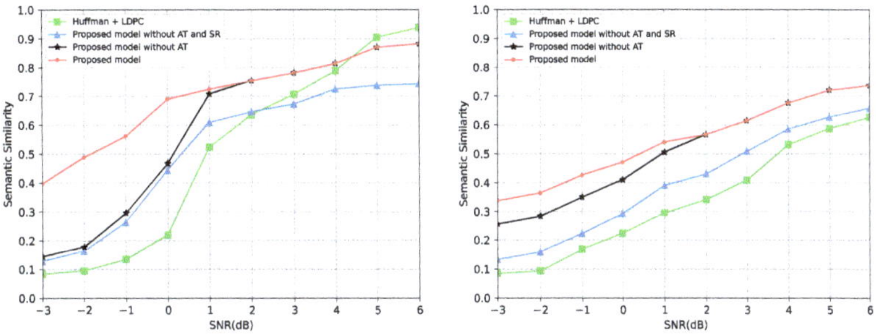

(a) (b)

Figure 11. (**a**) Semantic similarity versus the SNR over the AWGN channel. (**b**) Semantic similarity versus the SNR over the Rayleigh fading channel.

To ensure the fairness of the comparison of experimental results, we computed the time complexities of all strategies. We transmitted 1000 sentences from the transmitter to the receiver by using different strategies and calculated the average execution time. All tests were run on Python and were performed by the computer with AMD Ryzen 7 4800H and NVIDIA GeForce GTX 3060. The results are shown in Table 4. From Table 4, our proposed model increases the computational complexity and improves communication reliability.

Table 4. The time complexity of all strategies.

Strategies	Time Complexity/s
Huffman + LDPC	2.7324
Proposed model without AT and SR	3.1638
Proposed model without AT	3.7742
Proposed model	3.8539

4.2.2. Comparison with Other Semantic Communication Models

To validate that our proposed model is more competitive than existing research, we compared it with the scheme from [23], which adopts an end-to-end deep learning-based communication system for text transmission (named DeepNN). Figure 12 shows the relationship between the SNR and the semantic similarity performance over the AWGN channel. From Figure 12, our proposed model outperforms DeepNN across the entire SNR region. The reasons are two-fold. First, by using triplets as semantic basic symbols, our proposed model can extract lossless semantics. Moreover, the important triplets are allocated more transmission resources in our proposed model, which effectively protects the importance of the semantics. However, DeepNN uses a fixed bit length to encode sentences of different lengths, resulting in a partial loss of semantics.

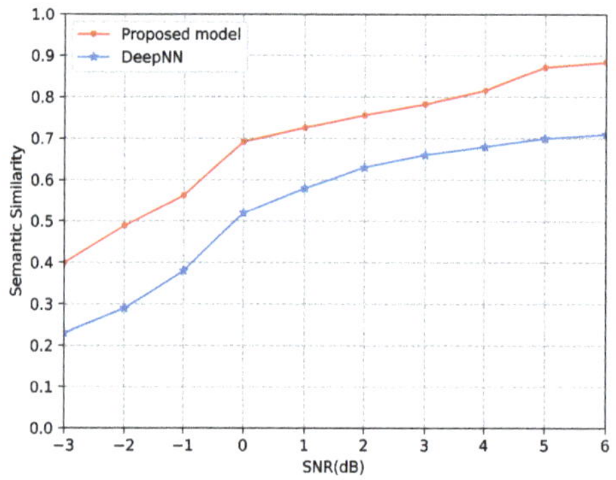

Figure 12. Semantic similarity of our proposed model and DeepNN versus the SNR over the AWGN channel.

5. Conclusions

In this paper, the reliable semantic communication assisted by the knowledge graph was studied, which overcomes the problem that the meaning of data represented by the features of the deep learning model cannot be explainable [26,28]. Specifically, we proposed a semantic extraction scheme that transforms the transmitted sentence into multiple triplets with semantic importance. Moreover, an adaptive transmission scheme is proposed, in which the important triplets are allocated more communication resources to combat channel distortion. Moreover, a semantic restoration scheme was designed to reconstruct the sentence and recover the whole semantic at the receiver. The simulation results show that the proposed system outperforms the traditional schemes in improving communication reliability, especially in the low SNR regime. However, the optimal number of triplets transmitted over a specific channel is still an 'open question'. In the future, more work is needed to analyze the relationship between the number of triplets and the channel quality.

Author Contributions: Conceptualization, S.J.; methodology, S.J. and Y.L.; formal analysis, Y.Z. and P.L.; investigation, K.C. and J.X.; supervision, H.Z.; writing—original draft preparation, S.J. and Y.L.; writing—review and editing, K.C., H.Z. and J.W. All authors have read and agreed to the published version of the manuscript.

Funding: This research was funded in part by the National Natural Science Foundation of China under grant nos. 61931020, U19B2024, and 62001483, and in part by the science and technology innovation Program of Hunan Province under grant no. 2021JJ40690.

Institutional Review Board Statement: Not applicable.

Informed Consent Statement: Not applicable.

Data Availability Statement: Data are available from the authors, on request.

Conflicts of Interest: The authors declare no conflict of interest.

References

1. Sah, D.K.; Kumar, D.P.; Shivalingagowda, C.; Jayasree, P.V.Y. 5G applications and architectures. In *5G Enabled Secure Wireless Networks*; Jayakody, D., Srinivasan, K., Sharma, V., Eds.; Springer: Cham, Switzerland, 2019; pp. 45–68.
2. Zhang, Y.; Zhang, P.; Wei, J. Semantic communication for intelligent devices: Architectures and a paradigm. *Sci. Sin. Inform.* **2022**, *52*, 907–921. [CrossRef]
3. International Telecommunication Union. *Report on the Implementation of the Strategic Plan and the Activities of the Union for 2019–2020*; ITU: Geneva, Switzerland, 2020.
4. Shannon, C.E. A mathematical theory of communication. *Bell Syst. Tech. J.* **1948**, *27*, 379–423. [CrossRef]
5. Pencheva, E.; Atanasov, I.; Asenov, I. Toward network intellectualization in 6G. In Proceedings of the 2020 XI National Conference with International Participation (ELECTRONICA), Sofia, Bulgaria, 23–24 July 2020; pp. 1–4.

6. Khan, L.U.; Saad, W.; Niyato, D.; Han, Z.; Hong, C.S. Digital-Twin-Enabled 6G: Vision, architectural trends, and future directions. *IEEE Commun. Mag.* **2022**, *60*, 74–80. [CrossRef]
7. Zhang, P.; Xu, W.J.; Gao, H.; Niu, K.; Xu, X.D.; Qin, X.Q.; Yuan, C.X.; Qin, Z.J.; Zhao, H.T.; Wei, J.B.; et al. Toward wisdom-evolutionary and primitive-concise 6G: A new paradigm of semantic communication networks. *Engineering* **2021**, *8*, 60–73. [CrossRef]
8. Shi, G.M.; Gao, D.H.; Song, X.D.; Chai, J.X.; Yang, M.X.; Xie, X.M.; Li, L.D.; Li, X.Y. A new communication paradigm: From bit accuracy to semantic fidelity. *arXiv* **2021**, arXiv:2101.12649.
9. Weaver, W. Recent contributions to the mathematical theory of communication. *ETC: Rev. Gen. Semant.* **1953**, *10*, 261–281.
10. Güler, B.; Yener, A.; Swami, A. The semantic communication game. *IEEE Trans. Cogn. Commun. Netw.* **2018**, *4*, 787–802. [CrossRef]
11. Popovski, P.; Simeone, O.; Boccardi, F.; Gündüz, D.; Sahin, O. Semantic-effectiveness filtering and control for post-5G wireless connectivity. *J. Indian Inst. Sci.* **2020**, *100*, 435–443. [CrossRef]
12. Weng, Z.Z.; Qin, Z.J.; Li, G.Y. Semantic communications for speech signals. In Proceedings of the ICC 2021-IEEE International Conference on Communications, Montreal, QC, Canada, 14–23 June 2021.
13. Ji, S.X.; Pan, S.R.; Cambria, E.; Marttinen, P.; Yu, P.S. A survey on knowledge graphs: Representation, acquisition and applications. *IEEE Trans. Neural Netw. Learn. Syst.* **2021**, *33*, 494–514. [CrossRef]
14. Jaradeh, M.Y.; Oelen, A.; Farfar, K.E.; Prinz, M.; D'Souza, J.; Kismihók, G.; Stocker, M.; Auer, S. Open research knowledge graph: Next generation infrastructure for semantic scholarly knowledge. In Proceedings of the 10th International Conference on Knowledge Capture, CA, USA, 19–21 November 2019; pp. 243–246.
15. Atef Mosa, M. Predicting semantic categories in text based on knowledge graph combined with machine learning techniques. *Appl. Artif. Intell.* **2021**, *35*, 933–951. [CrossRef]
16. Zhou, F.H.; Li, Y.H.; Zhang, X.Y.; Wu, Q.H.; Lei, X.F.; Hu, R.Q. Cognitive semantic communication systems driven by knowledge graph. *arXiv* **2022**, arXiv:2022.11958v1.
17. Shi, G.M.; Xiao, Y.; Li, Y.Y.; Xie, X.M. From semantic communication to semantic-aware networking: Model, architecture, and open problems. *IEEE Commun. Mag.* **2021**, *59*, 44–50. [CrossRef]
18. Rudolf, C.; Bar-Hillel, Y. An outline of a theory of semantic information. *J. Symb. Log.* **1954**, *19*, 230–232.
19. Floridi, L. Outline of a theory of strongly semantic information. *Minds Mach.* **2004**, *14*, 197–221. [CrossRef]
20. Bao, J.; Basu, P.; Dean, M.; Partridge, C.; Swami, A.; Leland, W.; Hendler, J. Towards a theory of semantic communication. In Proceedings of the IEEE Network Science Workshop, West Point, NY, USA, 22–24 June 2011; pp. 110–117.
21. Basu, P.; Bao, J.; Dean, M.; Hendler, J. Preserving quality of information by using semantic relationships. In Proceedings of the 2012 IEEE International Conference on Pervasive Computing and Communications Workshops, Lugano, Switzerland, 19–23 March 2012; pp. 58–63.
22. Lan, Q.; Wen, D.; Zhang, Z.; Zeng, Q.; Chen, X.; Popovski, P.; Huang, K. What is semantic communication? A view on conveying meaning in the era of machine intelligence. *arXiv* **2021**, arXiv:2110.00196.
23. Farsad, N.; Rao, M.; Goldsmith, A. Deep learning for joint source-channel coding of text. In Proceedings of the 2018 IEEE International Conference on Acoustics Speech and Signal Processing (ICASSP), Calgary, AB, Canada, 15–20 April 2018; pp. 2326–2330.
24. Rao, M.; Farsad, N.; Goldsmith, A. Variable length joint source-channel coding of text using deep neural networks. In Proceedings of the 2018 IEEE 19th International Workshop on Signal Processing Advances in Wireless Communications (SPAWC), Kalamata, Greece, 25–28 June 2018.
25. Liu, Y.L.; Zhang, Y.Z.; Luo, P.; Jiang, S.T.; Cao, K.; Zhao, H.T.; Wei, J.B. Enhancing communication reliability from the semantic level under low SNR. *Electronics* **2022**, *11*, 1358. [CrossRef]
26. Xie, H.Q.; Qin, Z.J.; Li, G.Y.; Juang, B.H. Deep learning enabled semantic communication systems. *IEEE Trans. Signal Process.* **2021**, *69*, 2663–2675. [CrossRef]
27. Vaswani, A.; Shazeer, N.; Parmar, N.; Uszkoreit, J.; Jones, L.; Gomez, A.N.; Kaiser, L.; Polosukhin, I. Attention is all you need. *Adv. Neural Inf. Process. Syst.* **2017**, *30*, 5998–6008.
28. Xie, H.Q.; Qin, Z.J. A lite distributed semantic communication system for Internet of Things. *IEEE J. Sel. Areas Commun.* **2021**, *39*, 142–153. [CrossRef]
29. Lu, K.; Li, R.P.; Chen, X.F.; Zhao, Z.F.; Zhang, H.G. Reinforcement learning-powered semantic communication via semantic similarity. *arXiv* **2021**, arXiv:2108.12121.
30. Weng, Z.Z.; Qin, Z.J. Semantic communication systems for speech transmission. *IEEE J. Sel. Areas Commun.* **2021**, *39*, 2434–2444. [CrossRef]
31. Hu, Q.; Zhang, G.; Qin, Z.; Cai, Y.; Yu, G. Robust semantic communications against semantic noise. *arXiv* **2022**, arXiv:2202.03338v1.
32. Xie, H.Q.; Qin, Z.J.; Li, G.Y. Task-oriented multi-user semantic communications for VQA task. *arXiv* **2021**, arXiv:2108.07357.
33. Zhou, Q.Y.; Li, R.P.; Zhao, Z.F.; Peng, C.H.; Zhang, H.G. Semantic communication with adaptive universal transformer. *IEEE Wirel. Commun. Le.* **2022**, *11*, 453–457. [CrossRef]
34. Papineni, K.; Roukos, S.; Ward, T.; Zhu, W.J. BLEU: A method for automatic evaluation of machine translation. In Proceedings of the 40th Annual Meeting on Association for Computational Linguistics, Philadelphia, PA, USA, 7–12 July 2002; pp. 311–318.
35. Banerjee, S.; Lavie, A. METEOR: An automatic metric for MT evaluation with improved correlation with human judgments. In Proceedings of the Second Workshop on Statistical Machine Translation, Prague, Czech Republic, 23 June 2007; pp. 228–231.

36. Agirre, E.; Banea, C.; Cer, D.; Diab, M.; Gonzalez-Agirre, A.; Mihalcea, R.; Rigau, G.; Wiebe, J. SemEval-2016 Task 1: Semantic textual similarity, monolingual and cross-lingual evaluation. In Proceedings of the 10th International Workshop on Semantic Evaluation (SemEval-2016), San Diego, CA, USA, 16–17 June 2016; pp. 497–511.
37. Mathur, N.; Baldwin, T.; Cohn, T. Tangled up in BLEU: Reevaluating the evaluation of automatic machine translation evaluation metrics. *arXiv* **2020**, arXiv:2006.06264.
38. Kilgarriff, A.; Fellbaum, C. WordNet: An electronic lexical database. *Language* **2000**, *76*, 706–708. [CrossRef]
39. Devlin, J.; Chang, M.W.; Lee, K.; Toutanova, K. BERT: Pre-training of deep bidirectional transformers for language understanding. In Proceedings of the 2019 Annual Conference of the North American Chapter of the Association for Computational Linguistics: Human Language Technologies (NAACL-HLT 2019), Minneapolis, MN, USA, 2–7 June 2019.
40. Qi, R.; Zhang, Y.H.; Zhang, Y.H.; Bolton, J.; Manning, C.D. Stanza: A python natural language processing toolkit for many human languages. In Proceedings of the 58th Annual Meeting of the Association for Computational Linguistics: System Demonstrations, Online, 5–10 July 2020; pp. 101–108.
41. Greff, K.; Srivastava, R.K.; Koutník, J.; Steunebrink, B.R.; Schmidhuber, J. LSTM: A search space odyssey. *IEEE Trans. Neural Netw. Learn. Syst.* **2017**, *28*, 2222–2232. [CrossRef]
42. Velickovic, P.; Cucurull, G.; Casanova, A.; Romero, A.; Lio, P.; Bengio, Y. Graph attention networks. In Proceedings of the 6th International Conference on Learning Representations, Vancouver, BC, Canada, 30 April–3 May 2018.
43. Huffman, D.A. A method for the construction of minimum-redundancy codes. *Proc. IRE* **1952**, *40*, 1098–1101. [CrossRef]
44. Gallager, R. Low-density parity-check codes. *IRE Trans. Inf. Theory* **1962**, *8*, 21–28. [CrossRef]
45. Gardent, C.; Shimorina, A.; Narayan, S.; Perez-Beltrachini, L. Creating training corpora for NLG micro-planners. In Proceedings of the 55th Annual Meeting of the Association for Computational Linguistics (Volume 1: Long Papers), Vancouver, BC, Canada, 30 July–4 August 2017; pp. 179–188.

entropy

Article

Coded Caching for Broadcast Networks with User Cooperation †

Zhenhao Huang [1], Jiahui Chen [1], Xiaowen You [1], Shuai Ma [2] and Youlong Wu [1,*]

1 School of Information Science and Technology, ShanghaiTech University, No. 393 Huaxia Middle Road, Pudong, Shanghai 201210, China; huangzhh@shanghaitech.edu.cn (Z.H.); chenjh1@shanghaitech.edu.cn (J.C.); youxw@shanghaitech.edu.cn (X.Y.)
2 Information Processing and Communications Laboratory, Telecom Paris, IP Paris, 91120 Palaiseau, France; ma@telecom-paris.fr
* Correspondence: wuyl1@shanghaitech.edu.cn
† This paper was in part presented at the IEEE Information Theory Workshop, Visby, Gotland, Sweden, 2019 and at the IEEE 57th Annual Allerton Conference on Communication, Control, and Computing (Allerton), Monticello, IL, USA, 24–27 September 2019.

Abstract: Caching technique is a promising approach to reduce the heavy traffic load and improve user latency experience for the Internet of Things (IoT). In this paper, by exploiting edge cache resources and communication opportunities in device-to-device (D2D) networks and broadcast networks, two novel coded caching schemes are proposed that greatly reduce transmission latency for the centralized and decentralized caching settings, respectively. In addition to the multicast gain, both schemes obtain an additional *cooperation gain* offered by user cooperation and an additional *parallel gain* offered by the parallel transmission among the server and users. With a newly established lower bound on the transmission delay, we prove that the centralized coded caching scheme is *order-optimal*, i.e., achieving a constant multiplicative gap within the minimum transmission delay. The decentralized coded caching scheme is also order-optimal if each user's cache size is larger than a threshold which approaches zero as the total number of users tends to infinity. Moreover, theoretical analysis shows that to reduce the transmission delay, the number of users sending signals simultaneously should be appropriately chosen according to the user's cache size, and always letting more users send information in parallel could cause high transmission delay.

Keywords: coded cache; cooperation; device-to-device; transmission delay

Citation: Huang, Z.; Chen, J.; You, X.; Ma, S.; Wu, Y. Coded Caching for Broadcast Networks with User Cooperation. *Entropy* **2022**, *24*, 1034. https://doi.org/10.3390/e24081034

Academic Editors: H. Vincent Poor, Holger Boche, Rafael F. Schaefer and Onur Günlü

Received: 22 June 2022
Accepted: 25 July 2022
Published: 27 July 2022

1. Introduction

With the rapid development of Internet of Things (IoT) technologies, IoT data traffic, such as live streaming and on-demand video streaming, has grown dramatically over the past few years. To reduce the traffic load and improve the user latency experience, the caching technique has been viewed as a promising approach that shifts the network traffic to low congestion periods. In the seminal paper [1], Maddah-Ali and Niesen proposed a coded caching scheme based on centralized file placement and coded multicast delivery that achieves a significantly larger global multicast gain compared to the conventional uncoded caching scheme.

The coded caching scheme has attracted wide and significant interest. The coded caching scheme was extended to a setup with decentralized file placement, where no coordination is required for the file placement [2]. For the cache-aided broadcast network, ref. [3] showed that the rate–memory tradeoff of the above caching system is within a factor of 2.00884. For the setting with uncoded file placement where each user stores uncoded content from the library, refs. [4,5] proved that Maddah-Ali and Niesen's scheme is optimal. In [6], both the placement and delivery phases of coded caching are depicted using a placement delivery array (PDA), and an upper bound for all possible regular PDAs was established. In [7], the authors studied a cached-aided network with heterogeneous setting where the user cache memories are unequal. More asymmetric network settings have been discussed, such as coded caching with heterogeneous user profiles [8], with distinct sizes of files [9], with asymmetric cache sizes [10–12] and with distinct link qualities [13]. The settings with varying file popularities have been discussed in [14–16]. Coded caching that jointly considers various heterogeneous aspects was studied in [17]. Other works on coded caching include, e.g., cache-aided noiseless multi-server network [18], cache-aided wireless/noisy broadcast networks [19–22], cache-aided relay networks [23–25], cache-aided interference management [26,27], coded caching with random demands [28], caching in combination networks [29], coded caching under secrecy constraints [30], coded caching with reduced subpacketization [31,32], the coded caching problem where each user requests multiple files [33], and a cache-aided broadcast network for correlated content [34], etc.

A different line of work is to study the cached-aided networks without the presence of a server, e.g., the device-to-device (D2D) cache-aided network. In [35], the authors investigated coded caching for wireless D2D network [35], where users locate in a fixed mesh topology wireless D2D network. A D2D system with selfish users who do not participate in delivering the missing subfiles to all users was studied in [36]. Wang et al. applied the PDA to characterize cache-aided D2D wireless networks in [37]. In [38], the authors studied the spatial D2D networks in which the user locations are modeled by a Poisson point process. For heterogeneous cache-aided D2D networks where users are equipped with cache memories of distinct sizes, ref. [39] minimized the delivery load by optimizing over the partition during the placement phase and the size and structure of D2D during the delivery phase. A highly dense wireless network with device mobility was investigated in [40].

In fact, combining the cache-aided broadcast network with the cache-aided D2D network can potentially reduce the transmission latency. This hybrid network is common in many practical distributed systems such as cloud network [41], where a central cloud server broadcasts messages to multiple users through the cellular network, and meanwhile users communicate with each other through a fiber local area network (LAN). A potential scenario is that users in a moderately dense area, such as a university, want to download files, such as movies, from a data library, such as a video service provider. It should be noted that the user demands are highly redundant, and the files need not only be stored by a central server but also partially cached by other users. Someone can attain the desired content through both communicating with the central server and other users such that the communication and storage resources can be used efficiently. Unfortunately, there is very little research investigating the coded caching problem for this hybrid network. In this paper, we consider such hybrid cache-aided network where a server consisting of $N \in \mathbb{Z}^+$ files connects with $K \in \mathbb{Z}^+$ users through a broadcast network, and meanwhile the users can exchange information via a D2D network. Unlike the settings of [35,38], in which each user can only communicate with its neighboring users via spatial multiplexing, we consider the D2D network as either an error-free shared link or a flexible routing network [18]. In particular, for the case of the shared link, all users exchange information via a shared link. In the flexible routing network, there exists a routing strategy adaptively partitioning all users into multiple groups, in each of which one user sends data packets error-free to the remaining users in the corresponding group. Let $\alpha \in \mathbb{Z}$ be the number of groups who send signals at the same time, then the following fundamental questions arise for this hybrid cache-aided network:

- *How does α affect the system performance?*
- *What is the (approximately) optimal value of α to minimize the transmission latency?*
- *How can communication loads be allocated between the server and users to achieve the minimum transmission latency?*

In this paper, we try to address these questions, and our main contributions are summarized as follows:

- We propose novel coded caching schemes for this hybrid network under centralized and decentralized data placement. Both schemes efficiently exploit communication opportunities in D2D and broadcast networks, and appropriately allocate communication loads between the server and users. In addition to multicast gain, our schemes achieve much smaller transmission latency than both that of Maddah-Ali and Niesen's scheme for a broadcast network [1,2] and the D2D coded caching scheme [35]. We characterize a *cooperation gain* and a *parallel gain* achieved by our schemes, where the cooperation gain is obtained through cooperation among users in the D2D network, and the parallel gain is obtained through the parallel transmission between the server and users.
- We prove that the centralized scheme is order-optimal, i.e., achieving the optimal transmission delay within a constant multiplicative gap in all regimes. Moreover, the decentralized scheme is also optimal when the cache size of each user M is larger than the threshold $N(1-\sqrt[K-1]{1/(K+1)})$ that is approaching zero as $K \to \infty$.
- For the centralized data placement case, theoretical analysis shows that α should decrease with the increase of the user caching size. In particular, when each user's caching size is sufficiently large, only one user should be allowed to send information, indicating that the D2D network can be just a simple shared link connecting all users. For the decentralized data placement case, α should be dynamically changing according to the sizes of subfiles created in the placement phase. In other words, always letting more users parallelly send information can cause a high transmission delay.

Please note that the decentralized scenario is much more complicated than the centralized scenario, since each subfile can be stored by $s = 1, 2, \ldots, K$ users, leading to a dynamic file-splitting and communication strategy in the D2D network. Our schemes, in particular the decentralized coded caching scheme, differ greatly with the D2D coded caching scheme in [35]. Specifically, ref. [35] considered a fixed network topology where each user connects with a fixed set of users, and the total user cache sizes must be large enough to store all files in the library. However, in our schemes, the user group partition is dynamically changing, and each user can communicate with any set of users via network routing. Moreover, our model has the server share communication loads with the users, resulting in an allocation problem on communication loads between the broadcast network and D2D network. Finally, our schemes achieve a tradeoff between the cooperation gain, parallel gain and multicast gain, while the schemes in [1,2,35] only achieve the multicast gain.

The remainder of this paper is as follows. Section 2 presents the system model, and defines the main problem studied in this paper. We summarize the obtained main results in Section 3. Following that is a detailed description of the centralized coded caching scheme with user cooperation in Section 4. Section 5 extends the techniques we developed for the centralized caching problem to the setting of decentralized random caching. Section 6 concludes this paper.

2. System Model and Problem Definition

Consider a cache-aided network consisting of a single server and K users as depicted in Figure 1. The server has a library of N independent files $W_1, \ldots, W_N$. Each file W_n, $n = 1, \ldots, N$, is uniformly distributed over

$$[2^F] \triangleq \{1, 2, \ldots, 2^F\},$$

for some positive integer F. The server connects with K users through a noisy-free shared link but rate-limited to a network speed of C_1 bits per second (bits/s). Each user $k \in [K]$ is equipped with a cache memory of size MF bits, for some $M \in [0, N]$, and can communicate with each other via a D2D network.

We mainly focus on two types of D2D networks: a shared link as in [1,2] and a flexible routing network introduced in [18]. In the case of a shared link, all users connect with each other through a shared error-free link but rate-limited to C_2 bits/s. In the flexible routing network, K users can arbitrarily form multiple groups via network routing, in each of which at most one user can send error-free data packets at a network speed C_2 bits/s to the remaining users within the group. To unify these two types of D2D networks, we introduce an integer $\alpha_{\max} \in \{1, \lfloor \frac{K}{2} \rfloor\}$, which denotes the maximum number of groups allowed to send data parallelly in the D2D network. For example, when $\alpha_{\max} = 1$, the D2D network degenerates into a shared link, and when $\alpha_{\max} = \lfloor \frac{K}{2} \rfloor$, it turns to be the flexible network.

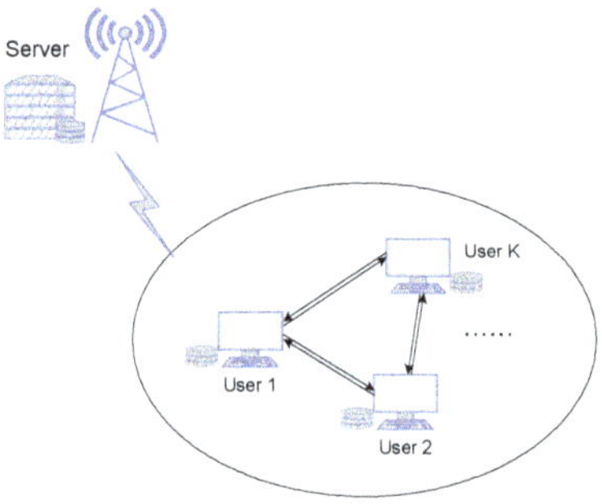

Figure 1. Caching system considered in this paper. A server connects with K cache-enabled users and the users can cooperate through a flexible network.

The system works in two phases: a placement phase and a delivery phase. In the placement phase, all users will access the entire library $W_1, \dots, W_N$ and fill the content to their caching memories. More specifically, each user k, for $k \in [K]$, maps $W_1, \dots, W_N$ to its cache content:

$$Z_k \triangleq \phi_k(W_1, \dots, W_N), \tag{1}$$

for some caching function

$$\phi_k : [2^F]^N \to [\lfloor 2^{MF} \rfloor]. \tag{2}$$

In the delivery phase, each user requests one of the N files from the library. We denote the demand of user k as $d_k \in [N]$, and its desired file as W_{d_k}. Let $\mathbf{d} \triangleq (d_1, \dots, d_K)$ denotes the request vector. In this paper, we investigate the worst request case where each user makes a unique request.

Once the request vector $\mathbf{d}$ is informed to the server and all users, the server produces the symbol

$$X \triangleq f_{\mathbf{d}}(W_1, \dots, W_N), \tag{3}$$

and broadcasts it to all users through the broadcast network. Meanwhile, user $k \in \{1, \dots, K\}$ produces the symbol (Each user k can produce X_k as a function of Z_k and the received signals sent by the server, but because all users can access to the server's signal due to the fact that the server broadcasts its signals to the network, it is equivalent to generating X_k as a function Z_k).

$$X_k \triangleq f_{k,\mathbf{d}}(Z_k), \tag{4}$$

and sends it to a set of intended users $\mathcal{D}_k \subseteq [K]$ through the D2D network. Here, $\mathcal{D}_k$ represents the set of destination users served by node k, $f_{\mathbf{d}}$ and $f_{k,\mathbf{d}}$ are some encoding functions

$$f_{\mathbf{d}} : [2^F]^N \to [\lfloor 2^{R_1 F} \rfloor], \ f_{k,\mathbf{d}} : [\lfloor 2^{MF} \rfloor] \to [\lfloor 2^{R_2 F} \rfloor], \tag{5}$$

where R_1 and R_2 denote the *transmission rate* sent by the server in the broadcast network and by each user in the D2D network, respectively. Here we focus on the symmetric case where all users have the same transmission rate. Due to the constraint of $\alpha_{\max}$, at most

$\alpha_{\max}$ users can send signals parallelly in each channel use. The set of $\alpha_{\max}$ users who send signals in parallel could be adaptively changed in the delivery phase.

At the end of the delivery phase, due to the error-free transmission in the broadcast and D2D networks, user k observes symbols sent to them, i.e., $(X_j : j \in [K], k \in \mathcal{D}_j)$, and decodes its desired message as $\hat{W}_{d_k} = \psi_{k,\mathbf{d}}(X, (X_j : j \in [K], k \in \mathcal{D}_j), Z_k)$, where $\psi_{k,\mathbf{d}}$ is a decoding function.

We define the worst-case probability of error as

$$P_e \triangleq \max_{\mathbf{d} \in \mathcal{F}^n} \max_{k \in [K]} \Pr\big(\hat{W}_{d_k} \neq W_{d_k}\big). \tag{6}$$

A coded caching scheme (M, R_1, R_2) consists of caching functions $\{\phi_k\}$, encoding functions $\{f_{\mathbf{d}}, f_{k,\mathbf{d}}\}$ and decoding functions $\{\psi_{k,\mathbf{d}}\}$. We say that the rate region (M, R_1, R_2) is *achievable* if for every $\epsilon > 0$ and every large enough file size F, there exists a coded caching scheme such that P_e is less than ϵ.

Since the server and the users send signals in parallel, the total transmission delay, denoted by T, can be defined as

$$T \triangleq \max\{\frac{R_1 F}{C_1}, \frac{R_2 F}{C_2}\}. \tag{7}$$

The *optimal* transmission delay is $T^* \triangleq \inf\{T : T \text{ is achievable}\}$. For simplicity, we assume that $C_1 = C_2 = F$, and then from (7) we have

$$T = \max\{R_1, R_2\}. \tag{8}$$

When $C_1 \neq C_2$, e.g., $C_1 : C_2 = 1/k$, one small adjustment allowing our scheme to continue to work is multiplying λ by $1/(k(1-\lambda)+\lambda)$, where λ is a devisable parameter introduced later.

Our goal is to design a coded caching scheme to minimize the transmission delay. Finally, in this paper we assume $K \leq N$ and $M \leq N$. Extending the results to other scenarios is straightforward, as mentioned in [1].

3. Main Results

We first establish a general lower bound on the transmission delay for the system model described in Section 2, then present two upper bounds of the optimal transmission delay achieved by our centralized and decentralized coded caching schemes, respectively. Finally, we present the optimality results of these two schemes.

Theorem 1 (Lower Bound). *For memory size $0 \leq M \leq N$, the optimal transmission delay is lower bounded by*

$$T^* \geq \max\left\{\frac{1}{2}\left(1 - \frac{M}{N}\right), \max_{s \in [K]}\left(s - \frac{KM}{\lfloor N/s \rfloor}\right), \max_{s \in [K]}\left(s - \frac{sM}{\lfloor N/s \rfloor}\right)\frac{1}{1+\alpha_{\max}}\right\}. \tag{9}$$

Proof. See the proof in Appendix A. □

3.1. Centralized Coded Caching

In the following theorem, we present an upper bound on the transmission delay for the centralized caching setup.

Theorem 2 (Upper Bound for the Centralized Scenario). *Let $t \triangleq KM/N \in \mathbb{Z}^+$, and $\alpha \in \mathbb{Z}^+$. For memory size $M \in \{0, \frac{N}{K}, \frac{2N}{K}, \ldots, N\}$, the optimal transmission delay T^* is upper bounded by $T^* \le T_{\text{central}}$, where*

$$T_{\text{central}} \triangleq \min_{\alpha \le \alpha_{\max}} K\Big(1-\frac{M}{N}\Big)\frac{1}{1+t+\alpha\min\{\lfloor\frac{K}{\alpha}\rfloor-1,t\}}. \tag{10}$$

For general $0 \le M \le N$, the lower convex envelope of these points is achievable.

Proof. See scheme in Section 4. □

The following simple example shows that the proposed upper bound can greatly reduce the transmission delay.

Example 1. *Consider a network described in Section 2 with $KM/N = K-1$. The coded caching scheme without D2D communication [1] has the server multicast an XOR message useful for all K users, achieving the transmission delay $K(1-\frac{M}{N})\frac{1}{1+t} = \frac{1}{K}$. The D2D coded caching scheme [35] achieves the transmission delay $\frac{N}{M}(1-\frac{M}{N}) = \frac{1}{K-1}$. The achievable transmission delay in Theorem 2 equals $\frac{1}{2K-1}$ by letting $\alpha = 1$, almost twice as short as the transmission delay of previous schemes if K is sufficiently large.*

From (10), we obtain that the optimal value of α, denoted by α^*, equals 1 if $t \ge K-1$ and to $\alpha_{\max}$ if $t \le \lfloor\frac{K}{\alpha_{\max}}\rfloor - 1$. When ignoring all integer constraints, we obtain $\alpha^* = \frac{K}{t+1}$. We rewrite this choice as follows:

$$\alpha^* = \begin{cases} 1, & t \ge K-1, \\ K/(t+1), & \lfloor K/\alpha_{\max}\rfloor - 1 < t < K-1, \\ \alpha_{\max}, & t \le \lfloor K/\alpha_{\max}\rfloor - 1. \end{cases} \tag{11}$$

Remark 1. *From (11), we observe that when M is small such that $t \le \lfloor K/\alpha_{\max}\rfloor - 1$, we have $\alpha^* = \alpha_{\max}$. As M is increasing, α^* becomes $K/(t+1)$, smaller than $\alpha_{\max}$. When M is sufficiently large such that $M \ge (K-1)N/K$, only one user should be allowed to send information, i.e., $\alpha^* = 1$. This indicates that letting more users parallelly send information could be harmful. The main reason for this phenomenon is the existence of a tradeoff between the multicast gain,* cooperation gain *and* parallel gain, *which will be introduced below in this section.*

Comparing T_{central} with the transmission delay achieved by Maddah-Ali and Niesen's scheme for the broadcast network [1], i.e., $K(1-\frac{M}{N})\frac{1}{1+t}$, T_{central} consists of an additional factor

$$G_{\text{central,c}} \triangleq \frac{1}{1+\frac{\alpha}{1+t}\min\{\lfloor\frac{K}{\alpha}\rfloor-1,t\}}, \tag{12}$$

referred to as *centralized cooperation gain*, as it arises from user cooperation. Comparing T_{central} with the transmission delay achieved by the D2D coded caching scheme [35], i.e., $\frac{N}{M}(1-\frac{M}{N})$, T_{central} consists of an additional factor

$$G_{\text{central,p}} \triangleq \frac{1}{1+\frac{1}{t}+\frac{\alpha}{t}\min\{\lfloor\frac{K}{\alpha}\rfloor-1,t\}}, \tag{13}$$

referred to as *centralized parallel gain*, as it arises from parallel transmission among the server and users. Both gains depend on K, M/N and $\alpha_{\max}$.

Substituting the optimal α^* into (12), we have

$$G_{\text{central,c}} = \begin{cases} \dfrac{1+t}{K+t}, & t \geq K-1, \\ \dfrac{1+t}{K-\frac{K}{t+1}+t}, & \lfloor \dfrac{K}{\alpha_{\max}} \rfloor - 1 < t < K-1, \\ \dfrac{1+t}{\alpha_{\max}t+t+1}, & t \leq \lfloor \dfrac{K}{\alpha_{\max}} \rfloor - 1. \end{cases} \tag{14}$$

When fixing $(K, N, \alpha_{\max})$, $G_{\text{central,c}}$ in general is not a monotonic function of M. More specifically, when M is small enough such that $t < \lfloor \frac{K}{\alpha_{\max}} \rfloor - 1$, the function $G_{\text{central,c}}$ is monotonically decreasing, indicating that the improvement caused by introducing D2D communication. This is mainly because relatively larger M allows users to share more common data with each other, providing more opportunities on user cooperation. However, when M grows larger such that $t \geq \lfloor \frac{K}{\alpha_{\max}} \rfloor - 1$, the local and global caching gains become dominant, and less improvement can be obtained from user cooperation, turning $G_{\text{central,c}}$ to a monotonic increasing function of M,

Similarly, substituting the optimal α^* into (13), we obtain

$$G_{\text{central,p}} = \begin{cases} \dfrac{t}{K+t}, & t \geq K-1, \\ \dfrac{t}{\frac{t \cdot K}{t+1}+t+1}, & \lfloor \dfrac{K}{\alpha_{\max}} \rfloor - 1 < t < K-1, \\ \dfrac{t}{\alpha_{\max}t+t+1}, & t \leq \lfloor \dfrac{K}{\alpha_{\max}} \rfloor - 1. \end{cases} \tag{15}$$

Equation (15) shows that $G_{\text{central,p}}$ is monotonically increasing with t, mainly due to the fact that when M increases, more content can be sent through the D2D network without the help of the central server, decreasing the improvement from parallel transmission between the server and users.

The centralized cooperation gain (12) and parallel gain (13) are plotted in Figure 2 when $N = 40$, $K = 20$ and $\alpha_{\max} = 5$.

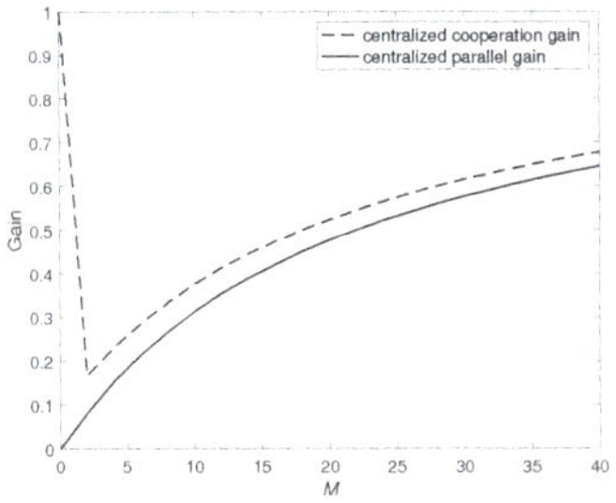

Figure 2. Centralized cooperation gain and parallel gain when $N = 40$, $K = 20$ and $\alpha_{\max} = 5$.

Remark 2. *Larger α could lead to better parallel and cooperation gain (more uses can concurrently multicast signals to other users), but will result in worse multicast gain (signals are multicast to fewer users in each group). The choice of α in (11) is in fact a tradeoff between the multicast gain, parallel gain and cooperation gain.*

The proposed scheme achieving the upper bound in Theorem 2 is order-optimal.

Theorem 3. *For memory size $0 \leq M \leq N$,*

$$\frac{T_{\text{central}}}{T^*} \leq 31. \tag{16}$$

Proof. See the proof in Appendix B. □

The exact gap of T_{central}/T^* could be much smaller. One could apply the method proposed in [3] to obtain a tighter lower bound and shrink the gap. In this paper, we only prove the order optimality of the proposed scheme, and leave the work of finding a smaller gap as the future work.

Figure 3 plots the lower bound (9) and upper bounds achieved by various schemes, including the proposed scheme, the scheme *Maddah-Ali 2014* in [1] which considers the broadcast network without D2D communication, and the scheme *Ji 2016* in [35], which considers the D2D network without server. It is obvious that our scheme outperforms the previous schemes and approaches closely to the lower bound.

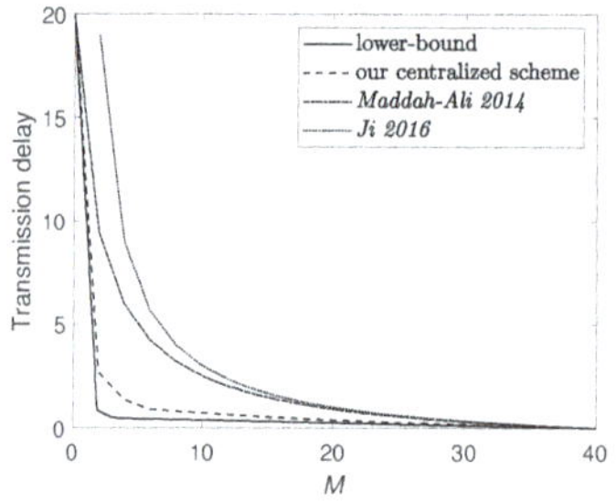

Figure 3. Transmission delay when $N = 40$, $K = 20$ and $\alpha_{\max} = 5$. The upper bounds are achieved under the centralized caching scenario.

3.2. Decentralized Coded Caching

We exploit the multicast gain from coded caching, D2D communication, and parallel transmission between the server and users, leading to the following upper bound.

Theorem 4 (Upper Bound for the Decentralized Scenario). *Define $p \triangleq M/N$. For memory size $0 \le M \le N$, the optimal transmission delay T^* is upper bounded by*

$$T^* \le T_{\text{decentral}} \triangleq \max\left\{R_\emptyset, \frac{R_\text{s} R_\text{u}}{R_\text{s} + R_\text{u} - R_\emptyset}\right\}, \tag{17}$$

where

$$R_\emptyset \triangleq K(1-p)^K, \tag{18}$$

$$R_\text{s} \triangleq \frac{1-p}{p}\left(1-(1-p)^K\right), \tag{19}$$

$$R_\text{u} \triangleq \frac{1}{\alpha_{\max}} \sum_{s=2}^{\lceil \frac{K}{\alpha_{\max}} \rceil - 1} \left(\frac{s\binom{K}{s}}{s-1} p^{s-1}(1-p)^{K-s+1}\right) + \sum_{s=\lceil \frac{K}{\alpha_{\max}} \rceil}^{K} \left(\frac{K\binom{K-1}{s-1}}{f(K,s)} p^{s-1}(1-p)^{K-s+1}\right), \tag{20}$$

with

$$f(K,s) \triangleq \begin{cases} \lfloor \frac{K}{s} \rfloor (s-1), & (K \bmod s) < 2, \\ K - 1 - \lfloor K/s \rfloor, & (K \bmod s) \ge 2. \end{cases} \tag{21}$$

Proof. Here, $R_\emptyset$ represents the transmission rate of sending contents that are not cached by any user, R_s and R_u represent the transmission rate sent by the server via the broadcast network, and the transmission rate sent by users via the D2D network, respectively. Equation (17) balances the communication loads assigned to the server and users. See more detailed proof in Section 5. □

The key idea of the scheme achieving (17) is to partition K users into $\lceil \frac{K}{s} \rceil$ groups for each communication round $s \in [K-1]$, and let each group perform the D2D coded caching scheme [35] to exchange information. The main challenge is that that among all $\lceil \frac{K}{s} \rceil$ groups, there are $\lfloor \frac{K}{s} \rfloor$ groups of the same size s, and an *abnormal* group of size $(K \bmod s)$ if $(K \bmod s) \neq 0$, leading to an asymmetric caching setup. One may use the scheme [35] for the groups of size s, for the group of size $(K \bmod s) \geq 2$, but how to exploit the caching resource and communication capability of all groups while balancing communication loads among the two types of groups to minimize the transmission delay remains elusive and needs to be carefully designed. Moreover, this challenge poses complexities both in establishing the upper bound and in optimality proof.

Remark 3. *The upper bound in Theorem 4 is achieved by setting the number of users that exactly send signals in parallel as follows:*

$$\alpha_{\mathrm{D}} = \begin{cases} \alpha_{\max}, & \textit{case 1}, \\ \lfloor \frac{K}{s} \rfloor, & \textit{case 2}, \\ \lceil \frac{K}{s} \rceil, & \textit{case 3}. \end{cases} \tag{22}$$

If $\lceil \frac{K}{s} \rceil > \alpha_{\max}$, the number of users who send data in parallel is smaller than α_{max}, indicating that always letting more users parallelly send messages could cause higher transmission delay. For example, when $K \geq 4$, $s = K-1$ and $\alpha_{max} = \lfloor \frac{K}{2} \rfloor$, we have $\alpha_D = 1 < \alpha_{max}$.

Remark 4. *From the definitions of $T_{\mathrm{decentral}}$, R_{s}, R_{u} and $R_{\emptyset}$, it is easy to obtain that $R_{\emptyset} \leq T_{\mathrm{decentral}} \leq R_{\mathrm{s}}$,*

$$T_{\mathrm{decentral}} = \begin{cases} \frac{R_{\mathrm{s}} R_{\mathrm{u}}}{R_{\mathrm{s}} + R_{\mathrm{u}} - R_{\emptyset}}, & R_{\mathrm{u}} \geq R_{\emptyset}, \\ R_{\emptyset}, & R_{\mathrm{u}} < R_{\emptyset}, \end{cases} \tag{23}$$

$T_{\mathrm{decentral}}$ decreases as $\alpha_{\max}$ increases, and $T_{\mathrm{decentral}}$ increases as R_{u} increases if $R_{\mathrm{u}} \geq R_{\emptyset}$.

Due to the complex term R_{u}, $T_{\mathrm{decentral}}$ in Theorem 4 is hard to evaluate. Since $T_{\mathrm{decentral}}$ is increasing as R_{u} increases (see Remark 4), substituting the following upper bound of R_{u} into (17) provides an efficient way to evaluate $T_{\mathrm{decentral}}$.

Corollary 1. *For memory size $0 \leq p \leq 1$, the upper bound of R_{u} is given below:*

- $\alpha_{\max} = 1$ *(a shared link):*

$$R_{\mathrm{u}} \leq \frac{1-p}{p}\left[1 - \frac{5}{2}Kp(1-p)^{K-1} - 4(1-p)^{K} + \frac{3(1-(1-p)^{K+1})}{(K+1)p}\right]; \tag{24}$$

- $\alpha_{\max} = \lfloor \frac{K}{2} \rfloor$ *(a flexible network):*

$$R_{\mathrm{u}} \leq \frac{K(1-p)}{(K-1)}\left[1 - (1-p)^{K-1} - \frac{2/p}{K-2}\left(1-(1-p)^{K} - Kp(1-p)^{K-1}\right)\right]. \tag{25}$$

Proof. See the proof in Appendix C. □

Recall that the transmission delay achieved by the decentralized scheme without D2D communication [2] is equal to R_{s} given in (19). We define the ratio between $T_{\mathrm{decentral}}$ and R_{s} as *decentralized cooperation gain*:

$$G_{\mathrm{decentral,c}} \triangleq \max\left\{\frac{R_{\emptyset}}{R_{\mathrm{s}}}, \frac{R_{\mathrm{u}}}{R_{\mathrm{s}} + R_{\mathrm{u}} - R_{\emptyset}}\right\}, \tag{26}$$

with $G_{\text{decentral,c}} \in [0, 1]$ because of $R_{\varnothing} \leq R_s$. Similar to the centralized scenario, this gain arises from the coordination between users in the D2D network. Moreover, we also compare $T_{\text{decentral}}$ with the transmission delay $(1-p)/p$, achieved by the D2D decentralized coded caching scheme [35], and define the ratio between R_s and $(1-p)/p$ as *decentralized parallel gain*:

$$G_{\text{decentral,p}} \triangleq G_{\text{decentral,c}} \cdot \Big(1 - (1-p)^K\Big), \tag{27}$$

where $G_{\text{decentral,p}} \in [0, 1]$ arises from the parallel transmission between the server and the users.

We plot the decentralized cooperation gain and parallel gain for the two types of D2D networks in Figure 4 when $N = 20$ and $K = 10$. It can be seen that $G_{\text{decentral,c}}$ and $G_{\text{decentral,p}}$ in general are not monotonic functions of M. Here $G_{\text{decentral,c}}$ performs in a way similar to $G_{\text{central,c}}$. When M is small, the function $G_{\text{decentral,c}}$ is monotonically decreasing from value 1 until reaching the minimum. For larger M, the function $G_{\text{decentral,c}}$ turns to monotonically increase with M. The reason for this phenomenon is that in the decentralized scenario, when M increases, the proportion of subfiles that are not cached by any user and must be sent by the server is decreasing. Thus, there are more subfiles that can be sent parallelly via D2D network as M increases. Meanwhile, the decentralized scheme in [2] offers an additional multicasting gain. Therefore, we need to balance these two gains to reduce the transmission delay.

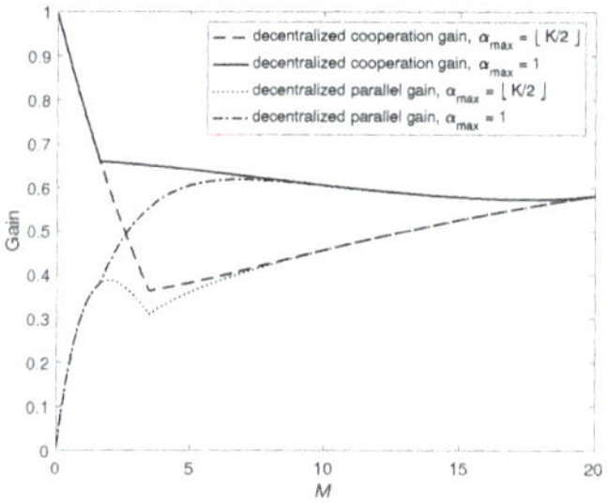

Figure 4. Decentralized cooperation gain and parallel gain when $N = 20$ and $K = 10$.

The function $G_{\text{decentral,p}}$ behaves differently as it monotonically increases when M is small. After reaching the maximal value, the function $G_{\text{decentral,p}}$ decreases monotonically until meeting the local minimum (The abnormal bend in parallel gain when $\alpha_{\max} = \lfloor \frac{K}{2} \rfloor$ comes from a balance effect between the $G_{\text{decentral,c}}$ and $1-(1-p)^K$ in (27)), then $G_{\text{decentral,p}}$ turns to be a monotonic increasing function for large M. Similar to the centralized case, as M increases, the impact of parallel transmission among the server and users becomes smaller since more data can be transmitted by the users.

Theorem 5. *Define* $p \triangleq M/N$ *and* $p_{\text{th}} \triangleq 1 - \left(\frac{1}{K+1}\right)^{\frac{1}{K-1}}$, *which tends to 0 as K tends to infinity. For memory size* $0 \leq M \leq N$,

- *if* $\alpha_{\max} = 1$ *(shared link), then*

$$\frac{T_{\text{decentral}}}{T^*} \leq 24;$$

- *if* $\alpha_{\max} = \lfloor \frac{K}{2} \rfloor$, *then*

$$\frac{T_{\text{decentral}}}{T^*} \leq \begin{cases} \max\left\{6, 2K\left(\dfrac{2K}{2K+1}\right)^{K-1}\right\}, & p < p_{\text{th}}, \\ 6, & p \geq p_{\text{th}}. \end{cases}$$

Proof. See the proof in Appendix D. □

Figure 5 plots the lower bound in (9) and upper bounds achieved by various decentralized coded caching schemes, including our scheme, the scheme *Maddah-Ali 2015* in [2] which considers the case without D2D communication, and the scheme *Ji 2016* in [35] which considers the case without server.

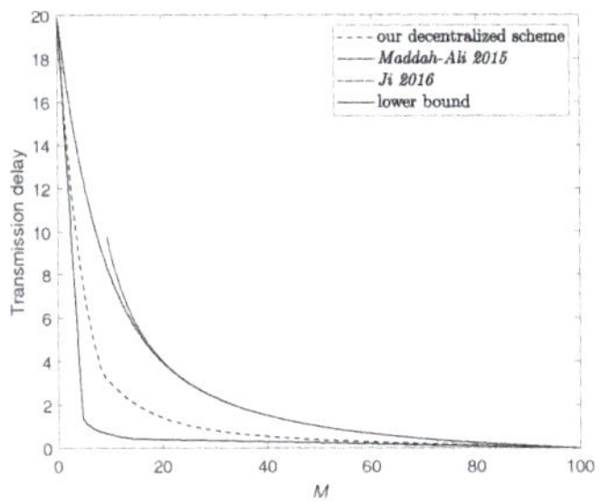

Figure 5. Transmission delay when $N = 100$, $K = 20$ and $\alpha_{\max} = 3$. The upper bounds are achieved under the decentralized random caching scenario.

4. Coding Scheme under Centralized Data Placement

In this section, we describe a novel centralized coded caching scheme for arbitrary K, N and M such that $t = KM/N$ is a positive integer. The scheme can be extended to the general case $1 \le t \le K$ by following the same approach as in [1].

We first use an illustrative example to show how we form D2D communication groups, split files and deliver data, and then present our generalized centralized coding caching scheme.

4.1. An Illustrative Example

Consider a network consisting of $K = 6$ users with cache size $M = 4$, and a library of $N = 6$ files. Thus, $t = KM/N = 4$. Divide all six users into two groups of equal size, and choose an integer $L_1 = 2$ that guarantees $\frac{K\binom{K-1}{t}L_1}{\min\{\alpha(\lfloor K/\alpha \rfloor - 1), t\}}$ to be an integer. (According to (11) and (29), one optimal choice could be ($\alpha = 1$, $L_1 = 4$, $\lambda = 5/9$), here we choose ($\alpha = 2$, $L_1 = 2$, $\lambda = 1/3$) for simplicity, and also in order to demonstrate that even with a suboptimal choice, our scheme still outperforms that in [1,35]). Split each file W_n, for $n = 1, \ldots, N$, into $3\binom{6}{4} = 45$ subfiles:

$$W_n = (W^l_{n,\mathcal{T}} : l \in [3], \mathcal{T} \subset [6], |\mathcal{T}| = 4).$$

We list all the requested subfiles uncached by all users as follows: for $l = 1, 2, 3$,

$$\begin{gathered}
W^l_{d_1,\{2,3,4,5\}}, W^l_{d_1,\{2,3,4,6\}}, W^l_{d_1,\{2,3,5,6\}}, W^l_{d_1,\{2,4,5,6\}}, W^l_{d_1,\{3,4,5,6\}};\\
W^l_{d_2,\{1,3,4,5\}}, W^l_{d_2,\{1,3,4,6\}}, W^l_{d_2,\{1,3,5,6\}}, W^l_{d_2,\{1,4,5,6\}}, W^l_{d_2,\{3,4,5,6\}};\\
W^l_{d_3,\{1,2,4,5\}}, W^l_{d_3,\{1,2,4,6\}}, W^l_{d_3,\{1,2,5,6\}}, W^l_{d_3,\{1,4,5,6\}}, W^l_{d_3,\{2,4,5,6\}};\\
W^l_{d_4,\{1,2,3,5\}}, W^l_{d_4,\{1,2,3,6\}}, W^l_{d_4,\{1,2,5,6\}}, W^l_{d_4,\{1,3,5,6\}}, W^l_{d_4,\{2,3,5,6\}};\\
W^l_{d_5,\{1,2,3,4\}}, W^l_{d_5,\{1,2,3,6\}}, W^l_{d_5,\{1,2,4,6\}}, W^l_{d_5,\{1,3,4,6\}}, W^l_{d_5,\{2,3,4,6\}};\\
W^l_{d_6,\{1,2,3,4\}}, W^l_{d_6,\{1,2,3,5\}}, W^l_{d_6,\{1,2,4,5\}}, W^l_{d_6,\{1,3,4,5\}}, W^l_{d_6,\{2,3,4,5\}}.
\end{gathered}$$

The users can finish the transmission in different partitions. Table 1 shows the transmission in four different partitions over the D2D network.

Table 1. Subfiles sent by users in different partition, $l = 1, 2$.

$\{1,2,3\}$	$\{4,5,6\}$
user 2: $W^1_{d_1,\{2,3,4,5\}} \oplus W^1_{d_3,\{1,2,4,5\}}$	user 5: $W^1_{d_4,\{2,3,5,6\}} \oplus W^1_{d_6,\{2,3,4,5\}}$
user 2: $W^1_{d_1,\{2,3,4,6\}} \oplus W^1_{d_3,\{1,2,4,6\}}$	user 5: $W^1_{d_4,\{1,2,5,6\}} \oplus W^1_{d_6,\{1,2,4,5\}}$
user 1: $W^1_{d_2,\{1,3,4,6\}} \oplus W^1_{d_3,\{1,2,5,6\}}$	user 4: $W^1_{d_5,\{2,3,4,6\}} \oplus W^1_{d_6,\{1,3,4,5\}}$
user 3: $W^1_{d_1,\{2,3,5,6\}} \oplus W^1_{d_2,\{1,3,5,6\}}$	user 6: $W^1_{d_4,\{1,3,5,6\}} \oplus W^1_{d_5,\{1,3,4,6\}}$
$\{1,2,4\}$	$\{3,5,6\}$
user 2: $W^l_{d_1,\{2,4,5,6\}} \oplus W^l_{d_4,\{1,2,3,5\}}$	user 5: $W^l_{d_3,\{1,4,5,6\}} \oplus W^l_{d_6,\{1,2,3,5\}}$
$\{1,4,6\}$	$\{2,3,5\}$
user 6: $W^l_{d_1,\{3,4,5,6\}} \oplus W^l_{d_4,\{1,2,3,6\}}$	user 3: $W^l_{d_2,\{3,4,5,6\}} \oplus W^l_{d_5,\{1,2,3,4\}}$
$\{1,2,5\}$	$\{3,4,6\}$
user 1: $W^l_{d_2,\{1,4,5,6\}} \oplus W^l_{d_5,\{1,2,3,6\}}$	user 4: $W^l_{d_3,\{2,4,5,6\}} \oplus W^l_{d_6,\{1,2,3,4\}}$
$\{1,2,3\}$	$\{4,5,6\}$
user 3: $W^2_{d_1,\{2,3,4,5\}} \oplus W^2_{d_2,\{1,3,4,5\}}$	user 4: $W^2_{d_5,\{2,3,4,6\}} \oplus W^2_{d_6,\{2,3,4,5\}}$
user 3: $W^2_{d_1,\{2,3,4,6\}} \oplus W^2_{d_2,\{1,3,4,6\}}$	user 4: $W^2_{d_5,\{1,2,4,6\}} \oplus W^2_{d_6,\{1,2,4,5\}}$
user 2: $W^2_{d_1,\{2,3,5,6\}} \oplus W^2_{d_3,\{1,2,4,5\}}$	user 5: $W^2_{d_4,\{1,3,5,6\}} \oplus W^2_{d_6,\{1,3,4,5\}}$
user 1: $W^2_{d_3,\{1,2,4,6\}} \oplus W^2_{d_2,\{1,3,5,6\}}$	user 6: $W^2_{d_4,\{1,2,5,6\}} \oplus W^2_{d_5,\{1,3,4,6\}}$
user 1: $W^2_{d_3,\{1,2,5,6\}} \oplus W^1_{d_2,\{1,3,4,5\}}$	user 6: $W^1_{d_5,\{1,2,4,6\}} \oplus W^2_{d_4,\{2,3,5,6\}}$

In Table 1, all users first send XOR symbols with superscript $l = 1$. Please note that the subfiles $W^1_{d_2,\{1,3,4,5\}}$ and $W^1_{d_5,\{1,2,4,6\}}$ are not delivered at the beginning since $\frac{K\binom{K-1}{t}}{\alpha(\lfloor K/\alpha \rfloor - 1)}$ is not an integer. Similarly, for subfiles with $l = 2$, $W^2_{d_3,\{1,2,5,6\}}$ and $W^2_{d_4,\{2,3,5,6\}}$ remain to be sent to user 3 and 4. In the last transmission, user 1 delivers the XOR message $W^2_{d_3,\{1,2,5,6\}} \oplus W^1_{d_2,\{1,3,4,5\}}$ to user 2 and 3, and user 6 multicasts $W^1_{d_5,\{1,2,4,6\}} \oplus W^2_{d_4,\{2,3,5,6\}}$ to user 5 and 6. The transmission rate in the D2D network is $R_2 = \frac{1}{3}$.

For the remaining subfiles with superscript $l = 3$, the server delivers them in the same way as in [1]. Specifically, it sends symbols $\oplus_{k \in \mathcal{S}} W^3_{d_k, \mathcal{S} \setminus \{k\}}$, for all $\mathcal{S} \subseteq [K] : |\mathcal{S}| = 5$. Thus, the rate sent by the server is $R_1 = \frac{2}{15}$, and the transmission delay $T_{\text{central}} = \max\{R_1, R_2\} = \frac{1}{3}$, which is less than the delay achieved by the coded caching schemes for the broadcast network [1] and the D2D communication [35], respectively.

4.2. The Generalized Centralized Coding Caching Scheme

In the placement phase, each file is first split into $\binom{K}{t}$ subfiles of equal size. More specifically, split W_n into subfiles as follows: $W_n = (W_{n,\mathcal{T}} : \mathcal{T} \subset [K], |\mathcal{T}| = t)$. User k caches all the subfiles if $k \in \mathcal{T}$ for all $n = 1, \ldots, N$, occupying the cache memory of MF bits. Then split each subfile $W_{n,\mathcal{T}}$ into two mini-files as $W_{n,\mathcal{T}} = \left(W^{\mathrm{s}}_{n,\mathcal{T}}, W^{\mathrm{u}}_{n,\mathcal{T}}\right)$, where

$$
\begin{aligned}
|W^{\mathrm{s}}_{n,\mathcal{T}}| &= \lambda \cdot |W_{n,\mathcal{T}}| = \lambda \cdot \frac{F}{\binom{K}{t}}, \\
|W^{\mathrm{u}}_{n,\mathcal{T}}| &= (1-\lambda) \cdot |W_{n,\mathcal{T}}| = (1-\lambda) \cdot \frac{F}{\binom{K}{t}},
\end{aligned} \tag{28}
$$

with

$$
\lambda = \frac{1+t}{\alpha \min\{\lfloor \frac{K}{\alpha} \rfloor - 1, t\} + 1 + t}. \tag{29}
$$

Here, the mini-file $W^{\mathrm{s}}_{n,\mathcal{T}}$ and $W^{\mathrm{u}}_{n,\mathcal{T}}$ will be sent by the server and users, respectively. For each mini-file $W^{\mathrm{u}}_{n,\mathcal{T}}$, split it into L_1 pico-files of equal size $(1-\lambda)\cdot\frac{F}{L_1\binom{K}{t}}$, i.e., $W^{\mathrm{u}}_{n,\mathcal{T}} = \left(W^{\mathrm{u},1}_{n,\mathcal{T}},\ldots,W^{\mathrm{u},L_1}_{n,\mathcal{T}}\right)$, where L_1 satisfies

$$\frac{K\cdot\binom{K-1}{t}\cdot L_1}{\alpha\min\{\lfloor\frac{K}{\alpha}\rfloor-1,t\}}\in\mathbb{Z}^+. \tag{30}$$

As we will see later, condition (29) ensures that communication loads can be optimally allocated between the server and the users, and (30) ensures that the number of subfiles is large enough to maximize multicast gain for the transmission in the D2D network.

In the delivery phase, each user k requests file W_{d_k}. The request vector $\mathbf{d}=(d_1,d_2,\ldots,d_K)$ is informed by the server and all users. Please note that different parts of file W_{d_k} have been stored in the user cache memories, and thus the uncached parts of W_{d_k} can be sent both by the server and users. Subfiles

$$\left(W^{\mathrm{u},1}_{d_k,\mathcal{T}},\ldots,W^{\mathrm{u},L_1}_{d_k,\mathcal{T}}:\mathcal{T}\subset[K],|\mathcal{T}|=t,k\notin\mathcal{T}\right)$$

are requested by user k and will be sent by the users via the D2D network. Subfiles

$$\left(W^{\mathrm{s}}_{d_k,\mathcal{T}}:\mathcal{T}\subset[K],|\mathcal{T}|=t,k\notin\mathcal{T}\right)$$

are requested by user k and will be sent by the server via the broadcast network.

First consider the subfiles sent by the users. Partition the K users into α groups of equal size:

$$\mathcal{G}_1,\ldots,\mathcal{G}_\alpha,$$

where for $i,j=1,\ldots,\alpha$, $\mathcal{G}_i\subseteq[K]:|\mathcal{G}_i|=\lfloor K/\alpha\rfloor$, and $\mathcal{G}_i\cap\mathcal{G}_j=\emptyset$, if $i\neq j$. In each group $\mathcal{G}_i$, one of $\lfloor K/\alpha\rfloor$ users plays the role of server and sends symbols based on its cached contents to the remaining $(\lfloor K/\alpha\rfloor-1)$ users within the group.

Focus on a group $\mathcal{G}_i$ and a set $\mathcal{S}\subset[K]:|\mathcal{S}|=t+1$. If $\mathcal{G}_i\subseteq\mathcal{S}$, then all nodes in $\mathcal{G}_i$ share subfiles

$$(W^{\mathrm{u},l}_{n,\mathcal{T}}:l\in[L_1],n\in[N],\mathcal{G}_i\subseteq\mathcal{T},|\mathcal{T}|=t).$$

In this case, user $k\in\mathcal{G}_i$ sends XOR symbols that contains the requested subfiles useful to all remaining $\lfloor K/\alpha\rfloor-1$ users in $\mathcal{G}_i$, i.e., $\oplus_{j\in\mathcal{G}_i\setminus\{k\}}W^{\mathrm{u},l(k,\mathcal{G}_i,\mathcal{S})}_{d_j,\mathcal{S}\setminus\{j\}}$, where $l(k,\mathcal{G}_i,\mathcal{S})\in[L_1]$ is a function of $(k,\mathcal{G}_i,\mathcal{S})$ which avoids redundant transmission of any fragments.

If $\mathcal{S}\subseteq\mathcal{G}_i$, then the nodes in $\mathcal{S}$ share subfiles

$$(W^{\mathrm{u},l}_{n,\mathcal{T}}:l\in[L_1],n\in[N],\mathcal{T}\subset\mathcal{S},|\mathcal{T}|=t).$$

In this case, user $k\in\mathcal{S}$ sends an XOR symbol that contains the requested subfiles for all remaining $t-1$ users in $\mathcal{S}$, i.e., $\oplus_{j\in\mathcal{S}\setminus\{k\}}W^{\mathrm{u},l(k,\mathcal{G}_i,\mathcal{S})}_{d_j,\mathcal{S}\setminus\{j\}}$. Other groups perform the similar steps and concurrently deliver the remaining requested subfiles to other users.

By changing group partition and performing the delivery strategy described above, we can send all the requested subfiles

$$(W^{\mathrm{u},1}_{d_k,\mathcal{T}},\ldots,W^{\mathrm{u},L_1}_{d_k,\mathcal{T}}:\mathcal{T}\subset[K],|\mathcal{T}|=t,k\notin\mathcal{T})_{k=1}^{K} \tag{31}$$

to the users.

Since α groups send signals in a parallel manner (α users can concurrently deliver contents), and each user in a group delivers a symbol containing $\min\{\lfloor K/\alpha\rfloor-1,t\}$ non-repeating pico-files requested by other users, in order to send all requested subfiles in (31), we need to send in total

$$\frac{K\cdot\binom{K-1}{t}\cdot L_1}{\alpha\min\{\lfloor\frac{K}{\alpha}\rfloor-1,t\}} \tag{32}$$

XOR symbols, each of size $\frac{1-\lambda}{\binom{K}{t}}F$ bits. Notice that L_1 is chosen according to (30), ensuring that (32) equals to an integer. Thus, we obtain R_2 as

$$\begin{aligned}R_2 &= \frac{KL_1\cdot\binom{K-1}{t}}{\alpha\min\{\lfloor\frac{K}{\alpha}\rfloor-1,t\}}\cdot\frac{1-\lambda}{L_1\binom{K}{t}}\\ &= K\Big(1-\frac{M}{N}\Big)\frac{1}{1+t+\alpha\min\{\lfloor\frac{K}{\alpha}\rfloor-1,t\}},\end{aligned} \tag{33}$$

where the last equality holds by (29).

Now consider the delivery of the subfiles sent by the server. Apply the delivery strategy as in [1], i.e., the server broadcasts

$$\oplus_{k\in\mathcal{S}}W^{\mathrm{s}}_{d_k,\mathcal{S}\backslash\{k\}}$$

to all users, for all $\mathcal{S}\subseteq[K]:|\mathcal{S}|=t+1$. We obtain the transmission rate of the server

$$\begin{aligned}R_1 =&\lambda\cdot K\left(1-\frac{M}{N}\right)\cdot\frac{1}{1+t}\\ =&K\Big(1-\frac{M}{N}\Big)\frac{1}{1+t+\alpha\min\{\lfloor\frac{K}{\alpha}\rfloor-1,t\}}.\end{aligned} \tag{34}$$

From (33) and (34), we can see that the choice λ in (29) guarantees equal communication loads at the server and users. Since the server and users transmit the signals simultaneously, the transmission delay of the whole network is the maximum between R_1 and R_2, i.e., $T_{\mathrm{central}}=\max\{R_1,R_2\}=\frac{K(1-M/N)}{1+t+\alpha\min\{\lfloor K/\alpha\rfloor-1,t\}}$, for some $\alpha\in[\alpha_{\max}]$.

5. Coding Scheme under Decentralized Data Placement

In this section, we present a novel decentralized coded caching scheme for joint broadcast network and D2D network. The decentralized scenario is much more complicated than the centralized scenario, since each subfile can be stored by $s=1,2,\ldots,K$ users, leading to a dynamic file-splitting and communication strategy in the D2D network. We first use an illustrative example to demonstrate how we form D2D communication groups, split data and deliver data, and then present our generalized coding caching scheme.

5.1. An Illustrative Example

Consider a joint broadcast and D2D network consisting of $K=7$ users. When using the decentralized data placement strategy, the subfiles cached by user k can be written as

$$\Big(W_{n,\mathcal{T}}:n\in[N],k\in\mathcal{T},\mathcal{T}\subseteq[7]\Big). \tag{35}$$

We focus on the delivery of subfiles $W_{n,\mathcal{T}}:n\in[N],k\in\mathcal{T},|\mathcal{T}|=s=4$, i.e., each subfile is stored by $s=4$ users. A similar process can be applied to deliver other subfiles with respect to $s\in[K]\backslash\{4\}$.

To allocate communication loads between the server and users, we divide each subfile into two mini-files $W_{n,\mathcal{T}}=\Big(W^{\mathrm{s}}_{n,\mathcal{T}},W^{\mathrm{u}}_{n,\mathcal{T}}\Big)$, where mini-files $\{W^{\mathrm{s}}_{n,\mathcal{T}}\}$ and $\{W^{\mathrm{u}}_{n,\mathcal{T}}\}$ will be sent by the server and users, respectively. To reduce the transmission delay, the size of $W^{\mathrm{s}}_{n,\mathcal{T}}$ and $W^{\mathrm{u}}_{n,\mathcal{T}}$ need to be chosen properly such that $R_1=R_2$, i.e., the transmission rate of the server and users are equal; see (37) and (39) ahead.

Divide all the users into two non-intersecting groups $(\mathcal{G}_1^r, \mathcal{G}_2^r)$, for $r \in [35]$ which satisfies

$$\mathcal{G}_1^r \subset [K], \mathcal{G}_2^r \subset [K], |\mathcal{G}_1^r| = 4, |\mathcal{G}_2^r| = 3, \mathcal{G}_1^r \cap \mathcal{G}_2^r = \emptyset.$$

There are $\binom{7}{4} = 35$ kinds of partitions in total, thus $r \in [35]$. Please note that for any user $k \in \mathcal{G}_i^r$, $|\mathcal{G}_i^r| - 1$ of its requested mini-files are already cached by the rest users in $\mathcal{G}_i^r$, for $i = 1, 2$.

To avoid repetitive transmission of any mini-file, each mini-file in

$$(W^{\mathrm{u}}_{d_k,\mathcal{T}\setminus\{k\}} : \mathcal{T} \subseteq [7], k \in [7])$$

is divided into non-overlapping pico-files $W^{\mathrm{u}_1}_{d_k,\mathcal{T}\setminus\{k\}}$ and $W^{\mathrm{u}_2}_{d_k,\mathcal{T}\setminus\{k\}}$, i.e.,

$$W^{\mathrm{u}}_{d_k,\mathcal{T}\setminus\{k\}} = (W^{\mathrm{u}_1}_{d_k,\mathcal{T}\setminus\{k\}}, W^{\mathrm{u}_2}_{d_k,\mathcal{T}\setminus\{k\}}).$$

The sizes of $W^{\mathrm{u}_1}_{n,\mathcal{T}}$ and $W^{\mathrm{u}_2}_{n,\mathcal{T}}$ need to be chosen properly to have equal transmission rate of group $\mathcal{G}_1^r$ and $\mathcal{G}_2^r$; see (51) and (52) ahead.

To allocate communication loads between the two different types of groups, split each $W^{\mathrm{u}_1}_{d_k,\mathcal{T}\setminus\{k\}}$ and $W^{\mathrm{u}_2}_{d_k,\mathcal{T}\setminus\{k\}}$ into 3 and two equal fragments, respectively, e.g.,

$$W^{\mathrm{u}_1}_{d_2,\{1,3,4\}} = \left(W^{\mathrm{u}_1,1}_{d_2,\{1,3,4\}}, W^{\mathrm{u}_1,2}_{d_2,\{1,3,4\}}, W^{\mathrm{u}_1,3}_{d_2,\{1,3,4\}}\right),$$
$$W^{\mathrm{u}_2}_{d_2,\{1,3,4\}} = \left(W^{\mathrm{u}_2,1}_{d_2,\{1,3,4\}}, W^{\mathrm{u}_2,2}_{d_2,\{1,3,4\}}\right).$$

During the delivery phase, in each round, one user in each group produces and multicasts an XOR symbol to all other users in the same group, as shown in Table 2.

Table 2. Parallel user delivery when $K = 7, s = 4, \mathcal{G}_1^r = 4$ and $\mathcal{G}_2^r = 3$, $r \in [35]$.

$\{1,2,3,4\}$	$\{5,6,7\}$
user 1: $W^{\mathrm{u}_1,1}_{d_2,\{1,3,4\}} \oplus W^{\mathrm{u}_1,1}_{d_3,\{1,2,4\}} \oplus W^{\mathrm{u}_1,1}_{d_4,\{1,2,3\}}$	user 5: $\bigcup_{x\in\{1,2,3,4\}} W^{\mathrm{u}_2,1}_{d_6,\{5,7,x\}} \oplus W^{\mathrm{u}_2,1}_{d_7,\{5,6,x\}}$
user 2: $W^{\mathrm{u}_1,1}_{d_1,\{2,3,4\}} \oplus W^{\mathrm{u}_1,2}_{d_3,\{1,2,4\}} \oplus W^{\mathrm{u}_1,2}_{d_4,\{1,2,3\}}$	user 6: $\bigcup_{x\in\{1,2,3,4\}} W^{\mathrm{u}_2,1}_{d_5,\{6,7,x\}} \oplus W^{\mathrm{u}_2,2}_{d_7,\{5,6,x\}}$
user 3: $W^{\mathrm{u}_1,2}_{d_2,\{1,3,4\}} \oplus W^{\mathrm{u}_1,2}_{d_1,\{2,3,4\}} \oplus W^{\mathrm{u}_1,3}_{d_4,\{1,2,3\}}$	user 7: $\bigcup_{x\in\{1,2,3,4\}} W^{\mathrm{u}_2,2}_{d_6,\{5,7,x\}} \oplus W^{\mathrm{u}_2,2}_{d_5,\{6,7,x\}}$
user 4: $W^{\mathrm{u}_1,3}_{d_2,\{1,3,4\}} \oplus W^{\mathrm{u}_1,3}_{d_3,\{1,2,4\}} \oplus W^{\mathrm{u}_1,3}_{d_1,\{2,3,4\}}$	
$\{1,2,3,5\}$	$\{4,6,7\}$
user 1: $W^{\mathrm{u}_1,1}_{d_2,\{1,3,5\}} \oplus W^{\mathrm{u}_1,1}_{d_3,\{1,2,5\}} \oplus W^{\mathrm{u}_1,1}_{d_5,\{1,2,3\}}$	user 4: $\bigcup_{x\in\{1,2,3,5\}} W^{\mathrm{u}_2,y_{(..)}}_{d_6,\{4,7,x\}} \oplus W^{\mathrm{u}_2,y_{(..)}}_{d_7,\{4,6,x\}}$
user 2: $W^{\mathrm{u}_1,1}_{d_1,\{2,3,5\}} \oplus W^{\mathrm{u}_1,2}_{d_3,\{1,2,5\}} \oplus W^{\mathrm{u}_1,2}_{d_5,\{1,2,3\}}$	user 6: $\bigcup_{x\in\{1,2,3,5\}} W^{\mathrm{u}_2,1}_{d_4,\{6,7,x\}} \oplus W^{\mathrm{u}_2,y_{(..)}}_{d_7,\{4,6,x\}}$
user 3: $W^{\mathrm{u}_1,2}_{d_2,\{1,3,5\}} \oplus W^{\mathrm{u}_1,2}_{d_1,\{2,3,5\}} \oplus W^{\mathrm{u}_1,3}_{d_5,\{1,2,3\}}$	user 7: $\bigcup_{x\in\{1,2,3,5\}} W^{\mathrm{u}_2,y_{(..)}}_{d_6,\{4,7,x\}} \oplus W^{\mathrm{u}_2,2}_{d_4,\{6,7,x\}}$
user 5: $W^{\mathrm{u}_1,3}_{d_2,\{1,3,5\}} \oplus W^{\mathrm{u}_1,3}_{d_3,\{125\}} \oplus W^{\mathrm{u}_1,3}_{d_1,\{235\}}$	
$\{1,2,3,6\}$	$\{4,5,7\}$
user 1: $W^{\mathrm{u}_1,1}_{d_2,\{1,3,6\}} \oplus W^{\mathrm{u}_1,1}_{d_3,\{1,2,6\}} \oplus W^{\mathrm{u}_1,1}_{d_6,\{1,2,3\}}$	user 4: $\bigcup_{x\in\{1,2,3,6\}} W^{\mathrm{u}_2,y_{(..)}}_{d_5,\{4,7,x\}} \oplus W^{\mathrm{u}_2,y_{(..)}}_{d_7,\{4,5,x\}}$
user 2: $W^{\mathrm{u}_1,1}_{d_1,\{2,3,6\}} \oplus W^{\mathrm{u}_1,2}_{d_3,\{1,2,6\}} \oplus W^{\mathrm{u}_1,2}_{d_6,\{1,2,3\}}$	user 5: $\bigcup_{x\in\{1,2,3,6\}} W^{\mathrm{u}_2,1}_{d_4,\{5,7,x\}} \oplus W^{\mathrm{u}_2,y_{(..)}}_{d_7,\{4,5,x\}}$
user 3: $W^{\mathrm{u}_1,2}_{d_2,\{1,3,6\}} \oplus W^{\mathrm{u}_1,2}_{d_1,\{2,3,6\}} \oplus W^{\mathrm{u}_1,3}_{d_6,\{1,2,3\}}$	user 7: $\bigcup_{x\in\{1,2,3,6\}} W^{\mathrm{u}_2,y_{(..)}}_{d_5,\{4,7,x\}} \oplus W^{\mathrm{u}_2,2}_{d_4,\{5,7,x\}}$
user 6: $W^{\mathrm{u}_1,3}_{d_2,\{1,3,6\}} \oplus W^{\mathrm{u}_1,3}_{d_3,\{1,2,6\}} \oplus W^{\mathrm{u}_1,3}_{d_1,\{2,3,6\}}$	
... .	... .

There should be 35 partitions in total while the table only shows three partitions.

Please note that in this example, each group only appears one time among all partitions. However, for some other values of s, each group could appear multiple times in different partitions. For example, when $s = 2$, group $\{1,2\}$ appears in both partitions

$\{\{1,2\},\{3,4\},\{5,6,7\}\}$ and $\{\{1,2\},\{3,5\},\{4,6,7\}\}$. To reduce the transmission delay, one should balance communication loads between all groups, and between the server and users as well.

5.2. The Generalized Decentralized Coded Caching Scheme

In the placement phase, each user k applies the caching function to map a subset of $\frac{MF}{N}$ bits of file $W_n, n = 1, ..., N$, into its cache memory at random: $W_n = \left(W_{n,\mathcal{T}} : \mathcal{T} \subseteq [K]\right)$. The subfiles cached by user k can be written as $\left(W_{n,\mathcal{T}} : n \in [N], k \in \mathcal{T}, \mathcal{T} \subseteq [K]\right)$. When the size of file F is sufficiently large, by the law of large numbers, the subfile size with high probability can be written by

$$|W_{n,\mathcal{T}}| \approx p^{|\mathcal{T}|}(1-p)^{K-|\mathcal{T}|}. \tag{36}$$

The delivery procedure can be characterized into three different levels: allocating communication loads between the server and user, inner-group coding (i.e., transmission in each group) and parallel delivery among groups.

5.2.1. Allocating Communication Loads between the Server and User

To allocate communication loads between the server and users, split each subfile $W_{n,\mathcal{T}}$, for $\mathcal{T} \subseteq [K] : \mathcal{T} \neq \emptyset$, into two non-overlapping mini-files

$$W_{n,\mathcal{T}} = \left(W^{\mathrm{s}}_{n,\mathcal{T}}, W^{\mathrm{u}}_{n,\mathcal{T}}\right),$$

where

$$\begin{aligned} |W^{\mathrm{s}}_{n,\mathcal{T}}| &= \lambda \cdot |W_{n,\mathcal{T}}|, \\ |W^{\mathrm{u}}_{n,\mathcal{T}}| &= (1-\lambda) \cdot |W_{n,\mathcal{T}}|, \end{aligned} \tag{37}$$

and λ is a design parameter whose value is determined in Remark 5.

Mini-files $(W^{\mathrm{s}}_{d_k,\mathcal{T}\setminus\{k\}} : k \in [K])$ will be sent by the server using the decentralized coded caching scheme for the broadcast network [2], leading to the transmission delay

$$\lambda R_{\mathrm{s}} = \lambda \frac{1-M/N}{M/N}\left(1-(1-\frac{M}{N})^K\right), \tag{38}$$

where R_{s} is defined in (19).

Mini-files $(W^{\mathrm{u}}_{d_k,\mathcal{T}\setminus\{k\}} : k \in [K])$ will be sent by users using *parallel user delivery* described in Section 5.2.3. The corresponding transmission rate is

$$R_2 = (1-\lambda)R_{\mathrm{u}}, \tag{39}$$

where R_{u} represents the transmission bits sent by each user normalized by F.

Since subfile $W_{d_k,\emptyset}$ is not cached by any user and must be sent exclusively from the server, the corresponding transmission delay for sending $(W_{d_k,\emptyset} : k \in [K])$ is

$$R_{\emptyset} = K(1-\frac{M}{N})^K, \tag{40}$$

where $R_{\emptyset}$ coincides with the definition in (18).

By (38)–(40), we have

$$R_1 = R_{\emptyset} + \lambda R_{\mathrm{s}}, \;\; R_2 = (1-\lambda)R_{\mathrm{u}}. \tag{41}$$

According to (8), we have $T_{\mathrm{decentral}} = \max\{R_1, R_2\}$.

Remark 5 (Choice of λ). *The parameter λ is chosen such that $T_{\text{decentral}}$ is minimized. If $R_{\text{u}} < R_{\emptyset}$, then the inequality $R_2 \leq R_1$ always holds and $T_{\text{decentral}}$ reaches the minimum $T_{\text{decentral}} = R_{\emptyset}$ with $\lambda = 0$. If $R_{\text{u}} \geq R_{\emptyset}$, solving $R_1 = R_2$ yields $\lambda = \frac{R_{\text{u}} - R_{\emptyset}}{R_{\text{s}} + R_{\text{u}}}$ and $T_{\text{decentral}} = \frac{R_{\text{s}} R_{\text{u}}}{R_{\text{s}} + R_{\text{u}} - R_{\emptyset}}$.*

5.2.2. Inner-Group Coding

Given parameters $(s, \mathcal{G}, \text{i}, \gamma)$ where $s \in [K-1]$, $\mathcal{G} \subseteq [K]$, $\text{i} \in \{\text{u}, \text{u}_1, \text{u}_2\}$ with indicators $\text{u}, \text{u}_1, \text{u}_2$ described in (37) and (51), and $\gamma \in \mathbb{Z}^+$, we present how to successfully deliver

$$(W^{\text{i}}_{d_k, \mathcal{S}\setminus\{k\}} : \forall \mathcal{S} \subseteq [K], |\mathcal{S}| = s, \mathcal{G} \subseteq \mathcal{S})$$

to every user $k \in \mathcal{G}$ via D2D communication.

Split each $W^{\text{i}}_{d_k, \mathcal{S}\setminus\{k\}}$ into $(|\mathcal{G}|-1)\gamma$ non-overlapping fragments of equal size, i.e.,

$$W^{\text{i}}_{d_k, \mathcal{S}\setminus\{k\}} = \left(W^{\text{i},l}_{d_k, \mathcal{S}\setminus\{k\}} : l \in [(|\mathcal{G}|-1)\gamma]\right), \tag{42}$$

and each user $k \in \mathcal{G}$ takes turn to broadcast XOR symbol

$$X^{\text{i}}_{k,\mathcal{G},s} \triangleq \oplus_{j \in \mathcal{G}\setminus\{k\}} W^{\text{i},l(j,\mathcal{G},\mathcal{S})}_{d_j, \mathcal{S}\setminus\{j\}}, \tag{43}$$

where $l(k, \mathcal{G}, \mathcal{S}) \in [(|\mathcal{G}|-1)\gamma]$ is a function of $(k, \mathcal{G}, \mathcal{S})$ which avoids redundant transmission of any fragments. The XOR symbol $X^{\text{i}}_{k,\mathcal{G},s}$ will be received and decoded by the remaining users in $\mathcal{G}$.

For each group $\mathcal{G}$, inner-group coding encodes in total $\binom{K-|\mathcal{G}|}{s-|\mathcal{G}|}$ of $W^{\text{i}}_{d_k, \mathcal{S}\setminus\{k\}}$, and each XOR symbol $X^{\text{i}}_{k,\mathcal{G},s}$ in (43) contains fragments required by $|\mathcal{G}|-1$ users in $\mathcal{G}$.

5.2.3. Parallel Delivery among Groups

The parallel user delivery consists of $(K-1)$ rounds characterized by $s = 2, \ldots, K$. In each round s, mini-files

$$(W^{\text{u}}_{d_k, \mathcal{T}\setminus\{k\}} : \forall \mathcal{T} \subseteq [K], |\mathcal{T}| = s, k \in [K])$$

are recovered through D2D communication.

The key idea is to partition K users into $\lceil \frac{K}{s} \rceil$ groups for each communication round $s \in \{2, ..., K\}$, and let each group perform the D2D coded caching scheme [35] to exchange information. If $(K \bmod s) \neq 0$, there will be $\lfloor \frac{K}{s} \rfloor$ numbers of groups of the same size s, and an *abnormal* group of size $(K \bmod s)$, leading to an asymmetric caching setup. We optimally allocate the communication loads between the two types of groups, and between the broadcast network and D2D network as well.

Based on K, s and $\alpha_{\max}$, the delivery strategy in the D2D network is divided into 3 cases:

- Case 1: $\lceil \frac{K}{s} \rceil > \alpha_{\max}$. In this case, $\alpha_{\max}$ users are allowed to send data simultaneously. Select $s \cdot \alpha_{\max}$ users from all users and divide them into $\alpha_{\max}$ groups of equal size s. The total number of such kinds of partition is

$$\beta_1 \triangleq \frac{\binom{K}{s}\binom{K-s}{s} \cdots \binom{K-s(\alpha_{\max}-1)}{s}}{\alpha_{\max}!}. \tag{44}$$

  In each partition, $\alpha_{\max}$ users, selected from $\alpha_{\max}$ groups, respectively, send data in parallel via the D2D network.

- Case 2: $\lceil \frac{K}{s} \rceil \leq \alpha_{\max}$ and $(K \bmod s) < 2$. In this case, choose $(\lfloor \frac{K}{s} \rfloor - 1)s$ users from all users and partition them into $(\lfloor \frac{K}{s} \rfloor - 1)$ groups of equal size s. The total number of such kind partition is

$$\beta_2 \triangleq \frac{\binom{K}{s}\binom{K-s}{s} \cdots \binom{K-s(\lfloor \frac{K}{s} \rfloor - 1)}{s}}{\lfloor \frac{K}{s} \rfloor !}. \tag{45}$$

In each partition, $(\lfloor \frac{K}{s} \rfloor - 1)$ users selected from $(\lfloor \frac{K}{s} \rfloor - 1)$ groups of equal size s, respectively, together with an extra user selected from the *abnormal* group of size $K - s(\lfloor \frac{K}{s} \rfloor - 1)$ send data in parallel via the D2D network.

- Case 3: $\lceil \frac{K}{s} \rceil \leq \alpha_{\max}$ and $(K \bmod s) \geq 2$. In this case, every s users form a group, resulting in $\lfloor \frac{K}{s} \rfloor$ groups consisting of $s \lfloor \frac{K}{s} \rfloor$ users. The remaining $(K \bmod s)$ users form an *abnormal* group. The total number of such kind of partition is

$$\beta_3 = \beta_2. \tag{46}$$

In each partition, $\lfloor \frac{K}{s} \rfloor$ users selected from $\lfloor \frac{K}{s} \rfloor$ groups of equal size s, respectively, together with an extra user selected from the abnormal group of size $(K \bmod s)$ send data in parallel via the D2D network.

Thus, the exact number of users who parallelly send signals can be written as follows:

$$\alpha_{\mathrm{D}} = \begin{cases} \alpha_{\max}, & \text{case 1,} \\ \lfloor \frac{K}{s} \rfloor, & \text{case 2,} \\ \lceil \frac{K}{s} \rceil, & \text{case 3.} \end{cases} \tag{47}$$

Please note that each group $\mathcal{G}$ re-appears

$$N_{\mathcal{G}} \triangleq \frac{\binom{K-s}{s} \cdots \binom{K-s\cdot(\alpha_{\mathrm{D}}-1)}{s}}{(\alpha_{\mathrm{D}}-1)!} \tag{48}$$

times among $[\beta_c]$ partitions.

Now we present the decentralized scheme for these three cases as follows.

Case 1 ($\lceil \frac{K}{s} \rceil > \alpha_{\max}$): Consider a partition $r \in [\beta_1]$, denoted by

$$\mathcal{G}_1^r, \ldots, \mathcal{G}_{\alpha_{\mathrm{D}}}^r,$$

where $|\mathcal{G}_i^r| = s$ and $\mathcal{G}_i^r \cap \mathcal{G}_j^r = \emptyset, \forall i, j \in [\alpha_{\mathrm{D}}]$ and $i \neq j$.

Since each group $\mathcal{G}_i^r$ re-appears $N_{\mathcal{G}_i^r}$ times among $[\beta_1]$ partitions, and $(|\mathcal{G}_i^r| - 1)$ users take turns to broadcast XOR symbols (43) in each group $\mathcal{G}_i^r$, in order to guarantee that each group can send a unique fragment without repetition, we split each mini-file $W^{\mathrm{u}}_{d_k, \mathcal{S}\backslash\{k\}}$ into $(|\mathcal{G}_i^r| - 1)N_{\mathcal{G}_i^r}$ fragments of equal size.

Each group $\mathcal{G}_i^r$, for $r \in [\beta_1]$ and $i \in [\alpha_{\mathrm{D}}]$, performs inner-group coding (see Section 5.2.2) with parameters

$$(s, \mathcal{G}_i^r, \mathrm{u}, N_{\mathcal{G}_i^r}),$$

for all s satisfying $\lceil \frac{K}{s} \rceil > \alpha_{\max}$. For each round r, all groups $\mathcal{G}_1^r, \ldots, \mathcal{G}_{\alpha_{\mathrm{D}}}^r$ parallelly send XOR symbols containing $|\mathcal{G}_i^r| - 1$ fragments required by other users of its group. By the fact that the partitioned groups traverse every set $\mathcal{T}$, i.e.,

$$\mathcal{T} \subseteq \{\mathcal{G}_1^r \cup \ldots \cup \mathcal{G}_{\alpha_{\mathrm{D}}}^r\}_{r=1}^{\beta_1}, \forall \mathcal{T} \subseteq [K] : |\mathcal{T}| = s,$$

and since inner-group coding enables each group $\mathcal{G}_i^r$ to recover

$$(W^{\mathrm{u}}_{d_k,\mathcal{S}\setminus\{k\}} : \forall \mathcal{S} \subseteq [K], |\mathcal{S}| = s, \mathcal{G}_i^r \subseteq \mathcal{S}, k \in [K]),$$

we can recover all required mini-files

$$(W^{\mathrm{u}}_{d_k,\mathcal{T}\setminus\{k\}} : \forall \mathcal{T} \subseteq [K], |\mathcal{T}| = s, k \in [K]).$$

The transmission delay of Case 1 in round s is thus

$$\begin{aligned} R^{\mathrm{u}}_{\mathrm{case1}}(s) &\triangleq \sum_{r\in[\beta_1]} \sum_{k\in\mathcal{G}_i^r} |X^{\mathrm{u}}_{k,\mathcal{G}_i^r,s}| \\ &\overset{(a)}{=} \frac{K\binom{K-1}{s-1}}{\alpha_{\mathrm{D}}(s-1)} |W^{\mathrm{u}}_{d_k,\mathcal{T}\setminus\{k\}}| \\ &= \frac{K\binom{K-1}{s-1}}{\alpha_{\max}(s-1)}(1-\lambda)p^{s-1}(1-p)^{K-s+1}, \end{aligned} \tag{49}$$

where (a) follows by (44) and (48).

Case 2 ($\lceil \frac{K}{s} \rceil \leq \alpha_{\max}$ and $(K \bmod s) < 2$): We apply the same delivery procedure as Case 1, except that β_1 is replaced by β_2 and $\alpha_{\mathrm{D}} = \lfloor \frac{K}{s} \rfloor$. Thus, the transmission delay in round s is

$$\begin{aligned} R^{\mathrm{u}}_{\mathrm{case2}}(s) &= \frac{K\binom{K-1}{s-1}}{\alpha_D(s-1)} |W^{\mathrm{u}}_{d_k,\mathcal{T}\setminus\{k\}}| \\ &= \frac{K\binom{K-1}{s-1}}{\lfloor \frac{K}{s} \rfloor (s-1)}(1-\lambda)p^{s-1}(1-p)^{K-s+1}. \end{aligned} \tag{50}$$

Case 3 ($\lceil \frac{K}{s} \rceil \leq \alpha_{\max}$ and $(K \bmod s) \geq 2$): Consider a partition $r \in [\beta_3]$, denoted as

$$\mathcal{G}_1^r, \ldots, \mathcal{G}_{\alpha_{\mathrm{D}}}^r,$$

where $\mathcal{G}_i^r \subseteq [K]$, $\mathcal{G}_i^r \cap \mathcal{G}_j^r = \emptyset$, $\forall i,j \in [\alpha_{\mathrm{D}}-1]$ and $i \neq j$ and $\mathcal{G}_{\alpha_{\mathrm{D}}}^r = [K]\setminus(\cup_{i=1}^{\alpha_{\mathrm{D}}-1}\mathcal{G}_i^r)$ with $|\mathcal{G}_i^r| = s$, $|\mathcal{G}_{\alpha_{\mathrm{D}}}^r| = (K \bmod s)$.

Since group $\mathcal{G}_i^r : i \in [\alpha_{\mathrm{D}}-1]$ and $\mathcal{G}_{\alpha_{\mathrm{D}}}^r$ have different group sizes, we further split each mini-file $W^{\mathrm{u}}_{d_k,\mathcal{T}\setminus\{k\}}$ into two non-overlapping fragments such that

$$\begin{aligned} |W^{\mathrm{u}_1}_{d_k,\mathcal{T}\setminus\{k\}}| &= \lambda_2 |W^{\mathrm{u}}_{d_k,\mathcal{T}\setminus\{k\}}|, \\ |W^{\mathrm{u}_2}_{d_k,\mathcal{T}\setminus\{k\}}| &= (1-\lambda_2)|W^{\mathrm{u}}_{d_k,\mathcal{T}\setminus\{k\}}|, \end{aligned} \tag{51}$$

where $\lambda_2 \in [0,1]$ is a designed parameter satisfying (52).

Split each mini-file $W^{\mathrm{u}_1}_{d_k,\mathcal{S}\setminus\{k\}}$ and $W^{\mathrm{u}_2}_{d_k,\mathcal{S}\setminus\{k\}}$ into fragments of equal size:

$$\begin{aligned} W^{\mathrm{u}_1}_{d_k,\mathcal{S}\setminus\{k\}} &= \left(W^{\mathrm{u}_1,l}_{d_k,\mathcal{S}\setminus\{k\}} : l \in [(s-1)N_{\mathcal{G}_i^r}]\right), \\ W^{\mathrm{u}_2}_{d_k,\mathcal{S}\setminus\{k\}} &= \left(W^{\mathrm{u}_2,l}_{d_k,\mathcal{S}\setminus\{k\}} : l \in \left[(|\mathcal{G}_{\alpha_{\mathrm{D}}}^r|-1)\binom{s-1}{|\mathcal{G}_{\alpha_{\mathrm{D}}}^r|-1}N_{\mathcal{G}_i^r}\right]\right). \end{aligned}$$

Following the similar encoding operation in (43), group $\mathcal{G}_i^r : i \in [\alpha_{\mathrm{D}}-1]$ and group $\mathcal{G}_{\alpha_{\mathrm{D}}}^r$ send the following XOR symbols, respectively:

$$(X^{\mathrm{u}_1}_{k,\mathcal{G}_i^r,s} : k \in \mathcal{G}_i^r)_{i=1}^{(\alpha_{\mathrm{D}}-1)}, \quad (X^{\mathrm{u}_2}_{k,\mathcal{G}_{\alpha_{\mathrm{D}}}^r,s} : k \in \mathcal{G}_{\alpha_{\mathrm{D}}}^r).$$

For each $s \in \{2, \ldots, K\}$, the transmission delay for sending the XOR symbols above by group $\mathcal{G}_i^r : i \in [\alpha_D - 1]$ and group $\mathcal{G}^r_{\lceil \frac{K}{s} \rceil}$ can be written as

$$R^{u_1}_{\text{case3}}(s) = \frac{\lambda_2 K\binom{K-1}{s-1}}{(\alpha_D - 1)(s-1)} \cdot |W^{u}_{d_k, \mathcal{T}\setminus\{k\}}|,$$
$$R^{u_2}_{\text{case3}}(s) = \frac{(1-\lambda_2) K\binom{K-1}{s-1}}{(K \bmod s) - 1} \cdot |W^{u}_{d_k, \mathcal{T}\setminus\{k\}}|,$$

respectively. Since $\mathcal{G}_i : i \in [\lfloor \frac{K}{s} \rfloor]$ and group $\mathcal{G}_{\lceil \frac{K}{s} \rceil}$ can send signals in parallel, by letting

$$R^{u_1}_{\text{case3}}(s) = R^{u_2}_{\text{case3}}(s), \tag{52}$$

we eliminate the parameter λ_2 and obtain the balanced transmission delay at users for Case 3:

$$R^{u}_{\text{case3}}(s) \triangleq \frac{K\binom{K-1}{s-1}}{K - 1 - \lfloor \frac{K}{s} \rfloor}(1-\lambda) p^{s-1}(1-p)^{K-s+1}. \tag{53}$$

Remark 6. *The condition $\lceil \frac{K}{s} \rceil > \alpha_{\max}$ in Case 1 implies that $s \leq \lceil \frac{K}{\alpha_{\max}} \rceil - 1$. In this regime, the transmission delay is given in (49). If $s \geq \lceil \frac{K}{\alpha_{\max}} \rceil - 1$ and $(K \mod s) < 2$, scheme for Case 2 starts to work and the transmission delay is given in (50); If $s \geq \lceil \frac{K}{\alpha_{\max}} \rceil - 1$ and $(K \mod s) \geq 2$, scheme for Case 3 starts to work and the transmission delay is given in (53).*

In each round $s \in \{2, \ldots, K\}$, all requested mini-files can be recovered by the delivery strategies above. By Remark 6, the transmission delay in the D2D network is

$$\begin{aligned} R_2 &= (1-\lambda)\frac{1}{\alpha_{\max}} \sum_{s=2}^{\lceil \frac{K}{\alpha_{\max}} \rceil - 1} \left[\frac{s\binom{K}{s}}{s-1} p^{s-1}(1-p)^{K-s+1}\right] + (1-\lambda) \sum_{s=\lceil \frac{K}{\alpha_{\max}} \rceil}^{K} \left[\frac{K\binom{K-1}{s-1}}{f(K,s)} p^{s-1}(1-p)^{K-s+1}\right] \\ &= (1-\lambda) R_u, \end{aligned} \tag{54}$$

where R_u is defined in (20) and

$$f(K,s) \triangleq \begin{cases} \lfloor \frac{K}{s} \rfloor (s-1), & (K \bmod s) < 2, \\ K - 1 - \lfloor K/s \rfloor, & (K \bmod s) \geq 2. \end{cases} \tag{55}$$

6. Conclusions

In this paper, we considered a cache-aided communication via joint broadcast network with a D2D network. Two novel coded caching schemes were proposed for centralized and decentralized data placement settings, respectively. Both schemes achieve a parallel gain and a cooperation gain by efficiently exploiting communication opportunities in the broadcast and D2D networks, and optimally allocating communication loads between the server and users. Furthermore, we showed that in the centralized case, letting too many users parallelly send information could be harmful. The information theoretic converse bounds were established, with which we proved that the centralized scheme achieves the optimal transmission delay within a constant multiplicative gap in all regimes, and the decentralized scheme is also order-optimal when the cache size of each user is larger than a small threshold which tends to zero as the number of users tends to infinity. Our work indicates that combining the cache-aided broadcast network with the cache-aided D2D network can greatly reduce the transmission latency.

Author Contributions: Project administration, Y.W.; Writing—original draft, Z.H., J.C. and X.Y.; Writing—review & editing, S.M. All authors have read and agreed to the published version of the manuscript.

Funding: This research was funded by National Natural Science Foundation of China grant number 61901267.

Conflicts of Interest: The authors declare no conflict of interest.

Appendix A. Proof of the Converse

Let T_1^* and T_2^* denote the optimal rate sent by the server and each user. We first consider an enhance system where every user is served by an exclusive server and user, which both store full files in the database, then we are easy to obtain the following lower bound:

$$T^* \geq \frac{1}{2}(1 - \frac{M}{N}). \tag{A1}$$

Another lower bound follows similar idea to [1]. However, due to the flexibility of D2D network, the connection and partitioning status between users can change during the delivery phase, prohibiting the direct application of the proof in [1] into the hybrid network considered in this paper. Moreover, the parallel transmission of the server and many users creates abundant different signals in the networks, making the scenario more sophisticated.

Consider the first s users with cache contents $Z_1, ..., Z_s$. Define $X_{1,0}$ as the signal sent by the server, and $X_{1,1}, \ldots, X_{1,\alpha_{\max}}$ as the signals sent by the $\alpha_{\max}$ users, respectively, where $X_{j,i} \in [\lfloor 2^{T_2^* F} \rfloor]$ for $j \in [s]$ and $i \in [\alpha_{\max}]$. Assume that $W_1, \ldots, W_s$ are determined by $X_{1,0}$, $X_{1,1}, \ldots, X_{1,\alpha_{\max}}$ and $Z_1, \ldots, Z_s$. Additionally, define $X_{2,0}$, $X_{2,1}, \ldots, X_{2,\alpha_{\max}}$ as the signals which enable the users to decode $W_{s+1}, ..., W_{2s}$. Continue the same process such that $X_{\lfloor N/s \rfloor,0}$, $X_{\lfloor N/s \rfloor,1}, \ldots, X_{\lfloor N/s \rfloor,\alpha_{\max}}$ are the signals which enable the users to decode $W_{s\lfloor N/s \rfloor - s+1}, ..., W_{s\lfloor N/s \rfloor}$. We then have $Z_1, \ldots, Z_s$, $X_{1,0}, \ldots, X_{\lfloor N/s \rfloor,0}$, and

$$X_{1,1}, \ldots, X_{1,\alpha_{\max}}, \ldots, X_{\lfloor N/s \rfloor,1}, \ldots, X_{\lfloor N/s \rfloor,\alpha_{\max}}$$

to determine $W_1, \ldots, W_{s\lfloor N/s \rfloor}$. Let

$$\mathbf{X}_{1:\alpha_{\max}} \triangleq (X_{1,1}, \ldots, X_{1,\alpha_{\max}}, \ldots, X_{\lfloor N/s \rfloor,1}, \ldots, X_{\lfloor N/s \rfloor,\alpha_{\max}}).$$

By the definitions of T_1^*, T_2^* and the encoding function (5), we have

$$H(X_{1,0}, \ldots, X_{\lfloor N/s \rfloor,0}) \leq \lfloor N/s \rfloor T_1^* F, \tag{A2}$$
$$H(\mathbf{X}_{1:\alpha_{\max}}) \leq \lfloor N/s \rfloor \alpha_{\max} T_2^* F, \tag{A3}$$
$$H(\mathbf{X}_{1:\alpha_{\max}}, Z_1, \ldots, Z_s) \leq KMF. \tag{A4}$$

Consider the cut separating $X_{1,0}, \ldots, X_{\lfloor N/s \rfloor,0}$, $\mathbf{X}_{1:\alpha_{\max}}$, and $Z_1, \ldots, Z_s$ from the corresponding s users. By the cut-set bound and (A2), we have

$$\lfloor \frac{N}{s} \rfloor sF \leq \lfloor \frac{N}{s} \rfloor T_1^* F + KMF, \tag{A5}$$
$$\lfloor \frac{N}{s} \rfloor sF \leq \lfloor \frac{N}{s} \rfloor T_1^* F + sMF + \lfloor \frac{N}{s} \rfloor \alpha_{\max} T_2^* F. \tag{A6}$$

Since we have $T^* \geq T_1^*$ and $T^* \geq \max\{T_1^*, T_2^*\}$ from the above definition, we obtain

$$T^* \geq \max_{s \in [K]} (s - \frac{KM}{\lfloor N/s \rfloor}), \tag{A7}$$
$$T^* \geq \max_{s \in [K]} (s - \frac{sM}{\lfloor N/s \rfloor}) \frac{1}{1 + \alpha_{\max}}. \tag{A8}$$

Appendix B

We prove that T_{central} is within a constant multiplicative gap of the minimum transmission delay T^* for all values of M. To prove the result, we compare them in the following regimes.

- If $0.6393 < t < \lfloor K/\alpha \rfloor - 1$, from Theorem 1, we have

$$\begin{aligned} T^* &\geq (s - \frac{Ms}{\lfloor N/s \rfloor})\frac{1}{1+\alpha_{\max}} \\ &\overset{(a)}{\geq} \frac{1}{12} \cdot K\Big(1 - \frac{M}{N}\Big)\frac{1}{1+t} \cdot \frac{1}{1+\alpha_{\max}}, \end{aligned} \tag{A9}$$

  where (a) follows from [1] [Theorem 3]. Then we have

$$\begin{aligned} \frac{T_{\text{central}}}{T^*} &\leq 12 \cdot \frac{(1+\alpha_{\max})(1+t)}{1+t+\alpha t} \\ &= 12 \cdot \frac{(1+\alpha_{\max})}{1+\alpha t/(1+t)} \\ &\leq 12 \cdot \frac{(1+\alpha_{\max})}{1+\alpha \cdot 0.6393/(1+0.6393)} \\ &\leq 31, \end{aligned} \tag{A10}$$

  where the last inequality holds by setting $\alpha = \alpha_{\max}$.
- If $t > \lfloor K/\alpha \rfloor - 1$, we have

$$\begin{aligned} \frac{T_{\text{central}}}{T^*} &\leq \frac{K(1-\frac{M}{N})\frac{1}{1+t+\alpha(\lfloor K/\alpha \rfloor - 1)}}{\frac{1}{2}(1-\frac{M}{N})} \\ &= \frac{2K}{1+t+\alpha(\lfloor K/\alpha \rfloor - 1)} \\ &\overset{(a)}{\leq} \frac{2K}{K+KM/N} \\ &\leq 2, \end{aligned} \tag{A11}$$

  where (a) holds by choosing $\alpha = 1$.
- If $t \leq 0.6393$, setting $s = 0.275N$, we have

$$\begin{aligned} T^* &\geq s - \frac{KM}{\lfloor N/s \rfloor} \\ &\overset{(a)}{\geq} s - \frac{KM}{N/s - 1} \\ &= 0.275N - t \cdot 0.3793N \\ &\geq 0.0325N > \frac{1}{31} \cdot N, \end{aligned} \tag{A12}$$

  where (a) holds since $\lfloor x \rfloor \geq x - 1$ for any $x \geq 1$. Please note that for all values of M, the transmission delay

$$T_{\text{central}} \leq \min\{K, N\}. \tag{A13}$$

  Combining with (A12) and (A13), we have $\frac{T_{\text{central}}}{T^*} \leq 31$.

Appendix C

Appendix C.1. Case $\alpha_{\max} = \lfloor \frac{K}{2} \rfloor$

When $\alpha_{\max} = \lfloor \frac{K}{2} \rfloor$, we have

$$R_{\mathrm{u}} = R_{\mathrm{u\text{-}f}} \triangleq \sum_{s=2}^{K} \frac{K\binom{K-1}{s-1}}{f(K,s)} p^{s-1} q^{K-s+1}, \tag{A14}$$

where $R_{\mathrm{u\text{-}f}}$ denotes the user's transmission rate for a flexible D2D network with $\alpha_{\max} = \lfloor \frac{K}{2} \rfloor$. In the flexible D2D network, at most $\lfloor \frac{K}{2} \rfloor$ users are allowed to transmit messages simultaneously, in which the user transmission turns to unicast.

Please note that in each term of the summation:

$$\begin{aligned} \frac{K\binom{K-1}{s-1}}{f(K,s)} &\le \frac{K\binom{K-1}{s-1}}{K-1-\frac{K}{s}} \\ &= \left(\frac{K}{K-1} + \frac{\left(\frac{K}{K-1}\right)^2}{s-\frac{K}{K-1}}\right) \cdot \binom{K-1}{s-1} \\ &\le \frac{K\binom{K-1}{s-1}}{K-1} + \frac{2K\binom{K}{s}}{(K-1)(K-2)}, \end{aligned} \tag{A15}$$

where the last inequality holds by $s \ge \frac{K}{K-1} + \frac{K-2}{K-1} = 2$ and

$$\begin{aligned} \frac{\left(\frac{K}{K-1}\right)^2}{s-\frac{K}{K-1}} \binom{K-1}{s-1} &= \frac{K^2\binom{K-1}{s-1}}{(K-1)(K-2)} \cdot \frac{\frac{K-2}{K-1}}{s-\frac{K}{K-1}} \\ &\le \frac{K^2\binom{K-1}{s-1}}{(K-1)(K-2)} \cdot \frac{\frac{K-2}{K-1}+\frac{K}{K-1}}{s-\frac{K}{K-1}+\frac{K}{K-1}} \\ &= \frac{2K}{(K-1)(K-2)} \cdot \binom{K}{s}. \end{aligned}$$

Therefore, by (A15), $R_{\mathrm{u\text{-}f}}$ can be rewritten as

$$\begin{aligned} R_{\mathrm{u\text{-}f}} &\le \frac{K}{K-1} \sum_{s=2}^{K} \binom{K-1}{s-1} p^{s-1} q^{K-s+1} + \frac{2K}{(K-1)(K-2)} \sum_{s=2}^{K} \binom{K}{s} p^{s-1} q^{K-s+1} \\ &= \frac{Kq}{K-1} \cdot \sum_{i=1}^{K-1} \binom{K-1}{i} p^i q^{K-1-i} + \frac{2Kq/p}{(K-1)(K-2)} \cdot \sum_{s=2}^{K} \binom{K}{s} p^s q^{K-s} \\ &= \frac{Kq}{K-1}\left(1-q^{K-1}\right) + \frac{2Kq/p}{(K-1)(K-2)} \cdot \left(1-q^K-Kpq^{K-1}\right). \end{aligned}$$

Appendix C.2. Case $\alpha_{\max} = 1$

When $\alpha_{\max} = 1$, the cooperation network degenerates into a shared link where only one user acts as the server and broadcasts messages to the remaining $K-1$ users. A similar derivation is given in [35]. In this case, R_{u} can be rewritten as

$$\begin{aligned}
R_{\mathrm{u}} &= \sum_{s=2}^{K} \frac{s\binom{K}{s}}{s-1} p^{s-1} q^{K-s+1} \\
&\leq \sum_{s=2}^{K} \left(1 + \frac{3}{s+1}\right) \binom{K}{s} p^{s-1} q^{K-s+1} \\
&= \sum_{s=2}^{K} \binom{K}{s} p^{s-1} q^{K-s+1} + \frac{3}{K+1} \sum_{s=2}^{K} \binom{K+1}{s+1} p^{s-1} q^{K-s+1} \\
&= \frac{q}{p}\left(1 - q^K - Kpq^{K-1}\right) + \frac{3q/p^2}{K+1}\left(1 - q^{K+1} - (K+1)pq^K - \frac{K(K+1)}{2} p^2 q^{K-1}\right) \\
&= \frac{q}{p}\left(1 - \frac{5}{2}Kpq^{K-1} - 4q^K + \frac{3(1-q^{K+1})}{(K+1)p}\right),
\end{aligned}$$

where the inequality holds by the fact that $s \geq 2$.

Appendix D

Appendix D.1. When $\alpha_{\max} = \lfloor \frac{K}{2} \rfloor$

Recall that $p_{\mathrm{th}} \triangleq 1 - \left(\frac{1}{K+1}\right)^{\frac{1}{K-1}}$, which tends to zero as K goes to infinity. We first introduce the following three lemmas.

Lemma A1. *Given arbitrary convex function $g_1(p)$ and arbitrary concave function $g_2(p)$, if they intersect at two points with $p_1 < p_2$, then $g_1(p) \leq g_2(p)$ for all $p \in [p_1, p_2]$.*

We omit the proof of Lemma A1 as it is straightforward.

Lemma A2. *For memory size $0 \leq p \leq 1$ and $\alpha_{\max} = \lfloor \frac{K}{2} \rfloor$, we have*

$$R_{\mathrm{u}} \geq R_{\emptyset},\ T_{\mathrm{decentral}} = \frac{R_{\mathrm{s}} R_{\mathrm{u}}}{R_{\mathrm{s}} + R_{\mathrm{u}} - R_{\emptyset}},\ \textit{for all } p \in [p_{\mathrm{th}}, 1].$$

Proof. When $\alpha_{\max} = \lfloor \frac{K}{2} \rfloor$, from Equation (20), we have

$$\begin{aligned}
R_{\mathrm{u}} &= \sum_{s=2}^{K} \frac{K\binom{K-1}{s-1}}{f(K,s)} p^{s-1} (1-p)^{K-s+1} \\
&\geq \frac{K}{K} \sum_{x=1}^{K-1} \binom{K-1}{x} p^x (1-p)^{K-x} \\
&= (1-p)(1-(1-p)^{K-1}),
\end{aligned} \tag{A16}$$

where the first inequality holds by letting $x = s-1$ and $\frac{K}{K-1-\lfloor \frac{K}{s} \rfloor} > \frac{K}{K-1}$. It is easy to show that $(1-p)(1-(1-p)^{K-1})$ is a concave function of p by verifying $\frac{\partial^2 (1-p)(1-(1-p)^{K-1})}{\partial p^2} \leq 0$. □

On the other hand, one can easily show that

$$R_{\emptyset} = K(1-p)^K$$

is a convex function of p by showing $\frac{\partial^2 R_\emptyset(p)}{\partial p^2} \geq 0$. Since the two functions $(1-p)(1-(1-p)^{K-1})$ and $R_\emptyset$ intersect at $p_{\text{th}} = 1 - \left(\frac{1}{K+1}\right)^{\frac{1}{K-1}}$ and $p_2 = 1$ with $p_{\text{th}} \leq p_2$, from Lemma A1 and (A16), we have

$$R_\text{u} \geq (1-p)(1-(1-p)^{K-1}) \geq R_\emptyset,$$

for all $p \in [p_{\text{th}}, 1]$. From Remark 4, we know that $T_{\text{decentral}} = \frac{R_\text{s} R_\text{u}}{R_\text{s}+R_\text{u}-R_\emptyset}$ if $R_\text{u} \geq R_\emptyset$

Lemma A3. *For memory size* $0 \leq p \leq 1$ *and* $\alpha_{\max} = \lfloor \frac{K}{2} \rfloor$, *we have*

$$\frac{R_\text{s} R_\text{u}}{R_\text{s} + R_\text{u} - R_\emptyset} \leq 6T^*.$$

Proof. From (25) and (19), we have

$$\begin{aligned} R_\text{u} &\leq \frac{K}{K-1} \cdot \left(q - q^K\right) + \frac{2K}{(K-1)(K-2)} \cdot \frac{q}{p}\left(1 - q^K - Kpq^{K-1}\right) \\ &\overset{(a)}{\leq} \frac{K}{K-1} \cdot \left(q - q^K\right) + \frac{2K}{(K-1)(K-2)} \cdot \frac{q}{p}\left(1 - (1-Kp) - Kpq^{K-1}\right) \\ &= \frac{K(3K-2)}{(K-1)(K-2)} \cdot \left(q - q^K\right), \end{aligned} \tag{A17}$$

$$R_\text{s} = \frac{q}{p}\left(1 - q^K\right) \overset{(b)}{\leq} \frac{q}{p}\left(1 - (1-Kp)\right) = Kq, \tag{A18}$$

where (a) and (b) both follow from inequality

$$(1-p)^K \geq (1-Kp). \tag{A19}$$

□

Then, by Remark 4 and (A17), (A18) and definition of $R_\emptyset$ in (18), if $\alpha_{\max} = \lfloor \frac{K}{2} \rfloor$, then

$$\begin{aligned} \frac{R_\text{s} R_\text{u}}{R_\text{s} + R_\text{u} - R_\emptyset} &\leq \frac{Kq \cdot \frac{K(3K-2)}{(K-1)(K-2)}(q - q^K)}{Kq + \frac{K(3K-2)}{(K-1)(K-2)}(q - q^K) - Kq^K} \\ &= \left(3 - \frac{2}{K}\right) \cdot q. \end{aligned} \tag{A20}$$

From Theorem 1, we have $T^* \geq \frac{1}{2}q$. Thus, we obtain

$$\frac{R_\text{s} R_\text{u}}{R_\text{s} + R_\text{u} - R_\emptyset} \cdot \frac{1}{T^*} \leq \frac{\left(3 - 2/K\right) \cdot q}{q/2} \leq 6 - \frac{4}{K} < 6.$$

Next, we use Lemmas A2 and A3 to prove that when $\alpha_{\max} = \lfloor \frac{K}{2} \rfloor$,

$$\frac{T_{\text{decentral}}}{T^*} \leq \begin{cases} \max\left\{6, 2K\left(\frac{2K}{2K+1}\right)^{K-1}\right\}, & p < p_{\text{th}}, \\ 6, & p \geq p_{\text{th}}. \end{cases}$$

Appendix D.1.1. Case $\alpha_{\max} = \lfloor \frac{K}{2} \rfloor$ and $p \geq p_{\text{th}}$

In this case, from Lemma A2, we have

$$T_{\text{decentral}} = \frac{R_\text{s} R_\text{u}}{R_\text{s} + R_\text{u} - R_\emptyset}.$$

Thus, from Lemma A3,

$$T_{\text{decentral}} = \frac{R_{\text{s}}R_{\text{u}}}{R_{\text{s}} + R_{\text{u}} - R_{\emptyset}} \leq 6T^*.$$

Appendix D.1.2. Case $\alpha_{\max} = \lfloor \frac{K}{2} \rfloor$ and $p \leq p_{\text{th}}$

From the definition of $T_{\text{decentral}}$ in (17), we have

$$\frac{T_{\text{decentral}}}{T^*} = \max\{\frac{R_{\emptyset}}{T^*}, \frac{R_{\text{s}}R_{\text{u}}}{R_{\text{s}} + R_{\text{u}} - R_{\emptyset}} \cdot \frac{1}{T^*}\}. \tag{A21}$$

From Lemma A3, we know that

$$\frac{R_{\text{s}}R_{\text{u}}}{R_{\text{s}} + R_{\text{u}} - R_{\emptyset}} \cdot \frac{1}{T^*} \leq 6, \tag{A22}$$

and thus only focus on the upper bound of $R_{\emptyset}/T^*$.

According to Theorem 1, T^* has the following two lower bounds: $T^* \geq \frac{1-p}{2}$, and

$$T^* \geq \max_{s\in[K]} \left(s - \frac{KM}{\lfloor N/s \rfloor}\right) \geq \max_{s\in[K]} \left(s - \frac{KM}{N/(2s)}\right).$$

Let $R_1^*(p) \triangleq \frac{1}{2}(1-p)$ and $R_2^*(p) \triangleq (K - 2K^2 p)$, then we have

$$T^* \geq \max\{R_1^*(p), R_2^*(p)\}.$$

Here $R_{\emptyset}/R_1^*(p)$ and $R_{\emptyset}/R_2^*(p)$ both are monotonic functions of p according to the following properties:

$$\begin{aligned}
\frac{\partial(R_{\emptyset}/R_1^*(p))}{\partial p} &= \frac{\partial(2K(1-p)^{K-1})}{\partial p} \leq 0, \\
\frac{\partial(R_{\emptyset}/R_2^*(p))}{\partial p} &= \frac{\partial(q^K/(1-2Kp))}{\partial p} \\
&= \frac{Kq^{K-1}(1+2(K-1)p)}{(1-2Kp)^2} \geq 0.
\end{aligned}$$

Additionally, notice that if $p = 0$, then $\frac{R_{\emptyset}}{R_2^*(p)} = 1 < \frac{R_{\emptyset}}{R_1^*(p)}$, and if $p = 1$, $\frac{R_{\emptyset}}{R_2^*(p)} > \frac{R_{\emptyset}}{R_1^*(p)} = 1$. Therefore, the maximum value of $R_{\emptyset}/\max\{R_1^*, R_2^*\}$ is chosen at $p = \frac{1}{2K+1}$ which satisfying $R_1^*(\frac{1}{2K+1}) = R_2^*(\frac{1}{2K+1})$, implying that

$$\frac{R_{\emptyset}}{T^*} \leq \frac{R_{\emptyset}(\frac{1}{2K+1})}{R_1^*(\frac{1}{2K+1})} = 2K\left(\frac{2K}{2K+1}\right)^{K-1}. \tag{A23}$$

From (A21)–(A23), we obtain the following equality:

$$\frac{T_{\text{decentral}}}{T^*} \leq \max\left\{2K\left(\frac{2K}{2K+1}\right)^{K-1}, 6\right\}.$$

Appendix D.2. When $\alpha_{\max} = 1$

From Equation (24), we obtain that

$$\begin{aligned}
R_{\mathrm{u}} &\leq \frac{q}{p}\left(1 - \frac{5}{2}Kpq^{K-1} - 4q^{K} + \frac{3(1-q^{K+1})}{(K+1)p}\right) \\
&\leq \frac{q}{p}\left(1 - \frac{5}{2}Kpq^{K-1} - 4q^{K} + \frac{3(K+1)p}{(K+1)p}\right) \\
&= \frac{q}{p}\left(4\cdot(1-q^{K}) - \frac{5}{2}Kpq^{K-1}\right) \\
&\leq \frac{q}{p}(4\cdot(1-q^{K})) \\
&= 4R_{\mathrm{s}},
\end{aligned} \tag{A24}$$

where the second inequality holds by (A19) and the last equality holds by the definition $R_s \triangleq \frac{q}{p}(1-q^K)$ in (19). On the other hand, rewrite the second lower bound of T^*:

$$T^* \geq \max_{s\in[K]}\left(s - \frac{sM}{\lfloor N/s \rfloor}\right)\frac{1}{1+\alpha_{\max}}. \tag{A25}$$

From the result in [2] (Appendix B), we have

$$\frac{R_{\mathrm{s}}}{\max_{s\in[K]}\left(s - \frac{sM}{\lfloor N/s\rfloor}\right)} \leq 12. \tag{A26}$$

Combining (A24)–(A26), we have

$$\frac{R_{\mathrm{s}}}{T^*} \leq 12(1+\alpha_{\max}),\ \frac{R_{\mathrm{u}}}{T^*} \leq 48(1+\alpha_{\max}). \tag{A27}$$

If $p \leq p_{\mathrm{th}}$, by (A27) and since $R_{\varnothing} \leq T_{\mathrm{decentral}} \leq R_{\mathrm{s}}$ (see Remark 4), we have

$$\frac{T_{\mathrm{decentral}}}{T^*} \leq \frac{R_{\mathrm{s}}}{T^*} \leq 12(1+\alpha_{\max}) = 24, \tag{A28}$$

the last equality holds by the fact $\alpha_{\max} = 1$.

If $p \geq p_{\mathrm{th}}$, from Lemma A2, we have $R_{\mathrm{u}} \geq R_{\varnothing}$ and

$$\begin{aligned}
\frac{T_{\mathrm{decentral}}}{T^*} &= \frac{\frac{R_{\mathrm{s}}R_{\mathrm{u}}}{R_{\mathrm{s}}+R_{\mathrm{u}}-R_{\varnothing}}}{T^*} \\
&\leq \frac{\min\{R_{\mathrm{u}}, R_{\mathrm{s}}\}}{T^*} \\
&\leq \min\{12(1+\alpha_{\max}), 48(1+\alpha_{\max})\} \\
&= 24,
\end{aligned} \tag{A29}$$

where the second inequality holds by (A27) and the last equality is from the fact $\alpha_{\max} = 1$ in this case.

References

1. Maddah-Ali, M.A.; Niesen, U. Fundamental limits of caching. *IEEE Trans. Inf. Theory* **2014**, *60*, 2856–2867. [CrossRef]
2. Maddah-Ali, M.A.; Niesen, U. Decentralized coded caching attains order-optimal memory-rate tradeoff. *IEEE/ACM Trans. Netw.* **2015**, *23*, 1029–1040. [CrossRef]
3. Yu, Q.; Maddah-Ali, M.A.; Avestimehr, A.S. Characterizing the Rate-Memory Tradeoff in Cache Networks within a Factor of 2. *IEEE Trans. Inf. Theory* **2019**, *65*, 647–663. [CrossRef]
4. Wan, K.; Tuninetti, D.; Piantanida, P. On the optimality of uncoded cache placement. In Proceedings of the IEEE Information Theory Workshop (ITW), Cambridge, UK, 11–14 September 2016; pp. 161–165.

5. Yu, Q.; Maddah-Ali, M.A.; Avestimehr, A.S. The exact rate-memory tradeoff for caching with uncoded prefetching. *IEEE Trans. Inf. Theory* **2018**, *64*, 1281–1296. [CrossRef]
6. Yan, Q.; Cheng, M.; Tang, X.; Chen, Q. On the placement delivery array design for centralized coded caching scheme. *IEEE Trans. Inf. Theory* **2017**, *63*, 5821–5833. [CrossRef]
7. Zhang, D.; Liu, N. Coded cache placement for heterogeneous cache sizes. In Proceedings of the IEEE Information Theory Workshop (ITW), Guangzhou, China, 25–29 November 2018; pp. 1–5.
8. Wang, S.; Peleato, B. Coded caching with heterogeneous user profiles. In Proceedings of the IEEE International Symposium on Information Theory (ISIT), France, Paris, 7–12 July 2019; pp. 2619–2623.
9. Zhang, J.; Lin, X.; Wang, C.C. Coded caching for files with distinct file sizes. In Proceedings of the IEEE International Symposium on Information Theory (ISIT), Hong Kong, China, 14–19 June 2015; pp. 1686–1690.
10. Ibrahim, A.M.; Zewail, A.A.; Yener, A. Centralized coded caching with heterogeneous cache sizes. In Proceedings of the IEEE Wireless Communications and Networking Conference (WCNC), San Francisco, CA, USA, 19–22 March 2017; pp. 1–6.
11. Ibrahim, A.M.; Zewail, A.A.; Yener, A. Coded caching for heterogeneous systems: An Optimization Perspective. *IEEE Trans. Commun.* **2019**, *67*, 5321–5335. [CrossRef]
12. Amiri, M.M.; Yang, Q.; Gündüz, D. Decentralized caching and coded delivery with distinct cache capacities. *IEEE Trans. Commun.* **2017**, *65*, 4657–4669. [CrossRef]
13. Cao, D.; Zhang, D.; Chen, P.; Liu, N.; Kang, W.; Gündüz, D. Coded caching with asymmetric cache sizes and link qualities: The two-user case. *IEEE Trans. Commun.* **2019**, *67*, 6112–6126. [CrossRef]
14. Niesen, U.; Maddah-Ali, M.A. Coded caching with nonuniform demands. *IEEE Trans. Inf. Theory* **2017**, *63*, 1146–1158. [CrossRef]
15. Zhang, J.; Lin, X.; Wang, X. Coded caching under arbitrary popularity distributions. *IEEE Trans. Inf. Theory* **2018**, *64*, 349–366. [CrossRef]
16. Pedarsani, R.; Maddah-Ali, M.A.; Niesen, U. Online coded caching. *IEEE/ACM Trans. Netw.* **2016**, *24*, 836–845. [CrossRef]
17. Daniel, A.M.; Yu, W. Optimization of heterogeneous coded caching. *IEEE Trans. Inf. Theory* **2020**, *66*, 1893–1919. [CrossRef]
18. Shariatpanahi, S.P.; Motahari, S.A.; Khalaj, B.H. Multi-server coded caching. *IEEE Trans. Inf. Theory* **2016**, *62*, 7253–7271. [CrossRef]
19. Zhang, J.; Elia, P. Fundamental limits of cache-aided wireless BC: Interplay of coded-caching and CSIT feedback. *IEEE Trans. Inf. Theory* **2017**, *63*, 3142–3160. [CrossRef]
20. Bidokhti, S.S.; Wigger, M.; Timo, R. Noisy broadcast networks with receiver caching. *IEEE Trans. Inf. Theory* **2018**, *64*, 6996–7016. [CrossRef]
21. Sengupta, A.; Tandon, R.; Simeone, O. Cache aided wireless networks: Tradeoffs between storage and latency. In Proceedings of the 2016 Annual Conference on Information Science and Systems (CISS), Princeton, NJ, USA, 15–18 March 2016; pp. 320–325.
22. Tandon, R.; Simeone, O. Cloud-aided wireless networks with edge caching: Fundamental latency trade-offs in fog radio access networks. In Proceedings of the IEEE International Symposium on Information Theory (ISIT), Barcelona, Spain, 10–15 July 2016; pp. 2029–2033.
23. Karamchandani, N.; Niesen, U.; Maddah-Ali, M.A.; Diggavi, S.N. Hierarchical coded caching. *IEEE Trans. Inf. Theory* **2016**, *62*, 3212–3229. [CrossRef]
24. Wang, K.; Wu, Y.; Chen, J.; Yin, H. Reduce transmission delay for caching-aided two-layer networks. In Proceedings of the IEEE International Symposium on Information Theory (ISIT), France, Paris, 7–12 July 2019; pp. 2019–2023.
25. Wan, K.; Ji, M.; Piantanida, P.; Tuninetti, D. Caching in combination networks: Novel multicast message generation and delivery by leveraging the network topology. In Proceedings of the IEEE International Conference on Communications (ICC), Kansas City, MO, USA, 20–24 May 2018; pp. 1–6.
26. Naderializadeh, N.; Maddah-Ali, M.A.; Avestimehr, A.S. Fundamental limits of cache-aided interference management. *IEEE Trans. Inf. Theory* **2017**, *63*, 3092–3107. [CrossRef]
27. Xu, F.; Tao, M.; Liu, K. Fundamental tradeoff between storage and latency in cache-aided wireless interference Networks. *IEEE Trans. Inf. Theory* **2017**, *63*, 7464–7491. [CrossRef]
28. Ji, M.; Tulino, A.M.; Llorca, J.; Caire, G. Order-optimal rate of caching and coded multicasting with random demands. *IEEE Trans. Inf. Theory* **2017**, *63*, 3923–3949. [CrossRef]
29. Ji, M.; Tulino, A.M.; Llorca, J.; Caire, G. Caching in combination networks. In Proceedings of the 2015 49th Asilomar Conference on Signals, Systems and Computers, Pacific Grove, CA, USA, 8–11 November 2015.
30. Ravindrakumar, V.; Panda, P.; Karamchandani, N.; Prabhakaran, V. Fundamental limits of secretive coded caching. In Proceedings of the IEEE International Symposium on Information Theory (ISIT), Barcelona, Spain, 10–15 July 2016; pp. 425–429.
31. Tang, L.; Ramamoorthy, A. Coded caching schemes with reduced subpacketization from linear block codes. *IEEE Trans. Inf. Theory* **2018**, *64*, 3099–3120. [CrossRef]
32. Cheng, M.; Li, J.; Tang, X.; Wei, R. Linear coded caching scheme for centralized networks. *IEEE Trans. Inf. Theory* **2021**, *67*, 1732–1742. [CrossRef]
33. Wan, K.; Caire, G. On coded caching with private demands. *IEEE Trans. Inf. Theory* **2021**, *67*, 358–372. [CrossRef]
34. Hassanzadeh, P.; Tulino, A.M.; Llorca, J.; Erkip, E. Rate-memory trade-off for caching and delivery of correlated sources. *IEEE Trans. Inf. Theory* **2020**, *66*, 2219–2251. [CrossRef]

35. Ji, M.; Caire, G.; Molisch, A.F. Fundamental limits of caching in wireless D2D networks. *IEEE Trans. Inf. Theory* **2016**, *62*, 849–869. [CrossRef]
36. Tebbi, A.; Sung, C.W. Coded caching in partially cooperative D2D communication networks. In Proceedings of the 9th International Congress on Ultra Modern Telecommunications and Control Systems and Workshops (ICUMT), Munich, Germany, 6–8 November 2017; pp. 148–153.
37. Wang, J.; Cheng, M.; Yan, Q.; Tang, X. Placement delivery array design for coded caching scheme in D2D Networks. *IEEE Trans. Commun.* **2019**, *67*, 3388–3395. [CrossRef]
38. Malak, D.; Al-Shalash, M.; Andrews, J.G. Spatially correlated content caching for device-to-device communications. *IEEE Trans. Wirel. Commun.* **2018**, *17*, 56–70. [CrossRef]
39. Ibrahim, A.M.; Zewail, A.A.; Yener, A. Device-to-Device coded caching with distinct cache sizes. *arXiv* **2019**, arXiv:1903.08142.
40. Pedersen, J.; Amat, A.G.; Andriyanova, I.; Brännström, F. Optimizing MDS coded caching in wireless networks with device-to-device communication. *IEEE Trans. Wirel. Commun.* **2019**, *18*, 286–295. [CrossRef]
41. Chiang, M.; Zhang, T. Fog and IoT: An overview of research opportunities. *IEEE Internet Things J.* **2016**, *3*, 854–864. [CrossRef]

entropy

MDPI

Article

Degrees of Freedom of a *K*-User Interference Channel in the Presence of an Instantaneous Relay

Ali H. Abdollahi Bafghi [1], Mahtab Mirmohseni [2,*] and Masoumeh Nasiri-Kenari [1]

1 Department of Electrical Engineering, Sharif University of Technology, Tehran P932+FM4, Iran
2 Institute for Communication Systems (ICS), University of Surrey, Guildford GU2 7XH, UK
* Correspondence: m.mirmohseni@surrey.ac.uk

Abstract: In this paper, we study the degrees of freedom (DoF) of a frequency-selective K-user interference channel in the presence of an instantaneous relay (IR) with multiple receiving and transmitting antennas. We investigate two scenarios based on the IR antennas' cooperation ability. First, we assume that the IR receiving and transmitting antennas can coordinate with each other and that the transmitted signal of each transmitting antenna can depend on the received signals of all receiving antennas, and we derive lower and upper bounds for the sum DoF of this model. In an interference alignment scheme, we divide receivers into two groups called clean and dirty receivers. We design our scheme such that a part of the messages of clean receivers can be de-multiplexed at the IR. Thus, the IR can use these message streams for an interference cancellation at the clean receivers. Next, we consider an IR, the antennas of which do not have coordination with each other and where the transmitted signal of each transmitting antenna depends only on the received signal of its corresponding receiving antenna. We also derive lower and upper bounds for the sum DoF for this model of IR. We show that the achievable sum DoF decreases considerably compared with the coordinated case. In both of these models, our schemes achieve the maximum K sum DoF if the number of transmitting and receiving antennas is more than a finite threshold.

Keywords: frequency-selective interference channel; K-user interference channel; DoF; instantaneous relay

Citation: Abdollahi Bafghi, A.H.; Mirmohseni, M.; Nasiri-Kenari, M. Degrees of Freedom of a K-User Interference Channel in the Presence of an Instantaneous Relay. *Entropy* **2022**, *24*, 1078. https://doi.org/10.3390/e24081078

Academic Editors: H. Vincent Poor, Holger Boche, Rafael F. Schaefer and Onur Günlü

Received: 6 June 2022
Accepted: 26 July 2022
Published: 4 August 2022

1. Introduction

Spectrum sharing in wireless networks seems to be an inevitable solution to increasing bandwidth demands. How to treat interference is one of the main challenges in these scenarios. Interference alignment has proved to be a useful solution that aligns all interference signals into a smaller subspace, allowing the remaining signal space to be used for the transmission of main signals. Thereby, it can achieve the maximum degrees of freedom (DoF) of $\frac{K}{2}$ in a K-user interference channel [1]. An interesting question would be to find tools that can improve this maximum value for the DoF. Instantaneous relay (relay-without-delay; IR) is one of these tools [2,3].

For an IR, a transmitted signal in a t-th time slot ($\mathbf{X}_{\mathrm{IR}}(t)$) is a function of all received signals ($\mathbf{Y}_{\mathrm{IR}}(t)$) from a first time slot up to a current (t-th) time slot, i.e., $\mathbf{Y}_{\mathrm{IR}}(t) = f_{\mathrm{IR}}(\mathbf{X}_{\mathrm{IR}}(1), \ldots, \mathbf{X}_{\mathrm{IR}}(t))$, while for a classic relay, a transmitted signal in a t-th time slot does not depend on a received signal in the t-th (current) time slot (it was shown in [4] that a classic relay cannot increase the DoF of a K-user interference channel), i.e., $\mathbf{Y}_{\mathrm{R}}(t) = f_{\mathrm{R}}(\mathbf{X}_{\mathrm{R}}(1), \ldots, \mathbf{X}_{\mathrm{R}}(t-1))$. Though for the current technology, an IR might seem impractical, there have been significant results on an IR, and active reconfigurable intelligent surface (RIS) is a promising technology that makes it possible to realize an IR in the near future [5]. An RIS is a special case of the IR model for which a transmitted signal in the t-th time slot ($\mathbf{X}_{\mathrm{RIS}}(t)$) is a function of the received signal ($\mathbf{Y}_{\mathrm{RIS}}(t)$) in the t-th time slot only, i.e., $\mathbf{Y}_{\mathrm{RIS}}(t) = f_{\mathrm{RIS}}(\mathbf{X}_{\mathrm{RIS}}(t))$.

The capacities of wireless networks in the presence of an IR were studied in [6–30]. El Gamal et al., in [6], showed that in the presence of an IR, rates higher than an existing cut-set bound for a classic relay can be achieved for a point-to-point channel. In [7], a new upper bound was derived for the capacity of a channel with an IR. The authors in [8] studied a two-user interference channel in the presence of an IR and derived an outer bound for the Gaussian case under strong and very strong interference conditions. They also introduced an achievable scheme based on instantaneous amplify-and-forward relaying. In [9], the authors studied a K-user interference channel in the presence of an IR in two scenarios, wherein transmitters and receivers were aware and not aware of the existence of an IR. It was shown that in both cases, an IR can enlarge the rate region and increase user fairness. In [10], the authors studied general networks in the presence of an IR and derived cut-set bounds for two cases of the IR having or not having its own message; they showed that the proposed bounds are tight in some cases. In [11], it was proven that the networks with an IR can be considered a channel with in-block memory. Then, a cut-set bound was characterized that generalizes existing cut-set bounds.

As we stated before, an RIS is a special case of the generic IR model; thus, we will review some related work on the capacities of RIS-assisted networks. In [12], the fundamental capacity limit of RIS-assisted multiple-input multiple-output (MIMO) communications systems was studied by using a joint optimization of a MIMO transmit covariance matrix and RIS phase shifts. In [13], RIS-assisted communication systems were studied wherein a transmitter could control an RIS with a finite-rate link and information-theoretic limits were derived. It was proven that the capacity is achievable if information is jointly encoded in a transmitted signal and RIS phase shifts. In [14], a downlink non-orthogonal multiple-access (NOMA) RIS-assisted communication system was studied wherein multiple users were served by only one base station (BS). The sum rate of the users was maximized by using a joint optimization of a beamforming vector at the BS and the phase shifts of the RIS, wherein a successive interference cancellation decoding rate and RIS scattering element constraints existed. In [15], the usage of an RIS was studied for a rank improvement of MIMO communication channels.

From a DoF perspective, an interference alignment signaling scheme for a MIMO X-channel, which outperforms the achievable DoF of previous signaling schemes, was proposed in [16]. It is well known that the DoF of the frequency or time-selective K-user interference channel is $\frac{K}{2}$ [1], which is an important result of the interference alignment technique. We remark that the DoF of interference channels is an important problem, which has been studied vastly in the literature; e.g., the DoF of a multi-input multi-output (MIMO) interference channel [17], the DoF region of an interference channel [18,19], and the DoF of an interference channel with a partial network topology [20–25]. Interference alignment is an important technique, which has a vital impact on proving DoF achievability theorems for multi-user wireless networks. A survey of the results available on the interference alignment technique was reviewed in [26]. For the DoF of networks in the presence of an IR, the sum DoF of a two-user interference channel assisted by an IR, with M antennas for all nodes, was studied in [3], and it was proven that the DoF of $\frac{3M}{2}$ can be achieved. The DoF of an M antenna three-user interference channel assisted by an IR was studied in [27], and it was shown that a DoF of $2M$ is achievable. The DoF of a two-way K-user IR-aided interference channel, when the IR is equipped with $2K$ antennas, was studied in [28]. It was demonstrated that the DoF of K can be achieved. The DoF of a two-user interference channel in the presence of an IR, when there is an arbitrary number of IR transmitting and receiving antennas, was studied in [29]. An inner and two outer bounds were obtained. For a K-user interference channel assisted by an IR wherein the IR can only instantaneously amplify and forward a received signal in a current channel use, with the same number of antennas at all nodes, an achievable scheme and an outer bound were proposed in [30]. Though the DoF in some special cases wherein $K = 2$ or $K(K-1)$ IRs was derived, a general achievable DoF was not obtained. For a K-user interference channel in the presence of active and passive RISs, inner and outer bounds on a DoF region and lower and upper bounds on a sum DoF were derived in [31]. For both active and passive RISs, it was shown that by employing a sufficient number of elements for RIS, a K sum DoFs can be achieved. In [32], it was shown that when there is a line-of-sight link between an RIS and transceivers and there is no direct link between the transceivers, the phases of RIS elements can be adjusted such that all interference can be canceled and a maximum K DoF can be achieved in a K-user interference channel if the number of RIS elements is more than a finite value.

The goal of this paper was to study the sum DoF of a frequency-selective K-user interference channel in the presence of an IR. To the best of our knowledge, although the DoF of two- and three-user interference channels and a scenario in which there are $K(K-1)$ IRs have been studied, the sum DoF of a frequency-selective K-user interference channel (wherein symbol extensions are in the frequency domain) in the presence of a multi-input multi-output (MIMO) IR has not been characterized. Our contributions are as follows:

- We provide lower and upper bounds for the sum DoF of a K-user interference channel in the presence of a MIMO IR with Q receiving antennas and W transmitting antennas, which can coordinate with each other, i.e., each transmit antenna has access to all receiving antennas. For this purpose, we propose an interference alignment-based coding scheme in which we divide the receivers into two groups called clean and dirty receivers. We design beamforming vectors such that some message symbols corresponding to the clean receivers can be de-multiplexed at the IR. By de-multiplexing, we mean that the IR separates only some of the message symbols using linear operations without removing additive noise. Then, the IR utilizes the de-multiplexed symbols for an interference cancellation at the clean receivers. Our proposed scheme increases the DoF for $W > \frac{K}{2}$ compared to a case without an IR. Moreover, we show that if the number of IR antennas exceeds a finite threshold, the maximum DoF of K can be achieved, and we characterize this threshold.
- Moreover, we derive lower and upper bounds for the sum DoF for a special kind of IR for which the IR has the same number of receiving and transmitting antennas and the antennas do not have coordination with each other, i.e., the i-th transmitting antenna has access to the i-th receiving antenna only. We extend the coding scheme for this case and derive an achievable DoF. Similar to a coordinated IR, we show that by considering a number of IR antennas more than a finite threshold, the maximum DoF of K can be achieved. Our derivations show that the achievable DoF decreases considerably compared with the coordinated IR.

This paper is organized as follows. In Section 2, we present the system model. In Sections 3 and 4, we discuss our main results for the coordinated and non-coordinated IRs, respectively. In Section 5, we present some numerical results to evaluate our proposed schemes. Finally, in Section 6, we conclude the paper.

Notations: Bold letters demonstrate matrices. Calligraphic uppercase letters denote sets and vector spaces. $\mathbb{R}$ is the set of real numbers. For the set $\mathcal{A}$, $|\mathcal{A}|$ indicates the cardinality of $\mathcal{A}$. $\mathbf{V}^T$ and $\mathbf{V}^H$ are the transposition and Hermitian of matrix $\mathbf{V}$, respectively. $\mathrm{diag}(\mathrm{a}_1, \ldots, \mathrm{a}_\mathrm{m})$ denotes a diagonal matrix with the diagonal elements $a_1, \ldots, a_m$. The function $f(\rho)$ is $o(\log(\rho))$ if

$$\lim_{\rho \to \infty} \frac{|f(\rho)|}{\log(\rho)} = 0.$$

Sequence $a(n)$ goes to infinity with $O(g(n))$ if

$$0 < \lim_{n \to \infty} \frac{|a(n)|}{|g(n)|} < \infty.$$

$\mathbb{N}$ is the set of natural numbers, and $\mathbb{W}$ is the set of non-negative integers.

2. System Model and Preliminaries

2.1. System Model

We consider a K-user interference channel with an IR in which K single-antenna transmitters send their messages to K single-antenna receivers. In this system, the i-th transmitter sends the message $w^{[i]} \in \mathcal{W}^{[i]} = \{1, \ldots, \lfloor 2^{Tr_i} \rfloor\}$ to the i-th receiver, where r_i is the transmission rate corresponding to the i-th transmitter and T is the number of channel uses (in this paper, each channel use corresponds to each frequency slot and all transmissions are in the same time cycle). We assume an IR with Q receiving antennas and W transmitting antennas. Figure 1 shows the system model.

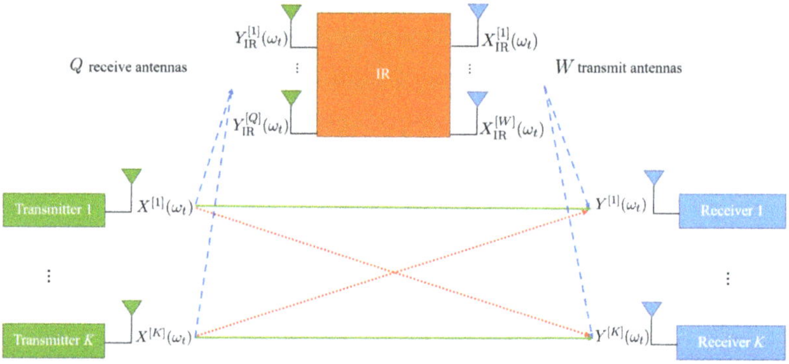

Figure 1. IR-assisted K-user interference channel. The IR has W transmitting antennas and Q receiving antennas. Direct links are shown by solid arrows, cross-links are shown by dotted arrows, and links between the IR and transmitters or receivers are shown by dashed arrows.

We consider a frequency-selective channel. Due to the instantaneity of the IR, it can process the signals received from all frequency slots in the current time cycle and transmit signals in different frequency slots in the same time cycle, which affects the received signals at the receivers in all frequency slots. The received signal at the j-th receiver in the t-th frequency slot ω_t is shown by $Y^{[j]}(\omega_t)$ and is presented as follows (note that in the general case, the IR-transmitted signal is a function of the received signal in the past time cycles in addition to the current time cycle. In the achievability proofs of this paper, the signals of past time cycles are not needed and transmissions in different frequency slots are at the same time cycle. However, for the upper bounds, the general case is considered.):

$$Y^{[j]}(\omega_t) = \sum_{i=1}^{K} H^{[ji]}(\omega_t) X^{[i]}(\omega_t) + \sum_{u=1}^{W} H_{\mathrm{IR-R}}^{[ju]}(\omega_t) X_{\mathrm{IR}}^{[u]}(\omega_t) + Z^{[j]}(\omega_t), \tag{1}$$

where $X^{[i]}(\omega_t)$ is the signal of the i-th transmitter, $H^{[ji]}(\omega_t)$ is the channel coefficient between the i-th transmitter and the j-th receiver, $X_{\mathrm{IR}}^{[u]}(\omega_t)$ is the transmitted signal of the u-th IR transmitting antenna, $H_{\mathrm{IR-R}}^{[ju]}(\omega_t)$ is the channel coefficient between the u-th IR transmitting antenna and the j-th receiver, and $Z^{[j]}(\omega_t)$ is additive white Gaussian noise (AWGN) at the j-th receiver in the t-th frequency slot ω_t, where $t \in \{1, 2, \ldots, T\}$. We assume a perfect self-interference cancellation at the IR; thus, the received signal at the q-th IR receiving antenna in the t-th frequency slot, which is shown by $Y_{\mathrm{IR}}^{[q]}(\omega_t)$, is given as follows:

$$Y_{\mathrm{IR}}^{[q]}(\omega_t) = \sum_{i=1}^{K} H_{\mathrm{T-IR}}^{[qi]}(\omega_t) X^{[i]}(\omega_t) + Z_{\mathrm{IR}}^{[q]}(\omega_t), \tag{2}$$

where $H_{\mathrm{T-IR}}^{[qi]}(\omega_t)$ is the channel coefficient from the i-th transmitter to the q-th IR receiving antenna (for an NC-IR, before a transmission begins, all required channel-state information and the transmission strategy are shared between all nodes and all receiving and transmitting antennas of the NC-IR. However, when the transmission begins, the i-th transmitting antenna of the NC-IR has access to the i-th receiving antenna only and its received signal cannot be exchanged between other transmitting antennas (the same holds for the active RIS [31])), $q \in \{1, \ldots, Q\}$, and $Z_{\mathrm{IR}}^{[q]}(\omega_t)$ are the AWGN at the q-th IR receiving antenna in the t-th frequency slot. We assume that the perfect channel-state information for all frequency slots is available at all nodes (this ideal assumption is vastly considered in the literature [1,33]. Noisy channel-state information will be an interesting subject of future work.). We consider two types of IR: (1) a MIMO IR, the antennas of which can have a coordination with each other, called MIMO-coordinated IR (C-IR) and (2) an IR with no coordination among its antennas because the u-th transmitting antenna has access to only the u-th receiving antenna ($W = Q$). We call this model non-coordinated IR (NC-IR). At each time cycle, for the MIMO C-IR, we have:

$$X_{\mathrm{IR}}^{[u]}(\omega_t) = f^{[u,\omega_t]}(Y_{\mathrm{IR}}^{[1]}(\omega_1), \ldots, Y_{\mathrm{IR}}^{[1]}(\omega_T), \ldots, Y_{\mathrm{IR}}^{[Q]}(\omega_1), \ldots, Y_{\mathrm{IR}}^{[Q]}(\omega_T)), \tag{3}$$

where $f^{[u,\omega_t]}$ indicates the encoding function of the IR for the u-th transmitting antenna at the t-th frequency slot ω_t. For the NC-IR, we have:

$$X_{\mathrm{IR}}^{[u]}(\omega_t) = f^{[u,\omega_t]}(Y_{\mathrm{IR}}^{[u]}(\omega_1), \ldots, Y_{\mathrm{IR}}^{[u]}(\omega_T)), u \in \{1, \ldots, Q\}. \tag{4}$$

We limit the functions $f^{[u,\omega_t]}$ to be linear. (1) and (2) can be rewritten into the following vector form:

$$\mathbf{Y}^{[j]} = \sum_{i=1}^{K} \mathbf{H}^{[ji]}\mathbf{X}^{[i]} + \sum_{u=1}^{W} \mathbf{H}_{\mathrm{IR-R}}^{[ju]}\mathbf{X}_{\mathrm{IR}}^{[u]} + \mathbf{Z}^{[j]}, \tag{5}$$

$$\mathbf{Y}_{\mathrm{IR}}^{[q]} = \sum_{i=1}^{K} \mathbf{H}_{\mathrm{T-IR}}^{[qi]}\mathbf{X}^{[i]} + \mathbf{Z}_{\mathrm{IR}}^{[q]}, \tag{6}$$

where $\mathbf{X}^{[i]}$ is a $T \times 1$ column vector including the channel inputs $X^{[i]}(\omega_t)$, i.e.,

$$\mathbf{X}^{[i]} = \begin{bmatrix} X^{[i]}(\omega_1) & X^{[i]}(\omega_2) & \cdots & X^{[i]}(\omega_T) \end{bmatrix}^T.$$

$\mathbf{Y}^{[i]}$, $\mathbf{Y}_{\mathrm{IR}}^{[q]}$, $\mathbf{X}_{\mathrm{IR}}^{[u]}$, $\mathbf{Z}^{[j]}$ and $\mathbf{Z}_{\mathrm{IR}}^{[q]}$ are also defined in the similar way. $\mathbf{H}^{[ji]}$ is a diagonal matrix defined as follows:

$$\mathbf{H}^{[ji]} = \mathrm{diag}\Big(H^{[ji]}(\omega_1), \ldots, H^{[ji]}(\omega_T)\Big).$$

$\mathbf{H}_{\mathrm{IR-R}}^{[ju]}$ and $\mathbf{H}_{\mathrm{T-IR}}^{[qi]}$ are also defined similarly. Considering functions $f^{[u,\omega_t]}$ to be linear, the operation of the the MIMO C-IR can be represented as follows:

$$\mathbf{X}_{\mathrm{IR}}^{[u]} = \sum_{q=1}^{Q} \mathbf{A}^{[uq]}\mathbf{Y}_{\mathrm{IR}}^{[q]}, \tag{7}$$

where $\mathbf{A}^{[uq]}$ are $T \times T$ matrices. Moreover, the linear operation of the NC-IR can be represented as follows:

$$\mathbf{X}_{\mathrm{IR}}^{[u]} = \mathbf{A}^{[u]}\mathbf{Y}_{\mathrm{IR}}^{[u]}. \tag{8}$$

Since we assume a frequency-selective K-user interference channel, $H^{[ji]}(\omega_t)$, $H_{\mathrm{IR-R}}^{[ju]}(\omega_t)$ and $H_{\mathrm{T-IR}}^{[qi]}(\omega_t)$ are independent random variables for different values of i, j, u, q and ω_t, whose cumulative distribution functions (CDFs) are continuous due to the frequency selectivity of the channel. In the case of complex channel coefficients, their real and imaginary parts are independent random variables , whose CDFs are continuous (e.g., complex Gaussian random variable).

Remark 1. *The assumption of frequency selectivity is essential for our coding scheme not only for the realization of independent channel coefficients for each channel use but also because if we assume the channel to be time selective and channel uses are in different time slots, by using (7) and (8), the matrices* $\mathbf{A}^{[uq]}$ *for the MIMO C-IR and the matrices* $\mathbf{A}^{[u]}$ *for the NC-IR must be lower triangular matrices due to the definition of the IR (the transmitted signal of an IR for the t-th time slot is a function of the received signals for the time slots* $t' \in \{1, \ldots, t\}$*). However, if we assume the channel to be frequency selective and consider our different channel uses in different frequency slots in the same time cycle, the transmitted signals of the IR for each frequency slot can be a function of all received signals for all frequency slots; thus, there would not be any constraint on the matrices* $\mathbf{A}^{[uq]}$ *and* $\mathbf{A}^{[u]}$ *and our proposed achievability schemes will be realizable.*

We assume that all transmitters can send a signal with a maximum average power of ρ, i.e., $\frac{1}{T}\sum_{t=1}^{T}\left|X^{[i]}(\omega_t)\right|^2 \leqslant \rho, \forall i \in \{1, \ldots, K\}$. We say the rate vector $\mathbf{r} = (r_1, \ldots, r_K)$ is achievable if $\lim_{T\to\infty} \Pr\left\{\bigcap_i \{\hat{w}^{[i]} \neq w^{[i]}\}\right\} = 0$, where $\hat{w}^{[i]}$ is the estimated message at the i-th receiver. In addition, $\mathcal{C}(\rho)$ indicates the closure of all the achievable rate vectors $\mathbf{r} = (r_1, \ldots, r_K)$.

2.2. Preliminaries

In the following section, we introduce some definitions that are used throughout this paper.

Degrees of freedom (DoF): Similar to [1], we define the DoF region $\mathcal{D}$ for a K-user interference channel as follows:

$$\mathcal{D} = \Big\{(d_1, \ldots, d_K) \in \mathbb{R}_+^K : \forall (w_1, \ldots, w_K) \in \mathbb{R}_+^K,$$

$$w_1 d_1 + \ldots + w_K d_K \le \limsup_{\rho\to\infty}\left(\frac{1}{\log(\rho)} \sup_{\mathbf{r}(\rho)\in\mathcal{C}(\rho)} (w_1 r_1 + \ldots + w_K r_K)\right)\Big\}. \tag{9}$$

Span: The span$(\mathbf{V})$ denotes the space spanned by the column vectors of the matrix $\mathbf{V}$.

Dimension: We define the number of dimensions of the span$(\mathbf{V})$ as the dimension of $\mathbf{V}$ and show it by using $d(\mathbf{V})$, which is equal to rank$(\mathbf{V})$.

Normalized asymptotic dimension: We will see in our analysis that for a given K, Q and for W, the dimensions of the beamforming matrices and the vector spaces will have an order of $O(n^l), l, n \in \mathbb{N}$. For the matrix $\mathbf{V}$, we define the normalized asymptotic dimension (D_N) as follows:

$$D_N(\mathbf{V}) = \lim_{n\to\infty} \frac{d(\mathbf{V})}{n^l}, \tag{10}$$

where l is the maximum integer number that satisfies $\lim_{n\to\infty} \frac{d(\mathbf{V})}{n^l} < \infty$.

These definitions are also used for the vector space $\mathcal{A}$; therefore, $d(\mathcal{A})$ indicates the dimension of $\mathcal{A}$, and $D_N(\mathcal{A})$ indicates the normalized asymptotic dimension of $\mathcal{A}$.

3. K-User Interference Channel in the Presence of MIMO C-IR

In this section, we present the lower and upper bounds for the sum DoF of the frequency-selective K-user interference channel with a MIMO C-IR. First, we introduce the lower bound as follows:

Theorem 1. *For a frequency-selective K-user interference channel with a MIMO C-IR, where* $\max\{W, Q\} \le K$*, the following DoF is achievable:*

$$\text{DoF} = \max\left\{\frac{K}{2} + \max\left\{0, K\frac{\frac{W}{K} - \frac{1}{2}}{1 + 2\left\lceil\frac{W}{Q}\right\rceil}\right\}, \min\{Q, W\}\right\}. \tag{11}$$

We can see from (11) that when $\frac{W}{K} > \frac{1}{2}$*, the DoF always increases over* $\frac{K}{2}$*, i.e., the DoF increases in the absence of an IR.*

Proof. We will prove the achievability of the first term $\frac{K}{2} + \max\left\{0, K\frac{\frac{W}{K}-\frac{1}{2}}{1+2\left\lceil\frac{W}{Q}\right\rceil}\right\}$ in (11) in the following. The proof of the second term, i.e., $\min\{Q, W\}$, is provided in Appendix A.

We present this proof in six steps. In Step 1, we divide the transmitters and the receivers into two groups (clean and dirty). In Step 2, some message streams are considered to have the capability of being de-multiplexed at the MIMO C-IR; thus, the MIMO C-IR can use them for an interference cancellation in the clean receivers. After the interference cancellation, the equivalent channel coefficients are derived for other receivers (dirty receivers). In Step 3, we introduce the interference alignment equations such that the assumption of the previous step (the de-multiplexing of some message streams) and the interference alignment for each receiver and MIMO C-IR receiving antenna are satisfied. In Step 4, we present the beamforming design for each symbol stream. In Step 5, we analyze the satisfaction of the interference alignment equations at each receiver and MIMO C-IR receiving antenna. Finally, in Step 6, we derive the achieved DoF, presented in the first term of (11).

Step 1: Partitioning the Transmitters and Receivers

We divide the transmitters into two partitions. For the transmitters $i \in \{1, \ldots, W\}$, we provide two sets of symbol streams: $\bar{\mathbf{x}}^{[i]}$ and $\tilde{\mathbf{x}}^{[i]}$ (each element of the vectors $\bar{\mathbf{x}}^{[i]}$ and $\tilde{\mathbf{x}}^{[i]}$ is the extended symbols). The matrices $\bar{\mathbf{V}}^{[i]}$ and $\tilde{\mathbf{V}}^{[i]}$ are the beamforming matrices, the columns of which are the beamforming vectors corresponding to the elements of $\bar{\mathbf{x}}^{[i]}$ and $\tilde{\mathbf{x}}^{[i]}$, respectively. We can write:

$$\mathbf{X}^{[i]} = \bar{\mathbf{V}}^{[i]}\bar{\mathbf{x}}^{[i]} + \tilde{\mathbf{V}}^{[i]}\tilde{\mathbf{x}}^{[i]}, i \in \{1, \ldots, W\}. \tag{12}$$

For the transmitters $i \in \{W+1, \ldots, K\}$, we only provide one set of extended symbols ($\bar{\mathbf{x}}^{[i]}$), and $\bar{\mathbf{V}}^{[i]}$ is the beamforming matrix for the symbols $\bar{\mathbf{x}}^{[i]}$. Thus, we have:

$$\mathbf{X}^{[i]} = \bar{\mathbf{V}}^{[i]}\bar{\mathbf{x}}^{[i]}, i \in \{W+1, \ldots, K\}. \tag{13}$$

Note that the matrices $\tilde{\mathbf{V}}^{[i]}$ and $\bar{\mathbf{V}}^{[i]}$ have T rows because we have T frequency slots. The dimensions of $\bar{\mathbf{x}}^{[i]}$ and $\tilde{\mathbf{x}}^{[i]}$ and the number of columns of $\bar{\mathbf{V}}^{[i]}$ and $\tilde{\mathbf{V}}^{[i]}$ are determined in the next steps.

In the following steps, we design the beamforming vectors $\tilde{\mathbf{V}}^{[i]}$ and $\bar{\mathbf{V}}^{[i]}$ such that the extended symbols $\tilde{\mathbf{x}}^{[i]}$ can be de-multiplexed at the MIMO C-IR. By de-multiplexing, we mean that the MIMO C-IR can separate each symbol of message streams $\tilde{\mathbf{x}}^{[i]}$ using zero forcing without decoding the symbol. The symbol streams $\bar{\mathbf{x}}^{[i]}$ act as interference signals, and their beamforming vectors align into a smaller subspace.

We also divide the receivers into clean and dirty sets. In the next steps, the signal transmitted by the MIMO C-IR is designed such that the interference induced by the symbols $\tilde{\mathbf{x}}^{[i]}$ will be removed at the receivers $j \in \{1, \ldots, W\}$, called clean receivers, but this interference will remain at the receivers $j \in \{W+1, \ldots, K\}$, called dirty receivers. The main reason for choosing these terms (clean and dirty receivers) is that in our scheme, the interference of some symbol streams is canceled at clean receivers by the MIMO C-IR (the MIMO C-IR can de-multiplex these symbols and use them for interference cancellation) and the clean receivers will observe fewer dimensions for the interference; however, all interference remains at the dirty receivers.

Step 2: Interference Cancellation at Clean Receivers and Equivalent Channel for Dirty Receivers

We design the beamforming vectors $\tilde{\mathbf{V}}^{[i]}$ and $\bar{\mathbf{V}}^{[i]}$ such that the interference induced by the symbols $\tilde{\mathbf{x}}^{[i]}$ will be removed at the clean receivers. We denote this interference as $\tilde{\mathbf{I}}^{[j]}$, which is written as follows:

$$\tilde{\mathbf{I}}^{[j]} = \sum_{i\in\{1,\ldots,W\},i\neq j} \mathbf{H}^{[ji]}\tilde{\mathbf{V}}^{[i]}\tilde{\mathbf{x}}^{[i]}, j \in \{1,\ldots,W\}, \tag{14}$$

The MIMO C-IR can de-multiplex the streams corresponding to $\tilde{\mathbf{x}}^{[i]}$ (this will be shown in Steps 3–5), which is only contaminated by an additive noise, i.e., it will separate them into the form of $\hat{\tilde{\mathbf{x}}}^{[i]} = \tilde{\mathbf{x}}^{[i]} + \tilde{\mathbf{z}}^{[i]}$. Thus, for the interference cancellation, the MIMO C-IR designs its transmitted signal such that:

$$\sum_{u\in\{1,\ldots,W\}} \mathbf{H}^{[ju]}_{\mathrm{IR-R}}\mathbf{X}^{[u]}_{\mathrm{IR}} =$$

$$- \sum_{i\in\{1,\ldots,W\},i\neq j} \mathbf{H}^{[ji]}\tilde{\mathbf{V}}^{[i]}\hat{\tilde{\mathbf{x}}}^{[i]} = - \sum_{i\in\{1,\ldots,W\},i\neq j} \mathbf{H}^{[ji]}\tilde{\mathbf{V}}^{[i]}\left(\tilde{\mathbf{x}}^{[i]} + \tilde{\mathbf{z}}^{[i]}\right) = -\tilde{\mathbf{I}}^{[j]} + \tilde{\mathbf{Z}}^{[j]}, \tag{15}$$

where

$$\tilde{\mathbf{Z}}^{[j]} = - \sum_{i\in\{1,\ldots,W\},i\neq j} \mathbf{H}^{[ji]}\tilde{\mathbf{V}}^{[i]}\tilde{\mathbf{z}}^{[i]}.$$

The vector Equation (15) generates a linear set of equations, an equation for each element of $\mathbf{X}^{[u]}_{\mathrm{IR}}$, which can be written for the t-th element as:

$$\sum_{u\in\{1,\ldots,W\}} H^{[ju]}_{\mathrm{IR-R}}(\omega_t)X^{[u]}_{\mathrm{IR}}(\omega_t) = -\tilde{I}^{[j]}(\omega_t) + \tilde{Z}^{[j]}(\omega_t), \quad \forall j \in \{1,\ldots,W\}, \quad \forall t \in \{1,\ldots,T\}, \tag{16}$$

which is a linear set of equations with W variables for each ω_t. This set of equations is almost surely solvable since the coefficients of the linear equations are drawn independently and their CDFs are continuous; thus, the determinant of the matrix of linear equations will be a non-zero polynomial in terms of independent random variables and by using ([34], Lemma 1), it will be a non-zero with a probability equal to 1. Applying (16), the interference cancellation will be conducted. Thus, for each ω_t, we will have:

$$X^{[u]}_{\mathrm{IR}}(\omega_t) = \sum_{j\in\{1,\ldots,W\}} H^{[ju]}_{\mathrm{inv}}(\omega_t)(-\tilde{I}^{[j]}(\omega_t)(\omega_t) + \tilde{Z}^{[j]}(\omega_t)), \tag{17}$$

where $H^{[ju]}_{\mathrm{inv}}(\omega_t)$, the factor of $-\tilde{I}^{[j]}(\omega_t) + \tilde{Z}^{[j]}(\omega_t)$ in (17), is a function of $H^{[j'u']}_{\mathrm{IR-R}}(\omega_t)$, $u', j' \in \{1,\ldots,W\}$ obtained by solving Equation (16). We can write Equation (17) in the vector form as follows:

$$\mathbf{X}^{[u]}_{\mathrm{IR}} = \sum_{j\in\{1,\ldots,W\}} \mathbf{H}^{[ju]}_{\mathrm{inv}}(-\tilde{\mathbf{I}}^{[j]} + \tilde{\mathbf{Z}}^{[j]}) \tag{18}$$

$$= \sum_{j\in\{1,\ldots,W\}} \sum_{i\in\{1,\ldots,W\},i\neq j} -\mathbf{H}^{[ju]}_{\mathrm{inv}}\mathbf{H}^{[ji]}\tilde{\mathbf{V}}^{[i]}\tilde{\mathbf{x}}^{[i]} + \sum_{j\in\{1,\ldots,W\}} \mathbf{H}^{[ju]}_{\mathrm{inv}}\tilde{\mathbf{Z}}^{[j]}, \tag{19}$$

where $\mathbf{H}^{[ju]}_{\mathrm{inv}}$ is a diagonal matrix as follows:

$$\mathbf{H}^{[ju]}_{\mathrm{inv}} = \mathrm{diag}\left(H^{[ju]}_{\mathrm{inv}}(\omega_1),\ldots,H^{[ju]}_{\mathrm{inv}}(\omega_T)\right).$$

We highlight two properties of $\mathbf{H}^{[ju]}_{\mathrm{inv}}$:

- Similar to $\mathbf{H}^{[ji]}$, diagonal elements $H^{[ju]}_{\mathrm{inv}}(\omega_t)$ are independent random variables for different $t \in \{1,\ldots,T\}$ because the channel coefficients are independent random variables for each $t \in \{1,\ldots,T\}$.

- Each diagonal element $H_{\text{inv}}^{[ju]}(\omega_t)$ is a fractional polynomial constructed by the matrices $H_{\text{IR-R}}^{[j'u']}(\omega_t), j', u' \in \{1, \ldots, W\}$. A fractional polynomial is the ratio of the polynomial $P_1(\cdot)$ to the non-zero polynomial $P_2(\cdot)$.

Although we cancel the interference $\tilde{\mathbf{I}}^{[j]}$ at the clean receivers, this interference remains at the dirty receivers with new equivalent channel coefficients. Now, we derive the new channel coefficients for $\tilde{\mathbf{V}}^{[i]}\tilde{\mathbf{x}}^{[i]}, \forall i \in \{1, \ldots, W\}$ at the dirty receivers $j \in \{W+1, \ldots, K\}$. By combining (5), (12), and (13), we have:

$$\mathbf{Y}^{[j]} = \sum_{i \in \{1,\ldots,K\}} \mathbf{H}^{[ji]}\bar{\mathbf{V}}^{[i]}\bar{\mathbf{x}}^{[i]} + \sum_{i \in \{1,\ldots,W\}} \mathbf{H}^{[ji]}\tilde{\mathbf{V}}^{[i]}\tilde{\mathbf{x}}^{[i]} + \sum_{u \in \{1,\ldots,W\}} \mathbf{H}_{\text{IR-R}}^{[ju]}\mathbf{X}_{\text{IR}}^{[u]} + \mathbf{Z}^{[j]} \tag{20}$$

$$= \sum_{i \in \{1,\ldots,K\}} \mathbf{H}^{[ji]}\bar{\mathbf{V}}^{[i]}\bar{\mathbf{x}}^{[i]} + \sum_{i \in \{1,\ldots,W\}} \mathbf{H}^{[ji]}\tilde{\mathbf{V}}^{[i]}\tilde{\mathbf{x}}^{[i]} + \sum_{u,d,i \in \{1,\ldots,W\}, i \neq d} \mathbf{H}_{\text{IR-R}}^{[ju]}\mathbf{H}_{\text{inv}}^{[du]}\mathbf{H}^{[di]}\tilde{\mathbf{V}}^{[i]}\tilde{\mathbf{x}}^{[i]} + \tilde{\tilde{\mathbf{Z}}}^{[j]}, \tag{21}$$

where (21) follows from (19) and:

$$\tilde{\tilde{\mathbf{Z}}}^{[j]} = \sum_{u,d} \mathbf{H}_{\text{IR-R}}^{[ju]}\mathbf{H}_{\text{inv}}^{[du]}\tilde{\mathbf{Z}}^{[d]} + \mathbf{Z}^{[j]}.$$

(21) can be rewritten as:

$$\mathbf{Y}^{[j]} = \sum_{i \in \{1,\ldots,K\}} \mathbf{H}^{[ji]}\bar{\mathbf{V}}^{[i]}\bar{\mathbf{x}}^{[i]} + \sum_{i \in \{1,\ldots,W\}} \tilde{\mathbf{H}}^{[ji]}\tilde{\mathbf{V}}^{[i]}\tilde{\mathbf{x}}^{[i]} + \tilde{\tilde{\mathbf{Z}}}^{[j]}, \tag{22}$$

$$\tilde{\mathbf{H}}^{[ji]} = \mathbf{H}^{[ji]} + \sum_{u,d \in \{1,\ldots,W\}, d \neq i} \mathbf{H}_{\text{IR-R}}^{[ju]}\mathbf{H}_{\text{inv}}^{[du]}\mathbf{H}^{[di]}, i \in \{1, \ldots, W\}, \tag{23}$$

where $\tilde{\mathbf{H}}^{[ji]}$ is the equivalent channel coefficient matrix from the transmitter $i \in \{1, \ldots, W\}$ to the receiver $j \in \{W+1, \ldots, K\}$ (dirty receivers) for $\tilde{\mathbf{V}}^{[i]}\tilde{\mathbf{x}}^{[i]}$. By using (23), we can see that $\tilde{\mathbf{H}}^{[ji]}$ has the following properties:

- $\tilde{\mathbf{H}}^{[ji]}$ is a diagonal matrix.
- $\tilde{\mathbf{H}}^{[ji]} = \mathbf{H}^{[ji]}, \forall j \in \{1, \ldots, W\}$.
- For $j \in \{W+1, \ldots, K\}$, its t-th diagonal element has the following form:

$$\tilde{H}^{[ji]}(\omega_t) =$$

$$\sum_{u,i',j' \in \{1,\ldots W\}, i' \neq j'} H_{\text{IR-R}}^{[ju]}(\omega_t) H^{[j'i']}(\omega_t) P^{[ui'j']}(\{H_{\text{IR-R}}^{[me]}(\omega_t) : m, e \in \{1, \ldots, W\}\}) + H^{[ji]}(\omega_t),$$

where $P^{[ui'j']}(\mathcal{S})$ indicates a fractional polynomial constructed from the variables $s \in \mathcal{S}$.

Step 3: Interference Alignment

In this step, we determine the interference alignment equations in the clean and dirty receivers and MIMO C-IR receiving antennas. In our interference alignment scheme, we align the subspace of the interference of each user into a bigger subspace with an equal normalized asymptotic dimension. Note that for the matrices $\mathbf{V}$ and $\mathbf{V}'$, we can have the following relations simultaneously: $d(\mathbf{V}) > d(\mathbf{V}')$, $D_N(\mathbf{V}) = D_N(\mathbf{V}')$, e.g., $d(\mathbf{V}) = (n+1)^l > d(\mathbf{V}') = n^l$, $D_N(\mathbf{V}) = D_N(\mathbf{V}') = 1$. We begin with clean receivers.

(1) Interference alignment at clean receivers: Consider the clean receiver $j \in \{1, \ldots, W\}$; for each $i \in \{1, \ldots, K\}, i \neq j$, we must have:

$$\text{span}\left(\mathbf{H}^{[ji]}\bar{\mathbf{V}}^{[i]}\right) \subseteq \bar{\mathcal{A}}_j, \tag{24}$$

where $\bar{\mathcal{A}}_j$ is considered a subspace that encompass all interference at the j-th receiver induced by $\bar{\mathbf{x}}^{[i]}, i \in \{1, \ldots, K\}, i \neq j$, for which we have:

$$\max_{i \in \{1,\ldots,K\}, i \neq j} D_N\left(\text{span}\left(\mathbf{H}^{[ji]}\bar{\mathbf{V}}^{[i]}\right)\right) = D_N(\bar{\mathcal{A}}_j), \tag{25}$$

which implies that the normalized asymptotic dimension of $\bar{\mathcal{A}}_j$ is equal to the maximum asymptotic dimension of $\text{span}\left(\mathbf{H}^{[ji]}\bar{\mathbf{V}}^{[i]}\right)$ for $\forall i \neq j$. Moreover, we define the message subspaces as:

$$\bar{\mathcal{C}}_j = \text{span}\left(\mathbf{H}^{[jj]}\bar{\mathbf{V}}^{[j]}\right),$$

$$\tilde{\mathcal{C}}_j = \text{span}\left(\tilde{\mathbf{H}}^{[jj]}\tilde{\mathbf{V}}^{[j]}\right).$$

and we require $\bar{\mathcal{C}}_j$, $\tilde{\mathcal{C}}_j$ and $\bar{\mathcal{A}}_j$ to be full-rank and linearly independent; thus, we can ensure the decodability of the message streams $\tilde{\mathbf{x}}^{[j]}$ and $\bar{\mathbf{x}}^{[j]}$ by using zero forcing at the j-th receiver.

(2) Interference alignment at dirty receivers: Consider the dirty receiver $j \in \{W+1,\ldots,K\}$. Here, we have two interference subspaces at each receiver j; the interference induced by $\bar{\mathbf{x}}^{[i]}$ aligns in subspace $\bar{\mathcal{A}}_j$, while the interference induced by $\tilde{\mathbf{x}}^{[i]}$ aligns in subspace $\tilde{\mathcal{A}}_j$. For each $i \in \{1,\ldots,K\}, i \neq j$, we must have:

$$\text{span}\left(\mathbf{H}^{[ji]}\bar{\mathbf{V}}^{[i]}\right) \subseteq \bar{\mathcal{A}}_j, \tag{26}$$

where $\bar{\mathcal{A}}_j$ is considered a subspace for which we have:

$$\max_{i \in \{1,\ldots,K\}, i \neq j} D_N\left(\text{span}\left(\mathbf{H}^{[ji]}\bar{\mathbf{V}}^{[i]}\right)\right) = D_N(\bar{\mathcal{A}}_j), \tag{27}$$

and for every $i \in \{1,\ldots,W\}$, we must have:

$$\text{span}\left(\tilde{\mathbf{H}}^{[ji]}\tilde{\mathbf{V}}^{[i]}\right) \subseteq \tilde{\mathcal{A}}_j, \tag{28}$$

where $\tilde{\mathcal{A}}_j$ is considered a subspace for which we have:

$$\max_{i \in \{1,\ldots,W\}} D_N\left(\text{span}\left(\tilde{\mathbf{H}}^{[ji]}\tilde{\mathbf{V}}^{[i]}\right)\right) = D_N(\tilde{\mathcal{A}}_j). \tag{29}$$

Moreover, we define the message subspace as:

$$\bar{\mathcal{C}}_j = \text{span}\left(\mathbf{H}^{[jj]}\bar{\mathbf{V}}^{[j]}\right),$$

and we want $\bar{\mathcal{C}}_j$, $\tilde{\mathcal{A}}_j$ and $\bar{\mathcal{A}}_j$ to be full-rank and linearly independent; hence, we can ensure the decodability of the message stream $\bar{\mathbf{x}}^{[j]}$ by using zero forcing in the j-th receiver.

(3) Interference alignment at the MIMO C-IR q-th receiving antenna: We assume that $W = QZ + P, 0 \leq P < Q$; we divide the transmitters $i \in \{1,\ldots,W\}$, into Q distinct sets, and the first P sets include $Z+1$ transmitters and the other $Q-P$ sets include Z transmitters. We name these sets $\mathcal{B}_q, q \in \{1,\ldots,Q\}$. We designed our interference alignment scheme such that the symbol streams $\tilde{\mathbf{x}}^{[i]}, i \in \mathcal{B}_q$ can be de-multiplexed at the q-th receiving antenna of the MIMO C-IR. To this end, all the interference induced by the symbol streams $\bar{\mathbf{x}}^{[i]}, i \in \{1,\ldots,K\}$ must align into a limited subspace at each receiving antenna of the MIMO C-IR. Thus, at each receiving antenna $q \in \{1,\ldots,Q\}$, and for each $i \in \{1,\ldots,K\}$, we must have:

$$\text{span}\left(\mathbf{H}_{\text{T-IR}}^{[qi]}\bar{\mathbf{V}}^{[i]}\right) \subseteq \bar{\mathcal{A}}_{r_q}, \tag{30}$$

where $\bar{\mathcal{A}}_{r_q}$ is considered a subspace for which we have:

$$\max_{i\in\{1,\ldots,K\}} D_N\left(\text{span}\left(\mathbf{H}^{[qi]}_{\text{T-IR}}\bar{\mathbf{V}}^{[i]}\right)\right) = D_N(\bar{\mathcal{A}}_{r_q}). \tag{31}$$

In addition, at the q-th receiving antenna of the MIMO C-IR, the interference induced by the symbol streams $\tilde{\mathbf{x}}^{[i]}, i \in \{1,\ldots,W\}, i \notin \mathcal{B}_q$ must align into a subspace named $\tilde{\mathcal{A}}_{r_q}$. Hence, for each $i \in \{1,\ldots,W\}, i \notin \mathcal{B}_q$, we must have:

$$\text{span}\left(\mathbf{H}^{[qi]}_{\text{T-IR}}\tilde{\mathbf{V}}^{[i]}\right) \subseteq \tilde{\mathcal{A}}_{r_q}, \tag{32}$$

where $\tilde{\mathcal{A}}_{r_q}$ is considered a subspace for which we have:

$$\max_{i\in\{1,\ldots,W\}, i\notin\mathcal{B}_q} D_N\left(\text{span}\left(\mathbf{H}^{[qi]}_{\text{T-IR}}\tilde{\mathbf{V}}^{[i]}\right)\right) = D_N(\tilde{\mathcal{A}}_{r_q}). \tag{33}$$

Furthermore, we define $\tilde{\mathcal{C}}_{i,r_q}, i \in \mathcal{B}_q$ as the message subspaces, which can be de-multiplexed at the q-th MIMO C-IR receiving antenna as follows:

$$\tilde{\mathcal{C}}_{i,r_q} = \text{span}\left(\mathbf{H}^{[qi]}_{\text{T-IR}}\tilde{\mathbf{V}}^{[i]}\right), i \in \mathcal{B}_q.$$

We want $\tilde{\mathcal{C}}_{i,r_q}, \forall i \in \mathcal{B}_q$, $\bar{\mathcal{A}}_{r_q}$ and $\tilde{\mathcal{A}}_{r_q}$ to be full-rank and linearly independent; thus, we can make sure that the message streams $\tilde{\mathbf{x}}^{[i]}, i \in \mathcal{B}_q$ can be de-multiplexed at the q-th MIMO C-IR receiving antenna by using zero forcing. Note that the q-th receiving antenna of the MIMO C-IR de-multiplexes the message streams $\tilde{\mathbf{x}}^{[i]}, i \in \mathcal{B}_q$ without having the coordination with other receiving antennas. After each antenna de-multiplexes its own message streams $\tilde{\mathbf{x}}^{[i]}, i \in \mathcal{B}_q$, all of these message streams are passed to the MIMO C-IR transmitting antennas so the transmitting antennas can have coordination with each other for an interference cancellation at the clean receivers (as in Equation (19)). A simple illustration of the interference alignment scheme is shown in Figure 2 for $K = 3$ and $W = 2$. In Steps 4 and 5, we prove the existence of such beamforming vectors, messages, and interference subspaces, which satisfies the previous interference alignment Equations (24)–(33) for the clean and dirty receivers and the MIMO C-IR. In Step 6, we analyze the achieved DoF by using these beamforming vector designs.

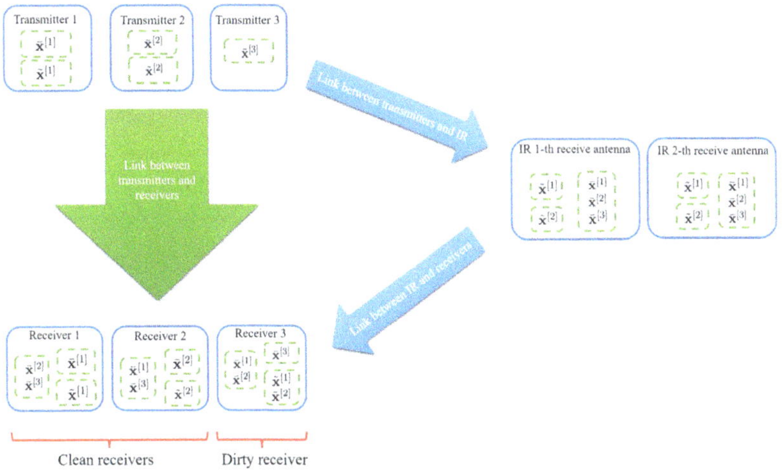

Figure 2. Interference alignment scheme for 3-user interference channel in the presence of MIMO C-IR with 2 receiving antennas. Subspaces corresponding to symbol streams in common dashed boxes align into a joint subspace at each node. We can see that the interference of the message streams $\tilde{\mathbf{x}}^{[1]}$ and $\tilde{\mathbf{x}}^{[2]}$ is canceled at clean receivers.

Step 4: Beamforming Matrix Design

In this step, we design beamforming matrices such that the alignment Equations (24)–(33) are satisfied and all users' message streams are decodable.

(1) Beamforming matrix design for $i \in \{1, \ldots, W\}$: To introduce the beamforming matrix design, we must define some new notations. First, we define set $\mathcal{F}(\mathcal{A}, \mathcal{B})$ as the set of all functions $g(x) : \mathcal{A} \to \mathcal{B}$, i.e.,

$$\mathcal{F}(\mathcal{A}, \mathcal{B}) = \{g(x) | g(x) : \mathcal{A} \to \mathcal{B}\}. \tag{34}$$

It is obvious that $|\mathcal{F}(\mathcal{A}, \mathcal{B})| = |\mathcal{A}|^{|\mathcal{B}|}$. Moreover, we define matrix $\mathbf{M}(g(x), \mathbf{N}^{[x]}, \mathcal{A})$ as follows:

$$\mathbf{M}(g(x), \mathbf{N}^{[x]}, \mathcal{A}) = \prod_{x \in \mathcal{A}} \left(\mathbf{N}^{[x]}\right)^{g(x)}. \tag{35}$$

Then, consider the vector $\mathbf{w} = \begin{bmatrix} 1 & 1 & \cdots & 1 \end{bmatrix}^H$. We design the beamforming matrices $\bar{\mathbf{V}}^{[i]}$ and $\tilde{\mathbf{V}}^{[i]}$ as the following:

$$\bar{\mathbf{V}}^{[i]} = \left\{ \left[\mathbf{M}(g_1(i,j), \mathbf{H}^{[ji]}, \bar{\mathcal{S}}_1)\right] \left[\mathbf{M}(g_2(i,q), \mathbf{H}^{[qi]}_{\text{T-IR}}, \bar{\mathcal{S}}_2)\right] \mathbf{w} : \right.$$
$$\left. g_1 \in \mathcal{F}(\bar{\mathcal{S}}_1, \{1, \ldots, n\}), g_2 \in \mathcal{F}(\bar{\mathcal{S}}_2, \{1, \ldots, sn\}) \right\}, \tag{36}$$

where

$$\bar{\mathcal{S}}_1 = \{(i,j) | i,j \in \{1, \ldots, K\}, i \neq j\}, \tag{37}$$
$$\bar{\mathcal{S}}_2 = \{(i,q) | i \in \{1, \ldots, K\}, q \in \{1, \ldots, Q\}\}, \tag{38}$$

where $n \in \mathbb{N}$ is an auxiliary variable that can go to infinity, and s is a parameter for controlling the dimension of $\bar{\mathbf{V}}^{[i]}$, i.e., $d(\bar{\mathbf{V}}^{[i]})$. This notation means that the right-hand side of (36) is the set of column vectors, which forms the beamforming matrix $\bar{\mathbf{V}}^{[i]}$. For $\tilde{\mathbf{V}}^{[i]}$, we have:

$$\tilde{\mathbf{V}}^{[i]} = \left\{ \left[\mathbf{M}(g_1(i,j), \tilde{\mathbf{H}}^{[ji]}, \bar{\mathcal{S}}_1)\right] \left[\mathbf{M}(g_2(i,q), \mathbf{H}^{[qi]}_{\text{T-IR}}, \tilde{\mathcal{S}}_2)\right] \left[\mathbf{M}(g_3(i,q), \mathbf{T}^{[qi]}, \tilde{\mathcal{S}}_3)\right] \mathbf{w} : \right.$$
$$\left. g_1 \in \mathcal{F}(\bar{\mathcal{S}}_1, \{1, \ldots, n\}), g_2 \in \mathcal{F}(\tilde{\mathcal{S}}_2, \{1, \ldots, sn\}), g_3 \in \mathcal{F}(\tilde{\mathcal{S}}_3, \{1, \ldots, vn\}) \right\}, \tag{39}$$

where $\bar{\mathcal{S}}_1$ is given in (37), and we have:

$$\tilde{\mathcal{S}}_2 = \left\{(i,q) \middle| i \in \{1, \ldots, K\}, i \notin \mathcal{B}_q, q \in \{1, \ldots, Q\}\right\}, \tag{40}$$
$$\tilde{\mathcal{S}}_3 = \left\{(i,q) \middle| i \in \mathcal{B}_q, q \in \{1, \ldots, Q\}\right\}, \tag{41}$$

$\mathbf{T}^{[qi]}$s are $T \times T$ diagonal random matrices for each i and q, where each of the diagonal elements for each matrix is drawn independently and its CDF is continuous.

(2) Beamforming matrix design for $i \in \{W+1, \ldots, K\}$: We consider the beamforming matrix $\bar{\mathbf{V}}^{[i]}$ as the following:

$$\bar{\mathbf{V}}^{[i]} = \left\{ \left[\mathbf{M}(g_1(i,j), \mathbf{H}^{[ji]}, \bar{\mathcal{S}}_1)\right] \left[\mathbf{M}(g_2(i,q), \mathbf{H}^{[qi]}_{\text{T-IR}}, \bar{\mathcal{S}}_2)\right] \mathbf{w} : \right.$$
$$\left. g_1 \in \mathcal{F}(\bar{\mathcal{S}}_1, \{1, \ldots, n\}), g_2 \in \mathcal{F}(\bar{\mathcal{S}}_2, \{1, \ldots, tn\}) \right\}, \tag{42}$$

where $\bar{\mathcal{S}}_1$ and $\bar{\mathcal{S}}_2$ are given by using (37) and (38), respectively. t is a parameter for controlling the dimension of $\bar{\mathbf{V}}^{[i]}$, i.e., $d(\bar{\mathbf{V}}^{[i]})$.

We note that each value of parameters s, v and t can be approximated by using rational numbers with arbitrarily small errors, and by choosing a sufficiently large n, parameters sn, vn and tn will be integers and our proposed scheme will be realizable.

Step 5: Validity of Interference Alignment Conditions and Decodability of Message Symbols

Now, we analyze the spaces of messages and interference.

(1) Validity of interference alignment conditions at the clean receivers $j \in \{1, \ldots, W\}$*:* For the clean receivers $j \in \{1, \ldots, W\}$, we have the following lemma:

Lemma 1. *For the clean receivers* $j \in \{1, \ldots, W\}$*, consider* $\bar{\mathcal{C}}_j$ *as the message subspace corresponding to the symbol stream* $\bar{\mathbf{x}}^{[j]}$*, consider* $\tilde{\mathcal{C}}_j$ *as the message subspace corresponding to the symbol stream* $\tilde{\mathbf{x}}^{[j]}$*, and consider* $\bar{\mathcal{A}}_j$ *as the interference subspace induced by the symbol stream* $\bar{\mathbf{x}}^{[j']}, j' \neq j$*. Then,* $\bar{\mathcal{C}}_j$*,* $\tilde{\mathcal{C}}_j$ *and* $\bar{\mathcal{A}}_j$ *are full-rank and linearly independent, i.e., all base vectors of these subspaces are linearly independent. Thus, the message streams* $\bar{\mathbf{x}}^{[j]}$ *and* $\tilde{\mathbf{x}}^{[j]}$ *are decodable by using zero forcing. In addition, we have:*

$$D_N(\bar{\mathcal{C}}_j) = \Gamma, \tag{43}$$

$$D_N(\tilde{\mathcal{C}}_j) = \chi, \tag{44}$$

$$D_N(\bar{\mathcal{A}}_j) = \max\{\Gamma, \zeta\}, \tag{45}$$

where

$$\Gamma = s^{QK}, \quad \chi = s^{QK-W} v^{W}, \quad \zeta = t^{QK}.$$

Proof. The proof is provided in Appendix B. □

(2) Validity of interference alignment conditions at the dirty receivers $j \in \{W+1, \ldots, K\}$*:* For the dirty receivers $j \in \{W+1, \ldots, K\}$, we have the following lemma:

Lemma 2. *For the dirty receivers* $j \in \{W+1, \ldots, K\}$*, consider* $\bar{\mathcal{C}}_j$ *the message subspace corresponding to the symbol stream* $\bar{\mathbf{x}}^{[j]}$*, consider* $\tilde{\mathcal{A}}_j$ *as the interference subspace corresponding to the symbol stream* $\tilde{\mathbf{x}}^{[j']}, j' \neq j$*, and consider* $\bar{\mathcal{A}}_j$ *as the interference subspace induced by the symbol streams* $\bar{\mathbf{x}}^{[j']}, j' \neq j$*. Then,* $\bar{\mathcal{C}}_j$*,* $\bar{\mathcal{A}}_j$ *and* $\tilde{\mathcal{A}}_j$ *are full-rank and linearly independent, i.e., all base vectors of these subspaces are linearly independent. Thus, the message stream* $\bar{\mathbf{x}}^{[j]}$ *is decodable by using zero forcing. In addition, we have:*

$$D_N(\bar{\mathcal{C}}_j) = \zeta, \tag{46}$$

$$D_N(\bar{\mathcal{A}}_j) = \max\{\Gamma, \zeta\}, \tag{47}$$

$$D_N(\tilde{\mathcal{A}}_j) = \chi. \tag{48}$$

Proof. The proof is provided in Appendix C. □

(3) Validity of interference alignment conditions at the MIMO C-IR q-th receiving antenna $q \in \{1, \ldots, Q\}$*:* For the q-th receiving antenna of the MIMO C-IR $q \in \{1, \ldots, Q\}$, we have the following lemma:

Lemma 3. *For the q-th receiving antenna of the MIMO C-IR* $q \in \{1, \ldots, Q\}$*, consider* $\tilde{\mathcal{C}}_{i,r_q}$ *the message subspace corresponding to the symbol streams* $\tilde{\mathbf{x}}^{[i]}, i \in \mathcal{B}_q$*, consider* $\tilde{\mathcal{A}}_{r_q}$ *the interference subspace corresponding to the symbol streams* $\tilde{\mathbf{x}}^{[j]}, j \neq \mathcal{B}_q$*, and consider* $\bar{\mathcal{A}}_{r_q}$ *the interference subspace induced by the symbol streams* $\bar{\mathbf{x}}^{[j]}, \forall j$*. Then,* $\tilde{\mathcal{C}}_{i,r_q}, i \in \mathcal{B}_q$*,* $\bar{\mathcal{A}}_{r_q}$*, and* $\tilde{\mathcal{A}}_{r_q}$ *are full-rank and linearly independent, i.e., all base vectors of these subspaces are linearly independent. Thus, the message stream* $\tilde{\mathbf{x}}^{[i]}, i \in \mathcal{B}_q$ *can be de-multiplexed by using zero forcing. In addition, we have:*

$$D_N(\tilde{\mathcal{C}}_{i,r_q}) = \chi, \tag{49}$$

$$\sum_{i \in \mathcal{B}_q} D_N(\tilde{\mathcal{C}}_{i,r_q}) = |\mathcal{B}_q| \chi, \tag{50}$$

$$D_N(\bar{\mathcal{A}}_{r_q}) = \max\{\Gamma, \zeta\}, \tag{51}$$

$$D_N(\tilde{\mathcal{A}}_{r_q}) = \chi. \tag{52}$$

Proof. The proof is provided in Appendix D. □

Now, we can calculate the dimension of the whole signal space at each receiver. We define $d_{t,j}$ as the total dimension at the j-th receiver and d_{t,r_q} as the total dimension at the q-th receiving antenna of the MIMO C-IR; thus, we have:

$$d_{t,j} = d(\bar{\mathcal{C}}_j) + d(\tilde{\mathcal{C}}_j) + d(\bar{\mathcal{A}}_j), \forall j \in \{1, \ldots, W\}, \tag{53}$$

$$d_{t,j} = d(\bar{\mathcal{C}}_j) + d(\bar{\mathcal{A}}_j) + d(\tilde{\mathcal{A}}_j), \forall j \in \{W+1, \ldots, K\}, \tag{54}$$

$$d_{t,r_q} = \sum_{i \in \mathcal{B}_q} d(\tilde{\mathcal{C}}_{i,r_q}) + d(\bar{\mathcal{A}}_{r_q}) + d(\tilde{\mathcal{A}}_{r_q}), \forall q \in \{1, \ldots, Q\}, \tag{55}$$

where the dimension of the message and the interference subspaces are derived in (A8)–(A10), (A20)–(A22), and (A26)–(A28) in Appendices B–D. Similarly, define $D_{N,t,j}$ as the total normalized asymptotic dimension at the j-th receiver and D_{N,t,r_q} as the total normalized asymptotic dimension at the q-th receiving antenna of the MIMO C-IR; thus, from (43)–(52), we have:

$$D_{N,t,j} = D_N(\bar{\mathcal{C}}_j) + D_N(\tilde{\mathcal{C}}_j) + D_N(\bar{\mathcal{A}}_j) = \Gamma + \chi + \max\{\Gamma, \zeta\}, \forall j \in \{1, \ldots, W\}, \tag{56}$$

$$D_{N,t,j} = D_N(\bar{\mathcal{C}}_j) + D_N(\bar{\mathcal{A}}_j) + D_N(\tilde{\mathcal{A}}_j) = \zeta + \chi + \max\{\Gamma, \zeta\}, \forall j \in \{W+1, \ldots, K\}, \tag{57}$$

$$D_{N,t,r_q} = \sum_{i \in \mathcal{B}_q} D_N(\tilde{\mathcal{C}}_{i,r_q}) + D_N(\bar{\mathcal{A}}_{r_q}) + D_N(\tilde{\mathcal{A}}_{r_q}) = |\mathcal{B}_q|\chi + \chi + \max\{\Gamma, \zeta\}, \forall q \in \{1, \ldots, Q\}. \tag{58}$$

Now, we determine the minimum value for the parameter T (for which the interference alignment equations are satisfied) as follows:

$$T = \max\left\{ \max_{j \in \{1,\ldots,K\}} \{d_{t,j}\}, \max_{q \in \{1,\ldots,Q\}} \{d_{t,r_q}\} \right\}, \tag{59}$$

and from (53)–(59), we have

$$\lim_{n \to \infty} \frac{T}{n^{K^2-K+QK}} = \chi + \max\{\Gamma, \zeta\} + \max\left\{ \max_{q \in \{1,\ldots,Q\}} |\mathcal{B}_q|\chi, \zeta, \Gamma \right\}. \tag{60}$$

However, we have:

$$\max_{q \in \{1,\ldots,Q\}} |\mathcal{B}_q| = \left\lceil \frac{W}{Q} \right\rceil,$$

so we conclude that:

$$\lim_{n \to \infty} \frac{T}{n^{K^2-K+QK}} = \chi + \max\{\Gamma, \zeta\} + \max\left\{ \left\lceil \frac{W}{Q} \right\rceil \chi, \zeta, \Gamma \right\}. \tag{61}$$

Up until now, we have considered any arbitrary real values for each parameter Γ, χ and ζ. Now, we make two additional assumptions for these parameters, which give us an achievable DoF. First, we set the normalized asymptotic dimension of the space at the clean receivers equal to that of the dirty receivers. Hence:

$$\Gamma = \zeta. \tag{62}$$

Second, we set the maximum normalized asymptotic dimension of the space at each MIMO C-IR receiving antenna to be less than or equal to that of the dirty receivers. Therefore, we have:

$$\zeta \geq \left\lceil \frac{W}{Q} \right\rceil \chi. \tag{63}$$

Having (62) and (63), (61) will have the following form:

$$\lim_{n\to\infty} \frac{T}{n^{K^2-K+QK}} = \chi + 2\Gamma. \tag{64}$$

Step 6: DoF Analysis

Now, we characterize the total DoF. As stated before, we have W clean receivers, each with a normalized message dimension equal to $\Gamma + \chi$, and $K - W$ dirty receivers, each with a normalized message dimension equal to ζ (note that we set $\zeta = \Gamma$).The total normalized transmission length is equal to $\chi + 2\Gamma$, so the total DoF has the following form:

$$\text{DoF} = \max_{\chi \geq 0, \Gamma \geq \left\lceil \frac{W}{Q} \right\rceil \chi} \frac{W(\chi + \Gamma) + (K - W)\Gamma}{\chi + 2\Gamma}, \tag{65}$$

and by assuming $\Gamma = \beta\chi$, we have:

$$\text{DoF} = \max_{\beta \geq \left\lceil \frac{W}{Q} \right\rceil} \frac{W(1+\beta) + (K - W)\beta}{1 + 2\beta} \tag{66}$$

$$= \frac{K}{2} + \max_{\beta \geq \left\lceil \frac{W}{Q} \right\rceil} K \frac{\frac{W}{K} - \frac{1}{2}}{1 + 2\beta} = \frac{K}{2} + \max\left\{ K \frac{\frac{W}{K} - \frac{1}{2}}{1 + 2\left\lceil \frac{W}{Q} \right\rceil}, 0 \right\}. \tag{67}$$

We remark that if $\frac{W}{K} > \frac{1}{2}$, we set $\beta = \left\lceil \frac{W}{Q} \right\rceil$, and if $\frac{W}{K} < \frac{1}{2}$, we tend β to ∞. This completes the proof of the achievability of the first term of (11). The proof of the second term, i.e., $\min\{Q, W\}$, is provided in Appendix A. □

Remark 2. *It is known that the DoF is an appropriate performance metric that provides a capacity approximation accurate within* $o(\log(\rho))$ *[1]. Therefore, Theorem 1 indicates that the approximate sum capacity of the K-user interference channel in the presence of a MIMO C-IR is lower bounded by* $\left(\max\left\{\frac{K}{2} + \max\left\{0, K\frac{\frac{W}{K}-\frac{1}{2}}{1+2\left\lceil\frac{W}{Q}\right\rceil}\right\}, \min\{Q, W\}\right\} - \epsilon\right) \log(1+\rho) + o(\log(\rho)), \forall\epsilon > 0$. *Now, we prove an improved achievable DoF for a special case of W and Q.*

Theorem 2. *Assume* $W = QZ + P, P = 1$. *Then, the achievable DoF (11) can be improved as follows:*

$$\text{DoF} = \max\left\{ \frac{K}{2} + \max\left\{ 0, K \frac{\frac{W}{K} - \frac{1}{2}}{1 + 2\left\lfloor \frac{W}{Q} \right\rfloor} \right\}, \min\{Q, W\} \right\}. \tag{68}$$

Proof. The proof is provided in Appendix E. □

Remark 3. *Theorem 2 shows that the approximate sum capacity of the K-user interference channel with a MIMO C-IR is lower bounded by* $\left(\max\left\{\frac{K}{2} + \max\left\{0, K\frac{\frac{W}{K}-\frac{1}{2}}{1+2\left\lfloor\frac{W}{Q}\right\rfloor}\right\}, \min\{Q, W\}\right\} - \epsilon\right)$ $\log(1+\rho) + o(\log(\rho)), \forall\epsilon > 0$, *where* $P = 1$ *(we have* $W = QZ + P, 0 \leq P < Q$*). From (11) and (68), we note that this lower bound is tighter than the previous bound.*

Remark 4. *As expected, if we set $Q = W = K$, the maximum K DoF, which is the DoF at the absence of interference, is achievable for the MIMO C-IR.*

Remark 5. *It was shown in [4] that an ordinary relay cannot increase the DoF of a K-user interference channel. The main difference here is that the instantaneity of the relay can significantly improve the DoF.*

Remark 6. *Although we derived the achievable DoF for the asymptotic case, the achievability results are also valid for finite values of the auxiliary variable n, which determines the dimensions of beamforming vectors (see Equations (36)–(42)). Thus, if all interference alignment conditions (24)–(33) are satisfied and T is sufficiently large (as in Equation (59), i.e., larger than the sum of the interference and message subspaces), then for each receiver $j \in \{1, \ldots, K\}$, there is the matrix $\mathbf{E}_j$ such that if we multiply the vector of received signals in all frequency slots ($\mathbf{Y}^{[j]}$) by $\mathbf{E}_j$, the transmitted streams will be separated at each receiver with additive noise. Then, for the clean receivers $j \in \{1, \ldots, W\}$, we have:*

$$\mathbf{E}_j \mathbf{Y}^{[j]} = \begin{bmatrix} \bar{\mathbf{x}}^{[j]} \\ \tilde{\mathbf{x}}^{[j]} \end{bmatrix} + \hat{\mathbf{n}}^{[j]}, \tag{69}$$

where $\hat{\mathbf{n}}^{[j]}$ is additive Gaussian noise, which is not necessarily white. Moreover, for the dirty receivers $j \in \{W+1, \ldots, K\}$, we have:

$$\mathbf{E}_j \mathbf{Y}^{[j]} = \bar{\mathbf{x}}^{[j]} + \hat{\mathbf{n}}^{[j]}. \tag{70}$$

Thus, the proposed achievability scheme can be used for resource allocation problems, such as sum-rate optimization problems. This kind of utilization of interference alignment coding schemes for optimization problems was used in [35]. However, finding the optimal input distributions for the symbol streams $\bar{\mathbf{x}}^{[i]}$ and $\tilde{\mathbf{x}}^{[i]}$ and the optimal values for other parameters (t, s, and v) in order to compare the performance of the proposed scheme with the performance of other signaling strategies (e.g., [36,37]) from the rate region perspective are still complicated problems and need complex optimization algorithms, which are directions for future research.

Next, we introduce an upper bound for the sum DoF of the frequency-selective K-user interference channel assisted by the MIMO C-IR.

Theorem 3. *Considering the functions $f^{[u,\omega_t]}$ to be linear in (3), the sum DoF of the frequency-selective K-user interference channel assisted by the MIMO C-IR can be upper-bounded as follows:*

$$\sum_{i=1}^{K} d_i \leq \min\left\{\frac{K}{2} + \frac{WQ}{2(K-1)}, K\right\}. \tag{71}$$

Proof. By using (5)–(7), we have:

$$\begin{aligned} \mathbf{Y}^{[j]} &= \sum_{i=1}^{K} \mathbf{H}^{[ji]}\mathbf{X}^{[i]} + \sum_{u=1}^{W} \mathbf{H}_{\text{IR-R}}^{[ju]} \sum_{q=1}^{Q} \mathbf{A}^{[uq]} \left(\sum_{i=1}^{K} \mathbf{H}_{\text{T-IR}}^{[qi]}\mathbf{X}^{[i]} + \mathbf{Z}_{\text{IR}}^{[q]} \right) + \mathbf{Z}^{[j]} \\ &= \sum_{i=1}^{K} \left(\mathbf{H}^{[ji]} + \sum_{u=1}^{W}\sum_{q=1}^{Q} \mathbf{H}_{\text{IR-R}}^{[ju]}\mathbf{A}^{[uq]}\mathbf{H}_{\text{T-IR}}^{[qi]} \right)\mathbf{X}^{[i]} + \hat{\mathbf{Z}}^{[j]} = \sum_{i=1}^{K} \hat{\mathbf{H}}^{[ji]}\mathbf{X}^{[i]} + \hat{\mathbf{Z}}^{[j]}, \end{aligned} \tag{72}$$

where

$$\hat{\mathbf{H}}^{[ji]} = \mathbf{H}^{[ji]} + \sum_{u=1}^{W}\sum_{q=1}^{Q} \mathbf{H}_{\text{IR-R}}^{[ju]}\mathbf{A}^{[uq]}\mathbf{H}_{\text{T-IR}}^{[qi]}, \tag{73}$$

$$\hat{\mathbf{Z}}^{[j]} = \sum_{u=1}^{W}\sum_{q=1}^{Q} \mathbf{H}_{\mathrm{IR-R}}^{[ju]}\mathbf{A}^{[uq]}\mathbf{Z}_{\mathrm{IR}}^{[q]} + \mathbf{Z}^{[j]}. \tag{74}$$

Now, consider the given $i, j \in \{1, \ldots, K\}, i \neq j$. The matrices $\mathbf{A}^{[uq]}$ must be chosen such that $\mathrm{rank}(\hat{\mathbf{H}}^{[ii]}) = T, \forall i$; otherwise, the messages of each transmitter cannot be transmitted completely and the resulting upper bound for the sum DoF will decrease. For more clarity of the proof, we eliminate messages $w^{[k]}, k \neq i, j$, and this causes the rates r_i and r_j to increase because of a data processing inequality [38] (Theorem 2.8.1). Hence, we have:

$$\mathbf{Y}^{[i]} = \hat{\mathbf{H}}^{[ii]}\mathbf{X}^{[i]} + \hat{\mathbf{H}}^{[ij]}\mathbf{X}^{[j]} + \hat{\mathbf{Z}}^{[i]}, \tag{75}$$

$$\mathbf{Y}^{[j]} = \hat{\mathbf{H}}^{[ji]}\mathbf{X}^{[i]} + \hat{\mathbf{H}}^{[jj]}\mathbf{X}^{[j]} + \hat{\mathbf{Z}}^{[j]}. \tag{76}$$

Now, we define new variables as follows:

$$\mathbf{Y}^{[j]\prime} = \hat{\mathbf{H}}^{[ij]}\left(\hat{\mathbf{H}}^{[jj]}\right)^{-1}\mathbf{Y}^{[j]} = \hat{\mathbf{H}}^{[ij]}\left(\hat{\mathbf{H}}^{[jj]}\right)^{-1}\left(\hat{\mathbf{H}}^{[ji]}\mathbf{X}^{[i]} + \hat{\mathbf{H}}^{[jj]}\mathbf{X}^{[j]}\right) + \hat{\mathbf{H}}^{[ij]}\left(\hat{\mathbf{H}}^{[jj]}\right)^{-1}\hat{\mathbf{Z}}^{[j]}, \tag{77}$$

$$\mathbf{Y}^{[j]\prime\prime} = \hat{\mathbf{H}}^{[ij]}\left(\hat{\mathbf{H}}^{[jj]}\right)^{-1}\left(\hat{\mathbf{H}}^{[ji]}\mathbf{X}^{[i]} + \hat{\mathbf{H}}^{[jj]}\mathbf{X}^{[j]}\right) + \hat{\mathbf{Z}}^{[i]}. \tag{78}$$

Then, we obtain:

$$Tr_i \leq I\left(w^{[i]}; \mathbf{Y}^{[i]}\right) + \varepsilon, \tag{79}$$

$$\begin{aligned} Tr_j &\leq I\left(w^{[j]}; \mathbf{Y}^{[j]}\right) + \varepsilon \leq I\left(w^{[j]}; \mathbf{Y}^{[j]}, \mathbf{Y}^{[j]\prime\prime}\right) + \varepsilon = I\left(w^{[j]}; \mathbf{Y}^{[j]\prime\prime}\right) + I\left(w^{[j]}; \mathbf{Y}^{[j]} \middle| \mathbf{Y}^{[j]\prime\prime}\right) + \varepsilon \\ &\leq I\left(w^{[j]}; \mathbf{Y}^{[j]\prime\prime} \middle| w^{[i]}\right) + I\left(w^{[j]}; \mathbf{Y}^{[j]} \middle| \mathbf{Y}^{[j]\prime\prime}\right) + \varepsilon \\ &= I\left(w^{[j]}; \mathbf{Y}^{[i]} \middle| w^{[i]}\right) + I\left(w^{[j]}; \mathbf{Y}^{[j]} \middle| \mathbf{Y}^{[j]\prime\prime}\right) + \varepsilon. \end{aligned} \tag{80}$$

Thus, we have:

$$T(r_i + r_j) \leq I\left(w^{[i]}, w^{[j]}; \mathbf{Y}^{[i]}\right) + I\left(w^{[j]}; \mathbf{Y}^{[j]} \middle| \mathbf{Y}^{[j]\prime\prime}\right) + 2\varepsilon \leq \left(2T - R^{[ij]}\right)\log(1+\rho) + o(\log(\rho)), \tag{81}$$

where $R^{[ij]} = \mathrm{rank}(\hat{\mathbf{H}}^{[ij]})$. By using the same argument, we obtain:

$$r_i + r_j \leq \left(2 - \frac{\max\left\{\mathrm{rank}\left(\hat{\mathbf{H}}^{[ij]}\right), \mathrm{rank}\left(\hat{\mathbf{H}}^{[ji]}\right)\right\}}{T}\right)\log(1+\rho) + o(\log(\rho)). \tag{82}$$

Therefore, we obtain:

$$\begin{aligned} (K-1)\sum_{i=1}^{K} r_i &= \sum_{i\neq j} r_i + r_j \\ &\leq \sum_{i\neq j}\left(2 - \frac{\max\left\{\mathrm{rank}\left(\hat{\mathbf{H}}^{[ij]}\right), \mathrm{rank}\left(\hat{\mathbf{H}}^{[ji]}\right)\right\}}{T}\right)\log(1+\rho) + o(\log(\rho)) \\ &= \left(K(K-1) - \sum_{i\neq j}\left(\frac{\max\left\{\mathrm{rank}\left(\hat{\mathbf{H}}^{[ij]}\right), \mathrm{rank}\left(\hat{\mathbf{H}}^{[ji]}\right)\right\}}{T}\right)\right)\log(1+\rho) + o(\log(\rho)). \end{aligned} \tag{83}$$

To minimize the term $\sum_{i\neq j}\left(\frac{\max\{\mathrm{rank}(\hat{\mathbf{H}}^{[ij]}), \mathrm{rank}(\hat{\mathbf{H}}^{[ji]})\}}{T}\right)$, there are WQT^2 variables in the matrices $\mathbf{A}^{[uq]}$. Every unit decrement of the rank of cross-link matrices requires T linear dependencies (T independent linear equations, which follow from the form of the arrangement of coefficients of equations); thus, we can see that:

$$\sum_{i \neq j} \left(\frac{\max\left\{ \text{rank}\left(\hat{\mathbf{H}}^{[ij]} \right), \text{rank}\left(\hat{\mathbf{H}}^{[ji]} \right) \right\}}{T} \right) \geq \frac{K(K-1)}{2} - \frac{WQ}{2}. \tag{84}$$

Considering (83) and (84), the upper bound (71) can be obtained. We note that $\sum_{i=1}^{K} d_i \leq K$ is obvious because of (79). □

Remark 7. *Theorem 3 indicates that the approximate sum capacity of the frequency-selective K-user interference channel assisted by the MIMO C-IR is upper-bounded by* $\min\{\frac{K}{2} + \frac{WQ}{2(K-1)}, K\}$ $\log(1+\rho) + o(\log(\rho))$.

4. *K*-User Interference Channel in the Presence of NC-IR

In this section, we provide the lower and upper bounds for the sum DoF of the frequency-selective *K*-user interference channel in the presence of an NC-IR as follows.

Theorem 4. *Consider* $U, p, e, e' \in \mathbb{W}$ *such that*

$$U = pe + e', 0 \leq e' < p, \frac{K}{2} < U \leq K. \tag{85}$$

Then, with an NC-IR with $W = Q = pU$ *antennas, the following DoF is achievable:*

$$\text{DoF} = \frac{K}{2} + \max\left\{ K \frac{\frac{U}{K} - \frac{1}{2}}{1 + 2\left\lceil \frac{U}{p} \right\rceil}, 0 \right\}. \tag{86}$$

Proof. The proof is provided in Appendix F. □

Remark 8. *Theorem 4 indicates that the approximate sum capacity of a frequency-selective K-user interference channel in the presence of the NC-IR is lower bounded by* $\left(\frac{K}{2} + \max\left\{ K \frac{\frac{U}{K} - \frac{1}{2}}{1+2\left\lceil \frac{U}{p} \right\rceil}, 0 \right\} - \epsilon \right)$ $\log(1+\rho) + o(\log(\rho)), \forall \epsilon > 0$.

Remark 9. *The active reconfigurable intelligent surface RIS can be modeled as a special case of an NC-IR [34]. It was proven in [34] that for an active RIS with* $Q = U(K-1) + U(K-U)$ *antennas, the following DoF is achievable:*

$$\text{DoF} = \frac{K+U}{2}, 0 \leq U \leq K. \tag{87}$$

Therefore, we can see that for $0 < Q < 2(K-1)$*, the achievable DoF (86) is dominant, and for* $Q \geq 2(K-1)$*, the maximums of (86) and (87) form the maximum achievable DoF for the NC-IR.*

Remark 10. *Considering Theorem 1, we can conclude that the maximum K DoF can be achieved by using* $Q = W = K$ *antennas for a MIMO C-IR, but* $Q = K(K-1)$ *antennas for achieving the maximum K DoF by an NC-IR is required, which grows quadratically and shows a loss of performance.*

Finally, we introduce an upper bound for the sum DoF of the frequency-selective *K*-user interference channel assisted by the NC-IR.

Theorem 5. *Considering the functions* $f^{[u,\omega_t]}$ *to be linear in (4), the sum DoF of the frequency-selective K-user interference channel assisted by the NC-IR can be upper-bounded as follows:*

$$\sum_{i=1}^{K} d_i \le \min\left\{\frac{K}{2} + \frac{Q}{2(K-1)}, K\right\} = \min\left\{\frac{K}{2} + \frac{W}{2(K-1)}, K\right\} = \min\left\{\frac{K}{2} + \frac{\sqrt{WQ}}{2(K-1)}, K\right\}. \quad (88)$$

Proof. This theorem can be proven by using the same argument given for Theorem 3, except for the fact that the linear operation of the NC-IR can be represented as (8). Thus, matrices $\mathbf{A}^{[u]}$ provide QT^2 variables, which changes (84) as follows:

$$\sum_{i \neq j} \left(\frac{\max\left\{\text{rank}\left(\hat{\mathbf{H}}^{[ij]}\right), \text{rank}\left(\hat{\mathbf{H}}^{[ji]}\right)\right\}}{T} \right) \ge \frac{K(K-1)}{2} - \frac{Q}{2}, \quad (89)$$

and which yields (88). □

Remark 11. *By considering Theorem 5, it can be seen that the approximate sum capacity of the frequency-selective K-user interference channel assisted by the NC-IR is upper-bounded by the expression* $\min\left\{\frac{K}{2} + \frac{Q}{2(K-1)}, K\right\} \log(1+\rho) + o(\log(\rho))$.

5. Numerical Results

In this section, we numerically evaluate the lower and upper bounds for the sum DoF provided in the previous sections by using some examples. We note that the proposed bounds of the DoF of the MIMO C-IR and NC-IR and the existing bounds for the active RIS [31] (Theorems 1–5) do not depend on the distribution of channel coefficients, and the only required properties are independence and being drawn from a CDF, which is continuous. In Figure 3, we compare the lower and upper bounds for the sum DoF of a six-user interference channel in the presence of the MIMO C-IR for different values of Q and W and the case without the MIMO C-IR. We see that the achievable DoF can approach only a maximum value ($K = 6$) when $W = K = 6$. Additionally, we can observe that the maximum achieved DoF is equal to W when $W \ge 4$. Moreover, the maximum K DoFs can be achieved when $Q = W$.

In Figure 4, we compare the lower and upper bounds for the sum DoF of four-user interference channels in the presence of the MIMO C-IR, NC-IR, and active RIS [34], and the case without an IR. We note that to have a fair comparison, we assume the same number of receiving and transmitting antennas for the MIMO C-IR ($W = Q$) as for the NC-IR and active RIS. These figures show that the maximum K DoF can be achieved by employing enough antennas for the MIMO C-IR, NC-IR, and active RIS. We see that the achievable DoF is considerably decreased for the NC-IR and active RIS, and this reduction is due to a lack of coordination between the antennas in the NC-IR and active RIS. Moreover, these figures show that the required number of antennas to allow the NC-IR and active RIS to achieve the maximum K DoF is quadratically larger than the required number of antennas for a MIMO C-IR, which shows a performance loss for the NC-IR due to a lack of coordination between the NC-IR antennas. In addition, the achievable DoF for the NC-IR is better than for the active RIS because the NC-IR can combine the received signals from different frequency slots (see Equation (4)); however, the model of the active RIS cannot conduct this operation.

In Figure 5, we compare the achievable sum DoF of a three-user interference channel in the presence of the MIMO C-IR (with $W = Q$), NC-IR, and active RIS, a time-selective channel without an IR [1], and a channel with constant coefficients using Improper Gaussian Signaling (IGS) [39] and Widely Linear Precoding (WLP) [40]. We can see that the proposed scheme for the MIMO C-IR has the best performance and the IGS and WLP schemes for the constant channel have the worst performance.

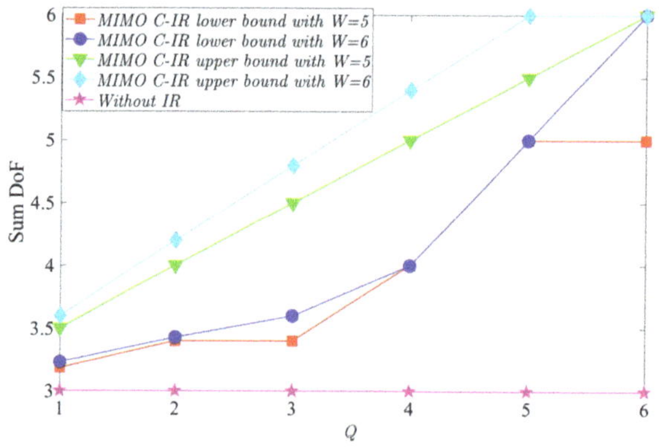

Figure 3. Comparison of lower and upper bounds for the sum DoF of the six-user interference channel in the presence of MIMO C-IR for the case without MIMO C-IR.

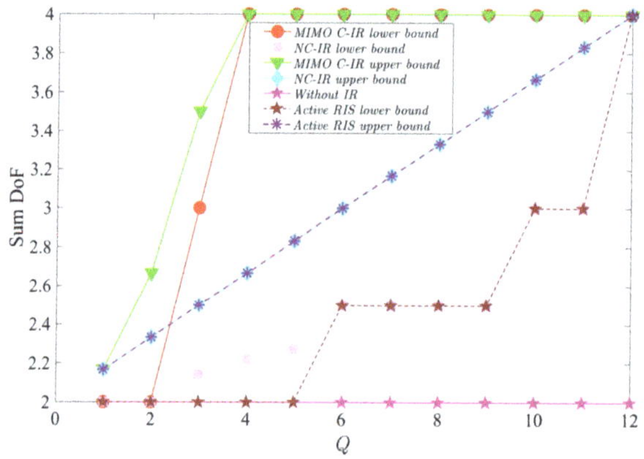

Figure 4. Comparison of lower and upper bounds for the sum DoF of the four-user interference channel in the presence of MIMO C-IR (with $W = Q$), NC-IR, active RIS and for the case without IR.

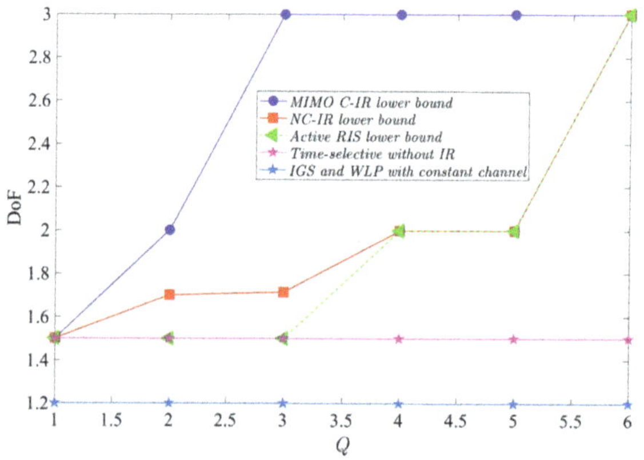

Figure 5. Comparison of the achievable sum DoF of the three-user interference channel in the presence of MIMO C-IR (with $W = Q$), NC-IR, and active RIS, the time-selective channel without IR [1], and the channel with constant coefficients using Improper Gaussian Signaling (IGS) [39] and Widely Linear Precoding (WLP) [40].

6. Conclusions

In this paper, we studied the lower and upper bounds for the sum DoF of the IR-assisted frequency-selective K-user interference channel and proposed novel interference alignment-based coding schemes. The main novelty of this work is proposing a new interference alignment-based coding scheme in which receivers are partitioned into two groups called clean and dirty receivers. In this scheme, a part of the message streams of transmitters corresponding to clean receivers is de-multiplexed at the IR, and the IR uses these streams for an interference cancellation at the clean receivers, which causes an improvement of the DoF. This DoF improvement is achieved because in the interference alignment scheme, the dimension of interference subspaces decreases and the dimension of message subspaces increases at the clean receivers. For a MIMO C-IR, the antennas of which can have coordination with each other, and for an NC-IR (an IR with no coordination between the antennas), we derived achievable DoFs and observed a performance loss for the NC-IR compared with the MIMO C-IR. Moreover, we showed that by considering a number of antennas more than a finite value, a maximum K DoF is achievable for both the MIMO C-IR and NC-IR. The directions of our future work will contains the following aspects: (1) Finding tight bounds for the DoF of a time-selective K-user interference channel in the presence of an IR; (2) Extending our proposed coding scheme for more general wireless channels, e.g., an X network; (3) Extending our coding scheme to a scenario with an imperfect CSI.

Author Contributions: Conceptualization, A.H.A.B.; Formal analysis, A.H.A.B. and M.M.; Supervision, M.M. and M.N.-K.; Validation, M.M. and M.N.-K.; Writing—original draft, A.H.A.B.; Writing—review & editing, M.M. and M.N.-K. All authors have read and agreed to the published version of the manuscript.

Funding: This research received no external funding.

Conflicts of Interest: The authors declare no conflict of interest.

Appendix A

In this scheme, we use only one frequency slot: ω_1. We set $L = \min\{W, Q\}$. We assume that only the transmitters $i \in \{1, \ldots, L\}$ send their messages to the receivers $j \in \{1, \ldots, L\}$ via the symbols $X^{[i]}(\omega_1), i \in \{1, \ldots, L\}$, and other transmitters are silent ($X^{[i]}(\omega_1) = 0, \forall i \in \{L+1, \ldots, K\}$). Considering (2), the MIMO C-IR can de-multiplex $X^{[i]}(\omega_1), \forall i \in \{1, \ldots, L\}$ by using L linear equations in the first L receiving antennas almost surely because the matrix of the coefficients is in terms of independent random variables; thus, the matrix's determinant is a non-zero polynomial of independent random variables with a continuous cumulative probability distribution, and considering [34] (Lemma 1), it is a non-zero with the probability 1. Then, the MIMO C-IR designs its transmitted signal to remove the interference in each receiver $j \in \{1, \ldots, L\}$ by solving the following linear equations:

$$-\sum_{i \in \{1,\ldots,L\}, i \neq j} H^{[ji]}(\omega_1)(X^{[i]}(\omega_1) + \tilde{Z}^{[i]}(\omega_t)) = \sum_{u=1}^{L} H_{\text{IR-R}}^{[ju]} X_{\text{IR}}^{[u]}, \forall j \in \{1, \ldots, L\}, \quad \text{(A1)}$$

$$\tilde{\tilde{Z}}^{[j]}(\omega_t) = -\sum_{i \in \{1,\ldots,L\}, i \neq j} H^{[ji]}(\omega_1)\tilde{Z}^{[i]}(\omega_t), \quad \text{(A2)}$$

where $\tilde{Z}^{[i]}(\omega_t)$ is the detection noise for symbol $X^{[i]}(\omega_t)$ at the MIMO C-IR. Note that by using this procedure, the interference cancellation is conducted, but we have the additional noise $\tilde{\tilde{Z}}^{[j]}(\omega_t)$, which is negligible in a high signal to noise ratio (SNR) regime. Therefore, L symbols can be transmitted in one frequency slot, and the total L DoF is achievable. Thus, the second term in (11) is achievable, which completes the proof.

Appendix B

Using (36) and (39), we characterize the message subspaces $\bar{\mathcal{C}}_j$ and $\tilde{\mathcal{C}}_j$ as follows:

$$\bar{\mathcal{C}}_j = \text{span}\left(\mathbf{H}^{[jj]}\bar{\mathbf{V}}^{[j]}\right) =$$

$$\text{span}\left\{\mathbf{H}^{[jj]}\left[\mathbf{M}(g_1(i,j),\mathbf{H}^{[ji]},\bar{\mathcal{S}}_1)\right]\left[\mathbf{M}(g_2(i,q),\mathbf{H}^{[qi]}_{\text{T-IR}},\bar{\mathcal{S}}_2)\right]\mathbf{w} : g_1 \in \mathcal{F}(\bar{\mathcal{S}}_1,\{1,\ldots,n\}), g_2 \in \mathcal{F}(\bar{\mathcal{S}}_2,\{1,\ldots,sn\})\right\}, \quad \text{(A3)}$$

where $\bar{\mathcal{S}}_1$, $\bar{\mathcal{S}}_2$, $\mathcal{F}(\cdot,\cdot)$, and $\mathbf{M}(\cdot,\cdot,\cdot)$ are given by using (37), (38), (34), and (35), respectively.

$$\tilde{\mathcal{C}}_j = \text{span}\left(\tilde{\mathbf{H}}^{[jj]}\tilde{\mathbf{V}}^{[j]}\right) =$$

$$\text{span}\left\{\tilde{\mathbf{H}}^{[jj]}\left[\mathbf{M}(g_1(i,j),\tilde{\mathbf{H}}^{[ji]},\tilde{\mathcal{S}}_1)\right]\left[\mathbf{M}(g_2(i,q),\mathbf{H}^{[qi]}_{\text{T-IR}},\tilde{\mathcal{S}}_2)\right]\left[\mathbf{M}(g_3(i,q),\mathbf{T}^{[qi]},\tilde{\mathcal{S}}_3)\right]\mathbf{w} :\right.$$

$$\left. g_1 \in \mathcal{F}(\tilde{\mathcal{S}}_1,\{1,\ldots,n\}), g_2 \in \mathcal{F}(\tilde{\mathcal{S}}_2,\{1,\ldots,sn\}), g_3 \in \mathcal{F}(\tilde{\mathcal{S}}_3,\{1,\ldots,vn\})\right\}, \quad \text{(A4)}$$

where $\tilde{\mathcal{S}}_2$ and $\tilde{\mathcal{S}}_3$ are given by using (40) and (41), respectively.

To satisfy interference alignment Equation (24), the subspace $\bar{\mathcal{A}}_j$ must be chosen such that:

$$\bigcup_{i\in\{1,\ldots,K\},i\neq j}\left\{\text{span}\left(\mathbf{H}^{[ji]}\bar{\mathbf{V}}^{[i]}\right)\right\} \subseteq \bar{\mathcal{A}}_j.$$

Therefore, we characterize $\bar{\mathcal{A}}_j$ as follows:

$$\bar{\mathcal{A}}_j =$$

$$\text{span}\left\{\left[\mathbf{M}(g_1(i,j),\mathbf{H}^{[ji]},\bar{\mathcal{S}}_1)\right]\left[\mathbf{M}(g_2(i,q),\mathbf{H}^{[qi]}_{\text{T-IR}},\bar{\mathcal{S}}_2)\right]\mathbf{w} : g_1 \in \mathcal{F}(\bar{\mathcal{S}}_1,\{1,\ldots,n+1\}), g_2 \in \mathcal{F}(\bar{\mathcal{S}}_2,\{1,\ldots,n\max\{s,t\}\})\right\}, \quad \text{(A5)}$$

where $\bar{\mathcal{S}}_1$ and $\bar{\mathcal{S}}_2$ are given by using (37) and (38), respectively. Note that to use the zero-forcing technique, the subspace of the interference must be a vector space, but the set of interference vectors, which is equal to $\bigcup_{i\in\{1,\ldots,K\},i\neq j}\left\{\text{span}\left(\mathbf{H}^{[ji]}\bar{\mathbf{V}}^{[i]}\right)\right\}$, is not a vector space; thus, we choose the subspace of interference (A5), which is easier to work with and includes $\bigcup_{i\in\{1,\ldots,K\},i\neq j}\left\{\text{span}\left(\mathbf{H}^{[ji]}\bar{\mathbf{V}}^{[i]}\right)\right\}$.

After that step, we analyze the dimension and the normalized asymptotic dimension of the messages and interference subspaces. First, we assume that the parameter T (the number of frequency slots) is sufficiently large, and at the end of Step 5 of the proof, we will choose the minimum value for T such that all message streams can be decodable and all interference alignment equations can be satisfied. Considering the natures of $\bar{\mathcal{A}}_j$ in (A5), $\bar{\mathcal{C}}_j$ in (A3), and $\tilde{\mathcal{C}}_j$ in (A4), we can see from a statement of [34] (Lemma 2) that if we choose the variables x_k as $H^{[ji]}(\omega_t), H^{[qi']}_{\text{T-IR}}(\omega_t), i, i', j \in \{1,\ldots,K\}, q \in \{1,\ldots,Q\}$, y_k as $H^{[ju]}_{\text{IR-R}}(\omega_t)$, $j \in \{W+1,\ldots,K\}, u \in \{1,\ldots,W\}$, and z_k as $H^{[ju]}_{\text{IR-R}}(\omega_t), j \in \{1,\ldots,W\}, u \in \{1,\ldots,W\}$, then by using [34] (Lemmas 1–3), the subspaces $\bar{\mathcal{A}}_j$, $\bar{\mathcal{C}}_j$ and $\tilde{\mathcal{C}}_j$ are almost surely full-rank and linearly independent (all base vectors of these subspaces are linearly independent). In fact, if we take the constructing base vectors of $\bar{\mathcal{A}}_j$, $\bar{\mathcal{C}}_j$ and $\tilde{\mathcal{C}}_j$ and construct a square matrix by choosing some rows of the matrix, we can see by using [34] (Lemmas 2–3) that the determinant of this square matrix will be a non-zero polynomial, and by using [34] (Lemma 1), it will be a non-zero with a probability equal to one; thus, all message streams are decodable at the clean receivers (by using zero forcing).

For more clarity, we will review [34] (Lemmas 1–3) as follows:

Ref. [34] (Lemma 1): Consider the k independent random variables $X_1,\ldots,X_k$, each constructed from a CDF, which is continuous. The probability of the event that the non-zero polynomial $P_k(X_1,\ldots,X_k)$, constructed from $X_1,\ldots,X_k$ with a finite degree, assumes the value zero is zero, i.e., $\Pr\{P_k(X_1,\ldots,X_k) = 0\} = 0$.

Ref. [34] (Lemma 2): Consider the three sets of variables $\{x_i, i \in \mathcal{A}_x, |\mathcal{A}_x| < \infty\}$, $\{y_i, i \in \mathcal{A}_y, |\mathcal{A}_y| < \infty\}$, and $\{z_i, i \in \mathcal{A}_z, |\mathcal{A}_z| < \infty\}$. Consider the following functions:

$$f_j = \prod_{i=1}^{|\mathcal{A}_x|} \left(x_i + \sum_{i' \in \mathcal{C}_j, i'' \in \mathcal{D}_j} x_{i'} y_{i''} P_1^{[i'i''j]}(z_k : k \in \mathcal{A}_z) + y_{i''} P_2^{[i'i''j]}(z_k : k \in \mathcal{A}_z) \right)^{a_i^j}, \tag{A6}$$

$$(a_1^j, \ldots, a_{|\mathcal{A}_x|}^j) \in \mathbb{W}^{|\mathcal{A}_x|}, j \in \{1, \ldots, J\},$$

where $P_1^{[i'i''j]}(\cdot)$ and $P_2^{[i'i''j]}(\cdot)$ are fractional polynomials and for $\forall j$, we have $|\mathcal{C}_j|, |\mathcal{D}_j| < \infty$. If for $\forall j, j'$ with $j \neq j'$, $(a_1^j, \ldots, a_{|\mathcal{A}_x|}^j) \neq (a_1^{j'}, \ldots, a_{|\mathcal{A}_x|}^{j'})$, then the functions f_j will be linearly independent.

Ref. [34] (Lemma 3): Consider the set of non-zero linearly independent fractional polynomials $\{P^{[j]}(\cdot), j \in \{1, \ldots, J\}\}$ and consider the J sets of variables $\mathcal{X}_j = \{x_i^j : i \in \mathcal{I}, \mathcal{I} \subseteq \mathbb{N}, |\mathcal{I}| < \infty\}$, $j \in \{1, \ldots, J\}$. The determinant of the following matrix will be a non-zero fractional polynomial:

$$\mathbf{A} = \begin{bmatrix} P^{[1]}(\mathcal{X}_1) & P^{[2]}(\mathcal{X}_1) & \cdots & P^{[J]}(\mathcal{X}_1) \\ P^{[1]}(\mathcal{X}_2) & P^{[2]}(\mathcal{X}_2) & \cdots & P^{[J]}(\mathcal{X}_2) \\ \vdots & \vdots & \ddots & \vdots \\ P^{[1]}(\mathcal{X}_J) & P^{[2]}(\mathcal{X}_J) & \cdots & P^{[J]}(\mathcal{X}_J) \end{bmatrix}. \tag{A7}$$

Now, we have to make sure that interference alignment Equations (24) and (25) are satisfied by analyzing the dimension of message streams and interference. The dimension of the message subspaces $\bar{\mathcal{C}}_j$ and $\tilde{\mathcal{C}}_j$, which is equal to the number of its base vectors in (A3) and (A4), can be characterized as follows:

$$d(\bar{\mathcal{C}}_j) = n^{K^2-K}(sn)^{QK}, \tag{A8}$$

$$d(\tilde{\mathcal{C}}_j) = n^{K^2-K}(sn)^{\varphi}(vn)^{\theta}, \tag{A9}$$

where

$$\varphi = \sum_{q'=1}^{Q} (K - |\mathcal{B}_{q'}|) = KQ - \sum_{q'=1}^{Q} |\mathcal{B}_{q'}| = KQ - W,$$

$$\theta = \sum_{q'=1}^{Q} |\mathcal{B}_{q'}| = W.$$

The dimension of the interference subspace $\bar{\mathcal{A}}_j$, which is equal to the number of its base vectors in (A5), is:

$$d(\bar{\mathcal{A}}_j) = (n+1)^{K^2-K}(\max\{sn, tn\})^{QK}. \tag{A10}$$

We can see from (A8)–(A10) and (10) that $l = K^2 - K + QK$. We define the following parameters:

$$\Gamma = s^{QK}, \tag{A11}$$

$$\chi = s^{QK-W} v^W, \tag{A12}$$

$$\zeta = t^{QK}. \tag{A13}$$

Considering (A8)–(A13) and (10), the normalized asymptotic dimensions of the message and interference subspaces are:

$$D_N(\bar{\mathcal{C}}_j) = \Gamma, \tag{A14}$$

$$D_N(\bar{\mathcal{C}}_j) = \chi, \tag{A15}$$

$$D_N(\bar{\mathcal{A}}_j) = \max\{\Gamma, \zeta\}. \tag{A16}$$

Interference alignment Equations (24) and (25) are satisfied because we can see that the normalized asymptotic dimension of the interference induced by $\bar{\mathbf{V}}^{[i]}\bar{\mathbf{x}}^{[i]}, i \in \{1, \ldots, W\}$, $i \neq j$ is Γ and the normalized asymptotic dimension of the interference induced by $\bar{\mathbf{V}}^{[i]}\bar{\mathbf{x}}^{[i]}, i \in \{W+1, \ldots, K\}$ is ζ.

Appendix C

Using (42), we can characterize the message subspace $\bar{\mathcal{C}}_j$ as follows:

$$\bar{\mathcal{C}}_j = \text{span}\left(\mathbf{H}^{[jj]}\bar{\mathbf{V}}^{[j]}\right) =$$

$$\text{span}\left\{\mathbf{H}^{[jj]}\left[\mathbf{M}(g_1(i,j), \mathbf{H}^{[ji]}, \bar{\mathcal{S}}_1)\right]\left[\mathbf{M}(g_2(i,q), \mathbf{H}^{[qi]}_{\text{T-IR}}, \bar{\mathcal{S}}_2)\right]\mathbf{w} : g_1 \in \mathcal{F}(\bar{\mathcal{S}}_1, \{1, \ldots, n\}), g_2 \in \mathcal{F}(\bar{\mathcal{S}}_2, \{1, \ldots, tn\})\right\}, \tag{A17}$$

where $\bar{\mathcal{S}}_1$, $\bar{\mathcal{S}}_2$, $\mathcal{F}(\cdot,\cdot)$, and $\mathbf{M}(\cdot,\cdot,\cdot)$ are given by using (37), (38), (34), and (35), respectively.

To satisfy interference alignment Equation (26), the subspace $\bar{\mathcal{A}}_j$ must be chosen such that:

$$\bigcup_{i \in \{1,\ldots,K\}, i \neq j} \left\{\text{span}\left(\mathbf{H}^{[ji]}\bar{\mathbf{V}}^{[i]}\right)\right\} \subseteq \bar{\mathcal{A}}_j.$$

Therefore, we characterize $\bar{\mathcal{A}}_j$ as follows:

$$\bar{\mathcal{A}}_j =$$

$$\text{span}\left\{\left[\mathbf{M}(g_1(i,j), \mathbf{H}^{[ji]}, \bar{\mathcal{S}}_1)\right]\left[\mathbf{M}(g_2(i,q), \mathbf{H}^{[qi]}_{\text{T-IR}}, \bar{\mathcal{S}}_2)\right]\mathbf{w} : g_1 \in \mathcal{F}(\bar{\mathcal{S}}_1, \{1, \ldots, n+1\}), g_2 \in \mathcal{F}(\bar{\mathcal{S}}_2, \{1, \ldots, n\max\{s,t\}\})\right\}, \tag{A18}$$

where $\bar{\mathcal{S}}_1$ and $\bar{\mathcal{S}}_2$ are given by (37) and (38), respectively. To satisfy interference alignment Equation (28), the subspace $\tilde{\mathcal{A}}_j$ must be chosen such that:

$$\bigcup_{i \in \{1,\ldots,W\}} \left\{\text{span}\left(\tilde{\mathbf{H}}^{[ji]}\tilde{\mathbf{V}}^{[i]}\right)\right\} \subseteq \tilde{\mathcal{A}}_j.$$

Therefore, we characterize subspace $\tilde{\mathcal{A}}_j$ as follows:

$$\tilde{\mathcal{A}}_j = \text{span}\left\{\left[\mathbf{M}(g_1(i,j), \tilde{\mathbf{H}}^{[ji]}, \bar{\mathcal{S}}_1)\right]\left[\mathbf{M}(g_2(i,q), \mathbf{H}^{[qi]}_{\text{T-IR}}, \tilde{\mathcal{S}}_2)\right]\left[\mathbf{M}(g_3(i,q), \mathbf{T}^{[qi]}, \tilde{\mathcal{S}}_3)\right]\mathbf{w} :\right.$$

$$\left. g_1 \in \mathcal{F}(\bar{\mathcal{S}}_1, \{1, \ldots, n+1\}), g_2 \in \mathcal{F}(\tilde{\mathcal{S}}_2, \{1, \ldots, sn\}), g_3 \in \mathcal{F}(\tilde{\mathcal{S}}_3, \{1, \ldots, vn\})\right\}, \tag{A19}$$

where $\tilde{\mathcal{S}}_2$ and $\tilde{\mathcal{S}}_3$ are given by using (40) and (41), respectively.

By using the same argument given for the clean receivers, subspaces $\bar{\mathcal{A}}_j$, $\tilde{\mathcal{A}}_j$, and $\bar{\mathcal{C}}_j$ are full-rank and linearly independent almost surely, i.e., all base vectors of these subspaces are linearly independent. Now, we analyze the dimensions of the message and interference subspaces. By calculating the number of base vectors of the message subspace $\bar{\mathcal{C}}_j$ in (A17), we have:

$$d(\bar{\mathcal{C}}_j) = n^{K^2-K}(tn)^{QK}, \tag{A20}$$

$$D_N(\bar{\mathcal{C}}_j) = \zeta,$$

and for the interference subspaces in (A18) and (A19), we have:

$$d(\bar{\mathcal{A}}_j) = (n+1)^{K^2-K}(\max\{sn, tn\})^{QK}, \tag{A21}$$

$$D_N(\bar{\mathcal{A}}_j) = \max\{\Gamma, \zeta\},$$

$$d(\tilde{\mathcal{A}}_j) = (n+1)^{K^2-K}(sn)^{QK-W}(vn)^{W}, \tag{A22}$$

$$D_N(\bar{\mathcal{A}}_j) = \chi.$$

Therefore, we can see that interference alignment Equations (26)–(29) are satisfied because the normalized asymptotic dimension of the interference subspace induced by $\tilde{\mathbf{V}}^{[i]}\tilde{\mathbf{x}}^{[i]}, i \in \{1,..,W\}$ is χ, the normalized asymptotic dimension of the interference subspace induced by $\tilde{\mathbf{V}}^{[i]}\tilde{\mathbf{x}}^{[i]}, i \in \{1,..,W\}$ is Γ, and the normalized asymptotic dimension of the interference subspace induced by $\tilde{\mathbf{V}}^{[i]}\tilde{\mathbf{x}}^{[i]}, i \in \{W+1,..,K\}, i \neq j$ is ζ.

Appendix D

Using (39), we can characterize the message subspaces $\tilde{\mathcal{C}}_{i,r_q}, i \in \mathcal{B}_q$ as follows:

$$\tilde{\mathcal{C}}_{i,r_q} = \text{span}\left(\mathbf{H}^{[qi]}_{\text{T-IR}}\tilde{\mathbf{V}}^{[i]}\right) =$$

$$\text{span}\left\{\mathbf{H}^{[qi]}_{\text{T-IR}}\left[\mathbf{M}(g_1(i,j),\tilde{\mathbf{H}}^{[ji]},\bar{\mathcal{S}}_1)\right]\left[\mathbf{M}(g_2(i,q),\mathbf{H}^{[qi]}_{\text{T-IR}},\tilde{\mathcal{S}}_2)\right]\left[\mathbf{M}(g_3(i,q),\mathbf{T}^{[qi]},\tilde{\mathcal{S}}_3)\right]\mathbf{w}:\right.$$

$$\left. g_1 \in \mathcal{F}(\bar{\mathcal{S}}_1,\{1,\ldots,n\}), g_2 \in \mathcal{F}(\tilde{\mathcal{S}}_2,\{1,\ldots,sn\}), g_3 \in \mathcal{F}(\tilde{\mathcal{S}}_3,\{1,\ldots,vn\})\right\}, \quad \text{(A23)}$$

where $\tilde{\mathcal{S}}_2$, $\tilde{\mathcal{S}}_3$, $\mathcal{F}(\cdot,\cdot)$, and $\mathbf{M}(\cdot,\cdot,\cdot)$ are given by using (40), (41), (34), and (35), respectively.

To satisfy interference alignment Equation (30), the subspace $\bar{\mathcal{A}}_{r_q}$ must be chosen such that:

$$\bigcup_{i\in\{1,\ldots,K\}} \left\{\text{span}\left(\mathbf{H}^{[qi]}_{\text{T-IR}}\bar{\mathbf{V}}^{[i]}\right)\right\} \subseteq \bar{\mathcal{A}}_{r_q}.$$

Therefore, we can characterize $\bar{\mathcal{A}}_j$ as follows:

$$\bar{\mathcal{A}}_{r_q} =$$

$$\text{span}\left\{\left[\mathbf{M}(g_1(i,j),\mathbf{H}^{[ji]},\bar{\mathcal{S}}_1)\right]\left[\mathbf{M}(g_2(i,q),\mathbf{H}^{[qi]}_{\text{T-IR}},\bar{\mathcal{S}}_2)\right]\mathbf{w}: g_1 \in \mathcal{F}(\bar{\mathcal{S}}_1,\{1,\ldots,n\}), g_2 \in \mathcal{F}(\bar{\mathcal{S}}_2,\{1,\ldots,n\max\{s,t\}+1\})\right\}, \quad \text{(A24)}$$

where $\bar{\mathcal{S}}_1$ and $\bar{\mathcal{S}}_2$ are given by using (37) and (38), respectively.

To satisfy interference alignment Equation (32), the subspace $\tilde{\mathcal{A}}_{r_q}$ must be chosen such that:

$$\bigcup_{i\in\{1,\ldots,W\}, i\notin\mathcal{B}_q} \left\{\text{span}\left(\mathbf{H}^{[qi]}_{\text{T-IR}}\tilde{\mathbf{V}}^{[i]}\right)\right\} \subseteq \tilde{\mathcal{A}}_{r_q}.$$

Therefore, we characterize $\tilde{\mathcal{A}}_j$ as follows:

$$\tilde{\mathcal{A}}_{r_q} = \text{span}\left\{\left[\mathbf{M}(g_1(i,j),\tilde{\mathbf{H}}^{[ji]},\bar{\mathcal{S}}_1)\right]\left[\mathbf{M}(g_2(i,q),\mathbf{H}^{[qi]}_{\text{T-IR}},\tilde{\mathcal{S}}_2)\right]\left[\mathbf{M}(g_3(i,q),\mathbf{T}^{[qi]},\tilde{\mathcal{S}}_3)\right]\mathbf{w}:\right.$$

$$\left. g_1 \in \mathcal{F}(\bar{\mathcal{S}}_1,\{1,\ldots,n\}), g_2 \in \mathcal{F}(\tilde{\mathcal{S}}_2,\{1,\ldots,sn+1\}), g_3 \in \mathcal{F}(\tilde{\mathcal{S}}_3,\{1,\ldots,vn\})\right\}, \quad \text{(A25)}$$

where $\tilde{\mathcal{S}}_2$ and $\tilde{\mathcal{S}}_3$ are given by using (40) and (41), respectively.

By using the same argument given for the clean receivers, subspaces $\bar{\mathcal{A}}_{r_q}$, $\tilde{\mathcal{A}}_{r_q}$ and $\tilde{\mathcal{C}}_{i,r_q}, i \in \mathcal{B}_q$ are full-rank and linearly independent almost surely, i.e., all base vectors of these subspaces are linearly independent. Now, by calculating the number of base vectors, we can analyze the dimensions of the subspaces $\tilde{\mathcal{C}}_{i,r_q}, i \in \mathcal{B}_q$, $\bar{\mathcal{A}}_{r_q}$ and $\tilde{\mathcal{A}}_{r_q}$:

$$d(\tilde{\mathcal{C}}_{i,r_q}) = n^{K^2-K}(sn)^{QK-W}(vn)^W, \forall i \in \mathcal{B}_q, \quad \text{(A26)}$$

$$D_N(\tilde{\mathcal{C}}_{i,r_q}) = \chi.$$

Thus, the normalized dimension of the total subspaces, the message symbols of which may be de-multiplexed ($\tilde{\mathbf{x}}^{[i]}, i \in \mathcal{B}_q$) at the MIMO C-IR q-th receiving antenna is:

$$\sum_{i\in\mathcal{B}_q} D_N(\tilde{\mathcal{C}}_{i,r_q}) = |\mathcal{B}_q|\chi.$$

For $\bar{\mathcal{A}}_{r_q}$, we have:

$$d(\bar{\mathcal{A}}_{r_q}) = n^{K^2-K}(\max\{sn, tn\}+1)^{KQ}, \tag{A27}$$
$$D_N(\bar{\mathcal{A}}_{r_q}) = \max\{\Gamma, \zeta\},$$

and for $\tilde{\mathcal{A}}_{r_q}$, we have:

$$d(\tilde{\mathcal{A}}_{r_q}) = n^{K^2-K}(sn+1)^{QK-W}(vn)^{W}, \tag{A28}$$
$$D_N(\tilde{\mathcal{A}}_{r_q}) = \chi.$$

Thus, we can see that interference alignment Equations (30)–(33) are satisfied.

Appendix E

The second term of (68) is exactly the same as the second term of (11) in Theorem 1. The proof of the first term is similar to the proof of the first term of (11) in Theorem 1 with a difference in the MIMO C-IR de-multiplexing method. In the proof of Theorem 1, each MIMO C-IR receiving antenna q de-multiplexes the message streams $\tilde{\mathbf{x}}_i, i \in \mathcal{B}_q$ separately without a coordination with other receiving antennas. However, in the proof of this theorem, we use a coordination between the MIMO C-IR receiving antennas. Without a loss of generality, assume that $|\mathcal{B}_1| = Z+1$ and $|\mathcal{B}_q| = Z, q \neq 1$. To de-multiplex the message streams $\tilde{\mathbf{x}}_i, i \in \{1, \ldots, W\}$ at the MIMO C-IR, first we de-multiplex the message streams $\tilde{\mathbf{x}}_i, i \in \mathcal{B}_q, q \neq 1$ at the q-th MIMO C-IR receiving antenna separately. Then, to de-multiplex the message streams $\tilde{\mathbf{x}}_i, i \in \mathcal{B}_1$, we first remove the interference induced by the message streams $\tilde{\mathbf{x}}_i, i \in \{1, \ldots, W\}, i \notin \mathcal{B}_1$. This results in a decrement in the total normalized asymptotic dimension at the first receiving antenna of the MIMO C-IR (the amount of decrement is χ), so (58) changes into the following form for $q = 1$:

$$D_{N,t,r_1} = \left\lfloor \frac{W}{Q} \right\rfloor \chi + \chi + \max\{\Gamma, \zeta\}, \tag{A29}$$

and the constraint (63) changes into the following form:

$$\zeta \geq \left\lfloor \frac{W}{Q} \right\rfloor \chi. \tag{A30}$$

Then, we see that the DoF (68) is achievable.

Appendix F

The proof of this theorem is similar to the first term in the proof of Theorem 1. Here, we use the variable U introduced in the statement of the theorem to denote the number of clean receivers. Note that to avoid several notations, we use the same notations (such as the name of sets and vector subspaces) used in the proof of Theorem 1. Thus, from now on, these notations belong to this theorem. Our proof has six steps as follows.

Step 1: Dividing Receivers, Transmitters, and NC-IR Antennas

Using the same method as Step 1 of the proof of the first term in Theorem 1, we divide the transmitters into two partitions. For the transmitters $i \in \{1, \ldots, U\}$, we provide two sets of symbol streams: $\bar{\mathbf{x}}^{[i]}$ and $\tilde{\mathbf{x}}^{[i]}$. The matrices $\bar{\mathbf{V}}^{[i]}$ and $\tilde{\mathbf{V}}^{[i]}$ are beamforming matrices, the columns of which are the beamforming vectors for each element of $\bar{\mathbf{x}}^{[i]}$ and $\tilde{\mathbf{x}}^{[i]}$, respectively. For the transmitters $i \in \{U+1, \ldots, K\}$, we provide only one set of the symbol stream $\bar{\mathbf{x}}^{[i]}$, and the matrix $\bar{\mathbf{V}}^{[i]}$ is the beamforming matrix for the symbols $\bar{\mathbf{x}}^{[i]}$. Hence, the vectors $\mathbf{X}^{[i]}$ will have the forms of (12) and (13) by using the setting $W = U$. The reason for this kind of partitioning is the same as in Theorem 1. The main difference here is in the interference alignment scheme used for de-multiplexing the message streams $\tilde{\mathbf{x}}^{[i]}, i \in \{1, \ldots, U\}$ in the NC-IR receiving antennas.

Next, we divide the transmitters $i \in \{1, \ldots, U\}$ into the p distinct sets $\mathcal{E}_l, l \in \{1, \ldots, p\}$ such that for $l \in \{1, \ldots, e'\}$, we have $|\mathcal{E}_l| = e + 1$, and for $l \in \{e' + 1, \ldots, p\}$, we have $|\mathcal{E}_l| = e$. Similarly, we divide the NC-IR antennas into the p distinct sets $\mathcal{F}_l, l \in \{1, \ldots, p\}$ such that $|\mathcal{F}_l| = U, \forall l \in \{1, \ldots, p\}$. Now, we design the beamforming matrices $\bar{\mathbf{V}}^{[i]}$ and $\tilde{\mathbf{V}}^{[i]}$ such that the message streams $\tilde{\mathbf{x}}^{[i]}, i \in \mathcal{E}_l$ may be de-multiplexed in each of the NC-IR antennas $u \in \mathcal{F}_l$ for $\forall l \in \{1, \ldots, p\}$.

Step 2: Interference Cancellation at the Clean Receivers and Equivalent Channel at the Dirty Receivers

For the interference cancellation, we design the outputs of antennas in the set $\mathcal{F}_l$ such that the interference induced by the message streams $\tilde{\mathbf{x}}^{[i]}, i \in \mathcal{E}_l$ is removed at the clean receivers $j \in \{1, \ldots, U\}$. Thus, the NC-IR antennas' transmitted signal must be designed such that they satisfy the following:

$$- \sum_{i \in \mathcal{E}_l, i \neq j} \mathbf{H}^{[ji]} \tilde{\mathbf{V}}^{[i]} \tilde{\mathbf{x}}^{[i]} = \sum_{u \in \mathcal{F}_l} \mathbf{H}^{[ju]}_{\mathrm{IR-R}} \mathbf{X}^{[u]}_{\mathrm{IR}}, \forall j \in \{1, \ldots, U\}, \forall l \in \{1, \ldots, p\}. \tag{A31}$$

The solution to (A31) can be derived as follows:

$$\mathbf{X}^{[u]}_{\mathrm{IR}} = \sum_{j \in \{1, \ldots, U\}} \sum_{i \in \mathcal{E}_l, i \neq j} \mathbf{H}^{[ju]}_{\mathrm{inv}} \mathbf{H}^{[ji]} \tilde{\mathbf{V}}^{[ji]} \tilde{\mathbf{x}}^{[i]}, \forall u \in \mathcal{F}_l, \tag{A32}$$

where $\mathbf{H}^{[ju]}_{\mathrm{inv}}$ is a $T \times T$ diagonal matrix and its t-th diagonal element is a fractional polynomial in terms of $H^{[j'u']}_{\mathrm{IR-R}}(\omega_t), u' \in \mathcal{F}_l, j' \in \{1, \ldots, U\}$. This solution exists almost surely because the matrix of the coefficients of the linear equations is in terms of independent random variables, its determinant is a non-zero polynomial in terms of these random variables drawn from a CDF, which is continuous, and by using [34] (Lemma 1), it is a non-zero with the probability 1. Note that each NC-IR receiving antenna de-multiplexes the symbol streams $\tilde{\mathbf{x}}^{[i]}$ with additive noise. This event does not disturb the equations above because if each symbol is replaced by a symbol with additive noise, the interference cancellation holds but we have additional noise, which is negligible in a high SNR regime. We can see that the received signals at the receivers have the same forms as (22) and $\mathbf{H}^{[ju]}_{\mathrm{inv}}$ and the equivalent channel matrix $\tilde{\mathbf{H}}^{[ji]}$ has the same properties introduced in Step 2 of the proof of the first term in Theorem 1.

Step 3: Interference Alignment Equations

The interference alignment equations and message and interference subspaces for the clean and dirty receivers are the same as in Step 3 of the proof of the first term in Theorem 1 ((24)–(29)) if we replace W with U. Consider $q \in \{1, \ldots, pU\}$: we define the function $L(q) = l$ if $q \in \mathcal{F}_l$ (l is unique because the sets $\mathcal{F}_l$ are disjointed). We designed the interference alignment scheme such that the symbol streams $\tilde{\mathbf{x}}^{[i]}, i \in \mathcal{E}_{L(q)}$ can be de-multiplexed at the q-th receiving antenna of the NC-IR. Thus, the interference alignment equations for the NC-IR change as follows.

To this end, all the interference induced by the symbol streams $\bar{\mathbf{x}}^{[i]}$ must align into a limited subspace. Therefore, at the q-th receiving antenna of the NC-IR and for each $i \in \{1, \ldots, K\}$, we must have:

$$\mathrm{span}\left(\mathbf{H}^{[qi]}_{\mathrm{T-IR}} \bar{\mathbf{V}}^{[i]}\right) \subseteq \bar{\mathcal{A}}_{r_q}, \tag{A33}$$

where $\bar{\mathcal{A}}_{r_q}$ is considered a subspace for which we have:

$$\max_{i \in \{1, \ldots, K\}} D_N\left(\mathrm{span}\left(\mathbf{H}^{[qi]}_{\mathrm{T-IR}} \bar{\mathbf{V}}^{[i]}\right)\right) = D_N(\bar{\mathcal{A}}_{r_q}). \tag{A34}$$

Then, for each $i \in \{1, \ldots, U\}, i \notin \mathcal{E}_{L(q)}$, we have:

$$\operatorname{span}\left(\mathbf{H}_{\mathrm{T-IR}}^{[qi]}\tilde{\mathbf{V}}^{[i]}\right) \subseteq \tilde{\mathcal{A}}_{r_q}, \tag{A35}$$

where $\tilde{\mathcal{A}}_{r_q}$ is considered a subspace for which we have:

$$\max_{i\in\{1,\dots,U\}, i\notin\mathcal{E}_{L(q)}} D_N\left(\operatorname{span}\left(\mathbf{H}_{\mathrm{T-IR}}^{[qi]}\tilde{\mathbf{V}}^{[i]}\right)\right) = D_N(\tilde{\mathcal{A}}_{r_q}). \tag{A36}$$

Moreover, we define $\tilde{\mathcal{C}}_{i,r_q}, i \in \mathcal{E}_{L(q)}$ as the message subspaces, which can be de-multiplexed at the NC-IR q-th antenna as follows:

$$\tilde{\mathcal{C}}_{i,r_q} = \operatorname{span}\left(\mathbf{H}_{\mathrm{T-IR}}^{[qi]}\tilde{\mathbf{V}}^{[i]}\right), i \in \mathcal{E}_{L(q)}. \tag{A37}$$

We want $\tilde{\mathcal{C}}_{i,r_q}, \forall i \in \mathcal{E}_{L(q)}, \tilde{\mathcal{A}}_{r_q}$ and $\tilde{\mathcal{A}}_{r_q}$ to be full-rank and linearly independent, so we can make sure that the message streams $\tilde{\mathbf{x}}^{[i]}, i \in \mathcal{E}_{L(q)}$ can be de-multiplexed at the q-th NC-IR antenna. In Steps 4 and 5, we prove the existence of such beamforming vectors, messages, and interference subspaces, which satisfies the previous interference alignment equations for the clean and dirty receivers and the MIMO C-IR. In Step 6, we analyze the achieved DoF by using the beamforming vectors' design.

Step 4: Beamforming Matrix Design

The beamforming matrices $\tilde{\mathbf{V}}^{[i]}, \forall i \in \{1,\dots,K\}$ are the same as (36) and (42) if we replace W with U. For $\tilde{\mathbf{V}}^{[i]}$, we have:

$$\tilde{\mathbf{V}}^{[i]} = \left\{\left[\mathbf{M}(g_1(i,j), \tilde{\mathbf{H}}^{[ji]}, \tilde{\mathcal{S}}_1)\right]\left[\mathbf{M}(g_2(i,q), \mathbf{H}_{\mathrm{T-IR}}^{[qi]}, \tilde{\mathcal{S}}_2)\right]\left[\mathbf{M}(g_3(i,q), \mathbf{T}^{[qi]}, \tilde{\mathcal{S}}_3)\right]\mathbf{w} : \right. \tag{A38}$$

$$\left. g_1 \in \mathcal{F}(\tilde{\mathcal{S}}_1, \{1,\dots,n\}), g_2 \in \mathcal{F}(\tilde{\mathcal{S}}_2, \{1,\dots,sn\}), g_3 \in \mathcal{F}(\tilde{\mathcal{S}}_3, \{1,\dots,vn\})\right\}, \tag{A39}$$

where $\tilde{\mathcal{S}}_1$, $\mathcal{F}(\cdot,\cdot)$ and $\mathbf{M}(\cdot,\cdot,\cdot)$ are given by using (37), (34), and (35), respectively, and we have:

$$\tilde{\mathcal{S}}_2 = \left\{(i,q)\middle| i \in \{1,\dots,K\}, i \notin \mathcal{E}_{L(q)}, q \in \{1,\dots,Q\}\right\}, \tag{A40}$$

$$\tilde{\mathcal{S}}_3 = \left\{(i,q)\middle| i \in \mathcal{E}_{L(q)}, q \in \{1,\dots,Q\}\right\}. \tag{A41}$$

$\mathbf{T}^{[q''i''']}$s are $T \times T$ diagonal random matrices for each (i,q), where each diagonal element for each matrix is drawn independently and its CDF is continuous.

Note that similar to the proof of Theorem 1, each value of the parameters s, v and t can be approximated by using rational numbers with arbitrarily small errors, and by choosing a sufficiently large n, the parameters sn, vn and tn will be integers.

Step 5: Validity of Interference Alignment Conditions and Decodability of Message Symbols

(1) Validity of Interference Alignment Conditions at Clean Receivers $j \in \{1,\dots,U\}$: The message subspace $\tilde{\mathcal{C}}_j$ and the interference subspace $\tilde{\mathcal{A}}_j$ will be exactly the same as (A3) and (A5). The message subspaces $\tilde{\mathcal{C}}_j$ will change as follows:

$$\tilde{\mathcal{C}}_j = \operatorname{span}\left(\tilde{\mathbf{H}}^{[jj]}\tilde{\mathbf{V}}^{[j]}\right) =$$

$$\operatorname{span}\left\{\tilde{\mathbf{H}}^{[jj]}\left[\mathbf{M}(g_1(i,j), \tilde{\mathbf{H}}^{[ji]}, \tilde{\mathcal{S}}_1)\right]\left[\mathbf{M}(g_2(i,q), \mathbf{H}_{\mathrm{T-IR}}^{[qi]}, \tilde{\mathcal{S}}_2)\right]\left[\mathbf{M}(g_3(i,q), \mathbf{T}^{[qi]}, \tilde{\mathcal{S}}_3)\right]\mathbf{w} : \right.$$

$$\left. g_1 \in \mathcal{F}(\tilde{\mathcal{S}}_1, \{1,\dots,n\}), g_2 \in \mathcal{F}(\tilde{\mathcal{S}}_2, \{1,\dots,sn\}), g_3 \in \mathcal{F}(\tilde{\mathcal{S}}_3, \{1,\dots,vn\})\right\}, \tag{A42}$$

where $\tilde{\mathcal{S}}_2$ and $\tilde{\mathcal{S}}_3$ are given by using (A40) and (A41).

Considering the natures of $\tilde{\mathcal{A}}_j$ in (A5), $\tilde{\mathcal{C}}_j$ in (A3), and $\tilde{\mathcal{C}}_j$ in (A42), we can see from a statement by [34] (Lemma 2) that if we choose the variables x_k as $H^{[ji]}(\omega_t), H_{\mathrm{T-IR}}^{[ri']}(\omega_t), i, i'$, $j \in \{1,\dots,K\}, u \in \{1,\dots,Q\}$, y_k as $H_{\mathrm{IR-R}}^{[ju]}(\omega_t), j \in \{U+1,\dots,K\}, u \in \{1,\dots,Q\}$, and z_k as $H_{\mathrm{IR-R}}^{[ju]}(\omega_t), j \in \{1,\dots,U\}, u \in \{1,\dots,Q\}$, then by using [34] (Lemmas 1–3), subspaces $\tilde{\mathcal{A}}_j$,

$\bar{\mathcal{C}}_j$ and $\tilde{\mathcal{C}}_j$ are full-rank and linearly independent (all base vectors of these subspaces are linearly independent) almost surely. The reason is that if we take the constructing base vectors of $\bar{\mathcal{A}}_j$, $\bar{\mathcal{C}}_j$, and $\tilde{\mathcal{C}}_j$ and construct a square matrix by choosing some rows of it, we can see by using [34] (Lemmas 2–3) that the determinant of this square matrix is a non-zero polynomial, which is non-zero with the probability 1 by using [34] (Lemma 1). Thus, all the message streams are decodable at the clean receivers (by using zero forcing). For more clarity, [34] (Lemmas 1–3) are reviewed in Appendix B.

Similar to the proof of Theorem 1, first we assume that the parameter T is sufficiently large, and at the end of this step, we determine the minimum required T. The dimensions of the subspaces $\bar{\mathcal{C}}_j$ and $\bar{\mathcal{A}}_j$ are the same as (A8) and (A10), respectively. Hence, we calculate the dimension of $\tilde{\mathcal{C}}_j$ by calculating the number of its base vectors in (A42) as follows:

$$d(\tilde{\mathcal{C}}_j) = n^{K^2-K}(sn)^{\varphi}(vn)^{\theta}, \tag{A43}$$

where

$$\varphi = \sum_{q'=1}^{Q}(K - \left|\mathcal{E}_{L(q')}\right|) = KQ - \sum_{q'=1}^{Q}\left|\mathcal{E}_{L(q')}\right| = KQ - U^2,$$

$$\theta = \sum_{q'=1}^{Q}\left|\mathcal{E}_{L(q')}\right| = U^2.$$

We can see from (10) that $l = K^2 - K + QK$. We can define the following parameters:

$$\Gamma = s^{QK},$$

$$\chi = s^{QK-U^2}v^{U^2},$$

$$\zeta = t^{QK}.$$

Therefore, the normalized asymptotic dimensions of the message and interference subspaces are:

$$D_N(\bar{\mathcal{C}}_j) = \Gamma, \tag{A44}$$

$$D_N(\tilde{\mathcal{C}}_j) = \chi, \tag{A45}$$

$$D_N(\bar{\mathcal{A}}_j) = \max\{\Gamma, \zeta\}. \tag{A46}$$

Thus, interference alignment Equations (24) and (25) are satisfied.

(2) Validity of interference alignment conditions at the dirty receivers $j \in \{U+1, \ldots, K\}$: For the dirty receivers, the message subspace $\bar{\mathcal{C}}_j$ and the interference subspace $\bar{\mathcal{A}}_j$ are exactly the same as (A17) and (A18). To satisfy interference alignment Equation (28) (if W is replaced with U), the subspace $\tilde{\mathcal{A}}_j$ must be chosen such that:

$$\bigcup_{i\in\{1,\ldots,U\}}\left\{\mathrm{span}\left(\tilde{\mathbf{H}}^{[ji]}\tilde{\mathbf{V}}^{[i]}\right)\right\} \subseteq \tilde{\mathcal{A}}_j.$$

Therefore, we can characterize subspace $\tilde{\mathcal{A}}_j$ as follows:

$$\tilde{\mathcal{A}}_j = \mathrm{span}\Big\{\Big[\mathbf{M}(g_1(i,j), \tilde{\mathbf{H}}^{[ji]}, \tilde{\mathcal{S}}_1)\Big]\Big[\mathbf{M}(g_2(i,q), \mathbf{H}^{[qi]}_{\text{T-IR}}, \tilde{\mathcal{S}}_2)\Big]\Big[\mathbf{M}(g_3(i,q), \mathbf{T}^{[qi]}, \tilde{\mathcal{S}}_3)\Big]\mathbf{w} :$$

$$g_1 \in \mathcal{F}(\tilde{\mathcal{S}}_1, \{1, \ldots, n+1\}), g_2 \in \mathcal{F}(\tilde{\mathcal{S}}_2, \{1, \ldots, sn\}), g_3 \in \mathcal{F}(\tilde{\mathcal{S}}_3, \{1, \ldots, vn\})\Big\}, \tag{A47}$$

where $\tilde{\mathcal{S}}_2$ and $\tilde{\mathcal{S}}_3$ are given by using (A40) and (A41).

By using the same argument given for $\bar{\mathcal{A}}_j$, $\bar{\mathcal{C}}_j$ and $\tilde{\mathcal{C}}_j$ at the clean receivers, subspaces $\bar{\mathcal{A}}_j$, $\tilde{\mathcal{A}}_j$ and $\bar{\mathcal{C}}_j$ are full-rank and linearly independent almost surely. Then, we have:

$$D_N(\bar{\mathcal{C}}_j) = \zeta, \tag{A48}$$

$$D_N(\bar{\mathcal{A}}_j) = \max\{\Gamma, \zeta\}, \tag{A49}$$

$$d(\tilde{\mathcal{A}}_j) = (n+1)^{K^2-K}(sn)^{QK-U^2}(vn)^{U^2}, \tag{A50}$$

$$D_N(\tilde{\mathcal{A}}_j) = \chi. \tag{A51}$$

Hence, we can see that interference alignment Equations (26)–(29) are satisfied.

(3) Validity of interference alignment conditions at the q-th antenna of the NC-IR $q \in \{1, \ldots, Q\}$*:*The interference subspace $\bar{\mathcal{A}}_{r_q}$ is exactly the same as (A24) if we replace W with U. The message subspaces $\tilde{\mathcal{C}}_{i,r_q}, i \in \mathcal{E}_{L(q)}$ and the interference subspace $\tilde{\mathcal{A}}_{r_q}$ will change as follows:

$$\tilde{\mathcal{C}}_{i,r_q} = \text{span}\left(\mathbf{H}^{[qi]}_{\text{T-IR}}\tilde{\mathbf{V}}^{[i]}\right) =$$

$$\text{span}\Big\{\mathbf{H}^{[qi]}_{\text{T-IR}}\Big[\mathbf{M}(g_1(i,j), \tilde{\mathbf{H}}^{[ji]}, \tilde{\mathcal{S}}_1)\Big]\Big[\mathbf{M}(g_2(i,q), \mathbf{H}^{[qi]}_{\text{T-IR}}, \tilde{\mathcal{S}}_2)\Big]\Big[\mathbf{M}(g_3(i,q), \mathbf{T}^{[qi]}, \tilde{\mathcal{S}}_3)\Big]\mathbf{w} :$$

$$g_1 \in \mathcal{F}(\tilde{\mathcal{S}}_1, \{1, \ldots, n\}), g_2 \in \mathcal{F}(\tilde{\mathcal{S}}_2, \{1, \ldots, sn\}), g_3 \in \mathcal{F}(\tilde{\mathcal{S}}_3, \{1, \ldots, vn\})\Big\}, \tag{A52}$$

where $\tilde{\mathcal{S}}_2$ and $\tilde{\mathcal{S}}_3$ are given by using (40) and (41), respectively.

$$\tilde{\mathcal{C}}_{i,r_q} = \text{span}\left(\mathbf{H}^{[qi]}_{\text{T-IR}}\tilde{\mathbf{V}}^{[i]}\right) =$$

$$\text{span}\Big\{\mathbf{H}^{[qi]}_{\text{T-IR}}\Big[\mathbf{M}(g_1(i,j), \tilde{\mathbf{H}}^{[ji]}, \tilde{\mathcal{S}}_1)\Big]\Big[\mathbf{M}(g_2(i,q), \mathbf{H}^{[qi]}_{\text{T-IR}}, \tilde{\mathcal{S}}_2)\Big]\Big[\mathbf{M}(g_3(i,q), \mathbf{T}^{[qi]}, \tilde{\mathcal{S}}_3)\Big]\mathbf{w} :$$

$$g_1 \in \mathcal{F}(\tilde{\mathcal{S}}_1, \{1, \ldots, n\}), g_2 \in \mathcal{F}(\tilde{\mathcal{S}}_2, \{1, \ldots, sn\}), g_3 \in \mathcal{F}(\tilde{\mathcal{S}}_3, \{1, \ldots, vn\})\Big\}, \tag{A53}$$

where $\tilde{\mathcal{S}}_2$ and $\tilde{\mathcal{S}}_3$ are given by using (A40) and (A41), respectively.

To satisfy interference alignment Equation (A35), the subspace $\tilde{\mathcal{A}}_{r_q}$ must be chosen such that:

$$\bigcup_{i \in \{1,\ldots,U\}, i \notin \mathcal{E}_{L(q)}} \left\{\text{span}\left(\mathbf{H}^{[qi]}_{\text{T-IR}}\tilde{\mathbf{V}}^{[i]}\right)\right\} \subseteq \tilde{\mathcal{A}}_{r_q}.$$

Therefore, we can characterize $\tilde{\mathcal{A}}_j$ as follows:

$$\tilde{\mathcal{A}}_{r_q} = \text{span}\Big\{\Big[\mathbf{M}(g_1(i,j), \tilde{\mathbf{H}}^{[ji]}, \tilde{\mathcal{S}}_1)\Big]\Big[\mathbf{M}(g_2(i,q), \mathbf{H}^{[qi]}_{\text{T-IR}}, \tilde{\mathcal{S}}_2)\Big]\Big[\mathbf{M}(g_3(i,q), \mathbf{T}^{[qi]}, \tilde{\mathcal{S}}_3)\Big]\mathbf{w} :$$

$$g_1 \in \mathcal{F}(\tilde{\mathcal{S}}_1, \{1, \ldots, n\}), g_2 \in \mathcal{F}(\tilde{\mathcal{S}}_2, \{1, \ldots, sn+1\}), g_3 \in \mathcal{F}(\tilde{\mathcal{S}}_3, \{1, \ldots, vn\})\Big\}, \tag{A54}$$

where $\tilde{\mathcal{S}}_2$ and $\tilde{\mathcal{S}}_3$ are given by using (A40) and (A41), respectively.

By using the same argument given before, subspaces $\bar{\mathcal{A}}_{r_q}$, $\tilde{\mathcal{A}}_{r_q}$, and $\tilde{\mathcal{C}}_{i,r_q}, i \in \mathcal{E}_{L(q)}$ are full-rank and linearly independent almost surely. We can see that:

$$d(\tilde{\mathcal{C}}_{i,r_q}) = n^{K^2-K}(sn)^{QK-U^2}(vn)^{U^2}, \forall i \in \mathcal{E}_{L(q)}, \tag{A55}$$

$$D_N(\tilde{\mathcal{C}}_{i,r_q}) = \chi, \tag{A56}$$

so the normalized dimension of the total subspaces that can be de-multiplexed at the NC-IR q-th antenna is:

$$\sum_{i \in \mathcal{E}_{L(q)}} D_N(\tilde{\mathcal{C}}_{i,r_q}) = \left|\mathcal{E}_{L(q)}\right|\chi. \tag{A57}$$

For $\bar{\mathcal{A}}_{r_q}$, the same as in the proof of Theorem 1, we have:

$$D_N(\bar{\mathcal{A}}_{r_q}) = \max\{\Gamma, \zeta\}. \tag{A58}$$

For $\tilde{\mathcal{A}}_{r_q}$, we have:

$$d(\tilde{\mathcal{A}}_{r_q}) = n^{K^2-K}(sn+1)^{QK-U^2}(vn)^{U^2}, \tag{A59}$$

$$D_N(\tilde{\mathcal{A}}_{r_q}) = \chi. \tag{A60}$$

Thus, we can see that interference alignment Equations (30)–(33) are satisfied.

The same as in the proof of scheme 1 in Theorem 1, we derive the dimension of the whole received signal space at each receiver. Therefore, if we define $d_{t,j}$ as the total dimension at the j-th receiver and d_{t,r_q} as the total dimension at the q-th receiving antenna of the NC-IR, then we can see (53)–(55) will be obtained if we replace W and $\mathcal{B}_q$ with U and $\mathcal{E}_{L(q)}$, respectively. Therefore, considering $D_{N,t,j}$ as the total normalized asymptotic dimension at the j-th receiver and D_{N,t,r_q} as the total normalized asymptotic dimension at the q-th antenna of the NC-IR, we have:

$$D_{N,t,j} = \Gamma + \chi + \max\{\Gamma, \zeta\}, \forall j \in \{1, \ldots, U\}, \tag{A61}$$

$$D_{N,t,j} = \zeta + \chi + \max\{\Gamma, \zeta\}, \forall j \in \{U+1, \ldots, K\}, \tag{A62}$$

$$D_{N,t,r_q} = \left|\mathcal{E}_{L(q)}\right|\chi + \chi + \max\{\Gamma, \zeta\}, \forall q \in \{1, \ldots, Q\}. \tag{A63}$$

Considering the parameter T as (59), we have:

$$\lim_{n\to\infty} \frac{T}{n^{K^2-K+QK}} = \chi + \max\{\Gamma, \zeta\} + \max\left\{\max_{q\in\{1,\ldots,Q\}} \left|\mathcal{E}_{L(q)}\right|\chi, \zeta, \Gamma\right\}. \tag{A64}$$

Moreover, we have:

$$\max_{q\in\{1,\ldots,Q\}} \left|\mathcal{E}_{L(q)}\right| = \left\lceil \frac{U}{p} \right\rceil. \tag{A65}$$

Therefore, from using (A64) and (A65), we can conclude that:

$$\lim_{n\to\infty} \frac{T}{n^{K^2-K+QK}} = \chi + \max\{\Gamma, \zeta\} + \max\left\{\left\lceil \frac{U}{p} \right\rceil \chi, \zeta, \Gamma\right\}. \tag{A66}$$

Moreover we let:

$$\Gamma = \zeta, \tag{A67}$$

$$\zeta \geq \left\lceil \frac{U}{p} \right\rceil \chi. \tag{A68}$$

By using assumptions (A67) and (A68), we can see that the total normalized length is:

$$\lim_{n\to\infty} \frac{T}{n^{K^2-K+QK}} = \chi + 2\Gamma. \tag{A69}$$

Step 6: DoF Analysis

Now, we can characterize the total DoF. As stated before, we have U clean receivers, each with a normalized message dimension equal to $\Gamma + \chi$, and $K - U$ dirty receivers, each with a normalized message dimension equal to ζ (note that we assumed $\zeta = \Gamma$). Therefore, the total normalized length of T is equal to $\chi + 2\Gamma$. Thus, the total DoF has the following form:

$$\text{DoF} = \max_{\chi\geq 0, \Gamma \geq \left\lceil \frac{U}{p} \right\rceil \chi} \frac{U(\chi + \Gamma) + (K-U)\Gamma}{\chi + 2\Gamma}. \tag{A70}$$

By assuming that $\Gamma = \beta\chi$, we have:

$$\text{DoF} = \max_{\beta \geq \left\lceil \frac{U}{p} \right\rceil} \frac{U(1+\beta) + (K-U)\beta}{1+2\beta} \tag{A71}$$

$$= \frac{K}{2} + \max_{\beta \geq \left\lceil \frac{U}{p} \right\rceil} K\frac{\frac{U}{K} - \frac{1}{2}}{1+2\beta} = \frac{K}{2} + \max\left\{K\frac{\frac{U}{K} - \frac{1}{2}}{1+2\left\lceil \frac{U}{p} \right\rceil}, 0\right\}, \tag{A72}$$

where (A72) follows from the fact that if $\frac{U}{K} > \frac{1}{2}$, we set $\beta = \left\lceil \frac{U}{p} \right\rceil$, and if $\frac{U}{K} < \frac{1}{2}$, we tend β to ∞. This completes the proof.

References

1. Cadambe, V.R.; Jafar, S.A. Interference alignment and the degrees of freedom of the K-User interference channel. *IEEE Trans. Inf. Theory* **2008**, *54*, 2334–2344. [CrossRef]
2. El Gamal, A.; Hassanpour, N. Relay-without-delay. In Proceedings of the International Symposium on Information Theory (ISIT), Adelaide, SA, Australia, 4–9 September 2005.
3. Lee, N.; Wang, C. Aligned interference neutralization and the degrees of freedom of the two-user wireless networks with an instantaneous relay. *IEEE Trans. Commun.* **2013**, *61*, 3611–3619. [CrossRef]
4. Cadambe, V.R.; Jafar, S.A. Degrees of freedom of wireless networks with relays, feedback, cooperation, and full duplex operation. *IEEE Trans. Inf. Theory* **2009**, *55*, 2334–2344. [CrossRef]
5. Di Renzo, M.; Debbah, M.; Phan-Huy, D.T.; Zappone, A.; Alouini, M.S.; Yuen, C.; Sciancalepore, V.; Alexandropoulos, G.C.; Hoydis, J.; Gacanin, H.; et al. Smart radio environments empowered by AI reconfigurable meta-surfaces: An idea whose time has come. *EURASIP J. Wirel. Commun. Netw.* **2019**, *2019*, 129. [CrossRef]
6. El Gamal, A.; Hassanpour, N.; Mammen, J. Relay networks with delays. *IEEE Trans. Inf. Theory* **2007**, *53*, 3413–3431. [CrossRef]
7. Salimi, A.; Mirmohseni, M.; Aref, M.R. A new capacity upper bound for "relay-with-delay" channel. In Proceedings of the International Symposium on Information Theory (ISIT), Seoul, Korea, 28 June–3 July 2009.
8. Chang, H.; Chung, S.-Y.; Kim, S. Interference channel with a causal relay under strong and very strong interference. *IEEE Trans. Inf. Theory* **2014**, *60*, 859–865. [CrossRef]
9. Ho, Z.K.M.; Jorswieck, E.A. Instantaneous relaying: Optimal strategies and interference neutralization. *IEEE Trans. Signal Process.* **2012**, *60*, 6655–6668. [CrossRef]
10. Baik, I.-J.; Chung, S.-Y. Causal relay networks. *IEEE Trans. Inf. Theory* **2015**, *61*, 5432–5440. [CrossRef]
11. Kramer, G. Information networks with in-block memory. *IEEE Trans. Inf. Theory* **2014**, *60*, 2105–2120. [CrossRef]
12. Zhang, S.; Zhang, R. Capacity characterization for intelligent reflecting surface aided MIMO communication. *IEEE J. Sel. Areas Commun.* **2020**, *38*, 1823–1838. [CrossRef]
13. Karasik, R.; Simeone, O.; Di Renzo, M.; Shamai, S. Beyond Max-SNR: Joint encoding for reconfigurable intelligent surfaces. In Proceedings of the International Symposium on Information Theory (ISIT), Los Angeles, CA, USA, 21–26 June 2020. [CrossRef]
14. Mu, X.; Liu, Y.; Guo, L.; Lin, J.; Al-Dhahir, N. Exploiting intelligent reflecting surfaces in NOMA networks: Joint beamforming optimization. *IEEE Trans. Wirel. Commun.* **2020**, *19*, 6884–6898.
15. Ozdogan, O.; Bjornson, E.; Larsson, E.G. Using intelligent reflecting surfaces for rank improvement in MIMO communications. In Proceedings of the IEEE International Conference on Acoustics, Speech and Signal Processing, Barcelona, Spain, 4–8 May 2020. [CrossRef]
16. Maddah-Ali, M.A.; Motahari, A.S.; Khandani, A.K. Communication over MIMO X channels: Interference alignment, decomposition, and performance analysis. *IEEE Trans. Inf. Theory* **2008**, *54*, 3457–3470.
17. Gou, T.; Jafar, S.A. Degrees of freedom of the K user $M \times N$ MIMO interference channel. *IEEE Trans. Inf. Theory* **2010**, *56*, 6040–6057. [CrossRef]
18. Ke, L.; Ramamoorthy, A.; Wang, Z.; Yin, H. Degrees of freedom region for an interference network with general message demands. *IEEE Trans. Inf. Theory* **2012**, *58*, 3787–3797. [CrossRef]
19. Khalil, M.; Khattab, T.; El-Keyi, A.; Nafie, M. On the degrees of freedom region of the $M \times N$ interference channel. In Proceedings of the IEEE Canadian Conference on Electrical and Computer Engineering, Vancouver, BC, Canada, 15–18 May 2016. [CrossRef]
20. Ruan, L.; Lau, V.K.N. Dynamic interference mitigation for generalized partially connected quasi-static MIMO interference channel. *IEEE Trans. Signal Process.* **2011**, *59*, 3788–3798.
21. Khatiwada, M.; Choi, S.W. On the interference management for K-user partially connected fading interference channels. *IEEE Trans. Commun.* **2012**, *60*, 3717–3725. [CrossRef]
22. Gou, T.; da Silva, C.R.C.M.; Lee, J.; Kang, I. Partially connected interference networks with No CSIT: Symmetric degrees of freedom and multicast across alignment blocks. *IEEE Commun. Lett.* **2013**, *17*, 1893–1896. [CrossRef]
23. Liu, T.; Yang, C. On the degrees of freedom of partially-connected symmetrically-configured MIMO interference broadcast channels. In Proceedings of the IEEE International Conference on Acoustics, Speech and Signal Processing, Florence, Italy, 4–9 May 2014. [CrossRef]
24. Liu, G.; Sheng, M.; Wang, X.; Jiao, W.; Li, Y.; Li, J. Interference alignment for partially connected downlink MIMO heterogeneous networks. *IEEE Trans. Commun.* **2015**, *63*, 551–564.
25. Liu, W.; Cai, J.; Li, J.; Sheng, M. Interference alignment with finite extensions in partially connected networks. *IEEE Trans. Commun.* **2017**, *65*, 851–862. [CrossRef]
26. Zhao, N.; Yu, F.R.; Jin, M.; Yan, Q.; Leung, V.C. Interference alignment and its applications: A survey, research issues, and challenges. *IEEE Commun. Soc. Mag.* **2016**, *18*, 1779–1803. [CrossRef]
27. Wang, Q.; Shu, Y.; Dong, M.; Xu, J.; Tao, X. Degrees of freedom of 3-user MIMO interference channels with instantaneous relay using interference alignment. *KSII Trans. Internet Inf. Syst.* **2015**, *9*, 1624–1641. [CrossRef]

28. Cheng, Z.; Devroye, N.; Liu, T. The degrees of freedom of fullduplex bidirectional interference networks with and without a MIMO relay. *IEEE Trans. Wirel. Commun.* **2016**, *15*, 2912–2924.
29. Liu, T.; Tuninetti, D.; Chung, S.Y. On the DoF region of the MIMO Gaussian two-user interference channel with an instantaneous relay. *IEEE Trans. Inf. Theory* **2017**, *63*, 4453–4471. [CrossRef]
30. Azari, A. On the DoF and secure DoF of K-user MIMO interference channel with instantaneous relays. *Wirel. Netw.* **2020**, *26*, 1921–1936. [CrossRef]
31. Abdollahi Bafghi, A.H.; Jamali, V.; Nasiri-Kenari, M.; Schober, R. Degrees of freedom of the K-user interference channel assisted by active and passive IRSs. *IEEE Trans. Commun.* **2022**, *70*, 3063–3080. [CrossRef]
32. Jiang, T.; Yu, W. Interference nulling using reconfigurable intelligent surface. *IEEE J. Sel. Areas Commun.* **2022**, *40*, 1392–1406. [CrossRef]
33. Cadambe, V.R.; Jafar, S.A. Interference alignment and the degrees of freedom of wireless X-networks. *IEEE Trans. Inf. Theory* **2009**, *55*, 3893–3908. [CrossRef]
34. Abdollahi Bafghi, A.H.; Jamali, V.; Nasiri-Kenari, M.; Schober, R. Degrees of freedom of the K-user interference channel in the presence of intelligent reflecting surfaces. *arXiv* **2020**, arXiv:2012.13787. Available online: https://arxiv.org/abs/2012.13787 (accessed on 26 December 2020). [CrossRef]
35. Abdollahi Bafghi, A.H.; Mirmohseni, M.; Ashtiani, F.; Nasiri-Kenari, M. Joint optimization of power consumption and transmission delay in a cache-enabled C-RAN. *IEEE Wirel. Commun. Lett.* **2020**, *9*, 1137–1140. [CrossRef]
36. Lagen, S.; Agustin, A.; Vidal, J. Coexisting linear and widely linear transceivers in the MIMO interference channel. *IEEE Trans. Signal Process.* **2016**, *64*, 652–664. [CrossRef]
37. Soleymani, M.; Santamaria, I.; Schreier, P.J. Improper Gaussian signaling for the K-user MIMO interference channels with hardware impairments. *IEEE Trans. Veh. Technol.* **2020**, *69*, 11632–11645.
38. Cover, T.; Thomas, J.A. *Elements of Information Theory*; Wiley-Interscience: Hoboken, NJ, USA, 2006. [CrossRef]
39. Cadambe, V.R.; Jafar, S.A.; Wang, C. Interference alignment with asymmetric complex signaling—Settling the Høst–Madsen–Nosratinia conjecture. *IEEE Trans. Inf. Theory* **2010**, *56*, 4552–4565. [CrossRef]
40. Medra, A.; Davidson, T.N. Widely linear interference alignment precoding. In Proceedings of the International Workshop on Signal Processing Advances in Wireless Communications (SPAWC), Toronto, ON, Canada, 22–25 June 2014. [CrossRef]

entropy

Review

Coding for Large-Scale Distributed Machine Learning

Ming Xiao * and Mikael Skoglund *

Division of Information Science and Engineering, Royal Institute of Technology, Malvinas Vag 10, KTH, 100-44 Stockholm, Sweden
* Correspondence: mingx@kth.se (M.X.); skoglund@kth.se (M.S.)

Abstract: This article aims to give a comprehensive and rigorous review of the principles and recent development of coding for large-scale distributed machine learning (DML). With increasing data volumes and the pervasive deployment of sensors and computing machines, machine learning has become more distributed. Moreover, the involved computing nodes and data volumes for learning tasks have also increased significantly. For large-scale distributed learning systems, significant challenges have appeared in terms of delay, errors, efficiency, etc. To address the problems, various error-control or performance-boosting schemes have been proposed recently for different aspects, such as the duplication of computing nodes. More recently, error-control coding has been investigated for DML to improve reliability and efficiency. The benefits of coding for DML include high-efficiency, low complexity, etc. Despite the benefits and recent progress, however, there is still a lack of comprehensive survey on this topic, especially for large-scale learning. This paper seeks to introduce the theories and algorithms of coding for DML. For primal-based DML schemes, we first discuss the gradient coding with the optimal code distance. Then, we introduce random coding for gradient-based DML. For primal–dual-based DML, i.e., ADMM (alternating direction method of multipliers), we propose a separate coding method for two steps of distributed optimization. Then coding schemes for different steps are discussed. Finally, a few potential directions for future works are also given.

Keywords: error-control coding; gradient coding; random codes; ADMM

Citation: Xiao, M.; Skoglund, M. Coding for Large-Scale Distributed Machine Learning. *Entropy* **2022**, *24*, 1284. https://doi.org/10.3390/e24091284

Academic Editor: H. Vincent Poor, Onur Günlü, Rafael F. Schaefer and Holger Boche

Received: 12 August 2022
Accepted: 8 September 2022
Published: 12 September 2022

1. Background and Motivations

With the fast development of computing and communication technologies, and emerging data-driven applications, e.g., IoT (Internet of Things), social network analysis, smart grids and vehicular networks, the volume of data for various intelligent systems with machine learning has increased explosively along with the number of involved computing nodes [1], i.e., in a large scale. For instance, learning systems based on MAPReduce [2] have been widely used and may often reach the data volume of petabytes (10^{15} bytes), which may be produced and stored in thousands of separated nodes [3,4]. Large-scale machine learning is pervasive in our societies and industries. Meanwhile, it is inefficient (sometimes even infeasible) to transmit all data to a central node for analysis. For the reason, distributed machine learning (DML), which stores and processes all or parts of data in different nodes, has attracted significant research interests and applications [1,3–16]. There are different methods of implementing DML, i.e., primal method (e.g., distributed gradient descend [4,7], federated learning [5,6]) and primal–dual method (e.g., alternating direction method of multipliers (ADMM)) [16]. In a DML system, participating nodes (i.e., agents or workers) normally process local data and send the learning model information to other nodes for consensus. For instance, in a typical federated learning system [5,6], worker nodes run multiple rounds of gradient descends (local epoch) with local data and received global models. Then, the updated local models are sent to the server for aggregating into new global models (normally weighted sum). The models are normally much shorter than raw data. Thus, significant communication costs are saved by federated learning, and meanwhile the transmission of models in general has better privacy than sending raw data over networks. Actually, in addition to federated learning, other DML also has the benefits of communication efficiency and improved privacy since model information has, in general, smaller volumes and better privacy than raw data.

Despite various benefits, there are severe challenges for the implementation of DML, especially for large-scale DML. Ideally, DML algorithms have speedup gains, which should scale linearly with the number of participating learning machines (computing nodes). However, the practical speedup gain of DML is limited by various bottlenecks, and is still far from the theoretical upper limits [17,18]. Among others, significant bottlenecks include communication loads, security, global convergence, synchronization, slow computing nodes, complex optimization functions, etc. For instance, due to the limitation of computing capability and communication networks, a part of the computing nodes may have slow response and become the bottleneck of DML systems if the fast-response nodes have to wait for them. These nodes are often referred to as straggler nodes [4], and also called system noise [19]. To efficiently combat the straggler nodes, many schemes have been proposed, such as repetition nodes [20,21], blacklisting straggler nodes [22] and error-control codes [4,8–14,23–25]. Blacklisting method detects the straggler nodes and will not schedule more tasks to them. Thus, it is a type of *after-event* approach. The repetition of computing nodes needs lots of resources and a suitable mechanism to detect straggler nodes and find corresponding repetition nodes. Moreover, it is rather expensive to repeat all computing tasks and related data. More recently, error-control coding was proposed for DML by regarding straggler nodes as erasure, which can be corrected by coded data from non-straggler nodes and are shown to be much more efficient than the schemes based on replication. Error-control coding can correct the loss by straggler nodes of current learning rounds and thus is a type of *current-event* approach.

In [8], more practical computing networks with hierarchical structures were studied. For such networks, hierarchical coding schemes based on multiple MDS codes were proposed to reduce computation time. In [9], each multiplication matrix was further divided into sub-matrices, and all sub-matrices were encoded by MDS codes (e.g., Reed–Solomon codes). Thus, the computed parts in straggler nodes can be exploited, and the computing time can be further reduced. However, as the number of nodes and sub-matrices increases, the complexity of the MDS codes will increase substantially. In [25], the deterministic construction of Reed–Solomon codes was proposed for gradient-based DML. The generator matrix of the codes in [25] is sparse and well balanced, and thus the waiting time is reduced for gradient computation. In [10], a new entangled polynomial coding scheme was proposed to minimize the recover threshold of master–worker networks with generalized configurations for matrix-multiplication-based DML. In [26,27], coding schemes are considered for matrix multiplication in heterogeneous computing networks. However, the complexity of coding in [26,27] is still very high for large-scale DML since matrix inversion is used for decoding, and moreover, the coding matrix is pre-fixed and is hard to adapt to varying networks. In [28], low-complexity decoding was proposed for matrix multiplication for DML. However, the results in [28] are preliminary and hard to be used for heterogeneous networks, and the communication load is still very high. In [11], coding schemes based on the Lagrange polynomial are proposed to encode blocks among worker nodes. The proposed codes may achieve optimal tradeoffs among redundancy (against straggler nodes), security (against Byzantine modification) and privacy. However, the coding scheme in [11] is also based on MDS codes, which may not be flexible and have high complexity for large-scale DML. Furthermore, the existing coding schemes are mostly for matrix multiplication (for distributed gradient descend), i.e., the primal method. Another important class of large-scale DML is based on primal-dual methods, i.e., ADMM [16], for which codes have seldom been studied. Thus, coding for ADMM based large-scale DML should be developed to combat straggler nodes, reduce communication loads and increase efficiency.

Despite the progress in coding for straggler nodes [4,8–14,24,25], the results are still preliminary and there are also various critical challenges for exploiting the advantages of DML, especially for *large-scale learning*: (1) Reliability and complexity—though coding has been proposed for addressing the straggler nodes to improve reliability, the existed schemes are mainly for the systems with a limited number of nodes or data. The coded DML schemes based on existing optimal error-control codes (i.e., maximum distance separable: MDS codes) [4,24,25] have very high encoding/decoding complexity when the number of involved nodes or the data volume scales up. Moreover, MDS codes treat every coding node equally and are not optimal for heterogeneous networks (e.g., IoT or mobile networks). (2) Communication loads—with increasing nodes or data volumes, the communication loads will quickly increase for exchanging model updates among learning nodes. Thus, coding schemes efficient in communication loads are critical for large-scale DML. (3) Limited learning functions—most of the existing coding schemes for DML are for gradient descend (primal method), i.e., combining coding with matrix multiplication and/or data shuffling [4,8–14,24,25]. Coding for many other important distributed learning functions, e.g., primal–dual optimization functions (also may be non-smooth or non-convex) in ADMM has seldom been explored. Moreover, existing coding for DML often runs in a master–worker structure, which may not be efficient (or even infeasible) for certain applications, e.g., those without master nodes. Thus, coding for fully decentralized DML should be also investigated. By encoding the messages to (or/and from) different destinations/sources in intermediate nodes, network coding shows the benefits of reducing information flow in the networks [29,30]. Moreover, it has been shown that network coding can improve the reliability and security of communication networks [12,31,32]. Thus, it is also valuable to discuss the applications of network coding to DML.

In what follows, we first introduce the basics on DML in Section 2. Then we discuss how error-control coding can help with the straggler problem in Section 3, the random coding construction in Section 4, and coding for primal–dual-based DML (ADMM) in Section 5. Finally, conclusions and discussion for future works are given in Section 6.

2. Introduction of Distributed Machine Learning

In general, DML will have two steps: (1) Agents learn local models from local data, maybe combining with global models. This step may iterate multiple rounds, i.e., local iterations, to produce a local model. (2) With local models, agents will reach consensus. These two steps may also iterate multiple rounds, i.e., global iterations. There are also different methods to implement the two steps, for instance, the primal and primal–dual methods as mentioned above. There are different ways to achieve consensus, for instance, through a central server, i.e., master–slave method or fully decentralized. For the former, the implementation is relatively straightforward. Yet, for the latter, there are also different approaches as will be discussed later on. For Step (1), the common local learning machine includes, for example, linear (polynomial) regressions, classification and neural networks. The common approach of these learning algorithms is to find the model parameters (e.g., weights in neural networks) that minimize the cost functions (such as mean-squared errors/L2 loss, hinge loss and cross-entropy loss). In general, convex cost functions should be chosen. For instance, for linear regression, we assume x, y as the input and output of the training data, respectively, and w (normally a matrix or a vector) as the weight to be optimized. If the mean-squared error cost functions are used, then the learning machine works as

$$\min_{w} \parallel xw - y \parallel^2 . \tag{1}$$

To find the optimal w, one common approach is to use gradient descend, which is a first-order iterative optimization algorithm for finding a local minimum of a differentiable function. If the cost function is convex, then the local minimum is also the global minimum [33]. For instance, in the training process of neural networks, gradient descend is commonly used to find the optimized weight and bias iteratively. The gradient is found by partial derivative of cost functions relative to optimizing variables (weight and bias of training examples). For instance, for node i, the optimizing variables can be updated by

$$w_{t+1}^i = w_t^i - \gamma \nabla F(w_t^i, D_i), \tag{2}$$

where t is the iteration step index, γ is the step size, D_i is the data set (training samples) in node i, $F(w_t^i)$ is the cost function with current optimizing variables, and $\nabla F(w_t^i, D_i)$ denotes the gradients for given (w_t^i, D_i) (by partial derivatives). The training process is normally performed in batches of data. D_i can be further divided into subsets, e.g., N subsets, i.e., $D_i = \{D_i^1, D_i^2, \cdots, D_i^N\}$. If subsets are exclusive, the gradients from different subsets are independent, i.e., $\nabla F(w_t^i, D_i) = \{\nabla F(w_t^i, D_i^1), \nabla F(w_t^i, D_i^2), \cdots, \nabla F(w_t^i, D_i^N)\}$. However, in many DML systems, e.g., those based on MAPReduce file systems, or sensor nodes in neighboring areas, there may be overlapping data subsets, i.e., $D_i^k = D_j^n$ for certain k, n and $i \neq j$. Therefore, there may be identical gradients in different nodes. These properties were recently exploited for coding. It it clear from (2) that for given gradients, the steps of finding optimal parameters are mainly linear matrix operations (matrix multiplications). Actually, in addition to neural networks, one core operation of many other learning algorithms is also matrix multiplications, such as regression, power-iteration-like algorithms, etc. [4]. Thus, one of the major coding schemes for DML is based on the matrix multiplication of the learning process [4,8–14,24,25]. Clearly, major coding schemes (forward error-control coding and network coding) are linear in terms of encoding and decoding operations, i.e., $C = M \times W$, where C, M and W are codeword (vectors), coding matrix and information message, respectively. Since both learning and coding operations are linear matrix operations, then the coding matrix and learning matrix can be *jointly* optimized. On the other hand, coding can be optimized to provide efficient and reliable information pipelines for DML systems. In such way, coding and DML matrices are *separately* optimized. Separate optimization actually has been widely studied for many years for existing systems due to the simpler design relative to joint design. There are many works in the literature on the separate optimization of learning systems and coding schemes. We will focus on joint design in this article.

3. Coding for Reliable Large-Scale DML

In this section, we will first give a review on the basic principles of coding for reliable DML. Then, we will discuss two optimal construction of codes for DML.

One toy example of how coding can help to deal with stragglers can be found in Figure 1 [34]. For instance, it can be a federated learning network with worker and server nodes. There is partial overlapping for data segments in different worker nodes and thus the partial overlapping of gradients. As in Figure 1, we divide the data set of a node into multiple smaller sets to denote the partial overlapping of different nodes. Meanwhile, multiple sets in a node are also necessary for encoding as shown in the figure since one data set corresponds to one source symbol of the code. In the server node, a weight sum of the gradient is needed. In the figure, three worker nodes have different data parts of D_1, D_2, D_3, which are used to compute gradients G_1, G_2, G_3, respectively. In the server, an individual gradient is not needed but only their sum $G_s = G_1 + G_2 + G_3$. We can easily see that gradients from *any* two nodes can calculate G_s. For instance, if worker3 is outage, then $G_s = 2(G_1/2 + G_2) - (G_2 - G_3)$ with two transmission coded blocks from worker1 and worker2. If there is no coding, then worker1 and worker2 have to transmit G_1, G_2, G_3 separately with three blocks after the coordination operations. Thus, coding can save the transmission and also coordination loads.

Though the idea of applying coding for DML is straightforward as shown in the above toy example, the code design will be rather challenging for large-scale DML, i.e., when the numbers of nodes and/or gradients per node are very large. One big challenge is how to construct encoding and decoding matrices, especially with limited complexity. In what follows, we will first give a brief introduction of the MAPReduce file systems, which are often used in DML. Then, we will discuss the coding schemes with deterministic construction [34]. The random construction based on fountain codes is given in the next section, which normally has lower complexity [13,14].

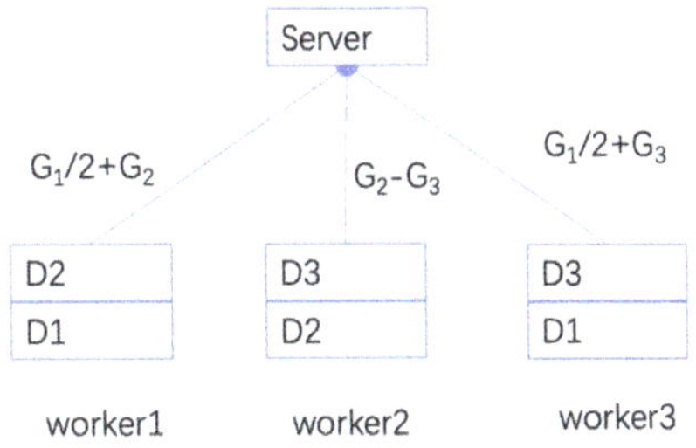

Figure 1. Coded DML with a master–worker structure can tolerate any of one straggler node.

In large DML systems, MAPReduce is a commonly used distributed file storage system. As shown in Figure 2, there are three stages for the MAPReduce file systems: map, shuffling and reduce. In the system, data are stored in different nodes. In the map stage, stored data are sent to different computing nodes (e.g., cloud computing nodes), according to pre-defined protocols. In the shuffling stage, the computed results (e.g., gradients) are exchanged among nodes. Finally, the end users will collect the computed results in the reduce stage. MAPReduce can be used in federated learning, which was originally proposed for the applications in mobile devices [5]. In such a scenario, data are first sent to different worker nodes in the map stage, according to certain design principles. Then in the shuffling stage, local model parameters are aggregated in the server node. Finally, the aggregated models are obtained in the final iteration at the server. In such a way, worker nodes have all necessary data for computing local models, sent from storage nodes. However, there may be straggling worker nodes, due to either slow computing at the node or transmission errors in the channels. In such scenario, gradient coding [34] can be used to correct the straggler nodes.

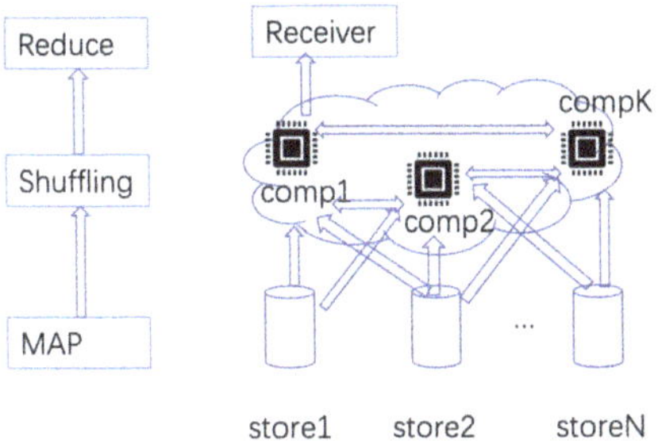

Figure 2. A common realization of DML based on MAPReduce.

To construct gradient coding, we use A to denote the possible straggler pattern multiplied by the corresponding decoding matrix, and B to denote how different gradients (or model parameters) are combined in the worker node. Thus, A denotes *transmission matrix multiplied by decoding* matrices in some sense (as they recover transmitting gradients from received coded symbols) and B can also be regarded as an *encoding* matrix. Assuming that k is the number of different gradients (data partitions) in all nodes and there are a total of n output channels in all nodes, the dimension of B is $n \times k$. Denoting $\bar{g} = [g_1, g_2, \cdots, g_k]^T$ as the vector of all gradients, then worker node i transmits $b_i\bar{g}$, where b_i is the i-th row of B and the encoding vector at node i. The dimension of A is $k \times n$. A row of A corresponds to an instance of straggling patterns, in which 0 means a straggler node and how the gradients are reproduced in the server. Thus, all rows in A denote all possible ways of straggling. Denoting f as the number of surviving workers (none-stragglers), there are at most $n - f$ 0s in each row of A. In the example of Figure 1, we only need the sum of gradients from worker nodes instead of the values of individual gradients. Thus, we have $AB = \mathbf{1}_{k\times k}$

and each row of $AB\bar{g}$ is identically $G_1 + G_2 + G_3$, where $\mathbf{1}_{k\times k}$ denotes all 1 matrix. For the example, we can easily see that

$$A = \begin{Bmatrix} 0 & 1 & 2 \\ 1 & 0 & 1 \\ 2 & -1 & 0 \end{Bmatrix}, \quad \text{and} \quad B = \begin{Bmatrix} 1/2 & 1 & 0 \\ 0 & 1 & -1 \\ 1/2 & 0 & 1 \end{Bmatrix}. \tag{3}$$

Clearly, if we want individual values of $\bar{g}$, we should redesign A, B such that AB is an identity matrix. Or if we want the weighted sum of gradients (weights more general than 1), A, B should be also redesigned. From the description, we can see that the main challenge of designing the gradient coding is to find suitable encoding matrix B such that it can correct the straggling loss defined by A. In [34], two different ways of finding B and corresponding A are given, i.e., fractional repetition and cyclic repetition schemes as detailed in the following.

We denote n and s as the number of worker nodes and straggler nodes, respectively, and assume n is a multiple of $s+1$. Then, fractional repetition construction is described as the following steps.

- Divide n workers into $s+1$ groups of size $n/(s+1)$;
- In each group, divide all the data equally and disjointly, assigning $s+1$ partitions to each worker;
- All the groups are replicas of each other;
- After local computing, every worker transmits the sum of its partial gradient.

By the second step, in a group, the first worker obtains the first $s+1$ partitions from the map stage and computes the first $s+1$ gradients, and the second worker obtains the second $s+1$ partition from the map stage and computes the second $s+1$ gradient and so on. The encoding of each group of workers can be denoted by a block matrix $\bar{B}_{block}(n,s) \in \mathbb{R}^{\frac{n}{s+1}\times n}$ with

$$\bar{B}_{block}(n,s) = \begin{bmatrix} \mathbf{1}_{1\times(s+1)} & \mathbf{0}_{1\times(s+1)} & \cdots & \mathbf{0}_{1\times(s+1)} \\ \mathbf{0}_{1\times(s+1)} & \mathbf{1}_{1\times(s+1)} & \cdots & \mathbf{0}_{1\times(s+1)} \\ \vdots & \vdots & \ddots & \vdots \\ \mathbf{0}_{1\times(s+1)} & \mathbf{0}_{1\times(s+1)} & \cdots & \mathbf{1}_{1\times(s+1)} \end{bmatrix}_{\frac{n}{s+1}\times n}. \tag{4}$$

Here $\mathbf{1}_{1\times(s+1)}$ and $\mathbf{0}_{1\times(s+1)}$ means $1\times(s+1)$ matrix of all 1 s and all 0 s (row vector), respectively. Then B is obtained by replicating $s+1$ copies of $\bar{B}_{block}(n,s)$, i.e.,

$$B = B_{frac} = \begin{bmatrix} \bar{B}^1_{block}(n,s) \\ \bar{B}^2_{block}(n,s) \\ \vdots \\ \bar{B}^{(s+1)}_{block}(n,s) \end{bmatrix}, \tag{5}$$

where $\bar{B}^i_{block}(n,s) = \bar{B}_{block}(n,s)$, for $i \in \{1,\cdots,s+1\}$. In addition to the encoding matrix B_{frac}, reference [34] also gives the algorithms of constructing the corresponding A matrix as follows.

It was shown in [34] that by fractional repetition schemes, $B = B_{frac}$ from (5) and A from Algorithm 1 can correct any s straggler. It can be more formally stated as the following theorem.

Algorithm 1 Algorithm to compute A for fractional repetition coding.

Input: $B = B_{frac}$;
$f \leftarrow \text{binom}(n,s)$ $\;A \leftarrow \text{zeros}(f,n)$ **for** $I \subseteq [n], s.t.|I| = (n-s)$ **do**
$\quad a = \text{zeros}(1,k)$ $\;x = \text{ones}(1,k)/B(I,:)$ $\;a(I) = x$ $\;A = [A;a]$
Output: A s.t. $AB = \underline{1}_{f\times k}$;

Theorem 1. *Consider $B = B_{frac}$ from (5) for a given number of workers n and stragglers $s(< n)$. Then, the scheme (A, B_{frac}), with A from Algorithm 1 is robust to any s straggler.*

Here, we refer the interested readers to [34] for the proof. In addition to fractional repetition construction, another way of finding the B matrix is the cyclic repetition scheme, which does not require n to be a multiple of $s+1$. The algorithm to construct the cyclic repetition B matrix is given as follows.

Actually, the resultant matrix $B = B_{cyc}$ from Algorithm 2 has the following support (non-zero parts):

$$supp(B_{cyc}) = \begin{bmatrix} * & * & \cdots & * & * & 0 & 0 & \cdots & 0 & 0 \\ 0 & * & * & \cdots & * & * & 0 & \cdots & 0 & 0 \\ \vdots & \vdots & \vdots & \vdots & \vdots & \vdots & \ddots & \ddots & \vdots & \vdots \\ 0 & 0 & \cdots & 0 & 0 & * & * & \cdots & * & * \\ \vdots & \vdots & \vdots & \vdots & \vdots & \vdots & \ddots & \ddots & \vdots & \vdots \\ * & \cdots & * & * & 0 & 0 & \cdots & 0 & 0 & * \end{bmatrix}, \quad (6)$$

where $*$ is the non-zero entries in B_{cyc}, and in each row of $supp(B_{cyc})$, there are $(s+1)$ non-zero entries. The position of non-zero entries is right shifted one step and cycled around until the last row. The construction of A matrix follows Algorithm 1 also for B_{cyc}. It was shown in [34] that cyclic repetition schemes can also correct any s stragglers:

Algorithm 2 Algorithm to construct $B = B_{cyc}$.

Input: $n, s(< n)$;
$H = \text{binom}(n, s)$ $H = -\text{sum}(H(:, 1 : n-1), 2)$ $B = \text{zeros}(n)$ **for** $i = 1 : n$ **do**
  $j = \text{mod}(i - 1 : s + i - 1, n) + 1$ $B(i, j) = [1; -H(:, j(2 : s+1))] \setminus H(:, j(1))]$
Output: $B \in \mathbb{R}^{n \times n}$ with $(s+1)$ non-zeros in each row.

Theorem 2. *Consider $B = B_{cyc}$ from Algorithm 2, for a given number of workers n and stragglers $s(< n)$. Then, the scheme (A, B_{cyc}), with A from Algorithm 1 is robust to any s straggler.*

Fractional repetition and cyclic repetition schemes provide specific methods of encoding and decoding for master–worker DML for tolerating any s stragglers. More generally, it was also shown in [34] the necessary conditions for matrix B for tolerating any s stragglers if the following conditions are satisfied.

Condition 1 (B-Span): Consider any scheme (A, B) robust to any s stragglers, given $n(s < n)$ workers, then every subset $(I) \subseteq \text{span}\{b_i | i \in (I)\}$ is satisfied, where $\text{span}\{\cdot\}$ is the span of vectors.

If A matrix is constructed by Algorithm 1, (A, B) with Condition 1 is also sufficient.

Corollary 1. *If A matrix is constructed by Algorithm 1 and B satisfies Condition 1, (A, B) can correct any s stragglers.*

Numerical results: In Figure 3, the average time per iteration for different schemes is compared from [34]. In *naive scheme*, the data are divided uniformly across all workers without replication, and the master just waits for all workers to send their gradients. In *ignoring the s straggler scheme*, the data distribution is the same as the naive scheme. However, the master node only waits until $n - s$ worker nodes successfully send their gradients (no need to wait for all gradients). Thus, as discussed in [34], ignoring the straggler scheme may lose in the generalization performance by ignoring a part of data sets of straggler nodes. The running learning algorithms are based on logistic regression. The training data are from the Amazon Employee Access dataset from Kaggle. The delay is introduced by the computing latency of AWS clusters, and there is no transmission error.

As shown in the figure, the naive scheme performs the worst. With increasing stragglers, coding schemes also perform better than ignoring straggler schemes as expected.

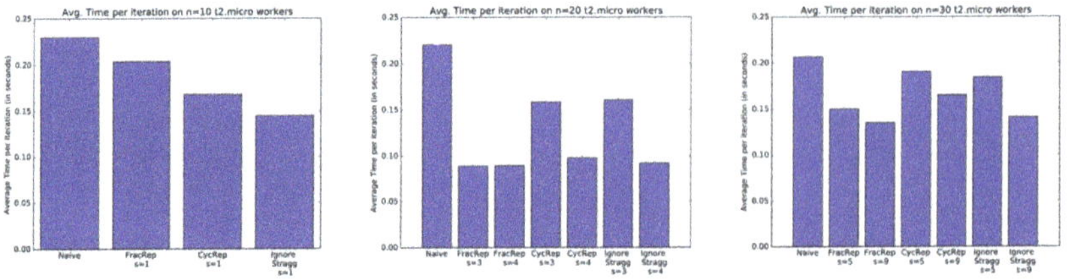

Figure 3. Comparison average time per iteration on Amazon employee access dataset [34].

4. Random Coding Construction for Large-Scale DML

The gradient coding in [34] works well for the DML scheme with a master–worker structure with limited sizes (finite number of nodes and limited data partitions). However, the deterministic construction of encoding and decoding matrices may be challenging when the number of nodes or data partitions (e.g., n or k) is large. The first challenge is the complexity of encoding and decoding, both of which are based on matrix multiplication, which may be rather complex, especially for decoding (e.g., based on Gaussian elimination). Though DML with MDS codes is optimal in terms of code distance (i.e., the degree of tolerance to the amount of straggler nodes), the coding complexity will be rather high with the increasing number of participating nodes, i.e., for hundreds or even thousands of computing nodes. For instance, Reed–Solomon codes normally need to run in non-binary fields, which are of high complexity. Another challenge is lack of flexibility. Both factional repetition and cyclic repetition coding schemes assume static networks (worker nodes and data). However, in practice, the participating nodes may be varying in mobile nodes or sensors, for example. In the mobile computing scenario, the number of participating nodes may be unknown. It will rather difficult to design deterministic coding matrices (A or B) in such a scenario. Similarly, if the data are from sensors, the amount of data may also be varying. Thus, the deterministic construction of coding is hard to adapt to these scenarios, which, however, are very common in large-scale learning networks. Thus, coding schemes efficient in varying networks and of low complexity are preferable for large-scale DML. In [13,14], we investigated the random coding for DML (or distributed computing in general) to address the problems. Our coding scheme is based on fountain codes [35–37]. The coding scheme is introduced as follows.

Encoding Phase: As shown in Figure 4, we consider a network with multiple storage and computing/fog nodes. Let FN_f denote the f-th fog node and let SU_s denote the s-th storage unit with $f \in \{1, 2, \cdots, F\}$ and $s \in \{1, 2, \cdots, S\}$, respectively. Let D_f denote the dataset node f needed to finish a learning task. D_f will be obtained from the storage units available to node f. For instance, in a DML with wireless links as in Figure 4, D_f means the data union for all the storage units within the communication range of FN_f (i.e., within R_f). Similar to federated learning, FN_f will use the current model parameters to calculate gradients, namely, intermediate gradients, denoted as $g_f = [g_{f,1}, g_{f,2}, \cdots, g_{f,|D_f|}]$, where $g_{f,a}$ means the gradient trained by data $a (a \in D_f)$ and $|D_f|$ is the size of D_f. Meanwhile, fog nodes need to calculate the intermediate model parameters (e.g., weight) $w_f = [w_{f,1}, w_{f,2}, \cdots, w_{f,|w_f|}]$, where $|w_f|$ is the length of model parameters learned at FN_f. Then the intermediate gradients and model parameters will be sent out to other fog nodes (or the central sever if there is one) for further processing after encoding. The coding process for g_f is as follows.

- A number d_g is selected according to degree distribution $\Omega(x) = \sum_{d_g=1}^{|D_f|} \Omega_{d_g} x^{d_g}$ with probability $\Omega_{d_g} x^{d_g}$;

- Then, d_g intermediate gradients are selected uniformly at random from g_f to encode into one coded intermediate gradient;
- The above two steps repeated until $Q_f^g = (1+\eta_f)|D_f|$ coded intermediate gradients are formed, where $\eta_f(\geq 0)$ is the expanding coefficient of the fountain codes (denoting redundancy).

$\Omega(x)$ can be optimized by the probability of straggling (regarded as erasure) due to channel errors, slow computing, etc. The optimization of the degree distribution for distributed fountain codes can be found in, for example, [38], and we will not discuss it here for space limitation. With the above coding process, the resulted coded intermediate gradients are

$$c_f^g = [g_{f,1}, g_{f,2}, \cdots, g_{f,|D_f|}]G_f^g = g_f G_f^g, \tag{7}$$

where G_f^g is the generator matrix at fog node FN_f. The encoding process for w_f is the same as that of g_f with a possibly different degree distribution $\mu(x) = \sum_{d_w=1}^{w_f} \mu_{d_w} x^{d_w}$. The formed $Q_f^w = (1+\eta_f)w_f$ coded intermediate parameters can be written as $c_f^w = w_f G_f^w$, where G_f^w is the generator matrix at FN_f for model parameters.

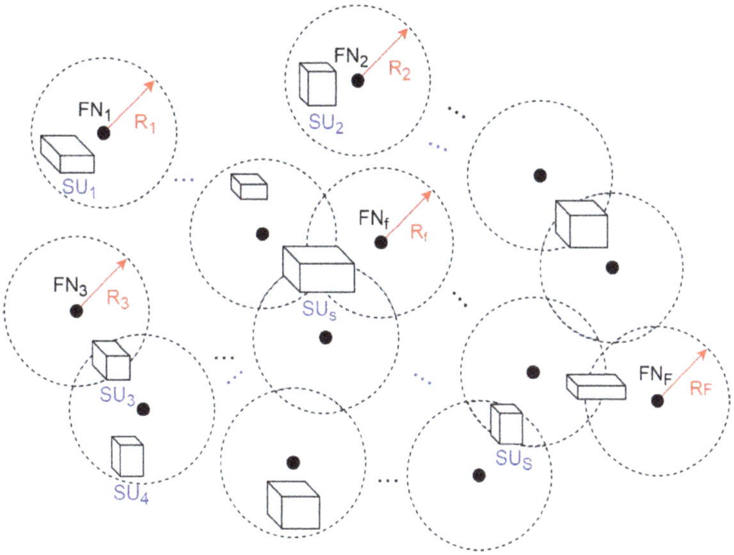

Figure 4. Distributed machine learning with multiple data storage and computing/fog nodes.

Exchanging Phase: The coded intermediate gradients c_f^g and model parameters c_f^w, $(f \in \{1,2,\cdots,N\})$ are exchanged among fog nodes. Let M be the total number of all different data in all F nodes, $M \leq \sum_{f=1}^{F} |D_f|$. The equality holds only if F datasets are disjoint.

Decoding Phase: The generator matrices for the received coded intermediate gradients and model parameters from fog node $FN_i(i \in \{1,2,\cdots,F\}) \setminus \{f\}$ at FN_f are $\tilde{G}_{i,f}^g$ with size $|G| \times Q_{i,f}^g$ and $\tilde{G}_{i,f}^w$ with size $w_i \times Q_{i,f}^w$, respectively, where $Q_{i,f}^g = (1-\epsilon_{i,f})Q_i^g$ and $Q_{i,f}^w = (1-\epsilon_{i,f})Q_i^w$. Here $\epsilon_{i,f}$ denotes the straggling probability from FN_i to FN_f due to various reasons, e.g., physical-layer erasure, slow computing, and congestion. Thus, the generator matrices corresponding to the received coded intermediate gradient and model parameters at FN_f can be written as $\tilde{G}_f^g = [\mathbf{1}_1\tilde{G}_{1,f}^g, \cdots, \mathbf{1}_{f-1}\tilde{G}_{f-1,f}^g, \mathbf{1}_{f+1}\tilde{G}_{f+1,f}^g, \cdots, \mathbf{1}_F\tilde{G}_{F,f}^g$ and $\tilde{G}_f^g = [\mathbf{1}_1\tilde{G}_{1,f}^g, \cdots, \mathbf{1}_{f-1}\tilde{G}_{f-1,f}^g, \mathbf{1}_{f+1}\tilde{G}_{f+1,f}^g, \cdots, \mathbf{1}_F\tilde{G}_{F,f}^g$ and $\tilde{G}_f^w = [\mathbf{1}_1\tilde{G}_{1,f}^w, \cdots, \mathbf{1}_{f-1}\tilde{G}_{f-1,f}^w,$

$\mathbf{1}_{f+1}\tilde{G}^{w}_{f+1,f}, \cdots, \mathbf{1}_F\tilde{G}^{w}_{F,f}$, respectively. Here $\mathbf{I} = \{\mathbf{1}_1, \cdots, \mathbf{1}_F\}$ is an indicator parameter. Let λ be the probability of straggling. Then, $\mathbf{I}_f, (f \in \{1, 2, \cdots, F\})$ can be evaluated as

$$\mathbf{I}_f = \begin{cases} 1, & \text{with probability} \quad 1 - \lambda, \\ 0, & \text{with probability} \quad \lambda. \end{cases} \tag{8}$$

Then fog node FN_f decodes the received coded intermediate parameters from $\tilde{G}^{g}_{i,f}$ and $\tilde{G}^{w}_{i,f}, (i \in \{1, 2, \cdots, F\} \setminus \{f\})$, and tried to decode $N - |D_f|$ new gradients and $\Gamma_w \sum_{i \in \{1,2,\cdots,F\} \setminus \{f\}} w_i$ model parameters, where $\Gamma_w \in [0, 1]$ is a parameter determined by specific learning algorithms. For the benefits of fountain codes (e.g., LT or Raptor codes), the iterative decoding is feasible if the numbers of received coded gradients or model parameters are slightly larger than those of gradients and models in transmitting fog nodes. Clearly, to optimize the code degree distribution and task allocation, it is critical for a node to know the number of received intermediate gradients and model parameters at the node. For the purpose, we have the following analysis.

Assume $\gamma_{a,b}$ as the overlapping ratio of the dataset in FN_a and FN_b, then for all fog nodes, we have the overlapping ratio as follows:

$$\gamma = \begin{bmatrix} 1 & \gamma_{1,2} & \cdots & \gamma_{1,F} \\ \gamma_{2,1} & 1 & \cdots & \gamma_{2,F} \\ \vdots & \vdots & \ddots & \vdots \\ \gamma_{F,1} & \gamma_{F,2} & \cdots & 1 \end{bmatrix}. \tag{9}$$

If $\gamma_{a,b} = 0$, then node FN_a and FN_b has disjoint datasets. At FN_f, $|D_f|$ intermediate gradients are known. Thus, $A = N - |D_f|$ new intermediate gradients are required for updating model parameters w_f. Then, we have the following result:

Theorem 3. *The total number of new intermediate gradients received from the other fog nodes at FN_f can be calculated by $\Delta = \sum_{\pi_i, i=1}^{F-1} \mathbf{1}_{\pi_i}((1 - \gamma_{\pi_i,f})\varphi(i,f)) \cdot |D_{\pi_i}|$, where $\varphi(i,f)$ can be written as*

$$\varphi(i,f)) = \begin{cases} 1, & \text{if} \quad i = 1, \\ \Pi_{a=1}^{i-1}(1 - \gamma_{\pi_i,\pi_i - \pi_a}|\Theta_{a,f}), & \text{if} \quad 2 \le i \le F-1, \end{cases} \tag{10}$$

where $\Theta_{a,f}$ is a set formed by the indices of fog nodes, and it can be evaluated by

$$\Theta_{a,f} = \begin{cases} \{f\}, & \text{if} \quad a = 1, \\ \{f, \pi_1, \cdots, \pi_{a-1}\}, & \text{if} \quad a > 1. \end{cases} \tag{11}$$

If γ is known at each fog node (or at least from the transmitted neighbors at each receiving node), then Δ can be evaluated, and the computation and communication loads can be optimized through proper task assignment and code degree optimization. Theorem 3 is for gradients, and a similar analysis also holds for model parameters. In Figure 5, we show the coding gains in terms of communication loads, which are defined as the ratio of the total number of data transmitted by all the fog nodes to the data required at these fog nodes. As we can see from the figure, if the number of nodes F or straggler probability increases, the coding gains increase as expected.

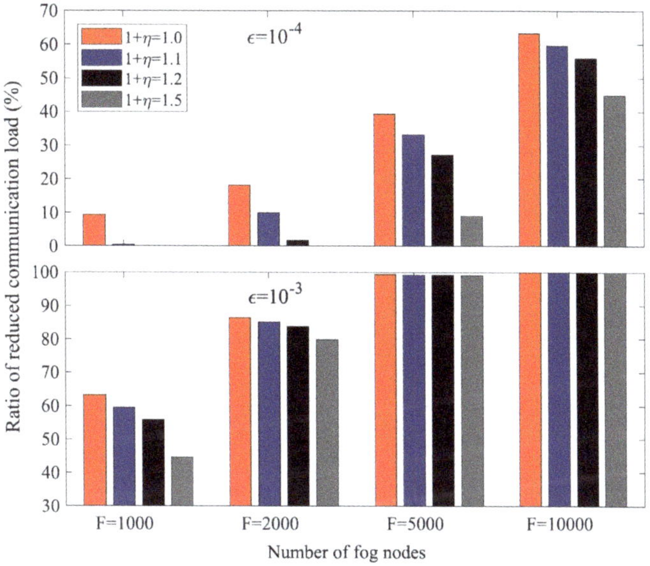

Figure 5. Ratio of coding gains relative to uncoded systems in communication loads.

We note that both deterministic codes in Section 3 and random construction coding here are actually a type of network coding [29,30], which can reduce communication loads by computing at intermediate nodes (fog nodes) [3,4]. More recently, one type of special network codes, i.e., BATS (batched sparse) codes, was proposed with two layered codes as shown in Figure 6. For outer codes, we can use error control codes such as fountain codes in MAP phase. For inner codes, network codes can be used such as random linear network codes in data shuffling stage. In [12], we studied BATS codes for fog computing networks. As shown in Figure 7, numerical results demonstrate that the BATS codes can achieve a lower communication load than uncoded and deterministic codes (network codes) if the computing load is lower than certain thresholds. Here, we skip further details and refer interested readers to [12].

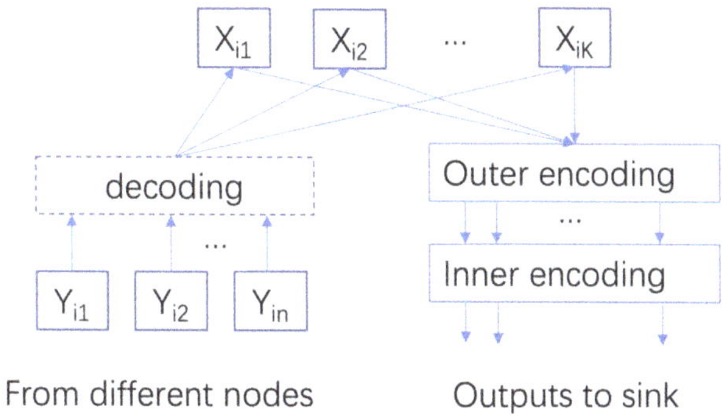

Figure 6. Large-scale distributed machine learning (DML) with BATS codes.

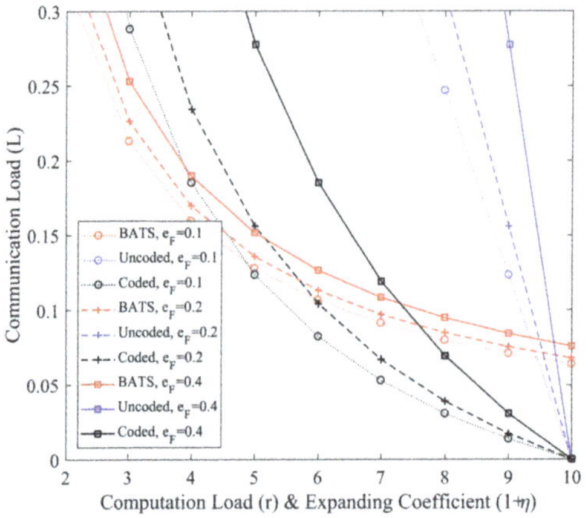

Figure 7. Communication load comparison among BATS codes, coded computing (deterministic codes) and uncoded [12]. e_F denotes the channel erasure probability and corresponds to straggling probability. The computing load is defined as involved computing nodes and thus corresponds to expanding coefficients.

5. Coding for ADMM

5.1. Introduction and System Setup

As a primal–dual optimization method, ADMM is shown to be able to generally converge at a rate of $\mathcal{O}(1/t)$ for convex functions, where t is the iteration number [16], which is often faster than the schemes based on primal methods. Meanwhile, ADMM also has the benefits of robustness to non-smooth/non-convex functions and being adaptive to fully decentralized implementation. Thus, ADMM is especially suitable for large-scale DML and has attracted substantial research interests. For DML, especially for the fully decentralized learning system without a central server, we can denote the learning network as $\mathcal{G} = (\mathcal{N}, \mathcal{E})$, where $\mathcal{N} = \{1, \ldots, N\}$ is the set of agents (computing nodes) and $\mathcal{E}$ is the set of links. For ADMM, agents aim at solving the following consensus optimization problem collaboratively:

$$\min_{x} \sum_{i=1}^{N} f_i(x; \mathcal{D}_i), \tag{12}$$

where $f_i : R^p \to R$ is the local optimization function of agent i, and $\mathcal{D}_i$ is the data set of agent i. All the agents share a global optimization variable $x \in R^n$. Data sets of different agent may have overlapping, i.e., $\mathcal{D}_i \cap \mathcal{D}_j \neq \emptyset$, for a part or all $i \neq j$. This can happen, for instance, among the sensors of nearby areas for weathers, traffic, smart grids, etc., or if MAPReduce is used, the same data are mapped to different agents. For ADMM, (12) is solved iteratively by a two-step process:

- Step (a), local optimization of f_i on receiving updated global variable and with $\mathcal{D}_i$ (normally by augmented Lagrangian as detailed below);
- Step (b), global variable x reaches consensus.

With DML, there are also straggler nodes and unreliable-link challenges for ADMM, especially for large-scale and heterogeneous networks or with wireless links. However, with primal–dual optimization, it is very hard (if possible) to transfer ADMM optimization process into a linear function (e.g., matrix multiplication as in gradient descend). Thus, coding schemes based on linear operations (e.g., matrix multiplication in [4,8–11,24,25]) are impossible to be directly used in ADMM and there are very few results on coding for ADMM so far, to our best knowledge. To address the problem, one solution is to use coding separately for two steps of ADMM. For instance, error control coding can be used for local optimization if the data are stored in different locations for an agent. For the global consensus, network coding can be used to reduce the communication loads and increase reliability. In [15], we preliminarily investigated how coding (MDS codes) can be used in local optimization (step (a)). A more detailed introduction is given as follows.

As depicted in Figure 8, a distributed computing system consists of multiple agents, each of which is connected with several edge computing nodes (ECNs). Agents can communicate with each other through links. ECNs are capable of processing data collected from sensors, and transferring desired messages (e.g., model updates) back to the connected agent. Based on the agent coverage and computing resources, the ECNs connected to agent $i(\in \mathcal{N})$ are denoted as $\mathcal{K}_i = \{1, \ldots, K_i\}$. This model is common in current intelligent systems, such as smart factories or homes.

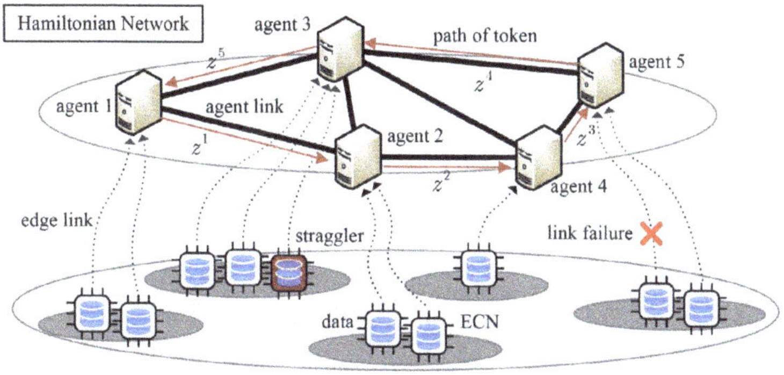

Figure 8. ADMM with multiple agents, each of which collect trained models from multiple ECNs with sensed data. Agents are connected via Hamiltonian networks.

The multi-agent system seeks to find out the optimal solution x^* by solving (12). $\mathcal{D}_i$ is allocated to dispersed ECNs K_i. The formulation of decentralized optimization problem can be described as follows. By defining $\boldsymbol{x} = [x_1, \ldots, x_N] \in \mathcal{R}^{pN \times d}$ and introducing a global variable $z \in \mathcal{R}^{p \times d}$, problem (12) can be reformulated as

$$(\text{P-1}) : \min_{\boldsymbol{x},z} \sum_{i=1}^{N} f_i(x_i; \mathcal{D}_i), \quad s.t. \, \mathbf{1} \otimes z - \boldsymbol{x} = \mathbf{0}, \tag{13}$$

where $\mathbf{1} = [1, \ldots, 1]^T \in \mathcal{R}^N$, and $\otimes$ is the Kronecker product. In the following, $f_i(x_i, \mathcal{D}_i)$ is denoted as $f_i(x_i)$ for simplifying illustration.

In what follows, we will present communication-efficient and straggler-tolerant decentralized algorithms, by which the agents can collaboratively find an optimal solution through local computations and limited information exchange among neighbors. In the scheme, local gradients are calculated in dispersed ECNs, while variables, including primal and dual variables and global variables z, are updated in the corresponding agent. For illustration purpose, we will first present stochastic ADMM (sI-ADMM) and then coded version of sI-ADMM (i.e., csI-ADMM). Both of them are proposed in [15]. The standard incremental ADMM iterations for decentralized consensus optimization will be reviewed first. The augmented Lagrangian function of problem (P-1) is

$$\mathcal{L}_\rho(\boldsymbol{x}, \boldsymbol{y}, z) = \sum_{i=1}^{N} f_i(x_i) + \langle \boldsymbol{y}, \mathbf{1} \otimes z - \boldsymbol{x} \rangle + \frac{\rho}{2} \|\mathbf{1} \otimes z - \boldsymbol{x}\|^2, \tag{14}$$

where $\boldsymbol{y} = [y_1, \ldots, y_N] \in \mathcal{R}^{pN \times d}$ is the dual variable, and $\rho > 0$ is a penalty parameter. With incremental ADMM (I-ADMM) [39,40], with guaranteeing $\sum_{i=1}^{N}(x_i^1 - \frac{y_i^1}{\rho}) = \mathbf{0}$ (e.g., initialize $x_i^1 = y_i^1 = \mathbf{0}$), the updates of $\boldsymbol{x}$, $\boldsymbol{y}$ and z at the $(k+1)$-th iteration follow:

$$x_i^{k+1} := \begin{cases} \arg\min_{x_i} f_i(x_i) + \frac{\rho}{2}\left\| z^k - x_i + \frac{y_i^k}{\rho} \right\|^2, \ i = i_k; \\ x_i^k, \text{ otherwise}; \end{cases} \tag{15a}$$

$$y_i^{k+1} := \begin{cases} y_i^k + \rho\left(z^k - x_i^{k+1}\right), \ i = i_k; \\ y_i^k, \text{ otherwise}; \end{cases} \tag{15b}$$

$$z^{k+1} := z^k + \frac{1}{N}\left[\left(x_{i_k}^{k+1} - x_{i_k}^k\right) - \frac{1}{\rho}\left(y_{i_k}^{k+1} - y_{i_k}^k\right)\right]. \tag{15c}$$

For ADMM, solving augmented Lagrangian especially for the x-update above may lead to rather high computational complexity. To achieve fast computation for x-update, *first-order* approximation and *mini-batch stochastic* optimization in (15a) can be adapted. Furthermore, a quadratic proximal term with parameter τ^k is proposed in [15] to stabilize the convergence behavior of the inexact augmented Lagrangian method. Ref. [15] also introduces the updating step-size γ^k for the dual update. Both parameters τ^k and γ^k can be adjusted with iteration k. Finally, the updates of $\boldsymbol{x}$ and $\boldsymbol{y}$ at the $(k+1)$-th iteration are presented as follows:

$$x_i^{k+1} := \begin{cases} \arg\min_{x_i} \left\langle \mathcal{G}_i(x_i^k; \boldsymbol{\xi}_i^k), x_i - x_i^k \right\rangle + \left\langle y_i^k, z^k - x_i \right\rangle \\ \quad + \frac{\rho}{2}\left\| z^k - x_i \right\|^2 + \frac{\tau^k}{2}\left\| x_i - x_i^k \right\|^2, \ i = i_k; \\ x_i^k, \text{ otherwise}; \end{cases} \tag{16a}$$

$$y_i^{k+1} := \begin{cases} y_i^k + \rho\gamma^k\left(z^k - x_i^{k+1}\right), \ i = i_k; \\ y_i^k, \text{ otherwise}; \end{cases} \tag{16b}$$

where $\mathcal{G}_i(x_i^k; \boldsymbol{\xi}_i^k)$ is the mini-batch stochastic gradient, which can be obtained through $\mathcal{G}_i(x_i^k; \boldsymbol{\xi}_i^k) = \frac{1}{M}\sum_{l=1}^{M} \nabla F_i(x_i^k; \xi_{i,l}^k)$. To be more specific, M is the mini-batch size of sampling data, $\boldsymbol{\xi}_i^k = \{\xi_{i,l}^k\}_M$ denotes a set of independent and identically distributed randomly selected samples in one batch, and $\nabla F_i(x_i^k; \xi_{i,l}^k)$ corresponds to the stochastic gradient of a single example $\xi_{i,l}^k$.

5.2. Mini-Batch Stochastic I-ADMM

For above setup of ADMM, *response time* is defined as the execution time for updating all variables in each iteration. In the updates, all steps, including x-update, y-update and z-update, are assumed to be in agents rather than ECNs. In practice, the update is often computed in a tandem order, which leads to a long response time. With the fast development of edge/fog computing, it is feasible to further reduce the response time since computing the local gradients can be dispersed to multiple edge nodes, as shown in Figure 8. Each ECN computes a gradient using local data and shares the result with its corresponding agent, and no information is directly exchanged among ECNs. Agents can be activated in a predetermined circulant pattern, e.g., according to a Hamiltonian cycle, and ECNs are activated whenever the connected agent is active, as shown in Figure 8. A Hamiltonian cycle based activation pattern is a cyclic pattern through a graph that visits each agent exactly once (i.e., $1 \to 2 \to 4 \to 5 \to 3$ in Figure 8). Correspondingly, the mini-batch stochastic incremental ADMM (sI-ADMM) [15] is presented in Algorithm 3. At agent i_k, global variable z^{k+1} gets updated and is passed as a token to the next agent i_{k+1} via a pre-determined traversing pattern, as shown in Figure 8. Specifically, in the k-th iteration with cycle index $m = \lfloor k/N \rfloor$, agent i_k is activated. Token z^k is first received and then the active agent broadcasts the local variable x_i^k to its attached ECNs $\mathcal{K}_i$. According to batch data with index $I_{i,j}^k$, new gradient $g_{i,j}$ is calculated in each ECN, followed by the gradient update, x-update, y-update and z-update in agent i_k, via steps 21–24 in Algorithm 3. At last, the global variable z^{k+1} is passed as a token to its neighbor i_{k+1}. In Algorithm 3, the stopping criterion is reached when $\left\| z^k - x_i^k \right\| \le \epsilon^{pri}$ and $\left\| \mathcal{G}_i(x_i^k;\xi_i^k) - y_i^k \right\| \le \epsilon^{dual}, \forall i \in \mathcal{N}$, where ϵ^{pri} and ϵ^{dual} are two pre-defined feasibility tolerances.

Algorithm 3 Mini-batch stochastic I-ADMM (sI-ADMM)

1: **initialize:** $\{z^1 = x_i^1 = y_i^1 = \mathbf{0}, | i \in \mathcal{N}\}$, batch size M;
2: **LocalDataAllocation:**
3: **for** agent $i \in \mathcal{N}$ **do**
4: **divide** $\mathcal{D}_i$ labeled data into K_i equally disjoint partitions and denote each partition as $\xi_{i,j}, j \in \mathcal{K}_i$;
5: **for** ECN $j \in \mathcal{K}_i$ **do**
6: **allocate** $\xi_{i,j}$ to ECN j;
7: **partition** $\xi_{i,j}$ examples into multiple batches with each size M/K_i;
8: **end for**
9: **end for**
10: **UpdatingProcess:**
11: **for** $k = 1, 2, \ldots$ **do**
12: **StepsofActiveAgent**$i = i_k = (k-1) \mod N + 1$**:**
13: **receive** token z^k;
14: **broadcast** local variable x_i^k to ECNs $\mathcal{K}_i$;
15: **ECN**$j \in \mathcal{K}_i$**computesgradientinparallel:**
16: **receive** local primal variable x_i^k;
17: **select** batch $I_{i,j}^k = m \mod \lfloor |\xi_{i,j}| \cdot K_i/M \rfloor$;
18: **update** gradient $g_{i,j} = \frac{K_i}{M} \sum_{l=1}^{\frac{M}{K_i}} \nabla F_i(x_i^k; \xi_{i,l}^k)$;
19: **transmit** $g_{i,j}$ to the connected agent;
20: **until** the K_i-th responded message is received;
21: **update** gradient via gradient summation:

$$\mathcal{G}_i(x_i^k; \xi_i^k) = \frac{1}{K_i} \sum_{j=1}^{K_i} g_{i,j}; \tag{17}$$

22: **update** $\boldsymbol{x}^{k+1}$ according to (16a);
23: **update** $\boldsymbol{y}^{k+1}$ according to (16b);
24: **update** z^{k+1} according to (15c);
25: **send** token z^{k+1} to agent i_{k+1} via link (i_k, i_{k+1});
26: **until** the stopping criterion is satisfied.
27: **end for**

5.3. Coding for Local Optimization for sI-ADMM

With less reliable and limited computing capability of ECNs, straggling nodes may be a significant performance bottleneck in the learning networks. To address this problem, error control codes can be used to mitigate the impact of the straggling nodes by leveraging data redundancy. Similar to Section 3, two MDS-based coding methods over real field $\mathcal{R}$, i.e., *fractional* repetition scheme and *cyclic* repetition scheme, can be adopted and integrated with sI-ADMM for reducing the responding time in the presence of straggling nodes. The coded sI-ADMM (csI-ADMM) approach is presented in Algorithm 4. Denote the minimum required ECNs number by R_i and the maximum number of stragglers the system can tolerate by S_i. Different from sI-ADMM, in csI-ADMM, encoding and decoding processes are used in each ECN $j \in \mathcal{K}_i$ and its corresponding agent i, respectively. $\mathcal{G}_i(x_i^k;\xi_i^k)$ will be updated via steps 15–20, where the local gradient is calculated in ECN $j \in \mathcal{K}_i$ in parallel via selected $(S_i+1)\overline{M}/K_i$ batch samples, and the gradient summation can be recovered in active agent i_k with the responded messages from any R_i out of K_i ECNs to combat slow links and straggler nodes. As in steps 22–26 of sI-ADMM, activated agent i_k then updates local variables successively. Computation redundancy is introduced, but agent i can tolerate any $(S_i = K_i - R_i)$ stragglers.

Algorithm 4 Coded sI-ADMM (csI-ADMM)

1: **initialize:** $\{z^1 = x_i^1 = y_i^1 = \mathbf{0} | i \in \mathcal{N}\}$, batch size $\overline{M}$;
2: **LocalDataAllocation:**
3: **for** agent $i \in \mathcal{N}$ **do**
4:   **divide** $\mathcal{D}_i$ labeled data based on repetition schemes in [34] and denote each partition as $\boldsymbol{\xi}_{i,j}, j \in \mathcal{K}_i$;
5:   **for** ECN $j \in \mathcal{K}_i$ **do**
6:     **allocate** $\boldsymbol{\xi}_{i,j}$ to ECN j;
7:     **partition** $\boldsymbol{\xi}_{i,j}$ examples into multiple batches with each size $(S_i+1)\overline{M}/K_i$;
8:   **end for**
9: **end for**
10: **UpdatingProcess:**
11: **for** $k = 1, 2, \ldots$ **do**
12:   **StepsofActiveAgent**$i = i_k = (k-1) \mod N + 1$**:**
13:   **run** steps 13–14 of Algorithm 3
14:   **ECN**$j \in \mathcal{K}_i$**computesgradientinparallel**:
15:     **run** step 16 of Algorithm 3
16:     **select** batch

$$I_{i,j}^k = m \mod \lfloor |\boldsymbol{\xi}_{i,j}| \cdot K_i/(S_i+1)\overline{M} \rfloor; \tag{18}$$

17:     **update** $g_{i,j}$ via encoding function $p_{enc}^j(\cdot)$;
18:     **transmit** $g_{i,j}$ to the connected agent;
19:   **until** the R_i-th fast responded message is received;
20:   **update** gradient via decoding function $q_{dec}^i(\cdot)$;
21:   **run** steps 22–26 of Algorithm 3;
22: **end for**

5.4. Simulations for Coded Local Optimization

Both computed-generated and real-world datasets are used to evaluate the performance of the coded stochastic ADMM algorithms. The experimental network $\mathcal{G}$ consists of N agents and $E = \frac{N(N-1)}{2}\eta$ links, where η is the network connectivity ratio. For agent i, $K_i = K$ ECNs with the same computing power (e.g., computing and memory) are attached. To reduce the impact of token traversing patterns, both the Hamiltonian cycle-based and non-Hamiltonian cycle-based (i.e., the shortest path cycle-based [41]) token traversing methods are evaluated for the proposed algorithms.

To demonstrate the advantages of the coding schemes, csI-ADMM algorithms are compared with uncoded sI-ADMM algorithms with respect to the accuracy [42], which is defined as

$$\text{accuracy} = \frac{1}{N}\sum_{i=1}^{N}\frac{\left\|x_i^k - x^*\right\|}{\left\|x_i^1 - x^*\right\|}, \tag{19}$$

where $x^* \in \mathcal{R}^{p\times d}$ is the optimal solution of (P-1), and the test error [43], which is defined as the mean square error loss. For demonstrating the robustness against straggler nodes, distributed coding schemes, including *cyclic* and *fractional* repetition methods and the uncode method, are used for comparison. For fair comparison, the parameters for algorithms are tuned and kept the same in different experiments. Moreover, unicast is considered among agents, and the communication cost per link is 1 unit. The consumed time for each communication among agents is assumed to follow a uniform distribution $\mathcal{U}(10^{-5}, 10^{-4})$ seconds. The response time of each ECN is measured by the computation time, and the overall response time of each iteration is equal to the execution time for updating all variables in each iteration. All experiments were performed using Python on an Intel CPU @2.3 GHz (16 GB RAM) laptop.

To show the benefit of coding, in Figure 9, we compare the accuracy vs. running time for both coded and uncoded sI-ADMM. In simulation, the maximum delay ϵ_i, $(i = 1, 2, 3)$ for stragglers in each iteration is considered. For illustration purpose, we set up different ϵ_i with $\epsilon_1 > \epsilon_2 > \epsilon_3$ in simulation. For showing the benefits of coding to the convergence rate, convergence vs. straggler nodes trade-off for csI-ADMM, the impact of the number of straggler nodes on the convergence speed is shown in Figure 10. In simulations, 10 independent experiment runs are performed with the same simulation setup on synthetic data and take an average for presentation. We can see that, with an increasing number of straggler nodes, the convergence speed decreases. This is because increasing the number of straggler nodes decreases the allowable mini-batch size allocated in each iteration and therefore affects the convergence speed.

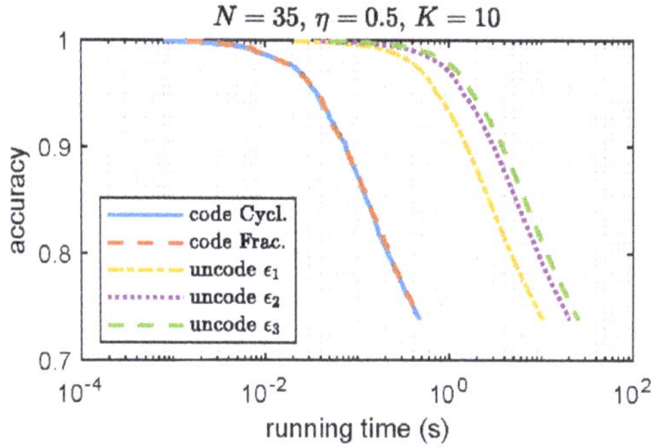

Figure 9. Comparison of coded and uncoded ADMM in accuracy and running time.

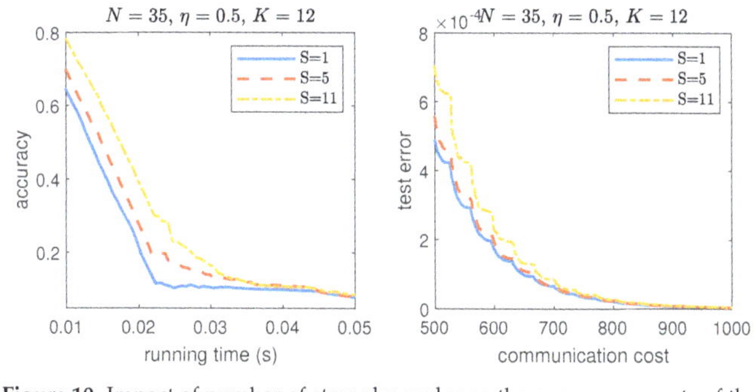

Figure 10. Impact of number of straggler nodes on the convergence rate of the proposed csI-ADMM on synthetic dataset.

5.5. Discussion

Above, we discuss the application of error-control coding in the local optimization step of ADMM. In the agent consensus step, there are also straggling or transmission errors for updating global variables. To improve reliability in the consensus step, we can use linear network error correction codes [31] or BATS codes [32] based on LT codes. For the latter, the global variable (vector) is divided into many smaller vectors. The encoding process continues until certain stopping criteria are reached (e.g., feedback from other nodes or time out). There are quite a few papers on applying network coding for consensus; see [44,45].

Since there is no significant difference between the consensus process of the global variables of ADMM or other types of messages, interested readers are referred to these papers for further reading. We note that network coding can improve both the reliability and security of the consensus, i.e., as secure network codes [46].

6. Conclusions and Future Work

We discussed how coding can be used to improve the reliability and reduce the communication loads for both primal- and primal–dual-based DML. We discussed both deterministic (and optimal) and random construction of error-control codes for DML. For the low-complexity and high flexibility, the latter may be more suitable for large-scale DML. For primal-dual based DML (i.e., ADMM), we discussed separate coding process for the two steps of ADMM, i.e., in local optimization and consensus processes separately. We introduced the algorithms on how to use codes for the local optimization of ADMM.

For emerging applications of increased interest, DML will be more and more common. Another interesting area for applying coding for DML is security. Though DML has a certain privacy-preserved capability (compared to transmit raw data), a higher security standard may be needed for sensitive applications. Secure coding has been an active topic for years; see [47]. We also have preliminary results on improving privacy by artificial noise in DML [40]. However, a further study is largely needed for improving performance and general scenarios.

Another interesting area for future work may be further studying coding for primal–dual methods. Though separate coding for the two steps of ADMM may solve the problem partly, the coding efficiency may be low and system complexity may be high. As discussed in Section 5, directly applying error control codes to ADMM may be infeasible. Another potential approach may be to simplify the optimization functions without significant performance loss, and error-control codes can be used.

Author Contributions: All authors have read and agreed to the published version of the manuscript.

Funding: This research is supported partly by Swedish Research Council (VR) project entitled "Coding for large-scale distributed machine learning" (Project ID: 2021-04772).

Institutional Review Board Statement: Not applicable.

Informed Consent Statement: Not applicable.

Data Availability Statement: Not applicable.

Acknowledgments: This is an invited contribution. The authors acknowledge the effort of Guest Editors and reviewers.

Conflicts of Interest: The authors declare no conflict of interest.

References

1. Wang, M.; Fu, W.; He, X.; Hao, S.; Wu, X. A Survey on Large-scale Machine Learning. *IEEE Trans. Knowl. Data Eng.* **2021**, *34*, 2574–2594. [CrossRef]
2. Dean, J.; Ghemawat, S. MapReduce: Simplified data processing on large clusters. In Proceedings of the 11th USENIX Symposium on Operating Systems Design and Implementation, Santa Clara, CA, USA, 10–12 July 2004; pp. 137–150.
3. Li, M.; Andersen, D.; Park, J.; Smola, A.J.; Ahmed, A.; Josifovski, V.; Long, J.; Shekita, E.J.; Su, B.-Y. Scaling Distributed Machine Learning with the Parameter Server. In Proceedings of the 6th Symposium on Operating Systems Design and Implementation (OSDI), Broomfield, CO, USA, 6–8 October 2014; pp. 137–150. Available online: http://www.usenix.org/events/osdi04/tech/dean.html (accessed on 7 September 2022).
4. Lee, K.; Lam, M.; Pedarsani, R.; Papailiopoulos, D.; Ramchandran, K. Speeding up distributed machine learning using codes. *IEEE Trans. Inf. Theory* **2018**, *64*, 1514–1529. [CrossRef]
5. Konecny, J.; McMahan, H.; Ramage, D.; Richtarik, P. Federated Optimization: Distributed Machine Learning for On-Device Intelligence. *arXiv* **2016**, arXiv:1610.02527.
6. McMahan, B.; Ramage, D. Federated Learning: Collaborative Machine Learning without Centralized Training Data. 2017. Available online: https://ai.googleblog.com/2017/04/federated-learning-collaborative.html (accessed on 7 September 2022).
7. Li, S.; Maddah-Ali, M.; Avestimehr, A. Coding for distributed fog computing. *IEEE Commun. Mag.* **2017**, *55*, 34–40. [CrossRef]

8. Park, H.; Lee, K.; Sohn, J.; Suh, C.; Moon, J. Hierarchical coding for distributed computing. In Proceedings of the IEEE International Symposium on Information Theory (ISIT), Vail, CO, USA, 17–22 June 2018; pp. 1630–1634.
9. Kiani, S.; Ferdinand, N.; Draper, S. Exploitation of stragglers in coded computation. In Proceedings of the IEEE International Symposium on Information Theory (ISIT), Vail, CO, USA, 17–22 June 2018; pp. 1988–1992.
10. Yu, Q.; Maddah-Ali, M.A.; Avestimehr, A.S. Straggler mitigation in distributed matrix multiplication: Fundamental limits and optimal coding. *arXiv* **2018**, arXiv:1801.07487v2.
11. Yu, Q.; Li, S.; Raviv, N.; Kalan, S.; Soltanolkotabi, M.; Avestimehr, A. Lagrange Coded Computing: Optimal Design for Resiliency, Security and Privacy. *arXiv* **2018**, arXiv:1801.07487v2.
12. Yue, J.; Xiao, M.; Pang, Z. Distributed Fog Computing Based on Batched Sparse Codes for Industrial Control. *IEEE Trans. Ind. Inform.* **2018**, *14*, 4683–4691. [CrossRef]
13. Yue, J.; Xiao, M. Coded Decentralized Learning with Gradient Descent for Big Data Analytics. *IEEE Commun. Lett.* **2020**, *24*, 362–366. [CrossRef]
14. Yue, J.; Xiao, M. Coding for Distributed Fog Computing in Internet of Mobile Things. *IEEE Trans. Mob. Comput.* **2021**, *20*, 1337–1350. [CrossRef]
15. Chen, H.; Ye, Y.; Xiao, M.; Skoglund, M.; Poor, H.V. Coded Stochastic ADMM for Decentralized Consensus Optimization with Edge Computing. *IEEE Internet Things J.* **2021**, *8*, 5360–5373. [CrossRef]
16. Boyd, S.; Parikh, N.; Chu, E.; Peleato, B.; Eckstein, J. Distributed optimization and statistical learning via the alternating direction method of multipliers. *Found. Trends Mach. Learn.* **2011**, *3*, 1–122.
17. Dean, J.; Corrado, G.; Monga, R.; Chen, K.; Devin, M.; Mao, M.; Ranzato, M.; Senior, A.; Tucker, P.; Ng, A.; et al. Large Scale Distributed Deep Networks. In *Advances in Neural Information Processing Systems 25*; Pereira, F., Burges, C.J.C., Bottou, L., Weinberger, K.Q., Eds.; Curran Associates, Inc.: Kottayam, India, 2012; pp. 1223–1231.
18. Grubic, D.; Tam, L.; Alistarh, D.; Zhang, C. Synchronous Multi-GPU Training for Deep Learning with Low-Precision Communications: An Empirical Study. In Proceedings of the 21st International Conference on Extending Database Technology, Vienna, Austria, 26–29 March 2018; pp. 145–156.
19. Dean, J.; Barroso, L.A. The tail at scale. *Commun. ACM* **2013**, *56*, 74–80. [CrossRef]
20. Ananthanarayanan, G.; Ghodsi, A.; Shenker, S.; Stoica, I. Effective straggler mitigation: Attack of the clones. In Proceedings of the 10th USENIX Symposium on Networked Systems Design and Implementation (NSDI '13), Lombard, IL, USA, 2–5 April 2013; Volume 13, pp. 185–198.
21. Wang, D.; Joshi, G.; Wornell, G. Using straggler replication to reduce latency in large-scale parallel computing. *ACM Sigmetrics Perform. Eval. Rev.* **2015**, *3*, 7–11. [CrossRef]
22. Yadwadkar, N.J.; Choi, W. Proactive straggler avoidance using machine learning. In *White Paper*; University of Berkeley: Berkeley, CA, USA, 2012; Volume 2012.
23. Karakus, C.; Sun, Y.; Diggavi, S.; Yin, W. Redundancy Techniques for Straggler Mitigation in Distributed Optimization and Learning. *J. Mach. Learn. Res.* **2019**, *20*, 2619–2665.
24. Li, S.; Maddah-Ali, M.; Avestimehr, A. A Fundamental Tradeoff Between Computation and Communication in Distributed Computing. *IEEE Trans. Inf. Theory* **2018**, *64*, 109–128. [CrossRef]
25. Halbawi, W.; Azizan, N.; Salehi, F.; Hassibi, B. Improving Distributed Gradient Descent Using Reed–Solomon Codes. In Proceedings of the IEEE International Symposium on Information Theory (ISIT), Vail, CO, USA, 17–22 June 2018; pp. 2027–2031.
26. Reisizadeh, A.; Prakash, S.; Pedarsani, R.; Avestimedhr, S. Coded Computation over Heterogeneous Clusters. In Proceedings of the IEEE International Symposium on Information Theory (ISIT), Aachen, Germany, 25–30 June 2017; pp. 2408–2412.
27. Fan, X.; Soto, P.; Zhong, X.; Xi, D.; Wang, Y.; Li, J. Leveraging Stragglers in Coded Computing with Heterogeneous Servers. In Proceedings of the IEEE/ACM 28th International Symposium on Quality of Service (IWQoS), Hang Zhou, China, 15–17 June 2020.
28. Wang, S.; Liu, J.; Shroff, N. Coded Sparse Matrix Multiplication. In Proceedings of the 35th International Conference on Machine Learning, Stockholm, Sweden, 10–15 July 2018; pp. 5152–5160.
29. Ahlswede, R.; Cai, N.; Li, S.Y.R.; Yeung, R.W. Network information flow. *IEEE Trans. Inf. Theory* **2000**, *46*, 1204–1216. [CrossRef]
30. Koetter, R.; Medard, M. An Algebraic Approach to Network Coding. *IEEE/ACM Trans. Netw. (TON)* **2003**, *11*, 782–795. [CrossRef]
31. Yeung, R.W.; Cai, N. Network Error Correction, Part I, Part II. *Commun. Inf. Syst.* **2006**, *6*, 37–54.
32. Yang, S.; Yeung, R. Batched sparse codes. *IEEE Trans. Inf. Theory* **2014**, *60*, 5322–5346. [CrossRef]
33. Boyd, S.; Vandenberghe, L. *Convex Optimization*; Cambridge University Press: Cambridge, UK, 2004.
34. Tandon, R.; Lei, Q.; Dimakis, A.; Karampatziakis, N. Gradient Coding: Avoiding Stragglers in Distributed Learning. In Proceedings of the 34th International Conference on Machine Learning, Sydney, Australia, 6–11 August 2017; Precup, D., Teh, Y.W., Eds.; Proceedings of Machine Learning Research, PMLR: Cambridge, MA, USA, 2017; Volume 70, pp. 3368–3376.
35. Byers, J.; Luby, M.; Mitzenmacher, M.; Rege, A. A digital fountain approach to reliable distribution of bulk data. *ACM SIGCOMM Comput. Commun. Rev.* **1998**, *28*, 56–67. [CrossRef]
36. Luby, M. LT codes. In Proceedings of the 43rd Annual IEEE Symposium on Foundations of Computer Science, Vancouver, BC, Canada, 16–19 November 2002; pp. 271–280.
37. Shokrollahi, A. Raptor codes. *IEEE Trans. Inform. Theory* **2006**, *52*, 2551–2567. [CrossRef]
38. Hussain, I.; Xiao, M.; Rasmussen, L. Buffer-based Distributed LT Codes. *IEEE Trans. Commu.* **2014**, *62*, 3725–3739. [CrossRef]
39. Ye, Y.; Xiao, M.; Skoglund, M. Randomized Neural Networks based Decentralized Multi-Task Learning via Hybrid Multi-Block ADMM. *IEEE Trans. Signal Process.* **2021**, *69*, 2844–2857. [CrossRef]

40. Ye, Y.; Chen, H.; Xiao, M.; Skoglund, M.; Poor, H.V. Privacy-preserving Incremental ADMM for Decentralized Consensus Optimization. *IEEE Trans. Signal Process.* **2020**, *68*, 5842–5854. [CrossRef]
41. Mao, X.; Gu, Y.; Yin, W. Walk Proximal Gradient: An Energy-Efficient Algorithm for Consensus Optimization. *IEEE Internet Things J.* **2018**, *6*, 2048–2060. [CrossRef]
42. Li, W.; Liu, Y.; Tian, Z.; Ling, Q. Communication-Censored Linearized ADMM for Decentralized Consensus Optimization. *IEEE Trans. Signal Inf. Process. Netw.* **2020**, *6*, 18–34. [CrossRef]
43. Hazan, E.; Levy, K.; Shalev-Shwartz, S. Beyond convexity: Stochastic quasi-convex optimization. *Adv. Neural Inf. Process. Syst.* **2015**, *28*, 1594–1602.
44. Cebe, M.; Kaplan, B.; Akkaya, K. A Network Coding Based Information Spreading Approach for Permissioned Blockchain in IoT Settings. In Proceedings of the 15th EAI International Conference on Mobile and Ubiquitous Systems: Computing, Networking and Services, New York, NY, USA, 5–7 November 2018.
45. Braun, M.; Wiesmaier, A.; Alnahawi, N.; Geibler, J. On Message-based Consensus and Network Coding. In Proceedings of the 12th International Conference on Network of the Future (NoF), Coimbra, Portugal, 6–8 October 2021.
46. Rouayheb, S.; Soljanin, E.; Sprintson, A. Secure network coding for wiretap networks of type II. *IEEE Trans. Inf. Theory* **2012**, *58*, 1361–1371. [CrossRef]
47. Cai, N.; Yeung, R.W. Secure Network Coding on a Wiretap Network. *IEEE Trans. Inf. Theory* **2011**, *57*, 424–435. [CrossRef]

entropy

Article

Bounds for Coding Theory over Rings

Niklas Gassner [1], Marcus Greferath [2], Joachim Rosenthal [1] and Violetta Weger [3,*]

1 Institute of Mathematics, University of Zurich, 8057 Zurich, Switzerland
2 School of Mathematics and Statistics, University College of Dublin, D04 V1W8 Dublin, Ireland
3 Department of Computer Engineering, Technical University of Munich, 80333 München, Germany
* Correspondence: violetta.weger@tum.de

Abstract: Coding theory where the alphabet is identified with the elements of a ring or a module has become an important research topic over the last 30 years. It has been well established that, with the generalization of the algebraic structure to rings, there is a need to also generalize the underlying metric beyond the usual Hamming weight used in traditional coding theory over finite fields. This paper introduces a generalization of the weight introduced by Shi, Wu and Krotov, called overweight. Additionally, this weight can be seen as a generalization of the Lee weight on the integers modulo 4 and as a generalization of Krotov's weight over the integers modulo 2^s for any positive integer s. For this weight, we provide a number of well-known bounds, including a Singleton bound, a Plotkin bound, a sphere-packing bound and a Gilbert–Varshamov bound. In addition to the overweight, we also study a well-known metric on finite rings, namely the homogeneous metric, which also extends the Lee metric over the integers modulo 4 and is thus heavily connected to the overweight. We provide a new bound that has been missing in the literature for homogeneous metric, namely the Johnson bound. To prove this bound, we use an upper estimate on the sum of the distances of all distinct codewords that depends only on the length, the average weight and the maximum weight of a codeword. An effective such bound is not known for the overweight.

Keywords: rings; coding theory; Johnson bound; Plotkin bound

Citation: Gassner, N.; Greferath, M.; Rosenthal, J.; Weger, V. Bounds for Coding Theory over Rings. *Entropy* **2022**, *24*, 1473. https://doi.org/10.3390/e24101473

Academic Editors: Onur Günlü, Rafael F. Schaefer, Holger Boche and H. Vincent Poor

Received: 15 September 2022
Accepted: 12 October 2022
Published: 16 October 2022

1. Introduction

Coding theoretic experience has shown that considering linear codes over finite fields often yields significant complexity advantages over the nonlinear counterparts, particularly when it comes to complex tasks such as encoding and decoding. On the other side, it was recognized early [1,2] that the class of binary block codes contains excellent code families, which were not linear (Preparata, Kerdock codes, Goethals and Goethals–Delsarte codes). For a long time, it could not be explained why these families exhibit formal duality properties in terms of their distance enumerators that occur only on those among linear codes and their duals.

A true breakthrough in the understanding of this behavior came in the early 1990s when, after preceding work by Nechaev [3], the paper by Hammons et al. [4] discovered that these families allow a representation in terms of $\mathbb{Z}_4$-linear codes.

A crucial condition for this ring-theoretic representation was that $\mathbb{Z}_4$ was equipped with an alternative metric, the Lee weight, rather than with the traditional Hamming weight, which only distinguishes whether an element is zero or non-zero. The Lee weight is finer, assigning 2 a higher weight than the other non-zero elements of this ring.

The fact that the traditional settings of linear coding theory (finite fields endowed with the Hamming metric) are actually too narrow, which suggests expanding the theory in at least two directions: on the algebraic part, the next more natural algebraic structure serving as alphabet for linear coding is that of finite rings (and modules). On the metrical part, the appropriateness of the Lee weight for $\mathbb{Z}_4$-linear coding suggests that the distance function for a generalized coding theory requires generalization as well.

Since these ground-breaking observations, an entire discipline arose within algebraic coding theory. A considerable community of scholars have been developing results in various directions, among them code duality, weight-enumeration, code equivalence, weight functions, homogeneous weights, existence bounds, code optimality and decoding schemes, to mention only a few.

The paper at hand aims at providing a further contribution to this discipline, by introducing the overweight on a finite ring. This weight is a generalization of the Lee weight over $\mathbb{Z}_4$, as well as of the weight introduced in [5] by Krotov over $\mathbb{Z}_{2^s}$ for any positive integer s, which was further generalized to $\mathbb{Z}_{p^k}$ in [6].

We study the relations of this new weight to other well-known weights over rings and state several properties of the overweight, such as its extremal property. We also develop a number of standard existence bounds, such as a Singleton bound, a sphere-packing bound, a Plotkin bound and a version of the (assertive) Gilbert–Varshamov bound.

In the final part of this article, we derive a general Johnson bound for the homogeneous weight on a finite Frobenius ring. This result is important, as it is closely connected to list decoding capabilities.

2. Preliminaries

Throughout this paper, we will consider R to be a finite ring with identity, denoted by 1. If R is a finite ring, we denote by $R^\times$ its group of invertible elements, also known as units.

Let us recall some preliminaries in coding theory, where we focus on ring-linear coding theory.

For a prime power q, let us denote by $\mathbb{F}_q$ the finite field with q elements and, for a positive integer m, we denote by $\mathbb{Z}_m$ the ring of integers modulo m.

In traditional coding theory, we consider a linear code to be a subspace of a vector space over a finite field.

Definition 1. *Let q be a prime power, and let $k \leq n$ be non-negative integers. A linear subspace C of $\mathbb{F}_q^n$ of dimension k is called a linear $[n,k]$ code.*

We define a weight in a general way.

Definition 2. *Let R be a finite ring. A real-valued function w on R is called a* weight *if it is a non-negative function that maps 0 to 0.*

It is natural to identify w with its additive extension to R^n, and so we will always write $w(x) = \sum_{i=1}^n w(x_i)$ for all $x \in R^n$. Every weight w on R induces a *distance* $d : R \times R \longrightarrow \mathbb{R}$ by $d(x,y) = w(x-y)$. Again, we will identify d with its natural additive extension to $R^n \times R^n$.

If the weight additionally is positive definite, symmetric and satisfies the triangular inequality, that is,

1. $w(0) = 0$ and $w(x) > 0$ for all $x \neq 0$,
2. $w(x) = w(-x)$ for all $x \in R$,
3. $w(x+y) \leq w(x) + w(y)$ for all $x, y \in R$,

then the induced distance inherits these properties, i.e.,

1. $d(x,y) \geq 0$ for all $x, y \in R$ and $d(x,y) = 0$ if and only if $x = y$.
2. $d(x,y) = d(y,x)$ for all $x, y \in R$,
3. $d(x,z) \leq d(x,y) + d(y,z)$ for all $x, y, z \in R$.

The most prominent and best studied weight in traditional coding theory is the Hamming weight.

Definition 3. *Let $n \in \mathbb{N}$. The Hamming weight of a vector $x \in R^n$ is defined as the size of its support*

$$w_H(x) = |\{i \in \{1, \dots, n\} \mid x_i \neq 0\}|,$$

and the Hamming distance between x and $y \in R^n$ is given by

$$d_H(x,y) = |\{i \in \{1, \dots, n\} \mid x_i \neq y_i\}| = w_H(x-y).$$

The minimum Hamming distance of a code is then defined as the minimum distance between two different codewords

$$d_H(C) = \min\{d_H(x,y) \mid x,y \in C,\ x \neq y\}.$$

Note that the concept of minimum distance can be applied for any underlying distance d.

In the paper at hand, we focus on a more general setting where the ambient space is a module over a finite ring.

Definition 4. *Let $n \in \mathbb{N}$ and let R be a finite ring. A submodule C of ${}_RR^n$ of size $M = |C|$ is called a left R-linear (n, M) code.*

The most studied ambient space for ring-linear coding theory is the integers modulo 4, denoted by $\mathbb{Z}_4$, endowed with the Lee metric.

Definition 5. *For $x \in \mathbb{Z}_m$, its Lee weight is defined as*

$$w_L(x) = \min\{x, \mid m - x \mid\}.$$

One of the most prominent generalizations of the Lee weight over $\mathbb{Z}_4$ is the homogeneous weight.

Definition 6. *Let R be a Frobenius ring. A weight $w : R \longrightarrow \mathbb{R}$ is called (left) homogeneous of average value $\gamma > 0$, if $w(0) = 0$ and the following conditions hold:*

(i) For all x, y with $Rx = Ry$, we have that $w(x) = w(y)$.
(ii) For every non-zero ideal $I \leq {}_RR$, it holds that

$$\frac{1}{|I|} \sum_{x \in I} w(x) \ = \ \gamma.$$

We will denote the homogeneous weight with wt.

The homogeneous weight was first introduced by Constantinescu and Heise in [7] in the context of coding over integer residue rings. It was later generalized by Greferath and Schmidt [8] to arbitrary finite rings, where the ideal I in Definition 6 was assumed to be a principal ideal. In its original form, however, the homogeneous weight only exists on finite Frobenius rings. It can be shown that a left homogeneous weight is at the same time right homogeneous, and for this reason, we will omit the reference to any side for the sequel. In [9], Honold and Nechaev finally generalized the notion of homogeneous weight to some finite modules, called weighted modules, over a (not necessarily commutative) ring R with identity.

Since we will establish a Plotkin bound for a new weight, let us recall here the Plotkin bound over finite fields equipped with the Hamming metric.

Theorem 1 (Plotkin bound). *Let C be an (n, M) block code over $\mathbb{F}_q$ with minimum Hamming distance d. If $d > \frac{q-1}{q}n$, then*

$$M \leq \frac{d}{d - \frac{q-1}{q}n}.$$

For the homogeneous weight, the following Plotkin bound was established in [10].

Theorem 2 (Plotkin bound for homogeneous weights, [10]). *Let wt be a homogeneous weight of average value γ on R, and let C be an (n, M) block code over R with minimum homogeneous distance d. If $\gamma n < d$, then*

$$M \leq \frac{d}{d - \gamma n}.$$

3. Overweight

As the Hamming weight defined over the binary can be generalized to larger ambient spaces in different ways resulting in different metrics, such as the Hamming weight over $\mathbb{F}_q$ or the Lee weight over $\mathbb{Z}_{p^s}$; in addition, the Lee weight over $\mathbb{Z}_4$ can be generalized in different ways. For example, the weight defined in [5] over $\mathbb{Z}_{2m}$ for any positive integer m is a possible generalization, but the most prominent generalization is the homogeneous weight (see for example [10]). In this section, we introduce a new generalization, called the *overweight*. This weight shows some interesting properties and relations to the homogeneous weight and can additionally be seen as a generalization of the weight defined in [5] over $\mathbb{Z}_{2^s}$ for any positive integer s and the weight defined in [6] over $\mathbb{Z}_{p^s}$.

Definition 7. *Let R be a finite ring. The* overweight *on R is defined as*

$$W : R \longrightarrow \mathbb{R}, \quad x \mapsto \begin{cases} 0 & \text{if } x = 0, \\ 1 & \text{if } x \in R^\times, \\ 2 & \text{otherwise.} \end{cases}$$

We also denote by W its additive expansion to R^n, given by $W(x) = \sum_{i=1}^n W(x_i)$.

Let us call the distance which is induced by the overweight the *overweight distance*, and denote it by D, i.e., $D(x, y) = W(x - y)$.

The motivation of introducing this new weight is twofold: on one hand, it is theoretically interesting to explore a new generalization of the Lee weight over $\mathbb{Z}_4$ and its connections to other known weights over rings. On the other hand, the overweight would also be perfectly suitable for a channel, where unit errors are more likely.

Note that the overweight is designed to satisfy the following criteria: it is positive definite, symmetric, satisfies the triangular inequality and distinguishes between units and non-zero non-units. Furthermore, it is extremal in the sense that, on a big family of rings, any increase of the weight of non-zero non-units would violate the triangular inequality, thus the name *overweight*. We will now study this extremal property in more details.

We can consider weights with values in $\{0, 1, \alpha\}$, for some $\alpha > 0$, without fixing the subsets of R where these values are attained. Thus, we are considering the generic weight function

$$f(x) = \begin{cases} 0 & \text{if } x = 0, \\ 1 & \text{if } x \in A_1, \\ \alpha & \text{if } x \in A_2, \end{cases}$$

where $A_1 \subset R \setminus \{0\}$ and $A_2 = R \setminus (A_1 \cup \{0\})$. Such a weight is always positive definite. In addition, the weight is symmetric if and only if A_1 and A_2 contain all additive inverses of their elements. Let us now consider the triangular inequality: if there exist $x, y \in A_1$ such that $x + y \in A_2$, then we must have

$$\alpha = f(x+y) \leq f(x) + f(y) = 2.$$

Thus, in order for f to be an extremal weight, one chooses $\alpha = 2$.

The overweight is a special case of such a weight function f with the choice $A_1 = R^\times$. The existence of elements $x, y \in R^\times$ such that $x + y \in R \setminus (\{0\} \cup R^\times)$ is satisfied for many rings—for example, for rings with a non-trivial Jacobson radical.

Relations to Other Weights

Clearly, the homogeneous weight and the overweight coincide with the Lee weight on $\mathbb{Z}_4$, with the Hamming metric on finite fields $\mathbb{F}_q$, and finally with the weight [6] on $\mathbb{Z}_{p^s}$.

Proposition 1. *The overweight over finite chain rings gives an upper bound on the normalized homogeneous weight.*

Proof. Over a finite chain ring with socle S and residue field size q, we have that the normalized homogeneous weight is defined as

$$wt(x) = \begin{cases} 0 & \text{if } x = 0, \\ \frac{q}{q-1} & \text{if } x \in S \setminus \{0\}, \\ 1 & \text{else.} \end{cases}$$

If $x \in S \setminus \{0\}$, then also $x \in R \setminus R^\times$, and

$$wt(x) = \frac{q}{q-1} \leq 2 = W(x).$$

If $x \in R^\times$, then $wt(x) = 1 = W(x)$ and finally, if $x \in R \setminus (S \cup R^\times)$, we have that

$$wt(x) = 1 \leq 2 = W(x),$$

which implies the result. □

In [11], Bachoc defines the following weight on $\mathbb{F}_p$-algebras A, with units $A^\times$ as follows:

$$w_B(x) = \begin{cases} 0 & \text{if } x = 0, \\ 1 & \text{if } x \in A^\times, \\ p & \text{else.} \end{cases}$$

This is in the same spirit as the overweight. The weight of Bachoc is, however, only assuming positive definiteness. We note that, whenever we have a $\mathbb{F}_2$-algebra, the two weights coincide. The overweight can thus also be seen as a generalization of Bachoc's weight to a general finite ring.

Let us illustrate this connection with some examples: we consider the ring $M_2(\mathbb{F}_p)$ of 2×2 matrices over $\mathbb{F}_p$ and the ring $\mathbb{F}_p[x]/(x^2)$. In both cases, the Bachoc weight only coincides with the homogeneous and the overweight in the case $p = 2$.

Finally, in [5], Krotov defines the following weight over $\mathbb{Z}_{2m}$, for any positive integer m:

$$w_K(x) = \begin{cases} 0 & \text{if } x = 0, \\ 2 & \text{if } 2 \mid x, x \neq 0, \\ 1 & \text{else.} \end{cases}$$

Clearly, this is a further generalization of the Lee weight over $\mathbb{Z}_4$ and thus coincides there with the homogeneous and the overweight. However, even more is true: the weight of Krotov and the overweight coincide over $\mathbb{Z}_{2^s}$, for any positive integer s. Thus, the overweight may be considered as a generalization of Krotov's weight over $\mathbb{Z}_{2^s}$ for any positive integer s.

Let us give some examples to illustrate the differences between the above-mentioned weights.

Example 1. *In the following table, w_H denotes the Hamming weight, wt the normalized homogeneous weight, w_L denotes the Lee weight, w_K denotes Krotov's weight, w_B denotes Bachoc's weight and finally W denotes the overweight. Let us consider two easy but pathological cases, namely $\mathbb{Z}_6$ for Table 1 and $\mathbb{Z}_2 \times \mathbb{Z}_2$ for Table 2.*

Table 1. Comparison of weights in $\mathbb{Z}_6$.

	w_H	wt	w_L	w_K	W
0	0	0	0	0	0
1	1	1/2	1	1	1
2	1	3/2	2	2	2
3	1	2	3	1	2
4	1	3/2	2	2	2
5	1	1/2	1	1	1

Table 2. Comparison of weights in $\mathbb{Z}_2 \times \mathbb{Z}_2$.

	w_H	wt	w_B	W
(0,0)	0	0	0	0
(0,1)	1	2	2	2
(1,0)	1	2	2	2
(1,1)	2	0	1	1

Finally, another interesting connection to the Hamming weight arises by considering the following linear injective isometry.

Lemma 1. *The map*

$$\begin{aligned} \psi : (\mathbb{F}_2[x]/(x^2), W) &\to (\mathbb{F}_2^2, w_H) \\ a + bx &\mapsto (a+b, b) \end{aligned}$$

is a linear isometry.

Recall that, over $\mathbb{F}_2[x]/(x^2)$, the overweight coincides with the weight of Bachoc and the homogeneous weight.

4. Bounds for the Overweight

In this section, we develop several bounds for the overweight, such as a Singleton bound, a sphere-packing bound, a Gilbert–Varshamov bound and a Plotkin bound.

For this, let us first define the minimum overweight distance of a code.

Definition 8. *Let $C \subseteq R^n$ be a code. The minimum overweight distance of C is then denoted by $D(C)$ and defined as*

$$D(C) = \min\{D(x, y) \mid x, y \in C, x \neq y\}.$$

4.1. A Singleton Bound

The Singleton bound usually follows a puncturing argument, which is possible for the overweight, but gives the same result as applying the following observation:

Remark 1. *For all $x \in R$, we have that*

$$0 \leq w_H(x) \leq W(x) \leq 2w_H(x) \leq 2n,$$

where w_H denotes the Hamming weight.

Hence, using the Singleton bound for the Hamming metric directly gives a Singleton bound for the overweight.

Proposition 2. *Let $C \subseteq R^n$ be a code of size M and minimum overweight distance d. Then,*

$$d \leq 2(n - \lceil \log_{|R|}(M) \rceil + 1).$$

Example 2. *A trivial example for a code achieving the Singleton bound in Proposition 2 is given by $C = \langle (p, \ldots, p) \rangle \subset \mathbb{Z}_{p^s}^n$, having $\log_{p^s}(| C |) = \frac{s-1}{s}$ and minimum overweight distance $d = 2n$.*

However, if we define the rank of a linear code C, denoted by $rk(C)$, to be the minimal number of generators of C, then the following bound is known for principal ideal rings [12,13]

$$d_H(C) \leq n - rk(C) + 1.$$

Codes achieving this bound are called Maximum Distance with respect to Rank (MDR) codes, in order to differentiate from MDS codes. This is a sharper bound than the usual Singleton bound, since for non-free codes we have $rk(C) > \log_{|R|}(M)$.

In the case of linear codes, the rank thus also leads to a sharper Singleton-like bound for the overweight.

Proposition 3. *Let R be a principal ideal ring. Let $C \subseteq R^n$ be a linear code of rank $rk(C)$ and minimum overweight distance d. Then,*

$$d \leq 2(n - rk(C) + 1).$$

Example 3. *As an example for a code, we can consider $C = \langle (3,6,3,0), (6,6,0,3) \rangle \subset \mathbb{Z}_9^4$, having minimum overweight distance $d = 6$.*

4.2. A Sphere-Packing Bound

The sphere-packing bound as well as the Gilbert–Varshamov bound are *generic* bounds, and we are able to provide them for the overweight in a simple form involving the volume of the balls in the underlying metric space.

We begin by defining balls with respect to the overweight distance.

Definition 9. *For a given radius $r \geq 0$, the* overweight ball *$B_{r,D}(x)$ of radius r centered in x is defined as*

$$B_{r,D}(x) := \{y \in R^n \mid D(x,y) \leq r\}.$$

Clearly, the volume of such a ball is invariant under translations, i.e.,

$$|B_{r,D}(x)| = |B_{r,D}(y)|,$$

for all $x, y \in R^n$.

Moreover, setting $u := |R^\times|$ and $v := |R| - 1 - u$, we have the generating function $f_W(z) = 1 + uz + vz^2$ for this weight function, so that the generating function for W on R^n takes the form

$$\begin{aligned} f_W^n(z) &= (1 + uz + vz^2)^n \\ &= \sum_{k_0+k_u+k_v=n} \binom{n}{k_0, k_u, k_v} 1^{k_0} (uz)^{k_u} (vz^2)^{k_v} \\ &= \sum_{k=0}^{n} \sum_{\ell=0}^{n-k} \binom{n}{k} \binom{n-k}{\ell} u^k v^\ell z^{k+2\ell}, \end{aligned}$$

where we have set $k = k_u$ and $\ell = k_v$, and where the condition $k_0 + k_u + k_v = n$ is transformed in $0 \le k \le n, 0 \le \ell \le n-k$. Now, setting $t = k + 2\ell$, we obtain the simplified expression for the generating function

$$f_W^n(z) = \sum_{t=0}^{2n} \sum_{\ell=0}^{\lfloor \frac{t}{2} \rfloor} \binom{n}{t-2\ell} \binom{n-t+2\ell}{\ell} u^{t-2\ell} v^\ell z^t.$$

Lemma 2. *The foregoing implies that the ball of radius e (centered in 0) has volume exactly*

$$|B_{e,D}(0)| = \sum_{t=0}^{e} \sum_{\ell=0}^{\lfloor \frac{t}{2} \rfloor} \binom{n}{t-2\ell} \binom{n-t+2\ell}{\ell} u^{t-2\ell} v^\ell. \tag{1}$$

We thus provided an explicit formula for the cardinality of balls in R^n with respect to the overweight distance.

We now obtain the sphere-packing bound for the overweight distance by combining the previous results. As before, R is a finite ring and $u = |R^\times|$, whereas $v = |R| - 1 - u$ represents the number of non-zero non-units.

Corollary 1 (Sphere-Packing Bound). *Let $C \subseteq R^n$ be a (not necessarily linear) code of length n, and minimum overweight distance $d = 2e + 1$. Then, we have*

$$|C| \le \frac{|R|^n}{|B_{e,D}(0)|},$$

where the cardinality of $B_{e,D}(0)$ is given in Equation (1).

If the minimum distance is even and R is a finite local ring with maximal ideal J, this bound can be adapted as follows.

Corollary 2. *Let R be a local ring with maximal ideal J, $q = |R/J|$ and $C \subseteq R^{n+1}$ be a (not necessarily linear) code of length $n+1$ and minimum overweight distance $d = 2e + 2$. Then,*

$$|C| \le \frac{|R|^{n+1}}{q|B_{e,D}(0)|},$$

where $B_{e,D}(0)$ is the overweight ball of radius e in R^n, and its volume is given in Equation (1).

Proof. Pick $x_1, \ldots, x_q$ such that the cosets $x_1 + J, \ldots, x_q + J$ form a partition of R. For all $m \in J$, define the set

$$S_m := \{x_1 + m, \ldots, x_q + m\}.$$

Notice that the sets S_m form a partition of R and that all elements of S_m have mutual overweight distance 1. Thus, given $r \in R$, we denote with $S(r)$ the unique set S_m that contains r. Furthermore, let

$$\pi : R^{n+1} \to R^n$$

be the projection that removes the $n+1$'th coordinate and

$$Z(x) := \{z \in R^{n+1} \mid D(\pi(z), \pi(x)) \leq e, \, z_{n+1} \in S(x_{n+1})\}.$$

Now, if $x \neq y \in R^{n+1}$ are two codewords, then $Z(x)$ and $Z(y)$ are disjoint. Indeed, if $z \in Z(x) \cap Z(y)$, then $S(x_{n+1}) = S(y_{n+1})$ as they cannot be disjoint. Hence, $D(x_{n+1}, y_{n+1}) \leq 1$. Furthermore, both $D(\pi(x), \pi(z))$ and $D(\pi(y), \pi(z))$ are less than or equal to e, implying that $D(\pi(x), \pi(y)) \leq 2e$. It follows that $D(x,y) \leq 2e+1$, which is a contradiction. □

To find non-trivial examples of perfect codes is as notoriously hard as over finite fields in the Hamming metric. Clearly, in the case $R = \mathbb{F}_q$, there are non-trivial perfect codes, as the overweight coincides with the Hamming weight. Examples of such codes can be found in [5] (Section IV). Furthermore, in the case $R = \mathbb{Z}_{p^k}$, linear 1-perfect codes are classified in terms of their parity-check matrix in [6] (Theorem IV.1).

4.3. A Gilbert–Varshamov Bound

With arguments similar to those for the sphere-packing bound, we can also obtain a lower bound on the maximal size of a code with a fixed minimum distance.

Proposition 4 (Gilbert–Varshamov bound)**.** *Let R be a finite ring, n a positive integer and $d \in \{0, \ldots, 2n\}$. Then, there exists a code $C \subseteq R^n$ of minimum overweight distance at least d satisfying*

$$|C| \geq \frac{|R|^n}{|B_{d-1,D}(0)|},$$

where the volume is given in Equation (1) for $e = d-1$, i.e.,

$$|B_{d-1,D}(0)| = \sum_{t=0}^{d-1} \sum_{\ell=0}^{\lfloor \frac{t}{2} \rfloor} \binom{n}{t-2\ell} \binom{n-t+2\ell}{\ell} u^{t-2\ell} v^{\ell}.$$

Proof. Assume $C \subseteq R^n$ of minimum overweight distance of at least d is a largest code of length n and minimum distance d. Then, the set of balls $B_{d-1,D}(x)$ centered in the codewords $x \in C$ must already cover the space R^n. Since, if this were not the case, one would find an element $y \in R^n$ that is not contained in the ball of radius $d-1$ around any element of C. This word y would have distance at least d to each of the words of C, and thus $C \cup \{y\}$ would be a code of properly larger size with distance at least d, a contradiction to the choice of C.

From the covering argument, we then see that

$$|C| \geq \frac{|R|^n}{|B_{d-1,D}(0)|},$$

as desired. □

Let us consider the special case where R is a finite chain ring. Since the overweight is an additive weight, and the conditions of [14] are easily verified, we can use [14] (Theorem 22) to obtain that random linear codes over R^n achieve the (asymptotic) Gilbert–Varshamov bound with high probability.

Example 4. *As an easy example, we can consider $R^n = \mathbb{Z}_8^2$. The maximal minimum overweight distance is given by $d = 2n = 4$. The Gilbert–Varshamov bound states for this example that* *there exists a code C with* $| C | > 1$, *as* $| B_{3,D}(0) | = 55$. *For example, the code* $C = \langle(2,2)\rangle$ *has four elements.*

4.4. A Plotkin Bound

Over a local ring, we can use methods similar to the ones used for the classical Plotkin bound to obtain an analogue of the Plotkin bound for (not necessarily linear) codes equipped with the overweight.

For the rest of this section, R is a finite local ring with maximal ideal J. The notation stems from the Jacobson radical of the ring R. Note that the factor ring R/J is a finite field, whose cardinality will be denoted by q.

Similarly to the Hamming case, for a subset $A \subseteq R$, we will denote by

$$\overline{W}(A) = \frac{\sum_{a\in A} W(a)}{|A|}$$

the average weight of the subset A.

Lemma 3. *Let* $I \subseteq R$ *be a left or right ideal. Then,*

$$\overline{W}(I) = \begin{cases} \frac{|R|+|J|-2}{|R|} & \text{if } I = R, \\ 2\left(1 - \frac{1}{|I|}\right) & \text{if } \{0\} \subsetneq I \subsetneq R, \\ 0 & \text{else.} \end{cases}$$

Proof. Note that the last case is trivial as $I = \{0\}$. If $\{0\} \subsetneq I \subsetneq R$, then all non-zero elements of I have weight 2, so this case follows as well.

Finally, if $I = R$, then there are $|R \setminus J| = |R| - |J|$ elements of weight 1 and $|J| - 1$ elements of weight 2. Hence, the total weight is $|R| - |J| + 2(|J| - 1)$ and dividing by $|R|$ yields the claim. □

Corollary 3. *Let* R *be a local ring with maximal ideal* J *and assume that* $|J| \geq 2$. *Then, we have that* $\overline{W}(J) \geq \overline{W}(I)$ *for all left or right ideals* $I \subseteq R$.

Proof. We immediately see that $\overline{W}(J) \geq \overline{W}(I)$ for all $I \subseteq J$. Now, consider the case $I = R$. We have that

$$\begin{aligned} \overline{W}(R) &= \frac{|R| + |J| - 2}{|R|} = \frac{|R \setminus J|}{|R|} + 2\frac{|J| - 1}{|R|} \\ &= \frac{|R \setminus J|}{|R|} + 2\frac{|J| - 1}{|J|} \cdot \frac{|J|}{|R|} \\ &\leq 2\frac{|J| - 1}{|J|} \cdot \frac{|R \setminus J|}{|R|} + 2\frac{|J| - 1}{|J|} \cdot \frac{|J|}{|R|} \\ &= 2\frac{|J| - 1}{|J|} = \overline{W}(J), \end{aligned}$$

where we used that $2\frac{|J|-1}{|J|} \geq 1$. □

To ease the notation, let us denote by η the following

$$\eta = \overline{W}(J) = 2\left(1 - \frac{1}{|J|}\right).$$

In what follows, we provide a Plotkin bound for the overweight over a local ring R with maximal ideal J. The case $|J| = 1$ is already well studied, since, in this case, R is a field and D is simply the Hamming distance. Hence, we will assume that $|J| \geq 2$.

We start with a lemma for the Hamming weight. The proof of it follows the idea of the classical Plotkin bound, which can be found in [15], and for the homogeneous weight in [10].

Lemma 4. *Let $I \subseteq R$ be a subset and P be a probability distribution on I. Then, we have that*

$$\sum_{x\in I}\sum_{y\in I} w_H(x-y)P(x)P(y) \leq 1 - \frac{1}{|I|}.$$

Proof. We have that

$$\sum_{x\in I}\sum_{y\in I} w_H(x-y)P(x)P(y) = \sum_{x\in I} P(x)(1-P(x)) = \sum_{x\in I} P(x) - \sum_{x\in I} P(x)^2.$$

If we apply the Cauchy–Schwarz inequality to the latter sum, we obtain that

$$\sum_{x\in I} P(x) - \sum_{x\in I} P(x)^2 \leq 1 - \frac{1}{|I|}\left|\sum_{x\in I} P(x)\right|^2 = 1 - \frac{1}{|I|}.$$

From which we can conclude. □

We are now ready for the most important step of the Plotkin bound. As before, R is a local ring with non-zero maximal ideal J and $\eta = \overline{W}(J)$.

Proposition 5. *Let P be a probability distribution on R. Then, it holds that*

$$\sum_{x\in R}\sum_{y\in R} W(x-y)P(x)P(y) \leq \eta.$$

Proof. Let $q = |R/J|$ and pick $x_1, \dots, x_q$ such that $x_i + J \neq x_j + J$ if $i \neq j$. Then, it follows that the cosets $\overline{x_i} := x_i + J$ form a partition of R. For all $k \in \{1, \dots, q\}$, we denote by

$$P_k = \sum_{x\in\overline{x_k}} P(x).$$

It follows that $\sum_{k=1}^{q} P_k = 1$. By rewriting the initial sum as sum over all cosets, we obtain that

$$\begin{aligned}
&\sum_{x\in R}\sum_{y\in R} W(x-y)P(x)P(y) \\
&= \sum_{k=1}^{q}\sum_{x\in\overline{x_k}}\sum_{y\in R} W(x-y)P(x)P(y) \\
&= \sum_{k=1}^{q}\sum_{x\in\overline{x_k}}\left(\sum_{y\in\overline{x_k}} 2w_H(x-y)P(x)P(y) + \sum_{z\in R\setminus\overline{x_k}} w_H(x-z)P(x)P(z)\right) \\
&= \sum_{k=1}^{q}\left(2\sum_{x\in\overline{x_k}}\sum_{y\in\overline{x_k}} w_H(x-y)P(x)P(y) + \sum_{x\in\overline{x_k}}\sum_{z\in R\setminus\overline{x_k}} P(x)P(z)\right) \\
&= \sum_{k=1}^{q}\left(2\sum_{x\in\overline{x_k}}\sum_{y\in\overline{x_k}} w_H(x-y)P(x)P(y) + \sum_{x\in\overline{x_k}} P(x)(1-P_k)\right).
\end{aligned}$$

If $P_k \neq 0$, then $\tilde{P}(x) := P(x)/P_k$ defines a probability distribution on $\overline{x_k}$. In this case, we apply Lemma 4 to obtain that

$$\begin{aligned} &\sum_{x\in\overline{x_k}}\sum_{y\in\overline{x_k}} w_H(x-y)P(x)P(y) \\ =&P_k^2\left(\sum_{x\in\overline{x_k}}\sum_{y\in\overline{x_k}} w_H(x-y)\frac{P(x)P(y)}{P_k^2}\right) \\ \leq&P_k^2\left(1-\frac{1}{|J|}\right). \end{aligned}$$

Note that the same inequality also trivially holds if $P_k = 0$. Applying this and using that $\sum_{x\in\overline{x_k}} P(x) = P_k$, we obtain that

$$\begin{aligned} &\sum_{k=1}^{q}\left(2\sum_{x\in\overline{x_k}}\sum_{y\in\overline{x_k}} w_H(x-y)P(x)P(y) + \sum_{x\in\overline{x_k}} P(x)(1-P_k)\right) \\ \leq&\sum_{k=1}^{q}\left(P_k^2\cdot 2\left(1-\frac{1}{|J|}\right)+P_k(1-P_k)\right) \\ \leq&\sum_{k=1}^{q} P_k\cdot 2\left(1-\frac{1}{|J|}\right) = 2\left(1-\frac{1}{|J|}\right) = \eta, \end{aligned}$$

where we used that $2\left(1-\frac{1}{|J|}\right) \geq 1$ since $|J| \geq 2$ in the last inequality. □

To complete the Plotkin bound for the overweight, we now follow the steps in [10]. Using Proposition 5, we obtain the following result:

Proposition 6. *Let $C \subseteq R^n$ be a (not necessarily linear) code of minimum overweight distance d. Then,*

$$|C|(|C|-1)d \leq \sum_{x\in C}\sum_{y\in C} D(x,y) \leq |C|^2 n\,\eta.$$

Proof. The first inequality follows since the distance between all distinct pairs of C is at least d.

For the second inequality, let $p_i : R^n \to R$ be the projection onto the ith coordinate. Note that

$$P_i(z) := \frac{|p_i^{-1}(z)\cap C|}{|C|}$$

defines a probability distribution on R for all $i \in \{1,\ldots,n\}$. Using Proposition 5, we obtain that

$$\begin{aligned} \sum_{x\in C}\sum_{y\in C} D(x,y) &= \sum_{i=1}^{n}\sum_{x\in C}\sum_{y\in C} W(x_i-y_i) \\ &= \sum_{i=1}^{n}\sum_{r\in R}\sum_{s\in R} W(r-s)P_i(r)P_i(s)|C|^2 \\ &\leq |C|^2\sum_{i=1}^{n}\eta = |C|^2 n\eta. \end{aligned}$$

Thus, we obtain the claim. □

From this inequality, we obtain a Plotkin bound for the overweight distance. As before, R is a local ring with non-zero maximal ideal J and $\eta = 2\left(1-\frac{1}{|J|}\right)$.

Theorem 3 (Plotkin bound for the overweight distance). *Let $C \subseteq R^n$ be a (not necessarily linear) code of minimum overweight distance $d = D(C)$ and assume that $d > n\eta$. Then,*

$$|C| \leq \frac{d}{d - n\eta}.$$

Proof. We divide both sides of the inequality in Proposition 6 by $|C|$ to obtain that

$$|C|(d - n\eta) \leq d.$$

The result then follows from the assumption that $d - n\eta > 0$. □

By rearranging the same inequality, we also obtain the following version of the Plotkin bound, which does not require the assumption that $d > n\eta$.

Corollary 4. *Let $C \subseteq R^n$ be a (not necessarily linear) code with $| C | \geq 2$ and let $d = D(C)$. Then,*

$$d \leq \frac{|C|n\eta}{|C| - 1}.$$

Proof. We obtain this by dividing both sides of the inequality in Proposition 6 by $|C|(|C| - 1)$, which is non-zero by assumption. □

Remark 2. *Note that W is a homogeneous weight on $\mathbb{Z}_4$, and thus our bound coincides with the bound from [10] for the homogeneous weight on $\mathbb{Z}_4$.*

Example 5. *If we consider codes over $\mathbb{Z}_9$ and fix $|C| = 9$, $n = 3$. We obtain that $d \leq 9/2$ and hence by the integrality that $d \leq 4$. The linear code*

$$C = \langle (1, 1, 3) \rangle$$

attains this bound.

5. A Johnson Bound for the Homogeneous Weight

Another interesting bound is the Johnson bound due to its relation with list-decodability. In the classical form, the Johnson bound gives an upper bound on the largest size $A_q(n, d, w)$ of a constant-weight w code over $\mathbb{F}_q$ of length n and minimum Hamming distance d. However, for the list-decodability of a code, we are interested in codes having codewords of weight *at most* w. In fact, if the largest size of such a code $A'_q(n, d, w)$ is small, e.g., at most a constant L, then every ball of radius w contains at most L codewords and hence one can decode a list of a size at most L. In more detail, the Johnson bound for list-decodability in the Hamming metric states that, if

$$\frac{w}{n} < (1 - \frac{1}{q})\left(1 - \sqrt{1 - \frac{q}{q-1}\delta}\right) = J_q(\delta),$$

where δ denotes the relative minimum distance, then $A'_q(n, d, w) \leq n(d - 1)$.

This famous bound is still missing for the well-studied homogeneous weight, which is, like the overweight, a generalization of the Lee weight over $\mathbb{Z}_4$. In this section, we prove a Johnson bound for the homogeneous weight from Definition 6, denoted by wt and let γ be its average weight on R. By abuse of notation, we denote with wt also the extension of wt to R^n, that is,

$$wt(x) = \sum_{i=1}^{n} wt(x_i).$$

Note that wt does not necessarily satisfy the triangle inequality. In [7] (Theorem 2), it is shown that the homogeneous weight on $\mathbb{Z}_m$ satisfies the triangle inequality if and only if m is not divisible by 6.

We define the ball of radius r with respect to a homogeneous weight wt to be the set of all elements having distance less than or equal to r.

Definition 10. *Let $y \in R^n$ and $r \in \mathbb{R}_{\geq 0}$. The ball $B_{r,wt}(y)$ of radius r centered in y is defined as*

$$B_{r,wt}(y) := \{x \in R^n \mid wt(x-y) \leq r\}.$$

Our aim is to provide a Johnson bound for the homogeneous weight over Frobenius rings. Thus, we begin by defining list-decodability.

Definition 11. *Let R be a finite ring. Given $\rho \in \mathbb{R}_{\geq 0}$, a code $C \subseteq R^n$ is called (ρ, L) list-decodable (with respect to wt) if, for every $y \in R^n$, it holds that*

$$|B_{\rho n,wt}(y) \cap C| \leq L.$$

Over Frobenius rings, the following result holds, which will play an important role in the proof of the Johnson bound.

Proposition 7 ([10] (Corollary 3.3))**.** *Let R be a Frobenius ring, $C \subseteq R^n$ a (not necessarily linear) code of minimum distance d and $\omega = \max\{wt(c) \mid c \in C\}$. If $\omega \leq \gamma n$, then*

$$|C|(|C|-1)d \leq \sum_{x,y \in C} wt(x-y) \leq 2|C|^2\omega - \frac{|C|^2\omega^2}{\gamma n}.$$

With this, we obtain an analogue of the Johnson bound for the homogeneous weight.

Theorem 4. *Let R be a Frobenius ring and $C \subseteq R^n$ be a (not necessarily linear) code of minimum distance d. Assume that $\rho \leq \gamma$. Then, it holds that C is $(\rho, d\gamma n)$ list-decodable if one of the following conditions is satisfied:*

(i) We have that $\gamma n(d - \gamma n) \geq 1$.

(ii) It holds that $\rho \leq \gamma - \sqrt{(\gamma - \frac{d}{n})\gamma + \frac{1}{n^2}}$.

Proof. Assume that $e \leq \rho n$ and let $y \in R^n$. We have to show that, under the given conditions, $|B_{e,wt}(y) \cap C| \leq d\gamma n$.

Note first that we may assume that $y = 0$; otherwise, simply consider the translate

$$C' = \{c - y \mid c \in C\}.$$

Assume that $x_1, \ldots, x_N$ are in $B_{e,wt}(0) \cap C$. We have that $wt(x_i - x_j) \geq d$ for $i \neq j$, thus using Proposition 7 and $wt(x-y) = wt(y-x)$, we obtain that

$$N(N-1)d \leq 2\sum_{i<j} wt(x_i - x_j) \leq 2N^2 e - \frac{N^2e^2}{\gamma n}.$$

Hence, it follows that

$$N(d\gamma n - 2e\gamma n + e^2) \leq d\gamma n.$$

It holds that

$$d\gamma n - 2e\gamma n + e^2 = (n\gamma - e)^2 - n\gamma(n\gamma - d).$$

If we assume that $n\gamma(n\gamma - d) \leq -1$, then we clearly have

$$(n\gamma - e)^2 - n\gamma(n\gamma - d) \geq 1.$$

If this is not the case, we see that $\sqrt{(\gamma - \frac{d}{n})\gamma + \frac{1}{n^2}}$ is well-defined. Thus, if

$$\frac{e}{n} \leq \gamma - \sqrt{\left(\gamma - \frac{d}{n}\right)\gamma + \frac{1}{n^2}},$$

then

$$n\gamma - e \geq \sqrt{(n\gamma - d)n\gamma + 1},$$

and hence

$$(n\gamma - e)^2 - n\gamma(n\gamma - d) \geq 1.$$

It follows that $N \leq d\gamma n$. □

Remark 3. *Note that the second condition already forces $\rho \leq \gamma$.*

Example 6. *As an easy example, we can consider the code $C = \langle(1,1),(4,0)\rangle \subset \mathbb{Z}_8^2$ of minimum homogeneous distance 2 and $\gamma = 1$. The second condition of Theorem 4 is clearly satisfied by choosing $\rho = 1/2$ since*

$$\gamma - \sqrt{\left(\gamma - \frac{d}{n}\right)\gamma + \frac{1}{n^2}} = \frac{1}{2},$$

implying that the code is $(1/2, 4)$ list decodable. For example, when setting $y = (1,2)$, we see that

$$B_{1,wt}(y) \cap C = \{(1,1),(2,2),(1,5),(6,2)\},$$

so the bound is attained.

6. Open Problems

We conclude this paper with some interesting open questions for the newly defined overweight that we have encountered.

Problem 1. *Classify the codes that attain the bounds derived in this paper.*

Problem 2. *Give a Griesmer bound, an Elias-Bassalygo and a Johnson bound for the overweight.*

Proving an analogue of a Griesmer, Elias-Bassalygo and Johnson bound poses a difficult challenge over rings and in particular for the overweight, due to the necessity of an effective upper bound on the sum of the distances.

Author Contributions: All authors contributed to the content of this article. Conceptualization, N.G., M.G., J.R. and V.W.; methodology, N.G., M.G., J.R. and V.W.; validation, N.G., M.G., J.R. and V.W.; formal analysis, N.G., M.G., J.R. and V.W.; investigation, N.G., M.G., J.R. and V.W.; data curation, N.G., M.G., J.R. and V.W.; writing—original draft preparation, N.G., M.G., J.R. and V.W.; writing—review and editing, N.G., M.G., J.R. and V.W.; visualization, N.G., M.G., J.R. and V.W. All authors have read and agreed to the published version of the manuscript.

Funding: The first and third author are supported by armasuisse Science and Technology (Project Nr.: CYD C-2020010) and were supported in part by the Swiss National Science Foundation Grant No. 188430. The fourth author is supported by the Swiss National Science Foundation Grant No. 195290 and by the European Union's Horizon 2020 research and innovation programme under the Marie Skłodowska-Curie grant agreement No. 899987.

Institutional Review Board Statement: Not applicable.

Data Availability Statement: Not applicable.

Conflicts of Interest: The authors declare no conflict of interest.

References

1. Kerdock, A.M. A class of low-rate nonlinear binary codes. *Inf. Control.* **1972**, *20*, 182–187. [CrossRef]
2. Preparata, F.P. A class of optimum nonlinear double-error-correcting codes. *Inf. Control.* **1968**, *13*, 378–400. [CrossRef]
3. Nechaev, A.A. Kerdock's code in cyclic form. *Diskret. Mat.* **1989**, *1*, 123–139. [CrossRef]
4. Hammons, A.R., Jr.; Kumar, P.V.; Calderbank, A.R.; Sloane, N.J.A.; Solé, P. The $\mathbb{Z}_4$-linearity of Kerdock, Preparata, Goethals, and related codes. *IEEE Trans. Inform. Theory* **1994**, *40*, 301–319. [CrossRef]
5. Krotov, D.S. On $\mathbb{Z}_{2^k}$-Dual Binary Codes. *IEEE Trans. Inf. Theory* **2007**, *53*, 1532–1537. [CrossRef]
6. Shi, M.; Wu, R.; Krotov, D.S. On $\mathbb{Z}_{p^k}$-Additive Codes and Their Duality. *IEEE Trans. Inf. Theory* **2019**, *65*, 3841–3847. [CrossRef]
7. Constantinescu, I.; Heise, W. A metric for codes over residue class rings. *Probl. Peredachi Informatsii* **1997**, *33*, 22–28.
8. Greferath, M.; Schmidt, S.E. Gray isometries for finite chain rings and a nonlinear ternary (36, 3^{12}, 15) code. *IEEE Trans. Inform. Theory* **1999**, *45*, 2522–2524. [CrossRef]
9. Nechaev, A.A.; Honold, T. Weighted modules and representations of codes. *Probl. Peredachi Informatsii* **1999**, *35*, 18–39.
10. Greferath, M.; O'Sullivan, M.E. On bounds for codes over Frobenius rings under homogeneous weights. *Discret. Math.* **2004**, *289*, 11–24. [CrossRef]
11. Bachoc, C. Applications of coding theory to the construction of modular lattices. *J. Comb. Theory Ser. A* **1997**, *78*, 92–119. [CrossRef]
12. Dougherty, S.T.; Kim, J.L.; Kulosman, H. MDS codes over finite principal ideal rings. *Des. Codes Cryptogr.* **2009**, *50*, 77–92. [CrossRef]
13. Norton, G.H.; Salagean, A. On the Hamming distance of linear codes over a finite chain ring. *IEEE Trans. Inf. Theory* **2000**, *46*, 1060–1067. [CrossRef]
14. Byrne, E.; Horlemann, A.L.; Khathuria, K.; Weger, V. Density of Free Modules over Finite Chain Rings. *arXiv* **2021**, arXiv:2106.09403.
15. van Lint, J. *Introduction to Coding Theory*; Graduate Texts in Mathematics; Springer: Berlin/Heidelberg, Germany, 1982.

entropy

Article

Gaussian Multiuser Wiretap Channels in the Presence of a Jammer-Aided Eavesdropper †

Rémi A. Chou [1,*] and Aylin Yener [2,*]

1 Department of Electrical Engineering and Computer Science, Wichita State University, Wichita, KS 67260, USA
2 Department of Electrical and Computer Engineering, The Ohio State University, Columbus, OH 43210, USA
* Correspondence: remi.chou@wichita.edu (R.A.C.); yener@ece.osu.edu (A.Y.)

† This paper is an extended version of our paper published in Chou, R.; Yener, A. The Gaussian multiple access wiretap channel when the eavesdropper can arbitrarily jam. In Proceedings of the IEEE International Symposium on Information Theory (ISIT), Aachen, Germany, 25–30 June 2017.

Abstract: This paper considers secure communication in the presence of an eavesdropper and a malicious jammer. The jammer is assumed to be oblivious of the communication signals emitted by the legitimate transmitter(s) but can employ any jamming strategy subject to a given power constraint and shares her jamming signal with the eavesdropper. Four such models are considered: (i) the Gaussian point-to-point wiretap channel; (ii) the Gaussian multiple-access wiretap channel; (iii) the Gaussian broadcast wiretap channel; and (iv) the Gaussian symmetric interference wiretap channel. The use of pre-shared randomness between the legitimate users is not allowed in our models. Inner and outer bounds are derived for these four models. For (i), the secrecy capacity is obtained. For (ii) and (iv) under a degraded setup, the optimal secrecy sum-rate is characterized. Finally, for (iii), ranges of model parameter values for which the inner and outer bounds coincide are identified.

Keywords: Gaussian wiretap channel; Gaussian multiple-access wiretap channel; Gaussian broadcast wiretap channel; jamming; secure communication

Citation: Chou, R.A.; Yener, A. Gaussian Multiuser Wiretap Channels in the Presence of a Jammer-Aided Eavesdropper. *Entropy* **2022**, *24*, 1595. https://doi.org/10.3390/e24111595

Academic Editor: Eduard Jorswieck

Received: 29 September 2022
Accepted: 28 October 2022
Published: 2 November 2022

1. Introduction

Consider secure communication over wireless channels between legitimate parties in the presence of an eavesdropper and a malicious jammer. The jammer is assumed to be oblivious of the legitimate users' communication but can employ any jamming strategy subject to a given power constraint. Consequently, the main channel between the legitimate users is arbitrarily varying [1]. Unlike most works that consider arbitrarily varying channels, however, pre-shared randomness is not available to the legitimate users in our scenario. Additionally, the jammer shares her jamming signal with the eavesdropper who can thus perfectly cancel the effect of the jamming signal on her channel. In this paper, we study the fundamental limits of secure communication rates in the presence of such a jammer-aided eavesdropper over four Gaussian wiretap channel models: the Gaussian wiretap channel [2], the Gaussian multiple-access wiretap channel [3], the Gaussian broadcast wiretap channel [4], and the Gaussian symmetric interference wiretap channel.

1.1. Contributions

Our contributions are summarized as follows.

- For secure communication over Gaussian point-to-point, multiple-access, broadcast, and symmetric interference wiretap channels in the presence of a jammer-aided eavesdropper as described above, we determine inner and outer bounds on the secrecy capacity region.
- We show that our bounds are tight for the point-to-point setting, tight for sum-rates for the multiple-access and interference settings under degraded setups, and tight for some ranges of model parameter values for the broadcast setting.

Our main strategy to handle our multiuser settings is to reduce the problem to single-user coding. Previous known techniques for such a reduction, such as rate-splitting [5] and successive cancellation decoding [5] [Appendix C], that have been developed for multiple-access settings without security constraints, do not easily apply to wiretap channel models. These techniques consist in achieving the corner points of achievability regions that can be described by polymatroids whose corner points have *positive components*. However, regions described by polymatroids whose corner points have *negative components*, as in our wiretap channel models, prevent the applications of these techniques. We overcome this roadblock by proposing novel time-sharing strategies coupled with appropriate secret-key exchanges between the legitimate users. As seen in the proofs of our results, eavesdropping and arbitrary jamming are not easy to decouple in the secrecy analysis. In particular, the analysis of the secrecy in our proposed model does not follow from a standard secrecy analysis in the absence of jamming, as we need to consider (i) codewords uniformly distributed over spheres, which we use to handle an arbitrarily varying main channel; and (ii) block-Markov coding and specific time-sharing strategies (to allow the reduction of multiuser coding to single-user coding) which create inter-dependencies between coding blocks. Note that our achievability schemes also rely on point-to-point codes developed in [1]. One of the benefits of reducing multiuser coding to point-to-point coding techniques is that despite the fact that our setting involves multiple transmitters and an arbitrarily varying channel between the legitimate users, *pre-shared randomness among the legitimate users will not be needed in our achievability schemes*. Our strategy for the converse consists of reducing the problem of determining a converse for our model to the problem of determining a converse for a related model in the absence of a jammer.

1.2. Related Works

Related works that consider simultaneous eavesdropping and oblivious jamming threats for the point-to-point discrete memoryless wiretap channel include [6–11]. The proof techniques used in these references to obtain security, such as random binning [12,13], resolvability/soft covering [10,14,15], or typicality arguments, are challenging to apply to a Gaussian setting in the absence of shared randomness at the legitimate user. Specifically, for the Gaussian point-to-point channel in the presence of an adversary that arbitrarily jams [1], the only known coding mechanism to obtain reliability in the absence of pre-shared randomness relies on codewords uniformly drawn on a unit sphere [1], which are challenging to integrate with the above techniques to obtain security because their components are not independent and identically distributed.

Another line of work [16] considers Gaussian channel models where the eavesdropper channel can vary arbitrarily, but the main channel is not. The setting considered in the present paper, where the main channel between the legitimate users is arbitrarily varying, prevents the use of analyses similar to those in [16] for the same reasons described above.

Several other works have considered continuous channel models, including the Gaussian MIMO wiretap channel [17], the Gaussian multiple-access wiretap channel [18], where deviating users can be viewed as active adversary, and continuous point-to-point wiretap channels [19,20], where the adversary can choose between eavesdropping or jamming. These references differ from the above-mentioned references on arbitrarily varying channels as they assume a specific signaling strategy for the jammer.

Finally, note that for point-to-point channels, stronger jamming strategies that depend on the signals of the legitimate transmitters have been studied in [21–23].

1.3. Organization of the Paper

The remainder of the paper is organized as follows. We describe the models in Section 2. We present our results for the Gaussian point-to-point wiretap channel, the Gaussian multiple-access wiretap channel, the Gaussian broadcast wiretap channel, and the Gaussian symmetric interference wiretap channel in Sections 3–6, respectively. We discuss in Section 4.2 a way to avoid, at least for some channel parameters, time-sharing for the multiple-access setting. We also discuss in Section 4.3 an extension of the multiple-access setting to more than two transmitters. We detail the proofs for the multiple-access setting in Sections 7 and 8. We end the paper with concluding remarks in Section 9.

2. Problem Statement

2.1. Notation

For $a, b \in \mathbb{R}$, define $[\![a,b]\!] \triangleq [\lfloor a \rfloor, \lceil b \rceil] \cap \mathbb{N}$, $]a,b[\triangleq [a,b] \backslash \{a,b\}$, $]a,b] \triangleq [a,b] \backslash \{a\}$, and $[a,b[\triangleq [a,b] \backslash \{b\}$. The components of a vector, X^n, of size $n \in \mathbb{N}$, are denoted by subscripts, i.e., $X^n \triangleq (X_1, X_2, \dots, X_n)$. For $x \in \mathbb{R}$, define $[x]^+ \triangleq \max(0, x)$. The notation $x \mapsto y$ describes a function that associates y to x when the domain and the image of the function are clear from the context. The power set of a finite set $\mathcal{S}$ is denoted by $2^{\mathcal{S}}$. The convex hull of a set $\mathcal{S}$ is denoted by $\text{Conv}(\mathcal{S})$. Unless specified otherwise, capital letters designate random variables, whereas lowercase letters designate realizations of associated random variables, e.g., x is a realization of the random variable X. For $R \in \mathbb{R}_+$, $\mathbb{B}_0^n(R)$ denotes the ball of radius R centered in 0 in $\mathbb{R}^n$ under the Euclidian norm.

2.2. Gaussian Multiuser Wiretap Channel in the Presence of a Jammer-Aided Eavesdropper

Consider the Gaussian memoryless wiretap channel model with two transmitters and two legitimate receivers

$$Y_1^n \triangleq \sqrt{g_{11}} X_1^n + \sqrt{g_{12}} X_2^n + \sqrt{g_{13}} S^n + N_1^n, \tag{1a}$$
$$Y_2^n \triangleq \sqrt{g_{21}} X_1^n + \sqrt{g_{22}} X_2^n + \sqrt{g_{23}} S^n + N_2^n, \tag{1b}$$
$$Z^n \triangleq \sqrt{h_1} X_1^n + \sqrt{h_2} X_2^n + N_Z^n, \tag{1c}$$

where Y_1^n, Y_2^n are the channel outputs observed by the legitimate receivers, and Z^n is the channel output observed by the eavesdropper. For $l \in \{1,2\}$, X_l^n is the signal emitted by Transmitter l satisfying the power constraint $\|X_l^n\|^2 \triangleq \sum_{i=1}^n (X_l)_i^2 \leq n\Gamma_l$, S^n is an arbitrary jamming sequence transmitted by the jammer that is oblivious of the communication of the legitimate users and satisfies the power constraint $\|S^n\|^2 \triangleq \sum_{i=1}^n S_i^2 \leq n\Lambda$, and $N_{Y_1}^n$, $N_{Y_2}^n$, N_Z^n are sequences of independent and identically distributed Gaussian noise with variances σ_1^2, σ_2^2, σ_Z^2, respectively. The channel coefficients g_{11}, g_{12}, g_{13}, g_{21}, g_{22}, g_{23}, h_1, h_2 are fixed and known to all parties. Note that we assume that the jammer helps the eavesdropper by sharing her jamming sequence, which allows the eavesdropper to perfectly cancel S^n from Z^n. Coding schemes and achievable rates are defined as follows.

Definition 1. *Let $n, k \in \mathbb{N}$. A $(2^{nR_1}, 2^{nR_2}, n, k)$ code C_n consists, for each block $j \in [\![1,k]\!]$, of*

- *Two message sets $\mathcal{M}_l^{(j)} \triangleq [\![1, 2^{nR_l^{(j)}}]\!]$, $l \in \{1,2\}$;*
- *Two stochastic encoders, $e_l^{(j)} : \mathcal{M}_l^{(j)} \to \mathbb{B}_0^n(\sqrt{n\Gamma_l})$, $l \in \{1,2\}$;*
- *Two decoders, $g_l^{(j)} : \mathbb{R}^n \to \mathcal{M}_l^{(j)}$, $l \in \{1,2\}$;*

where for any $l \in \{1,2\}$, $R_l = \frac{1}{k}\sum_{j=1}^k R_l^{(j)}$, and operates as follows. For each block $j \in [\![1,k]\!]$, transmitter $l \in \{1,2\}$ encodes with $e_l^{(j)}$ a uniformly distributed message $M_l^{(j)} \in \mathcal{M}_l^{(j)}$ to a codeword of length n, which is sent to the legitimate receiver over the channel described by Equation (1a), Equation (1b), Equation (1c) with the power constraint $n\Lambda$ for the jamming signal S_i^n. Note that all the power constraints at the transmitters and the jammer hold for a given transmission block of length n, which is relevant when the power constraints hold within any time window corresponding to n channel uses. Then, the legitimate receiver $l \in \{1,2\}$ forms an estimate $\widehat{M}_l^{(j)} \triangleq g_l^{(j)}(Y_l^n)$ of the message $M_l^{(j)}$. We define $\widehat{M} \triangleq \left(\widehat{M}_1^{(j)}, \widehat{M}_2^{(j)}\right)_{j \in [\![1,k]\!]}$, $M \triangleq \left(M_1^{(j)}, M_2^{(j)}\right)_{j \in [\![1,k]\!]}$, $S \triangleq (S_i^n)_{i \in [\![1,k]\!]}$, and $\mathcal{S} \triangleq \{(S_i^n)_{i \in [\![1,k]\!]} : \|S_i^n\|^2 \leq n\Lambda, \forall i \in [\![1,k]\!]\}$.

Definition 2. *A rate pair* (R_1, R_2) *is achievable, if there exists a sequence of* $(2^{nR_1}, 2^{nR_2}, n, k)$ *codes such that*

$$\lim_{n\to\infty} \sup_{S\in\mathcal{S}} \mathbb{P}[\widehat{M} \neq M] = 0 \text{ (reliability)}, \tag{2a}$$

$$\lim_{n\to\infty} \frac{1}{nk} H(M|Z^{kn}) \geq R_1 + R_2 \text{ (equivocation)}. \tag{2b}$$

2.3. Special Case 1: The Gaussian Wiretap Channel in the Presence of a Jammer-Aided Eavesdropper

Assume that the two transmitters are colocated and the two receivers are colocated in Section 2.2. More specifically, as depicted in Figure 1, the channel model of Section 2.2 becomes

$$Y^n \triangleq X^n + S^n + N_1^n, \tag{3a}$$

$$Z^n \triangleq \sqrt{h} X^n + N_Z^n, \tag{3b}$$

where $\sigma_1^2 = \sigma_Z^2 = 1$. We term this model as Gaussian Wiretap channel with Jammer-Aided eavesdropper (Gaussian WT-JA in short form). Note that this model recovers as a special case the Gaussian wiretap channel [2].

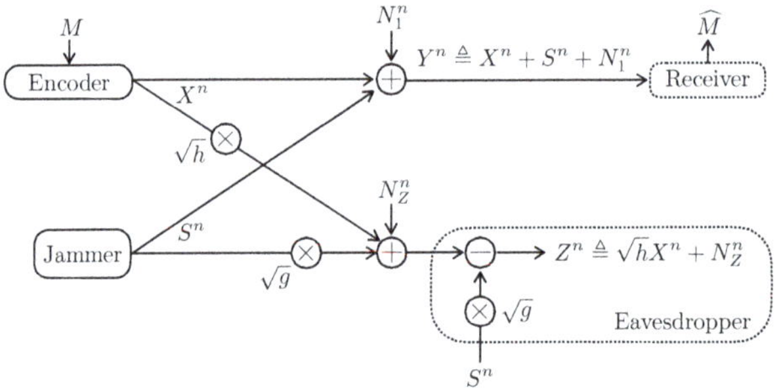

Figure 1. The Gaussian wiretap channel in the presence of a jammer-aided eavesdropper.

2.4. Special Case 2: The Gaussian Multiple-Access Wiretap Channel in the Presence of a Jammer-Aided Eavesdropper

Assume that the two receivers are colocated in Section 2.2. More specifically, as depicted in Figure 2, the channel model of Section 2.2 becomes

$$Y^n \triangleq X_1^n + X_2^n + S^n + N_1^n, \tag{4a}$$

$$Z^n \triangleq \sqrt{h_1} X_1^n + \sqrt{h_2} X_2^n + N_Z^n, \tag{4b}$$

where $\sigma_1^2 = \sigma_Z^2 = 1$. We term the model as Gaussian Multiple-Access Wiretap channel with Jammer-Aided eavesdropper (Gaussian MAC-WT-JA in short form) with the parameters $(\Gamma_1, \Gamma_2, h_1, h_2, \Lambda, \sigma_1^2, \sigma_Z^2)$. This model recovers as special cases the model in [24] in the absence of the security constraint (2b), and the Gaussian multiple-access wiretap channel [3]. Note that the model in [24] was introduced to study the presence of selfish transmitters via cooperative game theory, and that, similarly, the Gaussian MAC-WT-JA can be used to study the presence of selfish transmitters via coalitional game theory [25].

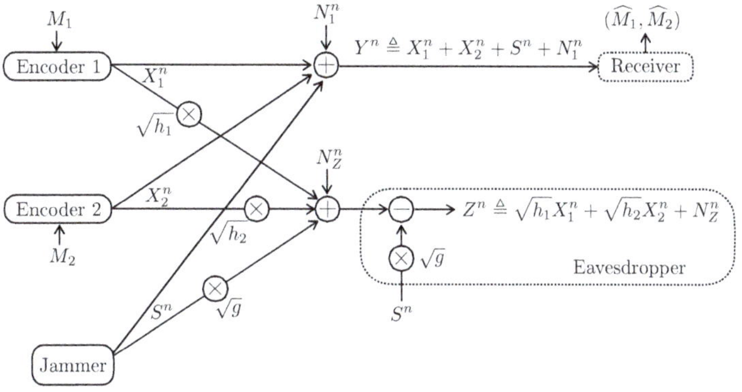

Figure 2. The Gaussian multiple-access wiretap channel in the presence of a jammer-aided eavesdropper.

2.5. Special Case 3: The Gaussian Broadcast Wiretap Channel in the Presence of a Jammer-Aided Eavesdropper

Assume that the two transmitters are colocated in Section 2.2. More specifically, as depicted in Figure 3, the channel model of Section 2.2 becomes

$$Y_1^n \triangleq X^n + \sqrt{g_1}S^n + N_1^n, \tag{5a}$$
$$Y_2^n \triangleq X^n + \sqrt{g_2}S^n + N_2^n, \tag{5b}$$
$$Z^n \triangleq \sqrt{h}X^n + N_Z^n, \tag{5c}$$

where $\sigma_Z^2 = 1$. We term the model as Gaussian Broadcast Wiretap channel with Jammer-Aided eavesdropper (Gaussian BC-WT-JA in short form). Note that this model recovers as special cases the multi-receiver wiretap channel [26] and the model in [27] in the absence of the security constraint (2b).

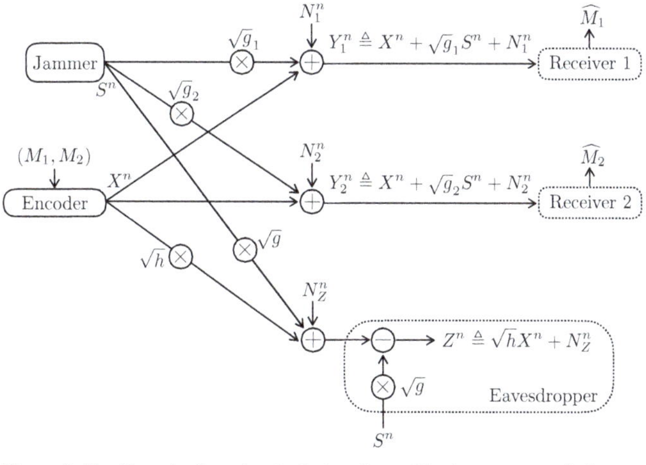

Figure 3. The Gaussian broadcast wiretap channel in the presence of a jammer-aided eavesdropper.

2.6. Special Case 4: The Gaussian Symmetric Interference Wiretap Channel in the Presence of a Jammer-Aided Eavesdropper

Consider the following special case of the channel model of Section 2.2

$$Y_1^n \triangleq X_1^n + X_2^n + S^n + N_1^n, \tag{6a}$$
$$Y_2^n \triangleq X_1^n + X_2^n + S^n + N_2^n, \tag{6b}$$
$$Z^n \triangleq \sqrt{h_1}X_1^n + \sqrt{h_2}X_2^n + N_Z^n, \tag{6c}$$

where $\sigma_1^2 = \sigma_2^2 = \sigma_Z^2 = 1$. We term the model as Gaussian Symmetric Interference Wiretap channel with Jammer-Aided eavesdropper (Gaussian SI-WT-JA in short form). In the absence of the security constraint (2b) and the jamming sequence, this model recovers a special case of the Gaussian interference channel under strong interference [28].

3. The Gaussian Wiretap Channel in the Presence of a Jammer-Aided Eavesdropper

We present a capacity result for the Gaussian WT-JA model described in Section 2.3.

Theorem 1. *The secrecy capacity of the Gaussian WT-JA is*

$$C(\Lambda) \triangleq \begin{cases} \left[\frac{1}{2}\log\left(\frac{1+(1+\Lambda)^{-1}\Gamma}{1+h\Gamma}\right)\right]^+ & \text{if } \Gamma > \Lambda \\ 0 & \text{if } \Gamma \leq \Lambda \end{cases}. \tag{7}$$

Observe that $C(\Lambda)$ is non-zero if and only if $\Gamma > \Lambda$ and $(1+\Lambda)^{-1} > h$. When $\Gamma > \Lambda$, Theorem 1 means that arbitrary oblivious jamming is no more harmful than Gaussian jamming, i.e., when the jamming sequence is obtained from independent and identical realizations of a zero-mean Gaussian random variable with variance equal to the power constraint Λ.

The proof of Theorem 1 follows as a special case of the achievability and converse bounds derived in the next section in Theorems 2 and 3, respectively, for the Gaussian MAC-WT-JA.

4. The Gaussian Multiple-Access Wiretap Channel in the Presence of a Jammer-Aided Eavesdropper

4.1. Inner and Outer Bounds for the Gaussian MAC-WT-JA

We derive inner and outer bounds for the Gaussian MAC-WT-JA in Theorems 2 and 3. Their proofs are provided in Sections 7 and 8, respectively.

Theorem 2 (Achievability). *We consider three cases.*

1. *When $\Gamma_1 > \Lambda$ and $\Gamma_2 \leq \Lambda$,*

$$\mathcal{R}_1^{\text{MAC}} \triangleq \left\{(R_1, 0) : R_1 \leq \max_{0\leq P_2\leq\Gamma_2}\left[\frac{1}{2}\log\left(\frac{1+\Gamma_1(1+\Lambda+P_2)^{-1}}{1+\Gamma_1 h_1(1+h_2P_2)^{-1}}\right)\right]^+\right\} \tag{8}$$

is achievable.

2. *When $\Gamma_2 > \Lambda$ and $\Gamma_1 \leq \Lambda$,*

$$\mathcal{R}_2^{\text{MAC}} \triangleq \left\{(0, R_2) : R_2 \leq \max_{0\leq P_1\leq\Gamma_1}\left[\frac{1}{2}\log\left(\frac{1+\Gamma_2(1+\Lambda+P_1)^{-1}}{1+\Gamma_2 h_2(1+h_1P_1)^{-1}}\right)\right]^+\right\} \tag{9}$$

is achievable.

3. *When $\min(\Gamma_1, \Gamma_2) > \Lambda$,*

$$\mathcal{R}^{\text{MAC}} \triangleq \text{Conv}\left(\mathcal{R}_1^{\text{MAC}} \cup \mathcal{R}_2^{\text{MAC}} \cup \bigcup_{\substack{\Lambda<P_1\leq\Gamma_1 \\ \Lambda<P_2\leq\Gamma_2}} \mathcal{R}_{1,2}^{\text{MAC}}(P_1, P_2)\right) \tag{10}$$

is achievable, where

$$\mathcal{R}_{1,2}^{\text{MAC}}(P_1,P_2) \triangleq \left\{(R_1,R_2) : R_1 \leq \left[\frac{1}{2}\log\left(\frac{1+P_1(1+\Lambda)^{-1}}{1+P_1h_1(1+h_2P_2)^{-1}}\right)\right]^+, \right.$$
$$R_2 \leq \left[\frac{1}{2}\log\left(\frac{1+P_2(1+\Lambda)^{-1}}{1+P_2h_2(1+h_1P_1)^{-1}}\right)\right]^+,$$
$$\left. R_1+R_2 \leq \left[\frac{1}{2}\log\left(\frac{1+(P_1+P_2)(1+\Lambda)^{-1}}{1+P_1h_1+P_2h_2}\right)\right]^+ \right\}. \quad (11)$$

Theorem 3 (Partial Converse)**.**

1. *If* $\max(\Gamma_1,\Gamma_2) \leq \Lambda$*, then no positive rate is achievable.*
2. *When* $\min(\Gamma_1,\Gamma_2) > \Lambda$ *and* $h_1 = h_2$*, the sum-rate bound of* $\mathcal{R}_{1,2}^{\text{MAC}}(\Gamma_1,\Gamma_2)$ *described in Equation (11) is tight by choosing* $(P_1,P_2) = (\Gamma_1,\Gamma_2)$*.*

Observe that in the achievability scheme for $\mathcal{R}_1^{\text{MAC}}$, choosing a transmission power smaller than Γ_1 for Transmitter 1 would result in a smaller region, since for a fixed P_2, $x \mapsto \log\left(\frac{1+x(1+\Lambda+P_2)^{-1}}{1+xh_1(1+h_2P_2)^{-1}}\right)$ is either negative when $(1+\Lambda+P_2)^{-1} \leq h_1(1+h_2P_2)^{-1}$, or non-decreasing when $(1+\Lambda+P_2)^{-1} > h_1(1+h_2P_2)^{-1}$. By exchanging the role of the transmitters, we have the same observation for $\mathcal{R}_2^{\text{MAC}}$.

4.2. Discussion of Rate-Splitting

Rate-splitting [5] can be adapted to the Gaussian MAC-WT-JA to avoid time-sharing, however, the entire region in Equation (11) cannot be achieved as splitting the power of one user precludes reliable communication. Assuming that

$$I(X_1X_2;Y) - I(X_1X_2;Z) \geq \max[I(X_1;Y|X_2) - I(X_1;Z), I(X_2;Y|X_1) - I(X_2;Z)], \quad (12)$$

then one can split the power of Transmitter 1 in $(P_1-\delta)$ and δ, where $\delta \in [0,P_1]$, and define the following functions from $[0,P_1]$ to $\mathbb{R}$

$$R_U : \delta \mapsto \frac{1}{2}\log\frac{1+(P_1-\delta)(1+\Lambda+\delta+P_2)^{-1}}{1+h_1(P_1-\delta)}, \quad (13a)$$
$$R_V : \delta \mapsto \frac{1}{2}\log\frac{1+\delta(1+\Lambda)^{-1}}{1+h_1\delta(1+h_1(P_1-\delta)+h_2P_2)^{-1}}, \quad (13b)$$
$$R_2 : \delta \mapsto \frac{1}{2}\log\frac{1+P_2(1+\Lambda+\delta)^{-1}}{1+h_2P_2(1+h_1(P_1-\delta))^{-1}}. \quad (13c)$$

Lemma 1. *For any* $\delta \in [0,P_1]$*, we have* $(R_U+R_V+R_2)(\delta) = I(X_1X_2;Y) - I(X_1X_2;Z)$*. Moreover, for any point* (x_0,y_0) *in*

$$\mathcal{D}(P_1,P_2) \triangleq \left\{(R_1,R_2) \in \mathcal{R}_{1,2}^{\text{MAC}}(P_1,P_2) : R_1+R_2 = \left[\frac{1}{2}\log\left(\frac{1+(P_1+P_2)(1+\Lambda)^{-1}}{1+P_1h_1+P_2h_2}\right)\right]^+\right\}, \quad (14)$$

there exists $\delta_0 \in [0,P_1]$ *such that* $x_0 = (R_U+R_V)(\delta_0)$ *and* $y_0 = R_2(\delta_0)$*.*

Proof. Define

$$Y \triangleq U+V+X_2+N_Y, \quad (15a)$$
$$Z \triangleq \sqrt{h_1}(U+V)+\sqrt{h_2}X_2+N_Z, \quad (15b)$$

where V, U, X_2, N_Y, N_Z are independent zero-mean Gaussian random variables with variances $\delta \in [0, P_1]$, $P_1 - \delta$, P_2, $(1 + \Lambda)$, 1, respectively. Additionally, define

$$R_U(\delta) \triangleq I(U;Y) - I(U;Z|VX_2) = \frac{1}{2}\log\frac{1 + (P_1 - \delta)(1 + \Lambda + \delta + P_2)^{-1}}{1 + h_1(P_1 - \delta)}, \tag{16a}$$

$$R_V(\delta) \triangleq I(V;Y|UX_2) - I(V;Z) = \frac{1}{2}\log\frac{1 + \delta(1 + \Lambda)^{-1}}{1 + h_1\delta(1 + h_1(P_1 - \delta) + h_2P_2)^{-1}}, \tag{16b}$$

$$R_2(\delta) \triangleq I(X_2;Y|U) - I(X_2;Z|V) = \frac{1}{2}\log\frac{1 + P_2(1 + \Lambda + \delta)^{-1}}{1 + h_2P_2(1 + h_1(P_1 - \delta))^{-1}}. \tag{16c}$$

By the chain rule, we have, for any $\delta \in [0, P_1]$, $(R_U + R_V + R_2)(\delta) = I(X_1X_2;Y) - I(X_1X_2;Z)$. Finally, since $(R_U + R_V)(0) = I(X_1;Y) - I(X_1;Z|X_2)$ and $(R_U + R_V)(P_1) = I(X_1;Y|X_2) - I(X_1;Z)$, by continuity of $\delta \mapsto (R_U + R_V)(\delta)$, there exists $\delta_0 \in [0, P_1]$ such that $x_0 = (R_U + R_V)(\delta_0)$ and $y_0 = R_2(\delta_0)$ for any point (x_0, y_0) in $\mathcal{D}(P_1, P_2)$. □

As remarked in [29], a potential issue is that $R_U(\delta_0)$ or $R_V(\delta_0)$ can be negative in Lemma 1. We have the following achievability result.

Proposition 1. *Let $(x_0, y_0) \in \mathcal{D}(P_1, P_2)$ and δ_0 be as in Lemma 1. Then, (x_0, y_0) can be achieved without time-sharing if $R_U(\delta_0) \geq 0$ and $R_V(\delta_0) \geq 0$ and $\min(\delta_0, P_1 - \delta_0) > \Lambda$. $(x_0, y_0) \in \mathcal{D}(P_1, P_2)$ can also be achieved without time-sharing if similar conditions (obtained by exchanging the role of the two transmitters) are satisfied when splitting the power of Transmitter 2.*

Proof idea: Transmitter 1 is split into two *virtual* users that transmit at rate $R_U(\delta)$ with power δ and at rate $R_V(\delta)$ with power $P_1 - \delta$. Encoding for User 2 and the two virtual users is similar to Case 1 in the proof of Theorem 2. The receiver adopts a minimum distance decoding rule as in Theorem 2 to first decode the message associated with the virtual user that transmits at rate R_V, then to decode the message associated with User 2, and finally, to decode the message associated with the virtual user that transmits at rate R_U. A similar procedure can be performed if one decides to split the power of Transmitter 2. □

An illustration of Proposition 1 is depicted in Figure 4. Note that for some model parameters, the set of points achievable with Proposition 1 can be empty and, unfortunately, it does not seem easy to obtain a simple analytical characterization of the rate pairs achievable with Proposition 1.

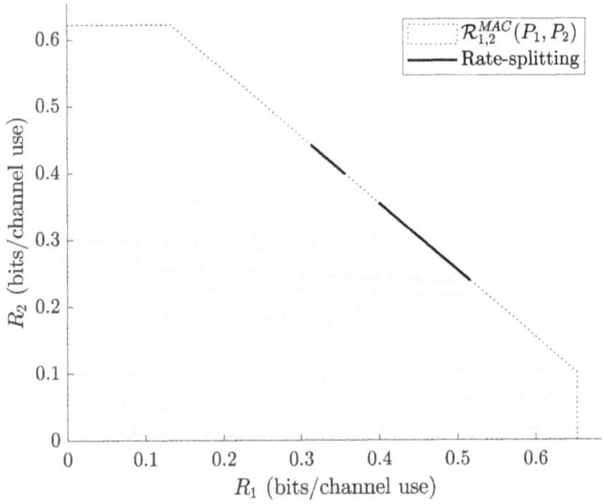

Figure 4. The shaded area represents $\mathcal{R}_{1,2}^{\text{MAC}}(P_1, P_2)$, where $(P_1, P_2, \Lambda, h_1, h_2) = (4, 3.3, 1.5, 0.12, 0.11)$. The solid segments represent the rate pairs achievable with Proposition 1.

4.3. Extension to More Than Two Transmitters

We extend our result for the MAC-WT-JA to the case of an arbitrary number of transmitters. The problem is more involved than the case of two transmitters and requires new time-sharing strategies that leverage extended polymatroid properties.

Consider the model of Section 2.4 with L transmitters instead of two transmitters. We let $\mathcal{L} \triangleq [\![1, L]\!]$ denote the set of transmitters. More specifically, the channel model of Section 2.4 becomes

$$Y^n \triangleq \sum_{l \in \mathcal{L}} X_l^n + S^n + N_1^n, \tag{17a}$$

$$Z^n \triangleq \sum_{l \in \mathcal{L}} \sqrt{h_l} X_l^n + N_Z^n, \tag{17b}$$

where $\sigma_1^2 = \sigma_Z^2 = 1$. We term the model as Gaussian MAC-WT-JA with parameters $((\Gamma_l)_{l\in\mathcal{L}}, (h_l)_{l\in\mathcal{L}}, \Lambda, \sigma_1^2, \sigma_Z^2)$. When the channel gains $(h_l)_{l\in\mathcal{L}}$ are all equal to $h \in [0,1[$, we refer to this model as the degraded MAC-WT-JA with parameters $((\Gamma_l)_{l\in\mathcal{L}}, h, \Lambda, \sigma_1^2, \sigma_Z^2)$. Given $\Lambda \in \mathbb{R}_+$ and $(\Gamma_l)_{l\in\mathcal{L}}$, we define $h_\Lambda \triangleq (1+\Lambda)^{-1}$, $\mathcal{L}(\Lambda) \triangleq \{l \in \mathcal{L} : \Gamma_l > \Lambda\}$, and $\mathcal{L}^c(\Lambda) \triangleq \mathcal{L} \backslash \mathcal{L}(\Lambda)$. The following achievability result is proven in Appendix B.

Theorem 4. *Assume that for all $l \in \mathcal{L}(\Lambda)$, $h_\Lambda > h_l$. The following region is achievable for the Gaussian MAC-WT-JA with parameters $((\Gamma_l)_{l\in\mathcal{L}}, (h_l)_{l\in\mathcal{L}}, \Lambda, 1, 1)$*

$$\mathcal{R} = \bigcup_{\substack{(P_l)_{l\in\mathcal{L}} \\ :\forall l \in \mathcal{L}(\Lambda), \Lambda < P_l \leq \Gamma_l}} \Bigg\{ (R_l)_{l\in\mathcal{L}} : \forall l \in \mathcal{L}^c(\Lambda), R_l = 0 \text{ and } \forall \mathcal{T} \subseteq \mathcal{L}(\Lambda), \; R_\mathcal{T} \leq \left[\frac{1}{2}\log\left(\frac{1+h_\Lambda P_\mathcal{T}}{1+(\sum_{l\in\mathcal{T}} h_l P_l)(1+\sum_{l\in\mathcal{T}^c} h_l P_l)^{-1}}\right)\right]^+ \Bigg\}, \tag{18}$$

where for any $(P_l)_{l\in\mathcal{L}}$ and $\mathcal{T} \subseteq \mathcal{L}$, we use the notation $P_\mathcal{T} \triangleq \sum_{l\in\mathcal{T}} P_l$.

We immediately obtain the following corollary.

Corollary 1. *The following region is achievable for the degraded Gaussian MAC-WT-JA with parameters $((\Gamma_l)_{l\in\mathcal{L}}, h, \Lambda, 1, 1)$*

$$\mathcal{R} = \bigcup_{\substack{(P_l)_{l\in\mathcal{L}} \\ :\forall l \in \mathcal{L}(\Lambda), \Lambda < P_l \leq \Gamma_l}} \Bigg\{ (R_l)_{l\in\mathcal{L}} : \forall l \in \mathcal{L}^c(\Lambda), R_l = 0 \text{ and } \forall \mathcal{T} \subseteq \mathcal{L}(\Lambda), \; R_\mathcal{T} \leq \left[\frac{1}{2}\log\left(\frac{1+h_\Lambda P_\mathcal{T}}{1+hP_\mathcal{T}(1+hP_{\mathcal{T}^c})^{-1}}\right)\right]^+ \Bigg\}. \tag{19}$$

Note that the achievability strategy used in the proof of Theorem 4 is different than the achievability strategy used in the proof of Theorem 2. While Theorem 4 gains in generality by considering an arbitrary number of users, it requires the assumption $\forall l \in \mathcal{L}(\Lambda), h_\Lambda > h_l$, which is not needed in Theorem 2. We also have the following optimality result, which is proven in Appendix C.

Theorem 5. *The maximal secrecy sum-rate $R_\mathcal{L} \triangleq \sum_{l\in\mathcal{L}} R_l$ achievable for the degraded Gaussian MAC-WT-JA with parameters $((\Gamma_l)_{l\in\mathcal{L}}, h, \Lambda, 1, 1)$ is*

$$\left[\frac{1}{2}\log\left(\frac{1+h_\Lambda \Gamma_{\mathcal{L}(\Lambda)}}{1+h\Gamma_{\mathcal{L}(\Lambda)}}\right)\right]^+. \tag{20}$$

Note that the optimal secrecy sum-rate is positive if and only if $h_\Lambda > h$ and $\mathcal{L}(\Lambda) \neq \emptyset$.

5. The Gaussian Broadcast Wiretap Channel in the Presence of a Jammer-Aided Eavesdropper

Theorems 6 and 7 provide inner and outer bounds, respectively, for the Gaussian BC-WT-JA.

Theorem 6 (Achievability). *We have the following inner bounds.*

1. *When* $g_2\Lambda \geq \Gamma$ *and* $g_1\Lambda < \Gamma$,

$$\mathcal{R}_1^{\mathrm{BC}} \triangleq \left\{ (R_1, 0) : R_1 \leq \left[\frac{1}{2} \log\left(\frac{1 + \frac{\Gamma}{\sigma_1^2 + g_1\Lambda}}{1 + h\Gamma} \right) \right]^+ \right\} \tag{21}$$

is achievable.

2. *When* $g_1\Lambda \geq \Gamma$ *and* $g_2\Lambda < \Gamma$,

$$\mathcal{R}_2^{\mathrm{BC}} \triangleq \left\{ (0, R_2) : R_2 \leq \left[\frac{1}{2} \log\left(\frac{1 + \frac{\Gamma}{\sigma_2^2 + g_2\Lambda}}{1 + h\Gamma} \right) \right]^+ \right\} \tag{22}$$

is achievable.

3. *When* $\max(g_1\Lambda, g_2\Lambda) < \Gamma$, *and, without loss of generality,* $\sigma_1^2 + g_1\Lambda \leq \sigma_2^2 + g_2\Lambda$ *(exchange the role of the receivers if* $\sigma_1^2 + g_1\Lambda > \sigma_2^2 + g_2\Lambda$*),*

$$\mathrm{Conv}\left(\mathcal{R}_1^{\mathrm{BC}} \cup \mathcal{R}_2^{\mathrm{BC}} \cup \bigcup_{\alpha \in]\max(g_1,g_2)\Lambda\Gamma^{-1}, 1]} \mathcal{R}^{\mathrm{BC}}(\alpha) \right), \tag{23}$$

is achievable where we have defined for $\alpha \in [0,1]$

$$\mathcal{R}^{\mathrm{BC}}(\alpha) \triangleq \left\{ (R_1, R_2) : R_1 \leq \left[\frac{1}{2} \log\left(\frac{1 + \frac{(1-\alpha)\Gamma}{\sigma_1^2 + g_1\Lambda}}{1 + h(1-\alpha)\Gamma} \right) \right]^+, \right.$$
$$\left. R_2 \leq \left[\frac{1}{2} \log\left(\frac{1 + \frac{\alpha\Gamma}{(1-\alpha)\Gamma + \sigma_2^2 + g_2\Lambda}}{1 + \frac{h\alpha\Gamma}{h(1-\alpha)\Gamma + 1}} \right) \right]^+ \right\}. \tag{24}$$

Note that $\mathcal{R}^{\mathrm{BC}}(\alpha = 0) = \mathcal{R}_1^{\mathrm{BC}}$ and $\mathcal{R}^{\mathrm{BC}}(\alpha = 1) = \mathcal{R}_2^{\mathrm{BC}}$. The achievability scheme of Theorem 6 is similar to the proof of Theorem 2 and [27] [Theorem 3].

Theorem 7 (Partial converse).

1. *If* $\Gamma \leq \min(g_1\Lambda, g_2\Lambda)$, *then no positive rate is achievable;*
2. *When* $g_2\Lambda \geq \Gamma$ *and* $g_1\Lambda < \Gamma$, *the achievability region* $\mathcal{R}_1^{\mathrm{BC}}$ *in Theorem 6 is tight;*
3. *When* $g_1\Lambda \geq \Gamma$ *and* $g_2\Lambda < \Gamma$, *the achievability region* $\mathcal{R}_2^{\mathrm{BC}}$ *in Theorem 6 is tight;*
4. *When* $\Gamma > \max(g_1\Lambda, g_2\Lambda)$, *the following region is an outer bound*

$$\bigcup_{\alpha \in [0,1]} \mathcal{R}^{\mathrm{BC}}(\alpha), \tag{25}$$

where $\mathcal{R}^{\mathrm{BC}}(\alpha)$ *has been defined in Theorem 6.*

The proof of Theorem 7 is similar to the proof of Theorem 3 using [26] in place of [30]. Observe that the gap between the inner and outer bounds of Theorems 6 and 7 when $\Gamma > \max(g_1\Lambda, g_2\Lambda)$ comes from the fact that our achievability scheme is limited to $\alpha \in]\max(g_1, g_2)\Lambda\Gamma^{-1}, 1] \cup \{0\}$.

6. The Symmetric Interference Wiretap Channel in the Presence of a Jammer-Aided Eavesdropper

By the symmetry in Equation (6a) and Equation (6b), a code for the Gaussian MAC-WT-JA allows Receiver $i \in \{1,2\}$ to securely recover the message of Transmitter i. Hence, from the achievability result for the Gaussian MAC-WT-JA, we have the following achievability result for the Gaussian SI-WT-JA.

Theorem 8 (Achievability). *We consider three cases.*

1. *When* $\Gamma_1 > \Lambda$ *and* $\Gamma_2 \leq \Lambda$, $\mathcal{R}_1^{\mathrm{SI}} \triangleq \mathcal{R}_1^{\mathrm{MAC}}$ *is achievable;*
2. *When* $\Gamma_2 > \Lambda$ *and* $\Gamma_1 \leq \Lambda$, $\mathcal{R}_2^{\mathrm{SI}} \triangleq \mathcal{R}_2^{\mathrm{MAC}}$ *is achievable;*
3. *When* $\min(\Gamma_1, \Gamma_2) > \Lambda$, $\mathcal{R}^{\mathrm{SI}} \triangleq \mathcal{R}^{\mathrm{MAC}}$ *is achievable;*

where $\mathcal{R}_1^{\mathrm{MAC}}$, $\mathcal{R}_2^{\mathrm{MAC}}$, *and* $\mathcal{R}^{\mathrm{MAC}}$ *are defined in Theorem 2.*

Next, by the symmetry in Equations (6a) and (6b), we have that any code for the Gaussian SI-WT-JA allows Receiver $i \in \{1,2\}$ to securely recover the messages from both transmitters, meaning that an outer bound for the Gaussian SI-WT-JA can be obtained by considering an outer bound for a Gaussian MAC-WT-JA. Hence, from the partial converse for the Gaussian MAC-WT-JA, we obtain the following partial converse for the Gaussian SI-WT-JA.

Theorem 9 (Partial converse).

1. *If* $\max(\Gamma_1, \Gamma_2) \leq \Lambda$, *then no positive rate is achievable.*
2. *When* $\min(\Gamma_1, \Gamma_2) > \Lambda$ *and* $h_1 = h_2$, *the sum-rate achieved in* $\mathcal{R}^{\mathrm{SI}}$ *is tight by choosing* $(P_1, P_2) = (\Gamma_1, \Gamma_2)$.

7. Proof of Theorem 2

To prove Theorem 2, it is sufficient to prove the achievability of the dominant face

$$\mathcal{D}(P_1,P_2) \triangleq \left\{ (R_1,R_2) \in \mathcal{R}_{1,2}^{\mathrm{MAC}}(P_1,P_2) : R_1 + R_2 = \left[\frac{1}{2} \log\left(\frac{1+(P_1+P_2)(1+\Lambda)^{-1}}{1+P_1h_1+P_2h_2} \right) \right]^+ \right\} \tag{26}$$

of $\mathcal{R}_{1,2}^{\mathrm{MAC}}(P_1,P_2)$ to prove the achievability of $\mathcal{R}_{1,2}^{\mathrm{MAC}}(P_1,P_2)$ when $\min(\Gamma_1,\Gamma_2) > \Lambda$ and where $(P_1,P_2) \in]\Lambda,\Gamma_1] \times]\Lambda,\Gamma_2]$. The achievability of $\mathcal{R}_i^{\mathrm{MAC}}$, $i \in \{1,2\}$, when $\Gamma_i > \Lambda$ and $\Gamma_{3-i} \leq \Lambda$ is obtained similarly by having Transmitter $\bar{i} \triangleq 3-i$ send Gaussian noise. Observe that the rate constraints in $\mathcal{R}_{1,2}^{\mathrm{MAC}}(P_1,P_2)$ can be expressed as

$$R_1 \leq [I(X_1;Y|X_2) - I(X_1;Z)]^+, \tag{27a}$$

$$R_2 \leq [I(X_2;Y|X_1) - I(X_2;Z)]^+, \tag{27b}$$

$$R_1 + R_2 \leq [I(X_1X_2;Y) - I(X_1X_2;Z)]^+, \tag{27c}$$

where

$$Y \triangleq X_1 + X_2 + N_Y, \tag{28a}$$

$$Z \triangleq \sqrt{h_1}X_1 + \sqrt{h_2}X_2 + N_Z, \tag{28b}$$

and X_1, X_2, N_Y, N_Z are independent zero-mean Gaussian random variables with variances P_1, P_2, $(1+\Lambda)$, 1, respectively. As remarked in [29], the set function $\mathcal{T} \mapsto I(X_{\mathcal{T}};Y|X_{\mathcal{T}^c}) - I(X_{\mathcal{T}};Z)$ is submodular but not necessarily non-decreasing, where $\forall \mathcal{T} \subseteq \{1,2\}$, $X_{\mathcal{T}} \triangleq (X_t)_{t \in \mathcal{T}}$. This is the main reason why achieving the corner points of $\mathcal{R}_{1,2}^{\mathrm{MAC}}(P_1,P_2)$ by means of point-to-point codes via the successive decoding method [5] [Appendix C] does not easily translate to our setting. Before we provide our solution, we summarize our proof strategy in the three cases below. Figure 5 illustrates these cases.

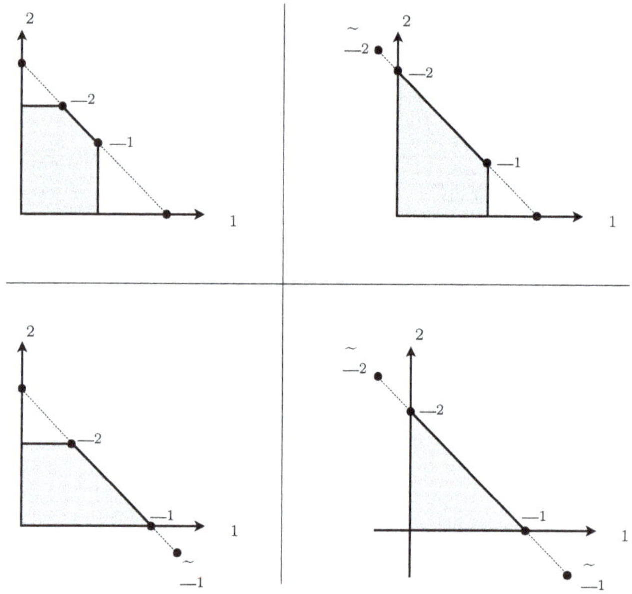

Figure 5. Region $\mathcal{R}_{1,2}(P_1, P_2)$.

Case 1: Assume

$$I(X_1X_2;Y) - I(X_1X_2;Z) \geq \max[I(X_1;Y|X_2) - I(X_1;Z), I(X_2;Y|X_1) - I(X_2;Z)]. \quad (29)$$

The corner points of $\mathcal{R}_{1,2}^{\text{MAC}}$ are given by

$$\underline{C}_1 \triangleq (I(X_1;Y|X_2) - I(X_1;Z), I(X_2;Y) - I(X_2;Z|X_1)), \quad (30a)$$

$$\underline{C}_2 \triangleq (I(X_1;Y) - I(X_1;Z|X_2), I(X_2;Y|X_1) - I(X_2;Z)). \quad (30b)$$

We will achieve each corner point with point-to-point coding techniques and perform time-sharing to achieve $\mathcal{D}(P_1, P_2)$. Specifically, to achieve $\underline{C}_i$, $i \in \{1,2\}$, the encoders will be designed such that the decoder can first estimate the codeword sent by Transmitter $\bar{i} \triangleq 3 - i$ (by considering the codewords of Transmitter i as noise), which is in turn used to estimate the codeword sent by Transmitter i. This approach is similar to the successive decoding method [5] [Appendix C] for a multiple-access channel in the absence of a security constraint.

Case 2.a: Assume

$$I(X_1X_2;Y) - I(X_1X_2;Z) \geq I(X_1;Y|X_2) - I(X_1;Z), \quad (31a)$$

$$I(X_1X_2;Y) - I(X_1X_2;Z) < I(X_2;Y|X_1) - I(X_2;Z). \quad (31b)$$

Hence,

$$\widetilde{\underline{C}}_2 \triangleq (I(X_1;Y) - I(X_1;Z|X_2), I(X_2;Y|X_1) - I(X_2;Z)) \quad (32)$$

has a negative x-coordinate and the method of Case 1 cannot be directly applied here. Now, the corner points of $\mathcal{R}_{1,2}^{\mathrm{MAC}}$ are

$$\underline{C}_1 \triangleq (I(X_1;Y|X_2) - I(X_1;Z), I(X_2;Y) - I(X_2;Z|X_1)), \tag{33a}$$
$$\underline{C}_2 \triangleq (0, I(X_1X_2;Y) - I(X_1X_2;Z))). \tag{33b}$$

The idea to achieve $\underline{C}_1$ is, as in Case 1, a successive decoding approach by decomposing the sum rate $I(X_1X_2;Y) - I(X_1X_2;Z)$ as the sum of $I(X_2;Y) - I(X_2;Z|X_1)$, which represents the secret message rate for Transmitter 2, and $I(X_1;Y|X_2) - I(X_1;Z)$, which represents the secret message rate for Transmitter 1. However, $\underline{C}_2$ cannot be decomposed in a similar manner and thus cannot be achieved with the same method. Instead, to achieve any point in $\mathcal{D}(P_1,P_2)$, we rely on a strategy over several transmission blocks. First, in an appropriate number of transmission blocks, the transmitters can send secret messages with rates $\underline{C}_1$ as in Case 1. Part of the secret messages of Transmitter 1, with a rate equal to the absolute value of the x-coordinate of the point $\widetilde{C}_2$, is dedicated to the exchange of a secret key between Transmitter 1 and the legitimate receiver. Then, for the remaining transmission blocks, Transmitter 2 transmits a secret message with rate $I(X_1X_2;Y) - I(X_1X_2;Z)$, while Transmitter 1 uses the previously generated secret key to produce a jamming signal, which can be canceled out by the legitimate receiver but not by the eavesdropper who does not know the secret key.

Case 2.b: Assume

$$I(X_1X_2;Y) - I(X_1X_2;Z) \geq I(X_2;Y|X_1) - I(X_2;Z), \tag{34a}$$
$$I(X_1X_2;Y) - I(X_1X_2;Z) < I(X_1;Y|X_2) - I(X_1;Z). \tag{34b}$$

This case is handled as Case 2.a by exchanging the role of the two transmitters.

Case 3: Assume

$$I(X_1X_2;Y) - I(X_1X_2;Z) < \min[I(X_1;Y|X_2) - I(X_1;Z), I(X_2;Y|X_1) - I(X_2;Z)]. \tag{35}$$

Hence,

$$\widetilde{C}_1 \triangleq (I(X_1;Y|X_2) - I(X_1;Z), I(X_2;Y) - I(X_2;Z|X_1)), \tag{36a}$$
$$\widetilde{C}_2 \triangleq (I(X_1;Y) - I(X_1;Z|X_2), I(X_2;Y|X_1) - I(X_2;Z)), \tag{36b}$$

have a negative y-component and a negative x-component, respectively, and the strategy of Case 1 or Case 2 cannot be directly applied here. The corner points of the region are

$$\underline{C}_1 \triangleq (I(X_1X_2;Y) - I(X_1X_2;Z), 0), \tag{37a}$$
$$\underline{C}_2 \triangleq (0, I(X_1X_2;Y) - I(X_1X_2;Z)). \tag{37b}$$

These corner points do not seem to be easily achievable using the method for Case 1. We will first show that it is possible to achieve a point $\underline{R} \in \mathcal{D}(P_1,P_2)$, where $\underline{R}$ has strictly positive components. All the other points in $\mathcal{D}(P_1,P_2)$ will then be achieved as in Case 2 by doing the substitutions $\underline{C}_1 \leftarrow \underline{R}$ and $\underline{C}_2 \leftarrow \underline{R}$ in Case 2.a and Case 2.b, respectively.

Note that it is sufficient to consider the case

$$\min[I(X_1;Y|X_2) - I(X_1;Z), I(X_2;Y|X_1) - I(X_2;Z)] \geq 0. \tag{38}$$

Indeed, for $i \in \{1,2\}$ and $\bar{i} \triangleq 3-i$, when $I(X_i;Y|X_{\bar{i}}) - I(X_i;Z) > 0$ and $I(X_{\bar{i}};Y|X_i) - I(X_{\bar{i}};Z) \leq 0$, we have $R_{\bar{i}} = 0$ and $R_i \leq I(X_1X_2;Y) - I(X_1X_2;Z) \leq I(X_i;Y|X_{\bar{i}}) - I(X_i;Z|X_{\bar{i}}) = \frac{1}{2}\log\left(\frac{1+P_i(1+\Lambda)^{-1}}{1+P_ih_i}\right)$. These cases correspond to Theorem 1 and can be treated as in Case 1.

7.1. Case 1

We show the achievability of $\underline{C}_2$. The achievability of $\underline{C}_1$ is obtained by exchanging the role of the transmitters.

Codebook construction: For Transmitter $i \in \{1,2\}$, construct a codebook $C_n^{(i)}$ with $\lceil 2^{nR_i} \rceil \lceil 2^{n\widetilde{R}_i} \rceil$ codewords drawn independently and uniformly on the sphere of radius $\sqrt{nP_i}$ in $\mathbb{R}^n$. The codewords are labeled $x_i^n(m_i, \widetilde{m}_i)$, where $m_i \in [\![1, 2^{nR_i}]\!]$, $\widetilde{m}_i \in [\![1, 2^{n\widetilde{R}_i}]\!]$. We define $C_n \triangleq (C_n^{(1)}, C_n^{(2)})$ and choose for $\delta > 0$

$$R_1 \triangleq I(X_1;Y) - I(X_1;Z|X_2) - \delta, \tag{39a}$$
$$\widetilde{R}_1 \triangleq I(X_1;Z|X_2) - \delta, \tag{39b}$$
$$R_2 \triangleq I(X_2;Y|X_1) - I(X_2;Z) - \delta, \tag{39c}$$
$$\widetilde{R}_2 \triangleq I(X_2;Z) - \delta. \tag{39d}$$

Encoding at Transmitter i $\in \{1,2\}$: Given $(m_i, \widetilde{m}_i)$, transmit $x_i^n(m_i, \widetilde{m}_i)$. In the remainder of the paper, we use the term randomization sequence for $\widetilde{m}_i$.

Decoding: The receiver performs minimum distance decoding to first estimate $(m_1, \widetilde{m}_1)$ and then to estimate $(m_2, \widetilde{m}_2)$, i.e., given y^n, it determines $(\hat{m}_1, \hat{\widetilde{m}}_1) \triangleq \phi_1(y^n, 0)$, and $(\hat{m}_2, \hat{\widetilde{m}}_2) \triangleq \phi_2(y^n, x_1^n(\hat{m}_1, \hat{\widetilde{m}}_1))$ where for $i \in \{1,2\}$

$$\phi_i(y^n, x) \triangleq \begin{cases} (m_i, \widetilde{m}_i) & \text{if } \|y^n - x - x_i^n(m_i, \widetilde{m}_i)\|^2 < \|y^n - x - x_i^n(m_i', \widetilde{m}_i')\|^2 \\ & \qquad \text{for } (m_i', \widetilde{m}_i') \neq (m_i, \widetilde{m}_i) \\ 0 & \text{if no such } (m_i, \widetilde{m}_i) \in [\![1, 2^{nR_i}]\!] \times [\![1, 2^{n\widetilde{R}_i}]\!] \text{ exists} \end{cases}. \tag{40}$$

Define $e(C_n, s^n) \triangleq \mathbb{P}\left[(\widehat{M}_1, \widehat{M}_2) \neq (M_1, M_2) | C_n\right]$. We now prove that $\mathbb{E}_{C_n}[\sup_{s^n} e(C_n, s^n)] + \frac{1}{n} I(M_1 M_2; Z^n | C_n) \xrightarrow{n \to \infty} 0$. We will thus conclude by Markov's inequality that there exists a sequence of realizations $(\mathcal{C}_n)_{n \geq 1}$ of $(C_n)_{n \geq 1}$ such that both $\sup_{s^n} e(\mathcal{C}_n, s^n)$ and $\frac{1}{n} I(M_1 M_2; Z^n | \mathcal{C}_n)$ can be made arbitrarily close to zero as $n \to \infty$.

Average probability of error: We have

$$\begin{aligned} e(C_n, s^n) &\leq \mathbb{P}\left[(\widehat{M}_1, \widehat{M}_2) \neq (M_1, M_2) \text{ or } (\hat{\widetilde{M}}_1, \hat{\widetilde{M}}_2) \neq (\widetilde{M}_1, \widetilde{M}_2) | C_n\right] & \text{(41a)} \\ &\leq e_1(C_n, s^n, x_2^n(M_2, \widetilde{M}_2)) + e_2(C_n, s^n, 0), & \text{(41b)} \end{aligned}$$

where for $i \in \{1,2\}$

$$\begin{aligned} e_i(C_n, s^n, x) \triangleq \frac{1}{\lceil 2^{nR_i} \rceil \lceil 2^{n\widetilde{R}_i} \rceil} \sum_{m_i} \sum_{\widetilde{m}_i} \mathbb{P}\Big[&\|x_i^n(m_i, \widetilde{m}_i) + s^n + x + N_Y^n - x_i^n(m_i', \widetilde{m}_i')\|^2 \\ &\leq \|s^n + x + N_Y^n\|^2 \text{ for some } (m_i', \widetilde{m}_i') \neq (m_i, \widetilde{m}_i) \Big]. \end{aligned} \tag{42}$$

Next, we have

$$\begin{aligned} \mathbb{E}_{C_n}[e_1(C_n, s^n, x_2^n(M_2, \widetilde{M}_2))] &\leq \mathbb{E}_{C_n}[e_1(C_n, s^n, x_2^n(M_2, \widetilde{M}_2)) | C_n^{(1)} \in \mathcal{C}_1^*] + \mathbb{P}[C_n^{(1)} \notin \mathcal{C}_1^*] & \text{(43a)} \\ &\xrightarrow{n \to \infty} 0, & \text{(43b)} \end{aligned}$$

where, in Equation (43a), $\mathcal{C}_1^*$ represents all the sets of unit norm vectors scaled by $\sqrt{nP_1}$ that satisfy the two conditions of Lemma A1 (in Appendix A), Equation (43b) holds because $\mathbb{P}[C_n^{(1)} \in \mathcal{C}_1^*] \xrightarrow{n \to \infty} 1$ by Lemma A1, and $\mathbb{E}_{C_n}[e_1(C_n, s^n, x_2^n(M_2, \widetilde{M}_2)) | C_n^{(1)} \in \mathcal{C}_1^*] \xrightarrow{n \to \infty} 0$ by Theorem A1 (in Appendix A) using that $R_1 + \widetilde{R}_1 < I(X_1;Y) = \frac{1}{2} \log\left(1 + \frac{P_1}{1 + \Lambda + P_2}\right)$ and by interpreting the signal of Transmitter 2 as noise. Then,

$$\mathbb{E}_{C_n}[e_2(C_n, s^n, 0)] \leq \mathbb{E}_{C_n}[e_2(C_n, s^n, 0)|C_n^{(2)} \in \mathcal{C}_2^*] + \mathbb{P}[C_n^{(2)} \notin \mathcal{C}_2^*] \tag{44a}$$

$$\xrightarrow{n\to\infty} 0, \tag{44b}$$

where, in Equation (44a), $\mathcal{C}_2^*$ represents all the sets of unit norm vectors scaled by $\sqrt{nP_2}$ that satisfy the two conditions of Lemma A1, Equation (44b) holds because $\mathbb{P}[C_n^{(2)} \in \mathcal{C}_2^*] \xrightarrow{n\to\infty} 1$ by Lemma A1, and $\mathbb{E}_{C_n}[e_2(C_n, s^n, 0)|C_n^{(2)} \in \mathcal{C}_2^*] \xrightarrow{n\to\infty} 0$ by Theorem A1 using that $R_2 + \widetilde{R}_2 < I(X_2; Y|X_1) = \frac{1}{2}\log\left(1 + \frac{P_2}{1+\Lambda}\right)$. Hence, by Equations (41b), (43b) and (44b), we have

$$\mathbb{E}_{C_n}[e(C_n, s^n)] \xrightarrow{n\to\infty} 0. \tag{45}$$

Equivocation: We first study the average error probability of decoding $(\widetilde{m}_1, \widetilde{m}_2)$ given (z^n, m_1, m_2) with the following procedure. Given (z^n, m_1, m_2), determine $\check{m}_2 \triangleq \psi_2(z^n, 0)$, and $\check{m}_1 \triangleq \psi_1(z^n, \sqrt{h_2}x_2^n(m_2, \check{m}_2))$ where

$$\psi_i(z^n, x) \triangleq \begin{cases} \widetilde{m}_i & \text{if } \|z^n - x - \sqrt{h_i}x_i^n(m_i, \widetilde{m}_i)\|^2 < \|z^n - x - \sqrt{h_i}x_i^n(m_i, \widetilde{m}_i')\|^2 \\ & \qquad \text{for } \widetilde{m}_i' \neq \widetilde{m}_i \\ 0 & \text{if no such } \widetilde{m}_i \in [\![1, 2^{n\widetilde{R}_i}]\!] \text{ exists} \end{cases}. \tag{46}$$

We define $\widetilde{e}(C_n) \triangleq \mathbb{P}\left[(\check{M}_1, \check{M}_2) \neq (\widetilde{M}_1, \widetilde{M}_2)|C_n\right]$ and for $i \in \{1, 2\}$,

$$\widetilde{e}_i(C_n, x) \triangleq \frac{1}{\lceil 2^{n\widetilde{R}_i} \rceil} \sum_{\widetilde{m}_i} \mathbb{P}\Big[\|\sqrt{h_i}x_i^n(m_i, \widetilde{m}_i) + x + N_Z^n - \sqrt{h_i}x_i^n(m_i, \widetilde{m}_i')\|^2 \leq \|x + N_Z^n\|^2 \text{ for some } \widetilde{m}_i' \neq \widetilde{m}_i\Big]. \tag{47}$$

Then, with the same notation as in Equations (43) and (44), we have

$$\mathbb{E}_{C_n}[\widetilde{e}(C_n)] \leq \mathbb{E}_{C_n}[\widetilde{e}_1(C_n, 0)] + \mathbb{E}_{C_n}[\widetilde{e}_2(C_n, \sqrt{h_1}x_1^n(M_1, \widetilde{M}_1))] \tag{48a}$$

$$\leq \mathbb{E}_{C_n}[\widetilde{e}_1(C_n, 0)|C_n^{(1)} \in \mathcal{C}_1^*] + \mathbb{P}[C_n^{(1)} \notin \mathcal{C}_1^*] + \mathbb{E}_{C_n}[\widetilde{e}_2(C_n, \sqrt{h_1}x_1^n(M_1, \widetilde{M}_1))|C_n^{(2)} \in \mathcal{C}_2^*] + \mathbb{P}[C_n^{(2)} \notin \mathcal{C}_2^*] \tag{48b}$$

$$\xrightarrow{n\to\infty} 0, \tag{48c}$$

where Equation (48c) holds because $\mathbb{P}[C_n^{(1)} \in \mathcal{C}_1^*] \xrightarrow{n\to\infty} 1$ and $\mathbb{P}[C_n^{(2)} \in \mathcal{C}_2^*] \xrightarrow{n\to\infty} 1$ by Lemma A1, $\mathbb{E}_{C_n}[\widetilde{e}_1(C_n, 0)|C_n^{(1)} \in \mathcal{C}_1^*] \xrightarrow{n\to\infty} 0$ by Theorem A1 using that $\widetilde{R}_1 < I(X_1; Z|X_2) = \frac{1}{2}\log(1 + h_1P_1)$, and $\mathbb{E}_{C_n}[\widetilde{e}_2(C_n, \sqrt{h_1}x_1^n(M_1, \widetilde{M}_1))|C_n^{(2)} \in \mathcal{C}_2^*] \xrightarrow{n\to\infty} 0$ by Theorem A1 using that $\widetilde{R}_2 < I(X_2; Z) = \frac{1}{2}\log\left(1 + \frac{h_2P_2}{1+h_1P_1}\right)$ and by interpreting the signal of Transmitter 1 as noise.

Define $M \triangleq (M_1, M_2)$, $\widetilde{M} \triangleq (\widetilde{M}_1, \widetilde{M}_2)$. Let the superscript T denote the transpose operation and define $\mathbf{X} \triangleq [\sqrt{h_1}(X_1^n)^T \quad \sqrt{h_2}(X_2^n)^T]^T \in \mathbb{R}^{2n\times 1}$, such that

$$Z^n = G\mathbf{X} + N_Z^n, \tag{49}$$

with $G \triangleq [I_n, I_n] \in \mathbb{R}^{n\times 2n}$ and I_n the identity matrix with dimension n. Let $K_{\mathbf{X}}$ denote the covariance matrix of $\mathbf{X}$. Note that, by independence between X_1^n and X_2^n, we have $K_{\mathbf{X}} = \begin{pmatrix} K_{\sqrt{h_1}X_1^n} & 0_n \\ 0_n & K_{\sqrt{h_2}X_2^n} \end{pmatrix}$, where $0_n \triangleq 0 \times I_n$ and $K_{\sqrt{h_i}X_i^n}$ is the covariance matrix of $\sqrt{h_i}X_i^n$, $i \in \{1, 2\}$. Then, for $i \in \{1, 2\}$, since X_i^n is chosen uniformly at random over a sphere of radius $\sqrt{nP_i}$, the off-diagonal elements of $K_{\sqrt{h_i}X_i^n}$ are all equal to 0 by symmetry, and the diagonal elements are all equal (also by symmetry) and sum to nh_iP_i. Hence, $K_{\sqrt{h_i}X_i^n} = h_iP_iI_n$, $i \in \{1,2\}$, and

$$K_{\mathbf{X}} = \begin{pmatrix} h_1P_1I_n & 0_n \\ 0_n & h_2P_2I_n \end{pmatrix}. \tag{50}$$

Then, we have

$$\begin{aligned}
I(M;Z^n|C_n) &= I(M\widetilde{M};Z^n|C_n) - I(\widetilde{M};Z^n|MC_n) && \text{(51a)}\\
&= I(M\widetilde{M};Z^n|C_n) - H(\widetilde{M}|C_n) + H(\widetilde{M}|Z^nMC_n) && \text{(51b)}\\
&\leq I(\mathbf{X};Z^n|C_n) - H(\widetilde{M}|C_n) + H(\widetilde{M}|Z^nMC_n) && \text{(51c)}\\
&\leq I(\mathbf{X};Z^n) - H(\widetilde{M}|C_n) + H(\widetilde{M}|Z^nMC_n) && \text{(51d)}\\
&= h(Z^n) - h(N_Z^n) - H(\widetilde{M}|C_n) + H(\widetilde{M}|Z^nMC_n) && \text{(51e)}\\
&\leq \frac{1}{2}\log|GK_{\mathbf{X}}G^T + I_n| - H(\widetilde{M}|C_n) + H(\widetilde{M}|Z^nMC_n) && \text{(51f)}\\
&= \frac{n}{2}\log(1 + h_1P_1 + h_2P_2) - H(\widetilde{M}|C_n) + H(\widetilde{M}|Z^nMC_n) && \text{(51g)}\\
&= nI(X_1X_2;Z) - H(\widetilde{M}|C_n) + H(\widetilde{M}|Z^nMC_n) && \text{(51h)}\\
&\leq nI(X_1X_2;Z) - n(I(X_1X_2;Z) - 2\delta) + O(n\mathbb{E}_{C_n}[\widetilde{e}(C_n)]) && \text{(51i)}\\
&= 2\delta n + o(n), && \text{(51j)}
\end{aligned}$$

where Equation (51b) holds by independence between M and $\widetilde{M}$; Equation (51c) holds because $(M,\widetilde{M}) - (\mathbf{X}, C_n) - Z^n$ forms a Markov chain; Equation (51d) holds because $C_n - \mathbf{X} - Z^n$ forms a Markov chain; Equation (51f) holds because $h(N_Z^n) = \frac{1}{2}\log((2\pi e)^n)$ and because $h(Z^n) \leq \frac{1}{2}\log((2\pi e)^n|GK_{\mathbf{X}}G^T + I_n|)$ by Equation (49) and the maximal differential entropy lemma (e.g., [31]) [Eq. (2.6)]; Equation (51g) holds by Equation (50); in Equation (51i), we used the definition of $\widetilde{R}_1 + \widetilde{R}_2$ and the uniformity of $\widetilde{M}$ to obtain the second term, and Fano's inequality to obtain the third term; Equation (51j) holds by Equation (48c).

Note that the idea of considering a fictitious decoder at the eavesdropper to use Fano's inequality in Equation (51i) is a standard technique that already appeared in [32].

7.2. Case 2

We only consider Case 2.a; Case 2.b is handled by exchanging the role of the transmitters. Let $\underline{R} \triangleq (R_1, R_2) \in \mathcal{D}(P_1, P_2)$. There exists $\alpha \in [0,1[$ such that $\underline{R} = (1-\alpha)\underline{C}_1 + \alpha\underline{\widetilde{C}}_2$. The corner point $\underline{C}_1$ is achievable by Case 1, however, recall that since the first component of $\underline{\widetilde{C}}_2$ is negative, it thus cannot be achieved as in Case 1, and one cannot perform time-sharing between $\underline{C}_1$ and $\underline{\widetilde{C}}_2$ to achieve $\underline{R}$. Instead, we achieve $\underline{R}$ as follows. We define $k, k' \in \mathbb{N}$ such that $k'/k = (1-\alpha)^{-1} - 1 + \epsilon$, $\epsilon > 0$, this is possible by density of $\mathbb{Q}$ in $\mathbb{R}$. We realize a first transmission T_1 as in Case 1 of a pair of confidential messages of length $nk\underline{C}_1$. Part of these confidential messages is dedicated to exchange a secret key of length $nk'(I(X_1;Z|X_2) - I(X_1;Y)) > 0$ between Transmitter 1 and the receiver, which is possible because $(1-\alpha)\underline{C}_1 + \alpha\underline{\widetilde{C}}_2 = \underline{R}$ has positive components. We then realize a second transmission T_2 of a pair of confidential messages of length $nk'(0, I(X_2;Y|X_1) - I(X_2;Z))$ assisted with the secret key that is shared between Transmitter 1 and the receiver. Hence, the overall transmission rate of confidential messages is $\frac{k}{k+k'}\underline{C}_1 + \frac{k'}{k+k'}\underline{\widetilde{C}}_2$, which is arbitrarily close to $\underline{R}$ by choosing a sufficiently small ϵ. We now explain how transmission T_2 is performed. We repeat k' times the following coding scheme.

Codebook construction: Perform the same codebook construction as in Case 1 for Transmitter 2. For Transmitter 1, construct a codebook with $\lceil 2^{n\check{R}_1}\rceil\lceil 2^{n\mathring{R}_1}\rceil$ codewords drawn independently and uniformly on the sphere of radius $\sqrt{nP_1}$ in $\mathbb{R}^n$. The codewords are labeled $x_1^n(\check{m}_1, \mathring{m}_1)$, where $\check{m}_1 \in [\![1, 2^{n\check{R}_1}]\!]$, $\mathring{m}_1 \in [\![1, 2^{n\mathring{R}_1}]\!]$. We define the rates $\check{R}_1 \triangleq I(X_1;Y) - \delta$, $\mathring{R}_1 \triangleq I(X_1;Z|X_2) - I(X_1;Y) - \delta$, and $\widetilde{R}_1 \triangleq \check{R}_1 + \mathring{R}_1 = I(X_1;Z|X_2) - 2\delta$.

Encoding at Transmitters: Encoding for Transmitter 2 is as in Case 1. Given $(\check{m}_1, \mathring{m}_1)$, Transmitter 1 forms $x_1^n(\check{m}_1, \mathring{m}_1)$, where $\mathring{m}_1$ is seen as a secret key known at the receiver and that has been shared through transmission T_1 described above. In the following, we define $\widetilde{m}_1 \triangleq (\check{m}_1, \mathring{m}_1)$.

Decoding and average probability of error: As in Case 1, using minimum distance decoding, one can show that on average over the codebooks, the receiver can reconstruct $x_1^n(\check{m}_1, \mathring{m}_1)$ with a vanishing average probability of error because $\mathring{m}_1$ is known at the receiver and because $\check{R}_1 < I(X_1;Y)$. The receiver can then reconstruct x_2^n as in Case 1.

Equivocation: The equivocation computation for transmission T_2 is as in Case 1 by remarking that it is possible on average over the codebooks to reconstruct with vanishing average probability of error first x_2^n given (z^n, m_2) and then x_1^n given (z^n, x_2^n) by using that $\widetilde{R}_1 < I(X_1;Z|X_2)$.

Finally, to conclude that $\underline{R}$ is achievable, we need to show that the secrecy constraint is satisfied for the joint transmissions T_1 and T_2. We use the superscript (T_i) to denote random variables associated with transmission T_i, $i \in \{1,2\}$. Define $M^{(T_1)} \triangleq \left(M_1^{(T_1)} \backslash \mathring{M}_1^{(T_1)}, M_2^{(T_1)}\right)$, the confidential messages sent during transmission T_1 excluding $\mathring{M}_1^{(T_1)}$, defined as all the confidential messages sent during transmission T_1 and used during transmission T_2. We define $M^{(T_2)} \triangleq \left(\emptyset, M_2^{(T_2)}\right)$ as the confidential messages sent during transmission T_2. We define $\widetilde{M}^{(T_i)} \triangleq \left(\widetilde{M}_1^{(T_i)}, \widetilde{M}_2^{(T_i)}\right)$ as the randomization sequences used by both transmitters in Transmission T_i, $i \in \{1,2\}$. We also define $\mathbf{X}^{(T_i)}$ as all the channel inputs from both transmitters in Transmission T_i, $i \in \{1,2\}$, and $\mathbf{Z}^{(T_i)}$ as all the channel outputs observed by the eavesdropper in Transmission $i \in \{1,2\}$. Finally, we define $M^{(T_1,T_2)} \triangleq \left(M^{(T_1)}, M^{(T_2)}\right)$, $\widetilde{M}^{(T_1,T_2)} \triangleq \left(\widetilde{M}^{(T_1)}, \widetilde{M}^{(T_2)}\right)$, $\mathbf{Z}^{(T_1,T_2)} \triangleq \left(\mathbf{Z}^{(T_1)}, \mathbf{Z}^{(T_2)}\right)$, $\mathbf{X}^{(T_1,T_2)} \triangleq \left(\mathbf{X}^{(T_1)}, \mathbf{X}^{(T_2)}\right)$, $C_n^{(T_1,T_2)} \triangleq \left(C_n^{(T_1)}, C_n^{(T_2)}\right)$. We have

$$
\begin{aligned}
& I(M^{(T_1,T_2)}; \mathbf{Z}^{(T_1,T_2)} | C_n^{(T_1,T_2)}) \\
&= I(M^{(T_1,T_2)} \widetilde{M}^{(T_1,T_2)}; \mathbf{Z}^{(T_1,T_2)} | C_n^{(T_1,T_2)}) - I(\widetilde{M}^{(T_1,T_2)}; \mathbf{Z}^{(T_1,T_2)} | M^{(T_1,T_2)} C_n^{(T_1,T_2)}) && \text{(52a)} \\
&= I(M^{(T_1,T_2)} \widetilde{M}^{(T_1,T_2)}; \mathbf{Z}^{(T_1,T_2)} | C_n^{(T_1,T_2)}) - H(\widetilde{M}^{(T_1,T_2)} | C_n^{(T_1,T_2)}) \\
&\quad + H(\widetilde{M}^{(T_1,T_2)} | \mathbf{Z}^{(T_1,T_2)} M^{(T_1,T_2)} C_n^{(T_1,T_2)}) && \text{(52b)} \\
&\leq I(\mathbf{X}^{(T_1,T_2)}; \mathbf{Z}^{(T_1,T_2)} | C_n^{(T_1,T_2)}) - H(\widetilde{M}^{(T_1,T_2)} | C_n^{(T_1,T_2)}) \\
&\quad + H(\widetilde{M}^{(T_1,T_2)} | \mathbf{Z}^{(T_1,T_2)} M^{(T_1,T_2)} C_n^{(T_1,T_2)}) && \text{(52c)} \\
&\leq I(\mathbf{X}^{(T_1,T_2)}; \mathbf{Z}^{(T_1,T_2)}) - H(\widetilde{M}^{(T_1,T_2)} | C_n^{(T_1,T_2)}) + H(\widetilde{M}^{(T_1,T_2)} | \mathbf{Z}^{(T_1,T_2)} M^{(T_1,T_2)} C_n^{(T_1,T_2)}) && \text{(52d)} \\
&\leq n(k+k') I(X_1 X_2; Z) - H(\widetilde{M}^{(T_1,T_2)} | C_n^{(T_1,T_2)}) + H(\widetilde{M}^{(T_1,T_2)} | \mathbf{Z}^{(T_1,T_2)} M^{(T_1,T_2)} C_n^{(T_1,T_2)}) && \text{(52e)} \\
&\leq 3n\delta(k+k') + H(\widetilde{M}^{(T_1,T_2)} | \mathbf{Z}^{(T_1,T_2)} M^{(T_1,T_2)} C_n^{(T_1,T_2)}) && \text{(52f)} \\
&\leq 3n\delta(k+k') + O\left(n \mathbb{E}_{C_n^{(T_1,T_2)}}[\widetilde{e}(C_n^{(T_1,T_2)})]\right), && \text{(52g)}
\end{aligned}
$$

where Equation (52b) holds because we defined $M^{(T_1,T_2)}$ such that $M^{(T_1,T_2)}$ is independent from $\widetilde{M}^{(T_1,T_2)}$, Equation (52c) holds because $(M^{(T_1,T_2)}, \widetilde{M}^{(T_1,T_2)}) - \left(C_n^{(T_1,T_2)}, \mathbf{X}^{(T_1,T_2)}\right) - \mathbf{Z}^{(T_1,T_2)}$ forms a Markov chain, Equation (52d) holds because $C_n^{(T_1,T_2)} - \mathbf{X}^{(T_1,T_2)} - \mathbf{Z}^{(T_1,T_2)}$ forms a Markov chain, Equation (52e) holds similar to Equation (51h), Equation (52f) holds because by definition $\widetilde{R}_1 + \widetilde{R}_2 \geq I(X_1 X_2; Z) - 3\delta$, Equation (52g) holds by Fano's inequality with $\widetilde{e}(\mathcal{C}_n^{(T_1,T_2)})$ defined as the probability of error to reconstruct $\widetilde{M}^{(T_1,T_2)}$ given $\left(\mathbf{Z}^{(T_1,T_2)}, M^{(T_1,T_2)}\right)$ using minimum distance decoding as in Case 1. Then, define $\widetilde{e}^{(1)}(\mathcal{C}_n^{(T_1,T_2)})$ as the error probability to reconstruct $\widetilde{M}^{(T_2)}$ from $\left(\mathbf{Z}^{(T_2)}, M^{(T_2)}\right)$ using minimum distance decoding, and $\widetilde{e}^{(2)}(\mathcal{C}_n^{(T_1,T_2)})$ as the error probability to reconstruct $\widetilde{M}^{(T_1)}$ from $\left(\mathbf{Z}^{(T_1)}, M^{(T_1)}, \widetilde{M}^{(T_2)}\right)$ using minimum distance decoding. As in the analysis of Case 1 and by observing that $\mathring{M}_1^{(T_1)}$ is included in $\widetilde{M}^{(T_2)}$, we have

$$\mathbb{E}_{\mathcal{C}_n^{(T_1,T_2)}}[\widetilde{e}(\mathcal{C}_n^{(T_1,T_2)})] \leq \mathbb{E}_{\mathcal{C}_n^{(T_1,T_2)}}[\widetilde{e}^{(1)}(\mathcal{C}_n^{(T_1,T_2)})] + \mathbb{E}_{\mathcal{C}_n^{(T_1,T_2)}}[\widetilde{e}^{(2)}(\mathcal{C}_n^{(T_1,T_2)})] \tag{53a}$$

$$\xrightarrow{n\to\infty} 0. \tag{53b}$$

We conclude from Equations (52g) and (53b)

$$I(M^{(T_1,T_2)}; \mathbf{Z}^{(T_1,T_2)} | \mathcal{C}_n^{(T_1,T_2)}) = 3n\delta(k+k') + o(n). \tag{54}$$

7.3. Case 3

We have $I(X_1;Z|X_2) - I(X_1;Y) > 0$ and $I(X_2;Z|X_1) - I(X_2;Y) > 0$ as depicted in Figure 5. Assume $I(X_1X_2;Y) - I(X_1X_2;Z) > 0$, otherwise $\mathcal{R}_{1,2}^{\mathrm{MAC}}(P_1,P_2) = \{(0,0)\}$. We will use the following lemma.

Lemma 2. *Define $h_\Lambda \triangleq (1+\Lambda)^{-1}$. We have*

1. $I(X_1;Z|X_2) - I(X_1;Y) \leq I(X_1;Y|X_2) - I(X_1;Z)$ *or* $I(X_2;Z|X_1) - I(X_2;Y) \leq I(X_2;Y|X_1) - I(X_2;Z)$.
2. $h_1 < h_\Lambda$ *or* $h_2 < h_\Lambda$.
3. *Assume* $I(X_1;Z|X_2) - I(X_1;Y) \leq I(X_1;Y|X_2) - I(X_1;Z)$. *There exists* $m, m' \in \mathbb{N}^*$, *such that*

$$m'(I(X_1;Y|X_2) - I(X_1;Z)) \geq m(I(X_1;Z|X_2) - I(X_1;Y)), \tag{55a}$$

$$m(I(X_2;Y|X_1) - I(X_2;Z)) > m'(I(X_2;Z|X_1) - I(X_2;Y)). \tag{55b}$$

Proof. (i) Assume that

$$I(X_1;Z|X_2) - I(X_1;Y) > I(X_1;Y|X_2) - I(X_1;Z), \tag{56a}$$

$$I(X_2;Z|X_1) - I(X_2;Y) > I(X_2;Y|X_1) - I(X_2;Z). \tag{56b}$$

Then,

$$\begin{aligned} &I(X_1;Z|X_2) - I(X_1;Y) + I(X_2;Z|X_1) - I(X_2;Y) \\ &> I(X_1;Y|X_2) - I(X_1;Z) + I(X_2;Y|X_1) - I(X_2;Z), \end{aligned} \tag{57}$$

which contradicts the fact that $I(X_1;Z|X_2) - I(X_1;Y) < I(X_2;Y|X_1) - I(X_2;Z)$ and $I(X_2;Z|X_1) - I(X_2;Y) < I(X_1;Y|X_2) - I(X_1;Z)$.

(ii) By contradiction, if $h_1 \geq h_\Lambda$ and $h_2 \geq h_\Lambda$, then $I(X_1X_2;Y) - I(X_1X_2;Z) \leq 0$.

(iii) Choose $m' \in \mathbb{N}^*$ such that

$$I(X_1;Z|X_2) - I(X_1;Y) \leq m'(I(X_1X_2;Y) - I(X_1X_2;Z)). \tag{58}$$

Then, there exists $m \in \mathbb{N}^*$ and $r \in [0, I(X_1;Z|X_2) - I(X_1;Y)[$ such that

$$m'(I(X_1;Y|X_2) - I(X_1;Z)) = m(I(X_1;Z|X_2) - I(X_1;Y)) + r. \tag{59}$$

Then, we have

$$
\begin{aligned}
& m(I(X_2;Y|X_1) - I(X_2;Z)) \\
&= m(I(X_1;Z|X_2) - I(X_1;Y)) + m(I(X_1X_2;Y) - I(X_1X_2;Z)) && \text{(60a)} \\
&= m'(I(X_1;Y|X_2) - I(X_1;Z)) + m(I(X_1X_2;Y) - I(X_1X_2;Z)) - r && \text{(60b)} \\
&= m'(I(X_2;Z|X_1) - I(X_2;Y)) + (m+m')(I(X_1X_2;Y) - I(X_1X_2;Z)) - r && \text{(60c)} \\
&> m'(I(X_2;Z|X_1) - I(X_2;Y)) + m(I(X_1X_2;Y) - I(X_1X_2;Z)) && \text{(60d)} \\
&> m'(I(X_2;Z|X_1) - I(X_2;Y)), && \text{(60e)}
\end{aligned}
$$

where Equation (60b) holds by Equation (59), and Equation (60d) holds because $r < I(X_1;Z|X_2) - I(X_1;Y) \leq m'(I(X_1X_2;Y) - I(X_1X_2;Z))$. □

By (i) in Lemma 2, assume without loss of generality that $I(X_1;Z|X_2) - I(X_1;Y) \leq I(X_1;Y|X_2) - I(X_1;Z)$ by exchanging the role of the transmitters if necessary. We let m, m' be as in (iii) of Lemma 2. $\mathcal{D}(P_1,P_2)$ is achieved in four steps.

Step 1. During a first transmission T_0, Transmitter 2 transmits a confidential message of length $nm'(I(X_2;Z|X_1) - I(X_2;Y))$ to the receiver. This is possible with a point-to-point wiretap code; as in Case 1, when Transmitter 1 remains silent and when $h_\Lambda > h_2$. If, on the other hand, $h_\Lambda \leq h_2$, then by (ii) in Lemma 2, $h_\Lambda > h_1$ and Transmitter 2 can transmit a confidential message of length $nm'(I(X_2;Z|X_1) - I(X_2;Y))$ as follows. Transmitter 1 transmits a confidential message of length $nk(I(X_1;Z|X_2) - I(X_1;Y))$, where $k \in \mathbb{N}^*$ is such that $nk(I(X_2;Y|X_1) - I(X_2;Z)) \geq nm'(I(X_2;Z|X_1) - I(X_2;Y))$. Using this secret key shared by Transmitter 1 and the receiver, Transmitter 2 can transmit a confidential message of length $nk(I(X_2;Y|X_1) - I(X_2;Z))$ as in Case 2. Note that Step 1 is operated in a fixed number of blocks of length n.

Step 2. As in Case 2, the transmitters achieve transmission T_1 of confidential messages of length $(nm'(I(X_1;Y|X_2) - I(X_1;Z)), 0)$ by using the secret key exchanged during T_0 between Transmitter 2 and the receiver. Then, as in Case 2 and because $m'(I(X_1;Y|X_2) - I(X_1;Z)) - m(I(X_1;Z|X_2) - I(X_1;Y)) \geq 0$ by (iii) in Lemma 2, the transmitters achieve a transmission T_2 of confidential messages of length $(0, nm(I(X_2;Y|X_1) - I(X_2;Z)))$ using a secret key of length $nm(I(X_1;Z|X_2) - I(X_1;Y))$ exchanged between Transmitter 1 and the receiver during T_1. Hence, after T_1 and T_2, the transmitters achieved the transmission of confidential messages of length $(nm'(I(X_1;Y|X_2) - I(X_1;Z)) - nm(I(X_1;Z|X_2) - I(X_1;Y)), nm(I(X_2;Y|X_1) - I(X_2;Z)))$.

Step 3. The transmitters repeat T_1 and T_2 t times, where t is arbitrary, since $m(I(X_2;Y|X_1) - I(X_2;Z)) - m'(I(X_2;Z|X_1) - I(X_2;Y)) > 0$ by (iii) in Lemma 2. After these t repetitions, the rate pair achieved is arbitrarily close to

$$
\begin{aligned}
\underline{R} = \frac{1}{m+m'}(&m'(I(X_1;Y|X_2) - I(X_1;Z)) - m(I(X_1;Z|X_2) - I(X_1;Y)), \\
&m(I(X_2;Y|X_1) - I(X_2;Z)) - m'(I(X_2;Z|X_1) - I(X_2;Y))) \qquad (61)
\end{aligned}
$$

provided that t is large enough since Step 1 only requires a fixed number of transmission blocks. Observe that $\underline{R} \in \mathcal{D}(P_1,P_2)$.

Step 4. Any point of $\mathcal{D}(P_1,P_2)$ can then be achieved as in Case 2 by doing the substitutions $\underline{C}_1 \leftarrow \underline{R}$ and $\underline{C}_2 \leftarrow \underline{R}$ in Case 2.a and Case 2.b, respectively.

The proof that secrecy holds over the joint transmissions is similar to Case 2 and thus omitted.

8. Proof of Theorem 3

We first show that determining a converse for our model reduces to determining a converse for a similar model when the jammer is inactive, i.e., when $\Lambda = 0$.

Lemma 3. *Let* $\mathcal{O} \triangleq \{(R_1, R_2) : R_1 \le B_1, R_2 \le B_2, R_1 + R_2 \le B_{1,2}\}$ *be an outer bound, i.e., a set that contains all possibly achievable rate pairs, for the Gaussian MAC-WT-JA with parameters* $(\Gamma_1, \Gamma_2, h_1, h_2, 0, \sigma_Y^2 + \Lambda, \sigma_Z^2)$. *Then,*

$$\left\{(R_1, R_2) : R_1 \le \begin{cases} B_1 & \text{if } \Gamma_1 > \Lambda \\ 0 & \text{if } \Gamma_1 \le \Lambda \end{cases}, R_2 \le \begin{cases} B_2 & \text{if } \Gamma_2 > \Lambda \\ 0 & \text{if } \Gamma_2 \le \Lambda \end{cases}, R_1 + R_2 \le B_{1,2}\right\}$$

is an outer bound for the Gaussian MAC-WT-JA with parameters $(\Gamma_1, \Gamma_2, h_1, h_2, \Lambda, \sigma_Y^2, \sigma_Z^2)$.

Proof. Consider any encoders and decoder for the Gaussian MAC-WT-JA with the parameters $(\Gamma_1, \Gamma_2, h_1, h_2, \Lambda, \sigma_Y^2, \sigma_Z^2)$ that achieve the rate pair (R_1, R_2). Note that by [24] [Theorem 2.3], for any $l \in \{1,2\}$ such that $\Gamma_l \le \Lambda$, we must have $R_l = 0$, since an outer bound for the model in [24] is also an outer bound for the Gaussian MAC-WT-JA, which has the additional security constraint (2b). Then, to derive an outer bound, it is sufficient to consider a specific jamming strategy and study the best achievable rates for this jamming strategy, since the boundaries of the capacity region correspond to the best (from the jammer's point of view) jamming strategies and any other jamming strategy can only enlarge the set of achievable rates. We assume that in each transmission block, the jamming sequence is S^n with the components independent and identically distributed according to a zero-mean Gaussian random variable with the variance $\Lambda' < \Lambda$. The average probability of error at the legitimate receiver is thus upper-bounded by $\sup_{S \in \mathcal{S}} \mathbb{P}[\widehat{M} \neq M] + k\mathbb{P}[\|S^n\|^2 > n\Lambda] \xrightarrow{n \to \infty} 0$ where we used the notation of Definition 1 and the fact that $k\mathbb{P}[\|S^n\|^2 > n\Lambda] \xrightarrow{n \to \infty} 0$ since $\Lambda' < \Lambda$. Hence, since the secrecy constraint is independent of Λ', we obtain the reliability and secrecy constraints for a Gaussian MAC-WT-JA with parameters $(\Gamma_1, \Gamma_2, h_1, h_2, 0, \sigma_Y^2 + \Lambda', \sigma_Z^2)$, meaning that $(R_1, R_2) \in \mathcal{O}'$, where $\mathcal{O}'$ is an outer bound for the Gaussian MAC-WT-JA with parameters $(\Gamma_1, \Gamma_2, h_1, h_2, 0, \sigma_Y^2 + \Lambda', \sigma_Z^2)$. Finally, we conclude the proof by choosing Λ' arbitrarily close to Λ. □

We now obtain Theorem 3 as follows. (i) holds from Lemma 3. (ii) holds from Lemma 3 and [33] [Theorem 6] by remarking that $x \mapsto \log\left(\frac{1+x(1+\Lambda)^{-1}}{1+xh}\right)$ is non-decreasing when $(1+\Lambda)^{-1} > h$ and negative when $(1+\Lambda)^{-1} \le h$.

9. Concluding Remarks

In this paper, we defined Gaussian wiretap channels in the presence of an eavesdropper aided by a jammer. The jamming signal is power-constrained and assumed to be oblivious of the legitimate users' communication but is not restricted to be Gaussian. We studied several models in this framework, namely point-to-point, multiple-access, broadcast, and symmetric interference settings. We derived inner and outer bounds for these settings, and identified conditions for these bounds to coincide. We stress that no shared randomness among the legitimate users is required in our coding schemes.

Our achievability scheme for the Gaussian MAC-WT-JA relies on novel time-sharing strategies and an extension of successive decoding for multiple-access channels to multiple-access wiretap channels via secret-key exchanges. An open problem remains to provide a scheme that avoids time-sharing. Section 4.2 provides such a scheme for some rate pairs and channel parameters; however, it might not be possible to achieve the entire region of Theorem 2 by solely relying on point-to-point codes, in which case the design of multi-transmitter codes for arbitrarily varying multiple-access channels would be necessary.

Finally, beyond proving the existence of achievability schemes for our models, finding explicit coding schemes largely remains an open problem. We note that [34] investigates this problem for short communication blocklengths over point-to-point channels via a practical approach that relies on deep learning. Another open problem is to achieve the same regions as that derived in this paper under strong and semantic security guarantees.

Author Contributions: The ideas in this work were formed by the discussions between R.A.C. and A.Y. Both authors collaborated on the writing of the manuscript. All authors have read and agreed to the published version of the manuscript.

Funding: This work was supported in part by NSF grants CIF-1319338, CNS-1314719, CCF-2105872, and CCF-2047913.

Institutional Review Board Statement: Not applicable.

Data Availability Statement: Not applicable.

Conflicts of Interest: The authors declare no conflict of interest.

Appendix A. Supporting Results

Lemma A1 ([1]). *Let $\epsilon > 0$, $\eta \in]8\sqrt{\epsilon}, 1[$, $K > 2\epsilon$, $R \in [2\epsilon, K]$, and $N \triangleq e^{nR}$. Let $X_1^n, \dots, X_N^n$ be independent random variables uniformly distributed on the unit sphere. With probability arbitrarily close to one as $n \to \infty$, we have*

1. $|\{j : \langle X_j^n, u^n \rangle \geq \alpha\}| \leq e^{n\left(\left[R+\frac{1}{2}\log(1-\alpha^2)\right]^+ + \epsilon\right)}$ *for any unit vector $u^n \in \mathbb{R}^n$, $\alpha > 0$.*
2. $\frac{1}{N}|\{i : |\langle X_j^n, X_i^n \rangle| \geq \alpha, |\langle X_j^n, u^n \rangle| \geq \beta$, *for some $j \neq i\}| \leq e^{-n\epsilon}$ for any unit vector $u^n \in \mathbb{R}^n$, $\alpha, \beta \in [0,1]$ such that $\alpha \geq \eta$, $\alpha^2 + \beta^2 > 1 + \eta - e^{-2R}$.*

Theorem A1 ([1,24]). *Consider a channel whose output is defined as $Y^n = X^n + V^n + s^n$, where X^n is the input such that $\|X^n\|^2 \leq n$, V^n represents noise (to be defined next), and s^n is a state unknown to the encoder and decoder such that $\|s^n\|^2 \leq n\Lambda$, $\Lambda < 1$. Let $\sigma, \delta > 0$. Consider a codebook $\mathcal{C}_n$ made of $N \triangleq e^{n(\frac{1}{2}\log(1+(\Lambda+\sigma^2)^{-1})-\delta)}$ codewords $(x_1^n, \dots, x_N^n)$ that satisfy the two conditions of Lemma A1, and define the average probability of error $e(\mathcal{C}_n)$ of a minimum distance decoder as $e(\mathcal{C}_n) \triangleq \frac{1}{N}\sum_{i=1}^N \mathbb{P}[\|x_i^n + s^n + V^n - x_j^n\|^2 \leq \|s^n + V^n\|^2$, for some $j \neq i]$.*

1. *(From [1]). If V^n is a vector with i.i.d. zero-mean Gaussian coordinates with variance σ^2, then $\lim_{n\to\infty} e(\mathcal{C}_n) = 0$.*
2. *(From [24]). If $V^n \triangleq W^n + U$, where W^n is a vector with i.i.d. zero-mean Gaussian coordinates with variance a^2 and U is independently distributed uniformly at random on a sphere with radius $\sqrt{nb^2}$ such that $a^2 + b^2 = \sigma^2$, then $\lim_{n\to\infty} e(\mathcal{C}_n) = 0$.*

Appendix B. Proof of Theorem 4

We first recall some definitions and results on polymatroids.

Definition A1 ([35]). *Let $f : 2^{\mathcal{M}} \to \mathbb{R}$. $\mathcal{P}(f) \triangleq \{(R_i)_{i\in\mathcal{M}} \in \mathbb{R}^{\mathcal{M}} : R_{\mathcal{S}} \leq f(\mathcal{S}), \forall \mathcal{S} \subseteq \mathcal{M}\}$ associated with the function f is an* extended polymatroid *if f is submodular, i.e., $\forall \mathcal{S}, \mathcal{T} \subseteq \mathcal{M}, f(\mathcal{S} \cup \mathcal{T}) + f(\mathcal{S} \cap \mathcal{T}) \leq f(\mathcal{S}) + f(\mathcal{T})$.*

Property A1 ([29] [Property 1]). *Define $g : 2^{\mathcal{L}(\Lambda)} \to \mathbb{R}, \mathcal{T} \mapsto I(X_{\mathcal{T}}; Y|X_{\mathcal{T}^c}) - I(X_{\mathcal{T}}; Z)$, where $Y \triangleq \sum_{l\in\mathcal{L}(\Lambda)} X_l + N_Y$, $Z \triangleq \sum_{l\in\mathcal{L}(\Lambda)} \sqrt{h_l} X_l + N_Z$, with $(X_l)_{l\in\mathcal{L}(\Lambda)}$, N_Y, N_Z independent zero-mean Gaussian random variables with variances $(P_l)_{l\in\mathcal{L}(\Lambda)}$, $(1+\Lambda)$, 1, respectively.*

$$C(\Lambda) \triangleq \left\{(R_l)_{l\in\mathcal{L}(\Lambda)} \in \mathbb{R}^{|\mathcal{L}(\Lambda)|} : \forall \mathcal{T} \subseteq \mathcal{L}(\Lambda), R_{\mathcal{T}} \leq g(\mathcal{T})\right\} \tag{A1}$$

associated with g is an extended polymatroid.

Property A2 ([35]). *Define the dominant face $D(\Lambda)$ of $C(\Lambda)$ as*

$$D(\Lambda) \triangleq \left\{(R_l)_{l\in\mathcal{L}(\Lambda)} \in C(\Lambda) : R_{\mathcal{L}(\Lambda)} = g(\mathcal{L}(\Lambda))\right\}. \tag{A2}$$

For $\pi \in Sym(|\mathcal{L}(\Lambda)|)$, where $Sym(|\mathcal{L}(\Lambda)|)$ is the symmetric group on $\mathcal{L}(\Lambda)$, for $i,j \in \mathcal{L}(\Lambda)$, define $\pi^{i:j} \triangleq (\pi(k))_{k\in[\![i,j]\!]}$. $D(\Lambda)$ is the convex hull of the vertices

$\mathcal{V} \triangleq \left\{(C_{\pi(i)})_{i\in[\![1,|\mathcal{L}(\Lambda)|]\!]} : \pi \in Sym(|\mathcal{L}(\Lambda)|)\right\}$, *where for* $\pi \in Sym(|\mathcal{L}(\Lambda)|)$, *for* $i \in [\![1,|\mathcal{L}(\Lambda)|]\!]$, $C_{\pi(i)} = g\left(\{\pi^{i:|\mathcal{L}(\Lambda)|}\}\right) - g\left(\{\pi^{i+1:|\mathcal{L}(\Lambda)|}\}\right)$.

Define $D_+(\Lambda) \triangleq D(\Lambda) \cap \mathbb{R}_+^{|\mathcal{L}(\Lambda)|}$. By Property A2, for any $\underline{R} \in D_+(\Lambda)$, for any $\underline{V} = (V_l)_{l\in\mathcal{L}(\Lambda)} \in \mathcal{V}$, there exists $\alpha_{\underline{V}} \in [0,1]$, such that $\sum_{\underline{V}\in\mathcal{V}} \alpha_{\underline{V}} = 1$ and $\underline{R} = \sum_{\underline{V}\in\mathcal{V}} \alpha_{\underline{V}}\underline{V}$. As remarked in [29], g is, in general, not non-decreasing; hence, some $\underline{V} \in \mathcal{V}$ might have negative components and the successive decoding method [5] [Appendix C] cannot be applied to the multiple-access wiretap channel. We show in the following how to overcome this issue. For $l \in \mathcal{L}(\Lambda)$, define $R_l^* \triangleq -\sum_{\underline{V}\in\mathcal{V}} \alpha_{\underline{V}}\mathbb{1}\{V_l < 0\}V_l$, and $\underline{R}^* \triangleq (R_l^*)_{l\in\mathcal{L}(\Lambda)}$. Our coding scheme operates in three steps, the idea of which is described below.

Step 1. For $l \in \mathcal{L}(\Lambda)$, a secret message of length nR_l^* is exchanged between Transmitter l and the receiver.

Step 2. For all $\underline{V} \in \mathcal{V}$, secret messages of length $n(\alpha_{\underline{V}}\mathbb{1}\{V_l > 0\}V_l)_{l\in\mathcal{L}(\Lambda)}$ are exchanged between the transmitters and the receiver, provided that secret sequences of length $n\underline{R}^*$ are shared between the transmitters and the receiver, which is ensured by Step 1. The overall length of secret communication is $n(\sum_{\underline{V}\in\mathcal{V}} \alpha_{\underline{V}}\mathbb{1}\{V_l > 0\}V_l)_{l\in\mathcal{L}(\Lambda)}$, i.e., $n(\underline{R} + \underline{R}^*)$.

Step 3. Repeat t times Step 2. It is possible to do so because secret sequences of length at least $n\underline{R}^*$ were exchanged between the transmitters and the receiver in Step 2. The overall rate of secret sequences exchanged between the transmitters and the receiver is thus $\underline{R}$, provided that t is large enough, since Step 1 only requires the transmission of a finite number of blocks.

The coding schemes and their analyses to realize Steps 1 and 2 are described in Appendix B.1 and Appendix B.2, respectively. In the remainder of the section, Y and Z are defined as in Property A1 with $(X_l)_{l\in\mathcal{L}(\Lambda)}$ zero-mean Gaussian random variables with variances $(P_l)_{l\in\mathcal{L}(\Lambda)}$.

Appendix B.1. Proof of Step 1

The proof of Step 1 directly follows from the point-to-point setting, i.e., Theorem 1, applied to each $l \in \mathcal{L}(\Lambda)$ since we assumed $h_l < h_\Lambda$.

Appendix B.2. Proof of Step 2

We fix $\underline{V} \in \mathcal{V}$. The following procedure must be reiterated for each $\underline{V} \in \mathcal{V}$ by applying a permutation $\pi \in Sym(|\mathcal{L}(\Lambda)|)$ on the labeling of the transmitters. For convenience, we relabel the transmitter from 1 to $|\mathcal{L}(\Lambda)|$ and redefine $\mathcal{L}(\Lambda)$ as $[\![1,|\mathcal{L}(\Lambda)|]\!]$. We show how to exchange secret messages with rate $(\mathbb{1}\{V_l > 0\}V_l)_{l\in\mathcal{L}(\Lambda)}$ between the transmitters and the receiver, when they have access to pre-shared secrets (obtained from Step 1) with rate $(-\mathbb{1}\{V_l < 0\}V_l)_{l\in\mathcal{L}(\Lambda)}$. Define $\mathcal{I} \triangleq \{l \in \mathcal{L}(\Lambda) : V_l \leq 0\}$ and $\mathcal{I}^c \triangleq \mathcal{L}(\Lambda)\backslash\mathcal{I}$. We also use the notation $X_{\mathcal{L}(\Lambda)} \triangleq (X_l)_{l\in\mathcal{L}(\Lambda)}$, $X^n_{\mathcal{L}(\Lambda)} \triangleq (X^n_l)_{l\in\mathcal{L}(\Lambda)}$, and for $i,j \in \mathcal{L}(\Lambda)$, $X_{i:j} \triangleq (X_l)_{l\in[\![i,j]\!]}$.

Codebook construction: For Transmitter $i \in \mathcal{I}^c$, construct a codebook $C_n^{(i)}$ with $\lceil 2^{nR_i}\rceil\lceil 2^{n\widetilde{R}_i}\rceil$ codewords drawn independently and uniformly on the sphere of radius $\sqrt{nP_i}$ in $\mathbb{R}^n$. The codewords are labeled $x_i^n(m_i,\widetilde{m}_i)$, where $m_i \in [\![1,2^{nR_i}]\!]$, $\widetilde{m}_i \in [\![1,2^{n\widetilde{R}_i}]\!]$. We choose the rates as $R_i \triangleq I(X_i;Y|X_{1:i-1}) - I(X_i;Z|X_{i+1:|\mathcal{L}(\Lambda)|}) - \delta$, $\widetilde{R}_i \triangleq I(X_i;Z|X_{i+1:|\mathcal{L}(\Lambda)|}) - \delta$. For Transmitter $i \in \mathcal{I}$, construct a codebook $C_n^{(i)}$ with $\lceil 2^{n\check{R}_i}\rceil\lceil 2^{n\mathring{R}_i}\rceil$ codewords drawn independently and uniformly on the sphere of radius $\sqrt{nP_i}$ in $\mathbb{R}^n$. The codewords are labeled $x_i^n(\check{m}_i,\mathring{m}_i)$, where $\check{m}_i \in [\![1,2^{n\check{R}_i}]\!]$, $\mathring{m}_i \in [\![1,2^{n\mathring{R}_i}]\!]$. We define the rates $\check{R}_i \triangleq I(X_i;Y|X_{1:i-1}) - \delta$, $\mathring{R}_i \triangleq I(X_i;Z|X_{i+1:|\mathcal{L}(\Lambda)|}) - I(X_i;Y|X_{1:i-1}) - \delta$, and $\widetilde{R}_i \triangleq \check{R}_i + \mathring{R}_i = I(X_i;Z|X_{i+1:|\mathcal{L}(\Lambda)|}) - 2\delta$. Define $C_n \triangleq (C_n^{(i)})_{i\in\mathcal{L}(\Lambda)}$.

Encoding at the transmitters: For Transmitter $i \in \mathcal{I}^c$, given $(m_i,\widetilde{m}_i)$, transmit $x_i^n(m_i,\widetilde{m}_i)$. For Transmitter $i \in \mathcal{I}$, given $(\check{m}_i,\mathring{m}_i)$, transmit $x_i^n(\check{m}_i,\mathring{m}_i)$, where $\check{m}_i$ is assumed to be known at the receiver by the transmissions in Step 1. In the following, we define for $i \in \mathcal{I}$,

$\widetilde{m}_i \triangleq (\check{m}_i, \mathring{m}_i)$. By convention, define for $i \in \mathcal{I}$, $m_i \triangleq \emptyset$. Also define $m \triangleq (m_i)_{i\in\mathcal{L}(\Lambda)}$, $\widetilde{m} \triangleq (\widetilde{m}_i)_{i\in\mathcal{L}(\Lambda)}$. In the following, we refer to $\widetilde{m}$ as randomization sequence.

Decoding: The receiver performs minimum distance decoding, i.e., given y^n, determine starting from $i = 1$ to $i = |\mathcal{L}(\Lambda)|$, $(\hat{m}_i, \hat{\widetilde{m}}_i) \triangleq \phi_i(y^n, \sum_{j=1}^{i-1} x_j^n(\hat{m}_j, \hat{\widetilde{m}}_j))$ where

$$\phi_i : (y^n, x) \mapsto \begin{cases} (m_i, \widetilde{m}_i) & \text{if } \|y^n - x - x_i^n(m_i, \widetilde{m}_i)\|^2 < \|y^n - x - x_i^n(m_i', \widetilde{m}_i')\|^2 \\ & \quad \text{for } (m_i', \widetilde{m}_i') \neq (m_i, \widetilde{m}_i) \\ 0 & \text{if no such } (m_i, \widetilde{m}_i) \in [\![1, 2^{nR_i}]\!] \times [\![1, 2^{n\widetilde{R}_i}]\!] \text{ exists} \end{cases}. \quad \text{(A3)}$$

Define $\hat{m} \triangleq (\hat{m}_i)_{i\in\mathcal{L}(\Lambda)}$, $\hat{\widetilde{m}} \triangleq (\hat{\widetilde{m}}_i)_{i\in\mathcal{L}(\Lambda)}$. Let $e(C_n, s^n) \triangleq \mathbb{P}\left[\widehat{M} \neq M | C_n\right]$, we now prove that on average on C_n, we have $\mathbb{E}_{C_n}[\sup_{s^n} e(C_n, s^n)] + \frac{1}{n} I(M; Z^n | C_n) \xrightarrow{n\to\infty} 0$. We will thus conclude that there exists a sequence of realizations $(\mathcal{C}_n)$ of (C_n) such that both $\sup_{s^n} e(\mathcal{C}_n, s^n)$ and $\frac{1}{n} I(M; Z^n | \mathcal{C}_n)$ can be made arbitrarily close to zero as $n \to \infty$.

Average probability of error: We have

$$e(C_n, s^n) \leq \mathbb{P}\left[\widehat{M} \neq M \text{ or } \widehat{\widetilde{M}} \neq \widetilde{M} \middle| C_n\right] \quad \text{(A4a)}$$

$$= \sum_{i\in\mathcal{L}(\Lambda)} e_i\left(C_n, s^n, \sum_{j=i+1}^{|\mathcal{L}(\Lambda)|} x_j^n(M_j, \widetilde{M}_j)\right), \quad \text{(A4b)}$$

where for $i \in \mathcal{L}(\Lambda)$

$$e_i(C_n, s^n, x) \triangleq \frac{1}{\lceil 2^{nR_i} \rceil \lceil 2^{n\widetilde{R}_i} \rceil} \sum_{m_i} \sum_{\widetilde{m}_i} \mathbb{P}\Big[\|x_i^n(m_i, \widetilde{m}_i) + s^n + x + N_Y^n - x_i^n(m_i', \widetilde{m}_i')\|^2 \leq \|s^n + x + N_Y^n\|^2 \text{ for some } (m_i', \widetilde{m}_i') \neq (m_i, \widetilde{m}_i)\Big]. \quad \text{(A5)}$$

Assume that the receiver has reconstructed $(m_j, \widetilde{m}_j)_{j\in[\![1,i]\!]}$, for $i \in \mathcal{L}(\Lambda)$. Assume first that $i + 1 \in \mathcal{I}^c$. Using minimum distance decoding, on average over the codebooks, we show that the receiver can reconstruct x_{i+1}^n. We have

$$\mathbb{E}_{C_n}\left[e_i\left(C_n, s^n, \sum_{j=i+1}^{|\mathcal{L}(\Lambda)|} x_j^n(M_j, \widetilde{M}_j)\right)\right]$$

$$\leq \mathbb{E}_{C_n}\left[e_i\left(C_n, s^n, \sum_{j=i+1}^{|\mathcal{L}(\Lambda)|} x_j^n(M_j, \widetilde{M}_j)\right) \middle| C_n^{(i)} \in \mathcal{C}_i^*\right] + \mathbb{P}\left[C_n^{(i)} \notin \mathcal{C}_i^*\right] \quad \text{(A6a)}$$

$$\xrightarrow{n\to\infty} 0, \quad \text{(A6b)}$$

where in Equation (A6a) $\mathcal{C}_i^*$ represents all the sets of unit norm vectors scaled by $\sqrt{nP_i}$ that satisfy the two conditions of Lemma A1 (in Appendix A), Equation (A6b) holds because $\mathbb{P}[C_n^{(i)} \in \mathcal{C}_i^*] \xrightarrow{n\to\infty} 1$ by Lemma A1, and $\mathbb{E}_{C_n}\left[e_i\left(C_n, s^n, \sum_{j=i+1}^{|\mathcal{L}(\Lambda)|} x_j^n(M_j, \widetilde{M}_j)\right) | C_n^{(i)} \in \mathcal{C}_i^*\right] \xrightarrow{n\to\infty} 0$ by Theorem A1 (in Appendix A) using the definition of $R_i + \widetilde{R}_i$ and by interpreting the signal of transmitters in $[\![i+1, |\mathcal{L}(\Lambda)|]\!]$ as noise.

Similarly, when $i + 1 \in \mathcal{I}$, using minimum distance decoding, on average over the codebooks, the receiver can reconstruct $x_{i+1}^n(\check{m}_{i+1}, \mathring{m}_{i+1})$ with a vanishing average probability of error because $\mathring{m}_{i+1}$ is known at the receiver and by definition of $\check{R}_{i+1}$, hence,

$$\mathbb{E}_{C_n}[e(C_n, s^n)] \xrightarrow{n\to\infty} 0. \quad \text{(A7)}$$

Equivocation: We first study the average error probability of decoding $\widetilde{m}$ given (z^n, m) with the following procedure. From $i = |\mathcal{L}(\Lambda)|$ to $i = 1$, given (z^n, m), determine $\dot{\widetilde{m}}_i \triangleq \psi_i\left(z^n, \sum_{j=i+1}^{|\mathcal{L}(\Lambda)|} \sqrt{h_j x_j^n(m_j, \dot{\widetilde{m}}_j)}\right)$, where for $i \in \mathcal{L}(\Lambda)$

$$\psi_i : (z^n, x) \mapsto \begin{cases} \widetilde{m}_i & \text{if } \|z^n - x - \sqrt{h_i} x_i^n(m_i, \widetilde{m}_i)\|^2 < \|z^n - x - \sqrt{h_i} x_i^n(m_i, \widetilde{m}_i')\|^2 \\ & \qquad \text{for } \widetilde{m}_i' \neq \widetilde{m}_i \\ 0 & \text{if no such } \widetilde{m}_i \in [\![1, 2^{n\widetilde{R}_i}]\!] \text{ exists} \end{cases}. \tag{A8}$$

We define $\widetilde{e}(C_n) \triangleq \mathbb{P}\left[\dot{\widetilde{M}} \neq \widetilde{M} \middle| C_n\right]$. We have

$$\widetilde{e}(C_n) = \sum_{i \in \mathcal{L}(\Lambda)} \widetilde{e}_i\left(C_n, \sum_{j=1}^{i-1} \sqrt{h_j x_j^n(M_j, \widetilde{M}_j)}\right), \tag{A9}$$

where for $i \in \mathcal{L}(\Lambda)$

$$\begin{aligned} \widetilde{e}_i(C_n, x) \triangleq \frac{1}{\lceil 2^{n\widetilde{R}_i} \rceil} \sum_{\widetilde{m}_i} \mathbb{P}\Big[& \|\sqrt{h_i} x_i^n(m_i, \widetilde{m}_i) + x + N_Z^n - \sqrt{h_i} x_i^n(m_i, \widetilde{m}_i')\|^2 \\ & \leq \|x + N_Z^n\|^2 \text{ for some } \widetilde{m}_i' \neq \widetilde{m}_i \Big]. \end{aligned} \tag{A10}$$

Similar to the justifications for obtaining Equation (A6b), $\mathbb{E}_{C_n}\left[\widetilde{e}_i(C_n, \sum_{j=1}^{i-1} \sqrt{h_j x_j^n(M_j, \widetilde{M}_j)})\right]$ vanishes to zero as $n \to \infty$ by interpreting the signal of transmitters in $[\![1, i-1]\!]$ as noise and by using the definition of $\widetilde{R}_i$. We thus obtain

$$\mathbb{E}_{C_n}[\widetilde{e}(C_n)] \xrightarrow{n \to \infty} 0. \tag{A11}$$

Let the superscript T denote the transpose operation and define $\mathbf{X} \triangleq [\sqrt{h_1}(X_1^n)^T \sqrt{h_2}(X_2^n)^T \ldots \sqrt{h_{|\mathcal{L}(\Lambda)|}}(X_{|\mathcal{L}(\Lambda)|}^n)^T]^T \in \mathbb{R}^{n|\mathcal{L}(\Lambda)| \times 1}$, such that

$$Z^n = G\mathbf{X} + N_Z^n, \tag{A12}$$

with $G \triangleq [I_n, I_n, \ldots, I_n] \in \mathbb{R}^{n \times n|\mathcal{L}(\Lambda)|}$ and I_n the identity matrix with dimension n. Let $K_{\mathbf{X}}$ denote the covariance matrix of $\mathbf{X}$. Similar to Equation (50), we have

$$K_{\mathbf{X}} = \mathrm{diag}(h_1 P_1 I_n, \ldots, h_{|\mathcal{L}(\Lambda)|} P_{|\mathcal{L}(\Lambda)|} I_n). \tag{A13}$$

Then, we have

$$\begin{aligned} I(M; Z^n | C_n) &\leq I(\mathbf{X}; Z^n) - H(\widetilde{M}|C_n) + H(\widetilde{M}|Z^n M C_n) && \text{(A14a)} \\ &\leq \frac{1}{2} \log |G K_{\mathbf{X}} G^T + I_n| - H(\widetilde{M}|C_n) + H(\widetilde{M}|Z^n M C_n) && \text{(A14b)} \\ &= \frac{n}{2} \log\left(1 + \sum_{l \in \mathcal{L}(\Lambda)} h_l P_l\right) - H(\widetilde{M}|C_n) + H(\widetilde{M}|Z^n M C_n) && \text{(A14c)} \\ &\leq nI(X_{\mathcal{L}(\Lambda)}; Z) - n(I(X_{\mathcal{L}(\Lambda)}; Z) - 2|\mathcal{L}(\Lambda)|\delta) + O(n\mathbb{E}_{C_n}[\widetilde{e}(C_n)]) && \text{(A14d)} \\ &= 2|\mathcal{L}(\Lambda)|\delta + o(n), && \text{(A14e)} \end{aligned}$$

where Equation (A14a) holds similar to Equation (51d), Equation (A14b) holds similar to Equation (51f), Equation (A14c) holds by Equation (A13), in Equation (A14d), we used the definition of $\sum_{i \in \mathcal{L}(\Lambda)} \widetilde{R}_i$ and the uniformity of $\widetilde{M}$ to obtain the second term, and Fano's inequality to obtain the third term, Equation (A14e) holds by Equation (A11).

The proof of joint secrecy for Step 1 and the repetitions of Step 2 is similar to the proof of Theorem 2.

Appendix C. Proof of Theorem 5

The proof that Equation (20) is an upper bound on the secrecy sum-rate is similar to the case $L = 2$ in Theorem 3.

Remark that from the statement of Corollary 1, it is unclear whether the sum-rate of Theorem 5 is achievable. However, by inspecting the proof of Theorem 4, observe that we achieve a point in $D_+(\Lambda) \triangleq D(\Lambda) \cap \mathbb{R}_+^{|\mathcal{L}(\Lambda)|}$, where $D(\Lambda)$ is defined in Equation (A2). Hence, the sum-rate of Theorem 5 is indeed achievable.

References

1. Csiszár, I.; Narayan, P. Capacity of the Gaussian arbitrarily varying channel. *IEEE Trans. Inf. Theory* **1991**, *37*, 18–26. [CrossRef]
2. Leung-Yan-Cheong, S.; Hellman, M. The Gaussian wire-tap channel. *IEEE Trans. Inf. Theory* **1978**, *24*, 451–456. [CrossRef]
3. Tekin, E.; Yener, A. The general Gaussian multiple-access and two-way wiretap channels: Achievable rates and cooperative jamming. *IEEE Trans. Inf. Theory* **2008**, *54*, 2735–2751. [CrossRef]
4. Bagherikaram, G.; Motahari, A.S.; Khandani, A.K. Secure broadcasting: The secrecy rate region. In Proceedings of the Communication, Control, and Computing, 2008 46th Annual Allerton Conference, Monticello, IL, USA, 23–26 September 2008; pp. 834–841.
5. Grant, A.; Rimoldi, B.; Urbanke, R.; Whiting, P. Rate-splitting multiple access for discrete memoryless channels. *IEEE Trans. Inf. Theory* **2001**, *47*, 873–890. [CrossRef]
6. MolavianJazi, E.; Bloch, M.; Laneman, J. Arbitrary jamming can preclude secure communication. In Proceedings of the 47th Annual Allerton Conference on Communication, Control, and Computing, Monticello, IL, USA, 1–3 October 2009; pp. 1069–1075.
7. Bjelaković, I.; Boche, H.; Sommerfeld, J. Capacity results for arbitrarily varying wiretap channels. In *Information Theory, Combinatorics, and Search Theory*; Springer: Berlin/Heidelberg, Germany, 2013; pp. 123–144.
8. Nötzel, J.; Wiese, M.; Boche, H. The Arbitrarily Varying Wiretap Channel: Secret Randomness, Stability, and Super-Activation. *IEEE Trans. Inf. Theory* **2016**, *62*, 3504–3531. [CrossRef]
9. Wiese, M.; Notzel, J.; Boche, H. A Channel Under Simultaneous Jamming and Eavesdropping Attack—Correlated Random Coding Capacities Under Strong Secrecy Criteria. *IEEE Trans. Inf. Theory* **2016**, *62*, 3844–3862. [CrossRef]
10. Goldfeld, Z.; Cuff, P.; Permuter, H.H. Arbitrarily varying wiretap channels with type constrained states. *IEEE Trans. Inf. Theory* **2016**, *62*, 7216–7244. [CrossRef]
11. Chou, R. Explicit Wiretap Channel Codes via Source Coding, Universal Hashing, and Distribution Approximation, When the Channels Statistics are Uncertain. *IEEE Trans. Inf. Forensics Secur.* **2022**, *17*. [CrossRef]
12. Csiszár, I. Almost Independence and Secrecy Capacity. *Probl. Inf. Transm.* **1996**, *32*, 40–47.
13. Yassaee, M.; Aref, M.; Gohari, A. Achievability proof via output statistics of random binning. *IEEE Trans. Inf. Theory* **2014**, *60*, 6760–6786. [CrossRef]
14. Hayashi, M. General nonasymptotic and asymptotic formulas in channel resolvability and identification capacity and their application to the wiretap channel. *IEEE Trans. Inf. Theory* **2006**, *52*, 1562–1575. [CrossRef]
15. Bloch, M.; Laneman, J.N. Strong secrecy from channel resolvability. *IEEE Trans. Inf. Theory* **2013**, *59*, 8077–8098. [CrossRef]
16. He, X.; Yener, A. MIMO wiretap channels with unknown and varying eavesdropper channel states. *IEEE Trans. Inf. Theory* **2014**, *60*, 6844–6869. [CrossRef]
17. Mukherjee, A.; Swindlehurst, A.L. Jamming games in the MIMO wiretap channel with an active eavesdropper. *IEEE Trans. Sig. Process.* **2013**, *61*, 82–91. [CrossRef]
18. Banawan, K.; Ulukus, S. Achievable secrecy rates in the multiple access wiretap channel with deviating users. In Proceedings of the IEEE International Symposium on Information Theory, Barcelona, Spain, 10–15 July 2016; pp. 2814–2818.
19. Amariucai, G.T.; Wei, S. Half-duplex active eavesdropping in fast-fading channels: A block-Markov Wyner secrecy encoding scheme. *IEEE Trans. Inf. Theory* **2012**, *58*, 4660–4677. [CrossRef]
20. Basciftci, Y.O.; Gungor, O.; Koksal, C.E.; Ozguner, F. On the secrecy capacity of block fading channels with a hybrid adversary. *IEEE Trans. Inf. Theory* **2015**, *61*, 1325–1343. [CrossRef]
21. Zhang, Y.; Vatedka, S.; Jaggi, S.; Sarwate, A.D. Quadratically constrained myopic adversarial channels. *IEEE Trans. Inf. Theory* **2022**, *68*, 4901–4948. [CrossRef]
22. Zhang, Y.; Vatedka, S.; Jaggi, S. Quadratically constrained two-way adversarial channels. In Proceedings of the IEEE International Symposium on Information Theory (ISIT), Los Angeles, CA, USA, 21–26 June 2020; pp. 1587–1592.
23. Li, T.; Dey, B.K.; Jaggi, S.; Langberg, M.; Sarwate, A.D. Quadratically constrained channels with causal adversaries. In Proceedings of the IEEE International Symposium on Information Theory (ISIT), Vail, CO, USA, 17–22 June 2018; pp. 621–625.
24. La, R.; Anantharam, V. A game-theoretic look at the Gaussian multiaccess channel. *DIMACS Ser. Discret. Math. Theor. Comput. Sci.* **2004**, *66*, 87–106.

25. Chou, R.A.; Yener, A. The degraded Gaussian multiple access wiretap channel with selfish transmitters: A coalitional game theory perspective. In Proceedings of the IEEE International Symposium on Information Theory (ISIT), Aachen, Germany, 25–30 June 2017; pp. 1703–1707.
26. Ekrem, E.; Ulukus, S. Secrecy capacity region of the Gaussian multi-receiver wiretap channel. In Proceedings of the IEEE International Symposium on Information Theory (ISIT), Seoul, Korea, 28 June–3 July 2009; pp. 2612–2616.
27. Sarwate, A.D.; Gastpar, M. Randomization Bounds on Gaussian arbitrarily varying channels. In Proceedings of the IEEE International Symposium on Information Theory (ISIT), Seattle, WA, USA, 9–14 July 2006; pp. 2161–2165.
28. Sato, H. The capacity of the Gaussian interference channel under strong interference. *IEEE Trans. Inf. Theory* **1981**, *27*, 786–788. [CrossRef]
29. Chou, R.; Yener, A. Polar coding for the multiple access wiretap channel via rate-splitting and cooperative jamming. *IEEE Trans. Inf. Theory* **2018**, *64*, 7903–7921. [CrossRef]
30. Ekrem, E.; Ulukus, S. On the secrecy of multiple access wiretap channel. In Proceedings of the Annual Allerton Conf. on Communication Control and Computing, Monticello, IL, USA, 23–26 September 2008; pp. 1014–1021.
31. El Gamal, A.; Kim, Y.H. *Network Information Theory*; Cambridge University Press: Cambridge, UK, 2011.
32. Wyner, A. The wire-tap channel. *Bell Syst. Tech. J.* **1975**, *54*, 1355–1387. [CrossRef]
33. Tekin, E.; Yener, A. The Gaussian multiple access wire-tap channel. *IEEE Trans. Inf. Theory* **2008**, *54*, 5747–5755. [CrossRef]
34. Rana, V.; Chou, R.A. Short Blocklength Wiretap Channel Codes via Deep Learning: Design and Performance Evaluation. *arXiv* **2022**, arXiv:2206.03477.
35. Schrijver, A. *Combinatorial Optimization: Polyhedra and Efficiency*; Springer Science & Business Media: Berlin/Heidelberg, Germany, 2003; Volume 24.

entropy

Article

Orthogonal Time Frequency Space Modulation Based on the Discrete Zak Transform

Franz Lampel *, Hamdi Joudeh, Alex Alvarado and Frans M. J. Willems

Information and Communication Theory Lab, Signal Processing Systems Group, Department of Electrical Engineering, Eindhoven University of Technology, 5600 MB Eindhoven, The Netherlands
* Correspondence: f.lampel@tue.nl

Abstract: In orthogonal time frequency space (OTFS) modulation, information-carrying symbols reside in the delay-Doppler (DD) domain. By operating in the DD domain, an appealing property for communication arises: time-frequency (TF) dispersive channels encountered in high-mobility environments become time-invariant. OTFS outperforms orthogonal frequency division multiplexing (OFDM) in high-mobility scenarios, making it an ideal waveform candidate for 6G. Generally, OTFS is considered a pre- and postprocessing step for OFDM. However, the so-called Zak transform provides the fundamental relation between the DD and time domain. In this work, we propose an OTFS system based on the discrete Zak transform (DZT). To this end, we discuss the DZT and establish the input–output relation for time-frequency (TF) dispersive channels solely by the properties of the DZT. The presented formulation simplifies the derivation and analysis of the input–output relation of the TF dispersive channel in the DD domain. Based on the presented formulation, we show that operating in the DD incurs no loss in capacity.

Keywords: orthogonal time frequency space modulation; discrete Zak transform; delay-Doppler channel; time-frequency dispersive channel; 6G

Citation: Lampel, F.; Joudeh, H.; Alvarado, A.; Willems, F.M.J. Orthogonal Time Frequency Space Modulation Based on the Discrete Zak Transform. *Entropy* **2022**, *24*, 1704. https://doi.org/10.3390/e24121704

Academic Editors: H. Vincent Poor, Holger Boche, Rafael F. Schaefer and Onur Günlü

Received: 16 October 2022
Accepted: 17 November 2022
Published: 22 November 2022

1. Introduction

Motivated by challenges encountered in wireless communication over time-variant channels, such as Doppler dispersion or equalization, a new modulation technique termed orthogonal time frequency space (OTFS) was introduced in [1]. The driving idea behind OTFS is to utilize the delay-Doppler (DD) domain to represent information-carrying symbols. The interaction of the corresponding OTFS waveform with a time-frequency (TF) dispersive channel results in a two-dimensional convolution of the symbols in the DD domain ([2], [Section III-A]). OTFS utilizes the time-invariant channel interaction in the DD domain and outperforms orthogonal frequency division multiplexing (OFDM) in high-mobility scenarios, as shown in [1–6], making it an ideal waveform candidate for 6G.

Most of the literature on OTFS considers OTFS as a pre- and postprocessing technique for OFDM systems, as described in [3,5,7]. However, the *continuous* Zak transform provides a more fundamental relationship between the DD and time domain, as pointed out in [2] and studied in [8]. In principle, OTFS describes a time domain signal by its DD representations in a similar way to OFDM, which defines a signal in the TF domain. The difference between the DD and TF domains is that the TF domain allows a continuous-time signal to be described by a discrete number of coefficients in the TF domain [9]. On the other hand, the *continuous* Zak transform maps a continuous-time signal to continuous values in the Zak domain. In [8], a discretization of the Zak representation was achieved using time and bandwidth limitations on the signal, represented by a point in the DD domain. However, depending on the domain of the signal under study, different variants of the Zak transform exists. The discrete-time version is referred to as the discrete-time Zak transform (DTZT) and the discrete (and finite) version is the discrete Zak transform (DZT) [10]. The DTZT is discrete in the delay and continuous in the frequency domain, while the DZT is discrete in both the delay and Doppler domains. Thus, an alternative description of OTFS can be provided by the DZT, as we show in this work.

Another motivation for using the DZT can be found by considering OFDM. The fundamental concept of OFDM, that is, mapping symbols onto a set of orthogonal signals in the frequency domain, dates back to 1966 [11]. The success of OFDM is based on its efficient *digital* implementation to compute the discrete Fourier transform (DFT) [12]. Equivalently, OTFS can be efficiently implemented using the *discrete* Zak transform (DZT). The DZT itself is based on the DFT, which allows for efficient implementation as well. Implementations of OTFS which resemble the DZT have been studied previously, in [13], for example. However, the proposed systems is based on OFDM that adds a cyclic prefix (CP) to every OFDM symbol. The CP adds additional signaling overhead and results in a different channel interaction in the DD domain.

DZT-based OTFS is closely related to radar processing in a pulse Doppler radar. A pulse radar transmits a pulse train with uniformly spaced and identical pulses. Target motion introduces a phase shift for each pulse, which is utilized at the receiver to extract the velocity information of a radar target. To this end, the sampled signal is arranged in a two-dimensional grid, and a DFT is applied along the so-called slow time to extract the velocity information of a target; see ([14], [Chapter 17]) or ([15], [Chapter 3]) for details. This variant of Doppler processing is equivalent to the DZT. Similarly, the radar transmitter of such a pulse Doppler radar can be described by the inverse DZT, as demonstrated in [16]. The close connection to radar makes OTFS an ideal waveform for joint communication and sensing, which has been explored by [6], among others.

A fundamental treatment of OTFS based on the DZT is currently absent from the literature. The aim of this work is to close this gap in the literature by providing a complete treatment of OTFS based solely on the DZT. Therefore, we discuss the DZT and its properties, then we derive the input–output relationship for TF dispersive channels in the DD using the DZT and its properties. Our DZT-based approach provides an intuitive understanding of OTFS and drastically simplifies its analysis. Based on our analysis, we further show that the capacity in the DD domain is equivalent to the capacity of the time-variant channel in the time domain (Parts of this work were presented at the 2022 IEEE International Conference on Communications Workshops (ICC Workshops) [17]).

The remainder of the paper is organized as follows. In Section 2, we provide an introduction to the DZT covering all properties needed for OTFS. The signal model based on the *DZT* is described in Section 3. Based on the presented signal model, we further establish the input–output relationship of OTFS based on the DZT in Section 4. In Section 5, we establish the connection between the DD and the TF domain, which allows the implementation of OTFS by an OFDM system. In Section 6, we demonstrate that operating in the DD incurs no loss in capacity. Finally, our conclusions are presented in Section 7.

2. Discrete Zak Transform

The *continuous* Zak transform is a mapping of a continuous-time signal onto a two-dimensional function. Implicit usage of the Zak transform can be traced back to Gauss [18]; however, it was Zak who formally introduced the transform in [19], and after whom it was named. An excellent paper from a signal theoretical point of view was provided by Janssen [20]. Later on, Bölcskei and Hlawatsch [10] provided an overview of the discrete versions of the transform, namely, the discrete-time Zak transform and the *discrete* Zak transform. This section is devoted to the DZT and its properties, which we use to describe OTFS and to establish the input–output relation of the TF dispersive channel discussed in Section 3.

2.1. Definition and Relations

In the following discussion, we treat finite-length sequences of length N as one period of a periodic sequence with period N, which we express as a product $N = KL$ with $K, L \in \mathbb{N}$.

Following the notation in [10], we use $Z_x^{(L,K)} \in \mathbb{C}^{\mathbb{Z}\times\mathbb{Z}}$ to denote the DZT of a sequence $x \in \mathbb{C}^{\mathbb{Z}}$ with a period KL. The DZT of x is defined as follows ([10], Equation (30)):

$$Z_x^{(L,K)}[n,k] \triangleq \frac{1}{\sqrt{K}} \sum_{l=0}^{K-1} \underbrace{x[n+lL]}_{x^{(n,L)}[l]} e^{-j2\pi\frac{k}{K}l}, \quad n,k \in \mathbb{Z}. \tag{1}$$

It follows from (1) that the DZT for a given n is the unitary discrete Fourier transform (DFT) of a subsampled sequence $x^{(n,L)} \triangleq \{x^{(n,L)}[l] = x[n+lL] : l \in \mathbb{Z}\}$. The variable n determines the starting phase of the downsampled sequence, whereas the variable k is the discrete frequency of its DFT. Thus, the variables n and k represent the time and frequency, respectively.

The *periodic* sequence x can be recovered from its DZT through the following sum relation:

$$x[n] = \frac{1}{\sqrt{K}} \sum_{k=0}^{K-1} Z_x^{(L,K)}[n,k], \tag{2}$$

which follows from the definition of the DZT in (1) and the relation

$$\sum_{k=0}^{K-1} e^{-j2\pi\frac{l}{K}k} = K \sum_{m=-\infty}^{\infty} \delta[l-mK], \tag{3}$$

where $\delta[n]$ denotes the Kronecker delta. We refer to (2) as the inverse discrete Zak transform (IDZT).

Remark 1. *Depending on the period N of the sequence under consideration, different choices of K and L are possible. We indicate the particular choice of L and K in the superscript of the DZT notation we use ($Z_x^{(L,K)}$). If the choice is not important for the context, we drop the superscript for brevity of notation (Z_x). Furthermore, the DZT is in general a complex-valued function. To illustrate the DZT, we often write the DZT in polar form, i.e.,*

$$Z_x[n,k] = |Z_x[n,k]| e^{j\varphi_x[n,k]}, \tag{4}$$

where $|Z_x[n,k]|$ and $\varphi_x[n,k]$ represent the magnitude and the phase of $Z_x^{(L,K)}[n,k]$, respectively. We restrict the phase to the principal values, i.e., to the interval $[-\pi,\pi)$.

Example 1 (DZT). *Consider the N-periodic sequence g with elements*

$$g[n] = \begin{cases} f[n], & 0 \le n \le L-1, \\ 0, & L \le n \le KL-1. \end{cases} \tag{5}$$

The sequence is zero, except possibly for the first L samples, where it takes the value of an arbitrary sequence f. The second condition in (5) implies that only one nonzero addend (for $l = 0$) exists in the summation (1). Thus, the elements of Z_g for $0 \le n \le L-1$ and $0 \le k \le K-1$ are

$$Z_g[n,k] = \frac{1}{\sqrt{K}} f[n]. \tag{6}$$

Example for a sequence f and the corresponding magnitude of the DZT Z_g are illustrated in Figure 1a,b, respectively.

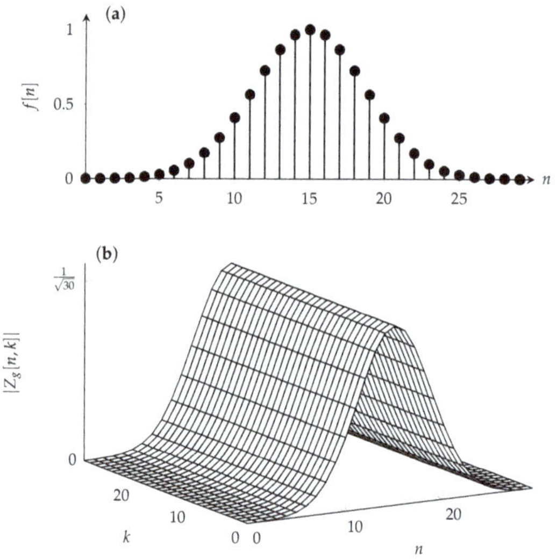

Figure 1. (**a**) Sequence $f[n] = e^{-\frac{1}{2}\left(\frac{n-L/2}{\sigma L/2}\right)^2}$ for $\sigma = 1/4$, $0 \leq n \leq L-1$ and $L = 30$. The sequence g has a period $KL = 900$. (**b**) Magnitude of the discrete Zak transform (DZT) Z_g with parameters $K = 30$, $L = 30$ in (6), for $0 \leq n \leq L-1$ and $0 \leq k \leq K-1$. The phase $\varphi_g[n,k]$ (not plotted) is zero for the presented values of n and k; see (6).

We express the period of the sequence x as a product KL with $K, L \in \mathbb{N}$. This factorization ensures that the sequence can be decomposed into L subsampled sequences with period K. In general, the product KL is not uniquely defined, as different choices of K and L result in the same product. Independent of the period, two choices are always possible and provide interesting insights. First, the choice $K = 1$ in (1) leads to

$$Z_x^{(L,1)}[n,k] = x[n], \tag{7}$$

i.e., the elements of DZT for a specific n and any k are the elements of the sequence x. Second, the case $L = 1$ results in

$$Z_x^{(1,K)}[n,k] = \frac{1}{\sqrt{K}} \sum_{l=0}^{K-1} x[n+l] e^{-j2\pi \frac{k}{K} l}. \tag{8}$$

For $n = 0$, we obtain

$$Z_x^{(1,K)}[0,k] = X[k] \tag{9}$$

where $X \in \mathbb{C}^{\mathbb{Z}}$ is the unitary DFT of the sequence x, i.e.,

$$X[k] \triangleq \frac{1}{\sqrt{K}} \sum_{l=0}^{K-1} x[l] e^{-j2\pi \frac{k}{K} l}. \tag{10}$$

It follows from (8) that $Z_x^{(1,K)}[n,k]$ represents the DFT of the circular shifted sequence x with shift parameter n. Using the circular shift property of the DFT provided in ([21], Equation (3.168))

$$x[n-n_0] \Leftrightarrow e^{-j2\pi \frac{k}{K} n_0} X[k], \tag{11}$$

we can express (8) equivalently as

$$Z_x^{(1,K)}[n,k] = e^{j2\pi \frac{k}{K} n} X[k] = e^{j2\pi \frac{k}{K} n} Z_x^{(1,K)}[0,k]. \tag{12}$$

Following the same approach used to obtain the DFT (9), we can obtain the inverse DFT (IDFT). Therefore, we consider (2) for the case $L = 1$, which is

$$x[n] \triangleq \frac{1}{\sqrt{K}} \sum_{k=0}^{K-1} X[k] e^{j2\pi \frac{k}{K} n}, \tag{13}$$

where (13) is obtained by substituting (12) in (2).

While the DZT Z_x of a sequence x can be obtained from a sequence x, it can additionally be obtained from its DFT X in (9) through

$$Z_x^{(L,K)}[n,k] = \frac{1}{\sqrt{L}} \sum_{l=0}^{L-1} X[k+lK] e^{j2\pi \frac{k+lK}{KL} n}. \tag{14}$$

Proof. See Appendix A. □

Equivalently, using (1), we recognize (14) as

$$Z_x^{(L,K)}[n,k] = e^{j2\pi \frac{n}{KL} k} Z_X^{(K,L)}[k,-n], \tag{15}$$

where $Z_X^{(K,L)}$ is the DZT of the DFT sequence X.

The corresponding inverse relation is

$$X[k] = \frac{1}{\sqrt{L}} \sum_{n=0}^{L-1} Z_x^{(L,K)}[n,k] e^{-2\pi \frac{k}{KL} n}. \tag{16}$$

Proof. See Appendix B. □

Figure 2 summarizes the relations between the sequence x, the DZT Z_x, and the DFT X. Note that the DFT X can be obtained in two ways: either directly via (10) or indirectly using (1) and (16). The later approach resembles the Cooley–Tukey algorithm, which is a fast Fourier transform algorithm [10].

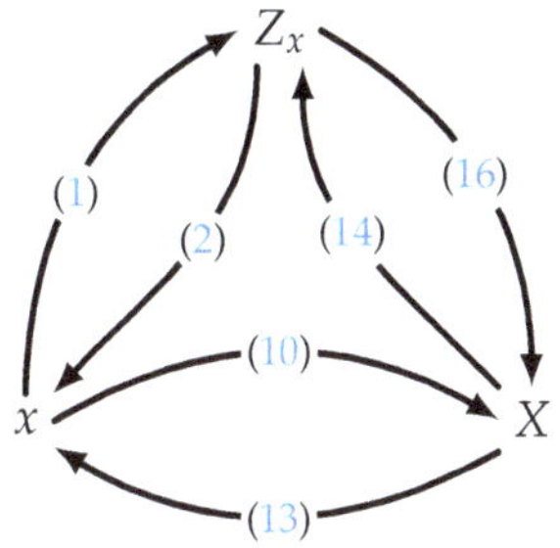

Figure 2. Different signal representations of a sequence x and its corresponding DZT Z_x and DFT X transforms.

2.2. Properties of the DZT

The DFT X of a sequence x with length K is periodic with period K, i.e., $X[k] = X[k+mK]$ with $m \in \mathbb{Z}$; see (10). The DZT possess similar properties, as the DZT is the DFT of the downsampled sequence $x^{(n,L)}$; see (1). Consequently, the DZT is periodic in the frequency variable k, i.e.,

$$Z_x^{(L,K)}[n,k+mK] = Z_x^{(L,K)}[n,k], \quad m \in \mathbb{Z}. \tag{17}$$

Using the circular shift property of the DFT in (11), we then have

$$Z_x^{(L,K)}[n+mL,k] = e^{j2\pi \frac{k}{K} m} Z_x^{(L,K)}[n,k], \quad m \in \mathbb{Z}, \tag{18}$$

i.e., the DZT is periodic in n with a period L up to a complex factor $e^{j2\pi(k/K)m}$. The DZT is therefore said to be *quasi*-periodic with *quasi*-period L. Due to the periodicity properties in (17) and (18), the DZT is fully determined by the DZT for $0 \le n \le L-1$ and $0 \le k \le K-1$, which is referred to as the fundamental rectangle [10].

The *quasi*-periodicity in (18) can be utilized to express the IDZT in (2) as follows:

$$x[n + lL] = \frac{1}{\sqrt{K}} \sum_{k=0}^{K-1} Z_x^{(L,K)}[n,k] e^{j2\pi \frac{k}{K} l}. \tag{19}$$

Here, we express the index of the sequence as sum of the form $n + lL$ with $0 \le n \le L-1$ and $l \in \mathbb{Z}$. Because the fundamental rectangle fully determines the DZT Z_x, we restrict ourselves to this fundamental rectangle when plotting the DZT. In fact, this is what is done in Figure 1b.

Example 2 (IDZT)**.** *Consider the DZT defined by a single nonzero coefficient on the fundamental rectangle of size* 4×6 *and provided by*

$$Z_x^{(4,6)}[n,k] = \delta[n]\delta[k]. \tag{20}$$

The fundamental rectangle and the DZT in (20) are illustrated in Figure 3a (left). One period of the sequence x obtained through (19) is

$$x[n] = \frac{1}{\sqrt{6}} \sum_{l=0}^{K-1} \delta[n - 6l], \tag{21}$$

i.e., a train of real Kronecker deltas starting at $n = 0$ *with spacing* $L = 6$*, as shown in Figure 3a (right). Now, consider the DZT*

$$Z_y^{(4,6)}[n,k] = \delta[n-3]\delta[k-5], \tag{22}$$

which is shown in Figure 3b. One period of the corresponding sequence y is

$$y[n] = \frac{1}{\sqrt{6}} \sum_{l=0}^{K-1} \delta[n - 3 - 6l] e^{j2\pi \frac{5}{6} l} \tag{23}$$

and is shown in Figure 3b. When compared to x, the sequence y is delayed by three samples and modulated with a discrete frequency $k = 5$.

In fact, a single coefficient at $Z_x[n,k]$ *maps onto a sequence*

$$v_{n,k}[n'] = \frac{1}{\sqrt{K}} \sum_{l=0}^{K-1} \delta[n' - n + lL] e^{j2\pi \frac{k}{K} l}. \tag{24}$$

The set of sequence $\{v_{n,k} : 0 \le n \le L-1, 0 \le k \le K-1\}$ *forms an orthonormal basis and* $Z_x[n,k]$ *are the* expansion coefficients *of a sequence x with respect to this orthonormal basis. We use this fact in Section 3, where we define a sequence by its corresponding DZT in the same way as OFDM defines the symbols in the DFT domain.*

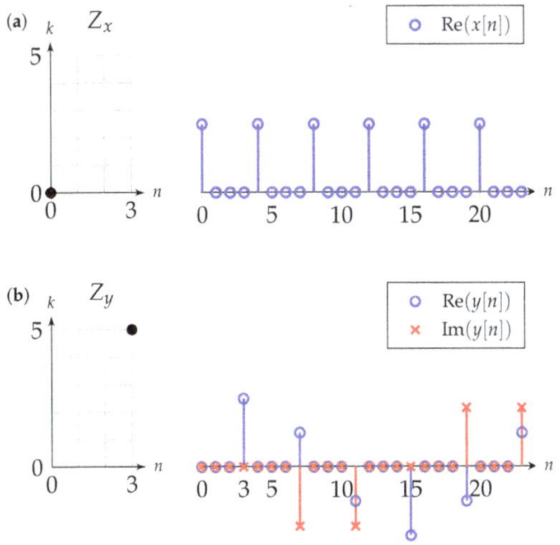

Figure 3. Two examples of DZTs (left) defined by a single nonzero coefficient on the fundamental rectangle (indicated by a dot) and the corresponding sequences (right) for (**a**) the DZT in (20) and (**b**) the DZT in (22).

Using the *quasi*-periodicity, we can further find that the elementwise product of a DZT Z_x with the complex conjugate DZT Z_y^* is periodic in n and k. Motivated by this periodicity, we apply a two-dimensional DFT, which turns out to be [10,22]

$$\sum_{n=0}^{L-1}\sum_{k=0}^{K-1} Z_x[n,k]Z_y^*[n,k]e^{j2\pi\left(\frac{m}{K}k-\frac{l}{L}n\right)} = \langle x, y_{m,l}\rangle, \tag{25}$$

where $y_{m,l} \triangleq y[n-mL]e^{j2\pi(l/L)n}$. Here, $\langle\cdot,\cdot\rangle$ is the inner product, defined as

$$\langle x, y\rangle = \sum_{n=0}^{N-1} x[n]y^*[n]. \tag{26}$$

Note that the Fourier kernel $e^{j2\pi\left(\frac{m}{K}k-\frac{l}{L}n\right)}$ in (25) has opposed signs for the two individual dimensions. Therefore, the two-dimensional discrete Fourier transform in (25) is usually referred to as the inverse *symplectic* finite Fourier transform (ISFFT).

Proof. See Appendix C. □

The inverse relation is provided by

$$Z_x[n,k]Z_y^*[n,k] = \frac{1}{KL}\sum_{m=0}^{K-1}\sum_{l=0}^{L-1}\langle x, y_{m,l}\rangle e^{-j2\pi\left(\frac{k}{K}m-\frac{n}{L}l\right)}, \tag{27}$$

which follows from applying the corresponding two-dimensional inverse transform on both sides of (25). The transform of the right-hand side of (27) is referred to as the symplectic finite Fourier transform (SFFT). The relations (25) and (27) provide a useful tool when considering the OTFS overlay for OFDM in Section 5.

2.3. Signal Transform Properties

Here, we list three signal transform properties that we use later when studying OTFS. A comprehensive overview of signal transform properties can be found in ([10], Table VII). Let x, y, and z be sequences with the same periods and let Z_x, Z_y, and Z_z be their respective DZTs. Then, the following properties hold:

1. *Shift:* Let y be the shifted version of x, i.e., $y[n] = x[n-m]$; then,

$$Z_y[n,k] = Z_x[n-m,k]. \tag{28}$$

A shift in the sequence causes a shift in the corresponding DZT. The proof follows from the definition of the DZT (1). For shifts of multiples of L, i.e., $m = lL$ with $l \in \mathbb{Z}$, we further have

$$Z_y[n,k] = e^{-j2\pi \frac{k}{K} m} Z_x[n,k], \tag{29}$$

which follows from the *quasi*-periodicity of the DZT in (18).

2. *Modulation:* Let $z = x \cdot y$ be the elementwise product of x and y, i.e., $z[n] = x[n]y[n]$. Then,

$$Z_z[n,k] = \frac{1}{\sqrt{K}} \sum_{l=0}^{K-1} Z_x[n,l] Z_y[n,k-l], \tag{30}$$

i.e., the DZT of the element-wise multiplication is a scaled convolution with respect to the variable k.

Proof. See Appendix D. □

3. *Circular Convolution:* Consider $z = x \circledast y$, i.e., the circular convolution of x and y. Then, the DZT Z_z is

$$Z_z[n,k] = \sqrt{K} \sum_{m=0}^{L-1} Z_x[m,k] Z_y[n-m,k], \tag{31}$$

i.e., the DZT of a circular convolution is the scaled convolution with respect to the variable n up to a constant.

Proof. See Appendix E. □

The shift property in (28) together with the *quasi*-periodicity in (18) has another important implication. In OTFS, as we show in Section 3, the received signal includes a superposition of delayed sequences that, in general, are not multiples of L. We discuss this further in Example 3.

Example 3 (Shifted DZT). *Consider a DZT Z_h with elements*

$$Z_h[n,k] = Z_g[n-10,k], \tag{32}$$

which is a shifted version of the DZT Z_g in Figure 1b of Example 1. To evaluate the DZT Z_h within the fundamental rectangle, we first make the observation that any index n can be expressed as $n = i + mL$ with $m = \lfloor n/L \rfloor$, where $\lfloor n/L \rfloor$ denotes the greatest integer less than or equal to n/L. In this example, the indices $n = 0$ to 9 of Z_h correspond to the indices $n = -10$ to -1 of Z_g. Expressing the latter indices in terms of i and m, we know $m = -1$ and i from 20 to 29. Thus, by the quasi-periodicity *property in (18), we have that $Z_h[n,k] = e^{-j2\pi k/K} Z_g[n+20,k]$ for $0 \le n \le 9$. On the other hand, the indices of $10 \le n \le 29$ of $Z_h[n,k]$ correspond to the indices $0 \le n \le 19$ of $Z_g[n,k]$. Therefore, $m = 0$ and Z_h is the shifted DZT Z_g within the fundamental rectangle. Thus,*

$$Z_h[n,k] = \begin{cases} e^{-j2\pi \frac{k}{K}} Z_g[n+20,k], & 0 \le n \le 9, \\ Z_g[n-10,k], & 10 \le n \le 29, \end{cases} \tag{33}$$

or more generally, $Z_h[n,k] = e^{j2\pi(k/K)\lfloor (n-10)/L \rfloor} Z_g[(n-10)_L, k]$. The DZT Z_h is depicted in Figure 4, which illustrates different phase behaviors as well.

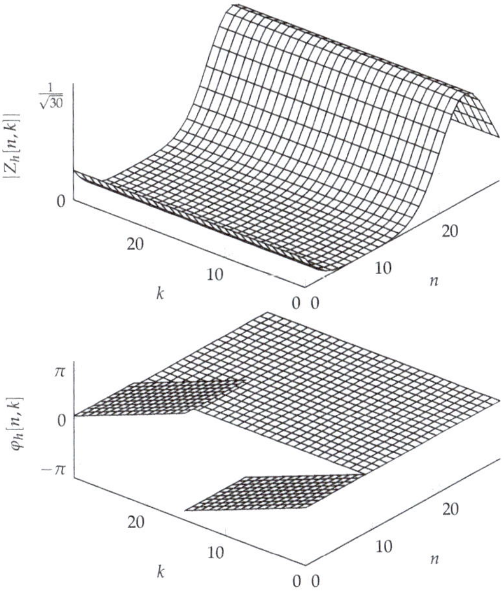

Figure 4. The DZT $Z_h[n,k] = Z_g[n-10,k]$ in Example 3, with $Z_g[n,k]$ being the DZT of Figure 1. The shift of the DZT with respect to n causes a circular shift of the magnitude $|Z_g[n,k]|$ of the DZT (**top**). The phase $\varphi_h[n,k]$ experiences an additional linear phase for indices smaller than 10 (**bottom**).

3. System Model

In this section, we use the IDZT/DZT to map the symbols in the DD domain directly to a time domain sequence and vice versa. We consider a pulse-amplitude modulation (PAM) system to map the discrete symbols onto continuous pulses, as schematically shown in Figure 5. This approach allows for the digital implementation of OTFS similar to the PAM implementation of OFDM presented in ([23] Chapter 6.4.2).

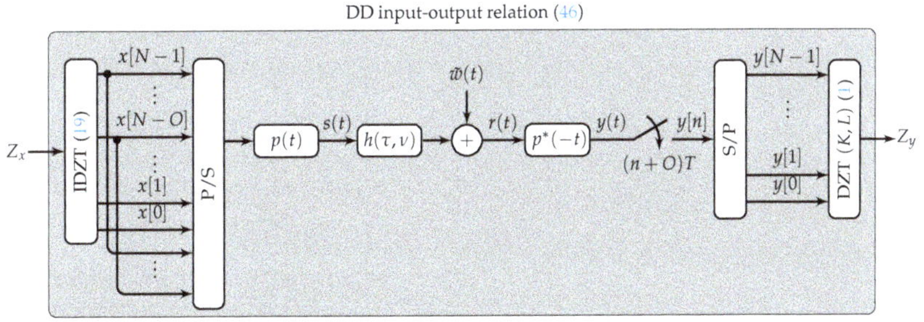

Figure 5. OTFS system model considered in this work. The IDZT maps a sequence consisting of the symbols defined in the DD domain to a discrete sequence. A CP is added by copying the last O samples. The resulting sequence x is converted to a serial stream by a parallel-to-serial converter (P/S) before being mapped onto a pulse $p(t)$ and sent over a noisy TF-dispersive channel $h(\tau,\nu)$. At the receiver, a sampled matched filter is applied before the serial stream is converted to a parallel stream by a serial-to-parallel (S/P) converter. Lastly, the sequence y is mapped to the DD domain using the DZT. The DD input–output relationship is provided by (46) and Theorem 1.

3.1. Transmitter

Similar to OFDM, which defines symbols in the frequency domain, OTFS defines $K \times L$ symbols on the fundamental rectangle in the Zak domain. The symbols in the Zak domain are mapped to a sequence in the time domain using the IDZT in (19). Prior to modulation, a CP of length O is added by copying the last O samples and inserting them at the beginning of the sequence (see Figure 5). As we show later, the CP turns the linear convolution of the channel into a circular convolution, allowing us to use the circular convolution property (47) of the DZT. The elements of the sequence x are then mapped onto time-shifted pulses $p(t)$ using PAM. The transmitted signal is provided as follows:

$$s(t) = \sum_{n=0}^{N+O-1} x[n-O]p(t-nT), \tag{34}$$

where T is the modulation interval and $p(t)$ is a square-root Nyquist pulse. Note that (34) is equivalent (up to the CP) to (21) of [8]. However, by considering the DZT and PAM, no discretization of the continuous Zak transform is required. Moreover, considering the class of Nyquist pulses in the modulation allows for more freedom in controlling the interference in the delay domain.

Remark 2. *In Section 2.1, we discussed the implications of the choice of the parameters K and L for the DZT. Similarly, the choice of K and L influences the OTFS system under study. For the case $K = 1$, the symbols of Z_x are arranged on a line along the delay axis. The IDZT does not alter the sequence and can be skipped; see (7). Thus, the system is a single carrier system. On the other hand, for $L = 1$, the symbols $Z_x^{(L,K)}[n,k]$ are arranged along the Doppler axis. The IDZT is simply the IDFT (see (13)), and (34) becomes an OFDM signal as in ([23] Chapter 6.4.2).*

3.2. Channel Model

We now consider TF dispersive channels and model the received signal as follows ([24] Chapter 1.3.1):

$$r(t) = \int_{-\infty}^{\infty}\int_{-\infty}^{\infty} h(\tau,\nu)s(t-\tau)e^{j2\pi\nu t}d\tau d\nu + \tilde{w}(t) \tag{35}$$

where $h(\tau,\nu)$ is the so-called DD spreading function. The complex noise $\tilde{w}(t)$ is assumed to be white and Gaussian with power spectral density N_0. We model the channel by P discrete scattering objects. Each scattering object is associated with a path delay τ_p, a Doppler shift ν_p, and a complex attenuation factor α_p. Thus, the spreading function $h(\tau,\nu)$ becomes

$$h(\tau,\nu) = \sum_{p=0}^{P-1} \alpha_p \delta(\tau-\tau_p)\delta(\nu-\nu_p). \tag{36}$$

Substituting (36) in (35) yields

$$r(t) = \sum_{p=0}^{P-1} \alpha_p s(t-\tau_p)e^{j2\pi\nu_p t} + \tilde{w}(t), \tag{37}$$

i.e., the received signal is a superposition of scaled, delayed, and Doppler-shifted replicas of the transmitted signal. The Doppler shift is provided by $\nu_p = v_p f_c / c$, where v_p, f_c, and c are the relative velocity of the pth scattering object, the carrier frequency, and the speed of light, respectively. The length of the CP in (34) is chosen such that OT is larger than or equal to the maximum delay.

Remark 3. *In the channel model in (36), it is assumed that the individual delays are independent of the absolute time. Strictly speaking, this is not the case, as the movement of a reflector affects the delay. However, (36) holds as long as the signal length NT is chosen such that the delay does not change significantly.*

Substituting (34) in (37), the received signal is

$$r(t) = \sum_{p=0}^{P-1} \alpha_p \sum_{n=0}^{N+O-1} x[n-O]p(t-nT-\tau_p)e^{j2\pi\nu_p t} + \tilde{w}(t). \tag{38}$$

3.3. Receiver

At the receiver, a matched filter with impulse response $p^*(-t)$ is applied. The output of the matched filter $y(t)$ is

$$y(t) = \sum_{p=0}^{P-1} \alpha_p \sum_{n=0}^{N+O-1} x[n-O] \int_{-\infty}^{\infty} p(\tau - nT - \tau_p)e^{j2\pi\nu_p \tau} p^*(\tau - t)d\tau + w(t), \tag{39}$$

where $w(t)$ is the filtered noise. Assuming that the pulse bandwidth is much larger than the maximum Doppler shift, we can approximate the integral in (39) as $e^{j2\pi\nu_p(nT+\tau_p)}h(t-nT-\tau_p)$, where $h(t)$ is the corresponding Nyquist pulse. The output of the matched filter is then

$$y(t) \approx \sum_{p=0}^{P-1} \alpha_p \sum_{n=0}^{N+O-1} x[n-O]e^{j2\pi\nu_p(nT+\tau_p)}h(t-nT-\tau_p) + w(t). \tag{40}$$

The matched filter output is sampled every T seconds and with an offset of OT to discard the CP. The sampled signal $y[m] = y((m+O)T)$ is

$$y[n] = \sum_{p=0}^{P-1} \alpha_p \sum_{m=-O}^{N-1} x[m]e^{j2\pi \frac{k_p}{KL} m} h_{\tau_p}[n-m] + w[n], \tag{41}$$

where $h_{\tau_p}[n] = h(nT - \tau_p)$ is the sampled Nyquist pulse and $w[m]$ are independent and identically distributed (i.i.d.) complex zero-mean Gaussian random variables with variance N_0. To shorten the notation, we combine the constant phase terms $e^{j2\pi\nu_p\tau_p}$ with the channel gain α_p in (41). Furthermore, we express ν_p as a multiple of the Doppler resolution, which we define as

$$\Delta\nu \triangleq 1/(KLT), \tag{42}$$

i.e., $\nu_p = \Delta\nu k_p$.

We can bound the interval for which $h(t)$ is significantly different from zero (for sufficient large L) to $\pm LT/2$. Thus, we can express $h_{\tau_p}[n]$ as

$$h_{\tau_p}[n] = \begin{cases} h(nT-\tau_p), & \text{for } -\frac{LT}{2} \leq nT - \tau_p < \frac{LT}{2}, \\ 0, & \text{else.} \end{cases} \tag{43}$$

The CP allows the linear convolution in (41) to be approximated by a circular convolution; the sample $y[n]$ is then provided by

$$y[n] = \sum_{p=0}^{P-1} \alpha_p y_p[n] + w[n], \tag{44}$$

where

$$y_p[n] = \sum_{m=0}^{KL-1} x[m]e^{j2\pi \frac{k_p}{N} m} h_{\tau_p}[n-m]. \tag{45}$$

Here, h_{τ_p} is periodicized over a period KL, i.e., $h_{\tau_p}[n] = h_{\tau_p}[n+KL]$. In a last step, the receiver computes the DZT of the sequence $y[m]$ before subsequent processing takes place.

4. Delay Doppler Input–Output Relationship

To express the input–output relationship in the DD domain for the system presented in Figure 5, we first note that the DZT is a linear transform; as such, we can write the DZT of (44) as

$$Z_y[n,k] = \sum_{p=0}^{P-1} \alpha_p Z_{y_p}[n,k] + Z_w[n,k], \tag{46}$$

where Z_{y_p} is the DZT of sequence y_p described in (45) and $Z_w[n,k]$ is the DZT of the noise. The elements of $Z_w[n,k]$ are i.i.d. zero-mean Gaussian random variables with variance N_0. This follows from the fact that the DZT is a unitary transform ([10], Section VI).

For the signal model of a single reflector in (45), we provide the following result for the input–output relationship in the DD domain for the OTFS system described in Section 3.

Theorem 1. *Considering the fundamental rectangle $Z_x \in \mathbb{C}^{L\times K}$ of complex symbols in the DD domain, the input–output relation for OTFS transmission over a time-frequency selective channel for a single reflector is*

$$Z_{y_p}[n,k] = \sum_{m=0}^{L-1}\left(\sum_{l=0}^{K-1} Z_x[m,l] Z_{\nu_p}[m,k-l]\right) Z_{\tau_p}[n-m,k], \tag{47}$$

where Z_{τ_p} and Z_{ν_p} are the delay and Doppler spreading functions, respectively. The delay spreading function Z_{τ_p} is the DZT of the shifted and sampled impulse $h_{\tau_p}[n]$ in (43), and the Doppler spreading functions is provided as follows:

$$Z_{\nu_p}[n,k] = \frac{1}{\sqrt{K}} e^{j2\pi \frac{k_p}{KL} n} e^{-j\pi \frac{K-1}{K}(k-k_p)} \frac{\sin\left(\pi(k-k_p)\right)}{\sin\left(\frac{\pi}{K}(k-k_p)\right)}. \tag{48}$$

Proof. See Appendix F. □

To illustrate the spreading of a single symbol in the DD domain, we consider the following example. Let $L = K = 30$ and

$$Z_x[n,k] = \begin{cases} 1 & \text{for } n = k = L/2, \\ 0 & \text{else.} \end{cases} \tag{49}$$

The fundamental rectangle with the only nonzero element is presented in Figure 6a. Furthermore, assume that $\tau = 0.5T$ and $\nu = 0.5\Delta\nu$. Note that this example causes the maximum spread of a single symbol in the DD domain. We can visualize the spreading of the symbol defined in (49) in two steps. Therefore, we define $Z_{\tilde{y}}$ as the DZT resulting from the inner convolution in (47), presented in Figure 6b, with respect to the Doppler index k. The resulting spread of the nonzero symbol is visualized in Figure 6c. Finally, the symbol that has been spread in the Doppler domain is spread in the delay domain by the delay spreading function Z_τ, which is illustrated in Figure 6d. Note that due to the limited support of h_τ (see (43)), the magnitude of Z_τ is independent of the index k. The resulting spread of the nonzero symbol in the DD domain is shown in Figure 6e.

For the particular case of $\tau_p = n_p T$ with $n_p = 0, 1, \ldots, O-1$ and $\nu_p = k_p/(KLT)$ with $k_p \in \mathbb{Z}$, Z_{y_p} simplifies to

$$Z_{y_p}[n,k] = e^{j2\pi \frac{k_p}{KL}(n-n_p)} Z_x[n-n_p, k-k_p], \tag{50}$$

i.e., the received symbols Z_{y_p} are in the DD domain displaced symbols Z_x.

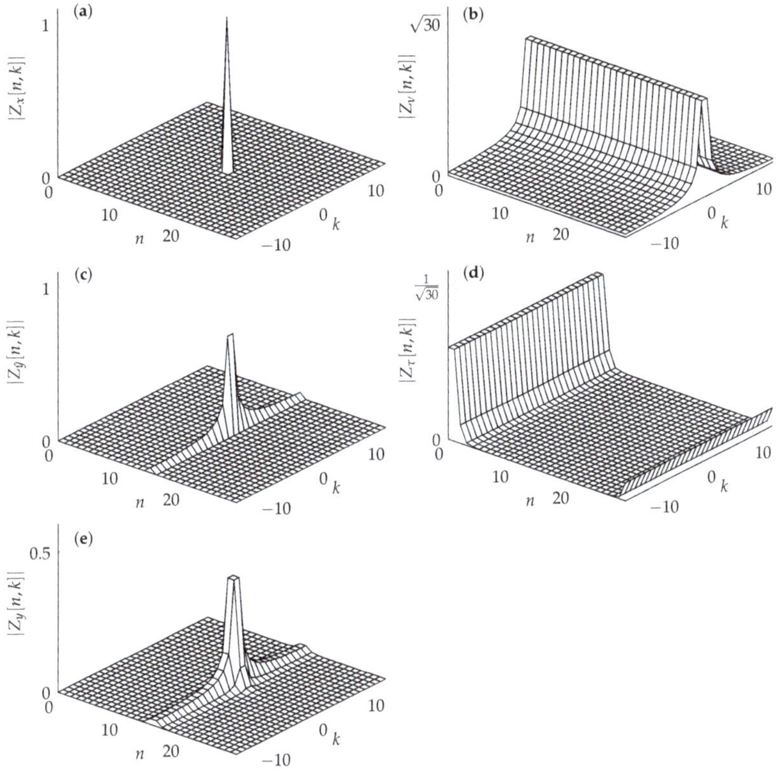

Figure 6. Example of the spread of a symbol (**a**) in the DD domain due to fractional delay and Doppler shift. The spread can be first evaluated in the Doppler domain (**c**) using the Doppler spreading function in (**b**). The spread symbol in the Doppler domain is further spread in the delay by the the delay spread function in (**d**). The overall spread in the DD domain is shown in (**e**).

Theorem 1 shows that the channel interaction with the symbols in the DD domain is time-invariant, neglecting the additional phase terms due to the quasi-periodicity and modulation. The invariance is helpful in the detection of the symbols. Consider a TDL-C channel with a delay spread of 300 ns, a carrier frequency of 4 GHz, and a maximum velocity of 120 kmph. Furthermore, assume an OTFS system with $K = 7$ and $L = 600$ and $1/T = 9$ MHz. The channel response $Z_h[n,k] = \sum_{l=0}^{K-1} Z_{v_p}[n,k-l]Z_{\tau_p}[n,k]$ in the DD domain is illustrated in Figure 7a. The magnitude of this channel stays approximately constant throughout the entire transmission of an OTFS frame. Figure 7b illustrates the equivalent OFDM channel. The variation of the channel along the subcarrier index k as well along the time index n can be seen. To keep track of the channel, additional pilots need to be used, and these cannot be used for communication.

In addition to constant channel interaction, OTFS offers the advantage of a concise and sparse channel description compared to OFDM. In an OFDM system, the channel coefficient for each subcarrier must be estimated for subsequent symbol detection. In contrast, for symbol detection in an OTFS system, knowledge of the interference introduced by each reflector is sufficient. The sparsity can be seen in Figure 7; the support of $|Z_h[n,k]|$ is limited to a small area, while the channel transfer function changes with each subcarrier and time index, that is, l and m, respectively.

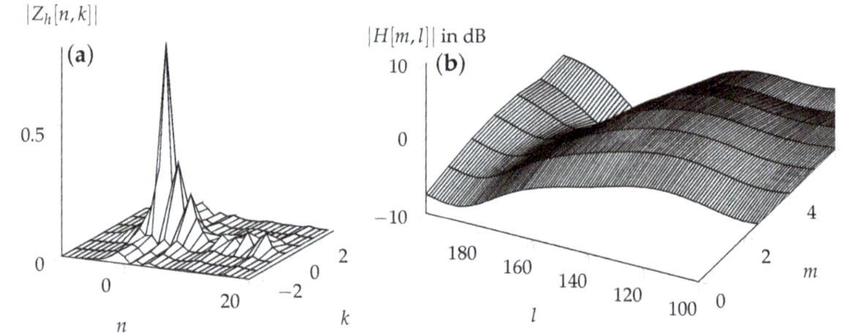

Figure 7. Two different representations of the time-variant channel: (**a**) DD representation and (**b**) TF representation. The DD domain representation is only nonzero for a small part of the domain, and stays constant throughout the transmission. On the other hand, the TF domain representation of the channel in the TF domain changes with respect to the time, and therefore needs to be tracked.

Remark 4. *The discrete two-dimensional convolution in (46) can be equivalently expressed in the form*

$$\mathbf{y} = \mathbf{H}\mathbf{x} + \mathbf{w}, \tag{51}$$

where $\mathbf{y}$, $\mathbf{x}$, *and* $\mathbf{w}$ *are the vectorized DTZs* Z_y, Z_x, *and* Z_w, *respectively. The vectors are all of length* KL. *The matrix* $\mathbf{H} \in \mathbb{C}^{KL \times KL}$ *describes the intersymbol interference in the DD domain. Because* Z_{τ_p} *and* Z_{ν_p} *have small support in the DD domain, the corresponding matrix* $\mathbf{H}$ *is sparse. The matrix-vector formulation of the input–output relationship is the basis for many works on OTFS; for example, see [5,6].*

5. OTFS Overlay for OFDM

Currently, orthogonal frequency division multiplexing (OFDM) is the dominant modulation scheme in wireless communication. For example, it is used in 5G and in several 802.11 standards. This section shows that DFT-based ODFM can be used for OTFS modulation and demodulation. In this context, OTFS is considered a pre- and postprocessing step for the OFDM system.

To derive the pre- and postprocessing step, we first derive an alternative way to compute the DZT. For this purpose, we consider (27). If we choose the sequence y such that its DZT $Z_y[n,k] = 1$, then we can obtain the DZT Z_x through the right-hand side of (27). The N periodic sequence y with DZT $Z_y[n,k] = 1$ is

$$y[n] = \begin{cases} \sqrt{K}, & 0 \leq n \leq L-1, \\ 0, & \text{elsewhere.} \end{cases} \tag{52}$$

With this particular choice of y, we recognize the inner product on the right-hand side of (27) as

$$\langle x, y_{m,l} \rangle = \sqrt{K} \sum_{n=0}^{L-1} x[n+mL] e^{j2\pi \frac{l}{L} n}, \tag{53}$$

which is the scaled L-point DFT of the samples $x[n]$ for $mL \leq n \leq (m+1)L - 1$. If we define

$$a_{m,l} \triangleq \langle x, y_{m,l} \rangle, \tag{54}$$

for $0 \leq m \leq K-1$ and $0 \leq l \leq L-1$, then the DZT of x is obtained through

$$Z_x[n,k] = \frac{1}{KL} \sum_{m=0}^{K-1} \sum_{l=0}^{L-1} a_{m,l} e^{-j2\pi \left(\frac{k}{K} m - \frac{n}{L} l\right)}, \tag{55}$$

i.e., by the SFFT of the coefficients $a_{m,l}$. Note that the set $a_{m,l}$ represents the Gabor expansion coefficients for the choice of a rectangular analysis window (see [25], Section 4), and thus a mixed TF representation of the sequence x.

The coefficients $a_{m,l}$, on the other hand, are obtained from $Z_x^{(L,K)}[n,k]$ using (25):

$$a_{m,l} = \sum_{n=0}^{L-1} \sum_{k=0}^{K-1} Z_x[n,k] e^{j2\pi\left(\frac{k}{K}m - \frac{n}{L}l\right)}. \tag{56}$$

The samples of the sequence x for $mL \leq n \leq (m+1)L - 1$ are obtained as follows:

$$x[n + mL] = \frac{1}{\sqrt{KL}} \sum_{l=0}^{L-1} a_{m,l} e^{j2\pi \frac{l}{L} n}, \tag{57}$$

which is the L-point IDFT of the coefficients $a_{m,l}$ for a fixed m. Thus, the DZT (IDZT) can be implemented by consecutive execution of the DFT (IDFT) and the SFFT (ISFFT).

The above-described two-step approach for the calculation of the DZT and IDZT can be used to implement OTFS using OFDM hardware, which is typically based on the IDFT/DFT (see ([26], Section 19.3), ([23], Section 6.4.2), ([27] Section 12.4.3), or ([28], Section 4.6)) by extending the transmitter and receiver by the ISFFT and SFFT, respectively. The coefficients $a_{m,l}$ then represent the coefficient in the TF domain. The index m refers to the mth OFDM symbol in the time domain, and l is the corresponding subcarrier index. Note that for the DZT, the parameter L the grid size in the delay domain. For DFT-SFFT implementation, on the other hand, L defines DFT size, which defines the number of points in the frequency domain. Thus, an $L \times K$ grid in the DD domain translates to a $K \times L$ grid in the TF domain.

Remark 5. *In CP-OFDM, a CP is added for each OFDM symbol by copying the last O samples of an OFDM symbol and inserting them in front of the corresponding OFDM symbol with length L. This symbol-wise CP is not required in the OFDM implementation of OTFS. Instead, a single CP is added by copying the last O samples of the entire sequence and inserting them in front of the sequence.*

6. DD Channel Capacity

The input–output relationship in (41) is equivalently expressed as

$$y[n] = \sum_{m \in \mathcal{L}} h[n,m] x[n-m] + w[n], \tag{58}$$

where $h[n,m]$ is the time-variant multi-tap channel response at time instance n and $\mathcal{L}$ is the support of $h[n,m]$ in m. This channel response is deterministic and periodic (considering $k_p \in \mathbb{Q}$) with some finite period M, i.e., $h[n,m] = h[n + bM, m]$ for any $n \in \{1,2,\ldots,M\}$ and $b \in \mathbb{Z}$. Upon using the channel N times, the input output relationship can be written in the following vector form:

$$\mathbf{Y}_N = \mathbf{H}_N \mathbf{X}_N + \mathbf{W}_N, \tag{59}$$

where $\mathbf{X}_N$ is the input block, $\mathbf{Y}_N$ is the corresponding output block, $\mathbf{W}_N$ is the block of noise samples (all column vectors), and $\mathbf{H}_N$ is the channel (convolution) matrix constructed from the time-varying channel response $h[n,m]$.

The above channel can be shown to be *information-stable* (see Section 3.9 in [29]); hence, its capacity is provided by the following multi-letter limiting expression [30]:

$$C = \lim_{N\to\infty} \sup_{f_{\mathbf{X}_N}} \frac{1}{N} I(\mathbf{X}_N; \mathbf{Y}_N), \tag{60}$$

where $f_{\mathbf{X}_N}$ is the multi-letter input distribution for block length N. For each block length N, the corresponding mutual information term in (60) is maximized by a Gaussian input [31]; hence, the capacity is provided by

$$C = \lim_{N\to\infty} \max_{\mathbf{Q}_N:\mathrm{tr}(\mathbf{Q}_N)\leq NP} \frac{1}{N}\log\det\left(\frac{1}{\sigma^2}\mathbf{H}_N\mathbf{Q}_N\mathbf{H}_N^{\mathsf{H}} + \mathbf{I}_N\right). \tag{61}$$

Let $\mathbf{H}_N = \mathbf{U}_N\mathbf{\Sigma}_N\mathbf{V}_N^{\mathsf{H}}$ be the SVD of $\mathbf{H}_N$. Then, the optimal input covariance matrix is provided by $\mathbf{Q}_N = \mathbf{V}_N\mathbf{D}_N\mathbf{V}_N^{\mathsf{H}}$, where $\mathbf{D}_N$ is a diagonal matrix obtained using water-filling [31]. The capacity-achieving strategy is characterized by a sequence $\{\mathbf{Q}_N\}_{N\in\mathbb{N}}$.

In case we do not wish to use the channel response matrix in the construction of input sequences, we may add the restriction that the multi-letter input distribution must be isotropic. In this case, we simply have $\mathbf{Q}_N = P\mathbf{I}_N$, and the capacity is provided by

$$C_{\text{iso}} = \lim_{N\to\infty} \frac{1}{N}\log\det\left(\frac{P}{\sigma^2}\mathbf{H}_N\mathbf{H}_N^{\mathsf{H}} + \mathbf{I}_N\right). \tag{62}$$

It is evident that C_{iso} is achieved by any input of the form $\mathbf{X}_N = \mathbf{B}_N\mathbf{S}_N$, where $\mathbf{B}_N$ is a set of orthonormal basis (i.e., $\mathbf{B}_N^{\mathsf{H}}\mathbf{B}_N = \mathbf{B}_N\mathbf{B}_N^{\mathsf{H}} = \mathbf{I}_N$) and $\mathbf{S}_N$ is a vector of zero-mean i.i.d. Gaussian symbols with covariance $\mathbb{E}\left[\mathbf{S}_N\mathbf{S}_N^{\mathsf{H}}\right] = P\mathbf{I}_N$. As shown in Section 2, the set of sequence $\{v_{n,k} : 0 \leq n \leq L-1, 0 \leq k \leq K-1\}$ forms an orthonormal basis. Thus, the capacity of the DD channel is provided by (62).

7. Conclusions

In this work, we have presented an OTFS based on the discrete Zak transform. The discrete Zak transform-based description allows for an efficient digital implementation of OTFS. Furthermore, we derived the input–output relation for the symbols in the delay-Doppler domain solely based on discrete Zak transform properties, which provides a concise description of OTFS compared to the pre- and postprocessing approaches for OFDM.

Our presented discrete Zak transform approach can be used to study and evaluate OTFS from a different perspectives, potentially leading to OTFS performance improvements. For example, considering Nyquist pulses $p(t)$ with larger roll-off factors allows the interference in the delay domain to be controlled. Additionally, applying windows to the subsampled sequences of the DZT reduces the interference in the Doppler domain.

Author Contributions: Conceptualization, F.L.; formal analysis, F.L.; H.J. and F.M.J.W.; writing—original draft preparation, F.L.; writing—review and editing, F.L, H.J., A.A. and F.M.J.W. All authors have read and agreed to the published version of the manuscript.

Funding: This research was funded by the Dutch Technology Foundation TTW, which is part of the Netherlands Organisation for Scientific Research (NWO), and which is partly funded by the Ministry of Economic Affairs under the project Integrated Cooperative Automated Vehicles (i-CAVE).

Institutional Review Board Statement: Not applicable.

Data Availability Statement: Not applicable.

Conflicts of Interest: The authors declare no conflict of interest.

Appendix A. Proof of Relation (14)

Substituting $x[n]$ in (1) by (13), we obtain

$$Z_x^{(L,K)}[n,k] = \frac{1}{K\sqrt{L}}\sum_{l=0}^{K-1}\sum_{k'=0}^{KL-1} X[k']e^{j2\pi\left(\frac{k'}{KL}(n+lL)-\frac{k}{KL}l\right)}. \tag{A1}$$

Note that in the derivation of (13), the case for $L=1$ was considered; thus, the sequence x has a period K. Here, on the other hand, we consider the sequence x to be KL-periodic.

Therefore, (13) is adopted accordingly by substituting K by KL. Next, we rearrange terms and obtain

$$Z_x^{(L,K)}[n,k] = \frac{1}{K\sqrt{L}} \sum_{k'=0}^{KL-1} X[k'] e^{j2\pi \frac{k'}{KL} n} \sum_{l=0}^{K-1} e^{-j2\pi \frac{k'-k}{K} l}, \tag{A2}$$

where we finally replace the last sum by relation (3) which, due to the sifting property of the Kronecker delta, leads to

$$Z_x^{(L,K)}[n,k] = \frac{1}{\sqrt{L}} \sum_{l=0}^{L-1} X[k + lK] e^{j2\pi \frac{k+lK}{KL} n}. \tag{A3}$$

Appendix B. Proof of Relation (16)

In a first step, we rewrite the summation in (10) as a double summation, i.e.,

$$X[k] = \frac{1}{\sqrt{KL}} \sum_{l=0}^{K-1} \sum_{n=0}^{L-1} x[n + lL] e^{-j \frac{k}{KL}(n+lL)}. \tag{A4}$$

Next, we use relation (19) to express $x[n + lL]$ through its IDZT, which leads to

$$X[k] = \frac{1}{K\sqrt{L}} \sum_{l=0}^{K-1} \sum_{n=0}^{L-1} \sum_{k'=0}^{K-1} Z[n,k'] e^{-j \frac{k-k'}{K} l} e^{-j \frac{k}{KL} n}, \tag{A5}$$

and in a final step we use relation (3) with respect to the summation over l, which results in

$$X[k] = \frac{1}{\sqrt{L}} \sum_{n=0}^{L-1} Z_x[n,k] e^{-j2\pi \frac{k}{KL} n}. \tag{A6}$$

Appendix C. Proof of Relation (25)

To prove the relation (25), we substitute the DZT Z_x and Z_y^* by their definition in (1). After rearranging terms, we obtain

$$\frac{1}{K} \sum_{n=0}^{L-1} \sum_{l'=0}^{L-1} \sum_{l''=0}^{L-1} x[n + l'L] y^*[n + l''L] e^{-j2\pi \frac{l}{L} n} \sum_{k=0}^{K-1} e^{-j2\pi \frac{k}{K}(l'-l''-m)}. \tag{A7}$$

We can us relation (3) to substitute the last summation. From the sifting property of the Kronecker delta (3), we have

$$\sum_{n=0}^{L-1} \sum_{l'=0}^{L-1} x[n + l'L] y^*[n + (l' - m)L] e^{-j2\pi \frac{l}{L} n}. \tag{A8}$$

Because the complex exponential sequence is periodic, with a period L, we can rewrite the double summation as a single summation, providing us with

$$\sum_{n=0}^{KL-1} x[n] y^*[n - mL] e^{-j2\pi \frac{l}{L} n} \tag{A9}$$

which can be recognized as the inner product between x and $y_{m,l}$.

Appendix D. Proof of the Modulation Property

To prove the modulation property, we can use the definition of the sequence $z = x \cdot y$ and the definition of the DZT in (1), which is

$$Z_z[n,k] = \frac{1}{\sqrt{K}} \sum_{l=0}^{K-1} x[n + lL] y[n + lL] e^{-j2\pi \frac{k}{K} l}. \tag{A10}$$

Now, expressing $x[n+lL]$ using (19), we have

$$Z_z[n,k] = \frac{1}{K}\sum_{m=0}^{K-1} Z_x[n,m]\sum_{l=0}^{K-1} y[n+lL]e^{-j2\pi\frac{(k-m)}{K}l}. \tag{A11}$$

Finally, using the DZT definition (1), we obtain

$$Z_z[n,k] = \frac{1}{\sqrt{K}}\sum_{m=0}^{K-1} Z_x[n,m]Z_y[n,k-m]. \tag{A12}$$

Appendix E. Proof of the Convolution Property

To prove relation (31), we first express the circular convolution as a multiplication in the DFT domain, i.e.,

$$Z[k] = \sqrt{KL}X[k]Y[k], \tag{A13}$$

where the factor $\sqrt{KL}$ is due to the unitary definition of the DFT. Using (14), we have

$$Z_z[n,k] = \sqrt{K}\sum_{l=0}^{L-1} X[k+lK]Y[k+lK]e^{j2\pi\frac{k+lK}{KL}n}. \tag{A14}$$

Now, using (16) to express the elements of the DFT through their DZT, we obtain

$$Z_z[n,k] = \frac{\sqrt{K}}{L}\sum_{n'=0}^{L-1}\sum_{n''=0}^{L-1} Z_x[n',k]Z_y[n'',k]\sum_{l=0}^{L-1} e^{-j2\pi\frac{k+lK}{KL}(n'+n''-n)}. \tag{A15}$$

Substituting the last sum by (3) and applying the sifting property of the Kronecker delta, we finally have

$$Z_z[n,k] = \sqrt{K}\sum_{n'=0}^{L-1} Z_x[n',k]Z_y[n-n',k]. \tag{A16}$$

Appendix F. Proof of Theorem 1

To prove Theorem 1, we start by expressing the sequence y in (45) as

$$y = \left(x \cdot u_{\nu_p}\right) \circledast h_{\tau_p}, \tag{A17}$$

where $u_{\nu_p}[n] = e^{j2\pi(k_p/N)n}$. Using the modulation property (30) and the convolution property (31), we can express the DZT of y as

$$Z_y[n,k] = \sum_{m=0}^{L-1}\left(\sum_{l=0}^{K-1} Z_x[m,l]Z_\nu[m,k-l]\right)Z_\tau[n-m,k]. \tag{A18}$$

Here, Z_ν is the DZT of sequence u_ν, which is

$$\begin{aligned} Z_\nu[n,k] &= \frac{1}{\sqrt{K}}\sum_{l=0}^{K-1} e^{j2\pi\frac{k_p}{KL}(n+lL)}e^{-j2\pi\frac{k}{K}l} \\ &= \frac{1}{\sqrt{K}}e^{j2\pi\frac{k_p}{KL}n}\sum_{l=0}^{K-1} e^{-j2\pi\frac{k-k_p}{K}l} \\ &= \frac{1}{\sqrt{K}}e^{j2\pi\frac{k_p}{KL}n}\frac{1-e^{-j2\pi(k-k_p)}}{1-e^{-j2\pi\frac{k-k_p}{K}}} \\ &= \frac{1}{\sqrt{K}}e^{j2\pi\frac{k_p}{KL}n}e^{-j\pi\frac{K-1}{K}(k-k_p)}\frac{\sin(2\pi(k-k_p))}{\sin\left(2\pi\frac{k-k_p}{K}\right)}. \end{aligned} \tag{A19}$$

References

1. Monk, A.; Hadani, R.; Tsatsanis, M.; Rakib, S. OTFS—Orthogonal Time Frequency Space. *arXiv* **2016**, arXiv:1608.02993.
2. Hadani, R.; Rakib, S.; Kons, S.; Tsatsanis, M.; Monk, A.; Ibars, C.; Delfeld, J.; Hebron, Y.; Goldsmith, A.J.; Molisch, A.F.; et al. Orthogonal Time Frequency Space Modulation. *arXiv* **2018** arXiv:1808.00519.
3. Hadani, R.; Rakib, S.; Tsatsanis, M.; Monk, A.; Goldsmith, A.J.; Molisch, A.F.; Calderbank, R. Orthogonal Time Frequency Space Modulation. In Proceedings of the 2017 IEEE Wireless Communications and Networking Conference (WCNC), San Francisco, CA, USA, 19–22 March 2017; pp. 1–6.
4. Hadani, R.; Rakib, S.; Molisch, A.F.; Ibars, C.; Monk, A.; Tsatsanis, M.; Delfeld, J.; Goldsmith, A.; Calderbank, R. Orthogonal Time Frequency Space (OTFS) modulation for millimeter-wave communications systems. In Proceedings of the 2017 IEEE MTT-S International Microwave Symposium (IMS), Honololu, HI, USA, 4–9 June 2017; pp. 681–683.
5. Raviteja, P.; Phan, K.T.; Hong, Y.; Viterbo, E. Interference Cancellation and Iterative Detection for Orthogonal Time Frequency Space Modulation. *IEEE Trans. Wirel. Commun.* **2018**, *17*, 6501–6515. [CrossRef]
6. Gaudio, L.; Kobayashi, M.; Caire, G.; Colavolpe, G. On the Effectiveness of OTFS for Joint Radar Parameter Estimation and Communication. *IEEE Trans. Wirel. Commun.* **2020**, *19*, 5951–5965. [CrossRef]
7. Murali, K.R.; Chockalingam, A. On OTFS Modulation for High-Doppler Fading Channels. In Proceedings of the 2018 Information Theory and Applications Workshop (ITA), San Diego, CA, USA, 11–16 February 2018; pp. 1–10.
8. Mohammed, S.K. Derivation of OTFS Modulation from First Principles. *IEEE Trans. Veh. Technol.* **2021**, *70*, 7619–7636. [CrossRef]
9. Matz, G.; Bolcskei, H.; Hlawatsch, F. Time-Frequency Foundations of Communications: Concepts and Tools. *IEEE Signal Process. Mag.* **2013**, *30*, 87–96. [CrossRef]
10. Bölcskei, H.; Hlawatsch, F. Discrete Zak transforms, polyphase transforms, and applications. *IEEE Trans. Signal Process.* **1997**, *45*, 851–866. [CrossRef]
11. Chang, R.W. Synthesis of band-limited orthogonal signals for multichannel data transmission. *Bell Syst. Tech. J.* **1966**, *45*, 1775–1796. [CrossRef]
12. Weinstein, S.; Ebert, P. Data Transmission by Frequency-Division Multiplexing Using the Discrete Fourier Transform. *IEEE Trans. Commun. Technol.* **1971**, *19*, 628–634. [CrossRef]
13. Farhang, A.; RezazadehReyhani, A.; Doyle, L.E.; Farhang-Boroujeny, B. Low Complexity Modem Structure for OFDM-Based Orthogonal Time Frequency Space Modulation. *IEEE Wirel. Commun. Lett.* **2018**, *7*, 344–347. [CrossRef]
14. Richards, M.; Scheer, J.; Holm, W. *Principles of Modern Radar*, 1st ed.; ASciTech Publishing: Edison, NJ, USA, 2010.
15. Skollnik, M. *Introduction to Radar Systems*, 3rd ed.; McGraw Hill Education: New York, NY, USA, 2001.
16. Bondre, A.S.; Richmond, C.D. Dual-Use of OTFS Architecture for Pulse Doppler Radar Processing. In Proceedings of the 2022 IEEE Radar Conference (RadarConf22), New York, NY, USA, 21–25 March 2022; pp. 1–6.
17. Lampel, F.; Avarado, A.; Willems, F.M. On OTFS using the Discrete Zak Transform. In Proceedings of the 2022 IEEE International Conference on Communications Workshops (ICC Workshops), Seoul, Republic of Korea, 16–20 May 2022; pp. 729–734.
18. Schempp, W. Radar ambiguity functions, the Heisenberg group, and holomorphic theta series. *Proc. Am. Math. Soc.* **1984**, *92*, 103–110. [CrossRef]
19. Zak, J. Finite Translation in Solid-State Physics. *Phys. Rev. Lett.* **1967**, *19*, 1385–1397. [CrossRef]
20. Janssen, A. The Zak Transform: A Signal Transform for Sampled Time-Continuous Signals. *Philips J. Res.* **1988**, *43*, 23–69.
21. Vetterli, M.; Kovačević, J.; Goyal, V.K. *Foundations of Signal Processing*, 1st ed.; Cambridge University Press: Cambridge, UK, 2014.
22. An, M.; Brodzik, A.; Gertner, I.; Tolimieri, R. Weyl-Heisenberg Systems and the Finite Zak Transform. In *Signal and Image Representation in Combined Spaces*; Coifman, Y.Z.R., Ed.; Wavelet Analysis and Its Applications; Academic Press: San Diego, CA, USA, 1998; Volume 7, pp. 3–21.
23. Barry, J.; Lee, E.; Messerschmitt, D. *Digital Communication*, 3rd ed.; Springer Science+Business Media: New York, NY, USA, 2004.
24. Hlawatsch, F.; Matz, G. (Eds.) *Wireless Communications Over Rapidly Time-Varying Channels*, 1st ed.; Academic Press: Oxford, UK, 2011.
25. Wexler, J.; Raz, S. Discrete Gabor expansions. *Signal Process.* **1990**, *21*, 207–220. [CrossRef]
26. Molisch, A. *Wireless Communications*, 2nd ed.; Wiley: Chichester, UK, 2011.
27. Goldsmith, A. *Wireless Communications*, 1st ed.; Cambridge University Press: New York, NY, USA, 2005.
28. Stüber, G.L. *Principles of Mobile Communications*, 4th ed.; Springer: Cham, Switzerland, 2017.
29. Han, T.S. *Information-Spectrum Methods in Information Theory*, 1st ed.; Springer: Berlin/Heidelberg, Germany, 2003.
30. Dobrushin, R. General formulation of Shannon's main theorem in information theory. *Am. Math. Sot. Trans.* **1963**, *33*, 323–438.
31. Telatar, E. Capacity of multi-antenna Gaussian channels. *Eur. Trans. Telecomm.* **1999**, *10*, 585–595. [CrossRef]

entropy

MDPI

Article

Private Key and Decoder Side Information for Secure and Private Source Coding †

Onur Günlü [1,*], Rafael F. Schaefer [2,3], Holger Boche [4,5,6,7] and Harold Vincent Poor [8]

1 Information Coding Division, Linköping University, 58183 Linköping, Sweden
2 Chair of Information Theory and Machine Learning, Technische Universität Dresden, 01062 Dresden, Germany
3 BMBF Research Hub 6G-life, Technische Universität Dresden, 01062 Dresden, Germany
4 Lehrstuhl für Theoretische Informationstechnik, TUM School of Computation, Information and Technology, Technical University of Munich, 80333 Munich, Germany
5 CASA: Cyber Security in the Age of Large-Scale Adversaries Exzellenzcluster, Ruhr-Universität Bochum, 44780 Bochum, Germany
6 BMBF Research Hub 6G-life, Technical University of Munich, 80333 Munich, Germany
7 Munich Center for Quantum Science and Technology (MCQST), Schellingstr. 4, 80799 Munich, Germany
8 Department of Electrical and Computer Engineering, Princeton University, Princeton, NJ 08544, USA
* Correspondence: onur.gunlu@liu.se
† This paper is an extended version of our paper that will be published in the 2022 IEEE Information Theory Workshop, Mumbai, India, November 2022.

Abstract: We extend the problem of secure source coding by considering a remote source whose noisy measurements are correlated random variables used for secure source reconstruction. The main additions to the problem are as follows: (1) all terminals noncausally observe a noisy measurement of the remote source; (2) a private key is available to all legitimate terminals; (3) the public communication link between the encoder and decoder is rate-limited; and (4) the secrecy leakage to the eavesdropper is measured with respect to the encoder input, whereas the privacy leakage is measured with respect to the remote source. Exact rate regions are characterized for a lossy source coding problem with a private key, remote source, and decoder side information under security, privacy, communication, and distortion constraints. By replacing the distortion constraint with a reliability constraint, we obtain the exact rate region for the lossless case as well. Furthermore, the lossy rate region for scalar discrete-time Gaussian sources and measurement channels is established. An achievable lossy rate region that can be numerically computed is also provided for binary-input multiple additive discrete-time Gaussian noise measurement channels.

Keywords: information theoretic security; secure source coding; remote source; private key; side information

Citation: Günlü, O.; Schaefer, R.F.; Boche, H.; Poor, H.V. Private Key and Decoder Side Information for Secure and Private Source Coding. *Entropy* **2022**, *24*, 1716. https://doi.org/10.3390/e24121716

Academic Editor: T. Aaron Gulliver

Received: 18 October 2022
Accepted: 18 November 2022
Published: 24 November 2022

Publisher's Note: MDPI stays neutral with regard to jurisdictional claims in published maps and institutional affiliations.

1. Introduction

Consider multiple terminals that observe correlated random sequences and wish to reconstruct these sequences at another terminal, called a decoder, by sending messages through noiseless communication links, i.e., the distributed source coding problem [1]. A sensor network where each node observes a correlated random sequence that needs to be reconstructed at a distant node is a classic example of this problem [2] (p. 258). Similarly, function computation problems in which a fusion center observes messages sent by other nodes to compute a function are closely related problems that can be used to model various recent applications [3,4]. Since messages sent over communication links can be public, security constraints are imposed on these messages against an eavesdropper in the same network [5]. If all sent messages are available to the eavesdropper, it is necessary to provide an advantage to the decoder over the eavesdropper to enable secure source coding. Providing side information that is correlated with the sequences that should be reconstructed to the decoder can provide such an advantage over the eavesdropper that can also have side information, as in [6–8]. Allowing for the eavesdropper to access only a strict subset of all messages is also a method to enable secure distributed source coding, which was considered in [9–11]; see also [12], in which a similar method was applied to enable secure remote source reconstruction. Similarly, a private key that is shared by legitimate terminals and hidden from the eavesdropper can also provide such an advantage, as in [13,14].

Source coding models in the literature commonly assume that dependent multiletter random variables are available and should be compressed. For secret-key agreement [15,16] and secure function computation problems [17,18], which are instances of the source coding with the side information problem [19] (Section IV-B), the correlation between these multiletter random variables was posited in [20,21] to stem from an underlying ground truth that is a remote source, such that its noisy measurements are these dependent random variables. Such a remote source allows one to model the cause of correlation in a network, so we also posit that there is a remote source whose noisy measurements are used in the source coding problems discussed below, which is similar to the models in [22] (p. 78) and [23] (Figure 9). Furthermore, in the chief executive officer (CEO) problem [24], there is a remote source whose noisy measurements are encoded, such that a decoder can reconstruct the remote source by using encoder outputs. Our model is different from the model in the CEO problem, since in our model, the decoder aims to recover encoder observations rather than the remote source that is considered mainly to describe the cause of correlation between encoder observations. Thus, we define the *secrecy leakage* as the amount of information leaked to an eavesdropper about encoder observations. Since the remote source is common for all observations in the same network, we impose a *privacy leakage* constraint on the remote source because each encoder output observed by an eavesdropper leaks information about unused encoder observations, which might later cause secrecy leakage when the unused encoder observations are employed [25–27]; see [28–30] for joint secrecy and joint privacy constraints imposed due to multiple uses of the same source.

1.1. Summary of Contributions

We extend the lossless and lossy source coding rate region analyses by considering a remote source that should be kept private, decoder and eavesdropper side information, and a private key shared by the encoder and decoder. Considering that one encoder provides insights with enough richness to extend the results to multiple encoders [31], in this work, we consider the single encoder case. A summary of the main contributions is as follows.

- We characterize the lossy secure and private source coding region when noisy measurements of a remote source are observed by all terminals, and there is one private key available.
- Requiring reliable source reconstruction, we also characterize the rate region for the lossless secure and private source coding problem.
- A Gaussian remote source and independent additive Gaussian noise measurement channels are considered to establish their lossy rate region under squared error distortion.
- We provide an achievable lossy secure and private source coding region for a binary remote source and its measurements through additive Gaussian noise channels, which includes computable differential entropy terms.

1.2. Organization

This paper is organized as follows. In Section 2, we introduce the lossless and lossy secure and private source coding problems with decoder and eavesdropper side information and a private key under storage, secrecy, privacy, and reliability or distortion constraints. In Section 3, we characterize the rate regions for the introduced problems, which include three parts that correspond to different private key rate regimes. In Section 4, we evaluate the lossy rate region for Gaussian sources and channels with squared error distortion. In Section 5, we consider a binary modulated remote source measured through additive Gaussian noise channels and provide an inner bound for the lossy rate region with Hamming distortion. In Section 6, we provide the proof for the lossy secure and and private source coding region.

1.3. Notation

Uppercase X represents random variables and lowercase x their realizations from a set $\mathcal{X}$, denoted by calligraphic letters. A discrete random variable X has probability distribution P_X and a continuous random variable X probability density function (pdf) p_X. A subscript i denotes the position of a variable in a length-n sequence $X^n = X_1, X_2, \ldots, X_i, \ldots, X_n$. Boldface uppercase $\mathbf{X} = [X_1, X_2, \ldots]^T$ represent vector random variables, where T denotes the transpose. $[1:m]$ denotes the set $\{1,2,\ldots,m\}$ for an integer $m \geq 1$. Define $[a]^- = \min\{a, 0\}$ for $a \in \mathbb{R}$. Function $H_b(x) = -x\log x - (1-x)\log(1-x)$ is the binary entropy function, where logarithms are to the base 2. A binary symmetric channel (BSC) with crossover probability ϵ is denoted by BSC(ϵ). $X \sim \text{Bern}(\beta)$ with $\mathcal{X} = \{0,1\}$ is a binary random variable with $\Pr[X=1] = \beta$. The $*$-operator represents $p * q = (1-2q)p + q$. Function $Q(\cdot)$ denotes the complementary cumulative distribution function of the standard Gaussian distribution. The function $\text{sgn}(\cdot)$ represents the signum function.

2. System Model

We consider the lossy source coding model with one encoder, one decoder, and an eavesdropper (Eve), depicted in Figure 1. The encoder $\mathsf{Enc}(\cdot,\cdot)$ observes a noisy measurement $\widetilde{X}^n$ of an i.i.d. remote source $X^n \sim P_X^n$ through a memoryless channel $P_{\widetilde{X}|X}$ in addition to a private key $K \in [1 : 2^{nR_0}]$. The encoder output is an index W that is sent over a link with limited communication rate. Decoder $\mathsf{Dec}(\cdot,\cdot,\cdot)$ observes index W, private key K, and another noisy measurement Y^n of the same remote source X^n through another memoryless channel $P_{YZ|X}$ in order to estimate $\widetilde{X}^n$ as $\widehat{\widetilde{X}^n}$. The other noisy output Z^n of $P_{YZ|X}$ is observed by Eve in addition to index W. Assume K is uniformly distributed, hidden from Eve, and independent of the source output and its noisy measurements. The source and measurement alphabets are finite sets.

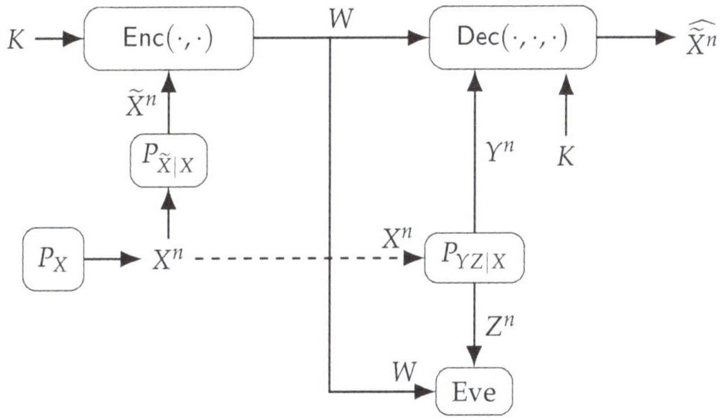

Figure 1. Source coding with noisy measurements $(\widetilde{X}^n, Y^n)$ of a remote source X^n and with a uniform private key K under privacy, secrecy, communication, and distortion constraints.

We next define the rate region for the lossy secure and private source coding problem defined above.

Definition 1. A *lossy* tuple $(R_{\rm w}, R_{\rm s}, R_\ell, D) \in \mathbb{R}^4_{\geq 0}$ is achievable given a private key with rate $R_0 \geq 0$, if for any $\delta > 0$ there exist $n \geq 1$, an encoder, and a decoder, such that

$$\frac{1}{n}\log|\mathcal{W}| \leq R_{\rm w} + \delta \qquad \text{(storage)} \tag{1}$$

$$\frac{1}{n}I(\widetilde{X}^n; W|Z^n) \leq R_{\rm s} + \delta \qquad \text{(secrecy)} \tag{2}$$

$$\frac{1}{n}I(X^n; W|Z^n) \leq R_\ell + \delta \qquad \text{(privacy)} \tag{3}$$

$$\mathbb{E}\Big[d\Big(\widetilde{X}^n, \widehat{\widetilde{X}^n}(Y^n, W, K)\Big)\Big] \leq D + \delta \qquad \text{(distortion)} \tag{4}$$

where $d(\widetilde{x}^n, \widehat{\widetilde{x}^n}) = \frac{1}{n}\sum_{i=1}^n d(\widetilde{x}_i, \widehat{\widetilde{x}}_i)$ is a per-letter bounded distortion metric. The *lossy* secure and private source coding region $\mathcal{R}_{\rm D}$ is the closure of the set of all achievable lossy tuples. ♢

In (2) and (3), we consider conditional mutual information terms to take account of unavoidable secrecy and privacy leakages due to Eve's side information, i.e., $I(\widetilde{X}^n; Z^n)$ and $I(X^n; Z^n)$, respectively; see also [21,32]. Furthermore, we consider conditional mutual information terms rather than corresponding conditional entropy terms, the latter of which is used in [6,14,33–35], to characterize the secrecy and privacy leakages simplifies our analysis.

We next define the rate region for the lossless secure and private source coding problem.

Definition 2. A *lossless* tuple $(R_{\rm w}, R_{\rm s}, R_\ell) \in \mathbb{R}^3_{\geq 0}$ is achievable given a private key with rate $R_0 \geq 0$, if for any $\delta > 0$ there exist $n \geq 1$, an encoder, and a decoder, such that we have (1)–(3) and

$$\Pr\Big[\widetilde{X}^n \neq \widehat{\widetilde{X}^n}(Y^n, W, K)\Big] \leq \delta \qquad \text{(reliability)}. \tag{5}$$

The *lossless* secure and private source coding region $\mathcal{R}$ is the closure of the set of all achievable lossless tuples. ♢

3. Secure and Private Source Coding Regions

3.1. Lossy Source Coding

The lossy secure and and private source coding region $\mathcal{R}_{\rm D}$ is characterized below; see Section 6 for its proof.

Define $[a]^- = \min\{a, 0\}$ for $a \in \mathbb{R}$.

Theorem 1. *For given P_X, $P_{\widetilde{X}|X}$, $P_{YZ|X}$, and R_0, the region $\mathcal{R}_D$ is the set of all rate tuples (R_w, R_s, R_ℓ, D) satisfying*

$$R_w \geq I(U; \widetilde{X}|Y) \tag{6}$$

and if $R_0 < I(U; \widetilde{X}|Y, V)$, then

$$R_s \geq I(U; \widetilde{X}|Z) + R' - R_0 \tag{7}$$

$$R_\ell \geq I(U; X|Z) + R' - R_0 \tag{8}$$

where we have

$$R' = [I(U; Z|V, Q) - I(U; Y|V, Q)]^- \tag{9}$$

and if $I(U;\widetilde{X}|Y,V) \leq R_0 < I(U;\widetilde{X}|Y)$, *then*

$$R_s \geq I(V;\widetilde{X}|Z) \tag{10}$$
$$R_\ell \geq I(V;X|Z) \tag{11}$$

and if $R_0 \geq I(U;\widetilde{X}|Y)$, *then*

$$R_s \geq 0 \tag{12}$$
$$R_\ell \geq 0 \tag{13}$$

for some

$$P_{QVU\widetilde{X}XYZ} = P_{Q|V}P_{V|U}P_{U|\widetilde{X}}P_{\widetilde{X}|X}P_X P_{YZ|X} \tag{14}$$

such that $\mathbb{E}\big[d\big(\widetilde{X},\widehat{\widetilde{X}}(U,Y)\big)\big] \leq D$ *for some reconstruction function* $\widehat{\widetilde{X}}(U,Y)$. *The region* $\mathcal{R}_D$ *is convexified by using the time-sharing random variable Q, required due to the* $[\cdot]^-$ *operation. One can limit the cardinalities to* $|\mathcal{Q}| \leq 2$, $|\mathcal{V}| \leq |\widetilde{\mathcal{X}}| + 3$, *and* $|\mathcal{U}| \leq (|\widetilde{\mathcal{X}}| + 3)^2$.

We remark that (12) and (13) show that one can simultaneously achieve *strong secrecy* and *strong privacy*, i.e., the conditional mutual information terms in (2) and (3), respectively, are negligible, by using a large private key K, which is a result missing in some recent works on secure source coding with a private key.

3.2. Lossless Source Coding

The lossless secure and and private source coding region $\mathcal{R}$ is characterized next; see below for a proof sketch.

Proposition 1. *For given* P_X, $P_{\widetilde{X}|X}$, $P_{YZ|X}$, *and* R_0, *the region* $\mathcal{R}$ *is the set of all rate tuples* (R_w, R_s, R_ℓ) *satisfying*

$$R_w \geq H(\widetilde{X}|Y) \tag{15}$$

and if $R_0 < H(\widetilde{X}|Y,V)$, *then*

$$R_s \geq H(\widetilde{X}|Z) + R'' - R_0 \tag{16}$$
$$R_\ell \geq I(\widetilde{X};X|Z) + R'' - R_0 \tag{17}$$

where we have

$$R'' = [I(\widetilde{X};Z|V,Q) - I(\widetilde{X};Y|V,Q)]^- \tag{18}$$

and if $H(\widetilde{X}|Y,V) \leq R_0 < H(\widetilde{X}|Y)$, *then*

$$R_s \geq I(V;\widetilde{X}|Z) \tag{19}$$
$$R_\ell \geq I(V;X|Z) \tag{20}$$

and if $R_0 \geq H(\widetilde{X}|Y)$, *then*

$$R_s \geq 0 \tag{21}$$
$$R_\ell \geq 0 \tag{22}$$

for some

$$P_{QV\widetilde{X}XYZ} = P_{Q|V}P_{V|\widetilde{X}}P_{\widetilde{X}|X}P_X P_{YZ|X}. \tag{23}$$

One can limit the cardinalities to $|\mathcal{Q}| \leq 2$ *and* $|\mathcal{V}| \leq |\widetilde{\mathcal{X}}| + 2$.

Proof Sketch. The proof for the lossless region $\mathcal{R}$ follows from the proof for the lossy region $\mathcal{R}_D$, given in Theorem 1 above, by choosing $U = \widetilde{X}$, such that we have reconstruction function $\widehat{\widetilde{X}}(\widetilde{X}, Y) = \widetilde{X}$, so we achieve $D = 0$. Thus, the reliability constraint in (5) is satisfied because $d(\cdot, \cdot)$ is a distortion metric. □

4. Gaussian Sources and Additive Gaussian Noise Channels

We evaluate the lossy rate region for a Gaussian example with squared error distortion by finding the optimal auxiliary random variable in the corresponding rate region. Consider a special lossy source coding case in which (i) there is no private key; (ii) the eavesdropper's channel observation Z^n is less noisy than the decoder's channel observation Y^n, such that we obtain a lossy source coding region with a single auxiliary random variable that should be optimized.

We next define less noisy channels, considering $P_{YZ|X}$.

Definition 3 ([36]). Z (or eavesdropper) is *less noisy* than Y (or decoder) if

$$I(L;Z) \geq I(L;Y) \tag{24}$$

holds for any random variable L, such that $L - X - (Y, Z)$ form a Markov chain. ◊

Corollary 1. *For given* P_X, $P_{\widetilde{X}|X}$, $P_{YZ|X}$, *and* $R_0 = 0$, *the region* $\mathcal{R}_D$ *when the eavesdropper is less noisy than the decoder is the set of all rate tuples* (R_w, R_s, R_ℓ, D) *satisfying*

$$R_w \geq I(U;\widetilde{X}|Y) = I(U;\widetilde{X}) - I(U;Y) \tag{25}$$

$$R_s \geq I(U;\widetilde{X}|Z) = I(U;\widetilde{X}) - I(U;Z) \tag{26}$$

$$R_\ell \geq I(U;X|Z) = I(U;X) - I(U;Z) \tag{27}$$

for some

$$P_{U\widetilde{X}XYZ} = P_{U|\widetilde{X}} P_{\widetilde{X}|X} P_X P_{YZ|X} \tag{28}$$

such that $\mathbb{E}\big[d(\widetilde{X}, \widehat{\widetilde{X}}(U, Y))\big] \leq D$ *for some reconstruction function* $\widehat{\widetilde{X}}(U, Y)$. *One can limit the cardinality to* $|\mathcal{U}| \leq |\widetilde{\mathcal{X}}| + 3$.

Proof Sketch. The proof for Corollary 1 follows from the proof for Theorem 1 by considering the bounds in (6)–(8) since $R_0 = 0$. Furthermore, R' defined in (9) is 0 for the less noisy condition considered, which follows because $(Q, V) - U - X - (Y, Z)$ form a Markov chain. □

Suppose the following scalar discrete-time Gaussian source and channel model for the lossy source coding problem depicted in Figure 1

$$X = \rho_x \widetilde{X} + N_x \tag{29}$$

$$Y = \rho_y X + N_y \tag{30}$$

$$Z = \rho_z X + N_z \tag{31}$$

where we have remote source $X \sim \mathcal{N}(0,1)$, fixed correlation coefficients $\rho_x, \rho_y, \rho_z \in (-1,1)$, and additive Gaussian noise random variables

$$N_x \sim \mathcal{N}(0, 1-\rho_x^2) \tag{32}$$
$$N_y \sim \mathcal{N}(0, 1-\rho_y^2) \tag{33}$$
$$N_z \sim \mathcal{N}(0, 1-\rho_z^2) \tag{34}$$

such that $(\widetilde{X}, N_x, N_y, N_z)$ are mutually independent, and we consider the squared error distortion, i.e., $d(\widetilde{x}, \widehat{\widetilde{x}}) = (\widetilde{x} - \widehat{\widetilde{x}})^2$. Note that (29) is an inverse measurement channel $P_{X|\widetilde{X}}$ that is a weighted sum of two independent Gaussian random variables, imposed to be able to apply the conditional entropy power inequality (EPI) [37] (Lemma II); see [20] (Theorem 3) and [38] (Section V) for binary symmetric inverse channel assumptions imposed to apply Mrs. Gerber's lemma [39]. Suppose $|\rho_z| > |\rho_y|$, such that Y is less stochastically degraded than Z, since then there exists a random variable $\widetilde{Y}$ such that $P_{\widetilde{Y}|X} = P_{Y|X}$ and $P_{\widetilde{Y}Z|X} = P_{Z|X}P_{\widetilde{Y}|Z}$ [40] (Lemma 6), so Z is also less noisy than Y since less noisy channels constitute a strict superset of the set of stochastically-degraded channels and both channel sets consider only the conditional marginal probability distributions [2] (p. 121).

We next take the liberty to use the lossy rate region in Corollary 1, characterized for discrete memoryless channels, for the model in (29)–(31). This is common in the literature since there is a discretization procedure to extend the achievability proof to well-behaved continuous-alphabet random variables and the converse proof applies to arbitrary random variables; see [2] (Remark 3.8). For Gaussian sources and channels, we use differential entropy and eliminate the cardinality bound on the auxiliary random variable. The lossy source coding region for the model in (29)–(31) without a private key is given below.

Proposition 2. *For the model in (29)–(31), such that $|\rho_z| > |\rho_y|$ and $R_0 = 0$, the region $\mathcal{R}_D$ with squared error distortion is the set of all rate tuples (R_w, R_s, R_ℓ, D) satisfying, for $\alpha \in (0,1]$,*

$$R_w \geq \frac{1}{2}\log\left(\frac{1-\rho_x^2\rho_y^2(1-\alpha)}{\alpha}\right) \tag{35}$$
$$R_s \geq \frac{1}{2}\log\left(\frac{1-\rho_x^2\rho_z^2(1-\alpha)}{\alpha}\right) \tag{36}$$
$$R_\ell \geq \frac{1}{2}\log\left(\frac{1-\rho_x^2\rho_z^2(1-\alpha)}{1-\rho_x^2(1-\alpha)}\right) \tag{37}$$
$$D \geq \frac{\alpha(1-\rho_x^2\rho_y^2)}{1-\rho_x^2\rho_y^2(1-\alpha)}. \tag{38}$$

Proof Sketch. For the achievability proof, let $U \sim \mathcal{N}(0, 1-\alpha)$ and $\Theta \sim \mathcal{N}(0,\alpha)$, as in [41] ([Equation (32)]) and [42] (Appendix B), be independent random variables for some $\alpha \in (0,1]$ such that $\widetilde{X} = U + \Theta$ and $U - \widetilde{X} - X - (Y,Z)$ form a Markov chain. Choose the reconstruction function $\widehat{\widetilde{X}}(U,Y)$ as the minimum mean square error (MMSE) estimator, and given any fixed $D > 0$, auxiliary random variables are chosen such that the distortion constraint is satisfied. We then have, for the squared error distortion,

$$D = \mathbb{E}\left[\left(\widetilde{X} - \widehat{\widetilde{X}}(U,Y)\right)^2\right] \overset{(a)}{=} \frac{1}{2\pi e}e^{2h(\widetilde{X}|U,Y)} \tag{39}$$

where equality in (a) is achieved because $\widetilde{X}$ is Gaussian and the reconstruction function is the MMSE estimator [43] (Theorem 8.6.6). Define the covariance matrix of the vector random variable $[\widetilde{X}, U, Y]$ as $\mathbf{K}_{\widetilde{X}UY}$ and of $[U, Y]$ as $\mathbf{K}_{UY}$, respectively. We then have

$$h(\widetilde{X}|U,Y) = h(\widetilde{X},U,Y) - h(U,Y)$$
$$= \frac{1}{2}\log\left(2\pi e \frac{\det(\mathbf{K}_{\widetilde{X}UY})}{\det(\mathbf{K}_{UY})}\right) \tag{40}$$

where $\det(\cdot)$ is the determinant of a matrix; see also [12] (Section F). Combining (39) and (40), and calculating the determinants, we obtain

$$D = \frac{\alpha(1-\rho_x^2\rho_y^2)}{1-\rho_x^2\rho_y^2(1-\alpha)}. \tag{41}$$

One can also show that

$$I(U;\widetilde{X}) = h(\widetilde{X}) - h(\widetilde{X}|U) = \frac{1}{2}\log\left(\frac{1}{\alpha}\right) \tag{42}$$
$$I(U;X) = h(X) - h(X|U) = \frac{1}{2}\log\left(\frac{1}{1-\rho_x^2(1-\alpha)}\right) \tag{43}$$
$$I(U;Y) = h(Y) - h(Y|U) = \frac{1}{2}\log\left(\frac{1}{1-\rho_x^2\rho_y^2(1-\alpha)}\right) \tag{44}$$
$$I(U;Z) = h(Z) - h(Z|U) = \frac{1}{2}\log\left(\frac{1}{1-\rho_x^2\rho_z^2(1-\alpha)}\right). \tag{45}$$

Thus, by calculating (25)–(27), the achievability proof follows.

For the converse proof, one can first show that

$$I(U;\widetilde{X}) - I(U;Y) = h(Y|U) - h(\widetilde{X}|U) \tag{46}$$
$$I(U;\widetilde{X}) - I(U;Z) = h(Z|U) - h(\widetilde{X}|U) \tag{47}$$
$$I(U;X) - I(U;Z) = h(Z|U) - h(X|U) \tag{48}$$

which follow since $h(\widetilde{X}) = h(X) = h(Y) = h(Z)$. Suppose

$$h(\widetilde{X}|U) = \frac{1}{2}\log(2\pi e\alpha) \tag{49}$$

for any $\alpha \in (0,1]$ that represents the unique variance of a Gaussian random variable; see [20] (Lemma 2) for a similar result applied to binary random variables. Thus, by applying the conditional EPI, we obtain

$$e^{2h(Y|U)} \overset{(a)}{=} e^{2h(\rho_x\rho_y\widetilde{X}|U)} + e^{2h(\rho_y N_x + N_y)}$$
$$= 2\pi e\left(\rho_x^2\rho_y^2\alpha + \rho_y^2(1-\rho_x^2) + 1 - \rho_y^2\right)$$
$$= 2\pi e\left(1-\rho_x^2\rho_y^2(1-\alpha)\right) \tag{50}$$

where (a) follows because $U - \widetilde{X} - (N_x, N_y)$ form a Markov chain and (N_x, N_y) are independent of $\widetilde{X}$, so (N_x, N_y) are independent of U, and equality is satisfied since, given U, $\rho_x\rho_y\widetilde{X}$ and $(\rho_y N_x + N_y)$ are conditionally independent and they are Gaussian random variables, as imposed in (49) above; see [20] (Lemma 1 and Equation (28)) for a similar result applied to binary random variables by extending Mrs. Gerber's lemma. Similarly, we have

$$e^{2h(Z|U)} = 2\pi e\left(1-\rho_x^2\rho_z^2(1-\alpha)\right) \tag{51}$$

which follows by replacing (Y, ρ_y, N_y) with (Z, ρ_z, N_z) in (50), respectively, because the channel $P_{Y|U}$ can be mapped to $P_{Z|U}$ with these changes due to (29)–(31) and the Markov chain relation $U - \widetilde{X} - X - (Y, Z)$. Furthermore, we have

$$\begin{aligned} e^{2h(X|U)} &\overset{(a)}{=} e^{2h(\rho_x \widetilde{X}|U)} + e^{2h(N_x)} \\ &= 2\pi e\big(\rho_x^2 \alpha + 1 - \rho_x^2\big) \\ &= 2\pi e\big(1 - \rho_x^2(1-\alpha)\big) \end{aligned} \tag{52}$$

where (a) follows because N_x is independent of U, and equality is achieved since, given U, $\rho_x \widetilde{X}$ and N_x are conditionally independent and are Gaussian random variables. Therefore, by applying (46)–(52) to (25)–(27), the converse proof for (35)–(37) follows.

Next, consider

$$\begin{aligned} h(\widetilde{X}|U,Y) &= -I(U;\widetilde{X}|Y) + h(\widetilde{X}|Y) \\ &\overset{(a)}{=} -h(Y|U) + h(\widetilde{X}|U) + h(Y|\widetilde{X}) \\ &\overset{(b)}{=} \frac{1}{2}\log\Big(\frac{\alpha}{1-\rho_x^2\rho_y^2(1-\alpha)}\Big) + h(\rho_x\rho_y\widetilde{X} + \rho_y N_x + N_y|\widetilde{X}) \\ &\overset{(c)}{=} \frac{1}{2}\log\Big(\frac{\alpha}{1-\rho_x^2\rho_y^2(1-\alpha)}\Big) + h(\rho_y N_x + N_y) \\ &= \frac{1}{2}\log\Big(2\pi e\frac{\alpha(\rho_y^2(1-\rho_x^2) + (1-\rho_y^2))}{1-\rho_x^2\rho_y^2(1-\alpha)}\Big) \\ &= \frac{1}{2}\log\Big(2\pi e\frac{\alpha(1-\rho_x^2\rho_y^2)}{1-\rho_x^2\rho_y^2(1-\alpha)}\Big) \end{aligned} \tag{53}$$

where (a) follows by (25) and (46), and since $h(Y) = h(\widetilde{X})$, (b) follows by (49) and (50), and (c) follows because (N_x, N_y) are independent of $\widetilde{X}$. Furthermore, for any random variable $\widetilde{X}$ and reconstruction function $\widehat{\widetilde{X}}(U, Y)$, we have [43] (Theorem 8.6.6)

$$\mathbb{E}\Big[\big(\widetilde{X} - \widehat{\widetilde{X}}(U,Y)\big)^2\Big] \geq \frac{1}{2\pi e} e^{2h(\widetilde{X}|U,Y)}. \tag{54}$$

Combining the distortion constraint given in Corollary 1 with (53) and (54), the converse proof for (38) follows. □

5. Multiple Binary-input Additive Gaussian Noise Channels

Consider next a binary remote source $X \in \{-1, 1\}$ and its binary noisy measurement $\widetilde{X} \in \{-1, 1\}$ observed by the encoder, which represents a practical setting with binary quantizations. For instance, a static random-access memory (SRAM) start-up output at a nominal temperature is a binary value obtained by quantizing sums of Gaussian random variables [28,44]. Suppose the noisy channel $P_{YZ|X}$ outputs consist of a single discrete-time additive Gaussian noise channel output Y observed by the decoder and two independent discrete-time additive Gaussian noise channel outputs $\mathbf{Z} = [Z_1, Z_2]^T$ observed by the eavesdropper, in which the eavesdropper obtains more information by measuring the remote source twice. Furthermore, assume that X is uniformly distributed, the binary channel $P_{\widetilde{X}|X}$ is symmetric such that $\Pr[\widetilde{X} \neq X] = p$ for $p \in [0, 1]$, and we also have

$$Y = \rho_y X + N_y \tag{55}$$

$$\mathbf{Z} = \begin{bmatrix} Z_1 \\ Z_2 \end{bmatrix} = \rho_z X \begin{bmatrix} 1 \\ 1 \end{bmatrix} + \begin{bmatrix} N_{z_1} \\ N_{z_2} \end{bmatrix} \tag{56}$$

where we have fixed correlation coefficients $\rho_y, \rho_z \in (-1, 1)$ and additive Gaussian noise random variables

$$N_y \sim \mathcal{N}(0, 1-\rho_y^2) \tag{57}$$
$$N_{z_1} \sim \mathcal{N}(0, 1-\rho_z^2) \tag{58}$$
$$N_{z_2} \sim \mathcal{N}(0, 1-\rho_z^2) \tag{59}$$

such that $(X, N_y, N_{z_1}, N_{z_2})$ are mutually independent. Consider the Hamming distortion, i.e., $d(\widetilde{x}, \widehat{\widetilde{x}}) = \mathbb{1}\{\widetilde{x} \neq \widehat{\widetilde{x}}\}$. Impose the condition $|\rho_z| > |\rho_y|$ such that Z_1 and Z_2 are less noisy than Y, so $\mathbf{Z}$ is also less noisy than Y, which follows by applying similar steps as being applied in Section 4. Thus, for $R_0 = 0$, the region $\mathcal{R}_D$ characterized in Corollary 1 is also valid for such binary-input additive Gaussian noise channels when one replaces Z with $\mathbf{Z}$. A computable achievable lossy secure and private source coding region for such channels is given next.

Proposition 3. *For the setting with multiple binary-input additive Gaussian noise channels, defined above, such that $|\rho_z| > |\rho_y|$ and $R_0 = 0$, the region $\mathcal{R}_D$ with Hamming distortion includes the set of all rate tuples (R_w, R_s, R_ℓ, D) satisfying, for an independent random variable $C \sim \mathrm{Bern}(p * q)$ with any $q \in [0, 0.5]$ and for any $\lambda \in [0, 1]$,*

$$R_w \geq \lambda\Big(1 - H_b(q) - h(\rho_y X + N_y) + h(\rho_y(1-2C) + N_y)\Big) \tag{60}$$

$$R_s \geq \lambda\left(1 - H_b(q) - h\left(\begin{bmatrix}\rho_z X + N_{z_1}\\ \rho_z X + N_{z_2}\end{bmatrix}\right) + h\left(\begin{bmatrix}\rho_z(1-2C) + N_{z_1}\\ \rho_z(1-2C) + N_{z_2}\end{bmatrix}\right)\right) \tag{61}$$

$$R_\ell \geq \lambda\left(1 - H_b(p*q) - h\left(\begin{bmatrix}\rho_z X + N_{z_1}\\ \rho_z X + N_{z_2}\end{bmatrix}\right) + h\left(\begin{bmatrix}\rho_z(1-2C) + N_{z_1}\\ \rho_z(1-2C) + N_{z_2}\end{bmatrix}\right)\right) \tag{62}$$

$$D \geq \lambda q + (1-\lambda)\left(p * Q\left(\frac{\rho_y}{\sqrt{1-\rho_y^2}}\right)\right) \tag{63}$$

where random variable $Y = (\rho_y X + N_y)$ has pdf

$$\frac{1}{2}\frac{\left(e^{-\frac{(y+\rho_y)^2}{2(1-\rho_y^2)}} + e^{-\frac{(y-\rho_y)^2}{2(1-\rho_y^2)}}\right)}{\sqrt{2\pi(1-\rho_y^2)}} \tag{64}$$

the random variable $\bar{Y} = (\rho_y(1-2C) + N_y)$ has pdf

$$(p*q)\frac{e^{-\frac{(\bar{y}+\rho_y)^2}{2(1-\rho_y^2)}}}{\sqrt{2\pi(1-\rho_y^2)}} + (1-(p*q))\frac{e^{-\frac{(\bar{y}-\rho_y)^2}{2(1-\rho_y^2)}}}{\sqrt{2\pi(1-\rho_y^2)}} \tag{65}$$

the vector random variable $\begin{bmatrix}Z_1\\ Z_2\end{bmatrix} = \left(\begin{bmatrix}\rho_z X + N_{z_1}\\ \rho_z X + N_{z_2}\end{bmatrix}\right)$ *has joint pdf*

$$\frac{1}{2}\frac{\left(e^{-\frac{\left((z_1+\rho_z)^2+(z_2+\rho_z)^2\right)}{2(1-\rho_z^2)}} + e^{-\frac{\left((z_1-\rho_z)^2+(z_2-\rho_z)^2\right)}{2(1-\rho_z^2)}}\right)}{2\pi(1-\rho_z^2)} \tag{66}$$

and the vector random variable $\begin{bmatrix}\bar{Z}_1\\ \bar{Z}_2\end{bmatrix} = \left(\begin{bmatrix}\rho_z(1-2C)+N_{z_1}\\ \rho_z(1-2C)+N_{z_2}\end{bmatrix}\right)$ *has joint pdf*

$$(p*q)\frac{e^{-\frac{\left((\bar{z}_1+\rho_z)^2+(\bar{z}_2+\rho_z)^2\right)}{2(1-\rho_z^2)}}}{2\pi(1-\rho_z^2)}+(1-(p*q))\frac{e^{-\frac{\left((\bar{z}_1-\rho_z)^2+(\bar{z}_2-\rho_z)^2\right)}{2(1-\rho_z^2)}}}{2\pi(1-\rho_z^2)}. \tag{67}$$

Proof. We first evaluate (25)–(27) by choosing a binary uniformly distributed U and a channel $P_{\widetilde{X}|U}$ such that $\Pr[\widetilde{X}\neq U]=q$ for any $q\in[0,0.5]$. We have

$$I(U;\widetilde{X}) = H(\widetilde{X}) - H(\widetilde{X}|U) \overset{(a)}{=} 1 - H_b(q) \tag{68}$$

$$I(U;X) = H(X) - H(X|U) \overset{(b)}{=} 1 - H_b(p*q) \tag{69}$$

where (a) and (b) follow by relabeling the input and output symbols to represent the channels $P_{\widetilde{X}|U}$ and $P_{X|\widetilde{X}}$ as BSC(q) and BSC(p), respectively, which follows since entropy is preserved under a bijective mapping for discrete random variables. For relabeled symbols, the channel $P_{X|U}$ is a BSC$(p*q)$ since it is a concatenation of two BSCs, so denote the independent random noise component in this channel as $C\sim$ Bern$(p*q)$. Then, we obtain

$$h(Y|U) = h(\rho_y X + N_y|U) \overset{(a)}{=} h(\rho_y(1-2C)+N_y) = h(\bar{Y}) \tag{70}$$

where (a) follows since symbols $\{-1,1\}$ correspond to the antipodal modulation of binary symbols, and since (C,N_y,U) are mutually independent. One can compute (70) numerically by using the pdf

$$p_{\bar{Y}}(\bar{y}) = \sum_{c=0}^{1} P_C(c)p_{\bar{Y}|C}(\bar{y}|c) = (p*q)\frac{e^{-\frac{(\bar{y}+\rho_y)^2}{2(1-\rho_y^2)}}}{\sqrt{2\pi(1-\rho_y^2)}} + (1-(p*q))\frac{e^{-\frac{(\bar{y}-\rho_y)^2}{2(1-\rho_y^2)}}}{\sqrt{2\pi(1-\rho_y^2)}}. \tag{71}$$

Similarly, we can compute

$$h(Y) = h(\rho_y X + N_y) \tag{72}$$

numerically by using the pdf

$$p_Y(y) = \sum_{x\in\{-1,1\}} P_X(x)p_{Y|X}(y|x) = \frac{1}{2}\frac{\left(e^{-\frac{(y+\rho_y)^2}{2(1-\rho_y^2)}}+e^{-\frac{(y-\rho_y)^2}{2(1-\rho_y^2)}}\right)}{\sqrt{2\pi(1-\rho_y^2)}}. \tag{73}$$

Next, consider

$$h(\mathbf{Z}|U) = h\left(\left(\rho_z X\begin{bmatrix}1\\1\end{bmatrix}+\begin{bmatrix}N_{z_1}\\N_{z_2}\end{bmatrix}\right)\Big|U\right) \overset{(a)}{=} h\left(\begin{bmatrix}\rho_z(1-2C)+N_{z_1}\\ \rho_z(1-2C)+N_{z_2}\end{bmatrix}\right) = h\left(\begin{bmatrix}\bar{Z}_1\\ \bar{Z}_2\end{bmatrix}\right) \tag{74}$$

where (a) follows since (C,N_{z_1},N_{z_2},U) are mutually independent. Denote

$$\bar{\mathbf{Z}} = [\bar{Z}_1,\bar{Z}_2]^T. \tag{75}$$

We can compute (74) numerically by using the joint pdf

$$p_{\bar{\mathbf{Z}}}(\bar{\mathbf{z}}) = p_{\bar{Z}_1\bar{Z}_2}(\bar{z}_1, \bar{z}_2) = \sum_{c=0}^{1} P_C(c) p_{\bar{Z}_1\bar{Z}_2|C}(\bar{z}_1, \bar{z}_2|c)$$
$$= (p*q)\frac{e^{-\frac{\left((\bar{z}_1+\rho_z)^2+(\bar{z}_2+\rho_z)^2\right)}{2(1-\rho_z^2)}}}{2\pi(1-\rho_z^2)} + (1-(p*q))\frac{e^{-\frac{\left((\bar{z}_1-\rho_z)^2+(\bar{z}_2-\rho_z)^2\right)}{2(1-\rho_z^2)}}}{2\pi(1-\rho_z^2)} \quad (76)$$

which follows since $\bar{\mathbf{Z}}|C$ is a jointly Gaussian vector random variable with independent components $\bar{Z}_1|C$ and $\bar{Z}_2|C$, since every scalar linear combination of the components is Gaussian; see [45] (Theorem 1). Similarly, we can compute

$$h(\mathbf{Z}) = h\left(\begin{bmatrix}\rho_z X + N_{z_1} \\ \rho_z X + N_{z_2}\end{bmatrix}\right) \quad (77)$$

numerically by using the joint pdf

$$p_{\mathbf{Z}}(\mathbf{z}) = p_{Z_1Z_2}(z_1, z_2) = \sum_{x\in\{-1,1\}} P_X(x) p_{Z_1Z_2|X}(z_1, z_2|x)$$
$$= \frac{1}{2}\frac{\left(e^{-\frac{\left((z_1+\rho_z)^2+(z_2+\rho_z)^2\right)}{2(1-\rho_z^2)}} + e^{-\frac{\left((z_1-\rho_z)^2+(z_2-\rho_z)^2\right)}{2(1-\rho_z^2)}}\right)}{2\pi(1-\rho_z^2)}. \quad (78)$$

Now, we consider the expected distortion. First, choose the reconstruction function

$$\hat{\widetilde{X}}_1(U, Y) = U \quad (79)$$

for the binary uniformly distributed U and the channel $P_{\widetilde{X}|U}$ such that $\Pr[\widetilde{X} \neq U] = q$ for any $q \in [0, 0.5]$, as considered above. For this reconstruction function and choices of U and $P_{\widetilde{X}|U}$, we obtain the expected distortion

$$\mathbb{E}\left[d(\widetilde{X}, \hat{\widetilde{X}}_1(U, Y))\right] = q. \quad (80)$$

Second, choose the reconstruction function

$$\hat{\widetilde{X}}_2(U, Y) = \mathrm{sgn}(Y) \quad (81)$$

and consider U. We then obtain

$$\mathbb{E}\left[d(\widetilde{X}, \hat{\widetilde{X}}_2(U, Y))\right] = p * Q\left(\frac{\rho_y}{\sqrt{1-\rho_y^2}}\right) \quad (82)$$

which follows since the channel $P_{\mathrm{sgn}(Y)|\widetilde{X}}$ can be considered as a concatenation of two BSCs with crossover probabilities p and $Q\left(\frac{\rho_y}{\sqrt{1-\rho_y^2}}\right)$, where the former follows since $\Pr[\widetilde{X} \neq X] = p$ and the latter because $X \in \{-1, 1\}$ and

$$\Pr[X \neq \mathrm{sgn}(Y)] = \Pr[X \neq \mathrm{sgn}(\rho_y X + N_y)] = \Pr[N_y > \rho_y]. \quad (83)$$

Therefore, the proof for the achievable lossy secure and private source coding region follows by combining (68)–(70), (72), (74), (77), (80), and (82) by applying time sharing, with time-sharing parameter $\lambda \in [0,1]$, between the two reconstruction functions in (79) and (81) with corresponding U and $P_{\widetilde{X}|U}$, since for constant U the terms in (25)–(27) are zero. □

Remark 1. *The proof of Proposition 3 follows similar steps as those in [46] (Section II) and it seems that the achievable lossy secure and private source coding region given in Proposition 3 is optimal. Considering* (R_w, R_s, R_ℓ)*, one can apply Mrs. Gerber's lemma to show that the choice of U such that* $P_{\widetilde{X}|U}$ *is a BSC(q) after relabeling the input and output symbols is optimal, since Mrs. Gerber's lemma is valid for all binary-input symmetric memoryless channels with discrete or continuous outputs [47]. This result follows because convexity is preserved; see also [48] (Appendix B) for an alternative proof of convexity preservation for independent BSC measurements. However, it is not entirely clear how to prove that the sign operation used for estimation suffices for the rate region.*

6. Proof for Theorem 1

6.1. Achievability Proof for Theorem 1

Proof Sketch. We leverage the output statistics of random binning (OSRB) method [16,49,50] for the achievability proof by following the steps described in [51] (Section 1.6).

Let $(V^n, U^n, \widetilde{X}^n, X^n, Y^n, Z^n)$ be i.i.d. according to $P_{VU\widetilde{X}XYZ}$ that can be obtained from (14) by fixing $P_{U|\widetilde{X}}$ and $P_{V|U}$, such that $\mathbb{E}[d(\widetilde{X}, \widehat{\widetilde{X}})] \le (D+\epsilon)$ for any $\epsilon > 0$. To each v^n assign two random bin indices $F_{\mathrm{v}} \in [1:2^{n\widetilde{R}_{\mathrm{v}}}]$ and $W_{\mathrm{v}} \in [1:2^{nR_{\mathrm{v}}}]$. Furthermore, to each u^n assign three random bin indices $F_{\mathrm{u}} \in [1:2^{n\widetilde{R}_{\mathrm{u}}}]$, $W_{\mathrm{u}} \in [1:2^{nR_{\mathrm{u}}}]$, and $K_{\mathrm{u}} \in [1:2^{nR_0}]$, where R_0 is the private key rate defined in Section 2. Public indices $F = (F_{\mathrm{v}}, F_{\mathrm{u}})$ represent the choice of a source encoder and decoder pair. Furthermore, we impose that the messages sent by the source encoder $\mathsf{Enc}(\cdot,\cdot)$ to the source decoder $\mathsf{Dec}(\cdot,\cdot,\cdot)$ are

$$W = (W_{\mathrm{v}}, W_{\mathrm{u}}, K + K_{\mathrm{u}}) \tag{84}$$

where the summation with the private key is in modulo- 2^{nR_0}, i.e., one-time padding.

The public index F_{v} is almost independent of $(\widetilde{X}^n, X^n, Y^n, Z^n)$ if we have [49] (Theorem 1)

$$\widetilde{R}_{\mathrm{v}} < H(V|\widetilde{X}, X, Y, Z) \overset{(a)}{=} H(V|\widetilde{X}) \tag{85}$$

where (a) follows since $(X, Y, Z) - \widetilde{X} - V$ form a Markov chain. The constraint in (85) suggests that the expected value, taken over the random bin assignments, of the variational distance between the joint probability distributions $\mathrm{Unif}[1{:}2^{n\widetilde{R}_{\mathrm{v}}}] \cdot P_{\widetilde{X}^n}$ and $P_{F_{\mathrm{v}}\widetilde{X}^n}$ vanishes when $n \to \infty$. Moreover, the public index F_{u} is almost independent of $(V^n, \widetilde{X}^n, X^n, Y^n, Z^n)$ if we have

$$\widetilde{R}_{\mathrm{u}} < H(U|V, \widetilde{X}, X, Y, Z) \overset{(a)}{=} H(U|V, \widetilde{X}) \tag{86}$$

where (a) follows from the Markov chain relation $(X, Y, Z) - \widetilde{X} - (U, V)$.

Using a Slepian–Wolf (SW) [1] decoder that observes $(Y^n, F_{\mathrm{v}}, W_{\mathrm{v}})$, one can reliably estimate V^n if we have [49] (Lemma 1)

$$\widetilde{R}_{\mathrm{v}} + R_{\mathrm{v}} > H(V|Y) \tag{87}$$

since then the expected error probability, taken over random bin assignments, vanishes when $n \to \infty$. Furthermore, one can reliably estimate U^n by using a SW decoder that observes $(K, V^n, Y^n, F_{\mathrm{u}}, W_{\mathrm{u}}, K + K_{\mathrm{u}})$ if we have

$$R_0 + \widetilde{R}_{\mathrm{u}} + R_{\mathrm{u}} > H(U|V, Y). \tag{88}$$

To satisfy (85)–(88), for any $\epsilon > 0$ we fix

$$\widetilde{R}_{\mathrm{v}} = H(V|\widetilde{X}) - \epsilon \tag{89}$$
$$R_{\mathrm{v}} = I(V;\widetilde{X}) - I(V;Y) + 2\epsilon \tag{90}$$
$$\widetilde{R}_{\mathrm{u}} = H(U|V,\widetilde{X}) - \epsilon \tag{91}$$
$$R_0 + R_{\mathrm{u}} = I(U;\widetilde{X}|V) - I(U;Y|V) + 2\epsilon. \tag{92}$$

Since all tuples $(v^n, u^n, \widetilde{x}^n, x^n, y^n, z^n)$ are in the jointly typical set with high probability, by the typical average lemma [2] (p. 26), the distortion constraint (4) is satisfied.

Communication Rate: (90) and (92) result in a communication (storage) rate of

$$R_{\mathrm{w}} = R_0 + R_{\mathrm{v}} + R_{\mathrm{u}} \overset{(a)}{=} I(U;\widetilde{X}|Y) + 4\epsilon \tag{93}$$

where (a) follows since $V - U - \widetilde{X} - Y$ form a Markov chain.

Privacy Leakage Rate: Since private key K is uniformly distributed, and is independent of source and channel random variables, we can consider the following virtual scenario to calculate the leakage. We first assume for the virtual scenario that there is no private key such that the encoder output for the virtual scenario is

$$\overline{W} = (W_{\mathrm{v}}, W_{\mathrm{u}}, K_{\mathrm{u}}). \tag{94}$$

We calculate the leakage for the virtual scenario. Then, given the mentioned properties of the private key and due to the one-time padding step in (84), we can subtract $H(K) = nR_0$ from the leakage calculated for the virtual scenario to obtain the leakage for the original problem, which follows from the sum of (91) and (92) if $\epsilon \to 0$ when $n \to \infty$. Thus, we have the privacy leakage

$$\begin{aligned}
I(X^n; W, F|Z^n) &= I(X^n; \overline{W}, F|Z^n) - nR_0 \\
&\overset{(a)}{=} H(\overline{W}, F|Z^n) - H(\overline{W}, F|X^n) - nR_0 \\
&\overset{(b)}{=} H(\overline{W}, F|Z^n) - H(U^n, V^n|X^n) + H(V^n|\overline{W}, F, X^n) + H(U^n|V^n, \overline{W}, F, X^n) - nR_0 \\
&\overset{(c)}{\leq} H(\overline{W}, F|Z^n) - nH(U, V|X) + 2n\epsilon_n - nR_0
\end{aligned} \tag{95}$$

where (a) follows because $(\overline{W}, F) - X^n - Z^n$ form a Markov chain, (b) follows since (U^n, V^n) determine $(F_{\mathrm{u}}, W_{\mathrm{u}}, K_{\mathrm{u}}, F_{\mathrm{v}}, W_{\mathrm{v}})$, and (c) follows since (U^n, V^n, X^n) is i.i.d. and for some $\epsilon_n > 0$ such that $\epsilon_n \to 0$ when $n \to \infty$ because $(F_{\mathrm{v}}, W_{\mathrm{v}}, X^n)$ can reliably recover V^n by (87) because of the Markov chain relation $V^n - X^n - Y^n$ and, similarly, $(F_{\mathrm{u}}, W_{\mathrm{u}}, K_{\mathrm{u}}, V^n, X^n)$ can reliably recover U^n by (88) because of $H(U|V,Y) \geq H(U|V,X)$ that is proved in [21] (Equation (55)) for the Markov chain relation $(V,U) - X - Y$.

Next, we consider the term $H(\overline{W}, F|Z^n)$ in (95) and provide single letter bounds on it by applying the six different decodability results given in [21] (Section V-A) that are applied to an entirely similar conditional entropy term in [21] (Equation (54)) that measures the uncertainty in indices conditioned on an i.i.d. multi-letter random variable. Thus, combining the six decodability results in [21] (Section V-A) with (95) we obtain

$$I(X^n; W, F|Z^n) \leq n\big([I(U;Z|V) - I(U;Y|V) + \epsilon]^- + I(U;X|Z) + 3\epsilon_n - R_0\big). \tag{96}$$

The equation (92) implicitly assumes that private key rate R_0 is less than $(I(U;\widetilde{X}|V) - I(U;Y|V) + 2\epsilon) = (I(U;\widetilde{X}|Y,V) + 2\epsilon)$, where the equality follows from the Markov chain relation $(V,U) - \widetilde{X} - Y$. The communication rate results are not affected by this assumption, since $\widetilde{X}^n$ should be reconstructed by the decoder. However, if the private key rate R_0 is greater than or equal to $(I(U;\widetilde{X}|Y,V) + 2\epsilon)$, then we can remove the bin index K_{u} from the code construction above and apply one-time padding to the bin index W_{u}, such that we have the encoder output

$$\overline{\overline{W}} = (W_{\mathrm{v}}, W_{\mathrm{u}} + K) \tag{97}$$

where the summation with the private key is in modulo- $2^{nR_{\mathrm{u}}} = 2^{n(I(U;\widetilde{X}|Y,V)+2\epsilon)}$. Thus, one then does not leak any information about W_{u} to the eavesdropper because of the one-time padding step in (97). We then have privacy leakage

$$\begin{aligned}
I(X^n;\overline{\overline{W}},F|Z^n) &= I(X^n;W_{\mathrm{v}},F|Z^n)\\
&\overset{(a)}{\leq} H(X^n|Z^n) - H(X^n|Z^n,W_{\mathrm{v}},F_{\mathrm{v}}) + \epsilon_n'\\
&\overset{(b)}{\leq} H(X^n|Z^n) - H(X^n|Z^n,V^n) + \epsilon_n'\\
&\overset{(c)}{=} nI(V;X|Z) + \epsilon_n'
\end{aligned} \tag{98}$$

where (a) follows for some ϵ_n' such that $\epsilon_n' \to 0$ when $n \to \infty$ since by (86) F_{u} is almost independent of (V^n, X^n, Z^n); see also [52] (Theorem 1), (b) follows since V^n determines $(F_{\mathrm{v}}, W_{\mathrm{v}})$, and (c) follows because (X^n, Z^n, V^n) are i.i.d.

Note we can reduce the privacy leakage given in (98) if $R_0 \geq (I(U;\widetilde{X}) - I(U;Y) + 4\epsilon) = (I(U;\widetilde{X}|Y) + 4\epsilon)$, where the equality follows from the Markov chain relation $U - \widetilde{X} - Y$, since then we can apply one-time padding to both bin indices W_{v} and W_{u} with the sum rate

$$\begin{aligned}
R_{\mathrm{v}} + R_{\mathrm{u}} &\overset{(a)}{=} I(V;\widetilde{X}) - I(V;Y) + 2\epsilon + I(U;\widetilde{X}|V) - I(U;Y|V) + 2\epsilon\\
&\overset{(b)}{=} I(U;\widetilde{X}) - I(U;Y) + 4\epsilon
\end{aligned} \tag{99}$$

where (a) follows by (90) and (92), and (b) follows from the Markov chain relation $V - U - \widetilde{X} - Y$. Thus, one then does not leak any information about $(W_{\mathrm{v}}, W_{\mathrm{u}})$ to the eavesdropper because of the one-time padding step, so we then obtain the privacy leakage of

$$I(X^n;F|Z^n) = I(X^n;F_{\mathrm{v}}|Z^n) + I(X^n;F_{\mathrm{u}}|Z^n,F_{\mathrm{v}}) \overset{(a)}{\leq} 2\epsilon_n' \tag{100}$$

where (a) follows since by (85) F_{v} is almost independent of (X^n, Z^n) and by (86) F_{u} is almost independent of (V^n, X^n, Z^n).

Secrecy Leakage Rate: Similar to the privacy leakage analysis above, we first consider the virtual scenario with the encoder output given in (94), and then calculate the leakage for the original problem by subtracting $H(K) = nR_0$ from the leakage calculated for the virtual scenario. Thus, we obtain

$$\begin{aligned}
I(\widetilde{X}^n;W,F|Z^n) &= I(\widetilde{X}^n;\overline{W},F|Z^n) - nR_0\\
&\overset{(a)}{=} H(\overline{W},F|Z^n) - H(\overline{W},F|\widetilde{X}^n) - nR_0\\
&\overset{(b)}{=} H(\overline{W},F|Z^n) - H(U^n,V^n|\widetilde{X}^n) + H(V^n|\overline{W},F,\widetilde{X}^n) + H(U^n|V^n,\overline{W},F,\widetilde{X}^n)\\
&\overset{(c)}{\leq} H(\overline{W},F|Z^n) - nH(U,V|\widetilde{X}) + 2n\epsilon_n' - nR_0\\
&\overset{(d)}{\leq} n([I(U;Z|V) - I(U;Y|V) + \epsilon]^- + I(U;\widetilde{X}|Z) + 3\epsilon_n' - R_0)
\end{aligned} \tag{101}$$

where (a) follows from the Markov chain relation $(\overline{W}, F) - \widetilde{X}^n - Z^n$, (b) follows since (U^n, V^n) determine $(\overline{W}, F)$, (c) follows because $(V^n, U^n, \widetilde{X}^n)$ are i.i.d. and because $(F_{\mathrm{v}}, W_{\mathrm{v}}, \widetilde{X}^n)$ can reliably recover V^n by (87) due to the Markov chain relation $V^n - \widetilde{X}^n - Y^n$ and, similarly, $(F_{\mathrm{u}}, W_{\mathrm{u}}, K_{\mathrm{u}}, V^n, \widetilde{X}^n)$ can reliably recover U^n by (88) due to $H(U|V,Y) \geq H(U|V,\widetilde{X})$ that can be proved as in [21] (Equation (55)) for the Markov chain relation $(V,U) - \widetilde{X} - Y$, and (d) follows by applying the six decodability results in [21] (Section V-A) that are applied to (95) with the final result in (96) by replacing X with $\widetilde{X}$.

Similar to the privacy leakage analysis above, if we have $R_0 \geq (I(U;\widetilde{X}|Y,V) + 2\epsilon)$, then we can eliminate $K_{\rm u}$ and apply one-time padding as in (97), such that no information about $W_{\rm u}$ is leaked to the eavesdropper, we have

$$\begin{aligned} I(\widetilde{X}^n;\overline{\overline{W}},F|Z^n) &= I(\widetilde{X}^n;W_{\rm v},F|Z^n) \\ &\overset{(a)}{\leq} H(\widetilde{X}^n|Z^n) - H(\widetilde{X}^n|Z^n,W_{\rm v},F_{\rm v}) + \epsilon_n' \\ &\overset{(b)}{\leq} H(\widetilde{X}^n|Z^n) - H(\widetilde{X}^n|Z^n,V^n) + \epsilon_n' \\ &\overset{(c)}{=} nI(V;\widetilde{X}|Z) + \epsilon_n' \end{aligned} \tag{102}$$

where (a) follows because by (86) $F_{\rm u}$ is almost independent of $(V^n,\widetilde{X}^n,Z^n)$, (b) follows since V^n determines $(F_{\rm v},W_{\rm v})$, and (c) follows because $(\widetilde{X}^n,Z^n,V^n)$ are i.i.d.

If $R_0 \geq (I(U;\widetilde{X}|Y) + 4\epsilon)$, we can apply one-time padding to hide $(W_{\rm v},W_{\rm u})$, as in the privacy leakage analysis above. We then have the secrecy leakage of

$$I(\widetilde{X}^n;F|Z^n) = I(\widetilde{X}^n;F_{\rm v}|Z^n) + I(\widetilde{X}^n;F_{\rm u}|Z^n,F_{\rm v}) \overset{(a)}{\leq} 2\epsilon_n' \tag{103}$$

where (a) follows since by (85) $F_{\rm v}$ is almost independent of $(\widetilde{X}^n,Z^n)$ and by (86) $F_{\rm u}$ is almost independent of $(V^n,\widetilde{X}^n,Z^n)$.

Suppose that public indices F are generated uniformly at random, and the encoder generates (V^n,U^n) according to $P_{V^nU^n|\widetilde{X}^nF_{\rm v}F_{\rm u}}$ that can be obtained from the proposed binning scheme above to compute the bins $W_{\rm v}$ from V^n and $W_{\rm u}$ from U^n, respectively. Such a procedure results in a joint probability distribution almost equal to $P_{VU\widetilde{X}XYZ}$ fixed above [51] (Section 1.6). The privacy and secrecy leakage metrics above are expectations over all possible public index realizations $F=f$. Therefore, using a time-sharing random variable Q for convexification and applying the selection lemma [53] (Lemma 2.2) to each decodability case separately, the achievability for Theorem 1 follows by choosing an $\epsilon > 0$ such that $\epsilon \to 0$ when $n \to \infty$. □

6.2. Converse Proof for Theorem 1

Proof Sketch. Assume that for some $\delta_n > 0$ and $n \geq 1$, there exist an encoder and a decoder, such that (1)–(4) are satisfied for some tuple $(R_{\rm w},R_{\rm s},R_\ell,D)$ given a private key with rate R_0.

Define $V_i \triangleq (W,Y_{i+1}^n,Z^{i-1})$ and $U_i \triangleq (W,Y_{i+1}^n,Z^{i-1},X^{i-1},K)$ that satisfy the Markov chain relation $V_i - U_i - \widetilde{X}_i - X_i - (Y_i,Z_i)$ by definition of the source statistics. We have

$$\begin{aligned} D+\delta_n &\overset{(a)}{\geq} \mathbb{E}\Big[d\Big(\widetilde{X}^n,\widehat{\widetilde{X}^n}(Y^n,W,K)\Big)\Big] \\ &\overset{(b)}{\geq} \mathbb{E}\Big[d\Big(\widetilde{X}^n,\widehat{\widetilde{X}^n}(Y^n,W,K,X^{i-1},Z^{i-1})\Big)\Big] \\ &\overset{(c)}{=} \mathbb{E}\Big[d\Big(\widetilde{X}^n,\widehat{\widetilde{X}^n}(Y_i^n,W,K,X^{i-1},Z^{i-1})\Big)\Big] \\ &\overset{(d)}{=} \frac{1}{n}\sum_{i=1}^{n}\mathbb{E}\Big[d\Big(\widetilde{X}_i,\widehat{\widetilde{X}_i}(U_i,Y_i)\Big)\Big] \end{aligned} \tag{104}$$

where (a) follows by (4), (b) follows since providing more information to the reconstruction function does not increase expected distortion, (c) follows from the Markov chain relation

$$Y^{i-1} - (Y_i^n,X^{i-1},Z^{i-1},W,K) - \widetilde{X}^n \tag{105}$$

and (d) follows from the definition of U_i.

Communication Rate: For any $R_0 \geq 0$, we have

$$
\begin{aligned}
n(R_w + \delta_n) &\stackrel{(a)}{\geq} \log|\mathcal{W}| \\
&\geq H(W|Y^n, K) - H(W|Y^n, K, \widetilde{X}^n) && (106)\\
&\stackrel{(b)}{=} \sum_{i=1}^{n} I(W; \widetilde{X}_i|\widetilde{X}^{i-1}, Y_{i+1}^n, Z^{i-1}, K, Y_i) && (107)\\
&\stackrel{(c)}{=} \sum_{i=1}^{n} I(\widetilde{X}^{i-1}, Y_{i+1}^n, Z^{i-1}, K, W; \widetilde{X}_i|Y_i) \\
&\stackrel{(d)}{\geq} \sum_{i=1}^{n} I(X^{i-1}, Y_{i+1}^n, Z^{i-1}, K, W; \widetilde{X}_i|Y_i) \\
&\stackrel{(e)}{=} \sum_{i=1}^{n} I(U_i; \widetilde{X}_i|Y_i) && (108)
\end{aligned}
$$

where (a) follows by (1), (b) follows from the Markov chain relation

$$
(Y^{i-1}, X^{i-1}, Z^{i-1}) - (\widetilde{X}^{i-1}, Y_i^n, K) - (\widetilde{X}_i, W) \quad (109)
$$

(c) follows because $(\widetilde{X}_i, Y_i)$ are independent of $(\widetilde{X}^{i-1}, Y_{i+1}^n, Z^{i-1}, K)$, (d) follows by applying the data processing inequality to the Markov chain relation in (109), and (e) follows from the definition of U_i.

Privacy Leakage Rate: We obtain

$$
\begin{aligned}
&n(R_\ell + \delta_n) \\
&\stackrel{(a)}{\geq} [I(W; Y^n) - I(W; Z^n)] + [I(W; X^n) - I(W; Y^n)] \\
&\stackrel{(b)}{=} [I(W; Y^n) - I(W; Z^n)] + I(W; X^n|K) - I(K; X^n|W) - I(W; Y^n|K) + I(K; Y^n|W) \\
&\stackrel{(c)}{=} [I(W; Y^n) - I(W; Z^n)] + [I(W; X^n|K) - I(W; Y^n|K)] - I(K; X^n|W, Y^n) \\
&\geq \sum_{i=1}^{n} \Big[I(W; Y_i|Y_{i+1}^n) - I(W; Z_i|Z^{i-1})\Big] \\
&\quad + \sum_{i=1}^{n} \Big[I(W; X_i|X^{i-1}, K) - I(W; Y_i|Y_{i+1}^n, K)\Big] - H(K) \\
&\stackrel{(d)}{=} \sum_{i=1}^{n} \Big[I(W; Y_i|Y_{i+1}^n, Z^{i-1}) - I(W; Z_i|Z^{i-1}, Y_{i+1}^n) - R_0\Big] \\
&\quad + \sum_{i=1}^{n} \Big[I(W; X_i|X^{i-1}, Y_{i+1}^n, K) - I(W; Y_i|Y_{i+1}^n, X^{i-1}, K)\Big] \\
&\stackrel{(e)}{=} \sum_{i=1}^{n} \Big[I(W; Y_i|Y_{i+1}^n, Z^{i-1}) - I(W; Z_i|Z^{i-1}, Y_{i+1}^n) - R_0\Big] \\
&\quad + \sum_{i=1}^{n} \Big[I(W; X_i|X^{i-1}, Y_{i+1}^n, Z^{i-1}, K) - I(W; Y_i|Y_{i+1}^n, X^{i-1}, Z^{i-1}, K)\Big] \\
&\stackrel{(f)}{=} \sum_{i=1}^{n} \Big[I(W, Y_{i+1}^n, Z^{i-1}; Y_i) - I(W, Z^{i-1}, Y_{i+1}^n; Z_i) - R_0\Big] \\
&\quad + \sum_{i=1}^{n} \Big[I(W, X^{i-1}, Y_{i+1}^n, Z^{i-1}, K; X_i) - I(W, Y_{i+1}^n, X^{i-1}, Z^{i-1}, K; Y_i)\Big]
\end{aligned}
$$

$$\overset{(g)}{=} \sum_{i=1}^{n} \Big[I(V_i;Y_i) - I(V_i;Z_i) - R_0 + I(U_i,V_i;X_i) - I(U_i,V_i;Y_i) \Big]$$
$$= \sum_{i=1}^{n} \Bigg[- I(U_i,V_i;Z_i) - R_0 + I(U_i,V_i;X_i) + (I(U_i;Z_i|V_i) - I(U_i;Y_i|V_i)) \Bigg]$$
$$\overset{(h)}{\geq} \sum_{i=1}^{n} \Big[I(U_i;X_i|Z_i) - R_0 + [I(U_i;Z_i|V_i) - I(U_i;Y_i|V_i)]^- \Big] \tag{110}$$

where (a) follows by (3) and from the Markov chain relation $W - X^n - Z^n$, (b) follows since K is independent of (X^n,Y^n), (c) follows from the Markov chain relation $(W,K) - X^n - Y^n$, (d) follows because $H(K) = nR_0$ and from Csiszár's sum identity [54], (e) follows from the Markov chain relations

$$Z^{i-1} - (X^{i-1}, Y_{i+1}^n, K) - (X_i, W) \tag{111}$$
$$Z^{i-1} - (X^{i-1}, Y_{i+1}^n, K) - (Y_i, W) \tag{112}$$

(f) follows because (X^n,Y^n,Z^n) are i.i.d. and K is independent of (X^n,Y^n,Z^n), (g) follows from the definitions of V_i and U_i, and (h) follows from the Markov chain relation $V_i - U_i - X_i - Z_i$.

Next, we provide the matching converse for the privacy leakage rate in (98), which is achieved when $R_0 \geq I(U;\widetilde{X}|Y,V)$. We have

$$n(R_\ell + \delta_n) \overset{(a)}{\geq} H(X^n|Z^n) - H(X^n|Z^n,W)$$
$$\overset{(b)}{=} H(X^n|Z^n) - \sum_{i=1}^{n} H(X_i|Z_i,Z^{i-1},X_{i+1}^n,W,Y_{i+1}^n)$$
$$\overset{(c)}{=} H(X^n|Z^n) - \sum_{i=1}^{n} H(X_i|Z_i,V_i,X_{i+1}^n)$$
$$\overset{(d)}{\geq} \sum_{i=1}^{n} [H(X_i|Z_i) - H(X_i|Z_i,V_i)]$$
$$= \sum_{i=1}^{n} I(V_i;X_i|Z_i) \tag{113}$$

where (a) follows by (3), (b) follows from the Markov chain relation

$$(Z_{i+1}^n, Y_{i+1}^n) - (X_{i+1}^n, W, Z^i) - X_i \tag{114}$$

(c) follows from the definition of V_i, and (d) follows because (X^n,Z^n) are i.i.d.

The matching converse for the privacy leakage rate in (100), achieved when $R_0 \geq I(U;\widetilde{X}|Y)$, follows from the fact that conditional mutual information is non-negative.

Secrecy Leakage Rate: We have

$$n(R_s + \delta_n)$$
$$\overset{(a)}{\geq} [I(W;Y^n) - I(W;Z^n)] + [I(W;\widetilde{X}^n) - I(W;Y^n)]$$
$$\overset{(b)}{=} [I(W;Y^n) - I(W;Z^n)] + I(W;\widetilde{X}^n|K) - I(K;\widetilde{X}^n|W) - I(W;Y^n|K) + I(K;Y^n|W)$$
$$\overset{(c)}{=} [I(W;Y^n) - I(W;Z^n)] + [I(W;\widetilde{X}^n|K) - I(W;Y^n|K)] - I(K;\widetilde{X}^n|W,Y^n)$$
$$\overset{(d)}{\geq} \sum_{i=1}^{n} \Big[I(W;Y_i|Y_{i+1}^n) - I(W;Z_i|Z^{i-1}) \Big] + I(W;\widetilde{X}^n|Y^n,K) - H(K)$$

$$
\begin{aligned}
&\stackrel{(e)}{=} \sum_{i=1}^{n} \Big[I(W;Y_i|Y_{i+1}^n,Z^{i-1}) - I(W;Z_i|Z^{i-1},Y_{i+1}^n) - R_0 \Big] \\
&\qquad + nH(\widetilde{X}|Y) - \sum_{i=1}^{n} H(\widetilde{X}_i|Y_i,Y_{i+1}^n,W,K,\widetilde{X}^{i-1}) \\
&\stackrel{(f)}{\geq} \sum_{i=1}^{n} \Big[I(W,Y_{i+1}^n,Z^{i-1};Y_i) - I(W,Z^{i-1},Y_{i+1}^n;Z_i) - R_0 \Big] \\
&\qquad + nH(\widetilde{X}|Y) - \sum_{i=1}^{n} H(\widetilde{X}_i|Y_i,Y_{i+1}^n,W,K,X^{i-1},Z^{i-1}) \\
&\stackrel{(g)}{=} \sum_{i=1}^{n} \Big[I(V_i;Y_i) - I(V_i;Z_i) - R_0 \Big] + nH(\widetilde{X}|Y) - \sum_{i=1}^{n} H(\widetilde{X}_i|Y_i,U_i,V_i) \\
&\stackrel{(h)}{=} \sum_{i=1}^{n} \Big[I(V_i;Y_i) - I(V_i;Z_i) - R_0 \Big] + \sum_{i=1}^{n} \Big[I(U_i,V_i;\widetilde{X}_i) - I(U_i,V_i;Y_i) \Big] \\
&= \sum_{i=1}^{n} \Big[-I(U_i,V_i;Z_i) - R_0 + I(U_i,V_i;\widetilde{X}_i) + (I(U_i;Z_i|V_i) - I(U_i;Y_i|V_i)) \Big] \\
&\stackrel{(i)}{\geq} \sum_{i=1}^{n} \Big[I(U_i;\widetilde{X}_i|Z_i) - R_0 + [I(U_i;Z_i|V_i) - I(U_i;Y_i|V_i)]^- \Big]
\end{aligned}
\tag{115}
$$

where (a) follows by (2) and from the Markov chain relation $W - \widetilde{X}^n - Z^n$, (b) follows because K is independent of $(\widetilde{X}^n, Y^n)$, (c) and (d) follow from the Markov chain relation $(W,K) - \widetilde{X}^n - Y^n$, (e) follows because $H(K) = nR_0$ and $(\widetilde{X}^n, Y^n)$ are i.i.d. and independent of K, and from the Csiszár's sum identity and the Markov chain relation

$$Y^{i-1} - (\widetilde{X}^{i-1}, W, K, Y_{i+1}^n, Y_i) - \widetilde{X}_i \tag{116}$$

(f) follows since (Y^n, Z^n) are i.i.d. and from the data processing inequality applied to the Markov chain relation

$$(X^{i-1}, Z^{i-1}) - (\widetilde{X}^{i-1}, W, K, Y_{i+1}^n, Y_i) - \widetilde{X}_i \tag{117}$$

(g) follows from the definitions of V_i and U_i, (h) follows from the Markov chain relation $(V_i, U_i) - \widetilde{X}_i - Y_i$, and (i) follows from the Markov chain relation $V_i - U_i - \widetilde{X}_i - Z_i$.

Next, the matching converse for the secrecy leakage rate in (102), achieved when $R_0 \geq I(U;\widetilde{X}|Y,V)$, is provided.

$$
\begin{aligned}
n(R_s + \delta_n) &\stackrel{(a)}{\geq} H(\widetilde{X}^n|Z^n) - H(\widetilde{X}^n|Z^n,W) \\
&\stackrel{(b)}{\geq} H(\widetilde{X}^n|Z^n) - \sum_{i=1}^{n} H(\widetilde{X}_i|Z_i,Z^{i-1},\widetilde{X}_{i+1}^n,W,Y_{i+1}^n) \\
&\stackrel{(c)}{=} H(\widetilde{X}^n|Z^n) - \sum_{i=1}^{n} H(\widetilde{X}_i|Z_i,V_i,\widetilde{X}_{i+1}^n) \\
&\stackrel{(d)}{\geq} \sum_{i=1}^{n} [H(\widetilde{X}_i|Z_i) - H(\widetilde{X}_i|Z_i,V_i)] = \sum_{i=1}^{n} I(V_i;\widetilde{X}_i|Z_i)
\end{aligned}
\tag{118}
$$

where (a) follows by (2), (b) follows from the Markov chain relation

$$(Z_{i+1}^n, Y_{i+1}^n) - (\widetilde{X}_{i+1}^n, W, Z^i) - \widetilde{X}_i \tag{119}$$

(c) follows from the definition of V_i, and (d) follows because $(\widetilde{X}^n, Z^n)$ are i.i.d.

Similar to the privacy leakage analysis above, the matching converse for the secrecy leakage rate in (103), achieved when $R_0 \geq I(U;\widetilde{X}|Y)$, follows from the fact that conditional mutual information is non-negative. □

Introduce a uniformly distributed time-sharing random variable $Q \sim \text{Unif}[1:n]$ that is independent of other random variables, and define $X = X_Q$, $\widetilde{X} = \widetilde{X}_Q$, $Y = Y_Q$, $Z = Z_Q$, $V = V_Q$, and $U = (U_Q, Q)$, so

$$(Q, V) - U - \widetilde{X} - X - (Y, Z) \tag{120}$$

form a Markov chain. The converse proof follows by letting $\delta_n \to 0$.

Cardinality Bounds: We use the support lemma [54] (Lemma 15.4) for the cardinality bound proofs, which is a standard step, so we omit the proof.

Author Contributions: Conceptualization, O.G., R.F.S., H.B. and H.V.P.; Methodology, O.G. and H.V.P.; Software, H.B.; Validation, R.F.S.; Formal analysis, O.G., R.F.S., H.B. and H.V.P.; Resources, H.B.; Data curation, O.G. and R.F.S.; Writing—original draft, O.G.; Writing—review & editing, R.F.S., H.B. and H.V.P.; Project administration, R.F.S. and H.V.P.; Funding acquisition, R.F.S. and H.B. All authors have read and agreed to the published version of the manuscript.

Funding: O. Günlü was supported by the ZENITH Research and Career Development Fund and the ELLIIT funding endowed by the Swedish government. R. F. Schaefer was supported in part by the German Federal Ministry of Education and Research (BMBF) within the national initiative for Post-Shannon Communication (NewCom) under grant no. 16KIS1004 and the National Initiative for 6G Communication Systems through the Research Hub 6G-life under grant no. 16KISK001K. H. Boche was supported in part by the BMBF within the National Initiative for 6G Communication Systems through the Research Hub 6G-life under grant no. 16KISK002 and within the national initiative for Information Theory for Post Quantum Crypto "Quantum Token Theory and Applications—QTOK" under grant no. 16KISQ037K, which has received additional funding from the German Research Foundation (DFG) within Germany's Excellence Strategy EXC-2092 CASA-390781972. H. V. Poor was supported in part by the U.S. National Science Foundation (NSF) under grant no. CCF-1908308.

Institutional Review Board Statement: Not applicable.

Informed Consent Statement: Not applicable.

Data Availability Statement: Not applicable.

Conflicts of Interest: The authors declare no conflict of interest. The funders had no role in the design of the study; in the collection, analyses, or interpretation of data; in the writing of the manuscript, or in the decision to publish the results.

References

1. Slepian, D.; Wolf, J. Noiseless coding of correlated information sources. *IEEE Trans. Inf. Theory* **1973**, *19*, 471–480. [CrossRef]
2. Gamal, A.E.; Kim, Y.H. *Network Information Theory*; Cambridge University Press: Cambridge, UK, 2011.
3. Orlitsky, A.; Roche, J.R. Coding for computing. *IEEE Trans. Inf. Theory* **2001**, *47*, 903–917. [CrossRef]
4. Günlü, O. Function computation under privacy, secrecy, distortion, and communication constraints. *Entropy* **2022**, *24*, 110. [CrossRef] [PubMed]
5. Prabhakaran, V.; Ramchandran, K. On secure distributed source coding. In Proceedings of the 2007 IEEE Information Theory Workshop, Solstrand, Norway, 1–6 July 2007; pp. 442–447.
6. Gündüz, D.; Erkip, E.; Poor, H.V. Secure lossless compression with side information. In Proceedings of the 2008 IEEE Information Theory Workshop, Porto, Portugal, 5–9 May 2008; pp. 169–173.
7. Tandon, R.; Ulukus, S.; Ramchandran, K. Secure source coding with a helper. *IEEE Trans. Inf. Theory* **2013**, *59*, 2178–2187. [CrossRef]
8. Gündüz, D.; Erkip, E.; Poor, H.V. Lossless compression with security constraints. In Proceedings of the 2008 IEEE Information Theory Workshop, Porto, Portugal, 5–9 May 2008; pp. 111–115.
9. Luh, W.; Kundur, D. Distributed secret sharing for discrete memoryless networks. *IEEE Trans. Inf. Forensics Secur.* **2008**, *3*, 1–7. [CrossRef]
10. Kittichokechai, K.; Chia, Y.K.; Oechtering, T.J.; Skoglund, M.; Weissman, T. Secure source coding with a public helper. *IEEE Trans. Inf. Theory* **2016**, *62*, 3930–3949. [CrossRef]
11. Salimi, S.; Salmasizadeh, M.; Aref, M.R. Generalised secure distributed source coding with side information. *IET Commun.* **2010**, *4*, 2262–2272. [CrossRef]
12. Naghibi, F.; Salimi, S.; Skoglund, M. The CEO problem with secrecy constraints. *IEEE Trans. Inf. Forensics Secur.* **2015**, *10*, 1234–1249. [CrossRef]

13. Yamamoto, H. Coding theorems for Shannon's cipher system with correlated source outputs, and common information. *IEEE Trans. Inf. Theory* **1994**, *40*, 85–95. [CrossRef]
14. Ghourchian, H.; Stavrou, P.A.; Oechtering, T.J.; Skoglund, M. Secure source coding with side-information at decoder and shared key at encoder and decoder. In Proceedings of the 2021 IEEE Information Theory Workshop (ITW) 2021, Virtual, 17–21 October 2021; pp. 1–6.
15. Maurer, U.M. Secret key agreement by public discussion from common information. *IEEE Trans. Inf. Theory* **1993**, *39*, 2733–2742. [CrossRef]
16. Ahlswede, R.; Csiszár, I. Common randomness in information theory and cryptography—Part I: Secret sharing. *IEEE Trans. Inf. Theory* **1993**, *39*, 1121–1132. [CrossRef]
17. Yao, A.C. Protocols for secure computations. In Proceedings of the 3rd Annual Symposium on Foundations of Computer Science (SFCS 1982), Chicago, IL, USA, 3–5 November 1982; pp. 160–164.
18. Yao, A.C. How to generate and exchange secrets. In Proceedings of the 3rd Annual Symposium on Foundations of Computer Science (SFCS 1982), Chicago, IL, USA, 3–5 November 1982; pp. 162–167.
19. Bloch, M.; Günlü, O.; Yener, A.; Oggier, F.; Poor, H.V.; Sankar, L.; Schaefer, R.F. An overview of information-theoretic security and privacy: Metrics, limits and applications. *IEEE J. Sel. Areas Inf. Theory* **2021**, *2*, 5–22. [CrossRef]
20. Günlü, O.; Kramer, G. Privacy, secrecy, and storage with multiple noisy measurements of identifiers. *IEEE Trans. Inf. Forensics Secur.* **2018**, *13*, 2872–2883. [CrossRef]
21. Günlü, O.; Bloch, M.; Schaefer, R.F. Secure multi-function computation with private remote sources. *arXiv* **2021**, arXiv:2106.09485.
22. Berger, T. *Rate Distortion Theory: A Mathematical Basis for Data Compression*; Prentice-Hall: Englewood Cliffs, NJ, USA, 1971.
23. Permuter, H.; Weissman, T. Source coding with a side information "Vending Machine". *IEEE Trans. Inf. Theory* **2011**, *57*, 4530–4544. [CrossRef]
24. Berger, T.; Zhang, Z.; Viswanathan, H. The CEO problem. *IEEE Trans. Inf. Theory* **1996**, *42*, 887–902. [CrossRef]
25. Günlü, O. Key Agreement with Physical Unclonable Functions and Biometric Identifiers. Ph.D. Thesis, Technical University of Munich, Munich, Germany , February 2019.
26. Ignatenko, T.; Willems, F.M.J. Biometric systems: Privacy and secrecy aspects. *IEEE Trans. Inf. Forensics Secur.* **2009**, *4*, 956–973. [CrossRef]
27. Lai, L.; Ho, S.W.; Poor, H.V. Privacy-security trade-offs in biometric security systems - Part I: Single use case. *IEEE Trans. Inf. Forensics Secur.* **2011**, *6*, 122–139. [CrossRef]
28. Kusters, L.; Günlü, O.; Willems, F.M. Zero secrecy leakage for multiple enrollments of physical unclonable functions. In Proceedings of the 2018 Symposium on Information Theory and Signal Processing in the Benelux, Enschede, The Netherlands, 31 May–1 June 2018; pp. 119–127.
29. Lai, L.; Ho, S.W.; Poor, H.V. Privacy-security trade-offs in biometric security systems—Part II: Multiple use case. *IEEE Trans. Inf. Forensics Secur.* **2011**, *6*, 140–151. [CrossRef]
30. Günlü, O. Multi-Entity and Multi-Enrollment Key Agreement with Correlated Noise. *IEEE Trans. Inf. Forensics Secur.* **2021**, *16*, 1190–1202. [CrossRef]
31. Günlü, O.; Schaefer, R.F.; Boche, H.; Poor, H.V. Secure and private source coding with private key and decoder side information. *arXiv* **2022**, arXiv:2205.05068.
32. Tu, W.; Lai, L. On function computation with privacy and secrecy constraints. *IEEE Trans. Inf. Theory* **2019**, *65*, 6716–6733. [CrossRef]
33. Villard, J.; Piantanida, P. Secure multiterminal source coding with side information at the eavesdropper. *IEEE Trans. Inf. Theory* **2013**, *59*, 3668–3692. [CrossRef]
34. Bross, S.I. Secure cooperative source-coding with side information at the eavesdropper. *IEEE Trans. Inf. Theory* **2016**, *62*, 4544–4558. [CrossRef]
35. Ekrem, E.; Ulukus, S. Secure lossy source coding with side information. In Proceedings of the 2011 49th Annual Allerton Conference on Communication, Control, and Computing (Allerton), Monticello, IL, USA, 28–30 September 2011; pp. 1098–1105.
36. Körner, J.; Marton, K. Comparison of two noisy channels. *Topics Inf. Theory* **1977**, 411–423.
37. Bergmans, P. A simple converse for broadcast channels with additive white Gaussian noise (Corresp.). *IEEE Trans. Inf. Theory* **1974**, *20*, 279–280. [CrossRef]
38. Günlü, O.; Schaefer, R.F.; Poor, H.V. Biometric and Physical Identifiers with Correlated Noise for Controllable Private Authentication. *arXiv* **2020**, arXiv:2001.00847.
39. Wyner, A.D.; Ziv, J. A theorem on the entropy of certain binary sequences and applications: Part I. *IEEE Trans. Inf. Theory* **1973**, *19*, 769–772. [CrossRef]
40. Watanabe, S.; Oohama, Y. Secret key agreement from correlated Gaussian sources by rate limited public communication. *IEICE Trans. Fundam. Electron., Commun. Comp. Sci.* **2010**, *93*, 1976–1983. [CrossRef]
41. Willems, F.M.; Ignatenko, T. Quantization effects in biometric systems. In Proceedings of the 2009 Information Theory and Applications Workshop, San Diego, CA, USA, 27 January–1 February 2009; pp. 372–379.
42. Yachongka, V.; Yagi, H.; Oohama, Y. Secret key-based authentication with passive eavesdropper for scalar Gaussian sources. *arXiv* **2022**, arXiv:2202.10018.
43. Cover, T.M.; Thomas, J.A. *Elements of Information Theory*, 2nd ed.; John Wiley & Sons: Hoboken, NJ, USA, 2012.

44. Maes, R. An accurate probabilistic reliability model for silicon PUFs. In *International Conference on Cryptographic Hardware and Embedded Systems*; Springer: Berlin/Heidelberg, Germany, 2013; pp. 73–89.
45. Anantharam, V. *Lecture Notes in Stochastic Estimation and Control: Jointly Gaussian Random Variables*; University California Berkeley: Berkeley, CA, USA, 2007.
46. Wyner, A.; Ziv, J. The rate-distortion function for source coding with side information at the decoder. *IEEE Trans. Inf. Theory* **1976**, *22*, 1–10. [CrossRef]
47. Chayat, N.; Shamai, S. Extension of an entropy property for binary input memoryless symmetric channels. *IEEE Trans. Inf. Theory* **1989**, *35*, 1077–1079. [CrossRef]
48. Günlü, O.; Kramer, G.; Skórski, M. Privacy and secrecy with multiple measurements of physical and biometric identifiers. In Proceedings of the 2015 IEEE Conference on Communications and Network Security (CNS), Florence, Italy, 28–30 September 2015; pp. 89–94.
49. Yassaee, M.H.; Aref, M.R.; Gohari, A. Achievability proof via output statistics of random binning. *IEEE Trans. Inf. Theory* **2014**, *60*, 6760–6786. [CrossRef]
50. Renes, J.M.; Renner, R. Noisy channel coding via privacy amplification and information reconciliation. *IEEE Trans. Inf. Theory* **2011**, *57*, 7377–7385. [CrossRef]
51. Bloch, M. *Lecture Notes in Information-Theoretic Security*; Georgia Institute of Technology: Atlanta, GA, USA, 2018.
52. Holenstein, T.; Renner, R. On the randomness of independent experiments. *IEEE Trans. Inf. Theory* **2011**, *57*, 1865–1871. [CrossRef]
53. Bloch, M.; Barros, J. *Physical-Layer Security*; Cambridge University Press: Cambridge, UK, 2011.
54. Csiszár, I.; Körner, J. *Information Theory: Coding Theorems for Discrete Memoryless Systems*, 2nd ed.; Cambridge University Press: Cambridge, UK, 2011.

entropy

Article

Broadcast Approach to Uplink NOMA: Queuing Delay Analysis

Maha Zohdy [1,†,‡], Ali Tajer [1,*,†] and Shlomo Shamai (Shitz) [2,†]

1 Department of Electrical, Computer, and Systems Engineering, Rensselaer Polytechnic Institute, Troy, NY 12180, USA
2 Faculty of Electrical Engineering, Technion—Israel Institute of Technology, Haifa 3200003, Israel
* Correspondence: tajer@ecse.rpi.edu; Tel.: +1-518-276-8237
† The authors contributed equally to this work.
‡ This author was with Rensselaer Polytechnic Institute when this work was completed. Currently, she is with MathWorks Inc., Natick, MA 01760, USA.

Abstract: Emerging wireless technologies are envisioned to support a variety of applications that require simultaneously maintaining low latency and high reliability. Non-orthogonal multiple access techniques constitute one candidate for grant-free transmission alleviating the signaling requirements for uplink transmissions. In open-loop transmissions over fading channels, in which the transmitters do not have access to the channel state information, the existing approaches are prone to facing frequent outage events. Such outage events lead to repeated re-transmissions of the duplicate information packets, penalizing the latency. This paper proposes a multi-access broadcast approach in which each user splits its information stream into several information layers, each adapted to one possible channel state. This approach facilitates preventing outage events and improves the overall transmission latency. Based on the proposed approach, the average queuing delay of each user is analyzed for different arrival processes at each transmitter. First, for deterministic arrivals, closed-form lower and upper bounds on the average delay are characterized analytically. Secondly, for Poisson arrivals, a closed-form expression for the average delay is delineated using the Pollaczek-Khinchin formula. Based on the established bounds, the proposed approach achieves less average delay than single-layer outage approaches. Under optimal power allocation among the encoded layers, numerical evaluations demonstrate that the proposed approach significantly minimizes average sum delays compared to traditional outage approaches, especially under high arrival rates.

Keywords: broadcast approach; channel state information; latency; multiple access

Citation: Zohdy, M.; Tajer, A.; Shamai, S. Broadcast Approach to Uplink NOMA: Queuing Delay Analysis. *Entropy* **2022**, *24*, 1757. https://doi.org/10.3390/e24121757

Academic Editors: Onur Günlü and Holger Boche

Received: 16 September 2022
Accepted: 15 November 2022
Published: 30 November 2022

1. Introduction

There is a growing need for maintaining low latency and high reliability in a wide range of wireless communication systems [1]. Among the recently proposed techniques for attaining the latency-reliability requirements is the power domain non-orthogonal multiple access (NOMA) [2–6]. Uplink power domain NOMA [5] facilitates simultaneous multi-user channel access, alleviating the traditional signaling period at the beginning of the transmission. Furthermore, by leveraging power control and adaptive decoding order among users, NOMA techniques enhance user fairness by taking into consideration the dissimilarities in the channel state of each user [7,8].

A fundamental challenge that NOMA faces in wireless networks is that its power control critically relies on the availability of full channel state information at each transmitter (CSIT). This assumption is generally unfeasible under the anticipated network scale growth. In the absence of CSIT, traditional NOMA occasionally suffers from outage events, which necessitate repeated re-transmissions and negatively affect the overall latency. To address this issue, we propose a non-orthogonal multi-access technique in which each transmitter splits its stream of information into multiple encoded layers, each adapted to a specific combination of all the network's channel states. Each user then transmits the superposition of all its encoded layers to the receiver. In particular, we approach the problem of minimizing the overall communication latency from a cross-layer resource allocation perspective by focusing on the dominant delay factor, i.e., the queuing delay [9]. The goal of the proposed approach is to minimize the average sum-queuing delay among users by optimally allocating power among the encoded layers at each transmitter in the physical layer.

Outage avoidance via multi-layer superposition coding was first proposed in [10,11] for the slowly fading single-user channels. This is generally referred to as the broadcast approach [12]. Furthermore, the studies in [13] extended the broadcast approach to the energy harvesting settings, those in [14–20] to random and multi-access channel models, and those in [21,22] to the multiuser interference channel. Aside from analyzing the achievable rate regions of multi-layer superposition coding [17,23], the average delay performance has only been studied for the single-user fading channel in [24]. However, under CSIT uncertainties, the advantages of adaptive multi-layer superposition coding for controlling the average queuing delay in multiple access channels are yet to be explored. Finally, we note that the broadcast approach is related to the studies on the "rate-splitting", the foundations of which rely on superposition coding of the layered information messages [25].

In this paper, we consider an N-user block fading multiple access channel (MAC) in which all transmitters are oblivious to their instantaneous channel state. Each user possesses an infinite capacity queue, occasionally holding the arriving information packets to be transmitted. A novel multi-layer superposition coding scheme is then employed, in which each transmitter adapts its message to the combined network state. Based on the proposed scheme, closed-form lower and upper bounds on the average delay are characterized analytically for deterministic arrivals. Furthermore, a closed-form expression for the average queuing delay is delineated for Poisson arrivals. Based on the derived bounds on average delay, the proposed approach is shown to outperform the single-layer outage approach. Finally, under optimal power allocation among the encoded layers, numerical evaluations demonstrate that the broadcast approach significantly reduces the average sum delays compared to traditional outage approaches under symmetric/asymmetric arrival rates and channel statistics among users.

A rich literature exists on minimizing the average delay through cross-layer resource allocation in MAC with full CSIT. Relevant studies include [26] in which the authors provide an optimal solution for minimizing average delays of two-user MAC channels by controlling the departure probability of each user's queue. In [27], an information-theoretic rate allocation policy is proposed to achieve a lower bound on the average delay of multi-access coding schemes. Dynamic power and rate control to minimize the average delay are studied for multi-access channels in [28]. The study in [28] provides a one-step value iteration policy for optimal scheduling in MAC fading channels. A lower bound on the LTE-A average delay is derived in [29] for random access channels under different arrival processes. The random access scheduling problem is addressed in [30] using a distributed virtual queue model facilitating a self-organizing policy. The study in [31] proposes a joint superposition coding and scheduling policy for the uplink NOMA by relying on user-pairing to reduce the complexity of analysis [32,33]. The accuracy of ranking users in NOMA techniques using distance-based measures versus instantaneous signal-to-noise ratio (SNR) is addressed in [34]. Joint scheduling and superposition coding in fading channels is studied in [35]. The effect of unsaturated traffic in uplink NOMA is studied in [36] using tools from queuing theory. Interaction between power control and queuing service rates in interference-limited channels is studied in [37]. Delay analysis of multi-point to multi-point networks is provided in [38] for spatial-temporal random arrival traffic. The problem of power control in delay-bounded applications is considered in [39], especially under the assumption of imperfect successive interference cancellation in uplink NOMA. The effective capacity of two-user uplink NOMA is characterized in [40] under quality-of-service delay constraints.

Energy-efficient transmission in uplink NOMA is studied in [41] under statistical delay constraints, where probabilistic upper bounds on queuing delays of NOMA are characterized. Resorting to the concept of effective capacity, the study in [42] proposes an optimized hybrid approach between non-orthogonal multiple access and orthogonal multiple access with different user pairing techniques in order to maximize the effective capacity under stringent delay constraints. Contention-based modified NOMA for uplink access is studied in [43], showing that exploiting collisions in the power domain can greatly reduce access delay. The throughput, access delay, and energy efficiency of NOMA uplink random access system are studied in [44]. Joint power control and user scheduling is considered in [45] to investigate the access delay minimization problem through an efficient sub-optimal iterative algorithm. Optimal power level partitioning to accommodate non-critical and high-priority messages is studied in [46]. A joint dynamic power control and user pairing algorithm is proposed in [47] to minimize long-term time average transmit power and queuing delay. Recent studies further includes [48] in which an adaptive rate NOMA with full CSIT is shown to provide better ergodic capacities for mobile users than OMA while satisfying strict local delay constraints for the internet of things (IoT) devices in cellular IoT networks. Opportunistic NOMA schemes are proposed in [49] for short message delivery with delay constraint based on which an upper bound on session error probability is derived, showing the impact of NOMA on session error under Rayleigh fading. A queuing delay analysis is presented in [50] for uplink NOMA with full CSIT, and the impact of channel estimation imperfections for finite-length channel coding is studied. Dynamic power allocation schemes with statistical delay quality-of-service (QoS) guarantees are shown in [51] to significantly improve the sum effective capacity and effective energy efficiency for an uplink NOMA system with paired users.

The rest of this paper is organized as follows. Section 2 presents the N-user multi-access channel model. The proposed multi-layer-based multi-access approach is outlined in Section 3 for the special case of the 2-state channel. The average delay achievable by the proposed approach is shown to outperform the average delay of the single-layer outage approach in Section 4 for deterministic and stochastic arrivals processes. The proposed multi-access approach is generalized to the case of finite arbitrary ℓ-state channel in Section 5. Finally, numerical evaluations are provided in Section 6, and the paper is concluded in Section 7.

2. Channel Model

Consider an N-user block fading MAC channel consisting of N transmitters and one receiver. The channel state is assumed to remain unchanged during the period of one transmission block of n channel uses and varies independently among consecutive blocks. We assume that the block length n is large enough to give rise to the notion of reliable communications but much shorter than the dynamics of the fading process [24]. Each transmitter is assumed to know the statistics of the channel state information (CSI) of its own link to the receiver but is oblivious to its instantaneous value. Complete CSI of all links is assumed to be available at the receiver. The input-output relationship of this channel is given by

$$Y = \sum_{i=1}^{N} h_i X_i + W , \tag{1}$$

where X_i denotes the transmitted signal from user i and W is the additive white Gaussian noise with zero mean and unit variance. Finally, h_i denotes the state of the fading channel between transmitter i and the receiver. The transmitted signal X_i is subject to an average power constraint P for all $i \in \{1, \ldots, N\}$, i.e., $\mathbb{E}\left[|X_i|^2\right] \leq P$. We consider a quantized model for the fading channel according to which h_i^2 takes one of two possible states, referred to as $\{\textit{weak}, \textit{strong}\}$, denoted by $\{\alpha_1, \alpha_2\}$, respectively. Without loss of generality, we assume $0 < \alpha_1 < \alpha_2 < +\infty$. User i experiences *strong* or *weak* channel states with probabilities $p_i \triangleq \mathbb{P}(h_i^2 = \alpha_2)$ and $\bar{p}_i \triangleq 1 - p_i$, respectively.

Each transmitter is assumed to possess an infinite-capacity queue. The queue at transmitter i receives random packets with an average arrival rate λ_i (bits/channel use). The size of the data queued at transmitter i at the beginning of any transmission block t is denoted by $\tilde{Q}_i(t),\ \forall i \in \{1,\ldots,N\}$. We define $A_i(t)$ as the total number of bits arriving in the queue at transmitter i during transmission block t. Finally, $r_i(t)$ (bits/channel use) denotes the service rate of the queue at transmitter i. Hence, the queue size at transmitter i at the end of any transmission block can be expressed using a recursive relationship as

$$\tilde{Q}_i(t+1) = \begin{cases} \tilde{Q}_i(t) + nA_i(t) - nr_i(t), & \tilde{Q}_i(t) + nA_i(t) - nr_i(t) \geq 0 \\ 0, & \text{otherwise} \end{cases}. \tag{2}$$

Accordingly, we define $Q_i(t)$ as queue size normalized by the number of transmission blocks n, i.e.,

$$Q_i(t+1) \triangleq \begin{cases} Q_i(t) + Z_i(t), & Q_i(t) + Z_i(t) \geq 0 \\ 0, & o.w. \end{cases}, \tag{3}$$

where the random variable $Z_i(t)$ is defined as $Z_i(t) \triangleq A_i(t) - r_i(t)$, and it captures the change in the queue size at transmitter i at the end of transmission block t. We remark that the number of bit arrivals $A_i(t)$ is random and does not necessarily fit into the exact size of the transmitted packet in a given transmission block. Therefore, if the backlogged data at any queue is less than a packet length, the data bits are zero-padded to form a complete packet for the encoder at each transmitter. Throughout the rest of the paper, we assume that the processing delay, i.e., encoding and decoding processes, as well as the transmission delay, are fixed and negligible with respect to the queuing delay. We use the concise notation $C(x,y) \triangleq \frac{1}{2}\log_2(1 + \frac{x}{\frac{1}{P}+y})$, $\{x_j^i\}_{j=1}^k \triangleq \{x_1^i, x_2^i, \ldots, x_k^i\}$. Finally, we denote the set of all users in the network by $\mathcal{N} \triangleq \{1,\ldots,N\}$.

3. 2-State Channel Multi-Access

In this section, we present a non-orthogonal multiple-access approach based on multi-layer encoding at each transmitter and successive interference cancellation (SIC) at the receiver. The underlying layering approach hinges on adapting the number of encoded layers at each transmitter to the combined fading state of the network, i.e., the fading states of all transmitters to the receiver. Owing to the arising interference in non-orthogonal multi-access channels with no CSIT, the channel state of each user directly affects the decoding success probabilities of all the other users. Motivated by this, the recent work in [17] proposed a multi-layer coding approach for the two-user multiple access channel with no CSIT, specially adapted to the combined network state resulting in an enlarged average achievable rate regions compared to the existing multi-layer coding approaches. In this section, we extend the layering approach in [17] to the general case of an arbitrary number of N-users. As shown in this paper, the proposed multi-access approach enjoys considerable advantages in reducing the queuing delay.

3.1. *Layering Approach*

At the beginning of each transmission block, user i aims to transmit all the data bits accumulated in its queue if the channel state allows it. Otherwise, it encodes a part of its data with the maximum allowable encoding rate. Towards this goal, user i encodes its data (fully or partially) using $2N$ independent messages generated from $2N$ Gaussian codebooks. These messages are denoted by $U_{jk}^i, \forall i \in \mathcal{N}, j \in \{1,2\}, k \in \{0 \cup \mathcal{N}\}$. Based on this decomposition

$$X_i = \sum_{j=1}^{2}\sum_{k=0}^{N} U_{jk}^i \,. \tag{4}$$

We consider an ordering of the network states based on the number of users with *strong* channel states denoted by k. We define $\mathcal{S}_k$ as the set of k users' indices that experience *strong* channel states. Accordingly, $\mathcal{E}_k$ denotes the event that exactly k users are experiencing a *strong* channel including.

The notation U^i_{jk} can be interpreted as follows. Superscript i denotes the user index $i \in \mathcal{N}$, subscript $j \in \{1,2\}$ refers to user i's channel state, where $j = 1$ if $h_i^2 = \alpha_1$ and otherwise $j = 2$. Finally, $k \in \{0 \cup \mathcal{N}\}$ represents the number of users in the network with a *strong* channel state, possibly including user i's channel. Therefore, for every value of k, user i adapts the rate of two codewords, $\{U^i_{jk}\}_{j=1}^2$, based on its own channel state resulting in a total of $2k$ layers. The correspondence between each channel state and the adapted layer is shown in Table 1 and summarized below:

- U^i_{10} is adapted to $\mathcal{E}_0$, where all channels are *weak*.
- U^i_{2N} is adapted to $\mathcal{E}_N$, where all channels are *strong*.
- When exactly k channels are *strong*:
  - U^i_{1k} is adapted to $\mathcal{N}\backslash\mathcal{E}_k$ if user i's channel is *weak*.
  - U^i_{2k} is adapted to $\mathcal{E}_k$ if user i's channel is *strong*.

The rate of codeword U^i_{jk} is denoted by R^i_{jk}. Finally, we define β^i_{jk} as the power fraction of the total power P allocated to codeword U^i_{jk}, such that

$$\sum_{j=1}^{2}\sum_{k=0}^{N} \beta^i_{jk} = 1\,.$$

For user i, the rate of each codebook is governed via the power allocation parameters β^i_{jk} such that at least one layer is successfully decoded in every possible network state.

Table 1. Layering and codebook assignments by user i.

h_i^2 \ k	0	1	2	...	$N-1$	N
α_1	U^i_{10}	U^i_{11}	U^i_{12}	...	U^1_{1N-1}	
α_2		U^i_{21}	U^i_{22}	...	U^i_{2N-1}	U^i_{2N}

3.2. Decoding Approach

Corresponding to the layering approach in Section 3.1, we propose a decoding algorithm with $2kN$ SIC stages for each combined channel state with k strong channels. The layers' decoding order is adapted to the combined channel states such that all the layers adapted to channel states with less than k strong users, $\{U^i_{j\ell}, \forall j \in \{1,2\}, \ell < k\}$, are first decoded and subtracted from the received signal. Afterwards, layers adapted to channel state with exactly k strong users, $\{U^i_{jk}, \forall j \in \{1,2\}\}$, are decoded.

When $|\mathcal{S}| = k$, the receiver employs $4k+1$ decoding stages. Each of the layers for any $j \in \{1,2\}$ and $\ell \in \{0,\ldots,k\}$, the set of codebooks $\{U^i_{j\ell} : i \in \mathcal{N}\}$ is partitioned to two sets

$$\mathcal{P}_{j\ell} \triangleq \{U^i_{j\ell} : i \in \mathcal{S}\} \qquad \text{and} \qquad \mathcal{Q}_{j\ell} \triangleq \{U^i_{j\ell} : i \notin \mathcal{S}\}\,, \tag{5}$$

rendering a total of $4k+1$ partitions for different $j \in \{1,2\}$ and $\ell \in \{0,\ldots,k\}$. The decoding strategy decodes one message from each of these, except for the partition $\{U^i_{2k} : i \notin \mathcal{S}\}$. The decoding strategy works as follows. We create the following two sequences of sets:

$$\mathcal{P} \triangleq \{\mathcal{P}_{10}, \mathcal{P}_{11}, \mathcal{P}_{21}, \ldots, \mathcal{P}_{2(k-1)}, \mathcal{P}_{1k}, \}\,, \tag{6}$$

$$\mathcal{Q} \triangleq \{\mathcal{Q}_{1k}, \mathcal{Q}_{2(k-1)}, \mathcal{Q}_{1(k-1)}, \ldots, \mathcal{Q}_{11}, \mathcal{Q}_{10}, \}\,. \tag{7}$$

The decoding strategy selects codebooks by alternating between $\mathcal{P}$ and $\mathcal{Q}$ in ascending order and decodes exactly one codebook from each. Specifically, the codebook sets are selected in the following order: $\{\mathcal{P}_{10}, \mathcal{Q}_{1k}, \mathcal{P}_{11}, \mathcal{Q}_{2(k-1)}, \mathcal{P}_{21}, \ldots, \mathcal{P}_{1k}, \mathcal{Q}_{10}\}$. This results in $4k$ coding stages. Finally, the codebooks in $\{U^i_{2k} : i \in \mathcal{S}\}$ are decoded as the last stage, i.e., stage $4k + 1$. Next, we describe the decoding stages and the set of codebooks decoded in each.

- **Decoding stage** 1**:** We start by decoding the layers $\mathcal{P}_{10} \triangleq \{U^i_{10} : i \in \mathcal{S}\}$, i.e., the codebooks U^i_{10} of only the k strong users in $\mathcal{S}$. We define $\mathcal{S}_k$ as an ordered set of these users, in which the users are ordered in an ascending order based on their indices. The codebooks will be decoded sequentially in this order.
- **Decoding stage** 2**:** Next, after decoding and removing the codebooks in $\mathcal{P}_{10}$, we sequentially decode the layers in $\mathcal{Q}_{1k} = \{U^i_{1k} : i \notin \mathcal{S}\}$, which involves layers U^i_{1k} of users with weak channels.
- **Decoding stage** 3**:** In the third stage, the codebooks in $\mathcal{P}_{10}$ and $\mathcal{Q}_{1k}$ are already decoded. We continue by sequentially decoding the set of codebooks in $\mathcal{P}_{11} \triangleq \{U^i_{11} : i \in \mathcal{S}\}$.
- **Decoding stage** 4**:** The decoding process continues by sequentially decoding the codebooks in $\mathcal{Q}_{2(k-1)} = \{U^i_{2(k-1)} : i \notin \mathcal{S}\}$, while the codebooks of $\mathcal{P}_{10}$, $\mathcal{Q}_{1k}$, and $\mathcal{P}_{11}$ are already decoded.
- **Decoding stage** 5**:** This stage sequentially decodes the codebooks $\mathcal{P}_{21}$.
- **Decoding stage** 6**:** This stage sequentially decodes the codebooks in $\mathcal{Q}_{1(k-1)}$.
- **Decoding stages** $\{2, \ldots, 4k + 1\}$**:** Following the pattern of the previous decoding stages, in general, in stage $\{2, \ldots, 4k\}$, we decode the codebooks according to the following schedule for $\ell \in \{1, \ldots, k\}$:

$$\begin{array}{ll} \text{codebooks in } \mathcal{Q}_{1(k-\ell+1)} & \text{stage} \;\; 4\ell - 2 \\ \text{codebooks in } \mathcal{P}_{1\ell} & \text{stage} \;\; 4\ell - 1 \\ \text{codebooks in } \mathcal{Q}_{2(k-\ell)} & \text{stage} \;\; 4\ell \\ \text{codebooks in } \mathcal{P}_{2\ell} & \text{stage} \;\; 4\ell + 1 \end{array} \tag{8}$$

The proposed decoding approach results in decoding more layers for a channel state with k strong users compared to a state with $k - 1$ strong users. In particular, the receiver decodes one extra layer for user i in channel state $\mathcal{E}_k$ as compared to state $\mathcal{E}_{k-1}$. Note that in both states, user i experiences a *weak* channel. On the other hand, the receiver decodes two extra layers for user i in channel state $\mathcal{E}_k$ as compared to state $\mathcal{E}_{k-1}$, note that user i experiences a *strong* channel in both states. Our intuition behind such a strategy hinges on two factors. First, that decoding and removing additional interfering users with strong channel states is expected to increase the achievable rate of user i. Secondly, when user i experiences a stronger channel, the receiver can possibly decode an additional layer from its message. The decoded layers for channel state $\mathcal{E}_k$ are shown in Table 2 for illustration.

Table 2. Decoded layers for channel state $\mathcal{E}_k$ where $h_i^2 = \alpha_j$.

Stage	**Stage 1**	**Stage 2**	**Stage 3**	**Stage 4**	...	**Stage $4k+1$**
Codebook	$\mathcal{P}_{10}$	$\mathcal{Q}_{1k}$	$\mathcal{P}_{11}$	$\mathcal{Q}_{2(k-1)}$	...	$\{U^1_{2k} : i \in \mathcal{S}_k\}$

Finally, the detailed steps of the proposed successive decoding algorithm are presented in Algorithm 1. We remark that the effect of the precedence of users with similar channel states within each decoding stage on the average achievable delay will be analyzed in the subsequent sections.

Algorithm 1: Successive Decoding for 2-state channel

```
input $(h_1^2, \ldots, h_N^2)$, $k$
for $\ell \in \{0, \ldots, k\}$
    if $\ell = 0$
        In stage 1 successively decode $\{U_{10}^i\}_{i=1}^N$
    else if $\ell \in \{1, \ldots, k\}$
        (1) In stage $4\ell - 2$ successively decode $\mathcal{Q}_{1(k-\ell+1)}$
        (2) In stage $4\ell - 1$ successively decode $\mathcal{P}_{1\ell}$
        (3) In stage $4\ell$ successively decode $\mathcal{Q}_{2(k-\ell)}$
        (4) In stage $4\ell + 1$ successively decode $\mathcal{P}_{2\ell}$
    end if
end for
```

Based on the multi-access approach outlined throughout this section, the service rate of the queue at transmitter i is determined by the total rates of the successfully decoded layers during each network state. Therefore, the service rate $r_i(t)$ during transmission block t varies randomly and is jointly determined by the states of all users as well as the power allocation among different layers at each transmitter, i.e., β_{jk}^i. The achievable rates for all the encoded layers are formally stated in the Theorem 1.

Theorem 1. *For the N-user MAC channel without CSIT, when exactly $k \in \mathcal{N} \cup \{0\}$ users have strong channels, the achievable rates of the layering approach in Section 3.1 and the decoding policy in Algorithm 1 are characterized by the set of rates $\left\{R_{jk}^i, \forall j \in \{1,2\}, i \in \mathcal{N}, \ell \in \{0 \cup \mathcal{N}\}\right\}$ that satisfy*

$$R_{j\ell}^i \leq \min_{\mathcal{S}:|\mathcal{S}|=k} d_{j\ell}^i(\mathcal{S}), \tag{9}$$

where constants $\left\{d_{jk}^i(\mathcal{S}), \forall k \in \{0 \cup \mathcal{N}\}, j \in \{1,2\}\right\}$ are defined in Appendix A.

Proof. See Appendix B. □

We remark that characterizing the achievable rate region of the proposed approach in the form of rate bounds on individual codebooks rates, rather than an average achievable rate region, will be instrumental to characterizing the average achievable delay analysis throughout the next section.

4. Average Queuing Delay

In this section, we investigate the average queuing delay achieved by the multi-access approach in Section 3 compared to the conventional single-layer (outage) multi-access approach. First, in Section 4.1, we focus on the case of the deterministic arrival process at each queue, for which we delineate lower and upper bounds on the average queuing delay. Furthermore, the case of stochastic arrivals is examined in Section 4.2 in which a closed-form expression for the average delay achievable by the proposed approach is characterized and compared to that of the single-layer transmission approach. To proceed, we define $\mathcal{E}_k^i$ as the event in which we have exactly k strong channels and they include the channel of user i. Accordingly, we define $\bar{\mathcal{E}}_k^i \triangleq \mathcal{N} \backslash \mathcal{E}_k^i$. We begin by computing the probabilities of the events $\mathcal{E}_k^i$ (and $\mathcal{E}(\bar{\mathcal{S}}_k^i)$) as follows.

$$\mathbb{P}\left[\mathcal{E}_k^i\right] = \sum_{\substack{\mathcal{I} \subseteq \mathcal{N} \\ |\mathcal{I}|=k}} \prod_{j \in \mathcal{I}} p_j \prod_{\substack{\ell \notin \mathcal{I} \\ \ell \neq i}} \bar{p}_\ell \quad \text{and} \quad \mathbb{P}\left[\bar{\mathcal{E}}_k^i\right] = \sum_{\substack{\mathcal{I} \subseteq \mathcal{N} \\ |\mathcal{I}|=k}} \prod_{\substack{j \in \mathcal{I} \\ j \neq i}} p_j \prod_{\ell \notin \mathcal{I}} \bar{p}_\ell \,. \tag{10}$$

where $\mathcal{I}$ denotes a subset of user indices.

4.1. Deterministic Arrivals

Throughout this subsection, we assume that the data arrival process at each queue is a deterministic process with an average arrival rate λ_i, i.e., $A_i(t) = \lambda_i$, $\forall i \in \mathcal{N}$. Note that as a result of the zero-padding applied by the encoder, whenever the available data bits are fewer than a transmission packet, a G/G/1 queuing model is generated at each transmitter. A closed-form expression characterizing the average delay of the G/G/1 queuing model is, in general, unknown. Therefore we resort to characterizing upper and lower bounds on the average queuing delay. These bounds are formally presented in Theorem 2. Before stating Theorem 2, we provide an outline of the main steps pertinent to deriving the characterized bounds, where the detailed proof can be found in Appendix C.

Establishing the desired bounds hinges on characterizing the average queue size at each transmitter i using the Laplace transform of the probability distribution function (PDF) of the queue size Q_i (moment generating function). Let the PDF of Q_i be denoted by $dF_i(q)$ and its associated Laplace transform be denoted by $L_i(s)$. Therefore, the average queue size at transmitter i is given by

$$\mathbb{E}[Q_i] = \lim_{s \to 0} -\frac{dL_i(s)}{ds} . \tag{11}$$

Recalling the recursive expression for Q_i in terms of the variable Z_i in (3), a recursive form of $F_i(q)$ can be expressed as follows [52,53]

$$F_i(q) = \begin{cases} \int_{-\infty}^{q} F_i(q-\tau) dF_{Z_i}(\tau) , & q \geq 0 \\ 0 , & q < 0 \end{cases} , \tag{12}$$

where $dF_{Z_i}(z)$ denote PDF of Z_i denoting change in queue size at user i. At the end of every transmission block, the change in queue size i, Z_i, is primarily determined by the difference between the data arrival λ_i and the total rate of all the layers successfully decoded by the receiver from user i's message stream, which in turn is determined by the combined network state. Consequently, $dF_{Z_i}(z)$ can be expressed as

$$\begin{aligned} dF_{Z_i}(z) = {} & \mathbb{P}\left[\mathcal{E}\left(\bar{\mathcal{S}}_0^i\right)\right]\delta\left(z - \lambda_i + R_{10}^i\right) + \mathbb{P}\left[\mathcal{E}\left(\mathcal{S}_N^i\right)\right]\delta\left(z - \lambda_i + \sum_{j=1}^{2}\sum_{k=1}^{N} R_{jk}^i\right) \\ & + \sum_{\ell=1}^{N-1} \mathbb{P}\left[\mathcal{E}\left(\mathcal{S}_\ell^i\right)\right]\delta\left(z - \lambda_i + \sum_{j=1}^{2}\sum_{k=0}^{\ell-1} R_{jk}^i + R_{2\ell}^i\right) \\ & + \sum_{\ell=1}^{N-1} \mathbb{P}\left[\mathcal{E}\left(\bar{\mathcal{S}}_\ell^i\right)\right]\delta\left(z - \lambda_i + \sum_{j=1}^{2}\sum_{k=0}^{\ell-1} R_{jk}^i + R_{1\ell}^i\right) . \end{aligned} \tag{13}$$

We remark that in order to guarantee the stability of the data queue at each transmitter, we assume that the arrival rate λ_i is less than the average achievable rate (service rate of the queue), i.e.,

$$\lambda_i < \mathbb{E}[r_i] , \qquad \forall i \in \mathcal{N} , \tag{14}$$

where the average service rate at queue i is given by

$$\begin{aligned} \mathbb{E}[r_i] = {} & \mathbb{P}\left[\mathcal{E}\left(\bar{\mathcal{S}}_0^i\right)\right] R_{10}^i + \mathbb{P}\left[\mathcal{E}\left(\mathcal{S}_N^i\right)\right] \cdot \sum_{j=1}^{2}\sum_{k=1}^{N} R_{jk}^i \\ & + \sum_{\ell=1}^{N-1} \mathbb{P}\left[\mathcal{E}\left(\mathcal{S}_\ell^i\right)\right] \cdot \left(\sum_{j=1}^{2}\sum_{k=0}^{\ell-1} R_{jk}^i + R_{2\ell}^i\right) + \sum_{\ell=1}^{N-1} \mathbb{P}\left[\mathcal{E}\left(\bar{\mathcal{S}}_\ell^i\right)\right] \cdot \left(\sum_{j=1}^{2}\sum_{k=0}^{\ell-1} R_{jk}^i + R_{1\ell}^i\right) . \end{aligned} \tag{15}$$

An explicit expression for $F_i(q), \forall i \in \mathcal{N}$, directly follows by combining (12) and (13)

$$F_i(q) = \begin{cases} 0\,, & \forall q \in \mathcal{R}_1 \\ \mathbb{P}\big[\mathcal{E}\big(\mathcal{S}_0^i\big)\big] F_i(q - \lambda_i + \sum_{j=1}^{2}\sum_{k=0}^{N} R_{jk}^i)\,, & \forall q \in \mathcal{R}_2 \\ \vdots & \\ \mathbb{P}\big[\mathcal{E}\big(\bar{\mathcal{S}}_0^i\big)\big] F_i(q - \lambda_i + R_{10}^i)\,, & \forall q \in \mathcal{R}_{2N-1} \end{cases}, \tag{16}$$

where the intervals $\mathcal{R}_i, \forall i \in \{1, \ldots, 2N-1\}$, are given by

$$\begin{aligned} \mathcal{R}_1 &\triangleq (-\infty, 0)\,, \\ \mathcal{R}_2 &\triangleq \left[0, \lambda_i - \sum_{j=1}^{2}\sum_{k=0}^{N} R_{jk}^i + R_{1(N-1)}^i\right], \\ &\vdots \\ \mathcal{R}_{2N-1} &\triangleq \left[\lambda_i - R_{10}^i, \infty\right). \end{aligned}$$

Finally, the Laplace transform of the queue size PDF is computed using (16), which in turn facilitates obtaining the average queue size at user i. Note that although $F_i(q)$ is expressed in (16), it is still a recursive form. Therefore, the obtained expression for the average queue size delay contains the unknown term $F_i(q)$, which is why a closed form cannot be obtained. Subsequently, an upper and a lower bound on the average queue size of user $i \in \mathcal{N}$ are formally characterized in the next theorem.

Theorem 2. *The average queue size of transmitter i under the multi-access policy in Section 3 is bounded by*

$$\frac{1}{2}\sum_{j=1}^{2}\sum_{k=0}^{N} R_{jk}^i - \frac{\lambda_i}{2} - \frac{N_i}{D_i} \le \mathbb{E}[Q_i] \le \sum_{j=1}^{2}\sum_{k=0}^{N} R_{jk}^i - \lambda_i - \frac{N_i}{D_i}\,, \tag{17}$$

where we have defined $D_i \triangleq 2(\mathbb{E}[r_i] - \lambda_i)$ *and*

$$\begin{aligned} N_i \triangleq &-\left(\sum_{j=1}^{2}\sum_{k=0}^{N} R_{jk}^i - \lambda_i\right)^2 + \mathbb{P}\left[\mathcal{E}\left(\bar{\mathcal{S}}_0^i\right)\right]\left(\sum_{j=1}^{2}\sum_{k=1}^{N} R_{jk}^i\right)^2 \\ &+ \sum_{\ell=1}^{N-1} \mathbb{P}\left[\mathcal{E}\left(\mathcal{S}_\ell^i\right)\right] \cdot \left(\sum_{j=1}^{2}\sum_{k=\ell+1}^{N} R_{jk}^i + R_{1\ell}^i\right)^2 + \sum_{\ell=1}^{N-1} \mathbb{P}\left[\mathcal{E}\left(\bar{\mathcal{S}}^i{}_\ell\right)\right] \cdot \left(\sum_{j=1}^{2}\sum_{k=\ell+1}^{N} R_{jk}^i + R_{2\ell}^i\right)^2 . \end{aligned} \tag{18}$$

Proof. See Appendix C. □

Using Little's law, upper and lower bounds on the average queuing delay at transmitter i under deterministic arrivals can directly be obtained by normalizing the bounds characterized in Theorem 2 $\mathbb{E}[Q_i]$ by λ_i.

In order to assess the performance of the proposed multi-layer superposition coding access approach, we compare the achievable average queuing delay to that of the conventional single-layer access (outage) approach. To this end, we first summarize the single-layer approach, and afterward, a lower bound on the average queuing delay achieved by the single-layer approach is characterized in Lemma 1. Finally, we compare the rate of increase of the average delay achieved by each policy with respect to the data arrival rate. As the arrival rate increases, the rate of increase of the average delay with respect to λ_i resulting from the proposed approach is lower than that resulting from the single-layer (outage) approach.

According to the single-layer (outage) transmission approach, each transmitter encodes the available data in its queue into one layer of a fixed rate irrespective of the unknown network state. For $i \in \mathcal{N}$, let R_i^s denote the rate of the single encoded layer transmitted by user i in the outage approach. In any given transmission block, if the rate R_i^s lies in the achievable rate region of the actual network state, it will be successively decoded by the receiver. Otherwise, an outage occurs where the receiver fails to decode the message of user i, and the transmitter attempts to re-transmit the same message in the subsequent transmission block using the same encoding rate R_i^s. We define $r_i^s(t)$ as the service rate of the queue at user i under the single-layer transmission, the encoding rate of the codeword transmitted by user i in transmission block t and successively decoded by the receiver, hence removed from user i's queue. Furthermore, we denote by p_i^s the probability of successfully decoding a message of rate R_i^s from user i. Accordingly, the service rate of the queue at transmitter i using the outage approach is given by

$$r_i^s(t) = \begin{cases} R_i^s, & \text{with probability} \quad p_i^s \\ 0, & \text{with probability} \quad 1 - p_i^s \end{cases} . \tag{19}$$

Finally, we define Q_i^s as the queuing size at transmitter i under the single-layer transmission approach summarized above. In Lemma 1, we characterize lower and upper bounds on the average $\mathbb{E}[Q_i^s]$ using an approach similar to that used to characterize the bounds in Theorem 2.

Lemma 1. *The average queue size of transmitter i under single layer (outage) approach is lower and upper bounded according to:*

$$\frac{1}{2}R_i^s - \frac{\lambda_i}{2} - \frac{(R_i^s - \lambda_i)^2 - R_i^s(1 - p_i^s)}{2(p_i^s R_i^s - \lambda_i)} \le \mathbb{E}[Q_i^s] \le R_i^s - \lambda_i - \frac{(R_i^s - \lambda_i)^2 - R_i^s(1 - p_i^s)}{2(p_i^s R_i^s - \lambda_i)} . \tag{20}$$

Proof. Follows the same argument as that in Appendix C. □

In Theorem 2 and Lemma 1, we remark that the characterized bounds on the average queuing delay at each transmitter depend only on the arrival rate at the same node. Therefore, the effect of the average arrival rate on the delay bounds in (17) or (20) can be analyzed for each node i independently. In Theorem 3, while fixing the average achievable rates at each user among both approaches, we show that as the arrival rate λ_i at each user increases, the proposed multi-access approach lower rate of increase in the average queuing delay with respect to that achieved by the single layer approach.

Theorem 3. *For the N-user multiple access channel, given that*

$$\mathbb{E}[r_i] = \mathbb{E}[r_i^s] , \tag{21}$$

the rate of increase of average delay with respect the arrival rate under the approach in Section 3 is lower than that achieved by single-layer outage approach, i.e., for every $i \in \mathcal{N}$

$$\frac{\partial \mathbb{E}[Q_i]}{\partial \lambda_i} \le \frac{\partial \mathbb{E}[Q_i^s]}{\partial \lambda_i} . \tag{22}$$

Proof. See Appendix D. □

4.2. Stochastic Arrivals

In this section, we consider the proposed multi-layer superposition coding policy presented in Section 3 under Poisson distributed random arrivals $A_i \sim Pois(\lambda_i)$. We adopt the same queuing model in which each transmitter applies zero-padding in case the available bits in its queue are fewer than the size of a transmitted packet. Therefore, under Poisson distributed arrivals, the considered model constitutes an $M/G/1$ queuing model with an average arrival rate λ_i and service rate r_i specified in (15). Furthermore, we denote the queue utilization at transmitter i by $\rho_i \triangleq \frac{\lambda_i}{\mathbb{E}[r_i]}$. The average queue length for an $M/G/1$

queue can be characterized in a closed form by directly applying the Pollaczek-Khinchin formula. Theorem 4 formally states the average queuing size under the proposed layering and decoding approach.

Theorem 4. *According to the multi-access approach outlined in Section 3, the average queue length at user i with Poisson distributed arrivals with the average rate λ_i is given by*

$$\mathbb{E}[Q_i] = \rho_i + \frac{\rho_i^2 + \lambda_i \mathbb{V}[r_i]}{2(1-\rho_i)}, \tag{23}$$

where the average service rate $\mathbb{E}[r_i]$ is given by (15) and the variance of the service rate $\mathbb{V}[r_i]$ is

$$\begin{aligned} \mathbb{V}[r_i] = &-\mathbb{E}[r_i] + \mathbb{P}\left[\mathcal{E}\left(\bar{\mathcal{S}}_0^i\right)\right](R_{10}^i)^2 + \mathbb{P}\left[\mathcal{E}\left(\mathcal{S}_N^i\right)\right] \cdot \left(\sum_{j=1}^{2}\sum_{k=1}^{N} R_{jk}^i\right)^2 \\ &+ \sum_{\ell=1}^{N-1} \mathbb{P}\left[\mathcal{E}\left(\mathcal{S}_\ell^i\right)\right] \cdot \left(\sum_{j=1}^{2}\sum_{k=0}^{\ell-1} R_{jk}^i + R_{2\ell}^i\right)^2 + \sum_{\ell=1}^{N-1} \mathbb{P}\left[\mathcal{E}\left(\bar{\mathcal{S}^i}_\ell\right)\right] \cdot \left(\sum_{j=1}^{2}\sum_{k=0}^{\ell-1} R_{jk}^i + R_{1\ell}^i\right)^2. \end{aligned} \tag{24}$$

Proof. Follows by applying Pollaczek-Khinchin formula for the M/G/1 average queue size [54], where the service rate of queue i is given by r_i. □

We remark that the proof of Theorem 3 implies that the proposed approach outperforms the single-layer outage approach in the case of Poisson arrivals as well, under equal average achievable rates. This result can be readily verified given that the proof in Appendix D essentially boils down to showing that the variance of the service rate (transmission rate) at each queue, $\mathbb{V}[r_i]$, is higher in the case of single-layer outage approach when compared to the proposed multi-layer approach.

5. ℓ-State Channel Multi-Access

In this section, we generalize the multi-access encoding and decoding approach outlined in Section 3 from the special case of 2-state channel, $\{$*weak*, *strong*$\}$, to channel with an arbitrary number of states ℓ. We denote the channel states by $\{\alpha_1, \ldots, \alpha_\ell\}$. Without loss of generality, we assume that $0 < \alpha_1 < \cdots < \alpha_\ell < +\infty$. Similarly to Section 2, we consider a slowly fading non-orthogonal multiple access channel model with N-transmitters and one receiver. The channel power gain of each user i can randomly take one of ℓ-states, i.e., $h_i^2 \in \{\alpha_1, \ldots, \alpha_\ell\}$.

In the layering approach in Section 3.1, we ordered the network state according to the number of users experiencing a *strong* channel state. Subsequently, each user splits its message into $2N$ layers, and the receiver decodes the layers adapted to the actual network state. Similarly, for the ℓ-state channel, we order the combined network state according to the number of users in the network sharing a particular state α_j as well as the value of such a state. In particular, a combined network state is degraded with respect to another state if it has a strictly smaller sum-rate capacity. We define the column vector $\boldsymbol{h} \triangleq [h_1^2, \ldots, h_N^2]^T$ as the the combined network state and consider that a network state $\boldsymbol{h}$ to be degraded with respect to network state $\tilde{\boldsymbol{h}}$ if and only if

$$\|\boldsymbol{h}\|_1 < \|\tilde{\boldsymbol{h}}\|_1. \tag{25}$$

The motivation of such ordering stems from the fact the condition in (25) indicates the state $\tilde{\boldsymbol{h}}$ allows higher sum-rate capacity in an N-user MAC with full CSIT. In order to overcome the absence of full CSIT at each user, a transmitter splits its message into a finite number of layers, each adapted to the combined network state to avoid complete outages. Similarly to Section 3.1, user i encodes an available message using $(\ell-1)N+1$ independent random Gaussian codebooks. The codewords of these codebooks are denoted by U_{jk}^i. For layer U_{jk}^i, $j \in \{1, \ldots, \ell\}$ denotes the channel state of user i, that is $h_i^2 = \alpha_j$, while

$k \in \{0, \ldots, N-1\}$ denotes the number of users in the network with stronger channel state, i.e., $k = \sum_{i=1}^{N} I(h_i^2 > \alpha_j)$ where $I(x)$ is the indicator function.

According to the layering approach outlined above, the receiver attempts to successively decode up to $N((\ell-1)N+1)$ depending on the exact combined network state $\boldsymbol{h}$. In particular, when the actual network state is $\boldsymbol{h}$, the receiver decodes for each user i layer U_{jk}^i adapted to network state $\boldsymbol{h}$ in addition to all the layers adapted to all degraded network states $\tilde{\boldsymbol{h}}$ such that (25) is satisfied. The number of layers decoded for user i at the receiver increases from network state $\boldsymbol{h}$ to network state $\hat{\boldsymbol{h}}$ either if its own channel state becomes stronger or if the number of users experiencing channels strictly stronger than h_i^2 increases.

Given a network state $\boldsymbol{h}$, the receiver employs up to M stages of successive decoding, where M denotes the argument of the strongest channel gain in the network, i.e., $M \triangleq \arg \| \boldsymbol{h} \|_\infty$. In stage $n \in \{1, \ldots, M\}$, the receiver successively decodes up to one layer for each user according to a descending order of the channel states among users. The details of the proposed decoding order for the ℓ-state channel are outlined in Algorithm 2.

Algorithm 2: Successive Decoding for ℓ-state channel

1: **input** $\boldsymbol{h}$
2: **set** $k_i = \sum_{d=1}^{N} I(h_d^2 > \alpha_i), \forall i \in \mathcal{N}, \quad M \triangleq \arg \| \boldsymbol{h} \|_\infty$
3: **for** $m \in \{1, \ldots, M\}$
4: Successively decode $\{U_{mk_i}^i : h_i^2 \geq \alpha_m, \ \forall i \in \mathcal{N}\}$.
5: **end for**

We remark that according to the proposed layering approach for the ℓ-state channel and decoding approach in Algorithm 2, the total number of layers decoded by the receiver from each user i is possibly different in certain network states. Although, one possible generalization of the layering policy in Section 3 is that each user adapts a different encoding layer to each possible combined channel state, which in turn requires each user to encode its message into ℓ^N layers. However, the computational complexity of the decoding process, in addition to determining the optimal power allocation among layers, is considerable as the number of users N grows larger. Therefore, we adopt the outlined layering approach where each user splits its message into $N(\ell-1)+1$ layers instead of ℓ^N layers.

6. Numerical Evaluations

In this section, we evaluate the average achievable queuing delay for each user in the MAC channel using the multi-access broadcast approach outlined in Section 3. In particular, we adopt a Monte-Carlo simulation to optimally allocate the transmission power among the encoded layers at each user such that the average queuing delay is minimized. We divide the comparison settings into two main parts according to the arrival process at each queue, where we set the arrival process to be the same among both users in each setting. The first considers deterministic arrivals with value λ. The second one considers the Poisson arrival process. Furthermore, we also consider symmetric and asymmetric channel distributions among users. Throughout this section, we set the channel gains to $\alpha_1 = 0.5$ for the weak channel and $\alpha_2 = 1$ for the strong channel gains. In the symmetric case, we set the channel probability distribution for each user as $p_1 = p_2 = 0.5$, and in the asymmetric case, we set the probabilities to $p_1 = 0.5$ and $p_2 = 0.1$. In the asymmetric model, user 2 encounters a weak channel with a high probability, i.e., $\bar{p}_2 = 0.9$. We set the objective function in this numerical simulation to minimize the sum average delays of users 1 and 2 for the broadcast approach. Subsequently, based on the obtained optimal power distribution among the layers at each user, we evaluate the resulting average delay for the outage approach such that the average rates for each user are equal across both approaches.

Figures 1 and 2 focus on deterministic arrivals in the symmetric and asymmetric channel settings. In these figures, we compare average delay versus varying arrival rate λ in the proposed broadcast approach (denoted by "Bc") and in the outage approach (denoted by "outage"). In these evaluations, we have set the SNR to $P = 10$ dB. Furthermore, in these figures, we provide upper bounds that we have characterized for the broadcast approach (denoted by "Bc_{UB}") and the outage approach (denoted by "$Outage_{UB}$"). Figures 3 and 4 depict the counterparts of these results for Poisson arrival processes. Finally, it is observed that introducing asymmetry in the models (i.e., unequal probabilities for encountering strong channels) slightly improves the average latency of the broadcast approach, whereas it does not have a notable effect in the outage approach.

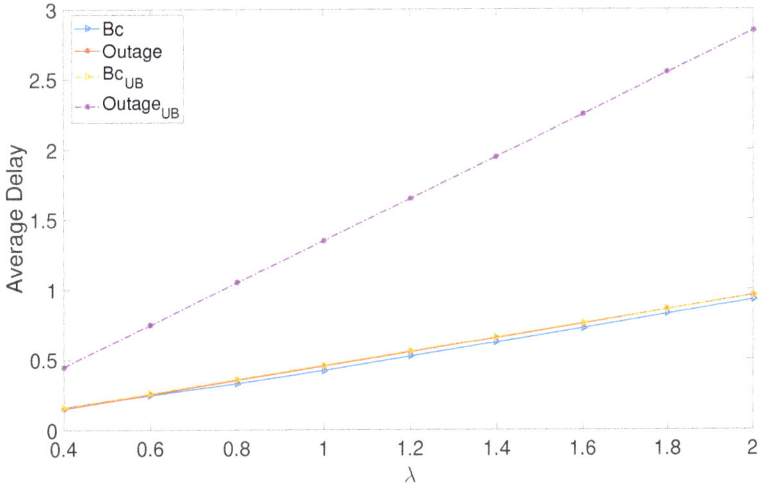

Figure 1. Deterministic: Symmetric.

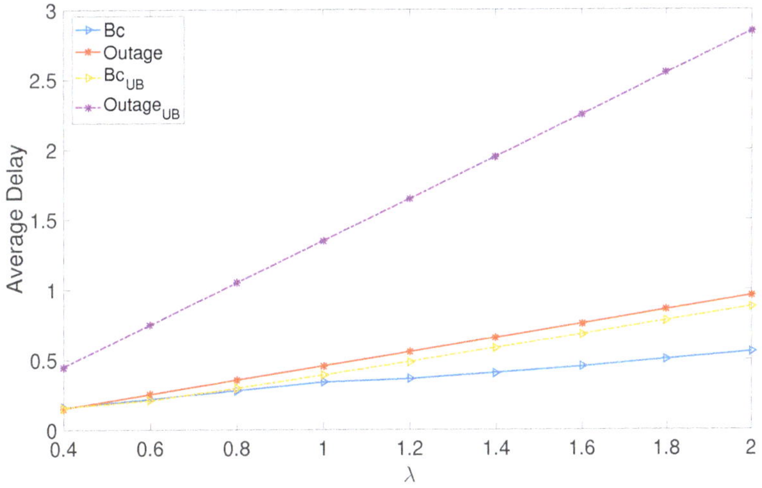

Figure 2. Deterministic: Asymmetric.

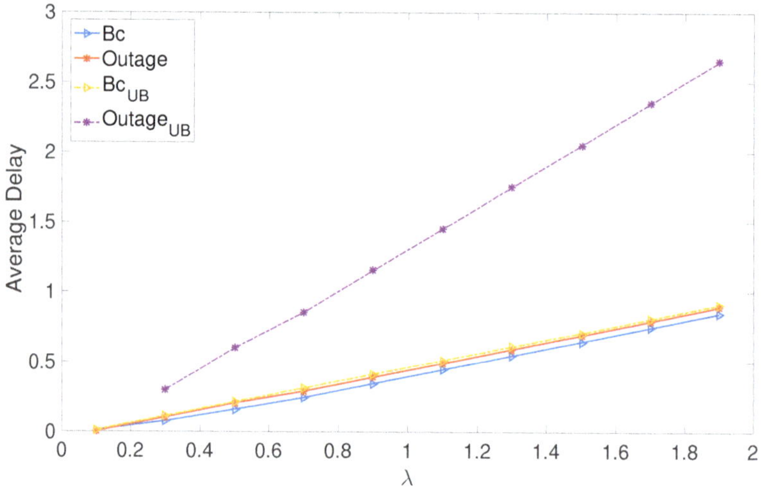

Figure 3. Poisson: Symmetric.

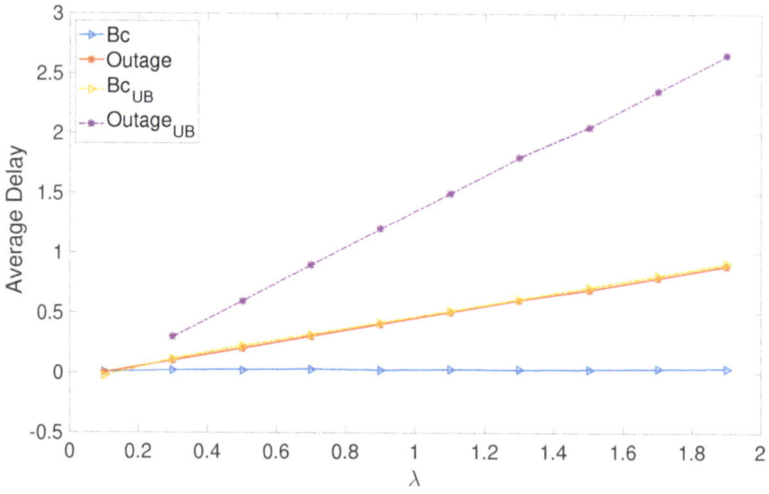

Figure 4. Poisson: Asymmetric.

The numerical evaluations support the analysis, demonstrating that the proposed broadcast approach significantly enhances the average delays of both users in the moderate and high SNR regimes for moderate and high arrival rates.

7. Concluding Remarks

In this paper, a non-orthogonal multi-access broadcast approach is employed, in which each user splits its information stream into a finite number of encoded layers, each adapted to one possible network state, serving as an outage-free low-latency transmission scheme. In particular, the average queuing delay of each user under the proposed multi-access approach is analyzed for different arrival processes at each transmitter. First, for deterministic arrivals, closed-form lower and upper bounds on the average delay are derived analytically. Secondly, for Poisson arrival rates, the average queuing delay is characterized in a closed form. The latency advantage of the proposed approach compared to the single-layer transmission is shown analytically. Finally, we note that in this paper, our focus has been on the discrete channel models since it provides a setting based on which the key ideas (specifically information layering and decoding strategy) can be described clearly and in detail. In order to gain insight into the behavior in the continuous channel models, by increasing the number of channel states in the limit of an infinite number of states, the models converge to a continuous model, and the codebook assignments and decoding strategy converge to their counterparts for continuous channels (larger number of codebooks with low rates).

Author Contributions: All authors have contributed equally to the manuscript. All authors have read and agreed to the published version of the manuscript.

Funding: The work of A. Tajer has been supported in part by the U.S. Nationa Science Foundation grant ECCS-1933107. The work of S. Shamai (Shitz) has been supported by the European Union's Horizon 2020 Research And Innovation Programme, grant agreement no. 694630.

Conflicts of Interest: The authors declare no conflict of interest.

Appendix A. Constants of Theorem 1

$\forall i \in \mathcal{N}:$

$$d^i_{10}(\phi) \triangleq C\left(\alpha_1\beta^i_{10}, N\alpha_1 - \sum_{j=1}^{i}\alpha_1\beta^j_{10}\right). \tag{A1}$$

$\forall m \in \mathcal{S}_k:$

$$d^m_{10}(\mathcal{S}_k) \triangleq C\left(\alpha_2\beta^m_{10}, (N-k)\alpha_1 + k\alpha_2 - \sum_{j\in\mathcal{S}_k, j\leq k(m)} \alpha_2(1-\beta^j_{10})\right), \tag{A2}$$

$$d^m_{11}(\mathcal{S}_k) \triangleq C\left(\alpha_2\beta^m_{11}, (N-k)\alpha_1 + k\alpha_2 - \sum_{j\in\mathcal{S}_k}\alpha_2\beta^j_{10} - \sum_{j\notin\mathcal{S}_k}\alpha_1\beta^j_{1k} - \sum_{j\in\mathcal{S}_k, j\leq k(m)} \alpha_2\beta^j_{11})\right), \tag{A3}$$

$$d^m_{21}(\mathcal{S}_k) \triangleq C\Bigg(\alpha_2\beta^m_{21}, (N-k)\alpha_1 + k\alpha_2 - \sum_{j\in\mathcal{S}_k}\alpha_2(\beta^j_{10}+\beta^j_{11})$$
$$- \sum_{j\notin\mathcal{S}_k}\alpha_1(\beta^j_{1k}+\beta^j_{2(k-1)}) - \sum_{j\in\mathcal{S}_k, j\leq k(m)} \alpha_2\beta^j_{21})\Bigg) \tag{A4}$$

$\forall m \in \mathcal{S}_k$ and $\ell \in \{1,\ldots,k\}$:

$$d^m_{1\ell}(\mathcal{S}_k) \triangleq C\Bigg(\alpha_2\beta^m_{1\ell}, (N-k)\alpha_1 + k\alpha_2 - \sum_{j\in\mathcal{S}_k}\alpha_2\beta^j_{10} - \sum_{j\in\mathcal{S}_k}\sum_{i=1}^{\ell-1}\alpha_2(\beta^j_{1i}+\beta^j_{2i})$$
$$- \sum_{j\notin\mathcal{S}_k}\alpha_1\sum_{i=1}^{\ell-1}(\beta^j_{1(k-i+1)}+\beta^j_{2(k-i+1)}) - \sum_{j\in\mathcal{S}_k, j\leq k(m)} \alpha_2\beta^j_{1\ell}\Bigg), \tag{A5}$$

$$d^m_{2\ell}(\mathcal{S}_k) \triangleq C\Bigg(\alpha_2\beta^m_{2\ell}, (N-k)\alpha_1 + k\alpha_2 - \sum_{j\in\mathcal{S}_k}\alpha_2\beta^j_{10} - \sum_{j\in\mathcal{S}_k}\sum_{i=1}^{\ell}\alpha_2\beta^j_{1i} - \sum_{j\in\mathcal{S}_k}\sum_{i=1}^{\ell-1}\alpha_2\beta^j_{2i}$$
$$- \sum_{j\notin\mathcal{S}_k}\alpha_1\sum_{i=1}^{\ell}(\beta^j_{1(k-i+1)}+\beta^j_{2(k-i+1)}) - \sum_{j\in\mathcal{S}_k, j\leq k(m)} \alpha_2\beta^j_{2\ell}\Bigg). \tag{A6}$$

$\forall n \notin \mathcal{S}_k$ and $\ell \in \{1, \ldots, k\}$:

$$d^n_{1(k-\ell+1)}(\mathcal{S}_k) \triangleq C\Bigg(\alpha_1 \beta^n_{1(k-\ell+1)}, (N-k)\alpha_1 + k\alpha_2 - \sum_{j\in\mathcal{S}_k} \alpha_2 \beta^j_{10} - \sum_{j\in\mathcal{S}_k}\sum_{i=1}^{\ell-1} \alpha_2(\beta^j_{1i} + \beta^j_{2i}) - \sum_{j\notin\mathcal{S}_k} \alpha_1 \sum_{i=1}^{\ell-1}(\beta^j_{1(k-i+1)} + \beta^j_{2(k-i+1)}) - \sum_{j\notin\mathcal{S}_k, j\leq \bar{k}(n)} \alpha_1 \beta^j_{1(k-\ell+1)})\Bigg), \tag{A7}$$

$$d^n_{2(k-\ell)}(\mathcal{S}_k) \triangleq C\Bigg(\alpha_1 \beta^n_{2(k-\ell)}, (N-k)\alpha_1 + k\alpha_2 - \sum_{j\in\mathcal{S}_k} \alpha_2 \beta^j_{10} - \sum_{j\in\mathcal{S}_k}\sum_{i=1}^{\ell} \alpha_2 \beta^j_{1i} - \sum_{j\in\mathcal{S}_k}\sum_{i=1}^{\ell-1} \alpha_2 \beta^j_{2i} - \sum_{j\notin\mathcal{S}_k}\sum_{i=1}^{\ell} \alpha_1 \beta^j_{1(k-i+1} - \sum_{j\notin\mathcal{S}_k}\sum_{i=1}^{\ell-1} \alpha_1 \beta^j_{2(k-i+1)} - \sum_{j\notin\mathcal{S}_k, j\leq \bar{k}(n)} \alpha_1 \beta^j_{2(k-\ell)})\Bigg). \tag{A8}$$

Appendix B. Proof of Theorem 1

The rate region characterized in Theorem 1 is achievable by employing the layering scheme in Section 3.1 at each transmitter combined with the successive decoding strategy in Algorithm 1. Recall that the maximum rate of codeword U^i_{jk}, for each user $i \in \mathcal{N}$ channel $j \in \{1, 2\}$, and $k \in \{0 \cup \mathcal{N}\}$, is bounded by the minimum achievable rate for that codebook in all combined network states during which it is decoded.

We define $\mathcal{S}$ as the set of users' indices that are experiencing a *strong* states. This set is known to the receiver. Accordingly, we define $\mathcal{S}_k$ as a realization of S that contains exactly k users, i.e., k users have strong channels and $N-k$ users have weak channels. Next, we discuss $\mathcal{S}_0$ and $\mathcal{S}_k$ for $k \in \mathcal{N}$, separately.

$|\mathcal{S}| = 0$: All channels are weak

In the event of a network state with all channels in the weak state, $h^2_i = \alpha_1$, $\forall i \in \mathcal{N}$, the receiver decodes only one layer per user. Specifically, it decodes $\{U^i_{10} : i \in \mathcal{N}\}$. It performs successive decoding, starting from user 1 and continuing in the ascending order of users' indices. In order to successfully decode layers $\{U^i_{10} : i \in \mathcal{N}\}$, the rate of each layer $i \in \mathcal{N}$ should satisfy:

$$\forall i \in \mathcal{N}: \qquad R^i_{10} \leq C\left(\alpha_1 \beta^i_{10}, N\alpha_1 - \sum_{j=1}^{i} \alpha_1 \beta^j_{10}\right) \triangleq d^i_{10}(\phi). \tag{A9}$$

Note that the second argument $C(x, y)$ represents the undecoded layers that will be treated as interference for layer U^i_{10}. Hence, based on the successive decoding procedure, when the receiver decodes U^i_{10}, layers U^i_{10} for users $j \in \{1, \ldots, i-1\}$ have already been decoded. Thus, their interference is subtracted from the total transmitted signal, accounted by the term $1 - \beta^j_{10}$. On the other hand, none of the layers transmitted by users $j \in \{i+1, \ldots, N\}$ have been decoded yet, which is accounted by the term $(N-i)\alpha_1$.

Next, we will characterize upper bounds on the achievable rates of all the layers decoded when there are exactly k users with strong channels, i.e., $|\mathcal{S}| = k$.

$|\mathcal{S}| = k$: k channels are strong

As discussed earlier, when $|\mathcal{S}| = k$, the receiver employs $4k+1$ decoding stages. For this purpose, the set of codebooks $\{U^i_{j\ell} : i \in \mathcal{N}\}$ is partitioned to two sets

$$\mathcal{P}_{j\ell} \triangleq \{U^i_{j\ell} : i \in \mathcal{S}\} \qquad \text{and} \qquad \mathcal{Q}_{j\ell} \triangleq \{U^i_{j\ell} : i \notin \mathcal{S}\}, \tag{A10}$$

rendering a total of $4k+1$ partitions for different $j \in \{1, 2\}$ and $\ell \in \{0, \ldots, k\}$. The decoding strategy, decodes one message from each of these, except for the partition $\{U^i_{2k} : i \notin \mathcal{S}\}$. The decoding strategy works as follows. We create the following two sequences of sets:

$$\mathcal{P} \triangleq \{\mathcal{P}_{10}, \mathcal{P}_{11}, \mathcal{P}_{21}, \ldots, \mathcal{P}_{2(k-1)}, \mathcal{P}_{1k}, \}, \tag{A11}$$

$$\mathcal{Q} \triangleq \{\mathcal{Q}_{1k}, \mathcal{Q}_{2(k-1)}, \mathcal{Q}_{1(k-1)}, \ldots, \mathcal{Q}_{11}, \mathcal{Q}_{10}, \}. \tag{A12}$$

The decoding strategy selects codebooks by alternating between $\mathcal{P}$ and $\mathcal{Q}$ an an ascending order and decodes exactly one codebook from each. This results in $4k$ coding stages. Finally, the codebooks in $\{U^i_{2k} : i \in \mathcal{S}\}$ are decoded as the last stage, i.e., stage $4k+1$.

- **Decoding stage** 1:
  We start by decoding the layers $\mathcal{P}_{10} \triangleq \{U^i_{10} : i \in \mathcal{S}\}$. Recall that $\mathcal{S}_k$ was defined as an ordered set of these users. The codebooks will be decoded sequentially in this order. When $m \in \mathcal{S}_k$, we denote the position of m in $\mathcal{S}_k$ by $k(m)$. Hence, $\forall m \in \mathcal{S}_k$

$$R^m_{10} \leq C\left(\alpha_2\beta^m_{10}, (N-k)\alpha_1 + k\alpha_2 - \sum_{j\in\mathcal{S}_k, j\leq k(m)} \alpha_2(1-\beta^j_{10})\right) \triangleq d^m_{10}(\mathcal{S}_k)\,. \tag{A13}$$

- **Decoding stage** 2:
  Next, we sequentially decode the layers in $\mathcal{Q}_{1k} = \{U^i_{1k} : i \notin \mathcal{S}\}$, which involves layers U^i_{1k} of users with weak channels. When $n \notin \mathcal{S}_k$, we denote the position of n in the ordered set $\mathcal{N}\backslash\mathcal{S}_k$ by $\bar{k}(n)$. Hence, $\forall n \notin \mathcal{S}_k$

$$R^n_{1k} \leq C\left(\alpha_1\beta^n_{1k}, (N-k)\alpha_1 + k\alpha_2 - \sum_{j\in\mathcal{S}_k} \alpha_2\beta^j_{10} - \sum_{j\notin\mathcal{S}_k, j<\bar{k}(n)} \alpha_1\beta^j_{1k}\right) \triangleq d^n_{1k}(\mathcal{S}_k)\,. \tag{A14}$$

- **Decoding stage** 3:
  In the third stage, the codebooks in $\mathcal{P}_{10}$ and $\mathcal{Q}_{1k}$ are already decoded. We continue by sequentially decoding the set of codebooks in $\mathcal{P}_{11} \triangleq \{U^i_{11} : i \in \mathcal{S}\}$. Hence, $\forall m \in \mathcal{S}_k$

$$R^m_{11} \leq C\left(\alpha_2\beta^m_{11}, (N-k)\alpha_1 + k\alpha_2 - \sum_{j\in\mathcal{S}_k} \alpha_2\beta^j_{10} - \sum_{j\notin\mathcal{S}_k} \alpha_1\beta^j_{1k} - \sum_{j\in\mathcal{S}_k, j\leq k(m)} \alpha_2\beta^j_{11})\right) \triangleq d^m_{11}(\mathcal{S}_k)\,. \tag{A15}$$

- **Decoding stage** 4:
  The decoding process continues by sequentially decoding the codebooks in $\mathcal{Q}_{2(k-1)} = \{U^i_{2(k-1)} : i \notin \mathcal{S}\}$, while the codebooks of $\mathcal{P}_{10}$, $\mathcal{Q}_{1k}$, and $\mathcal{P}_{11}$ are already decoded. Hence, for $n \notin \mathcal{S}_k$

$$\begin{aligned} R^n_{2(k-1)} \leq C\Bigg(&\alpha_1\beta^n_{2(k-1)}, (N-k)\alpha_1 + k\alpha_2 - \sum_{j\in\mathcal{S}_k} \alpha_2(\beta^j_{10} + \beta^j_{11}) \\ &- \sum_{j\notin\mathcal{S}_k} \alpha_1\beta^j_{1k} - \sum_{j\notin\mathcal{S}_k, j\leq\bar{k}(n)} \alpha_1\beta^j_{2(k-1)})\Bigg) \triangleq d^n_{2(k-1)}(\mathcal{S}_k)\,. \end{aligned} \tag{A16}$$

- **Decoding stage** 5:
  This stage sequentially decodes the codebooks $\mathcal{P}_{21}$. For all $m \in \mathcal{S}^i_k$ we have

$$\begin{aligned} R^m_{21} \leq C\Bigg(&\alpha_2\beta^m_{21}, (N-k)\alpha_1 + k\alpha_2 - \sum_{j\in\mathcal{S}_k} \alpha_2(\beta^j_{10} + \beta^j_{11}) \\ &- \sum_{j\notin\mathcal{S}_k} \alpha_1(\beta^j_{1k} + \beta^j_{2(k-1)}) - \sum_{j\in\mathcal{S}_k, j\leq k(m)} \alpha_2\beta^j_{21})\Bigg) \triangleq d^m_{21}(\mathcal{S}_k)\,. \end{aligned} \tag{A17}$$

- **Decoding stage** 6:
  This stage sequentially decodes the codebooks in $\mathcal{Q}_{1(k-1)}$. Hence, $\forall n \notin \mathcal{S}_k$ we have

$$R^n_{1(k-1)} \leq C\Bigg(\alpha_1\beta^n_{1(k-1)}, (N-k)\alpha_1 + k\alpha_2 - \sum_{j\in\mathcal{S}_k}\alpha_2(\beta^j_{10}+\beta^j_{11}+\beta^j_{21}) - \sum_{j\notin\mathcal{S}_k}\alpha_1(\beta^j_{1k}+\beta^j_{2(k-1)}) - \sum_{j\notin\mathcal{S}_k, j\leq\bar{k}(n)}\alpha_1\beta^j_{1(k-1)}\Bigg) \triangleq d^n_{1(k-1)}(\mathcal{S}_k)\,. \tag{A18}$$

- **Decoding stages $\{2,\ldots,4k+1\}$:**
  Following the pattern of the previous decoding stages, in general in the stage $\{2,\ldots,4k\}$, we decode the codebooks according to the following schedule, for $\ell \in \{1,\ldots,k\}$:

$$\begin{array}{ll} \text{codebooks in } \mathcal{Q}_{1(k-\ell+1)} & \text{stage} \quad 4\ell-2 \\ \text{codebooks in } \mathcal{P}_{1\ell} & \text{stage} \quad 4\ell-1 \\ \text{codebooks in } \mathcal{Q}_{2(k-\ell)} & \text{stage} \quad 4\ell \\ \text{codebooks in } \mathcal{P}_{2\ell} & \text{stage} \quad 4\ell+1 \end{array} \tag{A19}$$

  Accordingly, we obtain the following rate constraints.

- **Decoding stage $4\ell-2$:**

  By sequentially decoding the messages in $\mathcal{Q}_{1(k-\ell+1)}$, $\forall n \notin \mathcal{S}_k$ we have

$$R^n_{1(k-\ell+1)} \leq C\Bigg(\alpha_1\beta^n_{1(k-\ell+1)}, (N-k)\alpha_1 + k\alpha_2 - \sum_{j\in\mathcal{S}_k}\alpha_2\beta^j_{10} - \sum_{j\in\mathcal{S}_k}\sum_{i=1}^{\ell-1}\alpha_2(\beta^j_{1i}+\beta^j_{2i}) - \sum_{j\notin\mathcal{S}_k}\alpha_1\sum_{i=1}^{\ell-1}(\beta^j_{1(k-i+1)}+\beta^j_{2(k-i+1)}) - \sum_{j\notin\mathcal{S}_k, j\leq\bar{k}(n)}\alpha_1\beta^j_{1(k-\ell+1)}\Bigg) \triangleq d^n_{1(k-\ell+1)}(\mathcal{S}_k)\,. \tag{A20}$$

- **Decoding stage $4\ell-1$:**
  By sequentially decoding the messages in $\mathcal{P}_{1\ell}$, $\forall m \in \mathcal{S}_k$ we have

$$R^m_{1\ell} \leq C\Bigg(\alpha_2\beta^m_{1\ell}, (N-k)\alpha_1 + k\alpha_2 - \sum_{j\in\mathcal{S}_k}\alpha_2\beta^j_{10} - \sum_{j\in\mathcal{S}_k}\sum_{i=1}^{\ell-1}\alpha_2(\beta^j_{1i}+\beta^j_{2i}) - \sum_{j\notin\mathcal{S}_k}\alpha_1\sum_{i=1}^{\ell-1}(\beta^j_{1(k-i+1)}+\beta^j_{2(k-i+1)}) - \sum_{j\in\mathcal{S}_k, j\leq k(m)}\alpha_2\beta^j_{1\ell}\Bigg) \triangleq d^m_{1\ell}(\mathcal{S}_k)\,. \tag{A21}$$

- **Decoding stage 4ℓ:**

  By sequentially decoding the messages in $\mathcal{Q}_{1(k-\ell)}$, $\forall n \notin \mathcal{S}_k$ we have

$$R^n_{2(k-\ell)} \leq C\Bigg(\alpha_1\beta^n_{2(k-\ell)}, (N-k)\alpha_1 + k\alpha_2 - \sum_{j\in\mathcal{S}_k}\alpha_2\beta^j_{10} - \sum_{j\in\mathcal{S}_k}\sum_{i=1}^{\ell}\alpha_2\beta^j_{1i} - \sum_{j\in\mathcal{S}_k}\sum_{i=1}^{\ell-1}\alpha_2\beta^j_{2i} - \sum_{j\notin\mathcal{S}_k}\sum_{i=1}^{\ell}\alpha_1\beta^j_{1(k-i+1} - \sum_{j\notin\mathcal{S}_k}\sum_{i=1}^{\ell-1}\alpha_1\beta^j_{2(k-i+1)} - \sum_{j\notin\mathcal{S}_k, j\leq\bar{k}(n)}\alpha_1\beta^j_{2(k-\ell)}\Bigg) \triangleq d^n_{2(k-\ell)}(\mathcal{S}_k)\,. \tag{A22}$$

- **Decoding stage $4\ell+1$:**
  By sequentially decoding the messages in $\mathcal{P}_{2\ell}$, $\forall m \in \mathcal{S}_k$ we have

$$R^m_{2\ell} \leq C\Bigg(\alpha_2\beta^m_{2\ell},(N-k)\alpha_1 + k\alpha_2 - \sum_{j\in\mathcal{S}_k}\alpha_2\beta^j_{10} - \sum_{j\in\mathcal{S}_k}\sum_{i=1}^{\ell}\alpha_2\beta^j_{1i} - \sum_{j\in\mathcal{S}_k}\sum_{i=1}^{\ell-1}\alpha_2\beta^j_{2i}$$
$$- \sum_{j\notin\mathcal{S}_k}\alpha_1\sum_{i=1}^{\ell}(\beta^j_{1(k-i+1)} + \beta^j_{2(k-i+1)}) - \sum_{j\in\mathcal{S}_k, j\leq k(m)}\alpha_2\beta^j_{2\ell}\Bigg) \triangleq d^m_{2\ell}(\mathcal{S}_k)\,. \tag{A23}$$

Given the upper bounds on the individual achievable rates of $U^i_{jk}, \forall i \in \mathcal{N}, j \in 1,2,$ $k \in \{0 \cup \mathcal{N}\}$, the maximum achievable rate of U^i_{jk} is bounded my the minimum upper bound among all the network states within which it is decoded.

Appendix C. Proof of Theorem 2

By applying a change of variable to each term and taking the integral $\int_0^\infty e^{-sq}dF_1(q)$ as a common factor, $L_1(s)$ can be expressed as

$$L_1(s) = \frac{F_1(0) - \int_{0^+}^{(\sum_{ij}R^1_{ij}-\lambda_1)} e^{-s(q+(\lambda_1-\sum_{ij}R^1_{ij}))}dF_1(q)}{1-[\bar{p}_1\bar{p}_2e^{-s(\lambda_1-\sum_{ij}R^1_{ij})} + \bar{p}_1p_2e^{-s(\lambda_1-R^1_{11}-R^1_{21}))} + p_1\bar{p}_2e^{-s(\lambda_1-R^1_{11}-R^1_{12}))} + p_1p_2e^{-s(\lambda_1-R^1_{11}))}]} \tag{A24}$$

Further, by using the definition of $F_1(0) = \bar{p}_1\bar{p}_2F_1(q-(\lambda_1-\sum_{ij}R^1_{ij}))$ and multiplying the numerator and denominator of (A24) by a common factor, $e^{-s(\sum_{ij}R^1_{ij}-\lambda_1)}$, we have.

$$\begin{aligned} L_1(s) &= \frac{\bar{p}_1\bar{p}_2[\int_0^{(\sum_{ij}R^1_{ij}-\lambda_1)} e^{-s(\sum_{ij}R^1_{ij}-\lambda_1)} - e^{-sq}dF_1(q)]}{e^{-s(\sum_{ij}R^1_{ij}-\lambda_1)} - [\bar{p}_1\bar{p}_2 + \bar{p}_1p_2e^{-s(R^1_{12}+R^1_{22}))} + p_1\bar{p}_2e^{-s(R^1_{21}+R^1_{22}))} + p_1p_2e^{-s(R^1_{21}+R^1_{12}+R^1_{22}))}]} \\ &\triangleq \frac{D_1(s)}{N_1(s)}\,. \end{aligned} \tag{A25}$$

It can be readily noticed from (A25) that $\lim_{s\to0} D_1(s) = \lim_{s\to0} N_1(s) = 0$, therefore we apply L'hopital's limit rule on (A25) to arrive at

$$\mathbb{E}[Q_1] = \lim_{s\to0}\frac{D''_{Q_1}(s) - N''_{Q_1}(s)}{2D'_{Q_1}(s)}\,. \tag{A26}$$

Finally, we evaluate the terms $D''_{Q_1}(s)$, $N''_{Q_1}(s)$ and $D'_{Q_1}(s)$ where we have

$$\lim_{s\to0} D'_{Q_1}(s) = -(\sum_{ij}R^1_{ij}-\lambda_1) + \bar{p}_1p_2(R^1_{12}+R^1_{22}) + p_1\bar{p}_2(R^1_{12}+R^1_{22}) + p_1p_2(R^1_{12}+R^1_{21}+R^1_{22}) \tag{A27}$$

$$\lim_{s\to0} D''_{Q_1}(s) = (\sum_{ij}R^1_{ij}-\lambda_1)^2 - \bar{p}_1p_2(R^1_{12}+R^1_{22})^2 - p_1\bar{p}_2(R^1_{12}+R^1_{22})^2 - p_1p_2(R^1_{12}+R^1_{21}+R^1_{22})^2\,, \tag{A28}$$

and

$$\lim_{s\to0} N''_{Q_1}(s) = \bar{p}_1\bar{p}_2\int_0^{(\sum_{ij}R^1_{ij}-\lambda_1)}[(\sum_{ij}R^1_{ij}-\lambda_1)^2 - q^2]dF_1(q)\,. \tag{A29}$$

Finally, by using $\lim_{s\to0} D'_1(s) = \lim_{s\to0} N'_1(s)$, the second derivative of the numerator term can be upper bounded by replacing $(\sum_{ij}R^1_{ij}-\lambda_1+q)$ by $2(\sum_{ij}R^1_{ij}-\lambda_1)$ arriving at

$$\lim_{s\to 0} N''_{Q_1}(s) \leq 2(\sum_{ij} R^1_{ij} - \lambda_1)\Bigg(\sum_{ij} R^1_{ij} - \lambda_1$$
$$-\bar{p}_1 p_2(R^1_{12} + R^1_{22}) - p_1\bar{p}_2(R^1_{12} + R^1_{22}) - p_1 p_2(R^1_{12} + R^1_{21} + R^1_{22})\Bigg). \quad \text{(A30)}$$

Next, we leverage (A26) reaching

$$\mathbb{E}[Q_i] \geq \frac{1}{2}\sum_{j=1}^{2}\sum_{k=0}^{N} R^i_{jk} - \frac{\lambda_i}{2} - \frac{N_i}{D_i},$$
$$\mathbb{E}[Q_i] \leq \sum_{j=1}^{2}\sum_{k=0}^{N} R^i_{jk} - \lambda_i - \frac{N_i}{D_i}, \quad \text{(A31)}$$

where

$$N_i \triangleq -\left(\sum_{j=1}^{2}\sum_{k=0}^{N} R^i_{jk} - \lambda_i\right)^2$$
$$+\mathbb{P}\left[\mathcal{E}\left(\bar{\mathcal{S}}^i_0\right)\right]\left(\sum_{j=1}^{2}\sum_{k=1}^{N} R^i_{jk}\right)^2$$
$$+\sum_{\ell=1}^{N-1}\mathbb{P}[\mathcal{E}(\mathcal{S}^i_\ell)]\cdot\left(\sum_{j=1}^{2}\sum_{k=\ell+1}^{N} R^i_{jk} + R^i_{1\ell}\right)^2$$
$$+\sum_{\ell=1}^{N-1}\mathbb{P}\left[\mathcal{E}\left(\bar{\mathcal{S}^i}_\ell\right)\right]\cdot\left(\sum_{j=1}^{2}\sum_{k=\ell+1}^{N} R^i_{jk} + R^i_{2\ell}\right)^2$$
$$D_i \triangleq 2(\mathbb{E}[r_i] - \lambda_i). \quad \text{(A32)}$$

Appendix D. Proof of Theorem 3

In this Appendix, we base the proof of Theorem 3 on two main steps. First, we characterize a lower bound on the average achievable rate of each user i using a single layer per user (outage approach). Secondly, we derive the rate of increase of the average achievable delay with respect to the average arrival rate λ_i (first-order derivative) for the delay upper bound of the multi-layer approach to that of the delay lower bound of the outage approach. Finally, under a fixed average achievable rate among both approaches, we show that the proposed approach outperforms the single layer outage approach.

Recalling the recursive expression for Q_i in terms of the variable Z_i in (3), a recursive form of $F_i(q)$ can be expressed as follows [52,53]

$$F_i(q) = \begin{cases} 0, & q < 0 \\ \int_{-\infty}^{q} F_i(q-\tau)dF_{Z_i}(\tau), & q \geq 0, \end{cases} \quad \text{(A33)}$$

where $dF_{Z_i}(z)$ denote pdf of Z_i.

At the end of every transmission block, the change in queue size i, Z_i, is primarily determined by the difference between the data arrival λ_i and the fixed rate successfully decoded at the receiver, which in turn is determined by the combined network state. Consequently, $dF_{Z_i}(z)$ can be expressed by

$$dF_{Z_i}(z) = P_{\text{out}}\delta(z - \lambda_i + R_{\text{F}}). \quad \text{(A34)}$$

We remark that in order to guarantee the stability of every queue i, we assume that the arrival rate λ_i is less that the average achievable rate (service rate of the queue), i.e.,

$$\lambda_i < P_{\text{out}} R_{\text{F}},\ \forall i \in \mathcal{N}. \quad \text{(A35)}$$

Combining (12) and (13), an explicit expression for $F_i(q), \forall i \in \mathcal{N}$ is given by

$$F_i(q) =$$
$$\begin{cases} 0, & \forall q < 0 \\ P_{\text{out}} F_i(q - \lambda_i + R_{\text{F}}), & \forall q \geq 0 \end{cases}. \quad \text{(A36)}$$

Finally, we evaluate the terms $D''_{Q_1}(s)$ and $N''_{Q_1}(s)$ where we have

$$\lim_{s\to 0} D''_{Q_1}(s) = (R_F - \lambda_i)^2 - (1 - P_{out})R_F^2, \tag{A37}$$

and

$$\lim_{s\to 0} N''_{Q_1}(s) = P_{out} \int_0^{R_F - \lambda_1)} [(R_F - \lambda_1)^2 - q^2] dF_1(q). \tag{A38}$$

Finally, by using $\lim_{s\to 0} D'_1(s) = \lim_{s\to 0} N'_1(s)$, the second derivative of the numerator term can be lower bounded by replacing $(F_F - \lambda_1 + q)$ by $(R_F - \lambda_1)$ arriving at

$$\lim_{s\to 0} N''_{Q_1}(s) \geq (R_F - \lambda_1)(R_F - \lambda_1 - P_{out} R_F). \tag{A39}$$

and substitute (A26) reaching

$$\mathbb{E}[Q_i] \geq \frac{1}{2} R_F - \frac{\lambda_i}{2} - \frac{N_i}{D_i}, \tag{A40}$$

where

$$\begin{aligned} N_i &\triangleq -(R_F - \lambda_i)^2 + (1 - P_{out})R_F^2 \\ D_i &\triangleq P_{out} R_F - \lambda_i. \end{aligned} \tag{A41}$$

By taking the derivative of the upper/lower bounds derived above we reach

$$\frac{\partial U_B}{\partial \lambda_i} = -1 - \frac{\sum_{j=1}^{2} \sum_{k=0}^{N} R_{jk}^i - \lambda_i}{\mathbb{E}[r_i] - \lambda_i} - 2\frac{N_i}{D_i^2}, \tag{A42}$$

$$\frac{\partial L_B}{\partial \lambda_i} = -1 - \frac{R_F - \lambda_i}{P_{out} R_F - \lambda_i} - 2\frac{-(R_F - \lambda_i)^2 + (1 - P_{out})R_F^2}{P_{out} R_F - \lambda_i}. \tag{A43}$$

References

1. *Study on Scenarios and Requirements for Next Generation Access Technologies*; ETSI: Sophia Antipolis, France, 2017.
2. Ding, Z.; Liu, Y.; Choi, J.; Sun, Q.; Elkashlan, M.; Chih-Lin, I.; Poor, H.V. Application of non-orthogonal multiple access in LTE and 5G networks. *IEEE Commun. Mag.* **2017**, *55*, 185–191. [CrossRef]
3. Ding, Z.; Lei, X.; Karagiannidis, G.K.; Schober, R.; Yuan, J.; Bhargava, V.K. A survey on non-orthogonal multiple access for 5G networks: Research challenges and future trends. *IEEE J. Sel. Areas Commun.* **2017**, *35*, 2181–2195. [CrossRef]
4. Ding, Z.; Yang, Z.; Fan, P.; Poor, H.V. On the performance of non-orthogonal multiple access in 5G systems with randomly deployed users. *IEEE Signal Process. Lett.* **2014**, *21*, 1501–1505. [CrossRef]
5. Islam, S.R.; Avazov, N.; Dobre, O.A.; Kwak, K.-S. Power-domain non-orthogonal multiple access (NOMA) in 5G systems: Potentials and challenges. *IEEE Commun. Surv. Tutor.* **2016**, *19*, 721–742. [CrossRef]
6. Benjebbovu, A.; Li, A.; Saito, Y.; Kishiyama, Y.; Harada, A.; Nakamura, T. System-level performance of downlink NOMA for future LTE enhancements. In Proceedings of the IEEE Global Communications Conference Workshops, Atlanta, GA, USA, 9–13 December 2013; pp. 66–70.
7. Wang, W.; Liu, Y.; Luo, Z.; Jiang, T.; Zhang, Q.; Nallanathan, A. Toward cross-layer design for non-orthogonal multiple access: A quality-of-experience perspective. *IEEE Wirel. Commun.* **2018**, *25*, 118–124. [CrossRef]
8. Condoluci, M.; Dohler, M.; Araniti, G.; Molinaro, A.; Sachs, J. Enhanced radio access and data transmission procedures facilitating industry-compliant machine-type communications over LTE-based 5G networks. *IEEE Wirel. Commun.* **2016**, *23*, 56–63. [CrossRef]
9. Bennis, M.; Debbah, M.; Poor, H.V. Ultrareliable and low-latency wireless communication: Tail, risk, and scale. *Proc. IEEE* **2018**, *106*, 1834–1853. [CrossRef]
10. Shamai, S.; Steiner, A. A broadcast approach for a single-user slowly fading MIMO channel. *IEEE Trans. Inf. Theory* **2003**, *49*, 2617–2635. [CrossRef]
11. Shamai, S. A broadcast strategy for the Gaussian slowly fading channel. In Proceedings of the IEEE International Symposium Information Theory, Ulm, Germany, 29 June–4 July 1997; p. 150.
12. Tajer, A.; Steiner, A.; Shamai, S. The broadcast approach in communication networks. *Entropy* **2021**, *23*, 120. [CrossRef]
13. Zohdy, M.; Tajer, A. Broadcast Approach for the Single-user Energy Harvesting Channel. *IEEE Trans. Commun.* **2019**, *67*, 3192–3204. [CrossRef]

14. Shamai, S. A broadcast approach for the multiple-access slow fading channel. In Proceedings of the IEEE International Symposium Information Theory, Sorrento, Italy, 25–30 June 2000; p. 128.
15. Minero, P.; Tse, D.N.C. A broadcast approach to multiple access with random states. In Proceedings of the IEEE International Symposium Information Theory, Nice, France, 24–29 June 2007; pp. 2566–2570.
16. Minero, P.; David, N.; Franceschetti, M. A broadcast approach to random access. In Proceedings of the IEEE Information Theory Workshop, Taormina, Italy, 11–16 October 2009; pp. 615–619.
17. Kazemi, S.; Tajer, A. Multiaccess communication via a broadcast approach adapted to the multiuser channel. *IEEE Trans. Commun.* **2018**, *66*, 3341–3353. [CrossRef]
18. Zohdy, M.; Tajer, A.; Shamai, S. Broadcast Approach to Multiple Access with Local CSIT. *IEEE Trans. Commun.* **2019**, *67*, 7483–7498. [CrossRef]
19. Kazemi, S.; Tajer, A. A broadcast approach to multiple access adapted to the multiuser channel. In Proceedings of the IEEE International Symposium on Information Theory, Aachen, Germany, 25–30 June 2017.
20. Zohdy, M.; Kazemi, S.; Tajer, A. A broadcast approach to multiple access with partial CSIT. In Proceedings of the IEEE Global Communications Conference, Abu Dhabi, United Arab Emirates, 9–13 December 2018.
21. Zohdy, M.; Tajer, A.; Shamai, S. Interference Management without CSIT: A Broadcast Approach. In Proceedings of the IEEE International Symposium on Information Theory (ISIT), Los Angeles, CA, USA, 21–26 June 2020.
22. Zohdy, M.; Tajer, A.; Shamai, S. Distributed Interference Management: A Broadcast Approach. *IEEE Trans. Commun.* **2021**, *69*, 149–163. [CrossRef]
23. Ye, N.; Wang, A.; Li, X.; Liu, W.; Hou, X.; Yu, H. Rate-adaptive multiple access for uplink grant-free transmission. *Wirel. Commun. Mob. Comput.* **2018**, *2018*, 1–21. [CrossRef]
24. Steiner, A.; Shamai, S. On queueing and multilayer coding. *IEEE Trans. Inf. Theory* **2010**, *56*, 2392–2415. [CrossRef]
25. Clerckx, B.; Mao, Y.; Jorswieck, E.A.; Yuan, J.; Love, D.J.; Erkip, E.; Niyato, D. A primer on rate-splitting multiple access: Tutorial, myths, and frequently asked questions. *arXiv* **2022**, arXiv:2209.00491.
26. Yang, J.; Ulukus, S. Delay-minimal transmission for average power constrained multi-access communications. *IEEE Trans. Wirel. Commun.* **2010**, *9*, 2754–2767. [CrossRef]
27. Yeh, E. Delay-optimal rate allocation in multiaccess communications: A cross-layer view. In Proceedings of the IEEE Workshop on Multimedia Signal Processing, St.Thomas, VI, USA, 9–11 December 2002; pp. 404–407.
28. Goyal, M.; Kumar, A.; Sharma, V. Optimal cross-layer scheduling of transmissions over a fading multiaccess channel. *IEEE Trans. Inf. Theory* **2008**, *54*, 3518–3537. [CrossRef]
29. Koseoglu, M. Lower bounds on the LTE-A average random access delay under massive M2M arrivals. *IEEE Trans. Commun.* **2016**, *64*, 2104–2115. [CrossRef]
30. Awuor, F.M.; Wang, C.-Y. Massive machine type communication in cellular system: A distributed queue approach. In Proceedings of the IEEE International Conference on Communications, Kuala Lumpur, Malaysia, 22–27 May 2016; pp. 1–7.
31. Zhao, X.; Chen, W. Non-orthogonal multiple access for delay-sensitive communications: A cross-layer approach. *IEEE Trans. Commun.* **2019**, *67*, 5053–5068. [CrossRef]
32. Ding, Z.; Fan, P.; Poor, H.V. Impact of user pairing on 5G nonorthogonal multiple-access downlink transmissions. *IEEE Trans. Veh. Technol.* **2015**, *65*, 6010–6023. [CrossRef]
33. Sedaghat, M.A.; Müller, R.R. On user pairing in uplink NOMA. *IEEE Trans. Wirel. Commun.* **2018**, *17*, 3474–3486. [CrossRef]
34. Salehi, M.; Tabassum, H.; Hossain, E. Accuracy of distance-based ranking of users in the analysis of NOMA systems. *IEEE Trans. Commun.* **2019**, *67*, 5069–5083. [CrossRef]
35. Zhao, X.; Chen, W. Delay optimal non-orthogonal multiple access with joint scheduling and superposition coding. In Proceedings of the IEEE Global Communications Conference, Singapore, 4–8 December 2017; pp. 1–6.
36. Liu, L.; Sheng, M.; Liu, J.; Dai, Y.; Li, J. Stable throughput region and average delay analysis of uplink NOMA systems with unsaturated traffic. *IEEE Trans. Commun.* **2019**, *67*, 8475–8488. [CrossRef]
37. Sheng, M.; Jiao, W.; Wang, X.; Liu, G. Effect of power control on performance of users in an interference-limited network with unsaturated traffic. *IEEE Trans. Veh. Technol.* **2016**, *66*, 2740–2755. [CrossRef]
38. Zhong, Y.; Quek, T.Q.; Ge, X. Heterogeneous cellular networks with spatio-temporal traffic: Delay analysis and scheduling. *IEEE J. Sel. Areas Commun.* **2017**, *35*, 1373–1386. [CrossRef]
39. Xu, C.; Wu, M.; Xu, Y.; Fang, Y. Uplink low-power scheduling for delay-bounded industrial wireless networks based on imperfect power-domain NOMA. *IEEE Syst. J.* **2020**, *14*, 2443–2454. [CrossRef]
40. Nasfi, R.; Chorti, A. Performance analysis of the uplink of a two user NOMA network under QoS delay constraints. In Proceedings of the IEEE International Conference on Ubiquitous and Future Networks, Zagreb, Croatia, 2–5 July 2019; pp. 526–528.
41. Xiao, C.; Zeng, J.; Liu, B.; Su, X.; Wang, J. Cross-layer power control for uplink NOMA in IoT applications with statistical delay constraints. In Proceedings of the IEEE Global Communications Conference, Abu Dhabi, United Arab Emirates, 9–13 December 2018; pp. 1–7.
42. Bello, M.; Yu, W.; Pischella, M.; Chorti, A.; Fijalkow, I.; Musavian, L. Flexible multiple access enabling low-latency communications: Introducing NOMA-R. *arXiv* **2020**, arXiv:2001.10637.
43. Li, A.; Chen, X.; Jiang, H. Contention based uplink transmission with NOMA for latency reduction. In Proceedings of the IEEE Vehicular Technology Conference, Sydney, NSW, Australia, 4–7 June 2017; pp. 1–6.

44. Seo, J.-B.; Jung, B.C.; Jin, H. Performance analysis of NOMA random access. *IEEE Commun. Lett.* **2018**, *22*, 2242–2245. [CrossRef]
45. Zhai, D.; Zhang, R.; Cai, L.; Yu, F.R. Delay minimization for massive internet of things with non-orthogonal multiple access. *IEEE J. Sel. Top. Signal Process.* **2019**, *13*, 553–566. [CrossRef]
46. Park, T.; Lee, G.; Saad, W. Message-aware uplink transmit power level partitioning for non-orthogonal multiple access (NOMA). In Proceedings of the IEEE Global Communications Conference, Abu Dhabi, United Arab Emirates, 9–13 December 2018; pp. 1–6.
47. Choi, M.; Kim, J.; Moon, J. Dynamic power allocation and user scheduling for power-efficient and delay-constrained multiple access networks. *IEEE Trans. Wirel. Commun.* **2019**, *18*, 4846–4858. [CrossRef]
48. Sreya, G.; Saigadha, S.; Goutam, M.P.D.D.; S, D.H. Adaptive rate NOMA for cellular IoT networks. *Proc. IEEE Wirel. Commun. Lett.* **2021**, *11*, 478–482. [CrossRef]
49. Jinho, G. Opportunistic NOMA for uplink short-message delivery with a delay constraint. *IEEE Trans. Wirel. Commun.* **2020**, *19*, 3727–3737.
50. Schiessl, S.; Sebastian, M.; Skoglund, M.; Gross, J. NOMA in the uplink: Delay analysis with imperfect CSI and finite-length coding. *IEEE Trans. Wirel. Commun.* **2020**, *19*, 3879–3893. [CrossRef]
51. Zeng, J.; Xiao, C.; Li, Z.; Ni, W.; Liu, R. Dynamic Power Allocation for Uplink NOMA With Statistical Delay QoS Guarantee. *IEEE Trans. Wirel. Commun.* **2021**, *20*, 8191–8203. [CrossRef]
52. Kleinrock, L. *Queuing Systems, Volume I: Theory;* Wiley: New York, NY, USA, 1975.
53. Kleinrock, L. *Queuing Systems, Volume II: Computer Applications;* Wiley: New York, NY, USA, 1975.
54. Chan, W.; Lu, T.-C.; Chen, R.-J. Pollaczek-Khinchin formula for the M/G/1 queue in discrete time with vacations. *IEEE Proc. Comput. Digit. Tech.* **1997**, *144*, 222–226. [CrossRef]

entropy

MDPI

Article

Straggler- and Adversary-Tolerant Secure Distributed Matrix Multiplication Using Polynomial Codes

Eimear Byrne [1], Oliver W. Gnilke [2] and Jörg Kliewer [3,*]

1 School of Mathematics and Statistics, University College Dublin, D04 V1W8 Dublin, Ireland
2 Department of Mathematical Sciences, Aalborg University, 9220 Aalborg, Danmark
3 Department of Electrical and Computer Engineering, New Jersey Institute of Technology, Newark, NJ 07410, USA
* Correspondence: jkliewer@njit.edu; Tel.: +1-973-596-3519

Abstract: Large matrix multiplications commonly take place in large-scale machine-learning applications. Often, the sheer size of these matrices prevent carrying out the multiplication at a single server. Therefore, these operations are typically offloaded to a distributed computing platform with a master server and a large amount of workers in the cloud, operating in parallel. For such distributed platforms, it has been recently shown that coding over the input data matrices can reduce the computational delay by introducing a tolerance against straggling workers, i.e., workers for which execution time significantly lags with respect to the average. In addition to exact recovery, we impose a security constraint on both matrices to be multiplied. Specifically, we assume that workers can collude and eavesdrop on the content of these matrices. For this problem, we introduce a new class of polynomial codes with fewer non-zero coefficients than the degree $+1$. We provide closed-form expressions for the recovery threshold and show that our construction improves the recovery threshold of existing schemes in the literature, in particular for larger matrix dimensions and a moderate to large number of colluding workers. In the absence of any security constraints, we show that our construction is optimal in terms of recovery threshold.

Keywords: distributed computation; matrix multiplication; distributed learning; information theoretic security; polynomial codes

Citation: Byrne, E.; Gnilke, O.W.; Kliewer, J. Straggler- and Adversary-Tolerant Secure Distributed Matrix Multiplication Using Polynomial Codes. *Entropy* **2023**, *25*, 266. https://doi.org/10.3390/e25020266

Academic Editor: Syed A. Jafar

Received: 1 November 2022
Revised: 16 January 2023
Accepted: 20 January 2023
Published: 31 January 2023

1. Introduction

Recently, tensor operations have emerged as an important ingredient of many signal processing and machine learning applications [1]. These operations are typically complex due to the large size of the associated tensors. Therefore, in the interest of a low execution time, such computations are often performed in a distributed fashion and outsourced to a cloud of multiple workers that operate in parallel over the distributed data set. These workers in many cases consist of commercial off-the-shelf servers that are characterized by failures and varying execution times. Such straggling servers are handled by state-of-the art cloud computation platforms via a repetition of the computation task at hand. However, recent work has shown that encoding the input data may help alleviate the straggler problem and thus reduce the computation latency, which mainly depends on the amount of stragglers present in the cloud computing environment; see [2,3]. More generally, it has been shown that coding can control the trade-off between computational delay and communication load between workers and master server [3–6]. In addition, the workers in the cloud may not be trustworthy, so the input and output of the partial computations need to be protected against unauthorized access. To this end, it has been shown that stochastic coding can help keep both input and output data secure from eavesdropping and colluding workers (see, for example, [7–14]).

In this work, we focus on the canonical problem of distributing the multiplication of two matrices A and B, i.e., $C = AB$, whose content should be kept secret from a prescribed number of colluding workers in the cloud. Our goal is to minimize the number of workers from which the partial result must be downloaded, the so-called *recovery threshold*, to recover the correct matrix product C.

Coded matrix computation was first addressed in the non-secure case by applying separate MDS codes to encode the two matrices [3]. In [5], polynomial codes have been introduced, which improves on the recovery threshold of [3]. The recovery threshold was further improved by the so-called MatDot and PolyDot codes [15,16] at the expense of a larger download rate. In particular, PolyDot codes allow a flexible trade-off between the recovery threshold and the download rate, depending on the application at hand.

In [17,18] two different schemes are presented, an explicit scheme that improves on the recovery thereshold of PolyDot codes and a construction based on the tensor rank of matrix multiplication, which is optimal up to a factor of 2. In [19] a new construction for private and secure matrix multiplication is proposed based on entangled polynomial codes, which allows for a flexible trade-off between the upload rate and the download rate (equivalently, the recovery threshold). For small numbers of stragglers [20] constructs schemes that outperform the entangled polynomial scheme. Recently, several attempts have been made to design coding schemes to further reduce upload and download rates, the recovery threshold, and computational complexity for both workers and server (see, for example, [21–27]). For example, in [21], bivariate polynomial codes were used to reduce the recovery threshold in specific cases. In [22], the authors considered new schemes for the private and secure case which outperform [19] for specific parameter regions. The work in [23] considered distributed storage repair codes, so-called field-trace polynomial codes, to reduce the download rate for specific partitions of matrices A and B. Very recently, the authors in [24] proposed a black-box coding scheme based on star products, which subsumes several existing works as special cases. In [25], a discrete Fourier transform-based scheme with low upload rates and encoding complexity is proposed. The work in [26] focused on selecting the evaluation points for the polynomial codes, providing a better upload rate than [9], but worse than [25].

In the following, we propose a new scheme for secure matrix multiplication, which provides explicit evaluation points for the polynomial codes, but unlike the work in [26], is also able to tolerate stragglers. Specifically, we exploit gaps in the underlying polynomial code. This is motivated by the observation that the recovery threshold can be improved by selecting the number of evaluation points to be equal to the number of only the *non-zero* coefficients in the polynomial [9,19]. In addition, selecting dedicated evaluation points has the advantage that the condition for security against colluding workers is automatically satisfied (see, for example, condition C2 in [27]). As such, our approach is able to provide a constructive scheme with provable security guarantees. Further, our coding scheme provides an advantage in terms of download rate in some cases, and is both straggler-tolerant and robust against Byzantine attacks on the workers.

This paper is organized as follows. In Section 2, the problem statement and the background is highlighted. Section 3 discusses design and properties of our proposed scheme and provides performance guarantees with respect to the number of helper nodes needed for recovery, security, straggler tolerance and under Byzantine attacks. Section 4 extends the scheme of Section 4 by introducing gaps into the code polynomials and by studying its properties. Finally, Section 5 presents numerical results and comparisons with state-of-the-art schemes from the literature.

2. Problem Statement and Background

Let A and B be a pair of matrices over the finite field $\mathbb{F}_q$, whose product is well defined. We consider the problem of computing the product $C = AB$. The computation will be distributed among a number of helper nodes, each of which will execute a portion of the total calculation. We also assume that the user wishes to hide the data contained in the matrices A and B and that up to T honest but curious helper nodes may collude to deduce information about the contents of A and B. To divide the work among the helper nodes, the matrices A and B are each divided into KM and ML blocks, respectively, of compatible dimensions, say $a \times r$ and $r \times b$. The matrices are also assumed to have independent and identically distributed uniformly distributed entries from a sufficiently large field of cardinality $q > N$, where N denotes the number of servers to be employed (in fact, we will require q to exceed the degree of a polynomial $P(x)Q(x)$, central to this scheme). Hence, for given matrix partition of A and B according to

$$A = \begin{bmatrix} A_{1,1} & \cdots & A_{1,M} \\ \vdots & \ddots & \vdots \\ A_{K,1} & \cdots & A_{K,M} \end{bmatrix}, \quad B = \begin{bmatrix} B_{1,1} & \cdots & B_{1,L} \\ \vdots & \ddots & \vdots \\ B_{M,1} & \cdots & B_{M,L} \end{bmatrix},$$

we obtain

$$C = AB = \begin{bmatrix} C_{1,1} & \cdots & C_{1,L} \\ \vdots & \ddots & \vdots \\ C_{K,1} & \cdots & C_{K,L} \end{bmatrix} \text{ where } C_{i,j} = \sum_{m=1}^{M} A_{i,m} B_{m,j}.$$

The system model is displayed in Figure 1. We consider a distributed computing system with a master server and N helper nodes or workers. The master server is interested in computing the product $C = AB$. In Figure 1, the worker receives matrices A and B and T random uniformly independent and identically distributed matrices of size $R_t \in \mathbb{F}_q^{a \times r}$ and $S_t \in \mathbb{F}^{r \times b}$ for $t \in [T]$. To keep the data secure and to leverage possible computational redundancy at the workers, the server sends encoded versions of the input matrices to the workers. This security constraint imposes the mutual information condition

$$I(A_{\mathcal{T}}, B_{\mathcal{T}}; A, B) = 0 \tag{1}$$

between the pair (A, B) and their encodings $(A_{\mathcal{T}}, B_{\mathcal{T}})$ for all subsets $\mathcal{T} \subset [N]$ of maximum cardinality T. The server generates a polynomial representation of A and R_t by constructing a polynomial $P(x) \in \mathbb{F}_q^{a \times r}[x]$. Likewise, a polynomial representation of B and Q_t results in a polynomial $Q(x) \in \mathbb{F}_q^{r \times b}[x]$. The polynomial encodings that the p-th worker receives comprise the two polynomial evaluations $P(\alpha_p)$ and $Q(\alpha_p)$, for distinct evaluation points $\alpha_p \in \mathbb{F}_q$ with $p \in [N]$. It then computes the matrix product $P(\alpha_p)Q(\alpha_p)$ and sends it back to the server. The server collects a subset of $N_R \leq N$ outputs from the workers as defined by the evaluation points in the subset $\{P(\alpha_p)Q(\alpha_p)\}_{p \in \mathcal{N}_R}$ with $|\mathcal{N}_R| = N_R$. The size of the smallest possible subset N_R for which perfect recovery is obtained, i.e.,

$$H(AB | \{P(\alpha_p)Q(\alpha_p) : p \in \mathcal{N}_R\}) = 0, \tag{2}$$

where H denoted the entropy function, is defined as the *recovery threshold*. The server then interpolates the underlying polynomial such that the correct product $C = AB$ can be assembled from a combination of the interpolated polynomial coefficients $C_{i,j}$ (see Section 3 for details).

We further define the *upload rate* R_u per worker as the sum of the dimensions of $P(\alpha_p)$ and $Q(\alpha_p)$, i.e., $R_u = (a + b)r$ field elements of $\mathbb{F}_q$. Likewise, the *download rate* or *communication load* R_d is defined as the total number of field elements to be downloaded from the workers such that (2) is satisfied, i.e., $R_d = abN_R$.

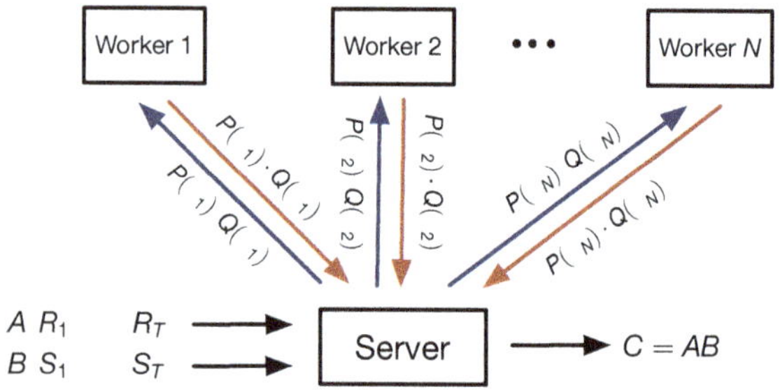

Figure 1. System model for secure matrix multiplication.

Notation. For the remainder, we fix A, B, C to be matrices over $\mathbb{F}_q$ such that $C = AB$, and we fix K, M, L, a, b, r to be the integers as defined above. We define $[n] := \{1, \ldots, n\}$ for any positive integer n. For each $k \in [K], \ell \in [L]$, and $m \in [M]$, we write $A_{k,m}$, $B_{m,\ell}$, and $C_{k,\ell}$ to denote the (k, m), (m, ℓ), and (k, ℓ) blocks of A, B, and C, respectively. The transpose of a matrix Z is denoted by Z^t.

3. Proposed Scheme

The scheme we propose uses a similar approach to the schemes in [9,19,27]. We will begin with the choices for exponents in $P(x)$ and $Q(x)$ and show that the desired blocks of C appear as coefficients of the product PQ. We discuss the maximum possible degree of PQ since it gives us an upper bound on the necessary evaluations, and hence workers, needed to interpolate PQ. In Section 3.3, we give explicit criteria for choices of evaluation points and prove that the scheme protects against collusion of up to T servers. Section 3.4 discusses the option to query additional servers to provide resilience against stragglers and Byzantine servers.

Section 4 uses ideas from the GASP scheme [9] to reduce the recovery threshold by examining how many coefficients in the product are already known to be zero.

3.1. Choice of Exponents and Maximal Degree

We propose the following scheme to outsource the computation among the worker servers. The model will incorporate methods to secure the privacy of the data held by the matrices A, B, and C.

Let $D := M + 2$. For the given A and B, we define the polynomials:

$$\bar{P}(x) := \sum_{k=1}^{K} x^{D(k-1)} \sum_{m=1}^{M} x^m A_{k,m} \quad \text{and} \quad \bar{Q}(x) := \sum_{\ell=1}^{L} x^{DK(\ell-1)} \sum_{m=1}^{M} x^{M+1-m} B_{m,\ell}.$$

We now define polynomials

$$P(x) := \bar{P}(x) + R(x) \quad \text{and} \quad Q(x) := \bar{Q}(x) + S(x),$$

where and $R(x), S(x)$ are a pair of matrix polynomials:

$$R(x) := \sum_{t=1}^{T} x^{D(t-1)} R_t \quad \text{and} \quad S(x) := \sum_{t=1}^{T} x^{D(t-1)} S_t,$$

whose coefficients are $a \times r$ and $r \times b$ matrices over $\mathbb{F}_q$, respectively, chosen uniformly at random.

In the next theorem, we show that the desired matrices $C_{k,\ell}$ appear as coefficients of the product PQ and can hence be retrieved by inspection of this product.

Theorem 1. *For each pair $(k, \ell) \in [K] \times [L]$, the block $C_{k,\ell}$ arising in the product $C = AB$ appears as the coefficient of $x^{D((k-1)+K(\ell-1))+M+1}$ in the product PQ.*

Proof. We calculate the product

$$
\begin{aligned}
PQ =& \bar{P}\bar{Q} + \bar{P}S + R\bar{Q} + RS \\
=& \sum_{k=1}^{K}\sum_{\ell=1}^{L} x^{D((k-1)+K(\ell-1))} \sum_{m=1}^{M}\sum_{m'=1}^{M} A_{k,m}B_{m',\ell}x^{M+1+m-m'} \\
&+ \sum_{k=1}^{K}\sum_{t'=1}^{T} x^{D(k+t'-2)} \sum_{m=1}^{M} A_{k,m}S_{t'}x^{m} \\
&+ \sum_{\ell=1}^{L}\sum_{t=1}^{T} x^{D(K(l-1)+(t-1))} \sum_{m'=1}^{M} R_t B_{m',\ell}x^{M+1-m'} \\
&+ \sum_{t=1}^{T}\sum_{t'=1}^{T} R_t S_{t'} x^{D(t+t'-2)}.
\end{aligned}
$$

Consider the exponents modulo D. The first term in the sum of terms above is the product $\bar{P}\bar{Q}$. Any of the exponents of x in this term are equal to $D-1 \equiv M+1 \mod D$ if and only if $m = m'$, in which case its corresponding coefficient is $C_{k,\ell}$. In particular, the matrix block $C_{k,\ell}$ appears in the product $\bar{P}\bar{Q}$ as the coefficient of $x^{D((k-1)+K(\ell-1))+M+1}$.

We claim that no other exponent of x in $PQ - \bar{P}\bar{Q}$ is equal to $M+1 \mod D$, from which the result will follow. Observe that the exponents in the second and third term of the product (i.e. those of $\bar{P}S + R\bar{Q}$) are all between 1 and M modulo D, while every exponent of x in the fourth term, which is RS, is a multiple of D. □

In order to retrieve the polynomial PQ, we may evaluate P and Q at a number of distinct values $\alpha_1, \ldots, \alpha_{N+1}$ in $\mathbb{F}_q^{\times}$. The values $P(\alpha_i)$ and $Q(\alpha_i)$ are found at a cost of zero non-scalar operations. Define

$$
V(\alpha_1,\ldots,\alpha_{N+1}) := \begin{pmatrix} 1 & \alpha_1 & \alpha_1^2 & \cdots & \alpha_1^N \\ 1 & \alpha_2 & \alpha_2^2 & \cdots & \alpha_2^N \\ \vdots & \ddots & \vdots & & \\ 1 & \alpha_N & \alpha_N^2 & \cdots & \alpha_N^N \\ 1 & \alpha_{N+1} & \alpha_{N+1}^2 & \cdots & \alpha_{N+1}^N \end{pmatrix}.
$$

The (i,j)-entries of the coefficients of $PQ \in \mathbb{F}_q^{a\times b}[x]$ can be retrieved by computing the product

$$
V(\alpha_1,\ldots,\alpha_{N+1})^{-1}((P(\alpha_1)Q(\alpha_1))_{i,j},\ldots,(P(\alpha_{N+1})Q(\alpha_{N+1}))_{i,j})^t,
$$

if the degree of PQ is at most N. Since this computation involves only $\mathbb{F}_q$-linear computations, the total non-scalar cost is the total cost of performing the $N+1$ matrix products $P(\alpha_i)Q(\alpha_i)$. In the distributed computation scheme as shown in Figure 1, the server uploads each pair of evaluations $P(\alpha_i), Q(\alpha_i)$ to the i-th worker node, which then computes the product $P(\alpha_i)Q(\alpha_i)$ and returns it to the server.

In this approach to reconstructing PQ, we require the participation of $N+1$ worker nodes, where N is the degree of PQ. For this reason, we study this degree. Since

$$
\deg(PQ) \leq \max(\deg(\bar{P}\bar{Q}), \deg(\bar{P}S), \deg(R\bar{Q}) \deg(RS)),
$$

we have the following result, wherein each of the values $N_1(K,L,M;T)$ to $N_4(K,L,M;T)$ correspond to the maximum possible degrees of $\bar{P}\bar{Q}, \bar{P}S, R\bar{Q}$, and RS, respectively. We write $N(A,B;K,L,M;T)$ to denote the maximum possible degree of the polynomial PQ, as the A,B,R,S range over all possible matrices of the stated sizes.

Proposition 1. *The degree of PQ is upper bounded by $N(A,B;K,L,M;T)$, where*

$$N(A,B;K,L,M;T) = \max \begin{cases} N_1(K,L,M;T) := D(KL-1) + 2M & (3) \\ N_2(K,L,M;T) := D(K+T-2) + M & (4) \\ N_3(K,L,M;T) := D(K(L-1)+T-1) + M & (5) \\ N_4(K,L,M;T) := 2D(T-1) & (6) \end{cases}$$

Proposition 2. *The following are equivalent.*

1. $T > K$,
2. $N_3(K,L,M;T) > N_1(K,L,M;T)$,
3. $N_4(K,L,M;T) > N_2(K,L,M;T)$.

Proof. First note that $T > K \Leftrightarrow T - K \geq 1$ and that $1 = \lceil \frac{M}{D} \rceil > \frac{M}{D}$. Since $T - K$ is an integer, we thus have that the following inequalities are equivalent to $T > K$:

$$T - K > \frac{M}{D},$$
$$D(T-K) > M,$$
$$D(K(L-1)+T-1) + M > D(KL-1) + 2M.$$

This shows that $N_3(K,L,M;T) > N_1(K,L,M;T)$ if and only if $T > K$. Similarly, using the 2nd and 3rd inequalities just above, we have

$$T > K \Leftrightarrow DT > DK + M,$$
$$\Leftrightarrow 2D(T-1) > D(T+K-2) + M,$$

from which we see that $N_4(K,L,M;T) > N_2(K,L,M;T)$ if and only if $T > K$. □

Proposition 3. *The following are equivalent.*

1. $T > K(L-1)+1$,
2. $N_4(K,L,M;T) > N_3(K,L,M;T)$,
3. $N_2(K,L,M;T) > N_1(K,L,M;T)$.

Proof. We have the following inequalities:

$$T > K(L-1)+1 \Leftrightarrow T - K(L-1) - 1 \geq 1 > \frac{M}{D},$$
$$\Leftrightarrow D(T - K(L-1) - 1) > M,$$
$$\Leftrightarrow D(2T-2) > D(K(L-1)+T-1) + M,$$

from which we deduce that $N_4(K,L,M;T) > N_3(K,L,M;T)$. We now show that $N_2(K,L,M;T) > N_1(K,L,M;T)$. We have:

$$T > K(L-1)+1 \Leftrightarrow D(T-K(L-1)-1) > M,$$
$$\Leftrightarrow D(K+T-2) + M > D(KL-1) + 2M.$$

□

We tabulate (see Table 1) the value of $N(K, L, M; T)$ based on the observations of Propositions 2 and 3.

Table 1. Summary table of maximal degree of PQ.

	$T > K(L-1)+1$		$T \leq K(L-1)+1$	
$T > K$	$2D(T-1)$	(6)	$D(K(L-1)+T-1)+M$	(5)
$T \leq K$	$D(K+T-2)+M$	(4)	$D(KL-1)+2M$	(3)

3.2. AB *versus* B^tA^t

We compare the recovery threshold cost of calculating B^tA^t rather than AB. It can be shown that it is always better to calculate AB whenever $K \geq L$. That is, we show that $N(A, B; K, L, M; T) \leq N(B^t, A^t; L, K, M; T)$ for $K \geq L$. We consider all possible cases for the maximal degree in the following two theorems and remarks.

Theorem 2. 1. *Let $T > K, L$. Suppose that $T < K(L-1)+1$ and $T < L(K-1)+1$. We have that*

$$N(A, B; K, L, M; T) = N_3(K, L, M; T) < N_3(L, K, M; T) = N(B^t, A^t; L, K, M; T),$$

if and only if $L < K$.

2. *Let $K \geq T > L$. Suppose that $T < K(L-1)+1$ and $T < L(K-1)+1$. We have that*

$$N(A, B; K, L, M; T) = N_1(K, L, M; T) < N_3(L, K, M; T) = N(B^t, A^t; L, K, M; T).$$

3. *Let $T > L, K$ and suppose that $L(K-1)+1 \geq T > K(L-1)+1$. We have that*

$$N(A, B; K, L, M; T) = N_4(K, L, M; T) < N_3(L, K, M; T) = N(B^t, A^t; L, K, M; T).$$

4. *Let $T > K \geq L$ and suppose that $T > L(K-1)+1$. We have that*

$$N(A, B; K, L, M; T) = N_4(K, L, M; T) = N_4(L, K, M; T) = N(B^t, A^t; L, K, M; T).$$

5. *Let $T \leq L \leq K$ and suppose that $T \leq K(L-1)+1$. We have that*

$$N(A, B; K, L, M; T) = N_1(K, L, M; T) = N_1(L, K, M; T) = N(B^t, A^t; L, K, M; T).$$

Proof. 1. Since $T > K$, and $T < K(L-1)+1$ by Propositions 2 and 3 we have that

$$N_3(K, L, M; T) > N_4(K, L, M; T) > N_2(K, L, M; T), N_1(K, L, M; T)$$

and so $N(A, B; K, L, M; T) = N_3(K, L, M; T)$.
Similarly, since $T > L$, and $T < L(K-1)+1$, we have that $N(B^t, A^t; L, K, M; T) = N_3(L, K, M; T)$. Clearly, $L < K$ if and only if:

$$\begin{aligned} N_3(K, L, M; T) &= D(K(L-1)+T-1)+M \\ &< D(L(K-1)+T-1)+M = N_3(L, K, M; T). \end{aligned}$$

2. By Propositions 2 and 3, the assumptions $K \geq T$ and $T < K(L-1)+1$ imply that $N(A, B; K, L, M; T) = N_1(K, L, M; T)$, while the assumptions $T > L$ and $T < L(K-1)+1$ yield that $N(B^t, A^t; K, L, M; T) = N_3(L, K, M; T)$.
Clearly, since $T > L$, we have $M < D(T-L)$ and

$$N_1(K, L, M; T) = D(KL-1)+2M < D(L(K-1)+T-1)+M = N_3(L, K, M; T).$$

3. From the given assumptions, by Propositions 2 and 3, we have $N(A, B; K, L, M; T) = N_4(K, L, M; T)$ and $N(B^t, A^t; L, K, M; T) = N_3(L, K, M; T)$. Since $L(K-1)+1 \geq T$, as in the proof of Proposition 3, we have
$$N_4(K, L, M; T) = 2D(T-1) = N_4(L, K, M; T) \leq N_3(L, K, M; T).$$
4. For the given assumptions the statement follows immediately from Propositions 2 and 3.
5. From the given assumptions, by Propositions 2 and 3, we have $N(A, B; K, L, M; T) = N_1(K, L, M; T)$ and $N(B^t, A^t; L, K, M; T) = N_1(L, K, M; T)$. The rest follows immediately from $N_1(K, L, M; T) = D(KL-1) + 2M = D(LK-1) + 2M = N_1(L, K, M; T)$. □

Remark 1. *Clearly, if $T \leq K$ and $T > K(L-1)+1$ then $L = 1$. In this case, from Propositions 3 and 2, we have that $N(A, B; K, 1, M; T) = N_2(K, 1, M; T)$.*

Theorem 3. *Let $T \leq K$ and $T > K(L-1)+1$.*

(i) Assume $T > L$ and $T \leq L(K-1)+1$ then $N(A, B; K, L, M; T) = N_2(K, 1, M; T) = N_3(1, K, M; T) = N(B^t, A^t; L, K, M; T)$.
(ii) Assume $T = 1 \leq L$ and $T \leq L(K-1)+1$ then $N(A, B; K, L, M; T) = N_2(K, 1, M; 1) < N_1(1, K, M; 1) = N(B^t, A^t; L, K, M; T)$.

Proof. (i) Since $L = 1$ we have that
$N_2(K, 1, M; T) = D(K+T-2) + M = D(L(K-1)+T-1) + M = N_3(1, K, M; T)$
and so the result follows.
(ii) We see that
$N_2(K, 1, M; 1) = D(K-1) + M < D(K-1) + 2M = N_1(1, K, M; 1)$
□

Remark 2. *The remaining two cases lead to a contradiction and can hence never occur. Let $T \leq K$ and $T > K(L-1)+1$ and $T > L(K-1)+1$. By Remark 1, we have that $L = 1$ and we obtain the contradiction $T \leq K < T$.*

3.3. T-Collusion

Each query is masked with a polynomial of the form $\sum_{i=0}^{T-1} x^{iD} R_i$, where R_i is chosen uniformly at random. A query is private in the case of T servers colluding if and only if the matrix
$$M(x_1, \ldots, x_T) := \begin{pmatrix} 1 & \cdots & 1 \\ x_1^D & \cdots & x_T^D \\ \vdots & \ddots & \vdots \\ x_1^{D(T-1)} & \cdots & x_T^{D(T-1)} \end{pmatrix}$$
has full rank for any subset of T evaluation points. This is the same as condition C2 in [27]. Because of the very specific set of exponents used, we can give a more explicit condition for the invertibility of this matrix.

Proposition 4. *The matrix $M(x_1, \ldots, x_T)$ is invertible if and only if the elements $x_1^D, \ldots, x_T^D$ are distinct.*

Proof. $M(x_1, \ldots, x_T)$ is a Vandermonde matrix with entries $x_1^D, \ldots, x_T^D$. □

Proposition 5. *A set of elements of $\mathbb{F}_q$ such that their D^{th} powers are pairwise different has size at most $N = \frac{q-1}{\gcd(q-1, D)} + 1$.*

Proof. Fix a generator γ of $\mathbb{F}_q^*$. Then the image of the map $x \mapsto x^D$ from $\mathbb{F}_q$ to $\mathbb{F}_q$ is given by 0 together with all powers γ^{Di} where $0 \leq i < q-1$. □

Corollary 1. *Let $T < q$. If $\gcd(q-1, D) = 1$, then the scheme in Section 3 is secure against T-collusion for any choice of evaluation points.*

3.4. Stragglers and Byzantine Servers

Considering the scheme as described in the previous section, we see that the responses are the coordinates of a codeword of a Reed–Solomon code. The polynomial that needs to be interpolated has degree at most $N = N(K, L, M; T)$, and hence $N+1$ evaluation points suffice for reconstruction. Any $N+1$ evaluation points are admissible and hence we have the following theorem.

Theorem 4. *The scheme in Section 3 is straggler resistant against S stragglers if $N+1+S$ helper nodes are used.*

Proof. The responses can be considered as a codeword in an $[N+1+S, N+1, S+1]$ RS code, with S erasures. Since S is smaller than the minimum distance of the code, the full codeword and hence the interpolating polynomial can be recovered. □

Similarly, we can use additional helper nodes to account for possible Byzantine servers whose responses are incorrect.

Theorem 5. *The scheme in Section 3 is resistant against Byzantine attacks of up to B helper nodes if $N+1+2B$ helper nodes are used.*

Proof. The responses can be considered as a codeword in an $[N+1+2B, N+1, 2B+1]$ RS code, with B errors. Since $2B$ is smaller than the minimum distance of the code, the full codeword and hence the interpolating polynomial can be recovered. □

Combining both theorems give us the following corollary.

Corollary 2. *The scheme in Section 3 is resistant against S stragglers and B Byzantine helper nodes if $N+1+S+2B$ helper nodes are used.*

4. Gaps in the Polynomial

The upper bound on the recovery threshold given by the maximum degree of the product PQ can actually be improved if we choose instead to use the fact that we need only as many servers as non-zero coefficients. Similar to considerations in [9], as a basic observation of linear algebra, we note that only as many evaluation points as there are possible non-zero coordinates are required to retrieve the required matrix coefficients of PQ. Let PQ have degree $r-1$ and suppose that $q \geq r+1$. Let $\alpha_1, \ldots, \alpha_r$ be distinct elements of $\mathbb{F}_q^{\times}$. Suppose that the zero coefficients of PQ are indexed by $\mathcal{I}$ and let $i = r - |\mathcal{I}|$. There exist $j_1, \ldots, j_i \in \{1, \ldots, r\}$ such that the $i \times i$ matrix V, found by deleting the columns of $V(\alpha_{j_1}, \ldots, \alpha_{j_i})$ indexed by $\mathcal{I}$, is invertible. Then, each (s,t)-entry of the unknown coefficients of the polynomial $PQ \in \mathbb{F}_q^{a \times b}[x]$ can be retrieved by computing the product

$$V^{-1}((P(\alpha_j)Q(\alpha_j))_{s,t} : j \in [r] \backslash \mathcal{I})^t.$$

Theorem 6. *Let $M \geq 2$, $D = M + 2$. Let*

$$\bar{P}(x) := \sum_{k=1}^{K} x^{D(k-1)} \sum_{m=1}^{M} x^m A_{k,m}, \quad R(x) := \sum_{t=1}^{T} x^{D(t-1)} R_t,$$
$$\bar{Q}(x) := \sum_{\ell=1}^{L} x^{DK(\ell-1)} \sum_{m=1}^{M} x^{M-m+1} B_{m,\ell}, \quad S(x) := \sum_{t=1}^{T} x^{D(t-1)} S_t.$$

The number N of non-zero terms in the product PQ satisfies

$$N \leq \begin{cases} N_1(K, L, M; T) + 1 & \text{if } M > 2, T \leq K, L \geq 2 \text{ or } L = 1, T = 1; \\ 3LK + K - T + LT + 1 & \text{if } M = 2, T \leq K, L \geq 2; \\ ((L-1)K + T)M + 2LK + 1 & \text{if } K + 1 \leq T \leq \lfloor LK/2 \rfloor + 1, L \geq 2; \\ ((L-1)K + T)M + LK + 2T - 1 & \text{if } T > \lfloor LK/2 \rfloor + 1, L \geq 2; \\ (K + T - 1)M + 2K + 1 & \text{if } 2 \leq T \leq \lfloor K/2 \rfloor + 1, L = 1; \\ (K + T - 1)M + K + 2T - 1 & \text{if } T > \lfloor K/2 \rfloor + 1, L = 1. \end{cases}$$

Proof. We have $P(x) = \bar{P}(x) + R(x)$ and $Q(x) = \bar{Q}(x) + S(x)$. Recall that $\bar{P}(x)$ and $R(x)$ have disjoint support, as do $\bar{Q}(x)$ and $S(x)$. From Theorem 1, for each each $k \in [K], \ell \in [L]$, the matrix

$$C_{k\ell} = A_{k,1}B_{1,\ell} + \cdots + A_{k,M}B_{M,\ell}$$

is the coefficient of x^h in $\bar{P}\bar{Q}$ for

$$h = (k-1)D + (\ell-1)KD + M + 1 = (k + (\ell-1)K)D - 1.$$

Clearly, each such coefficient $h \equiv M + 1 \mod D$. The degrees of terms arising in the product PQ are given by

$$(i + zK)D + j + y + 2, \tag{7}$$
$$(i + t)D + j + 1, \tag{8}$$
$$(u + zK)D + y + 1, \tag{9}$$
$$(u + t)D. \tag{10}$$

for $i \in \{0, ..., K-1\}, z \in \{0, ..., L-1\}, j, y \in \{0, ..., M-1\}$ and $u, t \in \{0, ..., T-1\}$. The sequence (7) corresponds to terms that appear in the product $\bar{P}\bar{Q}$. By inspection, we see that no element θ in any of the sequences (8)–(10) satisfies $\theta \equiv -1 \mod D$: in (8) this would require $j = M$ and in (9) this would require $y = M$, contradicting our choices of j, y. The total number of distinct terms to be computed is the number of distinct integers appearing in the union $\mathcal{T}$ of the elements of the sequences (7)–(10). Let $\mathcal{U}_0$ denote the set of integers appearing in (7). Observe that $\mathcal{U}_0 = \{2, \ldots, (LK+1)D - 4\}$, unless $M = 2$, in which case $\mathcal{U}_0 = \{j : 2 \leq j \leq 4LK, j \not\equiv 1 \mod 4\}$. Consider the set

$$\mathcal{U} := \{0, 1, 2, \ldots, (LK+1)D - 4\}.$$

We make the following observations with respect to $\mathcal{U}$.

- If $M > 2$, then $\mathcal{U} = \mathcal{U}_0 \cup \{0, 1\} \subset \mathcal{T}$,
- $\mathcal{U}$ contains the elements of (8) $\iff T \leq (L-1)K + 1$,
- $\mathcal{U}$ contains the elements of (9) $\iff T \leq K$,
- $\mathcal{U}$ contains the elements of (10) $\iff T \leq \lfloor LK/2 \rfloor + 1$.

Consider the following sets.

$$\begin{aligned} \mathcal{U}_1 &:= \{\alpha D + i : 0 \leq \alpha \leq K + T - 2, 1 \leq i \leq M\}, |\mathcal{U}_1| = (K + T - 1)M; \\ \mathcal{U}_2 &:= \{\beta D + j : 0 \leq \beta \leq T - 1 + (L-1)K, 1 \leq j \leq M\}, |\mathcal{U}_2| = ((L-1)K + T)M; \\ \mathcal{U}_3 &:= \{\gamma D : 0 \leq \gamma \leq 2T - 2\}, |\mathcal{U}_3| = 2T - 1. \end{aligned}$$

Clearly, $\mathcal{U}_1$ comprises the elements of the sequence (8) and the members of $\mathcal{U}_3$ are exactly those of the sequence (10). For $T \geq K+1$, we have

$$\{u + xK : 0 \leq u \leq T-1, 0 \leq x \leq L-1\} = \{\beta : 0 \leq \beta \leq T-1+(L-1)K\},$$

in which case $\mathcal{U}_2$ is exactly the set of elements of (9). It follows that $\mathcal{U}_1 \cup \mathcal{U}_2 \cup \mathcal{U}_3 \subseteq \mathcal{U}$ if and only if $T \leq \min\{(L-1)K+1, K, \lfloor LK/2 \rfloor + 1\}$. This minimum is K if $L \geq 2$ and is 1 if $L = 1$. Furthermore, $\mathcal{U}_3$ is disjoint from $\mathcal{U}_1$ and from $\mathcal{U}_2$. If $L \geq 2$ or if $L = K = 1$, then $\mathcal{U}_1 \subset \mathcal{U}_2$, while if $L = 1$, then $\mathcal{U}_2 \subset \mathcal{U}_1$.

Suppose first that $M > 2$. We thus have that $\mathcal{U} = \mathcal{T}$ if $L \geq 2$ and $T \leq K$, or if $L = T = 1$; in either of these cases, PQ has at most

$$|\mathcal{T}| = |\mathcal{U}| = (LK+1)D - 3 = (LK-1)D + 2M + 1 = N_1(K, L, M; T) + 1$$

non-zero terms. We summarize these observations as follows.

$$\mathcal{T} = \begin{cases} \mathcal{U} & \text{if } L \geq 2 \text{ and } T \leq K, \text{ or if } L = T = 1; \\ \mathcal{U} \cup \mathcal{U}_1 \cup \mathcal{U}_3 & \text{if } L = 1 \\ \mathcal{U} \cup \mathcal{U}_2 \cup \mathcal{U}_3 & \text{if } L \geq 2 \text{ or if } L = K = 1. \end{cases}$$

Furthermore,

$$\begin{aligned} \mathcal{U} \cap \mathcal{U}_3 &= \{\gamma D : 0 \leq \gamma \leq \min\{2T-2, LK\}\}, \\ \mathcal{U} \cap \mathcal{U}_2 &= \{\beta D + j : 0 \leq \beta \leq \min\{LK, T-1+(L-1)K\}, 1 \leq j \leq M\} \\ &\quad \setminus \{LKD + M - 1, LKD + M\}, \\ \mathcal{U} \cap \mathcal{U}_1 &= \{\alpha D + i : 0 \leq \alpha \leq \min\{LK, T+K-2\}, 1 \leq i \leq M\} \\ &\quad \setminus \{LKD + M - 1, LKD + M\} \end{aligned}$$

Hence $|\mathcal{U} \cap \mathcal{U}_3| = \min\{2T-1, LK+1\}$. If $T \geq K+1$ then $|\mathcal{U} \cap \mathcal{U}_2| = M(LK+1) - 2$ and so, applying inclusion–exclusion, we see that, if $L \geq 2$, then

$$|\mathcal{T}| = \begin{cases} |\mathcal{U}| = (LK+1)D - 3 = (LK+1)(M+2) - 3 & \text{if } K \geq T; \\ |\mathcal{U} \cup \mathcal{U}_2| = ((L-1)K+T)M + 2LK + 1 & \text{if } K+1 \leq T \leq \lfloor LK/2 \rfloor + 1; \\ |\mathcal{U} \cup \mathcal{U}_2 \cup \mathcal{U}_3| = ((L-1)K+T)M + LK + 2T - 1 & \text{otherwise}. \end{cases}$$

In the case $L = 1$, we have $\mathcal{U}_2 \subseteq \mathcal{U}_1$, while if $T \leq K$ then the elements of (9) are contained in $\mathcal{U}$. Therefore, $\mathcal{T} = \mathcal{U} \cup \mathcal{U}_1 \cup \mathcal{U}_3$ and so for $T \geq 2$ we have

$$|\mathcal{T}| = \begin{cases} (K+T-1)M + 2K + 1 & \text{if } T \leq \lfloor K/2 \rfloor + 1; \\ (K+T-1)M + K + 2T - 1 & \text{otherwise}. \end{cases}$$

Finally, suppose that $M = 2$. If $L = 1$ then, since $U_2 \subset \mathcal{U}_1$ we have $\mathcal{T} = \mathcal{U}_0 \cup \mathcal{U}_1 \cup \mathcal{U}_3$. Similar to previous computations, we see $|\mathcal{T}|$ takes the same values as in the case for $M > 2$. If $L \geq 2$ and $T \geq K+1$ then $\mathcal{T} = \mathcal{U}_0 \cup \mathcal{U}_2 \cup \mathcal{U}_3$. Again using similar computations as before, we see in this case that $|\mathcal{T}|$ takes the same values as in the case for $M > 2$. Suppose that $L \geq 2$ and $T \leq K$. In this case, the integers appearing in (9) comprise the set

$$\mathcal{U}_2' := \{4(u + zK) + j : 0 \leq u \leq T-1, 0 \leq z \leq L-1, 1 \leq j \leq 2\}, |\mathcal{U}_2'| = 2TL.$$

We have $|\mathcal{U}_0| = 3KL$ and moreover,

$$\begin{aligned}
\mathcal{U}_0 \cap \mathcal{U}_2' &= \{4(u+zK)+2 : 0 \le u \le T-1, 0 \le z \le L-1\}, |\mathcal{U}_0 \cap \mathcal{U}_2'| = TL;\\
\mathcal{U}_0 \cap \mathcal{U}_1 &= \{4\alpha+2 : 0 \le \alpha \le K+T-2\}, |\mathcal{U}_0 \cap \mathcal{U}_1| = K+T-1;\\
\mathcal{U}_0 \cap \mathcal{U}_3 &= \{4(\alpha+1) : 0 \le \alpha \le 2T-3\}, |\mathcal{U}_0 \cap \mathcal{U}_3| = 2T-2;\\
\mathcal{U}_1 \cap \mathcal{U}_2' &= \{4(u+zK)+j : 0 \le u \le T-1, 0 \le z \le 1, 1 \le j \le 2\}, |\mathcal{U}_1 \cap \mathcal{U}_2'| = 4T;\\
\mathcal{U}_0 \cap \mathcal{U}_1 \cap \mathcal{U}_2' &= \{4(u+zK)+2 : 0 \le u \le T-1, 0 \le z \le 1\}, |\mathcal{U}_0 \cap \mathcal{U}_1 \cap \mathcal{U}_2'| = 2T.
\end{aligned}$$

Therefore, $|\mathcal{T}| = 3LK + K - T + TL + 1$.
□

Example 1. *Let $M = 3, K = 3, L = 2$, that is:*

$$A = \begin{bmatrix} A_{1,1} & A_{1,2} & A_{1,3} \\ A_{2,1} & A_{2,2} & A_{2,3} \\ A_{3,1} & A_{3,2} & A_{3,3} \end{bmatrix}, \quad B = \begin{bmatrix} B_{1,1} & B_{1,2} \\ B_{2,1} & B_{2,2} \\ B_{3,1} & B_{3,2} \end{bmatrix}.$$

We will compute the product AB using 32 helper nodes, assuming that $T = 3$ servers may collude. Choose a pair of polynomials

$$R(z) = R_1 + R_6x^5 + R_{11}x^{10} \text{ and } S(z) = S_1 + S_6x^5 + S_{11}x^{10},$$

whose non-zero matrix coefficients are chosen uniformly at random over $\mathbb{F}_q$. We have

$$\begin{aligned}
\bar{P}(x) &= x(A_{1,1} + A_{1,2}x + A_{1,3}x^2) + x^6(A_{2,1} + A_{2,2}x + A_{2,3}x^2) + x^{11}(A_{3,1} + A_{3,2}z + A_{3,3}z^2)\\
\bar{Q}(x) &= x(B_{3,1} + B_{2,1}x + B_{1,1}x^2) + x^{16}(B_{3,2} + B_{2,2}x + B_{1,2}x^2).
\end{aligned}$$

Define $P(x) := \bar{P}(x) + R(x)$ and $Q(x) := \bar{Q}(x) + S(x)$. In Table 2, we show the exponents that arise in the product $P(x)Q(x)$. The monomials corresponding to the computed data are $4, 9, 14, 19, 24, 29$, shown in blue. The coefficients of $x^4, x^9, x^{14}, x^{19}, x^{24}$ and x^{29} are, respectively, given by

$$\begin{aligned}
C_{1,1} &= A_{1,1}B_{1,1} + A_{1,2}B_{2,1} + A_{1,3}B_{3,1},\\
C_{1,2} &= A_{1,1}B_{1,2} + A_{1,2}B_{2,2} + A_{1,3}B_{3,2},\\
C_{2,1} &= A_{2,1}B_{1,1} + A_{2,2}B_{2,1} + A_{2,3}B_{3,1},\\
C_{2,2} &= A_{2,1}B_{1,2} + A_{2,2}B_{2,2} + A_{2,3}B_{3,2},\\
C_{3,1} &= A_{3,1}B_{1,1} + A_{3,2}B_{2,1} + A_{3,3}B_{3,1},\\
C_{3,2} &= A_{3,1}B_{1,2} + A_{3,2}B_{2,2} + A_{3,3}B_{3,2}.
\end{aligned}$$

Note that the total number of non-zero terms in PQ is $LKD + M - 1 = 32$, as predicted by Theorem 6. This also corresponds to the case for which PQ has degree $N_1(K, L, M; T) = N_1(3, 2, 3; 3) = 31$, which is consistent with Theorem 2. Therefore, 32 helper nodes are required to retrieve PQ and hence the coefficients $C_{k,m}$. If the matrices have entries over $\mathbb{F}_q$ with $q = 64$, then since $\gcd(q-1, D) = \gcd(63, 5) = 1$, the user can retrieve the data securely in the presence of 3 colluding workers.

Suppose now that we have $T = 6$ colluding servers. In this case, we have $T = 6 > 4 = \lfloor LK/2 \rfloor + 1$ and $L > 1$ and so from Theorem 6, we expect the polynomial PQ to have at most $(LK + T)D - K(M + L) - 1 = 44$ non-zero coefficients. These exponents are shown in the corresponding degree table for our scheme (see Table 3). In this case, to protect against collusion by 6 workers, we require a total of 44 helpers. While the degree of PQ in this case is 50 (see Table 1), the coefficients corresponding to the exponents $E = \{34, 39, 44, 46, 47, 48, 49\}$ are zero, and hence known a priori to the user. Let α be a root of $x^6 + x^4 + x^3 + x + 1 \in \mathbb{F}_2[x]$, so that α generates $\mathbb{F}_{64}^{\times}$.

Let V be the 44×44 matrix obtained from $V(\alpha^i : i \in [63])$ by deleting the columns and rows indexed by $E \cup \{51, \ldots, 62\}$. It is readily checked (e.g., as here, using MAGMA [28]) that the determinant of V is α^{11} and in particular is non-zero. Therefore, we can solve the system to find the unknown coefficients of PQ via the computation $V^{-1}(P(\alpha^{ij})Q(\alpha^{ij}) : i, j \in [63] \backslash (E \cup \{51, \ldots, 62\}))^t$.

Table 2. Exponents of $P(x)Q(x)$ for $K = 3, L = 2, M = 3, T = 3$. The monomial exponents which correspond to the computed data are shown in blue. The grey background marks noise exponents.

	0	1	2	3	5	16	17	18	10
0	0	1	2	3	5	16	17	18	10
1	1	2	3	4	6	17	18	19	11
2	2	1	4	5	7	18	19	20	12
3	3	4	5	6	8	19	20	21	13
5	5	6	7	8	10	21	22	23	15
6	6	7	8	9	11	22	23	24	16
7	7	8	9	10	12	23	24	25	17
8	8	9	10	11	13	24	25	26	18
10	10	11	12	13	15	26	27	28	20
11	11	12	13	14	16	27	28	29	21
12	2	13	14	15	17	28	29	30	22
13	3	14	15	16	18	29	30	31	23

Table 3. Exponents of $P(x)Q(x)$ for $K = 3, L = 2, M = 3, T = 6$. The monomial exponents which correspond to the computed data are shown in blue. The grey background marks noise exponents.

	0	1	2	3	5	16	17	18	10	15	20	25
0	0	1	2	3	5	16	17	18	10	15	20	25
1	1	2	3	4	6	17	18	19	11	16	21	26
2	2	3	4	5	7	18	19	20	12	17	22	27
3	3	4	5	6	8	19	20	21	13	18	23	28
5	5	6	7	8	10	21	22	23	15	20	25	30
6	6	7	8	9	11	22	23	24	16	21	26	31
7	7	8	9	10	12	23	24	25	17	22	27	32
8	8	9	10	11	13	24	25	26	18	23	28	33
10	10	11	12	13	15	26	27	28	20	25	30	35
11	11	12	13	14	16	27	28	29	21	26	31	36
12	2	13	14	15	17	28	29	30	22	27	32	37
13	3	14	15	16	18	29	30	31	23	28	33	38
15	15	16	17	18	20	31	32	33	25	30	35	40
20	20	21	22	23	25	36	37	38	30	35	40	45
25	25	26	27	28	30	41	42	43	35	40	45	50

We remark that for the case of no collusion, Theorem 6 does not yield an optimal scheme. The proposition below outlines a modified scheme with a lower recovery threshold if secrecy is not a consideration.

Proposition 6. *Define the polynomials:*

$$\tilde{P}(x) := \sum_{k=1}^{K} x^{(k-1)M} \sum_{m=1}^{M} x^m A_{k,m},$$

$$\tilde{Q}(x) := \sum_{\ell=1}^{L} x^{(K+\ell-1)M} \sum_{m=1}^{M} x^{M+1-m} B_{m,\ell}.$$

The following hold:

1. *For each $(i, j) \in [K] \times [L]$, C_{ij} is the coefficient of $z^{M(i+j+K-1)+1}$ in $\tilde{P}\tilde{Q}$.*
2. *The number N of non-zero terms in the product $\tilde{P}\tilde{Q}$ satisfies*

$$N \leq KLM + M - 1.$$

Proof. For each $(i,j) \in [K] \times [L]$, define the following:

- $(c_{ij}) := (M(K+i+j-1)+1)$,
- $B_M(c_{ij}) := \{c_{ij} - M + 1, \dots, c_{ij} + M - 1\} = \{c_{ij} + u : -(M-1) \leq u \leq M-1\}$.

We have

$$\tilde{P}\tilde{Q} = \sum_{k=1}^{K} \sum_{\ell=1}^{L} \sum_{m=1}^{M} \sum_{m'=1}^{M} x^{M(K+\ell+k-1)+1+m-m'} A_{k,m} B_{m',\ell}.$$

The distinct monomials arising in the product $\tilde{P}\tilde{Q}$ are those indexed by the distinct elements of $\cup_{(i,j)\in[K]\times[L]} B_M(c_{ij})$. It is straightforward to check that for each $(i,j) \in [K] \times [L]$, the integer c_{ij} is not contained in $B_m(c_{ut})$ for any $(u,t) \neq (i,j)$ and hence the required coefficients C_{ij} that appear in the product $\tilde{P}\tilde{Q}$, which are indexed by the c_{ij}, can be uniquely retrieved. We compute the number of workers required by this scheme. We have

$$\begin{aligned} V &:= \left| \bigcup_{(i,j)\in[K]\times[L]} B_M(c_{ij}) \right| \\ &= KL(2M-1) - \sum_{(i,j)\neq(u,t)} \left| B_M(c_{ij}) \cap B_M(c_{st}) \right| \\ &= KL(2M-1) - (KL-1)(M-1) = KLM + M - 1. \end{aligned}$$

□

The recovery threshold of this scheme takes the same value as the recovery threshold of the poly-entangled scheme of Theorem 1 [18].

5. Results and Comparison with the State-of-the-Art

We provide some comparison plots that highlight parameter regions of interest. In Figure 2, we compare the two variants of our own scheme. The recovery threshold when considering the maximal degree of the resulting product polynomial is shown alongside the count of possibly non-zero coefficients. We see that significant gains can be achieved, especially in the higher collusion number region.

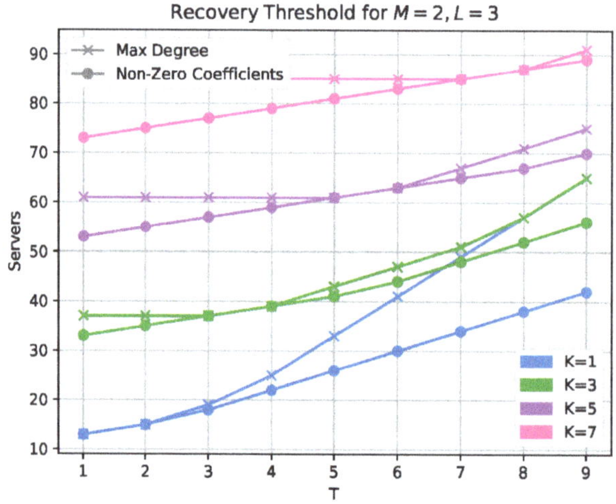

Figure 2. Comparison of maximal degree with non-zero coefficient.

In Figure 3, we compare our (non-zero coefficient) scheme with the SGPD scheme presented in [19]. For $K > 1$, we see that, except for very low values of T, our new scheme outperforms the SGPD scheme. This comparison of the recovery threshold for the two schemes is well justified since they use the same division of the matrices and will have identical upload and download costs per server.

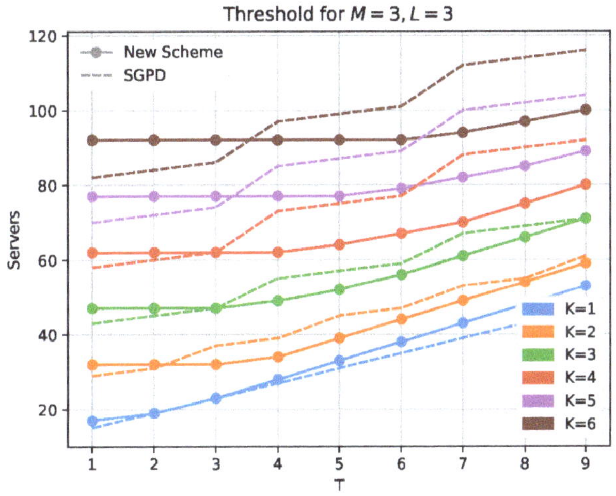

Figure 3. Comparison with [19].

The comparison in Figure 4 with the entangled codes scheme [17] and a newer scheme using roots of unity [26] shows that our new codes have lower recovery threshold for low number of colluding servers. Calculating the actual number of servers needed for the entangled scheme requires knowledge of the tensor rank of matrix multiplication. These ranks, or their best known upper bounds, are taken from [29,30]. It should be noted that the scheme in [26] requires that either $((L+1)(K+T)-1) \mid q$ or $(KML+LT+KM+T) \mid q$ where q is the field size. The requirements for our scheme outlined in Proposition 5 and Corollary 1 (i.e., that $\gcd(q-1, D) = 1, q > N$) are much less restrictive.

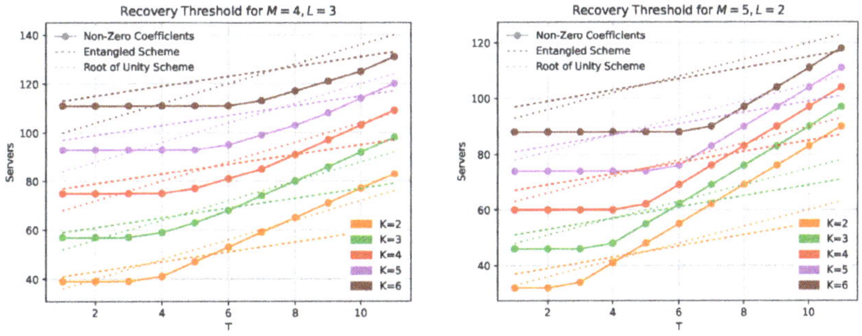

Figure 4. Comparison with [17,26] for the cases $M = 4, L = 3$ and $M = 5, L = 2$.

The comparison with the GASP scheme is less straightforward since the partitioning in GASP has a fixed value of $M = 1$. The plot in Figure 5 shows the recovery thresholds for the GASP scheme with partitioning $K = L = 3M$ as well as the recovery thresholds of our scheme for $K = L = 3$ and varying M from 1 to 5. We compare here with the maximal degree of our scheme, not the non-zero coefficients, to show that the variant of our scheme that is able to mitigate stragglers and Byzantine servers achieve much lower recovery thresholds. Fixing K and L to be the same value across this comparison means that the download cost per server is the same for all our schemes and the $K = L = 3$ GASP scheme. Note that in the $M = 1$ case, we have identical partition and hence upload cost per server as the $K = L = 3$ GASP scheme, while for $M = 2$, we have identical upload cost with the $K = L = 6$ GASP scheme, and $M = 5$ corresponds to the $K = L = 15$ GASP scheme. We can see that the grid partitioning allows for a much lower recovery threshold when the upload cost is fixed. The outer partitioning of the GASP scheme allows for low download cost per server that makes up for the higher recovery threshold. Explicitly, the outer partition into KM and LM blocks allows for a download rate of $N_{GASP}(\frac{ab}{M^2})$, where N_{GASP} is the recovery threshold for the GASP scheme. In contrast, the scheme presented in this paper will have a download rate of Nab if we partition into $K \times M$ and $M \times L$ blocks.

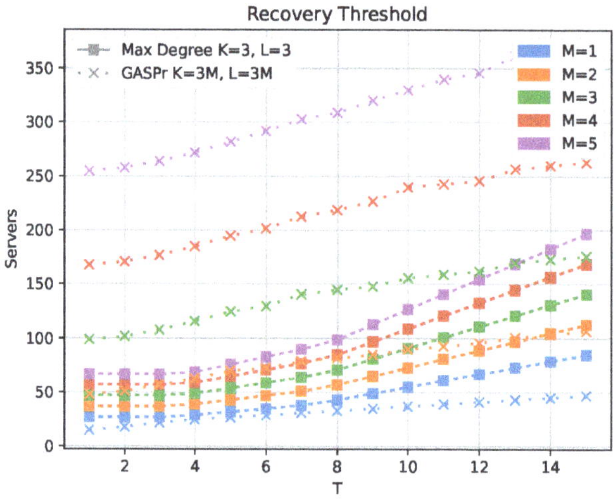

Figure 5. Comparison of the maximal degree with the $GASP_r$ scheme from [10].

It should be noted though that our construction allows to explicitly control the field size needed. In contrast, the GASP scheme might have to choose its evaluations points from an extension field Theorem 1 [9] if the base field is fixed by the entries of the matrices A and B, or just requires a very large base field. This would greatly increase the computational cost and the rates at all steps of the scheme. For example, for $K = 3, L = 3, T = 3$, GASP$_r$ uses $N = 22$ servers and the exponents for the randomness in one of the polynomials are $9, 10, 12$. Then, there are no suitable evaluation points for $q = 23, 25, 27, 29, 31, 32, 37, 41, 43$ and so for these values of q, an extension field is required.

Furthermore, the scheme presented in this paper can be used in situations where stragglers or Byzantine servers are expected as described in Corollary 2.

Complexity

We summarize the cost of $\mathbb{F}_q$-arithmetic operations and transmission of $\mathbb{F}_q$ elements associated with this scheme, using N servers. We refer the reader to ([25], Table 1) and ([26], Table 1) to view the complexity of other schemes in the literature (note that the costs defined in [25] are normalized). There are various trade-offs in costs depending on the partitioning chosen (the proposed scheme is completely flexible in this respect), ability to handle stragglers and Byzantine servers, and constraints on the field size q.

We remark that additions in general are much less costly than $\mathbb{F}_q$-multiplications in terms of space and time: for example, if $q = 2^\ell$, then an addition has space complexity (number of AND and XOR gates) $\mathcal{O}(\ell)$ and costs 1 clock in time, while multiplication has space complexity $\mathcal{O}(\ell^2)$ and time complexity $\mathcal{O}(\log_2(\ell))$ [31,32].

The encoding complexity of our scheme comes at the cost of evaluating the pair of polynomials $P(x)$ and $Q(x)$ each at N distinct elements of $\mathbb{F}_q$. This is equivalent to performing $Nr(a+b)$ (scalar) polynomial evaluations in $\mathbb{F}_q$. Given $\alpha \in \mathbb{F}_q$, the (i,j)-entry of $P(\alpha)$ is an evaluation of an $\mathbb{F}_q$-polynomial with $KM+T$ coefficients, while the (i,j)-entry of $Q(\alpha)$ is an evaluation of an $\mathbb{F}_q$-polynomial with $KL+T$ coefficients. The decoding complexity is the cost of interpolating the polynomial $PQ \in \mathbb{F}_q^{a\times b}[x]$ using N evaluation points, when PQ has at most N unknown coefficients.

The cost of either polynomial evaluation at N points or interpolation of a polynomial of degree at most $N-1$ has complexity $\mathcal{O}(N\log^2 N\log\log N)$. Therefore, we have the following statement.

Proposition 7.

1. *The encoding phase of the scheme presented in Section 3, using N servers, has complexity* $\mathcal{O}((a+b)rN\log^2 N\log\log N)$.
2. *The decoding phase of the scheme presented in Section 3, using N servers, has complexity* $\mathcal{O}(abN\log^2 N\log\log N)$.
3. *The total upload cost of the scheme presented in Section 3, using N servers, is* $r(a+b)N$.
4. *The total download cost of the scheme presented in Section 3, using N servers, is* abN.

6. Conclusions

In this work, we addressed the problem of secure distributed matrix multiplication for $C = AB$ in terms of designing polynomial codes for this setting. In particular, we assumed that A and B contain confidential data, which must be kept secure from colluding workers. Similar to some previous work also employing polynomial codes for distributed matrix multiplication, we proposed to deliberately leave gaps in the polynomial coefficients for certain degrees and provided a new code construction which is able to exploit these gaps to lower the recovery threshold. For this construction, we also presented new closed-form expressions for the recovery threshold as a function of the number of colluding workers and the specific number of submatrices that the matrices A and B are partitioned into during encoding. Further, in the absence of any security constraints, we showed that our construction is optimal in terms of recovery threshold. Our proposed scheme improves on the recovery threshold of existing schemes from the literature in particular for large dimensions of A and a larger number of colluding workers, in some cases, even by a large margin.

Author Contributions: Writing—original draft, E.B., O.W.G., and J.K. All authors have read and agreed to the published version of the manuscript.

Funding: This work was supported in part by U.S. National Science Foundation grants 1815322, 1908756, 2107370 in addition to the UCD Seed Funding- *Horizon Scanning* scheme (grant no. 54584).

Institutional Review Board Statement: Not applicable.

Data Availability Statement: Not applicable.

Conflicts of Interest: The authors declare no conflict of interest.

References

1. Janzamin, M.; Sedghi, H.; Anandkumar, A. Beating the perils of non-convexity: Guaranteed training of neural networks using tensor methods. *arXiv* **2015**, arXiv:1506.08473.
2. Joshi, G.; Soljanin, E.; Wornell, G. Efficient redundancy techniques for latency reduction in cloud systems. *ACM Trans. Model. Perform. Eval. Comput. Syst. (TOMPECS)* **2017**, *2*, 12:1–12:30. [CrossRef]
3. Lee, K.; Suh, C.; Ramchandran, K. High-dimensional coded matrix multiplication. In Proceedings of the IEEE International Symposium on Information Theory (ISIT), Aachen, Germany, 25–30 June 2017; pp. 2418–2422.
4. Lee, K.; Lam, M.; Pedarsani, R.; Papailiopoulos, D.; Ramchandran, K. Speeding Up Distributed Machine Learning Using Codes. *IEEE Trans. Inf. Theory* **2018**, *64*, 1514–1529. [CrossRef]

5. Yu, Q.; Maddah-Ali, M.; Avestimehr, S. Polynomial codes: An optimal design for high-dimensional coded matrix multiplication. In Proceedings of the Advances in Neural Information Processing Systems, Long Beach, CA, USA, 4–9 December 2017; pp. 4403–4413.
6. Li, S.; Maddah-Ali, M.A.; Yu, Q.; Avestimehr, A.S. A fundamental tradeoff between computation and communication in distributed computing. *IEEE Trans. Inform. Theory* **2017**, *64*, 109–128. [CrossRef]
7. Aliasgari, M.; Simeone, O.; Kliewer, J. Distributed and Private Coded Matrix Computation with Flexible Communication Load. *arXiv* **2019**, arXiv:1901.07705.
8. Yang, H.; Lee, J. Secure Distributed Computing With Straggling Servers Using Polynomial Codes. *IEEE Trans. Inf. Forensics Secur.* **2019**, *14*, 141–150. [CrossRef]
9. D'Oliveira, R.G.L.; El Rouayheb, S.; Karpuk, D. GASP Codes for Secure Distributed Matrix Multiplication. *IEEE Trans. Inf. Theory* **2020**, *66*, 4038–4050. [CrossRef]
10. D'Oliveira, R.G.L.; El Rouayheb, S.; Heinlein, D.; Karpuk, D. Degree Tables for Secure Distributed Matrix Multiplication. *IEEE J. Sel. Areas Inf. Theory* **2021**, *2*, 907–918. [CrossRef]
11. Yu, Q.; Raviv, N.; So, J.; Avestimehr, A.S. Lagrange Coded Computing: Optimal Design for Resiliency, Security and Privacy. *arXiv* **2018**, arXiv:1806.00939.
12. Kakar, J.; Ebadifar, S.; Sezgin, A. On the Capacity and Straggler-Robustness of Distributed Secure Matrix Multiplication. *IEEE Access* **2019**, *7*, 45783–45799. [CrossRef]
13. Chang, W.T.; Tandon, R. On the capacity of secure distributed matrix multiplication. In Proceedings of the 2018 IEEE Global Communications Conference (GLOBECOM), Abu Dhabi, United Arab Emirates, 9–13 December 2018; pp. 1–6.
14. Chang, W.T.; Tandon, R. On the Upload versus Download Cost for Secure and Private Matrix Multiplication. In Proceedings of the 2019 IEEE Information Theory Workshop (ITW), Gotland, Sweden, 25–28 August 2019; pp. 1–5.
15. Dutta, S.; Bai, Z.; Jeong, H.; Low, T.M.; Grover, P. A unified coded deep neural network training strategy based on generalized PolyDot codes. In Proceedings of the 2018 IEEE International Symposium on Information Theory (ISIT), Vail, CO, USA, 17–22 June 2018; pp. 1585–1589.
16. Dutta, S.; Fahim, M.; Haddadpour, F.; Jeong, H.; Cadambe, V.; Grover, P. On the Optimal Recovery Threshold of Coded Matrix Multiplication. *IEEE Trans. Inf. Theory* **2020**, *66*, 278–301. [CrossRef]
17. Yu, Q.; Avestimehr, A.S. Entangled Polynomial Codes for Secure, Private, and Batch Distributed Matrix Multiplication: Breaking the "Cubic" Barrier. In Proceedings of the 2020 IEEE International Symposium on Information Theory (ISIT), Los Angeles, CA, USA, 21–26 June 2020; pp. 245–250.
18. Yu, Q.; Maddah-Ali, M.A.; Avestimehr, A.S. Straggler Mitigation in Distributed Matrix Multiplication: Fundamental Limits and Optimal Coding. *IEEE Trans. Inf. Theory* **2020**, *66*, 1920–1933. [CrossRef]
19. Aliasgari, M.; Simeone, O.; Kliewer, J. Private and Secure Distributed Matrix Multiplication With Flexible Communication Load. *IEEE Trans. Inf. Forensics Secur.* **2020**, *15*, 2722–2734. [CrossRef]
20. Wang, H.-P.; Duursma, I. Parity-Checked Strassen Algorithm. *arXiv* **2020**, arXiv:2011.15082.
21. Hasirciolu, B.; Gomez-Vilardebo, J.; Gunduz, D. Bivariate Polynomial Codes for Secure Distributed Matrix Multiplication. *IEEE J. Sel. Areas Commun.* **2022**, *40*, 955–967. [CrossRef]
22. Li, J.; Hollanti, C. Private and Secure Distributed Matrix Multiplication Schemes for Replicated or MDS-Coded Servers. *IEEE Trans. Inf. Forensics Secur.* **2022**, *17*, 659–669. [CrossRef]
23. Machado, R.A.; D'Oliveira, R.G.L.; Rouayheb, S.E.; Heinlein, D. Field Trace Polynomial Codes for Secure Distributed Matrix Multiplication. In Proceedings of the 2021 XVII International Symposium "Problems of Redundancy in Information and Control Systems" (REDUNDANCY), Prague, Czech Republic, 23–25 November 2021.
24. Makkonen, O.; Hollanti, C. General Framework for Linear Secure Distributed Matrix Multiplication with Byzantine Servers. *arXiv* **2022**, arXiv:2205.07052.
25. Mital, N.; Ling, C.; Gündüz, D. Secure Distributed Matrix Computation With Discrete Fourier Transform. *IEEE Trans. Inf. Theory* **2022**, *68*, 4666–4680. [CrossRef]
26. Machado, R.A.; Manganiello, F. Root of Unity for Secure Distributed Matrix Multiplication: Grid Partition Case. *arXiv* **2022**, arXiv:2206.01559.
27. Zhu, J.; Li, S. A Systematic Approach towards Efficient Private Matrix Multiplication. *IEEE J. Sel. Areas Inf. Theory* **2022**, *3*, 257–274. [CrossRef]
28. Bosma, W.; Cannon, J.; Playoust, C. The Magma algebra system. I. The user language. *J. Symb. Comput.* **1997**, *24*, 235–265.
29. Sedoglavic, A. Yet Another Catalogue of Fast Matrix Multiplication Algorithms. Available online: https://fmm.univ-lille.fr/ (accessed on 28 October 2022).
30. Fawzi, A.; Balog, M.; Huang, A.; Hubert, T.; Romera-Paredes, B.; Barekatain, M.; Novikov, A.; Ruiz, F.J.; Schrittwieser, J.; Swirszcz, G.; et al. Discovering faster matrix multiplication algorithms with reinforcement learning. *Nature* **2022**, *610*, 47–53. [CrossRef] [PubMed]

31. Elia, M.; Leone, M. On the inherent space complexity of fast parallel multipliers for GF(2/sup m/). *IEEE Trans. Comput.* **2002**, *51*, 346–351. [CrossRef]
32. Elia, M.; Rosenthal, J.; Schipani, D. Polynomial evaluation over finite fields: New algorithms and complexity bounds. *Appl. Algebra Eng. Commun. Comput.* **2012**, *23*, 129–141. [CrossRef]

MDPI
St. Alban-Anlage 66
4052 Basel
Switzerland
Tel. +41 61 683 77 34
Fax +41 61 302 89 18
www.mdpi.com

Entropy Editorial Office
E-mail: entropy@mdpi.com
www.mdpi.com/journal/entropy

www.ingramcontent.com/pod-product-compliance
Lightning Source LLC
LaVergne TN
LVHW070457100526
838202LV00014B/1742